Puntos de partida

Puntos de partida

An Invitation to Spanish

MARTY KNORRE
University of Cincinnati

THALIA DORWICK

FRANCISCO R. FERRÁN
Oregon State University at Corvallis (emeritus)

WALTER LUSETTI
Oregon State University at Corvallis

WILLIAM F. RATLIFF
Marquette University

M. STANLEY WHITLEY
West Virginia University

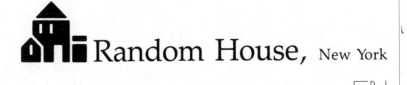 Random House, New York

This book was developed for Random House by Eirik Børve, Inc.

First Edition
98765
Copyright © 1981 by Random House, Inc.

Library of Congress Cataloging in Publication Data
Main entry under title:
Puntos de partida.
Includes index.
1. Spanish language—Grammar—1950–
I. Knorre, Marty.
PC4112.P8   468.2′421   80-25845
ISBN 0-394-32618-0

Manufactured in the United States of America

Text design: Meryl Sussman Levavi
Cover illustration: Susan Detrich
Line drawings: Axelle Fortier
Photo Editor: Lynn Goldberg

REPRINT ILLUSTRATIONS: SOURCES AND ACKNOWLEDGMENTS

Page 44 Courtesy of Cursos Internacionales de Verano de la Universidad de Salamanca **68, 289, 343, 423, 441, 479** Reprinted by permission of the artist, Mingote **110** *Semana*, N°. 2.062 (25 agosto 1979) **151** *Arriba, Domingo* (21 julio 1974): 5 **152, 208, 265, 419** Don Tobin, © King Features Syndicate, Inc., 1977/1978 **180, 235, 305** Copyright PIB Copenhagen **205, 207** Courtesy of Iberia **208** Reprinted as a courtesy of Aviaco Airlines **236** *Temas*, N°. 342 (30 agosto 1979): 78 **237** *Buena vida*, 2, N°. 22 (agosto 1979): 114 **256** *ABC, Domingo* (15 julio 1979): 55 **288** *La codorniz*, N°. 1393 (28 julio 1968): 13 **292 (left and center)** Copyright © 1980 Avis Rent-a-Car System, Inc.; Avis® and We Try Harder® **(right)** Courtesy of SEAT **342 (1, 2, 3, 4)** *Temas*, N°. 333 (30 noviembre 1978): 78; **(5)** *Temas*, N°. 328 (30 junio 1978): 71 **368** *Blanco y Negro*, N°. 3.248 (3 agosto 1974): 90 **379 (center)** *La codorniz*, N°. 1393 (28 julio 1968): 9 **397 (bottom)** *La codorniz*, N°. 1640 (26 agosto 1973): 17 **444** *La codorniz*, N°. 1393 (28 julio 1968): 13 **468** Copyright by A.L.I. **470 (bottom)** Reprinted courtesy of Consolidated Edison **490** Courtesy of Renfe

Preface

Puntos de partida: An Invitation to Spanish is a first-year program that emphasizes the four skills considered essential to a communicative approach to language learning. Each chapter has a cultural or practical theme, and grammar is introduced and practiced within that context. Written by a team of experienced language instructors, *Puntos de partida* provides a flexible framework that can be adapted to individual teaching situations and goals. The text was prepared with students in mind to help them learn how to learn a language and to give them the opportunity to use and enjoy it. The *Instructors' Edition*, which contains supplementary listening comprehension exercises, drills, and suggestions for enlivening classroom interaction, should be useful to experienced and inexperienced instructors alike.

ORGANIZATION

The main text consists of an opening chapter, **Ante todo,** which introduces students to the Spanish language and to the text itself, and twenty other chapters. Chapters 1–19 are each organized as follows:

1. **Objetivos,** which outline the grammar and culture presented in the chapter
2. **Vocabulario: Preparación,** which presents and practices the thematic vocabulary that will be emphasized in the rest of the chapter
3. **Pronunciación** (in the first fifteen chapters), which focuses on individual sounds that are particularly difficult for native speakers of English
4. **Minidiálogos y gramática,** three to five grammar points, each introduced by a minidialog or cartoon and followed by a series of exercises that progress from controlled (**Práctica**) to open-ended (**Conversación**); answers to most of the **Práctica** exercises are given in Appendix 2
5. **Diálogo y comentario cultural,** the main dialog, which focuses on the use of Spanish in everyday situations, in a cultural context
6. **Un poco de todo,** exercises that combine and review all of the grammar and vocabulary presented in the chapter
7. **Vocabulario,** the chapter vocabulary list, which includes all important words and expressions that are new to the chapter

Between chapters, an optional section called **Un paso más** presents activities that emphasize conversation, creativity, and humor, as well as a cultural reading with guided writing exercises. Instructors may use all, part, or none of this section, according to individual needs and schedules.

The text concludes with **Capítulo 20: En el extranjero,** which focuses on the study of Spanish abroad.

SUPPLEMENTARY MATERIALS

Puntos de partida may be used most successfully with any of the following components:

1. The *Workbook,* by Professors Alice and Oswaldo Arana (California State University, Fullerton), which provides additional practice with vocabulary and grammatical structures through a variety of written drills, including controlled and open-ended exercises, guided compositions, and activities.
2. The *Lab Manual* and *Tape Program,* by Professor María Sabló Yates (Central Michigan University), which offers pronunciation practice, listening comprehension exercises, dictations, pattern practice, and question-and-answer sequences; a *Tape Script* is available.
3. The *Instructors' Edition,* which contains on-page hints and suggestions, many supplementary exercises for developing listening and speaking skills, and variations and follow-ups on text exercises. There is also an *Instructors' Manual* with guidelines for instructors, suggestions for lesson planning, and more listening comprehension exercises.

AUTHORS

Professor Marty Knorre, of the University of Cincinnati, is the coordinator of the project (text and supplementary materials) and the author of the objectives, activities, on-page text in the *Instructors' Edition,* and *Instructors' Manual.* Dr. Thalia Dorwick is the author of the grammar explanations, exercises, and some of the minidialogs; she also served as project editor. Professors Walter Lusetti and Francisco Ferrán, of the University of Oregon, Corvallis, are the authors of the main dialogs, most of the minidialogs, and the cultural commentaries. Professor William F. Ratliff, of Marquette University, is the author of the cultural readings and the writing exercises that accompany them. Professor M. Stanley Whitley, of West Virginia University, is the author of the pronunciation sections.

While the coauthors are responsible primarily for their own sections of the book, all of them participated actively in the creation of the final manuscript, helping each other to realize their ideas.

ACKNOWLEDGMENTS

Puntos de partida was developed by the authors in consultation with over seventy coordinators of Spanish courses throughout the United States. The publishers would like to thank the following instructors who participated in a series of surveys, the results of which greatly influenced the scope, content, and format of this text. The appearance of their names does not necessarily constitute an endorsement of the text and its methodology.

Karen Odell Austin, *University of Southern Mississippi*

Milton M. Azevedo, *University of California, Berkeley*

Jack S. Bailey, *University of Texas, El Paso*

Clayton Baker, *Indiana University/ Purdue University, Indianapolis*

Sarah J. Banks, *Jackson State University*

Margaret E. Beeson, *Kansas State University*

Mary Lee Bretz, *Rutgers University, New Brunswick*

Joan Cain, *University of Southwestern Louisiana*

Emilie Cannon, *Wright State University*

Ezequiel Cárdenas, *Grossmont College*

John W. J. Davis, *William Rainey Harper College*

Patrick De Cicco, *Jersey City State College*

John J. Deveny, Jr., *Oklahoma State University*

R. Thomas Douglass, *University of Iowa*

Gilda Álvarez Evans, *Ohio State University*

James F. Ford, *University of Arkansas*

G. Ronald Freeman, *California State University, Fresno*

Herschel Frey, *University of Pittsburgh*

Roger H. Gilmore, *Colorado State University*

Helen D. Goode, *Southern Illinois University*

J. Ray Green, *University of Wisconsin, Milwaukee*

Vivian Gruber, *Stephen F. Austin State University*

Leonora Guinazzo, *Portland Community College*

Jorge Guitart, *State University of New York, Buffalo*

Violeta Gutiérrez, *California State University, Northridge*

Reginetta Haboucha, *Lehman College, City University of New York*

Gene M. Hammit, *Allegheny College*

Mathilda E. Harris, *Mt. Hood Community College*

William H. Heflin, Jr., *University of Tennessee*

James M. Hendrickson, *Lansing Community College*

Susana Hernández-Araico, *California State Polytechnic University, Pomona*

María C. Jiménez, *Sam Houston State University*

John F. Kellogg, *Golden West College*

Robert Kiekle, *Oregon State University*

Margaret S. Lara, *Santa Rosa Junior College*

Jerry W. Larson, *Northern Arizona University*

John M. Lipski, *Michigan State University*

Mary Loud, *Youngstown State University*

Ernest J. Lunsford, *Virginia Commonwealth University*

Mildred H. Lyon, *Central State University*

Martha Marks, *Northwestern University*

Claude G. Martin, *Rio Americano High School, Sacramento*

Jose G. Montero, *Northern Virginia Community College*

Thomas D. Morin, *University of Rhode Island*

Eunice D. Myers, *North Carolina State University*

Frank H. Nuessel, Jr., *University of Louisville*

Luis L. Pinto, *Bronx Community College, City University of New York*

Mary Plevich-Darretta, *Rutgers University, Newark*

Ransom H. Poythress, *California State University, Fresno*

Marcial Prado, *California State University, Fullerton*

Graciela Ramírez, *Washington Barrio Education Center, Sacramento*

María Rekowski, *Sacramento City College*

Marie S. Rentz, *University of Maryland*

Seymour Resnick, *Queens College, City University of New York*

Víctor J. Rojas, *State University of New York, Brockport*

William A. Rubio, *William Paterson College*

M. Louise Salstad, *University of Wyoming*

Lynn A. Sandstedt, *University of Northern Colorado*

Jorge Santana, *California State University, Sacramento*

Estela S. Serrano, *California State University, Sacramento*

Oscar U. Somoza, *University of Denver*

Luis Soto-Ruiz, *Marquette University*

John Staczek, *Florida International University, Tamiami Campus*

Alain Swietlicki, *University of Missouri, Columbia*

Irene Tenney, *University of California, Berkeley*

Luis Verano, *University of Oregon*

S. B. Vranich, *Lehmann College, City University of New York*

John G. Weiger, *University of Vermont*

M. Weissenrieder, *Ohio University*

Mildred Wilkinson, *Southern Illinois University*

John Zahner, *Montclair State College*

Sidney Zelson, *State University of New York, Buffalo*

Many other individuals as well deserve our thanks and appreciation for their help and support. Among them are the persons who, in addition to the coauthors, read the manuscript to help ensure its linguistic and cultural authenticity and pedagogical accuracy: Alice Arana (United States), Oswaldo Arana (Perú), Paul Figure (Chile), Aristóbulo Pardo (Colombia), María Sabló Yates (Panamá), and Begoña Zubiri (Spain). Special thanks are also due to Axelle Fortier, whose superb art has made our ideas come alive; to Mark Accornero, for his help in selecting and singing the songs that appear in the tape program; to Elena Keyser, who prepared the initial drafts of the **Vocabulario: Preparación** sections; to our editorial and production team at Random House: Tina Norum, Martha Leff, Elaine Romano, and Cele Gardner for their careful guidance of the project through the various stages of production, Meryl Sussman Levavi for her clear, functional, and attractive design, and Brent Collins and June Smith for their constant support; and to Marc Purtill, Kay Harden, Marsha McKay, and Félix Menchacatorre. Last but not least, special thanks to Eirik Børve, who inspired the project, and to Lesley Walsh, who helped carry it through to completion.

Contents

CAPÍTULO 4 LA VIDA SOCIAL 98

CAPÍTULO 5 EL TIEMPO 124

CAPÍTULO 6 EN UN RESTAURANTE ESPAÑOL 156

CAPÍTULO 18 DE VIAJE 474

CAPÍTULO 19 LOS HISPANOS EN LOS ESTADOS UNIDOS 498

CAPÍTULO 20 EN EL EXTRANJERO 526

Puntos de partida

Ante todo

Carlos Hernandez/EPA, Inc.

Puntos de partida means *points of departure, starting places.* As a textbook, its purpose is to provide you with a way to begin to learn the Spanish language and to become more familiar with the many people here and abroad who use it.

Language is the means by which humans communicate with one another. To learn a new language is to acquire another way of exchanging information and of sharing your thoughts, concerns, and opinions with others. *Puntos de partida* will help you use Spanish to communicate in various ways: to understand Spanish when others speak it, to speak it yourself, and to read and write it. This text will also help you to communicate in Spanish in nonverbal ways—via gestures and through an awareness of cultural differences. *Puntos de partida*, however, can only show you where to start. Look around you in your own community, and you will see that Spanish is not just a "foreign" language but truly a "living" language in the United States today.

Ante todo (*first of all*) is a preliminary chapter that will introduce you to the Spanish language and to the format of *Puntos de partida.*

SALUDOS° Y EXPRESIONES DE CORTESÍA   *Greetings*

1.

ANA: Hola, José.
JOSÉ: ¿Qué tal, Ana? (¿Cómo estás?)
ANA: Así así. ¿Y tú?
JOSÉ: ¡Muy bien! Hasta mañana, ¿eh?
ANA: Adiós.

¿Cómo estás? (¿Qué tal?) and **¿y tú?** are expressions used in informal situations with people you know well, on a first-name basis.

2.

SEÑOR ALONSO: Buenas tardes, señorita López.
SEÑORITA LÓPEZ: Muy buenas, señor Alonso. ¿Cómo está?
SEÑOR ALONSO: Bien, gracias. ¿Y usted?
SEÑORITA LÓPEZ: Muy bien, gracias. Adiós.
SEÑOR ALONSO: Hasta luego.

---

1. ANA: Hi, José. JOSÉ: How are you doing, Ana? (How are you?) ANA: So-so. And you? JOSÉ: Fine! See you tomorrow. OK? ANA: Bye.

2. MR. ALONSO: Good afternoon, Miss López. MISS LÓPEZ: 'Afternoon, Mr. Alonso. How are you? MR. ALONSO: Fine, thanks. And you? MISS LÓPEZ: Fine, thanks. Good-by. MR. ALONSO: See you later.

¿**Cómo está?** and ¿**y usted?** are used to address someone with whom you have a formal relationship.

3.

PROFESORA: ¿Cómo se llama usted?
      MARÍA: Me llamo María Sánchez.

¿**Cómo se llama usted?** is used in formal situations.   ¿**Cómo te llamas?** is used in informal situations, for example, with other students.

	Otras expresiones útiles°	*useful*
buenos días	good morning (used until lunchtime)	
buenas tardes	good afternoon (used until the evening meal)	
buenas noches	good evening, good night (used from the evening meal on)	
señor (Sr.)	Mr., sir	
señora (Sra.)	Mrs., ma'am ⎫ There is no standard Spanish equiva-	
señorita (Srta.)	Miss ⎬ lent for *Ms.* Use **Sra.** or **Srta.,** as ⎭ appropriate.	
gracias	thanks, thank you	
muchas gracias	thank you very much	
de nada	you're welcome	
por favor	please (also used to get someone's attention)	

---

3. PROFESSOR: What's your name?   MARÍA: My name is María Sánchez.

A propósito°...   *By the way*

Perdón (*pardon me, excuse me*) is used to attract someone's attention. It is also used—just as in English—to excuse yourself if you have made a mistake or bumped into someone, for example.

   Con permiso or simply **permiso**—not **perdón**—is used to request permission to pass by or through a group of people—for example, on a bus or in a line.

PRÁCTICA

A. *Practice dialogs 1 through 3 with another student, using his or her name and making other changes where appropriate.*

B. *How many different ways can you respond to the following greetings?*

1. —Buenas tardes.   4. —Hola.   7. —Muchas gracias.
2. —Adiós.   5. —¿Cómo está?   8. —Hasta mañana.
3. —¿Qué tal?   6. —Buenas noches.   9. —¿Cómo se llama usted?

C. *If the following persons met or passed each other at the given times, what would they say?*

1. Mr. Santana and Miss Pérez, at 5:00 P.M.
2. Mrs. Ortega and Pablo, at 10:00 A.M.
3. Ms. Hernández and Olivia, at 11:00 P.M.
4. you and a classmate, just before your Spanish class

CONVERSACIÓN

What are these people saying, ¿con permiso? or ¿perdón?

PRONUNCIACIÓN

There is a very close relationship between the way Spanish is written and the way it is pronounced. This makes it relatively easy to learn the basics of Spanish spelling and pronunciation.

Many Spanish sounds, however, do not have an exact equivalent in English; so you should not trust English to be your guide to Spanish pronunciation. Even words that are spelled the same in both languages are not pronounced in exactly the same way. It is important to become so familiar with Spanish sounds that you can pronounce them automatically, right from the beginning of your study of the language.

Vocales (*Vowels*): A, E, I, O, U

In English a vowel may stand for several different pronunciations. For example, the *a* represents a different sound in each of the following words: *far, fat, fate, fall,* and *sofa.* In English a vowel may also be silent, like the *e* in *make.*

Spanish vowels are always pronounced, and each vowel has one basic pronunciation (although vowel sounds may vary slightly, depending on the other sounds around them). Spanish vowel sounds are always short and tense. A single vowel is never drawn out into two sounds, like the *o* in the English word *go,* which really contains two separate vowel sounds: an *o* sound and a *u* sound (a glide).

SPANISH VOWEL SOUNDS
a pronounced like the *a* in *father*
e usually pronounced like the *e* in *they* but without the glide sound
i pronounced like the *i* in *machine*
o pronounced like the *o* in *home* but without the glide sound
u pronounced like the *u* in *rule*

Listen as your instructor contrasts the pronunciation of the following words in English and in Spanish: **olé, San Diego, burrito, San Antonio.** If you follow your English tendency to pronounce one vowel sound as two, you will have a very noticeable accent. Try to pronounce Spanish vowels with a steady, clipped pronunciation.

 Although the schwa ("uh" sound) is very common in English —*canal,* wai*t*ed, ev*i*l, *a*tom, s*u*fficient—it does not exist in Spanish.

PRÁCTICA

A. *Pronounce the following Spanish syllables, being careful to say each vowel with a clipped pronunciation.*

1. ma   fa   la   ta   pa
2. me   fe   le   te   pe
3. mi   fi   li   ti   pi
4. mo   fo   lo   to   po
5. mu   fu   lu   tu   pu
6. na   ne   ni   no   nu
7. su   do   be   sa   di

B. *Pronounce the following words, paying special attention to vowel sounds.*

1. hasta   tal   nada   mañana   gracias
2. de   qué   tres   Pérez   señor
3. así   señorita   día   permiso   así así
4. no   dos   con   cómo   noches
5. uno   usted   útil   tú   útiles

EL ALFABETO ESPAÑOL

There are thirty letters in the Spanish alphabet (alfabeto)—four more than in the English alphabet. The ch, ll, and rr are considered single letters even though they are two-letter groups; the ñ is the fourth extra letter. The letters k and w appear only in words borrowed from other languages.

Listen carefully as your instructor pronounces the words listed with the letters of the alphabet.

Letters	Names of Letters	Examples		
a	a	Antonio	Ana	la Argentina
b	be	Benito	Blanca	Bolivia
c	ce	Carlos	Cecilia	Cáceres
ch	che	Pancho	Concha	Chile
d	de	Domingo	Dolores	Durango
e	e	Eduardo	Elena	el Ecuador
f	efe	Felipe	Francisca	Florida
g	ge	Gerardo	Gloria	Guatemala
h	hache	Héctor	Hortensia	Honduras
i	i	Ignacio	Inés	Ibiza
j	jota	José	Juana	Jalisco

Letters	Names of Letters	Examples		
k	ka	(Karl)	(Kati)	(Kansas)
l	ele	Luis	Lola	Lima
ll	elle	Guillermo	Guillermina	Sevilla
m	eme	Manuel	María	México
n	ene	Noé	Nati	Nicaragua
ñ	eñe	Íñigo	Begoña	España
o	o	Octavio	Olivia	Oviedo
p	pe	Pablo	Pilar	Panamá
q	cu	Enrique	Raquel	Quito
r	ere	Álvaro	Clara	el Perú
rr	erre *or* ere doble	Rafael	Rosa	Monterrey
s	ese	Salvador	Sara	San Juan
t	te	Tomás	Teresa	Toledo
u	u	Agustín	Lucía	Uruguay
v	ve *or* uve	Víctor	Victoria	Venezuela
w	doble ve, ve doble, *or* uve doble	Oswaldo	(Wilma)	(Washington)
x	equis	Xavier	Ximena	Extremadura
y	i griega	Pelayo	Yolanda	Paraguay
z	zeta	Gonzalo	Esperanza	Zaragoza

PRÁCTICA

A. *Match the spelling with its pronunciation.*

Spelling

1. **ch**
2. **g** before **e** or **i;** also **j**
3. **h**
4. **g** before **a, o,** or **u**
5. **ll**
6. **ñ**
7. **r**
8. **r** at the beginning of a word or **rr** in the middle of a word
9. **v**

Pronunciation

a. like the *g* in English *garden*
b. similar to *dd* of *caddy* or *tt* of *kitty* when pronounced very quickly
c. like *ch* in English *cheese*
d. like Spanish **b**
e. similar to a "strong" English *h*
f. like *y* in English *yes* or like the *li* sound in *million*
g. a trilled sound, several Spanish **r**s in a row
h. similar to the *ny* sound in *canyon*
i. never pronounced

B. *Spell your own name and those of your classmates, using the Spanish alphabet.*

C. *Use the Spanish alphabet to spell these U.S. place names, all of which are of Hispanic origin:*

Toledo, Los Angeles, Montana, Lima, El Paso, Florida, Texas, Las Vegas, Amarillo, San Francisco

D. *Think of several other place names of Hispanic origin and spell them aloud, using the Spanish alphabet.*

Study Hint: Cognates

Many Spanish and English words are similar or identical in form and meaning. These related words are called *cognates* (**cognados**).

The existence of such a large number of cognates means that many Spanish words will be immediately recognizable to you. Although some cognates are spelled identically (*idea, general, gas, animal, motor*), most will differ slightly in spelling: *position*/**posición,** *secret*/**secreto,** *student*/**estudiante,** *rose*/**rosa,** *lottery*/**lotería,** *opportunity*/**oportunidad.**

What does each word in the following categories mean?

1. **Naciones:** Rusia, Japón, Italia, Francia, España, el Brasil
2. **Personas:** líder, profesor, actor, actriz, artista, turista, político
3. **Lugares** (*places*): restaurante, rancho, museo, garaje, banco, hotel
4. **Cosas** (*things*): teléfono, fotografía, sofá, televisión, lámpara
5. **Animales:** león, cebra, burro, elefante, chimpancé, hipopótamo
6. **Comidas y bebidas** (*food and drink*): tomate, cóctel, chocolate, vino, patatas
7. **Deportes** (*sports*): béisbol, tenis, golf, basquetbol, volibol
8. **Instrumentos musicales:** guitarra, piano, clarinete, trompeta, violín

---

FRASES ÚTILES PARA LA CLASE

Here are some phrases that you will hear and use frequently during class.

Los estudiantes	
Practice saying these sentences aloud. Then try to give the Spanish as you look at the English equivalents.	
¿Cómo se dice «page» en español?	How do you say *"page"* in Spanish?
Tengo una pregunta.	I have a question.
Otra vez, por favor. No entiendo. (No comprendo.)	(Say that) again, please. I don't understand.
No sé (la respuesta).	I don't know (the answer).
Cómo no.	Of course.

Hugh Rogers/Monkmeyer Press Photo

Los profesores

After you read these Spanish sentences, cover the English equivalents and tell what each expression means.

¿Hay preguntas?	Are there any questions?
Escuchen.	Listen.
Repitan.	Repeat.
Lean (en voz alta).	Read (aloud).
Escriban.	Write.
Contesten en oraciones completas, por favor.	Answer in complete sentences, please.
Dígale (Pregúntele) a otro estudiante _____.	Tell (Ask) another student _____.
Dé la respuesta correcta.	Give the right answer.
Cambie el verbo.	Change the verb.
Abran los libros, por favor, en la página _____.	Open your books, please, to page _____.

SPANISH TODAY

Spanish As a World Language

Although no one knows exactly how many languages are spoken around the world, linguists estimate that there are between 3,000 and 6,000. The following figures, reported by the 1980 *World Almanac*, indicate the number of native speakers of the twelve most important languages.

Chinese	846 million	Portuguese	141 million
English	380 million	**Bengali**	140 million
Hindi-Urdu	295 million	**German**	120 million
Russian	295 million	**Japanese**	115 million
Spanish	238 million	**Malay-Indonesian**	106 million
Arabic	142 million	**French**	100 million

Spanish, with 238 million native speakers, is among the top five languages. It is the national language in Spain, in all of South America except Brazil and Guyana, in most of Central America, in Mexico, Cuba, the Dominican Republic—in approximately twenty countries in all. These countries are on the map on this page.

Like all languages spoken by large numbers of people, Spanish varies from region to region. The Spanish of Madrid is noticeably different from that spoken in Mexico City or Buenos Aires, just as the English of London differs from that of Chicago or Dallas. Although these differences are most noticeable in pronunciation ("accent"), they are also found in the

Source: U.S. Bureau of Census.

vocabulary and special expressions used in different geographical areas. In Great Britain one hears the word *lift*, but the same apparatus is called an *elevator* in the United States. What is called an **autobús** (*bus*) in Spain may be called a **guagua** in the Caribbean. While such differences are noticeable, they result only rarely in misunderstandings among native speakers, since the majority of structures and vocabulary are common to the many varieties of each language.

Hispanics in the United States

The impact of Spanish is not limited to foreign countries. The Spanish language and people of Hispanic descent have been an integral part of United States life for centuries, and Hispanics are currently the fastest-growing cultural group in this country. The map on this page shows the number of Hispanics in the United States in 1976.

People of Hispanic origin were among the first colonizers of what is now the United States, and descendants of those early settlers live in all parts of this country today. Large groups of more recent arrivals can be found in New York (where there is a large Puerto Rican community), in Florida (the home of many Cubans and Central Americans), and in the Southwest,

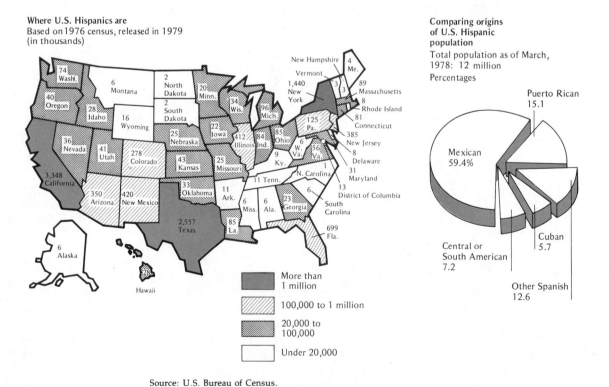

Where U.S. Hispanics are
Based on 1976 census, released in 1979
(in thousands)

Comparing origins of U.S. Hispanic population
Total population as of March, 1978: 12 million
Percentages

Puerto Rican 15.1

Mexican 59.4%

Cuban 5.7

Central or South American 7.2

Other Spanish 12.6

More than 1 million

100,000 to 1 million

20,000 to 100,000

Under 20,000

Source: U.S. Bureau of Census.

especially in California and Texas (where Mexican-Americans are the dominant Hispanic ethnic group).   And there has been a substantial increase in the number of Hispanics even in areas not usually thought of as having a large Hispanic population—Minneapolis–St. Paul, Seattle, New Orleans, to name only a few.

Hispanics in the United States come from many different ethnic and social backgrounds.   Their rich cultural heritage has helped to shape many aspects of life in this country, and they will continue to have considerable impact on daily life, culture, and business in the United States.   Clearly our second language, Spanish will be increasingly important in the future as a language for communication and commerce both in this country and abroad.

INTRODUCTION TO *PUNTOS DE PARTIDA*

Puntos de partida is divided into forty units: twenty basic chapters, alternating with twenty sections called **Un paso más** (*one more step*).   Each chapter has its own theme—university life here and abroad, travel, foods, and so on—as explained in the **Objetivos.** Important vocabulary and expressions related to the themes are included in **Vocabulario: preparación. Pronunciación** will introduce you to the Spanish sound system.

The grammar section, **Minidiálogos y gramática,** has two groups of exercises.   The first, **Práctica,** consists of drills and basic step-by-step practice with each new grammar point.   The second group, **Conversación,** is exactly that—a stimulus for speaking.   Here you can express yourself by answering questions, describing pictures and cartoons, completing sentences, and so on.   Throughout the grammar sections, the word ¡**Ojo!** (*watch out!*) will call your attention to areas where you should be especially careful when using Spanish.

The longer dialog that immediately follows the grammar section will be very easy to read because it is a combination of everything you have already learned in each chapter, as is the review section, **Un poco de todo** (*a little of everything*).   In **Vocabulario** you will find a complete list of all new words for the chapter.

Un paso más is very informal.   In the **Actividades,** you will use your new language skills to communicate your ideas and opinions to others.   In addition to cartoons, questionnaires, and suggestions for conversation, there will be materials that you would actually find in Spanish-speaking countries—ads, menus, tickets, forms, and the like—as well as hints on how to communicate more easily and more successfully with others in Spanish.   Finally, in the **Lectura cultural** (*cultural reading*) you will become acquainted with everyday life and important events in the Hispanic world.

capítulo 1 La universidad

Carlos Hernandez/EPA, Inc.

OBJETIVOS

In this chapter you will learn vocabulary and expressions related to the university (enrolling in the university, buying books, and so on), and to student life in general.

You will also learn about the following aspects of Spanish grammar:
1.* the gender of Spanish nouns and the formation of plurals, the definite articles (in English, *the*), and the indefinite articles (equivalent to *a, an* in English)

2. Spanish subject pronouns (the equivalents of *I, you, he, she, we,* and *they*)
3. how to form and use the present tense of regular **-ar** verbs, the first and largest of the three groups of regular Spanish verbs
4. how to ask questions that can be answered by *yes* or *no*
5. numbers from 1 to 30

Un paso más includes activities related to university life and a reading about gestures that speakers of Spanish use.

---

*The grammar sections of *Puntos de partida* are numbered consecutively throughout the book. If you need to review a particular grammar point, the index will refer you to its page number.

VOCABULARIO: PREPARACIÓN

La universidad

Lugares	Places
la biblioteca	the library
la clase	the class
la librería	the bookstore
la oficina	the office

Cosas	Things	Personas	People
el bolígrafo	the pen	el consejero	the counselor (*male*)
el cuaderno	the notebook	la consejera	the counselor (*female*)
el diccionario	the dictionary	el estudiante	the student (*male*)
el dinero	the money	la estudiante	the student (*female*)
el lápiz	the pencil	el profesor	the professor (*male*)
el libro	the book	la profesora	the professor (*female*)
la mesa	the table	el secretario	the secretary (*male*)
el papel	the paper	la secretaria	the secretary (*female*)
		el secretario general	the registrar (*male*)
		la secretaria general	the registrar (*female*)

A. *Identifique las cosas y las personas.*

1. En la clase
   la profesora _____
   la estudiante _____
   el papel _____
   el lápiz _____
   el bolígrafo _____
   la mesa _____

2. En la biblioteca
   el libro _____
   el diccionario _____
   el cuaderno _____
   el bolígrafo _____
   la mesa _____
   el estudiante _____

3. En la librería
   la estudiante _____
   el lápiz _____
   el cuaderno _____
   el bolígrafo _____
   el dinero _____

4. En la oficina
   la secretaria general _____
   el consejero _____
   la secretaria _____
   la mesa _____
   el diccionario _____

B. *¿Hombre o mujer?*   (Man or woman?)

MODELO   ¿La consejera? → *mujer*

1. ¿El profesor?   3. ¿El secretario?
2. ¿La estudiante?   4. ¿El estudiante?

Materias Subjects			
las ciencias	the sciences	**el inglés**	English
el español	Spanish	**las matemáticas**	mathematics
la historia	history	**la sicología**	psychology

C. **Asociaciones.**   *Which words do you associate with the numbered words on the left?*

1. las ciencias
2. la sicología
3. la biblioteca
4. el diccionario
5. el lápiz

las matemáticas	la librería	el papel
la universidad	el dinero	el cuaderno
la mesa	la historia	el libro
el bolígrafo	la estudiante	la historia
el secretario	la consejera	la clase
el español	el lápiz	el inglés

D. *Identifique los libros.*

MODELO   *Insectos de Norteamérica → Es para* (for) *la clase de ciencia.*

1. *El cálculo I*
2. *Romeo y Julieta*
3. *México en crisis*
4. *Puntos de partida*
5. *Skinner y Freud*

Study Hint: Learning New Vocabulary

Vocabulary is one of the most important tools for successful communication in a foreign language. What does it mean "to know vocabulary"? And what is the best way to learn vocabulary?

1. First, carefully study the words in the vocabulary list. If a word is a cognate or shares a root with an English word, be especially aware of differences in spelling and pronunciation. For example, note that **clase** is spelled with only one **s;** that there is no *th* in **matemáticas;** and that **ciencias** does not begin with an **s.** Keep in mind that an "almost but not quite perfect" spelling may lead to a miscommunication: **libro** (*book*) versus **libra** (*pound*); **mesa** (*table*) versus **mes** (*month*); **el consejero** (*male counselor*) versus **la consejera** (*female counselor*). You also need to remember which words require **el** and which require **la** to express *the,* as well as which words require a written accent—**lápiz, bolígrafo,**

for example—and where the accent occurs.

2. After studying the list, cover the English and give the English equivalent of each Spanish word.

3. When you are able to give the English without hesitation and without error, reverse the procedure; cover the Spanish and give the Spanish equivalent of each English word. Write out the Spanish words (using **el** or **la** where appropriate) once or several times and say them aloud.

4. Vocabulary lists and flash cards can be helpful tools in learning new vocabulary, and they are especially useful as a review or as a self-test.

5. Rote memorization, however, is only part of the learning process. Using new vocabulary to communicate requires practicing that vocabulary in context. What do you associate with this word? When might you want to use it?

Create a context—a place, a situation, a person or group of people—for the vocabulary that you want to learn or use a context from the text. The more associations you make with the word, the easier it will be to remember.

Practice useful words and phrases over and over—thinking about their meaning—until you can produce them automatically. You may find it useful to "talk to yourself," actually saying aloud the words you want to learn.

PRONUNCIACIÓN: Diphthongs and linking

Two successive weak vowels (**i, u**) or a combination of a strong vowel (**a, e,** or **o**) and a weak vowel (**i** or **u**) are pronounced as a single syllable, forming a *diphthong* (**diptongo**).

When words are combined to form phrases, clauses, and sentences, they are linked together in pronunciation. In spoken Spanish, it is usually impossible to hear the word boundaries—that is, where one word ends and another begins.

PRÁCTICA

A. *Más práctica con las vocales.* (More practice with vowels.)

1. hablar	pagar	cantar	trabajar
2. trece	clase	papel	general
3. dinero	oficina	bolígrafo	libro
4. hombre	profesor	dólares	los
5. universidad	matrícula	lugar	mujer

B. *Practique las siguientes palabras.* (Practice the following words.)

1. historia	secretaria	gracias	estudiante	Cecilia
2. bien	Oviedo	entiendo	ciencias	muy bien
3. secretario	biblioteca	adiós	diccionario	Antonio
4. cuaderno	Eduardo	el Ecuador	Guatemala	Managua
5. bueno	escuela	pues	Manuel	Venezuela

C. *Practice saying each phrase as if it were one long word, pronounced without a pause.*

1. el papel y el lápiz
2. la profesora y la estudiante
3. las ciencias y las matemáticas
4. la historia y la sicología
5. la secretaria general y el profesor
6. el inglés y el español
7. la clase en la biblioteca
8. el libro en la librería

MINIDIÁLOGOS Y GRAMÁTICA

1. NOUNS AND ARTICLES: GENDER AND NUMBER

En *una universidad* bilingüe: *la oficina del secretario* general

ESTUDIANTE:	...y *una clase* más, por *la mañana.*
	¿*El inglés* 4 (cuatro)?
SECRETARIO:	Hmm... no.
ESTUDIANTE:	¿*La sicología* 1 (uno)?
SECRETARIO:	¡Imposible, *señorita!*
ESTUDIANTE:	¿*El cálculo* 2 (dos)?
SECRETARIO:	Por *la noche*, sí. No hay por *la mañana.*
ESTUDIANTE:	Pues... ¿*el español* 10 (diez)?
SECRETARIO:	*El español*, sí.
ESTUDIANTE:	¡Bueno, por fin!

What did each person say—sí or no—*about the possibility or desirability of taking the following courses?*

EL SECRETARIO   1. *el inglés 4*

LA ESTUDIANTE   2. *la sicología 1*

3. *el cálculo 2*

4. *el español 10*

At a bilingual university: the registrar's office
STUDENT: . . . and one more class, in the morning. English 4? SECRETARY: Hmm . . . no. STUDENT:
Psychology 1? SECRETARY: Impossible, Miss! STUDENT: Calculus 2? SECRETARY: At night, yes.
There aren't [any sections] in the morning. STUDENT: Well . . . Spanish 10? SECRETARY: Spanish,
yes. STUDENT: Good, at last!

Gender of Nouns; Singular Articles

A *noun* (**sustantivo**) is a word that is the name of a person, place, thing, or idea. In English, nouns can be masculine, feminine, or neuter.

Masculine: man, grandfather, boy
Feminine: woman, grandmother, girl
Neuter: yard, tree, love

In Spanish, all nouns are either masculine or feminine in *gender* (**género**). This is a purely grammatical feature of nouns; it does not mean that Spanish speakers perceive things or ideas as having masculine or feminine attributes.

SINGULAR NOUNS AND ARTICLES			
	Masculine		Feminine
Definite	**el** hombre **el** libro	*the man* *the book*	**la** mujer *the woman* **la** mesa *the table*
Indefinite	**un** hombre **un** libro	*a (one) man* *a (one) book*	**una** mujer *a (one) woman* **una** mesa *a (one) table*

A. Nouns that refer to male beings and most nouns that end in **-o** are *masculine* (**masculino**) in gender: **hombre** (*man*), **libro** (*book*).

Nouns that refer to female beings and most nouns that end in **-a, -ión, -tad,** and **-dad** are *feminine* (**femenino**): **mujer** (*woman*), **mesa** (*table*), **nación** (*nation*), **libertad** (*liberty*), **universidad** (*university*).

¡OJO!   A common exception is the word **día** which ends in **-a** but is masculine in gender: **el día.**

Nouns that have other endings and that do not refer to either male or female beings may be masculine or feminine. Their gender must be memorized.

B. In English, *the* is the *definite article* (**artículo definido**). In Spanish, the definite article for masculine singular nouns is **el;** for feminine singular nouns it is **la.**

C. In English, the *singular indefinite article* (**artículo indefinido**) is *a* or *an*. In Spanish, the indefinite article, like the definite article, must agree with the gender of the noun: **un** for masculine nouns, **una** for feminine nouns. **Un** and **una** can also mean *one* as well as *a* or *an*. Context determines the meaning.

D. Some nouns that refer to persons indicate gender according to the following patterns:

If masculine ends in **-o**, the feminine changes **-o** to **-a**:

el niño   *the boy* →   **la** niña   *the girl*
el consejero   *the counselor* →   **la** consejera   *the counselor*
                     (male)   (female)

If masculine ends in a consonant, the feminine adds **-a**:

el profesor   *the professor* →   **la** profesora   *the professor*
                     (male)   (female)

Many other nouns that refer to people have a single form. Gender is indicated by the article: **el estudiante, la estudiante; el cliente** (*the male client*), **la cliente** (*the female client*).*

E. Since the gender of all nouns must be memorized, it is best to learn the definite article along with the noun; that is, learn **el lápiz** rather than just **lápiz**. The definite article will be given with nouns in vocabulary lists in this book.

[Práctica A, B]†

Plural Nouns and Articles

PLURAL NOUNS AND ARTICLES			
		Singular	Plural
Definite	Nouns ending in a vowel	**el** libro **la** mesa	**los** libros **las** mesas	*the books* *the tables*
	Nouns ending in a consonant	**la** universidad **el** papel	**las** universidades **los** papeles	*the universities* *the papers*
Indefinite		**una** mesa **un** papel	**unas** mesas **unos** papeles	*some tables* *some papers*

A. Spanish nouns that end in a vowel form plurals by adding **-s**. Nouns that end in a consonant add **-es**. Nouns that end in the consonant **-z** change the **-z** to **-c** before adding **-es**: lápiz → lápices.

B. The definite and indefinite articles must also agree in gender and number with the plural nouns they describe. **Unos** and **unas** mean *some, several,* or *a few.*

*A few nouns ending in -e reflect gender: **el dependiente** (*the male clerk*), **la dependienta** (*the female clerk*).
†This reference is a regular feature of the grammar sections of *Puntos de partida*. It means that you are now prepared to do exercises A and B in the **Práctica** section.

C. In Spanish, the masculine plural form of a noun is used to refer to a group that includes both males and females.

> **los** amigos   *the friends* (both male and female)
> **los** extranjer**os**   *the foreigners* (males and females)

Hay

Hay means *there is* or *there are.*

Hay un estudiante en la oficina.	*There is a student in the office.*
Hay unos estudiantes en la oficina.	*There are a few students in the office.*

[Práctica C, D, E]*

PRÁCTICA

A. *Dé* (give) *el artículo definido.*

1. consejero
2. biblioteca
3. hombre
4. inglés
5. niña
6. clase
7. dinero
8. nación

Dé el artículo indefinido.

9. momento
10. consejera
11. cuaderno
12. noche
13. papel
14. día
15. mujer
16. dependiente

B. *Cambie* (change):   *artículo definido → artículo indefinido*
                              artículo indefinido →artículo definido

1. el diccionario
2. la dependienta
3. el profesor
4. la mañana
5. el bolígrafo
6. una universidad
7. un día
8. un niño
9. una librería
10. una clase

C. *Dé la forma plural.*

1. la mesa
2. el libro
3. el amigo
4. la oficina
5. un cuaderno
6. un lápiz
7. una extranjera
8. un bolígrafo

---

*You are now prepared to do **Práctica C, D, E,** *and* **Conversación.**

Dé la forma singular.

9. los profesores
10. las secretarias
11. las niñas
12. unas tardes
13. unos lápices
14. unos papeles

D. *Which of the words listed to the right might be used to refer to the person(s) named to the left?*

1. Ana María: consejero mujer dependiente estudiante
2. Tomás: niño consejera profesor secretaria
3. Margarita y Juan: extranjeros amigos hombres estudiantes

E. *¿Cómo se dice en español?*

1. the students (*male and female*)
2. some universities
3. a clerk (*female*)
4. the foreigners
5. the secretaries (*male*)
6. some professors (*female*)

CONVERSACIÓN

A. *Give the male or female counterpart of each of the following persons.*

MODELO Marta, la secretaria → Pablo, *el secretario*
Carlos, un niño → Carlota, *una niña*

1. Carmen Castellano, la profesora César Cárdenas, _____
2. Camilo, un estudiante Conchita, _____
3. Juan Luis, el dependiente Juanita, _____
4. Josefina, una amiga Jorge, _____

B. *How many objects can you identify in this picture of a student's room? Begin each sentence with* **hay,** *and use the indefinite article with each noun that you mention.*

Hay _____ **en el cuarto** (*room*).

C. *Identifique las personas, las cosas y los lugares.*

MODELO   Hay ____ en ____. → Hay *un libro* en *la mesa.*

1.   2.   3.   4.   5.

2. SUBJECT PRONOUNS

Singular		Plural	
yo	*I*	**nosotros, nosotras**	*we*
tú	*you* (familiar)	**vosotros, vosotras**	*you* (familiar)
usted (Ud.)	*you* (formal)	**ustedes (Uds.)**	*you* (formal)
él	*he*	**ellos** ⎫	*they*
ella	*she*	**ellas** ⎭	

The *subject* **(sujeto)** of a sentence is the word or group of words about which something is said or asserted. Usually the subject indicates who or what performs the action of the sentence: *The **girl** threw the ball.*
    Indicate the subjects in the following sentences:

1. Olga is going to write a letter.
2. The car ran off the road.
3. Have Jack and Joyce arrived yet?
4. Love conquers all.

A *pronoun* (**pronombre**) is a word used in place of a noun: *She* [*the girl*] *threw the ball.* What English pronouns would you use in place of the subjects in the preceding four sentences?

Spanish subject pronouns are used as follows:

A. Several subject pronouns have masculine and feminine forms: **nosotros, nosotras; vosotros, vosotras; ellos, ellas.** The masculine plural form is used to refer to a group of males and females.

B. Note that, in general, the English subject pronoun *it* has no equivalent in Spanish: **Es para la clase** (*It is for the class*).

C. Spanish has two different words for *you* (singular): **tú** and **usted. Usted** is generally used to address persons with whom the speaker has a formal relationship. Use **usted** with people whom you call by their title and last name **(Sr. Gutiérrez, profesora Hernández),** or with people you don't know very well. Students generally address their teachers with **usted.** In some parts of the Spanish-speaking world, children use **usted** with their parents, in order to show respect.

   Tú implies a familiar relationship. Use **tú** when you would address a person by his or her first name, with close friends or relatives, and with children and pets. Students usually address each other as **tú.** If you are unsure about whether to use **tú** or **usted,** it is better to use **usted.** The native speaker can always suggest that you call him or her **tú** if that form is more appropriate.

D. The plural of **usted** is **ustedes.** In Latin America, as well as in the United States, **ustedes** also serves as the plural of **tú.** In Spain, however, the plural of **tú** is **vosotros/vosotras,** which is used when speaking to two or more persons whom you would call **tú** individually.

E. **Usted** and **ustedes** are frequently abbreviated in writing as **Ud.** or **Vd.,** and **Uds.** or **Vds.,** respectively. *Puntos de partida* will use **Ud.** and **Uds.**

PRÁCTICA

A. *What subject pronoun would you use to speak* about *the following persons?*

   1. yourself
   2. two men
   3. a female child
   4. yourself (*m.*) and a female friend
   5. yourself (*f.*) and a female friend
   6. your uncle Jorge
   7. your aunts Ana and Elena

B. *What subject pronoun would you use to speak* to *the following persons?*

   1. una profesora
   2. unos consejeros
   3. un niño

4. unas amigas
5. un dependiente
6. un estudiante
7. mamá

C. *What subject pronoun would you* substitute *for each of the following persons?*

1. Eva
2. Luis
3. Fausto y yo (*m.*)
4. tú (*m.*) y Cecilia
5. Vicente y David
6. Graciela y yo (*f.*)

3. PRESENT TENSE OF -AR VERBS

Una fiesta para los estudiantes internacionales

CARLOS: ¿No *desean* Uds. bailar?
ALFONSO: ¡Cómo no! Yo *bailo* con Mary. Ella *habla* inglés.
TERESA: Yo *hablo* francés y *bailo* con Jacques.
CARLOS: Y yo *bailo* con Gretchen.
GRETCHEN: Sólo si *pagas* las cervezas. ¡*Bailas* muy mal!

Who made—or might have made—each of the following statements?
1. Yo bailo con Jacques.
2. Yo hablo inglés.
3. Yo hablo alemán (German).
4. Nosotros hablamos francés.
5. Yo bailo con Alfonso.
6. ¡Yo no bailo mal!

HABLAR: *to speak*	
Singular	**Plural**
yo hablo	nosotros/as hablamos
tú hablas	vosotros/as habláis
Ud. ⎫	Uds. ⎫
él ⎬ habla	ellos ⎬ hablan
ella ⎭	ellas ⎭

A party for international students
CARLOS: Don't you want to dance? ALFONSO: Of course! I'll dance with Mary. She speaks English.
TERESA: I speak French and I'll dance with Jacques. CARLOS: And I'll dance with Gretchen.
GRETCHEN: Only if you buy (pay for) the beers! You dance very badly!

Infinitives and Personal Endings

A *verb* (**verbo**) is a word that indicates an action or a state of being: *We run, The house is in San Antonio.* The *infinitive* (**infinitivo**) of a verb indicates the action or state of being with no reference to who or what performs the action, or when it is done (present, past, or future). In English the infinitive is indicated by *to: to run, to be.* In Spanish all infinitives end in **-ar, -er,** or **-ir.** The regular **-ar** verbs, like **hablar,** are the first and largest group of Spanish verbs.

To *conjugate* (**conjugar**) a verb means to give the various forms of the verb with their subjects: *I speak, you speak, he (she, it) speaks, we speak, you speak, they speak.* In the English present tense, the conjugated forms of regular verbs vary little; there are only two forms: *run* and *runs.*

In Spanish, however, there are six forms, as shown in the conjugation of **hablar.** All regular Spanish verbs are conjugated by adding *personal endings* (**terminaciones personales**) that reflect the person doing the action. These are added to the *stem* (**raíz** or **radical**). The stem of a regular verb is the infinitive minus the infinitive ending: **habl̸a̸r̸ → habl-.**

The following personal endings are added to the stem of all regular **-ar** Spanish verbs: **-o, -as, -a, -amos, -áis, -an.** Notice that the vowel **-a** appears in all present tense endings except the first person singular, **yo hablo.**

Important **-ar** verbs in this chapter include:

bailar	to dance	**hablar**	to speak, talk
buscar	to look for	**necesitar**	to need
cantar	to sing	**pagar**	to pay (for)
comprar	to buy	**regresar**	to return
desear	to want	**tomar**	to take; to drink
enseñar	to teach	**trabajar**	to work
estudiar	to study		

¡OJO! In Spanish the meaning of the English word *for* is included in the verbs **pagar** (*to pay for*) and **buscar** (*to look for*).

As in English, when two Spanish verbs are used in sequence and there is no change of subject, the second verb is usually the infinitive.

Necesito **trabajar.** *I need to work.*
Desean **bailar.** *They want to dance.*

English Equivalents for Present Tense

In both English and Spanish, conjugated verb forms also indicate the *time* or *tense* (**tiempo**) of the action: *I run* (present), *I ran* (past).

The present tense forms of Spanish verbs correspond to three English equivalents.

hablo		
	I speak	Simple present tense
	I am speaking	Present progressive to indicate an action in progress
	I do speak	Emphatic present to give special emphasis

In Spanish, the present tense forms can also be used to indicate near future actions.

Hablo con Juan mañana.   *I'll speak with John tomorrow.*

[Práctica A]

Use and Omission of Subject Pronouns

In English, a verb must have an expressed subject (a noun or pronoun): *he/she/the train returns.* In Spanish, an expressed subject is not required; verbs are accompanied by a subject only for the sake of clarity, emphasis, or contrast.

1. *Clarification.* When the context does not make the subject clear, the subject pronoun is expressed: *usted/él/ella* **habla;** *ustedes/ellos/ellas* **hablan.**
2. *Emphasis.* Subject pronouns are used in Spanish to emphasize the subject when in English you would stress it with your voice.

Yo hablo bien.   *I* (not he, not you) *speak well.*

3. *Contrast.* Contrast is a special case of emphasis. Subject pronouns are used to contrast the actions of two individuals or groups.

Ellos hablan mucho; **nosotros**   *They talk a lot; we talk little.*
hablamos poco.

Negation

A Spanish sentence is made negative by placing the word **no** before the conjugated verb. No equivalent for the English words *do* or *does* is necessary.

El señor **no** habla inglés.   *The man doesn't speak English.*
No, **no** necesitamos dinero.   *No, we don't need money.*

¡OJO!   Notice the repetition of the word **no** in the previous sentence.
        The first **no** expresses the English word *no,* and the second **no**
        expresses the English word *not (don't).*

                                                            [Práctica B, C, D]

PRÁCTICA

A. *Dé Ud. frases nuevas según las indicaciones.*   (Give new sentences according to
   the cues.)

   1. —En la clase de español ¿quién (*who*) estudia español?
      —*Ud.* estudia español. (*nosotros, yo, ellos, Jacinto, tú, vosotras*)
   2. —¿Quién necesita un lápiz?
      —*Ella* necesita un lápiz. (*yo, Eugenio y tú, tú, nosotras, Ada, vosotros*)
   3. —¿Quién toma Coca-Cola en una fiesta?
      —*Clara* toma Coca-Cola. (*tú, Ud., él, Uds., Elena y yo, vosotras*)
   4. —¿Quién canta y baila en una fiesta?
      —*Tú* bailas y cantas. (*nosotros, los amigos, Uds., Irene y Diego, yo, vosotros*)

B. *Exprese en forma negativa.*

   1. Necesito el dinero.
   2. Ellos cantan en español.
   3. Paula desea tomar una cerveza.
   4. Yo trabajo todas las noches (*every night*).
   5. Ud. enseña muy bien.

C. *Form complete sentences by using one word or phrase from each column. Be sure
   to use the correct form of the verbs. Make any of the sentences negative, if you
   wish.*

   MODELO   *Jorge y yo regresamos por la noche.*
              Ud. trabaja en una oficina.

Jorge y yo		comprar	las cervezas
Ud.		regresar	francés
tú	(no)	buscar	la biblioteca
yo		trabajar	en una oficina
el dependiente		enseñar	por la noche
Uds.		pagar	lápices en la librería
		desear	hablar bien el español
		necesitar	trabajar más (*more*)
			estudiar más
			comprar unos cuadernos

D. *¿Cómo se dice en español?*

   1. We work in an office.
   2. *She* teaches French; *he* teaches English.

3. They're not buying the notebook.
4. John won't pay for the pens tomorrow.
5. *You (fam. s.)* are looking for the bookstore.
6. He's singing, but she's working.

CONVERSACIÓN

A. *Tell what these people are doing. Note that the definite article is used with titles—* **el señor, la señora, la señorita, el/la profesor(a)**—*when talking about a person.*

1. La Srta. Martínez _____.

2. Los estudiantes _____.

3. La estudiante _____.   4. La profesora Gil _____.   5. El Sr. Valdés _____.

6. El hombre _____.   7. Los alumnos _____.

B. *Preguntas. Conteste en oraciones completas.*

1. ¿Ud. estudia mucho o poco? ¿Estudia Ud. en la librería o en la biblioteca? ¿Canta Ud. muy bien o muy mal? ¿Toma mucho o poco? ¿Regresa a casa *(home)* por la tarde o por la noche?

2. ¿Uds. estudian español? ¿Hablan español en clase? ¿Hablan inglés en la clase de español? ¿Desean hablar español muy bien?

3. ¿El/la profesor(a) _____ habla español? ¿Enseña español? ¿Trabaja en una oficina de la universidad? ¿Un secretario trabaja aquí en la clase?

4. ¿La universidad paga la matrícula *(registration fees)*? ¿Los estudiantes necesitan pagar la matrícula? ¿los libros de texto? ¿Necesitan comprar lápices? ¿un diccionario? ¿Compran libros de texto en la biblioteca?

4. ASKING YES/NO QUESTIONS

There are two kinds of questions: information questions and yes/no questions. Questions that ask for new information or facts that the speaker does not know often begin with *interrogative words* such as *who*, *what*, etc. *Yes/no questions*, however, are those which require a simple *yes* or *no* answer.

Do you speak French? → No, I don't (speak French).

Rising Intonation

A common way to form yes/no questions in Spanish is simply to make your voice rise at the end of the question.

Statement:

Ud. trabaja aquí todos los días.   El niño regresa a casa hoy.
You work here every day.   *The boy is returning home today.*

Question:

¿Ud. trabaja aquí todos los días?   ¿El niño regresa a casa hoy?
Do you work here every day?   *Is the boy returning home today?*

There is no Spanish equivalent to English *do* or *does* in questions. Note also the use of an inverted question mark (¿) at the beginning of questions.

Inversion

Another way to form yes/no questions is to invert the order of the subject and verb, in addition to making your voice rise at the end of the question.

Statement:

    Ud. trabaja aquí todos los días.   **El niño** regresa a casa hoy.

Question:

    ¿Trabaja **Ud.** aquí todos los días?   ¿Regresa **el niño** a casa hoy?

PRÁCTICA

A. *Forme dos preguntas, según el modelo.*

    MODELO   Irma habla español. → *¿Habla Irma español?*

                          → *¿Irma habla español?*

    1. Ud. regresa a clase mañana.
    2. Elvira busca un cuaderno.
    3. Ramón toma cerveza.
    4. Ud. paga hoy.
    5. Uds. enseñan historia aquí.
    6. Ellos bailan todos los días.
    7. Ella trabaja mañana.

B. *Ask the questions that led to the following answers. Follow the model.*

    MODELO   Sí, bailo con Guillermo. → *¿Baila Ud. con Guillermo?*
                                    ¿Bailas (tú) con Guillermo?

    1. No, no regreso a casa hoy.
    2. Sí, estudiamos mucho.
    3. Sí, ella habla muy bien.
    4. No, no trabajo aquí todos los días.
    5. Sí, busco el diccionario.
    6. No, no necesitamos un lápiz.

CONVERSACIÓN

A. *Ask another student the following questions about what he or she is going to do tomorrow.*

    1. ¿Pagas la matrícula mañana?
    2. ¿Compras el texto en la librería mañana?
    3. ¿Tomas cerveza en clase?
    4. ¿Deseas bailar en clase?
    5. ¿Regresas a clase?

B. *Now ask your Spanish professor the preceding questions. Begin each question with*
    "Profesor(a) _____." Remember to use **usted.**

C. *Preguntas. Conteste en oraciones completas.*

    1. ¿Quién (*who*) enseña la clase mañana? ¿los estudiantes? ¿la consejera?
        ¿el presidente de la universidad? ¿el presidente de México?
    2. En una fiesta, ¿qué (*what*) no desean Uds. hacer (*to do*)? ¿estudiar? ¿pagar?
        ¿cantar? ¿trabajar? ¿bailar con el/la profesor(a)?

5. NUMBERS 1–30

Canción infantil
Dos y dos son cuatro,
cuatro y dos son seis,
seis y dos son ocho,
y ocho dieciséis.

© Marc & Evelyne Bernheim 1980/Woodfin Camp & Assoc.

0	cero				
1	uno	11	once	21	veintiuno
2	dos	12	doce	22	veintidós
3	tres	13	trece	23	veintitrés
4	cuatro	14	catorce	24	veinticuatro
5	cinco	15	quince	25	veinticinco
6	seis	16	dieciséis	26	veintiséis
7	siete	17	diecisiete	27	veintisiete
8	ocho	18	dieciocho	28	veintiocho
9	nueve	19	diecinueve	29	veintinueve
10	diez	20	**veinte**	30	**treinta**

A Child's Song   Two and two are four, four and two are six, six and two are eight, and eight are sixteen.

Uno is the form used in counting. It becomes **un** before masculine singular nouns, and its feminine form is **una**. Numbers that end in **-uno** also have masculine and feminine forms.

veinti**ún** niños	*twenty-one children*
veinti**una** personas	*twenty-one persons*

No other numbers from 0 to 30 show gender.

The numbers sixteen through nineteen may also be written as **diez y seis, diez y siete, diez y ocho,** and **diez y nueve.** The numbers twenty-one through twenty-nine have the same kind of alternate spelling: **veinte y uno, veinte y dos,** and so on. The combined form is somewhat more common in contemporary usage.

PRÁCTICA

A. *Practique los números.*

1. 19 señores	6. 16 papeles
2. 7 clases	7. 30 días
3. 4 señoras	8. 11 lápices
4. 14 fiestas	9. 21 profesoras
5. 12 amigos	10. 15 estudiantes

B. *Problemas de matemáticas.*

+ y	− menos	= son

MODELO $2 + 2 = ?$ → *Dos y dos son cuatro.*

1. $2 + 3 = ?$	5. $29 - 2 = ?$
2. $8 + 17 = ?$	6. $30 - 16 = ?$
3. $14 + 4 = ?$	7. $13 + 15 = ?$
4. $23 - 13 = ?$	8. $11 + 0 = ?$

CONVERSACIÓN

En la librería. *You have just asked the clerk the prices of three different models or brands of something you need to buy. In each case you want to buy the least expensive model. What is the price of the item you finally select?*

1. veintiséis pesos	trece pesos	treinta pesos
2. dieciocho dólares	veintiocho dólares	ocho dólares

3. dos pesos   doce pesos   un peso
4. seis pesetas   nueve pesetas   siete pesetas
5. veintiún dólares   diecisiete dólares diecinueve dólares

Now make up five similar choices between prices and present them orally to your classmates.

DIÁLOGO: En la universidad

A. *En la Oficina del° Secretario General, Universidad de Guadalajara,*   of the
   México

   David, estudiante extranjero
   La Sra. Jiménez, secretaria

DAVID:	Perdón, señora.	
SRA. JIMÉNEZ:	Buenos días. ¿Qué desea Ud.?	
DAVID:	Necesito los papeles de la matrícula, por favor.	
SRA. JIMÉNEZ:	¿Para° estudiantes extranjeros?	*for*
DAVID:	Sí. Hablo inglés y deseo estudiar español aquí en la universidad, en el curso para extranjeros.	
SRA. JIMÉNEZ:	Pues para extranjero Ud. habla muy bien el español. Un momento, por favor...	
DAVID:	Cómo no.°	**Cómo...** *Of course.*

(*Ella busca los papeles y regresa.*)

SRA. JIMÉNEZ:	Ahora bien°, para estudiantes extranjeros los papeles blancos°.	**Ahora...** *now then* *white*
DAVID:	Muchas gracias, señora.	
SRA. JIMÉNEZ:	De nada. ¿Por qué° no habla Ud. con la consejera para estudiantes extranjeros? Ella también° habla inglés.	**¿Por...** *why?* *also*

DAVID: Muy bien. Si es necesario, regreso mañana.
          Gracias, ¿eh? Hasta luego.
SRA. JIMÉNEZ: De nada. Adiós.

B. *En la librería*

David, estudiante extranjero
Marcos, dependiente de la librería y amigo de David

DAVID: Buenas tardes, Marcos.
MARCOS: Hola, David. ¿Qué tal?
DAVID: Bien, gracias. ¿Trabajas tú aquí en la librería?
MARCOS: Sí, yo trabajo aquí todas las tardes y tomo clases por la
          mañana. ¿Qué necesitas?
DAVID: Pues necesito un diccionario español-inglés, un dic-   *good / big / cheap*
          cionario bueno°, grande° y barato°.
MARCOS: Bueno y completo, sí, pero°... ¿barato? ¡No hay!   *but*
DAVID: También necesito dos cuadernos, un bolígrafo, un lápiz,
          un libro de texto y...
MARCOS: ¡Y el dinero para pagar! Por eso° trabajo, David, por eso   **Por...** *that's why*
          trabajo.

Comprensión

Conteste en oraciones completas.

A. 1. ¿Con quién (*whom*) habla David?
    2. ¿Qué desea David?
    3. ¿Habla David bien el español?
    4. ¿Qué papeles busca la Sra. Jiménez?
    5. ¿La consejera habla sólo español?

B. 1. ¿Quién trabaja en la librería?
    2. ¿Toma clases Marcos todas las tardes?
    3. ¿Qué típo de (*what kind of*) diccionario necesita David?
    4. ¿Qué más (*what else*) necesita David?
    5. ¿Y qué necesita para pagar?

Comentario cultural

The educational system in Hispanic countries differs considerably from that of the
United States. The **escuela primaria**—sometimes called the **colegio**—corresponds
to our elementary school and consists of from five to seven years of instruction.
The **escuela secundaria** (also called **liceo**, **instituto**, or **colegio**) provides secondary
education. Students who complete their secondary education receive the

bachillerato. In some countries, many students attend an additional year or two of **preparatoria** before entering the university.

At the university, students immediately begin specialized programs leading to a professional degree (**título**) in areas such as law, medicine, engineering, or the humanities. These university-level programs of study are established by ministries of education, and there are almost no electives. Students are required to take as many as eight different subjects in a single academic term. The lecture system is even more prevalent than it is in the United States, and university students take oral exams, as well as written ones. In most countries, performance is evaluated on a scale of one to ten, with seven considered passing.

A number of universities in Spain and Latin America have arranged special courses for foreign students (**cursos para extranjeros**). Such courses are designed for students whose special interest is the study of Spanish language, literature, and culture.

UN POCO DE TODO

A. *Cambie por el plural.*

MODELO   Ella paga el cuaderno. → *Ellas pagan los cuadernos.*

1. Él no desea tomar una cerveza.
2. Ud. baila con un estudiante.
3. ¿Compro el lápiz mañana?
4. Por eso hablas con la dependienta.
5. ¿Hay sólo una extranjera en el curso?

Cambie por el singular.

6. Ellas no buscan el dinero.
7. ¿Enseñan Uds. sólo dos clases de español?
8. Necesitamos unos libros de texto.
9. Las mujeres estudian sicología.
10. ¿Pagan Uds. sólo 30 pesos?

B. *Form complete sentences based on the words given, in the order given. Conjugate the verbs and add other words if necessary.*

MODELO   yo / hablar / español / clase → *Yo hablo español en clase.*

1. Uds. / comprar / papel / para / clase
2. ¿ / trabajar / Paco / aquí / librería / todas las noches / ?
3. Sr. Gil / yo / regresar / universidad / mañana
4. extranjero / no / hablar / bien / inglés
5. ¿ / hay / 21 / mujeres / y / sólo / 15 / hombres / ?

C. *Complete the following story by arranging the last five sentences in the proper order.*

Una noche hay una fiesta en la universidad. Marcos habla mucho con Ana y los dos cantan y bailan un poco. Pronto (*soon*) desean tomar una Coca-Cola...

   Marcos busca la Coca-Cola y regresa.
   Por eso regresa a la biblioteca y Ana baila hasta la mañana con Pablo.
   Toman la Coca-Cola y también bailan un poco más.
   Marcos no desea regresar pero necesita estudiar —toma seis clases.
   Desean bailar más, pero Marcos necesita regresar a la biblioteca para estudiar.

D. *Describe the following persons by telling what they do.*

   1. Un secretario _____.
   2. Una profesora _____.
   3. Un estudiante _____.
   4. Una dependienta _____.
   5. Vikki Carr _____.
   6. José Greco _____.

E. *Complete las oraciones en una forma lógica.*

   1. (No) Deseo bailar con _____.
   2. En clase (no) hay _____.
   3. En clase (no) necesitamos _____.
   4. En clase (no) deseamos _____.
   5. En la librería, busco _____.
   6. Regreso a _____ todos los días.
   7. (No) Deseo hablar con _____.
   8. El/la profesor(a) necesita _____.

VOCABULARIO

VERBOS
bailar to dance
buscar to look for
cantar to sing
comprar to buy
desear to want
enseñar to teach
estudiar to study
hablar to speak, talk
hay there is, there are
necesitar to need
pagar to pay (for)
regresar to return
 regresar a casa to go home
tomar to take; to drink
trabajar to work

SUSTANTIVOS
el **alemán** German (*language*)
el/la **amigo/a** friend
la **biblioteca** library
el **bolígrafo** pen
la **cerveza** beer
las **ciencias** sciences
la **clase** class
el/la **consejero/a** counselor
la **cosa** thing
el **cuaderno** notebook
el **curso** course
el/la **dependiente/a** clerk
el **día** day
el **diccionario** dictionary

el **dinero** money
el **dólar** dollar
el **español** Spanish (*language*)
el/la **estudiante** student
el/la **extranjero/a** foreigner
la **fiesta** party
el **francés** French (*language*)
la **historia** history
el **hombre** man
el **inglés** English (*language*)
el **lápiz** pencil
 (*pl.* **lápices**)
la **librería** bookstore
el **libro** book
el **libro de texto** textbook
el **lugar** place
la **mañana** morning
las **matemáticas** mathematics
la **materia** subject (*school*)
la **matrícula** registration fees
la **mesa** table
la **mujer** woman
el/la **niño/a** child; boy/girl
la **noche** night
la **oficina** office
el **papel** paper
la **persona** person
la **peseta** *unit of currency in Spain*
el **peso** *unit of currency in Mexico and several other Latin American countries*
el/la **profesor(a)** professor
el/la **secretario/a** secretary

el/la **secretario/a general** registrar
la **sicología** psychology
la **tarde** afternoon, evening
la **universidad** university

PALABRAS Y EXPRESIONES ÚTILES
a to
aquí here
con with
de of, from
en in; on; at
hoy today
mal badly
mañana tomorrow
más more
mucho much, a lot
no no; not
o or
para for; in order to
pero but
poco little; a little bit
por in (*the morning, evening, etc.*)
por eso that's why; therefore
pues... well . . .
¿qué? what?
¿quién? who? whom?
si if
sí yes
sólo only
también also
y and

Un paso más 1

Actividades

A. **¿Qué estudias?** The right-hand column lists a number of subjects **(materias)** that are studied at the university. The written forms of most of these are very similar to those of their English equivalents, but many of them *sound* very different. Tell about your academic interests and those of other people by creating sentences using one word or phrase from each column.

(No) Estudio _____.
(No) Deseo estudiar _____.
(No) Necesito estudiar _____.
_____ estudia _____.
  (estudiante)
El profesor _____
        (nombre)
  enseña _____.

La profesora _____
        (nombre)
  enseña _____.

español, francés, inglés
arte, filosofía, literatura, música
ciencias políticas, historia,
  sicología, sociología
biología, física, ingeniería,
  matemáticas, química

B. **Entrevista.** Interview another student by asking the following questions—or any others that occur to you—without taking notes. Then present as much of the information as you can to your classmates. (Use the **tú** form when speaking to another student.)

MODELO   *David estudia literatura, trabaja en McDonald's y baila mucho.*

1. ¿Estudias matemáticas? ¿literatura? ¿sicología? ¿química?
2. ¿Estudias en casa (*at home*) o en la biblioteca?
3. ¿Por la mañana tomas café o té?
4. ¿Trabajas? ¿Dónde (*where*)?
5. ¿En una fiesta bailas o hablas?
6. ¿En una fiesta tomas cerveza, vino o Coca-Cola?

A propósito...

When you first begin to study Spanish, you may think that you can speak only in very simple sentences because your knowledge of Spanish vocabulary and grammar seems limited. The following words can help you to form more complex sentences by linking together two or more words, phrases, or short sentences.

y	*and*
también	*also*
pero	*but*
por eso	*therefore*

Note the different impression made by the following sentences.

María enseña inglés. Estudia francés. → María enseña inglés *y* estudia francés.

Pepe canta bien. José canta mal. → Pepe canta bien *pero* José canta mal.

No bailo bien. No bailo con Juana. → No bailo bien, *por eso* no bailo con Juana.

C. **Las correcciones de la profesora.** As Professor Jiménez corrects the compositions of her first-year Spanish students, she finds that the following pairs of sentences are all grammatically correct, but they could be combined. Consider the probable relationship between the two sentences, and using the words given in **A propósito,** combine them as you think she might.

1. Hans habla alemán. Estudia inglés.
2. Gina habla italiano y francés. No habla español.
3. Necesitamos comprar un diccionario. Buscamos una librería.
4. Esteban toma Coca-Cola. Yo tomo cerveza.
5. Marta estudia ciencias. Necesita estudiar matemáticas.
6. Julio canta mal. Baila bien.
7. Necesito más dinero. Regreso a casa.
8. Ellos estudian el capítulo uno. Nosotros estudiamos el capítulo dos.
9. Delia necesita pagar la matrícula. Trabaja todas las tardes.
10. Anita baila bien la samba. No baila bien el chachachá.

	4 de octubre	5 de octubre
8:00	*Matemáticas I*	*Matemáticas I*
9:00	*Biblioteca*	
10:00		*Matemáticas II*
11:00		
12:00		
1:00	*Profª García*	*librería / bolígrafo (Pedro)*
2:00	*Biblioteca*	*diccionario*
3:00		
4:00		*Cálculo III*
5:00		
	Coctel - Dávila	*Fiesta - estudiantes internacionales*

D. **El profesor distraído.** Although he is an excellent teacher, Professor Ramírez is more than a bit absent-minded. Today, October 4, is the beginning of a new academic year, and he is particularly confused about what he has to do. You work part-time as an assistant to Professor Ramírez, and you correct him when he gets his schedule confused. Use the schedule given here to help him get to the right place at the right time.

MODELO   Profesor Ramírez: —Hoy hay un coctel (*cocktail party*) en casa de la profesora Gómez.

               Ud.:   —*Sí, hay un coctel, pero en casa de la profesora Dávila.*

1. Enseño Matemáticas I por la tarde.
2. Mañana necesito hablar con la profesora García.
3. Hoy por la noche hay una fiesta de los estudiantes internacionales.
4. Mañana enseño Matemáticas II por la tarde.
5. Hoy por la tarde regreso a la librería.
6. Mañana necesito comprar un diccionario y un lápiz para Pedro.

E. **¡No me diga!** (*You don't say!*) Your Spanish teacher has made the following statements. Do you believe him/her or not? Respond with **Es verdad** if you think the statement is true or **Es falso** if you believe it to be false.

1. Hablo español, inglés y francés.
2. Bailo muy bien.
3. No regreso a casa hoy.
4. Por la noche trabajo con estudiantes extranjeros.

Now create at least four original statements—true or false—about yourself for your classmates to react to.

F.

UNIVERSIDAD DE SALAMANCA
XIV CURSO DE VERANO PARA EXTRANJEROS

© Peter Menzel

The **Universidad de Salamanca** is an old and famous Spanish university. In addition to its regular course of studies for native students, it offers a number of **cursos para extranjeros.**

By looking at the form from the **Universidad de Salamanca,** match these English words with their Spanish equivalents.

1. size
2. please print
3. nationality
4. place of birth
5. month
6. beginning/elementary level
7. intermediate level
8. advanced level
9. lodging (note: **colegio** = *dormitory*)
10. medical insurance

a. alojamiento
b. nacionalidad
c. tamaño
d. Por favor, escriba con letra de imprenta
e. iniciación
f. mes
g. superior
h. seguro médico
i. medio
j. lugar de nacimiento

Cursos Internacionales de Verano · Universidad de Salamanca
HOJA DE INSCRIPCION

Acompañar 3 fotografías tamaño pasaporte

Por favor, escriba con letra de imprenta

Apellido (Nom, last name)

Nombre (Prénom, first name)

Nacionalidad

Lugar de nacimiento

Fecha de nacimiento — Día   Mes   Año

Dirección actual (Present adress)

Residencia habitual (Home adress)

Profesión (Ocupation)

CURSOS OFRECIDOS (¹)

I. Curso de lengua y cultura españolas:
   a) Iniciación
   b) Medio
   c) Superior

Julio   Agosto

II. Curso intensivo de lengua española:
   a) Iniciación
   b) Medio
   c) Superior

III. Curso Superior de filología:

INSCRIPCIONES OPCIONALES

Colegio   Familia   No desea

¿Alojamiento?¹ . . . .
¿Abono piscina?² . . . . . .
¿Seguro médico?² . . . . . .
¿Actividades culturales?² . . . .
¿Clases de guitarra?² . . . .
¿Bailes regionales?² . . . . .
¿Ha asistido a los Cursos de esta Universidad en años anteriores? . . . .

(1) Ponga una cruz en el recuadro que convenga (Write an X in the apropiate box)
(2) Póngase SI o NO en el recuadro correspondiente. (Write in SI or NO in the corresponding box)

ENVIESE ESTA HOJA DE INSCRIPCION A (SEND THIS APPLICATION TO): **CURSOS INTERNA-CIONALES DE VERANO. PATIO DE ESCUELAS MENORES. UNIVERSIDAD DE SALAMANCA**

Now ask another student for the required information. You don't need to ask complicated questions. To find out the other student's last name, simply ask, **¿Apellido?** using the rising intonation that tells the listener that you are asking a question.

Lectura cultural: Los gestos°

gestures

Hablamos con la boca° y también con el cuerpo°. Cada° nacionalidad expresa una parte de su° personalidad con los movimientos del cuerpo, con los gestos. Los italianos son famosos porque° hablan con las manos°; los ingleses, por lo general°, no usan muchos gestos. Aquí hay unos gestos hispánicos.

mouth / body / each
its
because
hands / **por...** generally

1. Adiós.

2. No.

3. Dinero.

4. Así así.

5. ¿Tomamos algo°?

6. Un momentito.

7. Es tacaño°.   *something/
tight, stingy*

Comprensión

A. Put the following words in order. Don't change the form of the words.

1. y / la / hablamos / boca / con / cuerpo / el
2. los / la / gestos / personalidad / expresan
3. las / manos / hablan / con / los / italianos
4. no / gestos / usan / ingleses / muchos / los

B. As one of your classmates or your instructor makes one of the gestures, write or say in Spanish its verbal equivalent.

Ejercicio escrito

Describe how we talk by forming original sentences with one word or phrase from each column.

yo		mucho
los profesores		poco
los estudiantes	hablo	con las manos
el/la consejero/a		demasiado (*too much*)
el señor _____	habla	por teléfono (todos los días)
la señorita/señora _____		en clase (todos los días)
nosotros los americanos	hablamos	ahora (*now*)
_____ y yo		mañana
los hombres/las mujeres	hablan	con _____
_____		_____

capítulo 2 La familia

Peter Menzel/Stock, Boston

OBJETIVOS

In this chapter you will learn vocabulary and expressions related to family relationships. And you will learn a variety of adjectives—many of which are very similar to English words—that you will be able to use to describe people, places, and things.

You will also learn about the following aspects of Spanish grammar:

6. the present tense of the irregular verb **ser,** one of the two Spanish verbs meaning *to be*

7. how to indicate possession and ownership
8. the contractions **del** (*of the*) and **al** (*to the*)
9. the forms and placement of adjectives
10. how to express the hour and to indicate at what time something takes place

Un paso más includes activities relating to the family and to Hispanic names, as well as a reading about **el compadrazgo** (the close relationship that exists between a child's parent and godparents).

VOCABULARIO: PREPARACIÓN

La familia y los parientes°   *relatives*

la madre (mamá)	mother (mom)	**la nieta**	granddaughter
el padre (papá)	father (dad)	**el nieto**	grandson
la hija	daughter	**la prima**	cousin (female)
el hijo	son	**el primo**	cousin (male)
la hermana	sister	**la tía**	aunt
el hermano	brother	**el tío**	uncle
la esposa	wife	**la sobrina**	niece
el esposo	husband	**el sobrino**	nephew
la abuela	grandmother		
el abuelo	grandfather		

A. *¿Quiénes son?*   (Who are they?)

los abuelos
(*grandparents*)

los padres
(*parents*)

los hijos
(*children*)

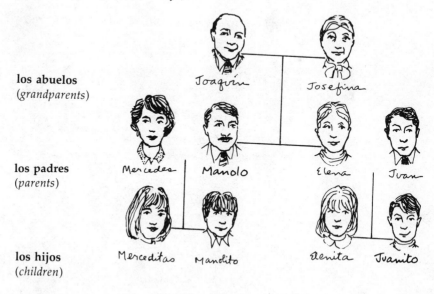

1. Los parientes de **Juanito:**

MODELO   Manolo es *el tío* de Juanito y Mercedes es *la tía.*

a. Juan es _____ y Elena es _____.

b. Joaquín es _____ y Josefina es _____.

c. Manolito es _____ y Merceditas es _____.

2. Los parientes de **Josefina:**
    a. Joaquín es _____ de Josefina.
    b. Manolo es _____; Elena es _____.
    c. Merceditas es _____ y Manolito es _____.
3. Los parientes de **Manolo:**
    a. Mercedes es _____ de Manolo.
    b. Elenita es _____ y Juanito es _____.
    c. Elena es _____.

Adjetivos

alto	tall	**joven**	young	**simpático**	nice;
bajo	short (in height)	**viejo**	old		likeable
grande	large, big	**nuevo**	new	**antipático**	unpleasant
pequeño	small	**bueno**	good	**trabajador**	hard-
guapo	handsome,	**malo**	bad		working
	good-looking	**listo**	smart,	**perezoso**	lazy
bonito	pretty		clever	**rico**	rich
feo	ugly	**tonto**	silly,	**pobre**	poor
corto	short (in		foolish	**alegre**	happy
	length)	**casado**	married	**triste**	sad
largo	long	**soltero**	single		

B. *Who is described by each of the following sentences?*

Einstein   el chimpancé

José   Roberto

1. _____ es listo.
   En comparación, _____ es tonto.

2. _____ es perezoso.
   _____ es trabajador.

1.95
1.60

Pepe   Pablo

Timoteo   Tomás

3. _____ es alto.
   _____ es bajo.

4. _____ es una persona alegre.
   _____ es una persona triste.

5. _____ es bueno y simpático.
   _____ es malo y antipático.
   _____ es guapo.
   _____ es feo.

6. _____ es un profesor joven.
   _____ es un profesor viejo.
   _____ es casado.
   _____ es soltero.

7. _____ es nuevo.
   _____ es viejo.
   _____ es largo.
   _____ es corto.

8. _____ es una familia grande y rica.
   _____ es una familia pequeña y pobre.

Más cognados

The following Spanish adjectives are cognates of English adjectives:
cruel, dramático, importante, inteligente, interesante, rebelde, religioso, responsable, romántico, sentimental, sincero.

C. *Describe* **Don Juan,** *the famous lover, in simple Spanish sentences that begin with* **Don Juan es . . .** *or* **Don Juan no es . . .,** *using some of the preceding adjectives.*

Now think of another well-known male figure—real or imaginary—and describe him. Try to describe as many qualities of the person as you can. For example:

El presidente es/no es...

Robert Redford es/no es...

PRONUNCIACIÓN: Stress and Written Accent Marks

In the words **hablar, papá, matrícula,** and **sobrino,** the italicized vowel is stressed (more prominent than the others). In Spanish, *stress* (**acentuación**) is predictable from the written form of the word.

1. If a word ends in a *vowel, n,* or *s,* stress normally falls on the next-to-the-last syllable.

   hablo   **ca**sa   **cla**se   **jo**ven   nece**si**tan   ha**bla**mos   **pri**mas

2. If a word ends in any other consonant, stress normally falls on the last syllable.

   traba**jar**   doc**tor**   espa**ñol**   us**ted**   ac**triz**

3. Any exception to these two rules will bear a written accent mark (**acento escrito**) on the stressed vowel.

   a**quí**   pa**pá**   na**ción**   fran**cés**   **lá**piz   **dó**lar   ma**trí**cula

4. When one-syllable words have accents, it is to distinguish them from *homonyms* (other words that sound like them). For example: **tú** (*you*)/**tu** (*your*); **él** (*he*)/**el** (*the*); **sí** (*yes*)/**si** (*if*).

5. Interrogative and exclamatory words carry a written accent on the stressed vowel. For example: **¿quién?** (*who?*), **¿dónde?** (*where?*), **¡cómo no!** (*of course!*).

PRÁCTICA

A. *Practique las siguientes palabras.*

1. hija alto bajo prima madre padre grande hermana bonito pequeño sobrina alegre interesante buscan cantan enseñan hablas pagas trabajas
2. pagar comprar desear regresar mujer trabajador libertad universidad papel español general sentimental
3. práctico matrícula romántico simpático antipático José así así Ramón nación perdón adiós francés inglés lápiz Gómez Pérez Ramírez Jiménez

B. *Indicate the stressed vowel of each word in the following list. Give the rule that determines the stress of each word.*

1. examen   2. lápiz   3. necesitar   4. perezoso   5. libertad   6. nación
7. hermana   8. compran   9. compramos   10. hombre   11. peso   12. mujer
13. matrícula   14. general   15. plástico   16. sobrinos

MINIDIÁLOGOS Y GRAMÁTICA

6. PRESENT TENSE OF *SER*

En la oficina de la profesora Castro

PROFESORA CASTRO: ¿*Es* éste el examen de Ud., Sr. Bermúdez?

RAÚL BERMÚDEZ: *Es* posible. ¿*Es* el examen de Raúl Bermúdez o de Jaime Bermúdez? *Somos* hermanos.

PROFESORA CASTRO: *Es* de Jaime Bermúdez, y *es* un suspenso.

RAÚL BERMÚDEZ: Pues *es* el suspenso de Jaime. ¡Yo *soy* Raúl!

1. *¿Con quién habla Raúl Bermúdez?*
2. *¿Raúl y Jaime son sobrinos?*
3. *¿Es Jaime profesor o estudiante?*
4. *¿Es el examen de Raúl o de Jaime?*

There are two Spanish verbs that mean *to be:* **ser** and **estar.** They are not interchangeable in any given context; the meaning that the speaker wishes to convey determines their use. In this section you will learn the forms of the irregular verb **ser** and some of its uses.

SER: *to be*			
yo	**soy**	nosotros/as	**somos**
tú	**eres**	vosotros/as	**sois**
usted		ustedes	
él	**es**	ellos	**son**
ella		ellas	

Uses of *Ser*

A. **Ser** is used to link the subject of a sentence to another NOUN.

Alicia y yo somos **amigos.**   *Alicia and I are friends.*
Cecilia es **profesora.**   *Cecilia is a professor.*

Note that in Spanish the indefinite article is not used after **ser** before unmodified (undescribed) nouns of profession.

[Práctica A]

In Professor Castro's office **PROFESSOR:** Is this your exam, Mr. Bermúdez? **RAÚL:** It's possible. Is it Raúl Bermúdez's exam or Jaime Bermúdez's? We're brothers. **PROFESSOR:** It's Jaime Bermúdez's, and it's an F. **RAÚL:** Well, the F is Jaime's. I'm Raúl!

B. **Ser** is used to express NATIONALITY; **ser** with **de** (*from*) is used to express national ORIGIN.

Juan es **peruano.**	*Juan is Peruvian.*
Somos **de los Estados Unidos.**	*We're from the United States.*
El dependiente es **de Cuernavaca.**	*The clerk is from Cuernavaca.*

[Práctica B]

C. **Ser** with **de** is used to express the MATERIAL something is made of.

La mesa es **de plástico.**	*The table is (made) of plastic.*
El coche es **de metal.**	*The car is (made) of metal.*

[Práctica C]

D. **Ser** with **para** is used to tell WHOM SOMETHING IS FOR.

La comida es **para Andrés.**	*The food is for Andrés.*
El regalo es **para usted.**	*The present is for you.*

[Práctica D]

E. **Ser** is used to form many IMPERSONAL EXPRESSIONS.

Es importante estudiar.	*It's important to study.*
No **es necesario** trabajar todos los días.	*It's not necessary·to work every day.*

Note the use of the infinitive after impersonal expressions.

[Práctica E, F, G]

PRÁCTICA

A. *Dé Ud. frases nuevas según las indicaciones.*

—¿Quién es estudiante?
—Ana es estudiante.   (*yo, Mario y Juan, Uds., Lilia y yo, tú, vosotros*)

B. *¿De dónde son?*   (Where are they from?)

Francia	Italia	Inglaterra (*England*)
México	los Estados Unidos	Alemania (*Germany*)

1. John Doe   2. Karl Lotze   3. Graziana Lazzarino
4. María Gómez   5. Claudette Moreau   6. Timothy Windsor

C. *¿De qué son estos* (these) *objetos?   ¿de metal?   ¿de plástico?   ¿de madera* (wood)? *¿de papel?*

1. el dinero   2. el lápiz   3. el libro
4. el cuaderno   5. el bolígrafo   6. la mesa

D. *¿Para quién son estas cosas? Conteste según el modelo.*

MODELO   el cuaderno / la profesora → *El cuaderno es para la profesora.*

1. la comida / los hijos
2. los papeles de la matrícula / la secretaria general
3. el regalo / Uds.
4. el dólar / la sobrina
5. la fiesta / Evangelina
6. la cerveza / nosotros

E. *Preguntas. Conteste en oraciones completas.*

1. ¿Es importante hablar español en la clase? ¿Es necesario hablar inglés? ¿Es posible tomar cerveza? ¿Es necesario trabajar mucho?
2. En una fiesta, ¿es posible bailar? ¿cantar? ¿Es necesario pagar las bebidas (*drinks*)? ¿Es necesario tomar mucho?

F. *Form complete sentences by using one word or phrase from each column.*

el diccionario		para Ernesto
los tíos		un coche
yo	eres	de Chile
Uds.	soy	doctoras
Carla y yo	(no) es	una ciudad (*city*)
tú	son	de papel
la fiesta	somos	de San Francisco
Madrid		consejeros
esto (*this*)		
____	____	____

G. *¿Quiénes son, de dónde son y dónde trabajan ahora (now)?*

MODELO   Teresa: actriz / de Madrid / en Cleveland →
           Teresa es actriz. Es de Madrid. Trabaja en Cleveland ahora.

1. Carlos Miguel: doctor / de Cuba / en Milwaukee
2. Maripili: extranjera / de Burgos / en Miami
3. Mariela: dependienta / de Buenos Aires / en Nueva York
4. Juan: artista* / de Lima / en Los Ángeles

*A number of professions end in **-ista** in both masculine and feminine forms. The article indicates gender: **el/la artista.**

CONVERSACIÓN

A. *Exchange information with your classmates about yourself and where you are from.*

MODELO   *Yo soy Carlos.   Soy estudiante.   Soy de Garfield Heights.   ¿Quién eres?*

B. *Can you identify the following figures—past and present—of the Spanish-speaking world?   Use the list of professions in the right-hand column as a guide.*

Eva Perón   artista
Roberto Clemente   soldado / soldada
Fidel Castro   conquistador / conquistadora
Hernán Cortés   actor / actriz
Pablo Neruda   político / política
Rita Moreno   beisbolista
Salvador Dalí   poeta / poetisa
Emiliano Zapata
Cantinflas

Study Hint: Learning Grammar

Learning a language is similar to learning any other skill; knowing *about* it is only part of what is involved.   Consider how you would acquire another skill, swimming, for example.   If you read all the available books on swimming, you will probably become an expert in talking *about* swimming and you will know what you *should* do in a pool.   Until you actually get into a pool and practice swimming, however, you will probably not swim very well.   In much the same way, if you memorize all the grammar rules but spend little time *practicing* them, you will not be able to communicate very well in Spanish.

As you study each grammar point in *Puntos de partida,* you will learn how the structure works; then you need to put your knowledge into practice.   First, read the grammar discussion, study and analyze the examples, and pay special attention to any **¡OJO!** sections, which will call your attention to problem areas.   Then begin to practice, first in the **Práctica** section.   Do the exercises and check your answers.   When you are certain that your answers are correct, practice doing each exercise several times until the answers sound and "feel" right to you.   As you do each item, think about what you are conveying and the context in which you could use each sentence, as well as about spelling and pronunciation.   Then move on to the **Conversación** section and continue to practice, this time in a more open-ended situation in which there are no "right" or "wrong" answers.

Always remember that language learning is cumulative.   This means that you are not finished with a grammar point when you go on to the next chapter.   Even though you are now studying the material in Chapter 2, you must remember how to conjugate **-ar** verbs and how to form *yes/no* questions, for example, because Chapter 2 builds on what you have learned in Chapter 1, just as all subsequent chapters will build on the material leading up to them.   A few minutes spent each day reviewing "old" topics will increase your confidence—and success— in communicating in Spanish.

7. POSSESSION WITH *DE*

In English **possession** (ownership) is expressed by *'s*. In Spanish possession is expressed by the word **de** (*of*). There is no *'s* in Spanish.

Es el dinero **de Carla.**	*It's Carla's money.*
Son los abuelos **de Jorge.**	*They're Jorge's grandparents.*
¿De quién es este examen?	*Whose exam is this?*

PRÁCTICA

¿De quién son estas cosas?

MODELO   el coche / Carlos → *¿De quién es el coche?*
                                          Es el coche de Carlos.

1. la Coca-Cola / Jesús
2. la idea / Paquita
3. las pesetas / Rodrigo
4. el cuaderno / Soledad
5. la clase / Lorenzo
6. el cuarto / Antonia

CONVERSACIÓN

Aquí, la familia de Luisa. ¿Quiénes son los parientes?

MODELO   *Alfonso es el abuelo de Luisa.*

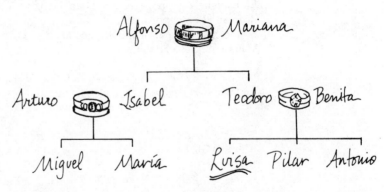

8. CONTRACTIONS *DEL* AND *AL*

A *contraction* (**contracción**) is the joining of two words that may also be said or written separately. In English, contractions are optional: *Pam is not/isn't a student, They are not/aren't here.*

In Spanish there are only two contractions, and they are obligatory. **De** and **el** contract to **del,** and **a** and **el** contract to **al.** No other articles contract with **de** or with **a.**

Es la casa **del** niño.	*It is the child's house.*
Es la casa **de los** niños.	*It is the children's house.*
Regreso **al** mercado mañana.	*I'll go back to the market tomorrow.*
Regreso **a la** tienda mañana.	*I'll go back to the store tomorrow.*

PRÁCTICA

Dé Ud. frases nuevas según las indicaciones.

1. —¿De quién son estas cosas?
   —Es *la peseta* del hombre.   (*el coche, la casa, el peso, el bolígrafo*)
2. —¿De quién es el libro?
   —Es el libro *del niño.*   (*la mujer, los abuelos, el tío, las amigas, el primo Juan*)
3. —Marcos necesita regresar a muchos lugares.   ¿Adónde regresa Marcos mañana?
   —Mañana Marcos regresa a *la biblioteca.*   (*el mercado, el hotel, la tienda, el hospital, el cuarto del abuelo, la casa de la tía*)

CONVERSACIÓN

A. *¿Por qué* (why) *necesita Ud. regresar a estos lugares?*

   1. Mañana regreso a la universidad porque (*because*) _____.
   2. En España siempre regreso al Hotel Fénix porque _____.
   3. Regreso al baile porque _____.
   4. El doctor regresa al hospital todos los días porque _____.
   5. Mañana regreso al/a la _____.

B. *¿Cuál* (what) *es la capital del estado de Colorado?   ¿del estado de Nuevo México? ¿del estado de Arizona?   ¿del estado de Montana?   ¿del estado de Nevada?   ¿del estado de Florida?   ¿del estado de California?*

Sacramento	Denver	Phoenix	Carson City
Tallahassee	Helena	Santa Fe	

9. ADJECTIVES: GENDER, NUMBER, AND POSITION

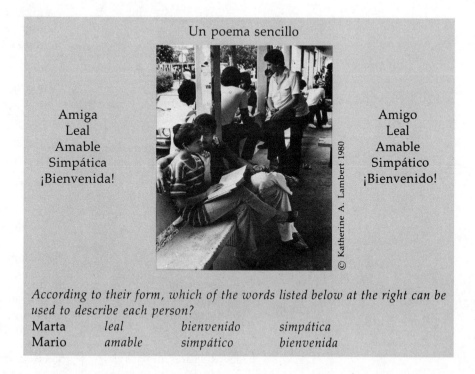

Un poema sencillo

Amiga
Leal
Amable
Simpática
¡Bienvenida!

Amigo
Leal
Amable
Simpático
¡Bienvenido!

© Katherine A. Lambert 1980

According to their form, which of the words listed below at the right can be used to describe each person?

| Marta | *leal* | *bienvenido* | *simpática* |
| Mario | *amable* | *simpático* | *bienvenida* |

An *adjective* (**adjetivo**) is a word that describes a noun or a pronoun. Adjectives may describe (*large* desk, *tall* woman) or tell how many there are (*a few* desks, *several* women).

Adjectives with *Ser*

In Spanish, forms of **ser** are used with adjectives that describe basic, inherent qualities or characteristics of the nouns they modify.

Antonio **es alegre.**   *Antonio is happy. (He is a happy person.)*
Tú **eres amable.**   *You're nice. (You're a nice person.)*

Forms of Adjectives

Spanish adjectives agree in gender and number with the noun or pronoun they modify. Each adjective has more than one form.

A Simple Poem. Friend Loyal Kind Nice Welcome!

	Masculine	Feminine
Singular	amigo inteligente amigo leal amigo alto	amiga inteligente amiga leal amiga alta
Plural	amigos inteligentes amigos leales amigos altos	amigas inteligentes amigas leales amigas altas

Adjectives that end in **-e (inteligente)** or in most consonants **(leal)** have only two forms, a singular form and a plural. Adjectives that end in **-o (alto)** show gender, as well as number.*

[Práctica A, B, C]

Adjectives of nationality have four forms:

	Masculine	Feminine
Singular	el doctor mexicano el doctor español el doctor alemán el doctor inglés	la doctora mexicana la doctora española la doctora alemana la doctora inglesa
Plural	los doctores mexicanos los doctores españoles los doctores alemanes los doctores ingleses	las doctoras mexicanas las doctoras españolas las doctoras alemanas las doctoras inglesas

The names of many languages—which are masculine in gender—are the same as the masculine singular form of the corresponding adjective of nationality: **el español, el inglés, el francés,** and so on. Note that in Spanish the names of languages and adjectives of nationality are not capitalized, but the names of countries are: **español** but **España.**

[Práctica D]

Mucho *and* Poco

The words **mucho** and **poco** can be used as adjectives or as *adverbs* (**adverbios**). Adverbs—words that modify verbs, adjectives, or other adverbs—are invariable in form.

Rosa trabaja **mucho/poco.**   *Rosa works a lot/little.*

[Práctica E]

---

*Adjectives that end in **-dor, -ón, -án,** and **-ín** also have four forms: **trabajador, trabajadora, trabajadores, trabajadoras.**

Placement of Adjectives

Adjectives that describe qualities of a noun generally follow the noun they modify. Adjectives of quantity precede the noun.

Hay **muchos** edificios **altos** en la ciudad.	*There are many tall buildings in the city.*
Necesito **otro** carro.*	*I need another car.*

Bueno, malo, and **grande** may precede the nouns they modify. When **bueno** and **malo** precede a masculine singular noun, they shorten to **buen** and **mal** respectively.

un recuerdo **bueno**/un **buen** recuerdo	*a good (pleasant) memory*
una niña **buena**/una **buena** niña	*a good girl*

When **grande** appears after a noun, it means *large* or *big*. When it precedes a singular noun—masculine or feminine—it shortens to **gran** and means *great* or *impressive*.

una mujer **grande**	*a big woman*
una **gran** mujer	*a great woman*

[Práctica F, G, H, I]

PRÁCTICA

A. *Dé Ud. frases nuevas según las indicaciones.*

1. —¿Cómo es su clase de español? (*What is your Spanish class like?*)
   —(No) Es una clase *alegre.* (*inteligente, interesante, importante, triste, amable, internacional, ¡imposible!*)
2. —¿Cómo son los perros (*dogs*)?
   —Los perros (no) son *valientes.* (*leal, impaciente, inteligente, importante*)
3. —¿Cómo es su (*your*) universidad?
   —La universidad (no) es *nueva.* (*viejo, grande, pequeño, bueno, malo*)

B. *Complete each sentence with all the adjectives that are appropriate according to form and meaning.*

1. La doctora es _____.	alta lista	casado bonito	jóvenes trabajadora
2. El hotel es _____.	viejo grande	alto fea	nueva interesante
3. Los abuelos son _____.	joven viejos	antipático religiosos	inteligentes práctica
4. Las niñas son _____.	malo buenas	cortas casadas	sentimental interesante

* The indefinite article is not used with **otro.**

C. *Juan and Juana, fraternal twins, are totally different. Tell what Juana is like.*

Juan es soltero. Es alto. Es guapo. Es perezoso. Es simpático.

D. *Tell what nationality the following persons could be.*

1. Monique habla francés; es _____.
2. José habla español; es _____.
3. Greta y Hans hablan alemán; son _____.
4. Gilberto habla portugués; es _____.
5. Gina y Sofía hablan italiano; son _____.
6. Winston habla inglés; es _____.

E. *Dé Ud. frases nuevas según las indicaciones.*

1. —Como (*as a*) estudiante, ¿qué necesita Ud.?
   —Necesito muchos/pocos *textos*. (*lápices, mesas, cuadernos, papel, ideas, dinero, clases*)
2. —¿Qué necesitan hacer (*to do*) Uds. para ser buenos estudiantes?
   —Necesitamos *estudiar* mucho/poco. (*trabajar, pagar, tomar, hablar en clase*)

F. *Use the adjectives in parentheses to describe the nouns opposite them. Be sure to use the proper form of each adjective. Use only one adjective at a time.*

1. libros   (nuevo / tres / barato)
2. una mesa   (bajo / pequeño / largo)
3. unas ciudades   (viejo / interesante / grande)
4. un carro   (pequeño / francés / largo)

Follow the same procedure in these sentences:

5. Por favor, deseo comprar un   (completo / barato / nuevo)
   diccionario.
6. Unos profesores enseñan bien.   (viejo / simpático / norteamericano)
7. Desean hablar con la hermana.   (casado / otro / joven)
8. Busco una casa.   (nuevo / bueno / blanco)

G. *Create new phrases by changing the position of the adjectives. Be sure to use the appropriate form of the adjective.*

1. un recuerdo bueno
2. una comida grande
3. unos tíos buenos
4. un hotel malo
5. unas actrices malas

H. *¿Cómo se dice en español?*

1. It's a great idea!
2. He's buying a big car.
3. We need another dictionary.
4. There are some nice students in the class.
5. You (**Uds.**) talk a lot.

I. *Cambie: Miguel → María.*

Miguel es un buen estudiante; pues estudia mucho. Es listo y amable. Es peruano; por eso habla español. Es alto y guapo; también es muy alegre. ¡Es una persona ideal!

CONVERSACIÓN

A. *Describa Ud. las diferencias.*

MODELO   *En el dibujo A, hay un perro grande.*   *En el dibujo B, hay un perro pequeño.*

A.   B.

B. *Use adjetivos para completar las oraciones en una forma lógica.*

1. El/la profesor(a) es _____.
2. Por lo general (*in general*) las mujeres son _____.
3. Por lo general los hombres son _____.
4. Los amigos son _____.
5. El español es una lengua (*language*) _____.
6. Los actores son _____.
7. Yo soy _____.

10. TELLING TIME

En el baile. Cenicienta y el Príncipe bailan.
CENICIENTA: *¿Qué hora es?*
  PRÍNCIPE: *Son las doce menos diez,* princesa.
CENICIENTA: ¡Por Dios! *Es hora de* regresar a casa. *Si no llego a las doce en punto . . .*

At the dance. Cinderella and the Prince are dancing. CINDERELLA: What time is it? PRINCE: It's ten of twelve, Princess. CINDERELLA: My goodness! It's time to return home. If I don't arrive exactly at twelve . . .

1. *¿Qué hora es?*
2. *¿Es tarde o temprano (early) para Cenicienta?*
3. *¿Es hora de bailar más?*
4. *¿A qué hora desea llegar a casa Cenicienta?*

Es la una.

Son las dos.

Son las cinco.

¿Qué hora es? is used to ask *What time is it?*.   In telling time, one says *Es la una* but *Son* **las dos (las tres, las cuatro,** and so on**).**   The feminine form of the definite article **(la, las)** is used; similarly, the feminine form **una** is used for one o'clock (agreeing with **hora**).

Es la una **y** { **cuarto.** **quince.**

Son las dos **y** { **media.** **treinta.**

Son las cinco **y diez.**

Son las ocho **y veinticinco.**

From the hour to the half-hour, Spanish, like English, expresses time by adding minutes or a portion of an hour to the hour.

Son las dos **menos** { **cuarto.** **quince.**

Son las ocho **menos diez.**

Son las once **menos veinte.**

From the half-hour to the hour, Spanish usually expresses time by subtracting minutes or a part of an hour from the *next* hour.

A.M. and P.M. are expressed by the phrase **de la mañana, de la tarde,** and **de la noche.**   When the hour is not expressed, concepts such as *in the morning* are expressed with the prepositions **por** or **en.**

Son las once **de** la noche.   *It's eleven P.M.*
Regreso **por (en)** la noche.   *I return at night.*

Otras expresiones útiles	
Es la una **en punto**.	It's exactly 1 o'clock. (It's one on the dot.)
¿A qué hora llegas?	(At) What time are you arriving?
Llego **a** la una (**a** las siete).	I'm arriving at one (at seven).
Es **hora de** estudiar (**de** regresar).	It's time to study (to return).

PRÁCTICA

A. *¿Qué hora es?*

1. 1:00	6. 6:45	11. 2:20 P.M.
2. 6:00	7. 4:15	12. 2:40 P.M.
3. 11:00	8. 11:45	13. 5:07 P.M.
4. 1:30	9. 9:10	14. 10:55 P.M.
5. 3:15	10. 9:50 P.M.	15. 8:00 A.M.

B. *¿A qué hora llega el tren? El tren llega a* _____ .

1. 2:19 P.M.	5. 1:59 A.M.
2. 5:15 P.M.	6. 10:22 P.M.
3. 9:30 A.M.	7. 1:07 P.M.
4. 11:40 P.M.	8. 6:16 A.M.

CONVERSACIÓN

A. *You are a travel agent. Your clients want to know when they are going to get to their destinations.*

MODELO   a Guanajuato / 9:00 A.M. →
        CLIENTES: ¿A qué hora llegamos *a Guanajuato?*
        AGENTE: Uds. llegan *a Guanajuato a las nueve de la mañana.*

1. a Sevilla	11:00 A.M.
2. a Buenos Aires	11:54 P.M.
3. a Los Ángeles	1:15 P.M.
4. a Miami	8:31 P.M.
5. a Málaga	5:35 A.M.

B. *Pregúntele a otro estudiante.*

1. ¿Tomas café en la cafetería en la mañana?
2. ¿A qué hora enseña el/la profesor(a)?
3. ¿Regresas a casa por la tarde o por la noche?
4. ¿Llegas a la universidad en la mañana o en la tarde?
5. ¿A qué hora estudias en la biblioteca?

DIÁLOGO: La familia de Gloria Gómez Pereda[1]*

En casa de Gloria

DOÑA[2] MARÍA:	*(Desde° el patio.)* Gloria, ¿quién llega?	*from*
GLORIA:	Es José, mamá.	

(Gloria y José pasan al patio.)

DOÑA MARÍA:	Bienvenido, José. Mucho gusto°.	**Mucho...** *Pleased to meet you.*
JOSÉ:	Igualmente, señora.	
DOÑA MARÍA:	Gloria, ¿por qué no presentas tú a la familia?°	**¿por...** *why don't you introduce the family?*
GLORIA:	¡Cómo no! Les presento a° un buen amigo, José Núñez Sandoval. Somos compañeros de clase en la universidad. Y ahora, Pepe, presento al número uno de la familia, mi abuelo Antonio. Es un profesor retirado.	**Les...** *let me introduce you to*
JOSÉ:	Encantado, don Antonio.	
ABUELO:	Igualmente, José. Bienvenido a esta° casa.	*this*
JOSÉ:	Muy amable, señor.	
GLORIA:	Y ahora, papá.	
JOSÉ:	Mucho gusto, don Luis. Papá habla mucho de usted y manda recuerdos° a toda la familia.	**manda...** *he sends his regards*
DON LUIS:	Somos muy buenos amigos. Bienvenido, hijo.	
GLORIA:	Y ahora, Carlos María.	
JOSÉ:	Encantado. ¿Es Ud. el hermano de Gloria?	
CARLOS MARÍA:	Sí, soy uno de los hermanos. Mucho gusto.	
GLORIA:	También hay dos hermanos solteros en la capital y una hermana casada que° llega más tarde. Somos una familia grande.	*who*
JOSÉ:	¡Y muy simpática!	
GLORIA:	Gracias, Pepe, pero hay más todavía°: con padres, abuelos, tíos y primos, llegamos a veintisiete.	*still, yet*
DOÑA MARÍA:	Bueno, hijos, basta° de matemáticas. Es hora de comer°.	*enough* / *to eat*
GLORIA:	Pues, ¡todos a la mesa!	

© Peter Menzel

*Footnotes in the dialog refer to the **Comentario cultural**.

Comprensión

¿Cierto (true) *o falso?   Corrija* (correct) *las oraciones falsas.*

1. José es el amigo de Gloria.
2. Doña María es la madre de José.
3. José es muy cortés (*courteous*).
4. Doña María presenta a la familia.
5. El padre de don Luis es un profesor retirado.
6. El padre de José manda regalos a la familia de don Luis.
7. El padre de José y el abuelo de Gloria son buenos amigos.
8. José es el hijo de don Luis.
9. Hay veintisiete hijos en total en la familia.
10. La familia de Gloria es pequeña y simpática.

Comentario cultural

1. In Hispanic cultures the extended family—made up of grandparents, parents, and children—is the most important social unit to which a person belongs. Very close relationships exist between parents and children, brothers and sisters, and grandparents and grandchildren.   Close ties are also maintained with aunts, uncles, and cousins.

   Because of strong family ties and also economic considerations, two or even three generations may live together in one household.   It is not uncommon to find grandparents living with their children and grandchildren.
2. **Don** and **doña** are titles of respect.   Because they are used with someone's first name, they are less formal than the titles **Sr., Sra.,** and **Srta.,** and they communicate a feeling of warmth, as well as respect.

UN POCO DE TODO

A. *Form complete sentences based on the words given, in the order given.   Conjugate the verbs and add other words if necessary.*

1. hay / mucho / ciudad / interesante / en / Honduras
2. hay / veintiuno / mesa / largo / en / cafetería
3. ser / bueno / recuerdo
4. madre / de / niñas / ser / doctora / bueno
5. don Carlos / ser / malo / actor / pero / ser / amable
6. yo / llegar / a casa / seis / de / mañana
7. hay / veinticuatro / hora / en / día
8. ser / libros / de / estudiante
9. Carmen / regresar / a / mercado / en / tarde

B. ¿Quién es? ¿un hermano? ¿una tía? ¿un abuelo? ¿un padre? ¿una prima?

1. Es viejo y retirado. Es casado y es padre de tres hijos; los hijos son padres también. Es _____.
2. Es joven. Es la hija de tío Carlos y tía Matilde. Es _____.
3. Es el hijo de los señores Pérez. Hay otros hijos en la familia también. Es _____.
4. Es el esposo de la señora. Hay hijos en la familia. Es _____.
5. Es la hija de los abuelos. También, es la hermana del padre. Es _____.

C. Working with two other students, ask and answer questions according to the model.

MODELO   Atlanta → ENRIQUETA: ¿De dónde eres tú?
                        AGUSTÍN: Soy de *Atlanta.*
                            EVA: Ah, eres *norteamericano.*
                        AGUSTÍN: Sí, por eso hablo *inglés.*

1. Guadalajara   5. Madrid
2. París   6. Londres
3. Roma   7. Berlín
4. San Francisco   8. Lima (peruano)

D. Using the following schedule of re-runs, explain to a friend what programs are on and at what time. You may use the titles more than once.

7:00	El show de Carol Burnett	8:30	Dibujos animados (*cartoons*)
7:30	El Zoo de Barcelona	9:00	Barnaby Jones
8:00	Yo canto	10:00	Cine Club: Historia de amor (*Love Story*)

1. Hay un programa cómico a _____.
2. Hay un programa romántico a _____.
3. Hay un programa dramático a _____.
4. Hay un programa de animales a _____.
5. Hay otro programa cómico a _____.
6. Hay un programa de música a _____.
7. Hay un programa para toda la familia a _____.
8. Hay un programa interesante a _____.

E. Complete las oraciones en una forma lógica.

1. En clase somos _____.   5. Mi madre es _____.
2. En mi familia hay _____.   6. En México hay _____.
3. Mi familia es _____.   7. La clase de español es a _____.
4. Mi padre es _____.   8. El coche de mi profesor(a) es _____.

VOCABULARIO

VERBOS

llegar   to arrive
ser   to be (*irreg.*)

SUSTANTIVOS

el/la **abuelo/a**   grandfather/
  grandmother
los **abuelos**   grandparents
el **actor**   actor
la **actriz**   actress
    (*pl.* **actrices**)
el **baile**   dance
la **bebida**   drink
el **café**   coffee
la **casa**   house
la **ciudad**   city
el **coche**   car
la **comida**   food
el **cuarto**   room
el/la **esposo/a**   husband/wife
el **estado**   state
los **Estados Unidos**   United States
el **examen**   exam
la **familia**   family
el/la **hermano/a**   brother/sister
el/la **hijo/a**   son/daughter
los **hijos**   children
la **hora**   hour
la **madre (mamá)**   mother (mom)
el/la **nieto/a**   grandson/
  granddaughter
el **padre (papá)**   father (dad)
los **padres**   parents
el **pariente**   relative
el/la **primo/a**   cousin

el **recuerdo**   memory; *pl.* regards
el **regalo**   present, gift
el/la **sobrino/a**   niece/nephew
el/la **tío/a**   uncle/aunt

ADJETIVOS

alegre   happy
alemán, alemana   German
alto/a   tall
amable   kind; nice
antipático/a   unpleasant
bajo/a   short (*in height*)
barato/a   inexpensive
bienvenido/a   welcome
bonito/a   pretty
bueno/a   good
casado/a   married
corto/a   short (*in length*)
español(a)   Spanish
feo/a   ugly
francés(a)   French
grande   large, big; great
guapo/a   handsome, good-looking
inglés, inglesa   English
joven   young
largo   long
leal   loyal
listo/a   smart, clever
malo/a   bad
mexicano/a   Mexican
mucho   a lot of, many
necesario/a   necessary
norteamericano/a   North American;
  from the United States

nuevo/a   new
otro/a   other, another
pequeño/a   small
perezoso/a   lazy
pobre   poor
poco/a   little, few
posible   possible
rico/a   rich
simpático/a   nice; likeable
soltero/a   single (*not married*)
todo/a   all, every
tonto/a   silly, foolish
trabajador(a)   hard-working
triste   sad
viejo/a   old

PALABRAS Y EXPRESIONES ÚTILES

ahora   now
¿de dónde es Ud.?   where are
  you from?
de la mañana   in the morning
de la noche   in the evening
de la tarde   in the afternoon
¿de quién?   whose?
¿dónde?   where?
en punto   exactly, on the dot
  (*with time*)
hora de + *inf.*   time to
  (*do something*)
¿qué hora es?   what time is it?
tarde   late
temprano   early

Un paso más 2

Actividades

SÓLO PAPÁ

A. **¿Una familia típica?** Describa la familia en el dibujo (*cartoon*).

1. ¿Es grande o pequeña la familia?
2. ¿Cuántas niñas hay? ¿Cuántos niños? ¿Cuántos hijos en total?
3. ¿Cómo es el papá? ¿Es trabajador? ¿egoísta (*egotistical, selfish*)?
4. ¿Cómo son los hijos? ¿Son serios? ¿Estudian mucho? ¿Trabajan mucho? ¿Hablan con el padre? ¿Habla el padre con ellos?
5. ¿La familia en el dibujo es similar a una familia norteamericana?

A propósito...

The importance of family ties and family identity in Hispanic cultures is revealed in the pattern of Spanish names. Hispanic individuals have two last names (surnames): the first is the first of their father's surnames, the second is the first of their mother's surnames. Thus, the son of **Antonio** *Gómez* **Ruiz** and **Elena** *Tovar* **Espinosa** is **Luis** *Gómez Tovar.* Although in everyday practice one may use only the first surname (the father's), both names are required for official purposes.

When women marry, they regularly retain their own surnames and add their husband's first surname. When **Elena Tovar Espinosa** marries **Antonio** *Gómez* **Ruiz,** her name becomes **Elena Tovar Espinosa** *de Gómez.* She would normally be known as **la señora de Gómez.**

Children are customarily given more than one Christian name. While **María** is a name often given to girls, it is frequently given to boys as a *second* Christian name: **Carlos María** in the dialog in this chapter, for example.

B. **¿Cómo se llaman?** What are the names of the following people?

1. The son of Luis Zamora Vicente y Adela Gómez Estrada is named Tomás
   _____.

2. The full legal name of Margarita Sandoval Pérez after she marries Manuel Martínez Delgado will be _____.

3. The grandfathers of Carmen García Pidal are Federico Pidal Borbón and Domingo García Núñez. Which is Carmen's paternal grandfather? Which is her maternal grandfather?

4. Ramón Gómez Jiménez and Esteban Gómez Solano are related. Could they be brothers? Father and son?

5. Pedro Rodríguez Jerez, Ana Rodríguez Salas, Antonio Rodríguez Salas, and Teresa Salas Zapata are at a family get-together. Which two are brother and sister? Which are their parents?

© Katherine A. Lambert 1980

C. **Entre amigos.** Among friends, nicknames are used just as frequently in Spanish as in English. They are often shortened forms of the name, sometimes based on the first part, sometimes on the last. For example, **Natividad** becomes **Nati** and **Enrique** becomes **Quique.** Other nicknames differ quite a bit from the formal name, as when **José** becomes **Pepe.** Women having compound names beginning with **María** are frequently called by their second name, by its nickname, or by a compound nickname. For example, **María del Pilar** may be called **Pilar, Pili,** or **Maripili.**

You have received postcards from a number of your Hispanic friends, and each of them has signed only his or her nickname (given in the left-hand column). Find the formal first name of each from the list in the right-hand column.

1. Pepa   Francisca
2. Berto   Francisco
3. Merche or Mercha   María Teresa
4. Paco or Pancho   Mercedes

5. Paca or Pancha   Josefa
6. Teresa, Tere, or Maritere   María de la Concepción
7. Lola   Guillermo
8. Concha   Alberto
9. Memo   Dolores

D. **Antónimos.** Sometimes Spanish *antonyms* (words that are opposite in meaning) are not at all similar in form: **bueno/malo, trabajador/perezoso.** In Spanish, as in English, however, many antonyms are formed by adding negative prefixes, such as **ir-, des-, in-, im-,** and **anti-,** to the adjective.

Antónimos

(ir)regular	(ir)reverente	(ir)religioso/a	(ir)responsable
(ir)racional	(des)agradable	(des)leal	(des)cortés
(in)justo/a	(in)activo/a	(in)competente	(in)discreto/a
(in)útil	(im)perfecto/a	(im)probable	(im)práctico/a
(im)paciente	(anti)comunista	(anti)patriótico/a	(anti)poético/a

Autodefiniciones. Describe yourself, using as many adjectives as possible.

MODELO   Soy **religiosa.** No soy **irreverente.**

Opiniones. ¿Sí o no?

1. Mi madre (hermano, tía, abuelo) es impaciente.
2. Es necesario ser rico/a para ser alegre.
3. Mis clases este (*this*) semestre son desagradables.
4. Los estudiantes son irresponsables.
5. Un americano comunista es un americano leal.
6. Los ejercicios (*exercises*) de este libro son útiles.
7. Es importante ser religioso/a.
8. La clase de español es muy grande.
9. El/la esposo/a ideal es feo/a y rico/a.
10. El mejor automóvil es práctico y pequeño.

E. **Las presentaciones.** The following phrases are frequently used in making introductions.

Sra. Aguilar, le presento a Adolfo Álvarez Montes.	*Mrs. Aguilar, may I introduce you to Adolfo Álvarez Montes.*
Benito, te presento a Adela.	*Benito, let me introduce you to Adela.*
Mucho gusto.	*Pleased to meet you.*
Encantado/a.	
Igualmente.	*Likewise.*
Bienvenido/a.	*Welcome.*

When introductions are made, Spanish speakers—both men and women—almost always shake hands.

With other students, practice making the following introductions, using **le** or **te,** as appropriate. Tell something about the person you are introducing.

1. You are at home, and a good friend stops by for a few minutes. Introduce him/her to your family.
2. You are in the library and happen to run into two of your professors at the circulation desk. Introduce them to each other.
3. You are at a party. Introduce one good friend to another.

Lectura cultural: El compadrazgo

En las culturas hispánicas —como en otras naciones de religión católica— el compadrazgo° tiene° mucha importancia. El compadrazgo resulta en un sistema de "familia extendida," donde un niño tiene, en efecto, dos padres y dos madres. Tiene padres biológicos y también padrinos°, los padres espirituales que recibe° en el bautismo.

    Por lo general los padrinos son otros miembros de la familia —un tío y una tía, quizá°— o unos íntimos amigos de la familia. El compadrazgo, pues, ofrece° más seguridad al ahijado°. Garantiza° otra familia al niño si una tragedia ocurre a los padres del ahijado.

    La relación entre los padrinos y el ahijado es una relación íntima. Los padrinos ayudan al° ahijado durante toda la vida°, y el ahijado ofrece a los padrinos el respeto y el amor que da a° los padres.

relationship between parents and god-parents / has godparents receives

perhaps offers / godchild / it guarantees

ayudan... *help the / life* **que...** *that he gives to*

© Peter Menzel

Comprensión

¿Cierto o falso? Corrija las oraciones falsas.

1. El compadrazgo existe sólo en las naciones hispánicas.
2. Cuando usamos la palabra *compadrazgo* hablamos de un tipo de familia extendida.
3. Un ahijado es el padre espiritual de los padrinos.
4. Los padrinos siempre (*always*) son un tío y una tía.
5. Si tiene padrinos, un niño tiene más seguridad.
6. Los padrinos aman (*love*) al ahijado.

Ejercicio escrito

Write a brief paragraph about the concept of the "extended family" as it may apply to your own family background. Use the following questions as a guide in developing your paragraph.

1. ¿Quiénes son los parientes o amigos que son como padres para Ud.? ¿Son padrinos? ¿abuelos? ¿tíos? ¿amigos mayores (*older*)? ¿vecinos (*neighbors*)?
2. ¿De dónde son? ¿Cómo son?
3. ¿Habla Ud. mucho con ellos? ¿De qué hablan Uds.?

capítulo 3 De compras

Jerry Frank/DPI

OBJETIVOS

In this chapter you will learn vocabulary and expressions related to articles of clothing and colors, as well as other words and phrases that are useful for shopping.

You will also learn about the following aspects of Spanish grammar:

11. how to use the word **se** to express passive voice (as in English *is sold* and *are needed*) and impersonal subjects, such as *one, you, they,* and *people*
12. the present tense of regular **-er** and **-ir** verbs
13. the present tense of four very common

Spanish irregular verbs: **tener** (*to have*), **venir** (*to come*), **querer** (*to want, to wish*), and **poder** (*to be able to, can*)

14. a number of expressions that use the Spanish verb **tener** (*to have*) where English uses *to be,* such as *to be hungry, thirsty, sleepy, in a hurry*
15. numbers from 31 to 100

Un paso más includes activities dealing with getting along in a Spanish-speaking country—shopping, using the phone, and so on—and a reading about styles of dress in the Hispanic world.

VOCABULARIO: PREPARACIÓN

De compras°			shopping
comprar	to buy	**el almacén**	department store
regatear	to haggle, to bargain	**el mercado**	market
		la tienda	shop, store
vender	to sell	**el precio**	price
venden de todo	they sell everything	**el precio fijo**	fixed (set) price

La ropa°			clothing
llevar	to wear; to carry	**los calcetines**	socks
la blusa	blouse	**las medias**	stockings
la camisa	shirt	**las botas**	boots
la camiseta	T-shirt	**un par de**	a pair of
el suéter	sweater	**zapatos/sandalias**	shoes/sandals
la falda	skirt	**el abrigo**	coat
el vestido	dress	**el impermeable**	raincoat
el traje	suit; costume	**la bolsa**	purse
los pantalones	pants	**la cartera**	wallet
la chaqueta	jacket		

A. *¿Qué llevan?*

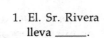

1. El. Sr. Rivera lleva _____.
2. La Srta. Alonso lleva _____.
3. El estudiante lleva _____.
4. La estudiante lleva _____.

B. *¿Qué artículos de ropa asocia Ud. con...*

¿las mujeres? ¿los hombres? ¿una fiesta formal? ¿el dinero? ¿el estado de Alaska?

C. *Llene los espacios con las palabras apropiadas.*

    1. El ____ es una tienda grande.
    2. No es posible ____ cuando (*when*) hay precios fijos.
    3. Deseo ____ el carro, pero el ____ es muy alto.
    4. En la librería ____ de todo: textos y otros libros, cuadernos, lápices.
    5. Nunca (*never*) llevo ____ a la clase.
    6. En casa siempre (*always*) llevo ____.

Los colores

amarillo/a	yellow	**negro/a**	black
anaranjado/a	orange	**pardo/a**	brown
azul	blue	**rojo/a**	red
blanco/a	white	**rosado/a**	pink
gris	gray	**verde**	green
morado/a	purple		

D. *¿Qué colores asocia Ud. con...?*

    ¿el dinero? ¿la una de la mañana? ¿una mañana bonita? ¿una mañana fea?
    ¿Satanás? ¿los Estados Unidos? ¿una jirafa? ¿un pingüino? ¿un limón?
    ¿una naranja? ¿las flores (*flowers*)?

E. *¿De qué color es?* Tell the color of things in your classroom.

    MODELOS   *Los pantalones de Roberto son azules.*
                      El bolígrafo de Anita es amarillo.

Now describe what someone is wearing without revealing his or her name.
Using your clues, can your classmates guess whom you are describing?

Tag Questions

Venden de todo aquí, **¿no?/ ¿verdad?**	They sell everything here, right? (don't they?)
No necesito impermeable hoy, **¿verdad?**	I don't need a raincoat today, do I? (right?)

In English and in Spanish, questions are frequently formed by adding
tags or phrases to the end of statements. Two of the most common
question tags in Spanish are **¿verdad?**, found after affirmative or negative statements, and **¿no?**, usually found after positive statements. The
inverted question mark comes immediately before the tag question, not
at the beginning of the sentence.

F. *Using question tags, ask another student questions based on the following statements:*

    1. Las mujeres no llevan pantalones.
    2. En un almacén hay precios fijos.
    3. No regateamos en los Estados Unidos.
    4. Una naranja es amarilla.
    5. El precio de unas botas elegantes es muy alto.
    6. En los almacenes no venden de todo.
    7. El/la profesor(a) lleva ropa fea hoy.

PRONUNCIACIÓN: P, T, and K

In English, the [p], [t], [k] sounds at the beginning of a word are *aspirated*—that is, they are released with a small puff of air. In Spanish, [p], [t], [k] are never aspirated.

Spanish [t] differs from English [t] in another respect. The English [t] is pronounced with the tip of the tongue on the alveolar ridge, just behind the upper teeth (see below). The Spanish [t] is a *dental* sound; it is pronounced with the tongue against the back of the upper teeth.

The Spanish [k] sound is like English [k], but is not aspirated. The [k] sound is written as **c** before a consonant (**clase**) or the vowels **a, o,** and **u (casado, cómico, matrícula),** and as **qu** before **e** or **i (que, quien).**

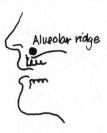

PRÁCTICA

Practique las siguientes palabras, frases y oraciones.

1. pasar presentar peseta peso pintor político padre programa
2. tienda tener todos traje todavía tío trabajador tía
3. camisa quince coche calcetín conquistador qué casado corto
4. una tía trabajadora
    una chaqueta corta
    un tío tonto
    un pintor casado
    todos los políticos
    casas y tiendas
5. Tomás toma té.
    También toma café.
    Paquito paga el papel.
    Pero Pablo paga el periódico.
    Cuco trabaja aquí.
    Quico trabaja con Carmen.

MINIDIÁLOGOS Y GRAMÁTICA

11. USES OF *SE:* IMPERSONAL *SE* AND THE PASSIVE REFLEXIVE

En una tienda

TURISTA: Buenos días. ¿*Se habla* inglés aquí?
EMPLEADO: Claro. *Se hablan* muchos idiomas.
TURISTA: ¿Y qué idiomas habla Ud.?
EMPLEADO: Pues en realidad yo hablo muy poco, pero el dinero habla
           siempre.

1. ¿*Se habla inglés en la tienda?*
2. ¿*Qué idiomas se hablan allí* (there)*?*
3. ¿*Habla mucho el empleado?*
4. ¿*Qué lengua ''habla'' más?*

Impersonal Se

In English there are several subjects—*you, one, people, they*—that refer
to people in general instead of to one person in particular.

> *You can get good bargains there.*   ***People** will talk.*

In Spanish these impersonal subjects are commonly expressed by using
the word **se** followed by the third person singular of the verb; there is no
expressed subject.

Se habla mucho en la clase de español.	*One talks a lot in Spanish class.*
Se trabaja mucho aquí.	*You work a lot here.*

[Práctica A, B]

Active versus Passive Voice

Active Voice
John threw the ball.

Passive Voice
The ball was thrown (by John).

In the *active voice* **(voz activa)** in English and in Spanish, the subject of
the verb performs the action. In the *passive voice* **(voz pasiva),** the subject
is acted on. The *agent* **(agente)** of the action is sometimes expressed in a
passive voice sentence: *by John.*

In a shop TOURIST: Good morning. Is English spoken here? CLERK: Of course. Many languages are
spoken. TOURIST: What languages do you speak? CLERK: Well, really, I talk very little, but money
always talks.

Passive Reflexive

In Spanish, when the agent is not expressed, the *passive reflexive* (**pasiva refleja)** is used. It consists of **se** plus the third person singular or plural of the verb. The form of the verb is determined by the subject, which usually follows the verb in this construction.

Se necesita un diccionario bilingüe.	*A bilingual dictionary is needed.*
Se necesita secretaria.	*Secretary needed.*
Se compran libros en la librería.	*Books are bought in the bookstore.*

[Práctica C, D]

PRÁCTICA

A. *Preguntas. Conteste en oraciones completas.*

MODELO   ¿Qué lengua se habla en Francia? → En Francia se habla *francés.*

1. ¿en México?
2. ¿en el Brasil?
3. ¿en Alemania?
4. ¿en Inglaterra?
5. ¿en los Estados Unidos?

B. *Dé Ud. frases nuevas según las indicaciones.*

—¿Cómo se viaja (*does one travel*) a México?
—Se viaja a México en _____ (*avión, carro, tren, autobús*).

C. *Hay un estudiante nuevo en la universidad. Explíquele* (explain to him) *qué se necesita para las clases.*

—Se necesita *papel. (lápices, un cuaderno, un diccionario, un libro de texto, ideas buenas)*

D. *¿Cómo se dice en español? Use la pasiva refleja o el* se *impersonal.*

1. You work a lot.
2. T-shirts are bought at **(en)** the bookstore.
3. You don't arrive late to Spanish class.
4. Spanish is spoken there.
5. Clerks needed.
6. You study a lot at **(en)** the university.

CONVERSACIÓN

A. Complete las oraciones en una forma lógica.

1. Se lleva(n) _____ a una fiesta.
2. Se trabaja mucho en _____.
3. Se busca un diccionario barato y bueno en _____.
4. Se baila en _____.
5. En la universidad se enseña(n) _____.

B. ¿Qué se hace _____? (What does one do _____?)

1. ¿Qué se hace en la biblioteca?
2. ¿Qué se hace en la clase?
3. ¿Qué se hace en un mercado?
4. ¿Qué se hace en un almacén?
5. ¿Qué se hace en una discoteca?
6. ¿Qué se hace en un avión?

C. ¿Qué se compra en una tienda de ropa?

12. PRESENT TENSE OF -*ER* AND -*IR* VERBS

En casa, antes del baile de máscaras
CECILIA: Pero hombre, es necesario llevar traje y máscara. ¿No *comprendes?*
PABLO: Bueno, si *insistes.*
CECILIA: *¡Insisto!*
PABLO: Muy bien. Pero todavía *creo* que yo *debo* llevar el traje de ángel.

1. *¿Qué deben llevar todos al baile?*
2. *¿Quién insiste?*
3. *¿Cecilia lleva el traje de Satanás?*
4. *¿Quién desea llevar el traje de ángel?*

At home, before the costume party CECILIA: But, man, you've got to (it's necessary to) wear a costume and a mask. Don't you understand? PABLO: Well, if you insist. CECILIA: I insist! PABLO: Okay. But I still think I should wear the angel costume.

COMER: *to eat*	VIVIR: *to live*
como com**emos**	vivo viv**imos**
com**es** com**éis**	viv**es** viv**ís**
com**e** com**en**	viv**e** viv**en**

The present tense of **-er** and **-ir** verbs is formed by adding personal endings to the stem of the verb (the infinitive minus its **-er/-ir** ending). The personal endings for **-er** and **-ir** verbs are the same except for the first and second person plural.

Remember that the Spanish present tense has three present tense equivalents in English and can also be used to express future meaning:

como	*I eat*	Simple present
	I do eat	Emphatic present
	I am eating	Present progressive
	I will eat	Future

Important **-er** and **-ir** verbs in this chapter include:

aprender	to learn	**abrir**	to open
beber	to drink	**asistir (a)**	to attend, go to
comer	to eat	**escribir**	to write
comprender	to understand	**insistir**	to insist (on do-
creer (en)	to think,	**(en** + *inf.*)	ing something)
	believe (in)	**recibir**	to receive
deber	should, must, ought	**vivir**	to live
(+ *inf.*)	to (do something)		
leer	to read		
vender	to sell		

PRÁCTICA

A. *Dé Ud. frases nuevas según las indicaciones.*

   1. —Hay una fiesta en casa hoy y los parientes comen y beben mucho. ¿Quién come y bebe mucho?
      —*Yo como y bebo en la fiesta.* (*los tíos, tú, Uds., la prima y yo, Ud., vosotras*)

2. —Hay muchos estudiantes en la clase de español. ¿Quién aprende español
   en clase?
   —*Tú* aprendes español en clase. (*nosotros, yo, Ud., la estudiante francesa,
   Uds., vosotros*)
3. —Es Navidad (*Christmas*) y todos reciben regalos. ¿Quién recibe regalos?
   —*Los hijos* reciben regalos. (*papá, tú, nosotras, los nietos, Alicia, vosotros*)
4. —Es importante asistir a clase hoy. ¿Quién asiste a clase?
   —*Yo* asisto a clase hoy. (*tú, nosotros, Ud., todos los estudiantes, Carlos,
   vosotras*)

B. *Form complete sentences by using one word or phrase from each column. Be sure
to use the correct forms of the verbs. Make any of the sentences negative, if you
wish.*

Ud.	vender	Coca-Cola, café antes de la clase
yo	abrir	un periódico (*newspaper*), un poema,
Rosendo	escribir	un telegrama, una carta (*letter*)
nosotros (no)	deber	la situación, el problema
ellas	leer	la puerta (*door*), el regalo
tú	beber	ropa cara (*expensive*)
_____	comprender	regatear en el mercado, llegar temprano,
		llevar un suéter
		_____

C. *Conteste en oraciones completas.*

1. Vivimos en Nueva York, ¿no?
2. Los estudiantes no beben en clase, ¿verdad?
3. Siempre recibes un suspenso en los exámenes, ¿no?
4. Escribo los ejercicios (*exercises*) todos los días, ¿no?
5. Muchos mexicanos viven en los Estados Unidos, ¿no?
6. Aprendemos francés en clase, ¿no?
7. Los profesores no insisten en recibir muchos regalos, ¿verdad?
8. El profesor no comprende árabe, ¿verdad?
9. Todos los niños creen en Santa Claus, ¿no?

D. *¿Cómo se dice en español?*

1. They sell a lot of shoes here.
2. I should write the letter today.
3. We're living here in San Rafael.
4. He understands Italian (**italiano**), doesn't he?
5. She doesn't understand French.

CONVERSACIÓN

A. *¿Qué hacen?*   (What are they doing?)

1.
2.
3.
4.
5.
6.

B. *En clase, ¿qué deben hacer* (do) *Uds.?*

1. ¿Deben entrar a la hora en punto?
2. ¿Deben hablar inglés?
3. ¿Deben escribir los ejercicios?
4. ¿Deben llevar regalos para el/la profesor(a)?
5. ¿Deben aprender las palabras (*words*) nuevas?
6. ¿Deben asistir a clase todos los días?

C. *Preguntas.   Conteste en oraciones completas.*

1. ¿Insiste Ud. en hablar inglés en clase?   ¿en comprender todo?   ¿en cantar en clase?
2. ¿En qué o en quién cree Ud.?   ¿en Santa Claus?   ¿en Dios (*God*)?   ¿en Alá?

13. *TENER, VENIR, QUERER,* AND *PODER*

TENER: *to have*	VENIR: *to come*	QUERER: *to want*	PODER: *to be able, can*
tengo	vengo	quiero	puedo
tienes	vienes	quieres	puedes
tiene	viene	quiere	puede
tenemos	venimos	queremos	podemos
tenéis	venís	queréis	podéis
tienen	vienen	quieren	pueden

Querer es poder

Yo forms of **tener** and **venir** are irregular: **tengo, vengo.**   In other forms of **tener, venir,** and **querer,** when the stem vowel **e** is stressed, it becomes **ie: tienes, vienes, quieres,** and so on.   Similarly, the stem vowel **o** in **poder** becomes **ue** when stressed.

PRÁCTICA

A. *Dé Ud. frases nuevas según las indicaciones.*

    1. —Es la semana (*week*) de exámenes.   ¿Quién tiene muchos exámenes?
       —*Sara* tiene muchos exámenes.   (*Pepe, nosotros, Alicia y Carlos, yo, tú, vosotras*)
    2. —Hay una fiesta del Club de Español a las nueve mañana.   ¿Quién viene?
       —*Ramón* viene a la fiesta mañana. (*yo, los estudiantes, tú, Uds., nosotras, vosotros*)
    3. —¿Quién quiere viajar (*travel*) a Sud América?
       —*Ana* quiere viajar a Sud América, pero no puede.   (*yo, ella, nosotros, todos los estudiantes, tú, vosotros*)

B. *Form complete sentences by using one word or phrase from each column.   Be sure to use the correct forms of the verbs.   Make any of the sentences negative, if you wish.*

tú		tener	pagar la comida
el profesor	(no)	venir	tarde a clase
yo		querer	un traje muy elegante
Uds.		poder	al restaurante a comer
_____ y yo			comprar un regalo para _____
_____			unos padres muy generosos
			a las siete de la noche
			_____

CONVERSACIÓN

Complete las oraciones en una forma lógica.

    1. En mi familia, tengo _____.
    2. Vengo a la clase de español de (*from*) _____.
    3. Un día, quiero viajar a _____ porque (*because*) _____.
    4. Puedo hablar _____.
    5. En la clase de español se puede (*one can*) _____.
    6. En clase mañana, queremos _____.
    7. Tengo muchos/as _____ en casa.
    8. Muchos extranjeros vienen a los Estados Unidos de (*from*) _____.

Study Hint: Studying and Learning Verbs

Knowing how to use verb forms quickly and accurately is one of the most important parts of learning how to communicate in a foreign language. The following suggestions will help you recognize and use verb forms in Spanish.

1. Study carefully any new grammar section that deals with verbs. Are the verbs regular? What is the stem? What are the personal endings? Don't just memorize the endings (**-o, -as, -a,** and so on). Practice the complete forms of each verb (**hablo, hablas, habla,** and so on) until they are "second nature" to you. Be sure that you are using the appropriate endings: **-ar** endings with **-ar** verbs, for example. Be especially careful when you write and pronounce verb endings, since a misspelling or mispronunciation can convey inaccurate information. Even though there is only a one-letter difference between **hablo** and **habla** or between **habla** and **hablan,** for example, that single letter makes a big difference in the information communicated.

2. Are you studying irregular verbs? If so, what are the irregularities? Practice the irregular forms many times so that you "overlearn"

them and will not forget them: **tengo, tienes, tiene, tienen.**

3. Once you are familiar with the forms, practice asking short conversational questions using **tú/Ud.** and **vosotros/Uds.** Answer each question, using the appropriate **yo** or **nosotros** form.

¿Hablas español? }
¿Habla español? } Sí, hablo español.

¿Comen Uds. en clase? } No, no comemos
¿Coméis en clase? } en clase.

4. It is easy to become so involved in mastering the *forms* of new verbs that you forget their *meanings.* However, being able to recite verb forms perfectly is useless unless you also understand what you are saying. Be sure that you always know both the spelling *and* the meaning of all verb forms, just as you must for any new vocabulary word. Practice using new verb forms in original sentences to reinforce their meaning.

5. Practice the forms of all new verbs given in the vocabulary lists in each chapter. Any special information that you should know about the verbs will be indicated either in the vocabulary list or in a grammar section.

14. *TENER* IDIOMS

La noche antes del examen

ELENA: *Tengo sueño.* Necesito descansar. ¡Ya es la una de la mañana!

CARLOS: ¿Por qué no tomas una taza de café? Todavía *tenemos que* estudiar más.

ELENA: Pero hombre, no *tengo sed. Tengo sueño.*

CARLOS: Sí, pero la cafeína...

ELENA: ¡...es mala para la salud!

CARLOS: ¡...y buena para las notas!

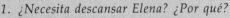

1. ¿Necesita descansar Elena? ¿Por qué?
2. ¿Quién debe tomar una taza de café?
3. ¿Qué tienen que hacer (do) Elena y Carlos?
4. ¿Es buena la cafeína para la salud? ¿para las notas?

The night before the exam ELENA: I'm sleepy. I need to rest. It's already one in the morning! CARLOS: Why don't you have a cup of coffee? We still have to study more. ELENA: But, man, I'm not thirsty. I'm sleepy. CARLOS: Yes, but caffein... ELENA: ...is bad for your health! CARLOS: ...and good for your grades!

An *idiom* (**modismo**) is a group of words that has meaning to speakers of a language but does not necessarily appear to make sense when examined word by word. Idiomatic expressions are often different from one language to another. For example, in English, *to pull Mary's leg* usually means to tease her, not to grab her leg and pull it. In Spanish one says **tomarle el pelo a María** (literally, *to take María's hair*).

Many ideas expressed in English with the verb *to be* are expressed in Spanish with **tener** idioms.

tener (18, 20) **años**	*to be* (18, 20) *years old*
tener calor	*to be warm* (*hot*), *feel warm* (*hot*)
tener frío	*to be cold, feel cold*
tener hambre	*to be hungry*
tener miedo (de)	*to be afraid* (*of*)
tener prisa	*to be in a hurry*
tener razón	*to be right*
no tener razón	*to be wrong*
tener sed	*to be thirsty*
tener sueño	*to be sleepy*

Other **tener** idioms include **tener ganas de** (*to feel like*) and **tener que** (*to have to*). The infinitive is always used after these two idiomatic expressions.

Tengo ganas de trabajar	*I feel like working.*
Tienen que ser prácticos.	*They have to be practical.*

PRÁCTICA

A. Dé Ud. frases nuevas según las indicaciones.

1. —¡Hoy es un día terrible! ¿Qué sensaciones tiene Ud.?
   —Tengo *hambre.* (*sed, sueño, miedo, frío, ganas de descansar*)
2. —¿Qué tiene Ud. que hacer esta noche (*do tonight*)?
   —Tengo que *llegar a casa temprano.* (*asistir a una clase a las siete, aprender unas palabras en español, leer la lección 3, estudiar toda la noche, hablar con un amigo*)
   —Pero... ¿qué tiene ganas de hacer?
   —Tengo ganas de *descansar.* (*abrir una botella de cerveza, vender todos los libros de texto, vivir en otra ciudad, mirar* (watch, look at) *la televisión, comer en un buen restaurante*)

B. Complete los párrafos (paragraphs) *siguientes con los modismos apropiados.*

1. Alfonso llega al aeropuerto de Nueva York. Es el 4 de septiembre, y Alfonso lleva un suéter y un abrigo. Alfonso tiene _____. No tiene _____.

2. De repente (*suddenly*) una serpiente enorme entra en la clase. Todos tienen _____.

3. Amanda trabaja todos los días y estudia todas las noches. Es una estudiante fenomenal, pero no descansa mucho y siempre tiene _____. Y no tiene tiempo para comer bien; por eso siempre tiene _____.

4. Ernesto regresa a la universidad. Son las tres menos cinco, y tiene clase de matemáticas a las tres. Ernesto tiene _____.

5. Hay una fiesta porque hoy es el cumpleaños (*birthday*) del primo Antonio. Tiene 29 _____.

6. Profesor: ¿Y la capital de la Argentina?
   Mariela: Buenos Aires.
   Celia: Cuzco.
   Mariela tiene _____ y Celia no tiene _____.

7. ¡Qué horrible! No hay bebidas en casa y yo tengo _____.

C. *¿Cómo se dice en español?*

1. Alice feels like buying a new T-shirt.
2. We have to study for the exam.
3. Are you afraid of snakes?
4. I don't feel like watching **(mirar)** television.
5. I have to go home now.

CONVERSACIÓN

A. *Describa los dibujos.*

1.
2.
3.
4.

B. *Preguntas.   Conteste en oraciones completas.*

1. ¿Qué tiene Ud. ganas de comer? ¿de tomar? ¿de hacer ahora?
2. ¿De qué o de quién tiene Ud. miedo?
3. ¿Cuántos (*how many*) años tiene Ud.? ¿Y el/la profesor(a)?
4. ¿Tiene Ud. razón siempre? En clase, ¿quién siempre tiene razón?
5. ¿Qué tiene Ud. que hacer ahora mismo (*right now*)? ¿Y mañana?

15. NUMBERS 31 THROUGH 100

¿Mi edad correcta? Pues... treinta y cinco años... no... ¿treinta y nueve? Ah, sí, cuarenta y dos. Sí, eso es.

1. *¿Quién busca trabajo (work, a job)?*
2. *¿Qué lleva el hombre? ¿y la mujer?*
3. *¿Cuántos años tiene él?*

31	treinta y uno		40	cuarenta
32	treinta y dos		50	cincuenta
33	treinta y tres		60	sesenta
34	treinta y cuatro		70	setenta
35	treinta y cinco		80	ochenta
36	treinta y seis		90	noventa
37	treinta y siete		100	cien, ciento
38	treinta y ocho			
39	treinta y nueve			

Beginning with thirty-one, Spanish numbers may not be written in combined form; thus **treinta y uno** must be three separate words.

Remember that when **uno** is part of a compound number (**treinta y uno, cuarenta y uno,** and so on), it becomes **un** before a masculine noun and **una** before a feminine noun.

cincuenta y **una** mesas	*fifty-one tables*
setenta y **un** coches	*seventy-one cars*

The short form **cien** is used before all nouns and is frequently used in counting.

cien casas	*a (one) hundred houses*
noventa y ocho, noventa y nueve, **cien**	*ninety-eight, ninety-nine, one hundred*

Ciento is used to express numbers above 100: **ciento uno, ciento dos,** and so on.

"My correct age? Well . . . thirty-five . . . no . . . thirty-nine? Oh, yes, forty-two. Yes, that's right."

PRÁCTICA

A. *Más problemas de matemáticas*

1. 30 + 50 = ?   5. 100 − 40 = ?
2. 45 + 45 = ?   6. 99 − 39 = ?
3. 32 + 58 = ?   7. 84 − 34 = ?
4. 77 + 23 = ?   8. 78 − 36 = ?

B. *Practique los números.*

1. 63 sombreros   6. 82 ciudades
2. 91 pesos   7. 61 pesetas
3. 44 calcetines   8. 39 almacenes
4. 100 bebidas   9. 75 personas
5. 76 abrigos   10. 57 parientes

CONVERSACIÓN

A. *¿Cuántos* (how many) *segundos hay en un minuto?   ¿Cuántos minutos hay en una hora?   ¿Cuántas horas en un día?   ¿Cuántos días en una semana?   ¿Cuántas semanas en un mes?   ¿Cuántos meses en un año?*

B. It is inventory time at the local department store. The following items are left over from last season's merchandise. Read the list to your supervisor, who will write it down.

50	faldas	49	pares de zapatos
100	pantalones	91	sombreros
71	blusas	64	medias
30	camisas	87	calcetines

DIÁLOGO: La visita de Lola

Los señores° Canales viven en Los Ángeles, California, con sus° tres hijos, Ceci, Emilio y Pepe. Lola, sobrina de los señores Canales, es de México y viene a Los Ángeles a visitar a sus° tíos.

Los... *Mr. and Mrs. / their*

her

A. *En el aeropuerto de Los Ángeles*
   SR. CANALES: ¡Bienvenida, Lola!

Frank Lesciandro/EPA, Inc.

SRA. CANALES:	¡Bienvenida, hija! ¿Qué tal el viaje°?
LOLA:	Excelente. Se viaja de prisa° y se come bien. Ya no° tengo miedo de los aviones.
SRA. CANALES:	¡Qué bien! Ahora puedes venir todos los años, ¿no?
LOLA:	Pues, no quiero ser una molestia° para Uds.
SR. CANALES:	¡Qué manera de hablar! Vivimos en una casa bastante° grande y tenemos un cuarto preparado.
LOLA:	Gracias. Y los primos, ¿qué tal?
SRA. CANALES:	Pues, muy bien todos. Ceci asiste a la universidad... tiene exámenes hoy. Pepe estudia en la escuela secundaria° y también tiene clases hoy.
LOLA:	¿Y Emilio?
SR. CANALES:	Él trabaja en uno de los grandes almacenes.
LOLA:	¡Qué conveniente! Antes de regresar necesito comprar unos regalos y otros recuerdos° para la familia.
SRA. CANALES:	Muy bien. Un día tienes que visitar el almacén de Emilio. Allí puedes comprar de todo.
LOLA:	Bueno... Sólo si Ud. viene también. No hablo muy bien el inglés.
SRA. CANALES:	No hay problema. Aquí se habla español en todas partes°.
SR. CANALES:	Por fin° las maletas°. Yo busco el carro y en cuarenta y cinco minutos llegamos a casa.

trip

de... *fast*
Ya... *no longer*

bother

quite

escuela.. *high school*

souvenirs

en... *everywhere*

Por... *finally / suitcases*

B. *Lola y Ceci de compras*

LOLA: Tienes razón, Ceci. Hay de todo, pero también es muy caro. En pesos es un horror y no puedo gastar° mucho.   *to spend (money)*

CECI: Pues, hay artículos de todo precio°. ¿Qué quieres comprar?   *de... in all price ranges*

LOLA: Es difícil... pues... una cartera para papá.

CECI: Perfecto. Donde trabaja Emilio se vende ropa para señores. ¿Qué más quieres?

LOLA: Una blusa o un suéter para mamá. ¿Qué crees?

CECI: Podemos decidir luego°. ¿Por qué no hablamos con Emilio ahora?   *later*

Comprensión

¿Cierto o falso? Corrija las oraciones falsas.

A. 1. Lola es la prima de los señores Canales.
   2. Los señores Canales viven en los Estados Unidos.
   3. Ellos tienen una casa muy pequeña.
   4. Ceci tiene tres hermanos.
   5. Emilio asiste a la universidad.
   6. Se habla español muy poco en Los Ángeles.
   7. La familia Canales vive muy cerca del (*close to*) aeropuerto.

B. 1. En el almacén venden de todo y muy barato.
   2. En pesos los precios son muy altos.
   3. Lola tiene mucho dinero en la cartera.
   4. Lola quiere comprar ropa para la familia.
   5. Emilio vende blusas.

Comentario cultural

In general, Hispanic tourists are as interested in shopping in the United States as North American tourists are in shopping abroad. Large department stores (**almacenes**) are more common in the United States than in Latin America and Spain. Conversely, in Hispanic countries small shops that specialize in particular products are much more common. A **zapatería** sells **zapatos,** a **papelería** is a stationery store, and so on. Frequently, many small shops or stalls are found in one area or building, which is called a **mercado.**

As you have seen in the dialog, many Mexicans come to the United States as tourists or to visit relatives who are living in the United States. They may be surprised to discover the large number of Hispanics living in the United States, particularly in the Southwest, California, New York, and, Florida, and the extent to which Spanish is spoken as a native language in this country, as the ads from the phone book on the next page show.

UN POCO DE TODO

A. *Cambie por el plural.*

1. No quieres vender el abrigo del abuelo, ¿verdad?
2. Se aprende una palabra importante todos los días.
3. No debes mirar la televisión si tienes sueño.
4. ¿Puede Ud. aprender cien palabras en una semana?
5. Tengo frío. Quiero regresar.

Cambie por el singular.

6. Queremos asistir a la clase.
7. ¿Por qué insisten Uds. en llevar cinco maletas? ¿Qué tienen allí?
8. Nosotros venimos tarde, pero se debe llegar temprano.
9. Se abren los libros en clase, ¿no?
10. Insisten en comer ahora porque tienen hambre.

B. *Form complete sentences based on the words given, in the order given. Conjugate the verbs and add other words if necessary.*

1. tú / siempre / tener / prisa; / deber / descansar / más
2. no / se / vender / trajes / vestidos / aquí / ¿verdad?
3. ella / poder / entrar / a / ocho / porque / se / abrir / temprano
4. Ud. / comprender / español / de / el Perú / ¿no?
5. se / vivir / bien / Guatemala

C. *Working with another student, ask and answer questions according to the model.*

MODELO   la fiesta / trabajar / ir (*to go*) a una fiesta →
ALFONSO: Vienes a *la fiesta,* ¿no?
CAROLINA: No puedo porque tengo que *trabajar,* pero creo que Anita tiene ganas de *ir a una fiesta.*

1. el baile / estudiar / bailar
2. el almacén / escribir una composición / comprar zapatos
3. el restaurante / leer una novela para la clase de inglés / comer
4. el mercado / aprender unas palabras para el examen / comprar una blusa
5. la clase / regresar a casa temprano hoy / aprender unas palabras de español

D. *Compose a want ad (un anuncio) for your local newspaper. Keep it simple and short, and avoid complete sentences—you're paying by the word! Use the model as a guide.*

MODELO   **SE BUSCA SECRETARIA.** *Inteligente y con experiencia. Trabajo diario* (daily work schedule) *de 8 a 6. 35 dólares el día. Referencias necesarias.*

Unas posibilidades:

1. **SE BUSCA PROFESOR(A) DE ESPAÑOL...**
2. **SE VENDEN LIBROS...**
3. **SE NECESITA EMPLEADO/A...**
4. **SE VENDE ROPA...**

E. *Complete las oraciones en una forma lógica.*

1. (No) Comprendo _____.
2. En clase escribimos _____.
3. Se vive bien en _____ porque hay _____.
4. Para ser buen(a) estudiante, se debe _____.
5. Se come bien en _____.
6. Se entra en la clase de español a la(s) _____.
7. Hoy quiero _____.
8. Para Ud., profesor(a), aquí tengo _____.
9. El/la profesor(a) puede _____ muy bien.
10. Vengo a la clase con _____.

VOCABULARIO

VERBOS

abrir   to open
aprender   to learn
asistir (a)   to attend, go to
beber   to drink
comer   to eat
comprender   to understand
creer (en)   to think, believe (in)
deber (+ *inf.*)   should, must,
   ought to (*do something*)
descansar   to rest
entrar (en)   to enter, go in
escribir   to write
insistir (en + *inf.*)   to insist
   (*on doing something*)
leer   to read
llevar   to wear; to carry
mirar   to look (at), watch
poder (ue)   to be able, can
querer (ie)   to want
recibir   to receive
regatear   to haggle,
   bargain
tener (ie)   to have
vender   to sell
venir (ie)   to come
viajar   to travel
visitar   to visit
vivir   to live

SUSTANTIVOS

el abrigo   coat
el almacén   department store
la blusa   blouse
la bolsa   purse

la bota   boot
los calcetines   socks
la camisa   shirt
la camiseta   T-shirt
la carta   letter
la cartera   wallet
el color   color
la chaqueta   jacket
el ejercicio   exercise
la falda   skirt
el impermeable   raincoat
la lengua   language
la maleta   suitcase
las medias   stockings
el mercado   market
la palabra   word
los pantalones   pants
el par   pair
el periódico   newspaper
el precio (fijo)   (fixed) price
la puerta   door
la ropa   clothing, clothes
la sandalia   sandal
el suéter   sweater
la tienda   shop, store
el traje   suit; costume
el vestido   dress
el zapato   shoe

ADJETIVOS

amarillo/a   yellow
anaranjado/a   orange
azul   blue
blanco/a   white
caro/a   expensive

gris   gray
morado/a   purple
negro/a   black
pardo/a   brown
rojo/a   red
rosado/a   pink
verde   green

PALABRAS Y EXPRESIONES ÚTILES

allí   there
de compras   shopping
de todo   everything
en casa   at home
¿no?   right? don't they (you, etc.)?
¿por qué?   why?
porque   because
que   that
tener
   ...años   to be . . . years old
   calor   to be warm (hot),
      feel warm (hot)
   frío   to be cold, feel cold
   ganas de (+ *inf.*)   to feel like
      (*doing something*)
   hambre   to be hungry
   miedo (de)   to be afraid (of)
   prisa   to be in a hurry
   que + *inf.*   to have to (*do some-
      thing*)
   razón   to be right
   sed   to be thirsty
   sueño   to be sleepy
siempre   always
¿verdad?   right? do they (you, etc.)?

Un paso más 3

Actividades

A. **¿Cómo usa Ud. su tiempo?** How frequently do you do each of the following things?

todos los días	every day
con frecuencia	frequently
una vez/dos veces a la semana/al mes	once/twice a week/a month
casi nunca	almost never
nunca	never

1. Leo novelas.
2. Miro la televisión.
3. Escribo una carta.
4. Como en un restaurante.
5. Aprendo palabras nuevas en español.
6. Leo el periódico.
7. Bebo Coca-Cola.
8. Compro un par de zapatos.
9. Llevo zapatos sin calcetines.
10. Llevo una camisa/blusa roja.
11. Vendo mis libros viejos.
12. Hablo con una persona de habla española (*a Spanish-speaking person*).

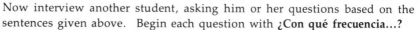

Now interview another student, asking him or her questions based on the sentences given above. Begin each question with **¿Con qué frecuencia...?**

MODELO   ¿Con qué frecuencia *lees novelas?*

B. **Lavandería y tintorería.** You are staying at a hotel in Mexico City, and you need to have laundry and dry cleaning done. A person from the hotel staff comes to pick up your clothing and to fill out the laundry form (p. 94). Working with another student, play the roles of hotel guest and staff member.

Frases útiles:

Su nombre, por favor.	*Your name, please.*
¿El número de su habitación?	*Your room number?*
¿Cuántos/as _____ hay?	*How many _____ are there?*
Muy bien, señor/señora/señorita.	*Fine, sir/ma'am/miss. I'll return*
Regreso mañana.	*tomorrow.*

LAVANDERÍA — TINTORERÍA			LAUNDRY — DRY CLEANING	
Cuenta del Húesped	Nuestra Cuenta		Tarifa	TOTAL
Guest's Count	Our Count		Rates Pesos	
		Batas—Robes	36.00	
		Blusas—Blouses	20.00	
		Calcetines—Socks	7.00	
		Camisones—Nightgowns	23.00	
		Camisas—Shirts	18.00	
		Camisas sport—Sport shirts	18.00	
		Corbatas—Neckties	14.00	
		Chaquetas—Jackets	30.00	
		Faldas—Skirts	28.00	
		Impermeables—Raincoats	45.00	
		Pantalones—Slacks	28.00	
		Pañuelos—Handkerchiefs	5.00	
		Pijamas—Pajamas	23.00	
		Ropa interior—Underwear	10.00	
		Sacos—Coats	28.00	
		Smoking—Tuxedos	65.00	
		Suéteres—Sweaters	28.00	
		Trajes—Suits	56.00	
		Trajes de noche—Evening dresses	CONVENCIONAL	
		Vestidos—Dresses	49.00	

C. **La guía telefónica.** You are traveling in Mexico and need the phone numbers of several Mexican friends. One of your classmates is the information operator, and you call him/her to get the numbers you need. Notice how phone numbers are grouped.

MODELO   2-23-45-75 →
           dos-veintitrés-cuarenta y cinco-setenta y cinco

Your conversation may begin something like this:

OPERADORA: Información.
  TURISTA: El número de la familia _____, por favor.
OPERADORA: Cómo no. ¿Dónde vive(n)?
  TURISTA: En la calle/avenida _____.
OPERADORA: Muy bien, señor/señora/señorita. El número es el _____-_____-
            _____-_____.
  TURISTA: Muchas gracias, _____. También necesito el número de _____.

After the operator has given you several numbers, change roles and begin again.

LA GUÍA TELEFÓNICA

Fierro Aguilar	Amalia	Avenida Juárez 86	7-65-03-91
Fierro Navarro	Teresa	Calle Misterios 45	5-86-58-16
Fierro Reyes	Gilberto	Avenida Miraflores 3	5-61-12-78
Figueroa López	Alberto	Calle Zaragoza 33	5-32-97-77
Figueroa Pérez	Julio	Avenida Iglesias 15	5-74-55-34
Gómez Pérez	Ana María	Calle Madero 7	7-94-43-88
Gómez Valencia	Javier	Avenida Córdoba 22	3-99-45-52
Guzmán Ávila	José Luis	Avenida Montevideo 4	6-57-29-40
Guzmán Martínez	Josefina	Avenida Independencia 25	2-77-22-70

D. **Ojo alerta.** ¿Cuáles (*what*) son las diferencias entre el dibujo (*drawing*) A y el dibujo B? Hay ocho diferencias en total.

MODELO   En el dibujo A hay ____;   en el dibujo B hay ____.

A.   B.

A propósito...

Here are a number of phrases that will be useful when you go shopping.
Vendedor(a):

¿Qué desea Ud.?	
¿En qué puedo servirle?	*Can I help you?*
Dígame.	
¿Qué talla necesita?	*What size do you need?* (clothing)
¿Qué número necesita?	*What size do you need?* (shoes)
¿De qué color?	*What color?*
No hay.	*We don't have any.*
No tenemos.	
Lo siento.	*I'm sorry.*
No nos quedan.	*We don't have any left.*

Cliente:

Deseo comprar un regalo para...	*I want to buy a gift for . . .*
¿Tienen Uds....?	*Do you have . . .?*
¿Cuánto es/son?	
¿Cuánto vale(n)?	*How much is it/are they?*
¿Qué precio tiene(n)?	
Es muy caro/a.	*It's very expensive.*
Necesito algo más barato.	*I need something cheaper.*

E. **De compras.** Although it is often possible—and lots of fun—to bargain over the price of an item in a shop or open-air market, for example, merchandise is normally sold at a fixed price in many, if not most, Hispanic stores.

   With another student take the roles of customer and salesperson in the following situations. Use the preceding phrases and the model, along with variations of them, to help you make your sales and purchases. Try to vary the conversation between salesperson and customer with each purchase.

MODELO   VENDEDOR: ¿Qué desea Ud., señorita?

            CLIENTE: Necesito comprar un diccionario español-inglés.

          VENDEDOR: Muy bien, señorita. Aquí tenemos un diccionario grande y completo.

            CLIENTE: Es un diccionario excelente pero es muy caro, ¿no?

          VENDEDOR: Ud. tiene razón, señorita. El otro diccionario es bueno y barato.

            CLIENTE: ¿Cuánto es, por favor?

          VENDEDOR: Cuesta 90 pesos.

            CLIENTE: Perfecto. Aquí tiene Ud. los 90 pesos.

          VENDEDOR: Muy bien, señorita.

            CLIENTE: Adiós, Sr. Ramírez.

          VENDEDOR: Adiós, señorita. Muy buenas.

1. En la librería de la universidad: Ud. desea comprar dos cuadernos pequeños.
2. En una tienda pequeña: Ud. desea comprar una blusa azul para su hermana (madre, amiga, tía).
3. En un almacén: Ud. quiere comprar un regalo para un amigo.
4. En una tienda de flores: Ud. necesita comprar seis rosas rojas.

Lectura cultural: Las modas°

fashions

Por lo general los hispanos no se visten° muy informalmente. Es cierto que los jóvenes llevan ropa de última moda° y las personas mayores° ropa más conservadora, pero también es cierto que todos se visten más elegantemente que° aquí en los Estados Unidos.

    La tendencia hispánica es parecer° elegante en casi° todas las ocasiones. Es verdad que los *bluejeans* son la moda en muchas partes —especialmente

se.. dress

de... fashionable / older

than

to seem, appear / almost

Michael D. Sullivan

Sybil Shelton/Peter Arnold, Inc.

entre los jóvenes— pero es preferible estar° elegante cuando uno no está°   *to be / is*
en casa.   Por ejemplo, para los hombres, se considera mala costumbre°   *custom*
estar en la calle° con camisa de manga corta° y sin chaqueta.   Tampoco°   *street /* **de..** *short sleeve /*
llevan ropa de colores brillantes.   Los pantalones, las camisas y las   *neither*
chaquetas de color azul, negro o gris son preferibles.

Se cree que hay pocas mujeres tan elegantes como las hispánicas, y es
verdad.   En las ciudades grandes como Madrid, Barcelona, Buenos Aires,
Lima, Caracas y Bogotá hay mujeres tan bien vestidas y peinadas como°   **tan...** *as well dressed*
las mujeres de París.   *and coiffed as*

Comprensión

Check your comprehension of the reading selection by matching the sentence fragments in the two columns to form complete sentences.   Then indicate whether
each statement is true or false.

1. Ud. debe saber (*to know*)
2. Los jóvenes y los viejos
3. Los norteamericanos llevan ropa
4. En la calle un hombre hispano
   tiene que llevar
5. Muchos hombres hispanos llevan
6. Las mujeres hispanas no

a. llevan el mismo estilo de ropa
b. que los hispanos no se visten
   (*dress*) exactamente como los
   norteamericanos
c. camisa de manga corta
d. más elegante que los hispanos
e. camisas rojas en todas las oca-
   siones
f. son tan elegantes como las fran-
   cesas

Ejercicios escritos

A. ¿Qué lleva Ud.?

1. Llevo _____ a una fiesta.
2. Llevo _____ cuando paso el día en casa.
3. Cuando asisto a mis clases, llevo _____.
4. Cuando voy (*I go*) de compras, llevo _____.

B. Complete el párrafo siguiente sobre las modas en los Estados Unidos.

En los Estados Unidos la individualidad es importante en las modas.   Por
ejemplo, los estudiantes llevan _____, pero los profesores _____.   También
son diferentes los estilos de los jóvenes y los viejos.   Las madres llevan _____
y los padres _____.   Pero yo, cuando bailo en una discoteca (estudio en la
biblioteca, trabajo en casa) llevo _____.

capítulo 4 La vida social

© Peter Menzel

OBJETIVOS

In this chapter you will learn the days of the week, and vocabulary and expressions related to friend-ship, dating, and marriage.

You will also learn about the following aspects of Spanish grammar:

16. three irregular verbs, **dar** (*to give*), **estar** (*to be*), and **ir** (*to go*), plus the use of **ir** to talk about what you are going to do in the future

17. the use of **estar** with the gerund (**tomando,** *taking*), to express an action that is in progress: **estoy hablando (comiendo, abriendo),** *I am talking (eating, opening)*

18. how to show possession or ownership by using possessive adjectives: **mi casa** (*my house*), **nuestro carro** (*our car*)

19. the pronouns used as objects of prepositions in expressions such as **para mí** (*for me*) and **con nosotros** (*with us*)

20. demonstrative adjectives and pronouns (words that express *this, that, these,* and *those,* as well as *this one* and *that one*)

Un paso más includes activities related to social life and social roles, and a reading about the social activities of Hispanic people.

VOCABULARIO: PREPARACIÓN

Los días de la semana

lunes	Monday	**viernes**	Friday
martes	Tuesday	**sábado**	Saturday
miércoles	Wednesday	**domingo**	Sunday
jueves	Thursday		

el lunes, el martes...	on Monday, on Tuesday . . .
los lunes, los martes...	on Mondays, on Tuesdays . . .
hoy (mañana) es viernes	today (tomorrow) is Friday
el fin de semana	the weekend

Except for **el sábado/los sábados** and **el domingo/los domingos**, all the days of the week use the same form for the plural as they do for the singular. The definite articles are used to express *on* with the days of the week. The days are not capitalized in Spanish.

A. Preguntas.

1. ¿Qué día es hoy? ¿mañana?
2. ¿Cuántos días hay en una semana?
3. ¿Qué días de la semana tenemos clase?
4. ¿Qué días de la semana no tenemos clase?
5. ¿Estudia Ud. mucho durante (*during*) el fin de semana? ¿Los domingos por la noche?

B. Tell at least one thing you want, need, have to do, or can do each day this week.

MODELO   *El lunes yo quiero* (necesito, tengo que, puedo) *asistir a clase.*

Las relaciones sentimentales

la amistad	friendship	**el noviazgo**	courtship,
la cita	date; appointment		engagement
el amor	love	**la boda**	wedding
		el matrimonio	marriage
		el divorcio	divorce

Andrew Sacks/EPA, Inc.

La boda

el novio	boyfriend; fiancé; groom	**el esposo**	husband
la novia	girlfriend; fiancée; bride	**la esposa**	wife

Adjetivos

moreno/a
trigueño/a } brunette   **rubio/a** blond
cariñoso/a affectionate

C. *¿Cierto o falso? Conteste cierto, falso o depende.*

1. El amor verdadero (*real*) no existe.
2. El noviazgo debe ser largo y formal.
3. El matrimonio es una obligación social necesaria.
4. Un novio/una novia es una limitación.
5. Las bodas grandes y formales son una tontería (*foolish thing*).
6. Un novio debe ser alto, moreno (trigueño) y guapo.
7. En una cita, la mujer debe pagar todo.
8. Las mujeres rubias no son muy inteligentes.
9. La amistad entre (*between*) los ex-esposos es posible después de (*after*) un divorcio.

D. *Unscramble the phrases in the right-hand column to form the definitions of the words on the left.*

1. el amor: relación / entre / cariñosa / novios / los
2. la amistad: dos / entre / amigos / relación
3. el divorcio: matrimonio / cuando / un / termina / se
4. el matrimonio: esposos / legal / entre / relación
5. el noviazgo: matrimonio / al / preludio
6. la cita: pasar tiempo / o / el novio / un amigo / con

Preposiciones			
cerca de	close to	**a la izquierda**	to the left
lejos de	far from	**(derecha) de**	(right) of
delante de	in front of	**entre**	between, among
detrás de	behind	**en**	on; in

A *preposition* or *prepositional phrase* is a word or group of words that expresses relationships in time or space—for example, **cerca de Juan** (*close to Juan*).

E. *¿Qué hay en el dibujo?*

MODELO   el hospital → *Hay un hospital a la derecha del bar.*

1. el bar
2. la ambulancia
3. el cine (*movie theater*)
4. la iglesia (*church*)
5. el cura (*priest*)
6. los novios
7. el niño
8. los árboles (*trees*)
9. la mamá
10. el parque pequeño

PRONUNCIACIÓN: B/V, F, and CH

Some sounds, such as English [b], are called *stops* because, as you pronounce them, you briefly stop the flow of air and then release it. Other sounds, such as English [f] and [v], pronounced by pressing the air out with a little friction, are called *fricatives*.

B/V In Spanish the pronunciation of the letters **b** and **v** is identical. At the beginning of a phrase or sentence, that is, after a pause, or after **m** or **n,** the letters **b** and **v** are pronounced just like the English stop [b]. Everywhere else they are pronounced like the fricative [ɓ], produced by creating friction when pressing the air through the lips. This sound has no equivalent in English.

F The letter **f** is pronounced as in English. Spanish always uses the letter **f**—never *ph*—to represent the sound [f]: **filosofía, fase, elefante.**

CH **Ch,** considered one letter in Spanish, is pronounced like the *ch* in English *chat, such.*

PRÁCTICA

Practique las siguientes palabras y frases.

1. [b]   bueno viejo verde venir barato Vicente boda viernes también hambre sombrero bienvenido hombre
2. [b̪]   novio llevar libro pobre abrir abrigo universidad
3. [b/b̪] bueno/es bueno un viaje/el viaje viajar/quiere viajar bien/muy bien en Venezuela/de Venezuela vende/se vende
4. [b/b̪] beber bebida vivir biblioteca
5. fin favor fiesta café francés Francia familia famoso
6. mucho chica chaqueta coche derecha *sándwich* chocolate Chile

---

MINIDIÁLOGOS Y GRAMÁTICA

---

16. PRESENT TENSE OF *DAR, ESTAR,* AND *IR; IR + A* + INFINITIVE

¿En la oficina del consejero matrimonial?

FEDERICO: ...y nunca *estás* en casa cuando yo regreso de la oficina.

MARICARMEN: *Estoy* de acuerdo, pero no puedo *estar* en casa con los niños todo el santo día. A veces *voy* al parque o a la...

SR. ALONSO: Perdón. El caso *está* muy claro. Un divorcio es la única solución.

MARICARMEN: Pero... un consejero debe *dar* consejos...

SR. ALONSO: Pero soy abogado. El consejero matrimonial *está* en la otra oficina.

1. ¿Dónde están Federico y Maricarmen?
2. ¿Cuál es la queja (complaint) de Federico? ¿Maricarmen está de acuerdo?
3. ¿Adónde va Maricarmen a veces? ¿Por qué?
4. ¿Cuál es la solución del Sr. Alonso? ¿Por qué da este (this) consejo?
5. ¿Dónde está el consejero matrimonial?

DAR: *to give*		ESTAR: *to be*		IR: *to go*	
doy	damos	estoy	estamos	voy	vamos
das	dais	estás	estáis	vas	vais
da	dan	está	están	va	van

At the marriage counselor's office? FEDERICO: . . . and you're never at home when I come back from the office. MARICARMEN: I agree, but I can't be at home with the kids the whole darned (blessed) day. Sometimes I go to the park or to the . . . ALONSO: Pardon me. The case is very clear. A divorce is the only solution. MARICARMEN: But . . . a counselor should give advice . . . ALONSO: But I'm a lawyer. The marriage counselor is in the other office.

Estar: ¿Dónde **está** el parque?   *Where is the park?*
             ¿Cómo **está** Ud.?   *How are you?*
             Estoy bien (mal, enfermo).   *I'm fine (not well, sick).*

Forms of **estar** are used to tell where someone or something is, and to talk about how someone is feeling, one's condition or state of health.*
  Estar de acuerdo (con) means *to be in agreement (with).*

   ¿No **están** Uds. **de acuerdo con** Pablo?   *Don't you agree with Pablo?*

Ir: Vamos a clase ahora mismo.   *Let's go to class right now.*

The first person plural of **ir, vamos** (*we go, are going, do go*), is also used to express *let's go.*
  Ir + **a** + *infinitive* is used to describe actions or events in the near future.

        Voy a estudiar esta tarde.   *I'm going to study this afternoon.*
        Van a venir a la fiesta esta   *They're going to come to the*
          noche.   *party tonight.*

PRÁCTICA

A. *Dé Ud. frases nuevas según las indicaciones.*

   1. —¿Quién da consejos?
      —*Nosotros* damos consejos.   (*Ud., yo, los abogados, Ud. y yo, la consejera, vosotros*)
   2. —¿Cómo están Uds.?
      —*Nosotros* estamos muy bien.   (*yo, ellos, Javier, tú, Rita, vosotros*)
   3. —Los viernes todos van a la cafetería después de la clase, ¿verdad?
      —Sí, *Fernando* va a la cafetería.   (*tú, Rosalba, yo, nosotras, Ud., vosotros*)
   4. —¿Quién va a asistir a la boda el sábado?
      —*Los novios* van a asistir a la boda.   (*yo, todos los amigos, nosotros, tú, los padres de los novios, vosotras*)

B. *Form complete sentences by using one word or phrase from each column.*

yo		al cine
Bolivia	dar	en Suramérica
mis compañeros de clase (no)	ir	muchas fiestas
tú	estar	a la boda con él
nosotros		muy mal hoy
_____		dinero a las causas políticas
		a la fiesta en Río
		_____

*The uses of **ser** and **estar** will be contrasted in grammar section 21 (Chapter 5).

C. *Exprese con **ir** + **a** + el infinitivo, según el modelo.*

MODELO   Raúl habla con Estela → Raúl *va a hablar* con Estela.

1. Los niños aprenden mucho.
2. Guillermina tiene una cita con Raúl el domingo.
3. Entramos en la iglesia a las ocho.
4. Tú vendes el coche el lunes, ¿no?
5. Termino los ejercicios y luego (*then*) vamos al cine.

D. *¿Cómo se dice en español?   Describa Ud. la luna de miel* (honeymoon) *de Juan y Marta.   Use Ud. **ir** + **a** + el infinitivo para expresar el tiempo futuro.*

On Monday at ten P.M. the plane arrives at the Mexico City airport. On Tuesday we'll visit the Cathedral **(la catedral)** and the Pyramids **(las pirámides)** of Teotihuacán. On Wednesday we'll go to the Anthropological Museum **(Museo de Antropología)**. On Thursday we'll buy presents at the Merced Market **(Mercado de la Merced),** and then **(luego)** we're going to go to the **Ballet Folklórico.** On Friday we return home.

CONVERSACIÓN

A. *¿Dónde están las ciudades siguientes* (following)*?*

1. ¿Amarillo? ¿Los Ángeles? ¿San Agustín? ¿Toledo? ¿Santa Fe? ¿Reno?
2. ¿Managua? ¿Guadalajara? ¿Buenos Aires? ¿La Habana? ¿Quito? ¿La Paz? ¿Bogotá?

B. *¿Con qué o con quién está Ud. de acuerdo?*

1. (No) Estoy de acuerdo con la política de... (el presidente, los republicanos, los demócratas, el senador _____, Karl Marx, los capitalistas, _____)
2. (No) Estoy de acuerdo con las ideas de... (mis padres, mis abuelos, mis profesores, todos mis amigos, las instituciones religiosas, _____)

C. *Complete las oraciones en una forma lógica.*

1. Este (*this*) año voy a viajar a _____.
2. Mañana voy a llevar _____ a la clase porque _____.
3. Un día voy a tener _____.
4. Un día voy a ser _____.
5. Un día voy a comprar _____.
6. Un día voy a poder _____.
7. Esta noche (*tonight*) voy a estudiar _____.
8. Esta noche voy a estar en _____.
9. Esta noche voy a comer en _____.
10. Mañana voy a entrar en clase a las _____.

D. **¿Qué vamos a hacer?** *Form sentences that tell where you are and one thing that you are going to do there. Follow the model.*

MODELO   en la clase → *Estamos en la clase.*
                          Vamos a cantar en español.

1. en la clase
2. en el parque
3. en casa
4. en una fiesta
5. en un restaurante o en un bar

17. PRESENT PROGRESSIVE: *ESTAR + -NDO*

The sentences in the left-hand column tell what the following persons are able to do.   Following the example, tell what they are doing right now.

Dolores puede bailar muy bien.   → Dolores **está bailando** ahora mismo.
Soledad puede cantar muy bien.   → Soledad **está** _____.
Yo puedo hablar español muy bien.   → Yo _____.
El/la profesor(a) puede enseñar muy bien. → Él/ella _____.

The sentences in the left-hand column tell what the following persons want to do. Following the example, tell what they are doing at the moment.

Santiago quiere comer.   → Santiago **está comiendo** en este momento.
Nati quiere beber.   → Nati **está** _____.
Yo quiero escribir una carta.   → Yo _____.
Tú quieres abrir el regalo.   → Tú _____.

Formation of the Progressive

In English the *present progressive* is formed with the verb *to be* and the *present participle*, the verb form that ends in *-ing: I am walking, we are driving, she is studying*.

The Spanish present progressive (**progresivo**) is formed with **estar** plus the present participle (**gerundio**), which is formed by adding **-ando** to the stem of **-ar** verbs and **-iendo** to the stem of **-er** and **-ir** verbs.* The present participle never varies; it always ends in **-o**.

tomar	→ **tomando**	*taking; drinking*
comprender	→ **comprendiendo**	*understanding*
abrir	→ **abriendo**	*opening*

When an unstressed **-i-** occurs between two vowels, it becomes a **-y-**.

leer	→ **leyendo**	*reading*
creer	→ **creyendo**	*believing*

Use of the Progressive

Ramón **está comiendo** ahora mismo.	*Ramón is eating right now.*
Compramos la casa mañana.	*We're buying the house tomorrow.*
Ella **estudia** química este semestre.	*She's studying chemistry this semester.*

In Spanish, the present progressive is used only to describe an action that is actually in progress, as in the first sentence above. The simple Spanish present is used to express other English usages of the present progressive: to tell what is going to happen (the second sentence) and to tell what someone is doing over a period of time but not necessarily at this very moment (the third sentence).

PRÁCTICA

A. Dé Ud. frases nuevas según las indicaciones.

—Todos los amigos de Ud. están en una fiesta. Ud. quiere asistir también. ¿Por qué?
—Todos están *bailando. (tomar, cantar, comer, abrir botellas de champán, hablar mucho)*
—Pero Ud. no puede ir. ¿Por qué no?
—Estoy *estudiando. (trabajar, escribir los ejercicios, leer el periódico, mirar un programa fascinante, aprender el vocabulario nuevo)*

---

*Ir, poder, and venir—as well as several other verbs that you will learn later—have irregular present participles: yendo, pudiendo, viniendo. However, these three verbs are seldom used in the progressive.

B. *Cambie por el progresivo, usando también las palabras entre paréntesis.*

1. Los estudiantes leen mucho. (en este momento)
2. Visitas la iglesia de San Pedro. (ahora)
3. Escribo en español. (ahora mismo)
4. Viajamos a Acapulco. (en este momento)
5. Venden fruta barata en el mercado. (hoy)

CONVERSACIÓN

¿Qué están haciendo (doing) *estas personas?   ¿Qué cree Ud.?   Use el progresivo de los verbos a la derecha.*

1. Vikki Carr   cocinar (*to cook*)
2. James Michener   buscar criminales
3. Julia Child   escribir
4. James Bond   bailar
5. los empleados de McDonald's   vender hamburguesas
6. el presidente de los Estados Unidos   cantar
7. Pablo Picasso   entrar en la Casa Blanca
8. José Greco   pintar

18. POSSESSIVE ADJECTIVES (UNSTRESSED)

En el periódico

Querida Antonia,
   Tengo un problema con *mis* padres. Creen que *mi* novio es demasiado pobre. *¡Nuestra* situación es imposible! ¿Qué debo hacer?
                                   Sola en *mi* tristeza

Querida Sola,
   Tu situación es difícil pero no es imposible. Debes contraer matrimonio con un ladrón; casi siempre son ricos los ladrones. Por otro lado, casi siempre ya tienen un par de esposas.*
                              Antonia

1. *¿Quién escribe y quién contesta* (answers)*?*
2. *¿Antonia tiene un problema con sus padres?*
3. *¿Cómo es el novio de Sola? (Su novio...)*
4. *¿Antonia cree que la situación de Sola es imposible? (Antonia cree que su situación...)*
5. *¿Con quién debe contraer matrimonio Sola? ¿Por qué?*

In the newspaper Dear Antonia, I have a problem with my parents. They think that my boyfriend is too poor. Our situation is impossible! What should I do? Alone in my sadness Dear Alone, Your situation is difficult, but it isn't impossible. You should marry a thief; thieves are almost always rich. On the other hand, they almost always have a couple of wives (handcuffs*) already. Antonia

*The plural form **esposas** means *handcuffs,* as well as *wives.*

POSSESSIVE ADJECTIVES				
my	**mi** libro/mesa **mis** libros/mesas	*our*	nuestro libro nuestros libros	nuestra mesa nuestras mesas
your	**tu** libro/mesa **tus** libros/mesas	*your*	vuestro libro vuestros libros	vuestra mesa vuestras mesas
your, his, *her, its*	**su** libro/mesa **sus** libros/mesas	*your,* *their*	**su** libro/mesa **sus** libros/mesas	

In Spanish, possessive adjectives agree in form with the person or thing possessed, not with the owner/possessor. Note that possessive adjectives are placed before the noun.

$$\text{Son} \begin{Bmatrix} \text{mis} \\ \text{tus} \\ \text{sus} \end{Bmatrix} \text{zapatos.} \qquad \text{Es} \begin{Bmatrix} \text{nuestra} \\ \text{vuestra} \\ \text{su} \end{Bmatrix} \text{casa.}$$

The possessive adjectives **mi(s), tu(s),** and **su(s)** show agreement with the noun they modify in number only. **Nuestro/a/os/as** and **vuestro/a/os/as,** like all adjectives that end in **-o,** show agreement in number and gender.

Su(s) can have several different equivalents in English: *your* (sing.), *his, her, its, your* (pl.), *their.* Usually, its meaning will be clear in context. For example, if you are admiring the car of someone whom you address as **Ud.** and ask, **¿Es nuevo su coche?,** it is clear from the context that you mean *Is your car new?* When context does not make the meaning of **su(s)** clear, **de** and a pronoun are used to indicate the possessor.

$$\left. \begin{matrix} \text{el coche} \\ \text{la casa} \\ \text{los libros} \\ \text{las mesas} \end{matrix} \right\} \text{de él (de ella, de Ud., de ellos, de ellas, de Uds.)}$$

¿Son jóvenes los hijos **de él?**   *Are his children young?*
¿Dónde vive el abuelo **de ellas?**   *Where does their grandfather live?*

PRÁCTICA

A. *Which nouns can these possessive adjectives modify without changing form?*

1. *su:* problema / pantalones / dinero / exámenes / amor / medias
2. *tus:* camisetas / idea / novias / falda / tazas / mercado

3. *mi:*   cita / ejercicios / suéter / carro / boda / amistad
4. *sus:*   trajes / periódico / limitaciones / zapato / televisión / boda
5. *nuestras:*   blusa / noviazgo / camisas / cine / tienda / nieta
6. *nuestro:*   tacos / calcetines / parientes / puerta / clase / sombrero

B. *Dé Ud. frases nuevas según las indicaciones.*

1. —¿Son cariñosos los parientes de Ud.?
   —Mi *primo* (no) es cariñoso.   (*hermanos, tíos, hija, primos, abuela, esposo/a*)
2. —María tiene mucha ropa.   ¿Cómo es su ropa?
   —Sus *blusas* son elegantes.   (*zapatos, faldas, abrigo, bolsas, ropa*)
3. —¿Cómo es la clase de Uds.?
   —Nuestra *clase* es magnífica.   (*profesor(a), compañeros, español, ideas*)

C. *Exprese según el modelo.*

MODELO   la casa de Paco → *su* casa
                        → *la* casa *de él*

1. los recuerdos de Paula
2. la profesión de mi novio
3. las ideas de mis amigas
4. el cuarto de Eugenia
5. los parientes de los empleados

D. *¿Cómo se dice en español?*

1. my shoes   4. their reason
2. his relatives 5. your wedding
3. our love   6. his fiancée

CONVERSACIÓN

A. *Tell the class about your family and friends.   Use the following questions as a guide when appropriate.*

1. ¿Su familia es grande?   ¿pequeña?
2. ¿Sus padres son norteamericanos?   ¿latinos?   ¿rubios?   ¿trigueños?
3. ¿Sus padres son simpáticos?   ¿cariñosos?   ¿generosos?
4. ¿Su padre/madre trabaja?   ¿Dónde?
5. ¿Cuántos hijos tienen sus padres?
6. ¿Sus hermanos son listos?   ¿jóvenes?   ¿trabajadores?   ¿Trabajan o estudian?
7. ¿Viven Uds. en una casa o en un apartamento?   ¿Cómo es su casa/apartamento?
8. ¿Sus abuelos/tíos viven en la casa/el apartamento también?
9. ¿Tiene Ud. esposo/a o novio/a?   ¿Quién es?   ¿Trabaja o estudia?

B. *¿Qué palabras asocia Ud. con las frases siguientes?*

1. nuestro país (*country*): Nuestro país _____; en nuestro país _____.
2. nuestra clase
3. nuestra universidad
4. el carro de Ud./de su familia

19. PRONOUN OBJECTS OF PREPOSITIONS

mí	*me*	nosotros/as	*us*
ti	*you* (fam.)	vosotros/as	*you* (fam.)
usted	*you* (form.)	ustedes	*you* (form.)
él	*him*	ellos	*them* (m. or m. + f.)
ella	*her*	ellas	*them* (f.)

The *object* **(complemento)** of a preposition is the noun or pronoun that follows it: *The book is for Tom/him.*

In Spanish, the pronouns that serve as objects of prepositions are identical in form to the subject pronouns, with the exception of **mí** and **ti**. Note the accent mark that distinguishes the pronoun object of a preposition **mí** from the possessive adjective **mi**.

The phrases **conmigo** and **contigo** are used to express the ideas *with me* and *with you* (familiar singular).

LÓGICO

Sabes, querida, he estado de compras.

Bien, ¿y qué has comprado?

Para ti, un tutú, y para mí un yoyó.

¿Estudias **conmigo** mañana?	*Will you study with me tomorrow?*
No, no puedo estudiar **contigo**.	*No, I can't study with you.*

Subject pronouns are used after the preposition **entre** (*between, among*).

Entre tú y yo, Horacio es un chico antipático.	*Between you and me, Horacio is an unpleasant guy.*

PRÁCTICA

A. *Working with another student, ask and answer questions according to the model.*

MODELO   el primo Jaime →
        ARTURO: ¿Para quién es el regalo? ¿Para *el primo Jaime*?
        BEATRIZ: Sí, es para *él*.

1. la novia   4. nosotros
2. mí   5. Uds.
3. las chicas   6. ti

Logical You know, dear, I've been shopping. Fine. What did you buy? For you, a tutu, and for me a yoyo.

B. *Complete Ud. la declaración de amor del novio a la novia.*

1. Nunca bailo con otra mujer. Siempre bailo con _____.
2. Nunca canto para otra mujer. Siempre canto para _____.
3. Nunca asisto a las fiestas sin (*without*) ti. Siempre asisto con _____.
4. No deseo vivir sin ti. Deseo vivir siempre con _____.

C. *¿Cómo se dice en español?*

1. They're talking about (**de**) her.
2. I'll study with you (*familiar*) on Friday.
3. Between you and me, the party is for him.
4. Are they coming with us?

CONVERSACIÓN

A. *Para Ud., ¿qué es difícil? ¿qué es fácil (easy)?*

Para mí, es _____.

B. *Hay muchos secretos en la clase. Cuente Ud. (tell) un secreto a otro/a estudiante.*

Entre tú y yo, _____.

20. DEMONSTRATIVE ADJECTIVES AND PRONOUNS

	DEMONSTRATIVE ADJECTIVES	
this	este libro	esta mesa
these	estos libros	estas mesas
that	ese libro aquel libro (allí)	esa mesa aquella mesa (allí)
those	esos libros aquellos libros (allí)	esas mesas aquellas mesas (allí)

Demonstrative Adjectives

Demonstrative adjectives (**adjetivos demostrativos**) are used to point out or indicate a specific noun or nouns. There are four demonstrative adjectives in English: *this* and its plural form *these, that* and its plural *those*. In English and in Spanish, demonstrative adjectives precede the noun they modify. In Spanish they also agree in number and gender with the noun.

A. **Este/a, estos/as** (*this, these*):

Este carro es de Francia.	*This car is from France.*
Estas señoritas son argentinas.	*These women are Argentinean.*

Forms of **este** are used to refer to nouns that are close to the speaker.

B. **Ese/a, esos/as** (*that, those*):

Ese hombre (cerca de Ud.) es abogado.	*That man (close to you) is a lawyer.*
Esas blusas son baratas.	*Those blouses are cheap.*

Forms of **ese** are used to refer to nouns that are near the person addressed.

C. **Aquel/la, aquellos/as** (*that* [over there], *those* [over there]):

Aquel coche (allí en la calle) es rápido.	*That car (there in the street) is fast.*
Aquella casa (en las montañas) es del hermano de Ramiro.	*That house (in the mountains) belongs to Ramiro's brother.*

Forms of **aquel** are used to refer to nouns that are distant from the speaker and the listener.

[Práctica A, B]

Demonstrative Pronouns

In English and in Spanish, the demonstrative adjectives can be used as pronouns, that is, in place of nouns. Note the use of the accent mark to distinguish demonstrative pronouns (**éste, ése, aquél**) from demonstrative adjectives (**este, ese, aquel**).

Necesito este diccionario y **ése.**	*I need this dictionary and that one.*
Estas señoras y **aquéllas** son las damas de honor, ¿verdad?	*These women and those (over there) are the bridesmaids, right?*

[Práctica C]

Neuter Demonstratives

The neuter demonstratives **esto, eso,** and **aquello** mean *this, that* (nearby), and *that* (far away) respectively.

¿Qué es **esto?**	*What is this?*
Eso es todo.	*That's all.*
¡Aquello es terrible!	*That's terrible.*

They refer to a whole idea, concept, situation, or statement, or to an as yet unidentified object. They never refer to a specific noun (**este libro, esa mesa,** and so on), and their form never changes.

[Práctica D, E]

PRÁCTICA

A. *Dé Ud. frases nuevas según las indicaciones.*

  1. —¿Qué se necesita para la clase hoy?
     —Se necesita este *libro.* (*papeles, mesa, exámenes, diccionario, lápices, ejercicios*)
  2. —¿De qué color es la ropa de los estudiantes?
     —Ese *sombrero* es azul. (*blusa, zapatos, pantalones, camisa, falda, calcetines*)

B. *Imagine that you have been to Mexico. Tell a friend about some of the people, places, and things you got to know. Follow the model.*

  MODELO   el restaurante Independencia / excelente →
             Aquel restaurante *es* excelente.

  1. la tienda de ropa en la calle Quince / barata
  2. los periódicos de la capital / magníficos
  3. el hotel Libertad / fenomenal
  4. los dependientes del hotel Libertad / simpáticos
  5. los precios en los almacenes / fijos

C. *Cambie los adjetivos demostrativos por pronombres demostrativos.*

  MODELO   Este libro es importante. → *Éste* es importante.

  1. Este joven es trigueño.
  2. Esas señoras son argentinas.
  3. Estos niños son rubios.
  4. Aquella actriz es una persona muy amable.
  5. Ese niño es muy listo.
  6. Aquellos cuadernos son para David.

D. *Match the questions or statements in the left-hand column with the situations described on the right.*

  1. ¿Qué es esto?
  2. ¿Todo eso?
  3. Eso es terrible.
  4. ¿Qué es aquello?

  a. En la montaña hay una cosa que Ud. no puede ver (*see*) muy bien.
  b. El profesor dice (*says*), «Uds. tienen que estudiar para un examen mañana y tienen que escribir una composición para el lunes.»
  c. Ud. abre el regalo y descubre una cosa interesante y curiosa.
  d. La hermana de un amigo está en el hospital por (*because of*) un accidente de carro.

E. *¿Cómo se dice en español?*

1. That suit is very expensive.
2. Those clients are very poor.
3. We need those pens over there, not these (**éstos no**).
4. He wants to buy that hotel in the mountains.
5. This store opens at 10:00, not that one.
6. Why are we studying this?

CONVERSACIÓN

A. *Describa Ud. los objetos y las personas de la clase de español. Siga el modelo.*

MODELO   **Esta mujer** *es rubia y* **aquélla** *es trigueña.*

B. *Preguntas.*

1. ¿Qué desea Ud. hacer esta noche? ¿Y este fin de semana?
2. ¿Cómo es esta universidad? ¿Cómo es esta clase? Y este libro, ¿cómo es?
3. ¿Cómo es esta ciudad? ¿y este estado?
4. ¿Quién es el presidente de este país? ¿Qué lenguas se hablan en este país?

DIÁLOGO: Tres perspectivas sobre° el amor   *about, on*

Aquí hay unos diálogos sobre varios aspectos del amor. ¿Cuál es la perspectiva de cada° persona? ¿Y cuál es la perspectiva de Ud.?   *each*

A. *El sábado en casa*

Amalia, una chica de quince años de edad
Margarita, su hermana, estudiante universitaria de veintiún años

AMALIA: ¡Ay, Margarita! Tengo un novio y...
MARGARITA: ¡Qué tonta eres!, Amalia. Sólo tienes quince años. Eres muy joven para tener un novio. Mira°, te° voy a   *look / to you* dar un buen consejo. Primero° tienes que terminar   *first* tus estudios y buscar un trabajo.
AMALIA: ¿Buscar un trabajo? Primero dices° que soy muy   *you say* joven para tener un novio y ahora dices que tengo que buscar un trabajo.
MARGARITA: Sí, eso es°. Un novio va a ser una limitación en todo   **eso...** *that's right* eso.

© Peter Menzel

B. *Delante de la iglesia*

    Panchito, un niño de siete años
    La señora Martínez, mamá de Panchito
    Don Federico, padre de la novia

        PANCHITO: Pero no tengo ganas de asistir a esta boda, mamá.
                  Las bodas son una tontería.

  SRA. MARTÍNEZ: Basta ya°, mi hijo. Todos están entrando ya en la   **Basta...** *that's enough*
                  iglesia. Tú vas a entrar conmigo.   *now*

    (*En la iglesia, un poco más tarde°.*)   **más...***later*

  SRA. MARTÍNEZ: Mira, Panchito, ésas son las damas de honor.
        PANCHITO: Y aquélla es la novia, ¿verdad? ¿Por qué está con
                  su padre?

  SRA. MARTÍNEZ: Porque es el padrino° y los padrinos llevan a la°   *best man* / **llevan...** *take*
                  novia al altar. Don Federico debe estar muy con-   *the*
                  tento hoy.

        PANCHITO: ¿Por qué?

  SRA. MARTÍNEZ: Porque el novio tiene una buena posición social y
                  está muy bien económicamente. ¿Qué más puede
                  desear un padre para su hija?

C. *Entrevista° con la familia Jiménez*   *interview*

    Entrevistadora° de la revista° *Mañana*   *interviewer* / *magazine*
    Raúl y Beatriz Jiménez, esposos jóvenes

  ENTREVISTADORA: Bueno, Raúl, ¿cuál es su profesión?
           RAÚL: ¿Mi profesión? La verdad es que tengo varias
              profesiones. Soy abogado primero, pero tam-
              bién doy clases particulares° por la tarde.   *private*

BEATRIZ: Además°, señorita, es un buen papá... muy cari- ‖ besides, in addition
ñoso con su hija... y también trabaja mucho en
casa... prepara la comida casi todas las noches.

ENTREVISTADORA: Y Ud., Beatriz, ¿cuál es su profesión... mejor
dicho°, sus profesiones? ‖ mejor... rather

BEATRIZ: Pues yo soy pintora. Trabajo aquí en mi estudio; así° puedo estar con nuestra hija. Pero ‖ so, that way
también doy clases en el instituto.

RAÚL: Por lo general dividimos el trabajo de la casa.
Por ejemplo, cuando Beatriz está en casa, hace° ‖ she does
el trabajo.

ENTREVISTADORA: ¿Y cuando los dos están en casa?

BEATRIZ Y RAÚL: ¡Terminamos en la mitad° del tiempo! ‖ half

Comprensión

*Which of the persons in the dialogs could be described by these statements? You may
mention more than one person for most statements.*

1. Es demasiado (*too*) joven para tener mucho interés en el amor.
2. Es una persona con ideas muy tradicionales.
3. Tiene un novio.
4. Es un esposo (*spouse*) modelo.
5. Es una persona con ideas muy modernas.
6. Tiene muchas ilusiones sobre el amor.
7. Combina su profesión y su vida (*life*) con su familia.
8. Cree que para una mujer es muy importante tener una buena educación y un
   buen trabajo.

Comentario cultural

The Spanish words **novio** and **novia** connote a relationship that is usually more
than that of *boyfriend* and *girlfriend* as these terms are used in the United States.
In Hispanic society, **novio** and **novia** generally imply the intention to marry.
A long **noviazgo** is expected, and that is usually the pattern.

In dialog A, Margarita represents the increasingly common Hispanic tendency
to place greater importance on the completion of a career than on an early marriage. Traditionally, the middle-class male in Hispanic society has tended not to
marry until he has completed his studies and is established in his career. That
pattern is becoming more usual for Hispanic women, as well, although traditional
ideas still prevail in some circles, as is true in many other parts of the world.

For most Hispanic couples the usual pattern of **noviazgo** and **boda** is still the
ideal. Wedding celebrations can be quite elaborate or quite simple, as in the
United States. A major difference is that it is not uncommon for the father of
the bride to serve as the **padrino de boda,** as you have seen in dialog B. Marital
relationships vary as much in Hispanic countries as they do in the United States,
and the couple in dialog C is typical of some younger couples, where the respon-
sibilities of careers and family life are shared equally.

UN POCO DE TODO

A. *Cambie por el plural.*

1. Voy a bailar contigo esta noche.
2. Ese chico está estudiando con su primo.
3. Mi padre nunca está de acuerdo conmigo.
4. El abogado está hablando con el padre de él.

Cambie por el singular.

5. Vamos a estudiar estas lecciones con ellos el domingo.
6. Las damas de honor están detrás de nosotros.
7. Damos clases de español a sus hijos.
8. Vamos a vender nuestros libros el lunes.

B. *Form complete sentences, based on the words given, in the order given. Conjugate the verbs and add other words if necessary.*

1. ella / estar / hablar / conmigo / este / momento
2. tú / ir / tener / hambre / si / no / comer / tu / hamburguesa
3. este / clase / se / dar / tres / en punto
4. este / tarde / ellos / ir / regresar / con / nuestro / tíos
5. este / noche / mi / primas / ir / fiesta / con / nuestro / abuelos

C. *Working with another student, ask and answer questions according to the model. Use the names of actual students in your class.*

MODELO   delante / detrás →
    ALFONSO: ¿Quién está *delante de ti?*
    CAROLINA: *Ernesto está delante de mí.*
    ALFONSO: No, Carolina. *Ernesto está detrás de ti. Juana está delante.*

1. a tu izquierda / a tu derecha
2. entre _____ y _____ / al lado (*side*) de ellos
3. detrás / delante
4. en el centro de la clase / delante de la clase
5. a tu derecha / delante

D. *Working with another student, play the roles of **los señores Gimeno**, a well-to-do Latin American couple. The two of you will be interviewed by the other members of the class, who will ask you about your possessions and about your family. Answer your classmates' questions by inventing details about yourselves and your married life together. You can talk about **los hijos de los señores Gimeno, sus otros parientes, sus casas, sus coches**, and so on.*

MODELO   Pregunta: *¿Cómo es su hijo Carlos?*
                 Respuesta: *Nuestro hijo es inteligente y guapo.*

E. *Complete las oraciones en una forma lógica.*

1. Esta tarde voy a _____.
2. Este semestre mis clases son _____ y mis profesores son _____.
3. En este momento estoy en _____ y estoy _____.
4. El sábado voy a _____.
5. Esta noche mi _____ y yo vamos a _____.
6. Para mí, esta clase es _____.
7. Este fin de semana mi familia y yo vamos a _____.
8. Para mí, el matrimonio (el amor, la amistad) es _____.

VOCABULARIO

VERBOS

contestar   to answer
dar (*irreg.*)   to give
estar (*irreg.*)   to be
ir (*irreg.*)   to go
terminar   to finish

SUSTANTIVOS

el/la **abogado/a**   lawyer
la **amistad**   friendship
el **amor**   love
la **boda**   wedding
la **calle**   street
el **cine**   movie theater
la **cita**   date, appointment
el **consejo**   advice
el/la **chico/a**   child, kid
el **divorcio**   divorce
domingo   Sunday
el/la **empleado/a**   employee
el **fin de semana**   weekend
la **idea**   idea
la **iglesia**   church
jueves   Thursday
lunes   Monday
martes   Tuesday
el **matrimonio**   marriage

miércoles   Wednesday
la **montaña**   mountain
el **noviazgo**   courtship, engagement
el/la **novio/a**   boy/girl friend; fiancé/
    fiancée; groom/bride
el **país**   country, nation
el **parque**   park
el **problema**   problem
la **profesión**   profession
el **restaurante**   restaurant
sábado   Saturday
la **semana**   week
el **tiempo**   time
la **tontería**   foolish thing
el **trabajo**   job; work; workday
la **vida**   life
viernes   Friday

ADJETIVOS

cariñoso/a   affectionate
difícil   difficult
enfermo/a   sick
fácil   easy
moreno/a   brunette
rubio/a   blond
siguiente   following, next
trigueño/a   brunette

PALABRAS Y EXPRESIONES ÚTILES

a la derecha de   to the right of
a la izquierda de   to the left of
ahora mismo   right now
casi   almost
cerca de   close to, near
¿cómo es...?   what is . . . like?
conmigo   with me
contigo   with you
¿cuál?   what? which?
cuando   when
¿cuántos/as?   how many?
de acuerdo con   in agreement with
delante de   in front of
después de   after
detrás de   behind
en este momento   at the moment,
    right now
entre   between, among
esta noche   tonight
lejos de   far from
luego   later; then, next
nunca   never
sin   without
ya   already

Un paso más 4

Actividades

A. **Limitaciones.** En el diálogo Margarita cree que un novio es «una limitación». Para otras personas, sin embargo (*however*), un novio no es una limitación. En la opinión de Ud., ¿cuáles de las personas o cosas siguientes son «una limitación»? ¿Cuáles no son una limitación? ¿Por qué?

un animal en casa
un coche
un(a) novio/a (esposo/a)
un hijo

el dinero

(no) es una
limitación
porque

no tengo que trabajar
necesita mucha atención
me da tiempo libre
es un buen amigo que «habla» conmigo cuando regreso a casa
los niños son estupendos
causa muchos problemas
puedo comprar las cosas que quiero
no tengo que caminar (*walk*) mucho

B. **Opiniones.** What percentage of your friends would agree with each of the following statements? Do you agree?

Preguntas	Por ciento			
	0–25	26–50	51–75	76–100
1. Es importante tener un noviazgo largo.				
2. Los hombres deben trabajar; las mujeres deben estar en casa con los niños.				
3. Un matrimonio no debe tener más de (*more than*) dos hijos.				
4. Vivir con el/la novio/a es una buena alternativa al matrimonio.				
5. Los novios deben practicar la misma religión.				
6. El divorcio es una solución buena y lógica para los problemas matrimoniales.				

Preguntas	Por ciento			
	0–25	26–50	51–75	76–100
7. La opinión que tienen los padres del novio (de la novia) es muy importante.				
8. Las mujeres deben tener los mismos derechos que (*same rights as*) los hombres.				

C. **Los novios.**   Prepare una descripción de lo que (*what*) pasa en el dibujo.   Ud. puede usar las siguientes preguntas como guía y debe inventar los detalles (*details*) necesarios.

Sin palabras

1. ¿Qué hora es?
2. ¿Quién es el novio? ¿Cómo es?
3. ¿Quién es la novia? ¿Cómo es ella?
4. ¿Por qué no quieren tener una boda grande?
5. ¿A quién lleva la novia? (Lleva a...) ¿Por qué?
6. ¿A dónde van después de la boda para su luna de miel (*honeymoon*)?
7. ¿Van a vivir felices (*happy*) para siempre o van a tener problemas? Explique.

A propósito...

Extending and accepting or rejecting invitations gracefully takes practice in any language. The following phrases will help you be prepared when the occasion arises.

¿Estás libre esta noche?	*Are you free tonight?*
¿Tienes tiempo para tomar un café (una copa)?	*Do you have time for a cup of coffee (a drink)?*
¿Quieres ir al cine esta noche?	*Do you want to go to the movies tonight?*
Tengo dos boletos para el concierto. ¿Puedes ir?	*I have two tickets for the concert. Can you go?*
Cómo no. Claro.	*Of course. Surely.*
Perfecto. De acuerdo.	*Perfect (OK, fine). Agreed.*
Lo siento, pero...	*I'm sorry, but . . .*
Es una lástima, pero...	*It's a pity (too bad), but . . .*
Es imposible porque...	*It's impossible because . . .*
...tengo un examen mañana.	*I have a test tomorrow.*
...ya tengo planes.	*I already have plans.*
...estoy invitado/a a comer en casa de unos amigos.	*I'm invited to eat at the house of some friends.*

D. **Invitaciones.** Using variations of the phrases in **A propósito,** as well as your own imagination, create a dialog illustrating one or more of the following situations:

1. Dos personas están en el museo. Los dos miran una pintura famosa. Él quiere hablar con ella y ella con él. Uno de ellos inicia la conversación y luego invita a tomar un café (una copa).
2. Un(a) estudiante invita a otro/a estudiante a ir al cine. Él/ella quiere ir, pero no puede.
3. Un joven de catorce años invita a una chica de trece años a una fiesta. Los dos están muy nerviosos.
4. Dos personas van a una fiesta. Tienen que arreglar (*to arrange*) todos los detalles: a qué hora van, qué ropa van a llevar, cómo van, etcétera.

E. **Querida Antonia...** Antonia offers free advice in her column to the lovelorn and to those with problems of almost all types (see Sola's letter on page 107). Write a letter to Antonia about one specific problem. Create an original problem or write about one of the following situations. Then write Antonia's answer to your letter, or trade letters with another student and write appropriate responses.

1. Ud. necesita hablar con sus padres sobre un problema, pero ellos no quieren hablar con Ud.
2. Su boda va a ser en tres meses. Su novio/a y Ud. quieren una boda familiar, con poca gente; sus padres quieren una boda grande, con unas quinientas (*five hundred*) personas.
3. Sus padres creen que su amigo/a es feo/a (que es perezoso/a, que no es muy inteligente, etcétera).
4. Su novio/a cree que el matrimonio es una tontería.
5. Sus padres creen que Ud. es muy joven para tener novio/a. Ud. tiene doce años.
6. Su novio/a quiere tener ocho o nueve niños. ¡Ud. no!

Lectura cultural: La vida social de los jóvenes

El paseo° es una de las actividades sociales de los jóvenes hispánicos, especialmente en los pueblos° pequeños. Cada domingo por la tarde los jóvenes —y muchas otras personas— van a la plaza principal donde pueden caminar° y conversar con los amigos mientras° escuchan° un concierto y comen de las muchas comidas ligeras° que se venden allí. Es una gran ocasión para todos los jóvenes.

El paseo no es la única actividad en la vida social de los jóvenes. El cine y las fiestas son actividades preferidas. En países como España, la Argentina y México siempre hay una variedad de películas° y dramas. En estos países y en los otros también hay películas de Europa y de los Estados Unidos. En cuanto a° las fiestas, los jóvenes hispánicos —como

stroll, promenade
towns

walk / while / they hear
comidas... *snacks, light meals*

movies

En... *regarding*

casi todos los jóvenes del mundo— no necesitan pretexto para pasarlo bien° bailando toda la noche.

Muchas de las actividades ocurren en grupos. Aunque° ahora no es necesario tener chaperona —especialmente en las ciudades grandes— frecuentemente las parejas salen° con otras parejas para así «evitar° el escándalo».

pasarlo... *to have a good time*
although

parejas... *couples go out/ avoid*

Comprensión

¿Cierto o falso? Corrija las oraciones falsas.

1. El paseo es una actividad muy particular de los países norteamericanos.
2. El paseo: Los jóvenes —y muchas otras personas— van a la plaza principal, pero no hablan con sus amigos.
3. El paseo es una actividad muy especial sólo para las chicas.
4. No hay muchas películas en México, la Argentina y España.
5. Las películas de Europa y de los Estados Unidos no llegan a Latinoamérica.
6. Los jóvenes hispánicos no bailan mucho.
7. Una pareja joven siempre necesita chaperona.

Ejercicio escrito

Use the following questions as a guide in writing a brief paragraph about **La vida social de los estudiantes norteamericanos.** Give some of your own responses to the questions, or use them to interview another student and then use his/her answers as a basis for your paragraph.

1. ¿Hay muchas actividades para estudiantes en la universidad?
2. ¿Hay muchos bailes? ¿Bailan mucho los estudiantes norteamericanos?
3. ¿Hay discotecas cerca de la universidad? ¿Cuáles son los bailes más populares? ¿los bailes modernos? ¿los bailes latinos?
4. ¿Hay muchos cines en su ciudad? ¿Hay muchas películas buenas? ¿muchas películas extranjeras? ¿películas en español?
5. ¿Cuáles son las películas favoritas de los estudiantes? ¿los actores favoritos? ¿las actrices?
6. ¿Dónde conversan los estudiantes con sus amigos? ¿en un bar? ¿en la residencia de estudiantes? ¿en la cafetería?
7. ¿Salen los estudiantes norteamericanos en grupos? ¿Salen las parejas con chaperona?

capítulo 5 El tiempo

Peter Menzel/Stock, Boston

OBJETIVOS

In this chapter you will learn vocabulary and expressions related to weather, seasons, and climates.

You will also learn about the following aspects of Spanish grammar:

21. more uses of the two Spanish verbs that mean *to be*, **ser** and **estar**
22. questions using interrogative words (*who? what?* and so on)
23. the present tense of the irregular verbs **hacer** (*to do; to make*), **poner** (*to put, place*), and **salir** (*to leave, go out*)

24. the present tense of verbs such as **pensar** (*to think*) that have systematic changes in their stem: **pienso, piensas, piensa, pensamos, pensáis, piensan**
25. how to express comparisons, such as *taller, more intelligent, less important,* and *as good as, better*

Un paso más includes activities related to sports, weather, and holidays, and it also contains a reading about the geography and climate of Latin America.

VOCABULARIO: PREPARACIÓN

Peter Menzel/Stock, Boston

EPA, Inc.

El tiempo° _weather_

¿Qué tiempo hace?	What's the weather like?
Hace (mucho) frío (calor, viento, sol).	It's (very) cold (hot, windy, sunny).
Hace fresco.	It's cool.
Hace (muy) buen/mal tiempo.	It's (very) good/bad weather.
Hay mucha contaminación.	There's a lot of pollution.
Llover	To rain
Llueve. Está lloviendo.	It rains. It's raining.
Nevar	To snow
Nieva. Está nevando.	It snows. It's snowing.

In Spanish many weather conditions are expressed with **hace.**   For example, **hace calor** literally means _it makes heat_.   Notice that the adjective **mucho** is used with the nouns **frío, calor, viento,** and **sol** to express _very_.

A. _¿Qué tiempo hace hoy?   Complete la oración en una forma lógica._

Hoy (no) hace mucho/muy _____ _(frío, sol, viento, mal tiempo, calor, buen tiempo)_

B. *Hoy es un día fatal...* Complete the phrases on the left with words or phrases from the columns on the right.

Hoy hace	mucha contaminación	nevando
Hoy está	fresco	lloviendo
Hoy hay	mucho frío	mucho viento

C. Describe the following weather conditions and tell how the people pictured are feeling. As in many weather expressions, very with some **tener** idioms is expressed with **mucho: Tengo mucho frío/calor.** In the context of weather **estar bien** means to be comfortable, neither hot nor cold.

1.   2.   3.   4.   5.   6.   7.

Los meses y las estaciones° del año   *seasons*

se(p)tiembre		marzo	
octubre	el otoño	abril	la primavera
noviembre		mayo	
diciembre		junio	
enero	el invierno	julio	el verano
febrero		agosto	

La fecha°   *date*

¿Cuál es la fecha de hoy? — What is today's date?
(Hoy) Es el primero de abril. — (Today) It is the first of April.
(Hoy) Es el cinco de febrero. — (Today) It is the fifth of February.

Primero is used to express the first day of the month. Cardinal numbers (**dos, tres,** and so on) are used for other days. The definite article **el** is used before the date. However, when the day of the week is expressed, **el** is omitted: **Hoy es jueves, tres de octubre.**

D. *Exprese estas fechas en español.*

1. March 7
2. August 24
3. December 1
4. June 5
5. September 19
6. May 30

E. *¿Qué día de la semana es el 12 (1, 20, 16, 11, 4, 29) de noviembre?*

F. *¿Cuándo se celebran?*

1. el Día de la Raza (*Columbus Day*)
2. el Día del Año Nuevo
3. el Día de los Enamorados (de San Valentín)
4. el Día de la Independencia de los Estados Unidos
5. el Día de los Inocentes (*Fools*)

G. *Preguntas*

1. ¿Cuál es la fecha de su cumpleaños? ¿del cumpleaños de su mejor (*best*) amigo/a? ¿la fecha de mañana? ¿la fecha de hoy?
2. ¿Cuáles son los meses de otoño? ¿de primavera? ¿Cuál es su mes favorito? ¿Por qué?
3. ¿Qué tiempo hace en invierno? ¿y en verano? ¿Cuál es su estación favorita? ¿Por qué?

PRONUNCIACIÓN: D, J, and G

D Spanish **d** has two basic sounds. At the beginning of a phrase or sentence or after **n** or **l**, it is pronounced as a stop: [d]. Like the Spanish [t], it is produced by putting the tongue against the back of the upper teeth. In all other cases, it is pronounced as a fricative [đ], that is, like the *th* sound in English *they, another.*

J Spanish **j** never has the sound of English *j,* as in *Jane* or *John.* In some dialects it is like English [h], but in most parts of the Spanish-speaking world, it has a rougher sound, a fricative. To make it, articulate a [k] sound, but with a light friction in the airflow instead of stopping it: **taco/Tajo, carro/jarro.**

G Spanish **g** before **e** or **i** is pronounced like the **j:** * **general, página.** Spanish **g** before **a, o,** or **u** is pronounced like the **g** in English *go* [g] at the beginning of a phrase or sentence or after **n: gas, gorila, gusto, inglés.** Elsewhere it is pronounced as a fricative [ǥ], with a very light friction: **el gas, el gorila, el gusto.**

PRÁCTICA

Practique las siguientes palabras y frases.

1. [d] ¿dónde? el doctor el dinero el domingo diez debe dos
2. [d̶] ¿adónde? la doctora mucho dinero este domingo adiós comida usted
3. taco/Tajo vaca/baja cura/jura roca/roja carro/jarro
4. jueves jirafa hijo joven extranjero adjetivo mujer viejo
5. general generoso inteligente geografía geología región sicología
6. [g] grande tengo gusto gracias ganas golf gramática gris
7. [ǥ] iglesia regalo amiga llegan diálogo telegrama alegre pagar

MINIDIÁLOGOS Y GRAMÁTICA

21. *SER* VERSUS *ESTAR*

Una conversación telefónica con un(a) esposo/a que *está* en un viaje de negocios.
Aló... ¿Cómo *estás*, mi amor?... ¿Dónde *estás* ahora?... ¿Qué hora *es* ahí? ¡Uyy!, *es* muy tarde. ¿Qué tiempo hace?... Y el hotel, ¿cómo *es?*... ¿Cuánto cuesta por noche?... *Es* bien barato. ¿Qué *estás* haciendo ahora?... Ay, pobre, *estás* muy ocupado/a. ¿Con quién vas a *estar* mañana?... ¿Quién *es* el dueño de esa compañía?... Ah, él *es* de Cuba, ¿verdad?... Bueno, mi vida, ¿adónde vas luego?... ¿Y cuándo vas a regresar?... *Está* bien, querido/a. Hasta luego, ¿eh?... Adiós.

¿Qué contesta la otra persona?
Aló... → **Aló.** →
¿Cómo estás, mi amor? . . . etcétera.

A phone conversation with a husband/wife who is on a business trip. Hello . . . How are you, dear? . . . Where are you now? . . . What time is it there? . . . My, it's very late. What's the weather like? . . . And how's the hotel? . . . How much is it per night? . . . It's very inexpensive. What are you doing now? . . . Poor dear, you're very busy. Whom are you going to be with tomorrow? . . . Who is the owner of that company? . . . Ah, he's from Cuba, isn't he? . . . Well, dear, where are you going next? . . . And when are you coming home? . . . OK, dear. Talk to you soon . . . Bye.

*In the words **México** and **mexicano** the letter **x** is also pronounced like the **j**.

SUMMARY OF THE USES OF **ESTAR**

1. to tell LOCATION   El libro **está en la mesa.**
2. with the present participle to form the PRESENT PROGRESSIVE   **Estamos tomando** una cerveza ahora.
3. to describe HEALTH   Paco **está enfermo.**
4. with ADJECTIVES that describe CONDITIONS   **Estoy** muy **ocupada.**
5. in a number of fixed EXPRESSIONS   **(No) Estoy de acuerdo. Está bien. Está claro.**

SUMMARY OF THE USES OF **SER**

1. to link the subject of a sentence to a NOUN   Ella **es doctora.**
2. to express NATIONALITY; with **de** to express ORIGIN   **Son cubanos. Son de Cuba.**
3. with **de** to tell what MATERIAL something is made of   Este bolígrafo **es de plástico.**
4. with **para** to tell WHOM SOMETHING IS FOR   El regalo **es para ti.**
5. to tell TIME   **Son las once. Es la una y media.**
6. with **de** to express POSSESSION   **Es de Carlota.**
7. with ADJECTIVES that describe BASIC, INHERENT CHARACTERISTICS   Ramona **es inteligente.**
8. in many IMPERSONAL EXPRESSIONS   **Es necesario** llegar temprano. **Es importante** estudiar.

Ser versus Estar with Adjectives

Ser is used with adjectives that describe the basic characteristics or inherent qualities of a person, place, or thing.

La amistad es **importante.**	*Friendship is important.*
Son **españoles.**	*They are Spanish.*
Aquella mujer es muy **baja.**	*That woman is very short.*

Estar is used with adjectives to express conditions. The following adjectives are commonly used with **estar:**

cansado/a	*tired*
ocupado/a // aburrido/a	*busy / bored*
sucio/a // limpio/a	*dirty / clean*
abierto/a // cerrado/a	*open / closed*
contento/a, alegre // triste	*happy / sad*

Some adjectives can be used with either **ser** or **estar,** depending on what the speaker intends to communicate. In general, when *to be* implies *looks, tastes, feels,* or *appears,* **estar** is used. Compare the following pairs of sentences:

¿Cómo **es** Amalia?	*What is Amalia like (as a person)?*
¿Cómo **está** Amalia?	*How is Amalia (feeling)?*
Daniel **es** guapo.	*Daniel is handsome. (He is a hand-some person.)*
Daniel **está** muy guapo esta noche.	*Daniel looks very nice (handsome) to-night.*
Este plato mexicano **es** muy famoso.	*This Mexican dish is very famous.*
Este plato mexicano **está** muy rico.	*This Mexican dish is (tastes) great.*

PRÁCTICA

A. *Por lo general, ¿se usa* **ser** *o* **estar** *con estas palabras?*

1. anglosajón   2. sucio   3. elegante   4. bien   5. viejo   6. claro
7. interesante   8. de acuerdo   9. rubio   10. abierto   11. rojo   12. difícil
13. cerrado   14. alegre   15. triste

B. *Form complete sentences by using one word or phrase from each column.*

1. El vaso (*glass*) es / está de cristal / en el apartamento / alto / de Pedro / verde / limpio / para mí

2. Los jóvenes son / están de acuerdo conmigo / cansados / anglosajones / a la derecha de sus abuelos / enfermos / simpáticos / muy tristes hoy / de San Francisco / amigos de nuestra familia / leyendo el texto / ocupados / en Los Ángeles / aburridos en este momento

C. *Complete las oraciones con la forma correcta de* **ser** *o* **estar.** *Explique por qué.*

1. Anita y Raúl _____ estudiantes.
2. _____ muy cansada, pero tengo que trabajar más.
3. La familia Martínez _____ de Chile.
4. _____ las ocho y cuarto.
5. Todo _____ bien, querido.

6. El abogado _____ cerca de su cliente.
7. Enero _____ un mes de invierno.
8. Bogotá _____ en Colombia.
9. Hoy _____ el veinte de noviembre.
10. ¿Cómo _____ hoy, Juanita?
11. _____ importante escuchar (*to listen*) bien.
12. Ahora yo _____ escribiendo los ejercicios.
13. El pasaporte _____ de Carmen.
14. Ese carro azul _____ para mi hermana.
15. La tienda de ropa _____ cerrada hoy.
16. El coche pequeño _____ de metal y plástico.
17. Los zapatos _____ negros.
18. Ahora _____ lloviendo.
19. Tú _____ peruano, ¿verdad?

D. *¿Cómo se dice en español?*

1. This book is for you.
2. It's necessary to listen well.   Is that clear?
3. These tacos are (*taste*) good.
4. You look very nice tonight.

CONVERSACIÓN

A. *Complete the following sentences by telling how you feel.*

1. Cuando recibo una A en un examen, estoy _____.
2. Cuando tengo mucho trabajo, estoy _____.
3. Cuando no puedo estar con mis amigos, estoy _____.
4. Cuando estoy en clase, _____.
5. Cuando llueve, _____.
6. Cuando hace mucho sol, _____.
7. Cuando nieva, _____.
8. Cuando hace calor, _____.

B. *Assume the identity of a famous person (television or movie personality, recording artist, or sports figure, for example). Your classmates will ask you yes/no questions in order to determine your identity. They may ask about your place of origin, your basic personal characteristics, your nationality, your profession, and so on. Here are some possible questions:*

1. **¿Es Ud. hombre? ¿mujer? ¿niño/a?**
2. **¿Es Ud. viejo/a? ¿joven? ¿guapo/a?**
3. **¿Es de los Estados Unidos? ¿del Canadá?**
4. **¿Está en nuestra ciudad?**
5. **¿Está jugando** (*playing*) **al béisbol ahora? ¿al fútbol? ¿al tenis?**

22. INTERROGATIVES

¿Cómo?	How?	¿Quién(es)?	Who?
¿Cuándo?	When?	¿De quién(es)?	Whose?
¿A qué hora?	At what time?	¿Dónde?	Where?
¿Qué?	What? Which?	¿De dónde?	From where?
¿Cuál(es)?	What? Which one/ones?	¿Adónde?	Where?
¿Por qué?	Why?	¿Cuánto/a?	How much?
		¿Cuántos/as?	How many?

In Spanish, *interrogative words* **(palabras interrogativas)** always have an accent over the stressed vowel. Remember to use an inverted question mark before each question. The interrogative word always comes first and is immediately followed by the verb: **¿Dónde vive Carlos?**

¿Qué? versus ¿Cuál?

¿Qué? asks for a definition or a explanation.

¿Qué es esto?	*What is this?*
¿Qué quieres?	*What do you want?*

¿Cuál(es)? asks the person who answers to make a choice or selection.*

¿Cuál es tu teléfono?	*What is your phone number?* (Which of the many possible numbers is yours?)
¿Cuáles son los países latinoamericanos?	*What are the Latin American countries?* (Which of all the countries of the world are Latin American?)
¿Cuál es la capital de Uruguay?	*What is the capital of Uruguay?* (Which of all its cities is the capital?)

¿Por qué?

¿Por qué?, written as two words and with an accent mark, means *why*? **Porque**, written as one word and with no accent, means *because*.

¿Por qué no escuchas?	*Why don't you listen?*
Porque no quiero.	*Because I don't want to.*

__¿Cuál(es)?__ is not generally used as an adjective.

¿Cuál de los dos libros quieres?	*Which of the two books do you want?*
but	
¿Qué libro quieres?	*Which (what) book do you want?*

Interrogatives with ¿Dónde?

¿**Dónde?** asks about location; ¿**de dónde?** asks about origin, and ¿**adónde?** asks about destination.

¿**Dónde** está Bolivia?	*Where is Bolivia?*
¿**De dónde** son esos estudiantes extranjeros?	*Where are those foreign students from?*
¿**Adónde** quieres ir?	*Where do you want to go?*

PRÁCTICA

A. *What interrogative words do you associate with the following information?*

1. A las doce.
2. Muy bien.
3. Mi esposo.
4. En la discoteca.
5. En primavera.
6. Porque no puedo.
7. Los novios.
8. Mucho dinero.
9. Cuatro hijos.

B. *Form the questions that result in the following answers:*
¿Qué/¿Cuál?

1. Éste es un peso mexicano.
2. Sacramento es la capital de California.
3. Es 2-75-40-19.
4. Necesito tu carro.
5. Quiero este vaso, no aquél.
6. El tango es un baile argentino.
7. Hace mucho frío en enero.

¿Quién/¿Quiénes/¿De quién?

1. Shirley MacLaine es una actriz muy famosa.
2. Las damas de honor son mis hermanas.
3. Es el examen de Arturo.
4. Sara siempre contesta todas las preguntas.

¿Dónde/¿De dónde/¿Adónde?

1. Son de Francia.
2. Quiero viajar a Colombia.
3. Los novios van a la iglesia.
4. El cine está en la calle Vallejo.
5. Hay mucha contaminación en las ciudades grandes.

¿Cuándo/¿A qué hora/¿Cuánto/a/¿Cuántos/as?

1. Pues tengo cuatro dólares.
2. Llegamos a las diez.
3. Tienen cuatro hijos.
4. Carlota tiene once blusas.
5. Hace frío en la Argentina en julio.
6. Voy a escuchar ese programa a las ocho.

CONVERSACIÓN

A. *What question is being asked by each of the following persons?*

1.
2.
3.

4.
5.
6.

B. *Use interrogatives to form as many questions as you can about each of the preceding pictures.*

> MODELO   dibujo 1:   *¿Dónde está el cine?*
> *¿Cuántas personas van al cine?*
> *¿Quién es el chico?*

C. *Guillermina es una niña de cinco años y, como todos los niños, siempre pregunta (asks) mucho.   ¿Qué puede preguntar Guillermina en estas situaciones?*

1.   MAMÁ: —Guillermina, éste es el señor Vargas.
   GUILLERMINA: —*¿Quién es el señor Vargas?   ¿De dónde...*
2.   PAPÁ: —Guillermina, tu primo Octavio viene mañana.
   GUILLERMINA: —_____
3.   ABUELA: —Guillermina, hay un regalo en la mesa.
   GUILLERMINA: —_____

23. PRESENT TENSE OF *HACER, PONER,* AND *SALIR*

En el hotel

FERNANDO: ¡Qué mañana más bonita! ¿Por qué no *salimos*?

FEDERICO: Yo no *salgo*. Seguro que *hace* mucho frío afuera. ¿Está bien si *pongo* la calefacción?

FERNANDO: Pero estamos en agosto.

FEDERICO: Sí, y estamos en Patagonia también.

1. *¿Quién quiere salir?*
2. *¿Por qué no quiere salir su amigo?*
3. *¿Quién va a poner la calefacción?*
4. *¿Dónde están Fernando y Federico?*
5. *¿Dónde está esa región?*
6. *¿Es invierno o verano allí en agosto? ¿Y aquí?*

HACER: *to do; to make*		PONER: *to put, place*		SALIR: *to leave, go out*	
hago	hacemos	pongo	ponemos	salgo	salimos
haces	hacéis	pones	ponéis	sales	salís
hace	hacen	pone	ponen	sale	salen

Hacer: ¿Por qué no **haces** los ejercios?   *Why don't you do the exercises?*

Estoy haciendo tortillas.   *I'm making tortillas.*

Hacer un viaje means *to take a trip.*

Quieren **hacer un viaje** al Perú.   *They want to take a trip to Peru.*

Poner: Siempre **pongo** mucho azúcar en el café.   *I always put a lot of sugar in my coffee.*

With appliances, **poner** means *to turn on.*

Voy a **poner** el radio.   *I'm going to turn on the radio.*

Salir: **Salen de** la clase ahora.   *They're leaving class now.*

At the hotel FERNANDO: What a pretty morning! Why don't we go out? FEDERICO: I'm not going out. It's sure to be cold out. Is it okay if I put on the heat? FERNANDO: But it's August. (But we're in the month of August.) FEDERICO: Yes, and we're in Patagonia, too.

Salir is always used with **de** when followed by a place.
Salir con can also mean *to go out with.*

Salgo con el hermano   *I'm going out with Cecilia's brother.*
de Cecilia.

Salir with **para** expresses destination.

Salimos para la playa   *We're leaving for the beach tomorrow.*
mañana.

PRÁCTICA

A. Dé Ud. frases nuevas según las indicaciones.

1. —Es importante ser muy activo. ¿Quién hace ejercicio todos los días?
   —*El profesor* hace ejercicio todos los días. (*tú, Raúl, yo, Lilia y yo, Uds., vosotros*)
2. —Todos entran en el teatro a las siete y media. ¿A qué hora salen?
   —*Susana* sale del teatro a las once. (*yo, tú, nosotros, el actor, Ud., vosotros*)
3. —Todos quieren escuchar (*to listen to*) un programa interesante. ¿Quién pone el radio?
   —*La tía* pone el radio. (*yo, Gabriela, tú, nosotros, Uds., vosotras*)

B. Form complete sentences by using one word or phrase from each column.

yo		en quince minutos
los policías	hacer	un viaje a Puerto Rico este otoño
el camarero (*waiter*) (no)	salir	con una latina
tú		los ejercicios en el cuaderno
Tito y yo	poner	la televisión
_____		de la estación (*station*)
		hielo (*ice*) en el vaso
		para Buenos Aires
		mucho azúcar en el café
		de casa a las cinco
		_____

CONVERSACIÓN

A. You're going to take a trip, and you have to pack your suitcase. Tell what you're going to pack, using the sentence given below. The next person will repeat what you said and add one item, and so on. How long can you keep the sentence going?

Hago un viaje y en mi maleta pongo _____.

B. Imagine que Ud. sale con una persona famosa. ¿Con quién sale y adónde van Uds. o qué van a hacer?

Salgo con _____.   Vamos a _____.

C. *Preguntas*

1. ¿Qué pone Ud. en el café? ¿en el té? ¿en una limonada? ¿Pone Ud. hielo en los refrescos (*soft drinks*) en invierno? ¿en verano?
2. ¿Qué hace Ud. en verano? ¿en invierno? ¿el día de su cumpleaños? ¿en setiembre? ¿los sábados?
3. ¿A qué hora sale Ud. de la clase de español? ¿de otras clases? ¿A qué hora sale Ud. para su primera clase?

24. PRESENT TENSE OF STEM-CHANGING VERBS

Un viaje con la familia

ESTEBAN: ¿Cómo *piensan* ir Uds., en tren o en avión?

MICAELA: Pensamos ir en tren.

ESTEBAN: ¿Por qué? Es más cómodo ir en avión y se llega antes.

MICAELA: Sí, pero no tenemos prisa. En realidad, los chicos *prefieren* ir en autobús. Creen que es más divertido.

ESTEBAN: ¡Hombre, eso es salir de Guatemala y entrar en Guatepeor! Por lo menos, ¿por qué no *vuelven* en avión?

1. *¿Cómo piensan ir Micaela y su familia?*
2. *¿Es más cómodo ir en tren o en avión?*
3. *¿Cómo se llega antes?*
4. *¿Cómo prefieren ir los niños? ¿Por qué?*
5. *¿Qué es Guatemala? Y Guatepeor, ¿existe?*

e → ie	o (u) → ue	e → i
PENSAR (IE): *to think*	VOLVER (UE): *to return*	PEDIR (I): *to ask for, order*
pienso pensamos piensas pensáis piensa piensan	vuelvo volvemos vuelves volvéis vuelve vuelven	pido pedimos pides pedís pide piden

You have already learned two *stem-changing verbs* (**verbos que cambian el radical**): **querer** and **poder.** In these verbs the stem vowels **e** and **o** be-

---

A trip with the family ESTEBAN: How do you plan to go, by train or by plane? MICAELA: We plan to go by train. ESTEBAN: Why? It's more comfortable to go by plane, and you get there sooner (before). MICAELA: Yes, but we're not in a hurry. In fact, the kids prefer to go by bus. They think that it's more fun. ESTEBAN: Good grief, that's going from bad to worse (to leave Guate**mala** [*bad*] and to enter Guate**peor** [*worse*])! Why don't you at least come back by plane?

come **ie** and **ue,** respectively, in stressed syllables. The stem vowels are stressed in all present-tense forms except **nosotros** and **vosotros.** All three classes of stem-changing verbs follow this regular pattern in the present tense. In vocabulary lists the stem change will always be shown in parentheses after the infinitive: **volver (ue).**

Stem-changing verbs practiced in this chapter include:

e → ie	o (u) → ue	e → i
cerrar to close **(ie)**	**almorzar** to have lunch **(ue)**	**pedir** to ask **(i)** for, order
empezar to begin **(ie)**	**dormir** to sleep **(ue)**	
pensar to think **(ie)**	**jugar** to play **(ue)*** (sports)	**servir** to serve **(i)**
preferir to prefer **(ie)**	**volver** to return **(ue)**	

When used with an infinitive, **empezar** is followed by **a.**

Uds. **empiezan a** hablar muy bien el español.   *You're beginning to speak Spanish very well.*

When followed by an infinitive, **pensar** means *to intend* or *plan to.*

¿Cuándo **piensas** contestar la carta?   *When do you intend to answer the letter?*

The stem vowels in the present participle of **-ir** stem-changing verbs also show a change. When listed in the vocabulary, all **-ir** stem-changing verbs will show two stem changes in parentheses: **dormir (ue, u).** The first stem change occurs in the present tense, the second in the present participle.

dormir (ue, **u**) → **d**urmiendo   preferir (ie, **i**) → prefiriendo
pedir (i, **i**) → pidiendo   servir (i, **i**) → sirviendo

PRÁCTICA

A. Dé Ud. frases nuevas según las indicaciones.

1. —¿Qué piden Uds. cuando hace mucho calor?
   —*Felipe* pide una cerveza bien fría. (*yo, nosotros, ellos, Lisa, tú, vosotros*)

***Jugar** is the only **u → ue** stem-changing verb in Spanish. **Jugar** is often followed by **al** when used with the name of a sport: **Juego *al* tenis.** Some Spanish-speakers, however, omit the **al.**

2. —¿Quién almuerza en el patio cuando hace buen tiempo?
   —*Ellas* almuerzan allí. (*Ud., los estudiantes, nosotros, tú, yo, vosotros*)
3. —¿Qué prefieren hacer Uds. en agosto, estudiar o descansar?
   —*Yo* prefiero descansar. (*Sergio, nosotros, Ana, ellas, tú, vosotras*)
4. —¿Qué están haciendo sus amigos en este momento?
   —Unos están estudiando; otros están _____. (*cerrar sus libros, pedir cerveza en un restaurante, volver a casa, servir refrescos, jugar al béisbol, dormir la siesta*)

B. *¿Qué prefieren?*

MODELO   Ignacio pide café, pero nosotros _____ un refresco. →
              Ignacio pide café, pero nosotros *pedimos* un refresco.

1. Tomás y Julia piensan viajar a Sudamérica este otoño, pero nosotros _____ viajar a España.
2. Tú vuelves a la estación mañana, pero nosotros _____ allí el jueves.
3. Nosotros empezamos a trabajar a las ocho, pero Reinaldo _____ a las nueve.
4. Nosotros dormimos ocho horas todas las noches, pero Lucía sólo _____ seis horas.
5. Nosotros servimos buena comida en nuestro restaurante y el Sr. Carrillo también _____ buena comida en su cafetería.
6. Nosotros jugamos al tenis hoy y Paula _____ con nosotros.
7. Tú cierras la tienda a las ocho, pero nosotros no _____ hasta las diez.

C. *Using the following verbs as a guide, tell about a visit to a restaurant. Use* **yo** *as the subject except where otherwise indicated.*

1. _____ pensar comer comida española
2. _____ entrar en un restaurante en la calle Bolívar
3. _____ pedir el menú
4. _____ preferir comer paella, un plato español
5. _____ no servir comida española (ellos)
6. _____ pedir tacos y una naranjada
7. _____ servir el almuerzo (el camarero)
8. _____ comer y volver a casa
9. _____ dormir la siesta porque hace calor

CONVERSACIÓN

A. *¿A qué hora...*

1. se cierra la biblioteca?
2. se cierran las tiendas en los Estados Unidos?
3. empieza Ud. a estudiar todas las noches?
4. empieza Ud. a comer?
5. vuelve Ud. a casa?
6. almuerza Ud.?

B. *Ask two other students the following questions. They should decide on an answer between them and reply using the* **nosotros** *form.*

1. ¿Qué prefieren Uds., preguntar o contestar en clase? ¿hablar en español o en inglés?
2. ¿Prefieren Uds. el tequila con limón o sin limón? ¿el café con azúcar o sin azúcar? ¿la Coca-Cola con hielo o sin hielo? ¿beber agua (*water*) o cerveza cuando hace muchísimo calor?
3. ¿Qué prefieren Uds., viajar en autobús o en tren? ¿tomar las vacaciones en verano o en invierno?
4. ¿Juegan Uds. al golf? ¿al fútbol? ¿al tenis? ¿al béisbol?
5. ¿Qué piensan Uds. de (*about*) la clase de español? (**Pensamos que** [*that*]...) ¿del profesor/de la profesora? ¿de su universidad? ¿de los Estados Unidos?

25. COMPARISONS

Regular Comparisons of Adjectives

Alicia es **más alta que** Marta.   *Alicia is taller than Marta.*
Marta es **menos alta que** Pablo.   *Marta is shorter (less tall) than Pablo.*
Pablo es **tan alto como** Alicia.   *Pablo is as tall as Alicia.*

The *comparative* (**comparativo**) of most English adjectives is formed by using the adverbs *more* or *less* (***more** intelligent,* **less** *important*), or by adding *-er* (*taller, longer*).

In Spanish, unequal comparisons are usually expressed with **más** (*more*)... **que** or **menos** (*less*)... **que** plus the adjective.*

Equal comparisons are expressed with **tan** _____ **como** plus the adjective.
[Práctica A, B]

*Más/menos *de* are used when the comparison is followed by a number: **Tengo más *de* un** hijo.

Irregular Comparative Forms

Spanish has the following irregular comparative forms:

mejor(es)	*better*	**mayor(es)**	*older*
peor(es)	*worse*	**menor(es)**	*younger*

Estos discos son **buenos,** pero ésos son **mejores.**

These records are good, but those are better.

[Práctica C]

Comparison of Nouns

Alicia tiene **más/menos** libros **que** Susana.

Alicia has more/fewer books than Susana.

Nosotros tenemos **tantas** pesetas **como** ellas.

We have as many pesetas as they (do).

Nouns are compared with the expressions **más/menos... que** and **tanto/a/os/as... como.** Tanto must agree in gender and number with the noun it modifies.

[Práctica D, E]

PRÁCTICA

A. Conteste según el dibujo.

1. ¿La biblioteca es más alta que la tienda?
2. ¿El museo es tan grande como el teatro?
3. ¿La tienda es menos alta que la biblioteca?
4. ¿La tienda es más alta que el museo?
5. ¿El teatro es tan alto como la biblioteca?
6. ¿El teatro es menos alto que la tienda?

B. Cambie: tan... como → más/menos... que.

1. Una limonada es tan ácida (*bitter*) como una naranjada.
2. Este periódico es tan interesante como ése.
3. Los tacos son tan deliciosos como las enchiladas.
4. Los niños son tan inteligentes como sus padres.
5. El matrimonio es tan importante como la amistad.

C. Complete, haciendo una comparación.

1. La comida italiana es buena, pero la comida mexicana es _____.
2. Las pruebas (*quizzes*) son malas, pero los exámenes son _____.

3. Pepito es grande ya; Demetrio, que tiene veinte años, es su hermano _____.
4. Luisita es muy joven; el bebé de la familia es su hermano _____.
5. La Argentina es grande, pero el Brasil es _____.
6. El elefante es grande, y el chimpancé es _____.

D. *Conteste, comparando las cosas de Alfredo con las* (those) *de Graciela.*

1. ¿Cuánto dinero tiene Alfredo?
2. ¿Cuánta cerveza tiene Graciela?
3. ¿Cuántos libros tiene Alfredo?
4. ¿Cuántos bolígrafos tiene Graciela?
5. ¿Cuántos cuadernos tiene Alfredo?
6. ¿Cuántas cartas tiene Graciela?

E. *Cambie: tanto... como → más/menos... que.*

1. Nicaragua tiene tantos lugares interesantes como Costa Rica.
2. Hay tantos compañeros como compañeras en esta clase.
3. Este pueblo tiene tantos habitantes como aquella ciudad.
4. Hay tantos coches en esta calle como en aquélla.
5. Hay tantos exámenes en la clase de español como en la clase de historia.
6. Estela bebe tanto café como yo.
7. Aquí hace tanto calor en verano como en invierno.

CONVERSACIÓN

A. *Conteste las preguntas en una forma lógica.*
   ¿Es Ud....

1. tan guapo/a como Burt Reynolds/Farrah Fawcett?
2. tan rico/a como Cristina Onassis?
3. tan leal como su mejor amigo/a?
4. tan inteligente como Einstein?
5. tan romántico/a como su novio/a o esposo/a?

¿Tiene Ud....

6. tanto dinero como los Rockefeller?
7. tantos tíos como tías?
8. tantos amigos como amigas?

9. tantas ideas buenas como _____?
10. tantos años como su profesor(a)?

B. *Comparative forms are used in many Spanish* sayings *(dichos). Several are given below. What are the English equivalents of these sayings? Can you think of another way to end them?*

1. Más feo que el coco (*bogeyman*).
2. Pesar (*to weigh*) menos que un mosquito.
3. Dormir como un tronco.
4. Más bueno que el pan (*bread*). [Note the special usage of **más bueno**.]

Study Hint: Using a Bilingual Dictionary

A Spanish–English/English–Spanish dictionary or vocabulary list is an excellent study aid, one that should be used very carefully. Follow these guidelines to minimize the pitfalls.

1. If you are looking for a Spanish word in the Spanish–English part of the dictionary, remember that in the Spanish alphabet the letters **ch, ll,** and **ñ** follow the letters **c, l,** and **n** respectively. The word **coche** will be found after the word **cocina; calle** will come after **calma;** and **caña** will follow **candidato.**

2. When you look in the English–Spanish section for the Spanish equivalent of an English word, keep in mind the part of speech— noun, verb, adjective, and so on—of the word you are looking for. By doing so, you will avoid many mistakes. Imagine the confusion that would arise if you chose the wrong word in the following cases:

   can: **lata** (noun, *tin can*) but **poder** (verb, *can, to be able*)

   light: **luz** (noun, *electric light, daylight*) but

   ligero (adjective, *light in color; light, not heavy*)

3. If the Spanish word that you find is not familiar to you, or if you simply want to check its meaning and usage, look up the new word in the Spanish–English section of the dictionary. Do the English equivalents given there correspond to the meaning you want to convey?

4. Remember that there is not always a one-to-one equivalency between Spanish and English words. **Jugar** means *to play* a sport or game, but the verb **tocar** must be used to talk about *playing* a musical instrument. **Un periódico** is a paper, a *news*paper, and **un papel** is a *sheet* of paper.

5. Minimize the number of "dictionary words" you use when writing in Spanish. It is best to limit yourself to words you know because you have used them in class. And when you do have to use the dictionary, try to check your word choice with your instructor or someone else who knows Spanish.

DIÁLOGO: Cartas de dos amigos

A.   Cerca de Ailigandí, 6 de agosto

Mi querido Héctor:

   Hago un alto° en mi viaje para escribir estas líneas. Hace calor, más   *pause*
de 45 grados° a la sombra°. Yo pido refresco tras° refresco. No hay   *45°C = 113°F / shade / after*

hielo.   El camarero viene con una naranjada tan ácida como un limón.
Pongo azúcar en el vaso y bebo, pero no tengo ganas, sólo sed.   Este
pueblo es más pequeño que el anterior° —¡y más aburrido!   el.. *the last one*

Salgo a la calle, donde hace un calor de mil° demonios.   Pregunto a   *a thousand*
un policía: —¿Cuándo es invierno en San Blas?   Él nota que estoy
sudando° tanto como un vaso de agua fría y contesta con buen humor: *sweating*
—Aquí es verano todo el año.   De nuevo° pregunto: —¿No hay esta-   **De...** *again*
ciones en este lugar? —¿Estaciones? ¡Oh, sí!   Hay dos: la estación de
verano y... la estación* de policía.   Yo vuelvo al hotel.   Pongo el radio
y escucho música de Buenos Aires.   Allá° es invierno ahora y hace frío. *there*
¡Cuántas ganas tengo de volver a mi patria!

Pensar que unos kilómetros más allá está Panamá con su alegría y...
con su aeropuerto.   Luego el avión y el vuelo° a casa.   *flight*

Pero ahora tengo que esperar° el autobús que sale los lunes, miércoles   *to wait for*
y viernes.   Es viejo, pero menos incómodo que el tren.

Hasta el domingo, si sobrevivo°.   *I survive*

Un saludo° cariñoso de tu compañero   *greeting*

Nicolás

B.   Mar del Plata, 31 de diciembre

Querido Nicolás:

Estoy contestando tu carta del seis de agosto.   Perdón por la demora°, *delay*
pero en julio, agosto y setiembre siempre salimos mi familia y yo de
Buenos Aires porque en aquellos meses hace mucho frío allí.

Ahora estamos esperando el Año Nuevo en la playa.   ¿Por qué no
vienes con nosotros?   Está haciendo un tiempo magnífico.

Un abrazo° de   *hug*

Héctor

---

*The police officer is making a play on the double meaning of **estación**: *season* and *station*.

P.D.* Todavía no comprendo la razón de tu viaje a Darién, Mosquitos y San Blas. ¿Tantos kilómetros para ir a sudar en Ailigandí? ¡Es más barato tomar un baño turco° en Buenos Aires!

baño... *Turkish bath*

Comprensión

¿Cierto o falso?   Corrija las oraciones falsas.

A. 1. Nicolás está en la Argentina.
    2. Pide pocos refrescos.
    3. La naranjada es muy ácida.
    4. Nicolás está muy contento en ese pueblo pequeño.
    5. Hace mucho calor, y Nicolás suda mucho.
    6. No hay verano en San Blas.
    7. En agosto hace frío en Buenos Aires.
    8. Nicolás quiere volver a la Argentina.
    9. El autobús es cómodo y sale todos los días.

B. 1. Héctor es muy puntual en contestar cartas.
    2. Hay demora de unos cuatro o cinco meses.
    3. Hace mucho frío en Mar del Plata en diciembre.
    4. La familia de Héctor va a la playa en diciembre.
    5. Héctor cree que es mejor —¡y más barato!— tomar un baño turco en Buenos Aires que sudar en Ailigandí.

Comentario cultural

Latinoamérica, Hispanoamérica, and **Iberoamérica** are some of the terms used to refer to the area that extends from the Rio Grande (or **Río Bravo,** as it is known in Mexico) to Cape Horn **(Cabo de Hornos).** Travelers in Latin America encounter a great variety of physical features and climates.

Although much of Latin America lies within the tropical zone, the climate is not tropical everywhere. Climate and temperatures vary considerably with elevation. Many of the large cities are located at high altitudes, where the climate is mild, with little variation in temperature throughout the year. Mexico City is at 7,800 feet; Bogotá, Colombia, at 8,500 feet; Cuzco, the ancient capital of the Incas, at

*Spanish uses **P.D.** (Latin *post data*) where English uses *P.S.* (Latin *post scriptum*).

11,200 feet; and La Paz, Bolivia, at 11,900 feet.   Seasons are marked mainly by changes in rainfall.

There are, however, areas of Latin America that are typically tropical in climate. In his letter to Héctor, Nicolás complains of the heat and humidity of Ailigandí (Panamá), a coastal city in the tropical rain forest that extends from the Caribbean coast of Central America to the equator.   The vast Amazon basin and a portion of the northeastern coast of Brazil have a similar climate.

Uruguay, a large portion of Paraguay, and almost all of Argentina and Chile are in the South Temperate Zone. Chile, with its 2,650-mile coastline, has deserts in the north and fjords and glaciers in the extreme south.   The geography of Argentina includes tropical zones in the north, immense pampas, and a wind-swept tableland that extends beyond the Strait of Magellan to Tierra del Fuego.

The seasons of the year are reversed in the Southern Hemisphere.   Nicolás, writing from Ailigandí in August, longs for his native Buenos Aires, where it is winter.   His friend Héctor, however, leaves Buenos Aires when he can during July, August, and September to escape the cold.

UN POCO DE TODO

A. *Cambie por el plural.*

1. ¿Por qué piensas que esta playa es mejor que aquélla?
2. Siempre sirvo una naranjada en verano.
3. Si no duermo ocho horas, estoy cansada todo el día.
4. ¿Cuándo hace calor en ese pueblo?
5. Mañana salgo para Panamá y pienso volver el sábado.

Cambie por el singular.

6. Preferimos almorzar con Uds. si no piensan salir temprano.
7. Siempre almorzamos en los buenos restaurantes que están en la Plaza de San Marcos.
8. Ponemos tanto dinero en el banco como Uds.
9. ¿Con quiénes jugamos el lunes?
10. Se cierran los mercados a las nueve los miércoles.

B. *Form complete sentences based on the words given, in the order given.   Conjugate the verbs, and add other words if necessary.*

1. Antonia / empezar / ser / estudiante / excelente
2. yo / no / volver / casa / con / tanto / trabajo / Elena
3. este / semana / yo / pensar / leer / tanto / lecciones / Estela
4. camarero / no / servir / tanto / cerveza / Coca-Cola
5. yo / hacer / peor / tacos / que / mi / hermanos

C. *Working with another student, ask and answer questions based on the places listed below. Follow the model, providing appropriate information.*

MODELO   SUSANA: ¿Piensas hacer un viaje a _____?
           PEDRO: Sí, salgo para _____ el (fecha o día).
           SUSANA: ¿No hace/hay _____ allá?
           PEDRO: Sí, por eso pienso poner _____ en mi maleta.

1. Mallorca / traje de baño
2. el Polo Norte / suéteres
3. San Juan / camisetas
4. Aspen / abrigo
5. Acapulco / raqueta de tenis

D. *Answer the following questions. Then ask the same questions of other students in the class to find at least one other person who answered a given question the way you did.*

1. ¿A qué hora almuerzas y dónde?
2. ¿Piensas que nuestro presidente es tan bueno como John F. Kennedy? ¿Por qué?
3. ¿De dónde (De qué estado) eres?
4. ¿Estás triste cuando llueve? ¿Qué haces cuando llueve?
5. ¿Adónde piensas ir después de la clase?
6. ¿Cuál prefieres, el verano o el invierno? ¿Por qué?
7. ¿Cuántos hermanos tiene Ud. en total?

E. *Complete las oraciones en una forma lógica.*

1. Cuando hace sol, prefiero _____.
2. Quiero salir con _____ porque es tan _____.
3. Pienso que _____ es más simpática que _____ porque _____.
4. Quiero salir para _____, donde hace/hay _____.
5. Este verano, (no) voy a hacer un viaje a _____; por eso estoy _____.
6. Mi padre/madre es _____; en este momento está _____.

VOCABULARIO

VERBOS

almorzar (ue)   to have lunch
cerrar (ie)   to close
dormir (ue, u)   to sleep
empezar (ie)   to begin
escuchar   to listen (to)
hacer (*irreg.*)   to do; to make
hacer un viaje   to take a trip
jugar (ue)   to play (sports)
llover (ue)   to rain
nevar (ie)   to snow
pedir (i, i)   to ask for, order
pensar (ie)   to think; to intend
poner (*irreg.*)   to put, place
preferir (ie, i)   to prefer
preguntar   to ask
salir (*irreg.*)   to leave, go out
servir (i, i)   to serve
volver (ue)   to return

SUSTANTIVOS

abril   April
agosto   August
el **agua** (*f.*)   water
el **azúcar**   sugar
el/la **camarero/a**   waiter/waitress
el/la **compañero/a**   companion,
   friend
el **cumpleaños** (*s.*)   birthday
diciembre   December

enero   January
la **estación**   season; station
febrero   February
la **fecha**   date
el **hielo**   ice
el **invierno**   winter
julio   July
junio   June
marzo   March
mayo   May
el **mes**   month
el **museo**   museum
noviembre   November
octubre   October
el **otoño**   fall
la **playa**   beach
el/la **policía**   police officer
la **primavera**   spring
el **pueblo**   town
el **refresco**   soft drink
se(p)tiembre   September
el **teatro**   theater
el **tiempo**   weather
el **vaso**   glass
el **verano**   fall

ADJETIVOS

abierto/a   open
aburrido/a   bored
cansado/a   tired

cerrado/a   closed
contento/a   happy
famoso/a   famous
limpio/a   clean
mayor   older
mejor   better
menor   younger
ocupado/a   busy
peor   worse
querido/a   dear
sucio/a   dirty

PALABRAS Y EXPRESIONES ÚTILES

¿a qué hora...?   at what time . . .?
¿adónde?   where?
allá   there
¿cuándo?   when?
¿cuánto/a?   how much?
está bien   it's okay (fine)
está claro   it's clear (obvious)
hace
   calor   it's hot
   fresco   it's cool
   frío   it's cold
   sol   it's sunny
   viento   it's windy
hay contaminación   there's
pollution
el primero de...   the first of . . .

Un paso más 5

Actividades

el basquetbol

el tenis

el golf

el hockey

el volibol

el béisbol

correr

el fútbol
norteamericano

nadar
(la natación)

el fútbol

el boxeo

pasear en
bicicleta
(el ciclismo)

patinar
(el patinaje de ruedas o sobre hielo)

el ping pong

esquiar

jugar en la nieve

remar

A. **Los deportes.** How interested are you and your classmates in sports? Interview another student to discover his or her interest(s) in sports.

1. ¿Juegas al béisbol? ¿al volibol? ¿al basquetbol? ¿al fútbol norteamericano? ¿al fútbol? De estos deportes, ¿cuál es tu favorito? ¿Con quién(es) practicas este deporte?
2. ¿Juegas al tenis? ¿al ping pong? ¿al golf? ¿Cuál prefieres?
3. En invierno, ¿qué prefieres —jugar en la nieve, patinar o esquiar?
4. ¿Prefieres correr o pasear en bicicleta? ¿remar o nadar?
5. En tu opinión, ¿cuál es más interesante —el boxeo o el hockey?
6. ¿Qué deportes se ven en la televisión? ¿Cuáles miras tú con frecuencia? ¿Cuál es tu favorito?
7. En tu opinión, ¿uno de los deportes es más peligroso (*dangerous*) que los otros? ¿Cuál? ¿Uno es más violento que los otros? ¿más interesante? ¿más aburrido que los otros?

B. **¿Es Ud. deportista?** What are you most likely to do on each of these occasions? Mark your answers and score yourself. Then refer to the **Interpretaciones,** which follow the test. Does the interpretation of your score describe you accurately?

1. El lunes por la noche prefiero _____
   a. mirar "El partido (*game*) de la semana" (fútbol norteamericano)
   b. escuchar música clásica   c. jugar al volibol con mis amigos/as
2. En verano si tengo un día libre (*free*) _____
   a. tomo el sol (*I sunbathe*) pero no nado   b. nado   c. paso unas horas bajo (*under*) un árbol, leyendo una novela
3. Es sábado y termino todas las cosas que tengo que hacer. Entonces yo _____
   a. juego al tenis   b. leo *Sports Illustrated*   c. escribo cartas
4. Es un día de invierno. Hace mucho frío y nieva. Prefiero _____
   a. esquiar o patinar   b. dormir una siesta   c. mirar los Juegos Olímpicos en la televisión
5. Es el 4 de julio y hace unos 40 grados (*104°F*) a la sombra. Voy a _____
   a. tomar limonada   b. jugar al béisbol   c. hablar de los deportes con los miembros de mi familia
6. Estoy mirando el *Superbowl* en la televisión. Estoy _____
   a. contento/a   b. descontento/a; prefiero estar en el estadio (*stadium*)   c. aburrido/a

   ☐ TOTAL

Interpretaciones
0–3 puntos   Para Ud. los deportes son de poco interés—quizá una pérdida (*waste*) de tiempo.
4–8 puntos   Los deportes tienen cierto interés para Ud., pero Ud. prefiere verlos, leer y hablar de ellos; Ud. participa poco.
9–12 puntos Ud. sí es muy deportista. Debe ser una persona muy activa.

C. **El 21 de julio en Europa.** El termómetro indica las equivalencias entre los grados Celsius, o centígrados de Europa, y los grados Fahrenheit de los Estados Unidos. Imagine que Ud. y sus compañeros de clase son habitantes de varias ciudades de Europa. A base de (*based on*) las temperaturas indicadas para el 21 de julio, ¿cómo van a contestar las siguientes preguntas para las ciudades indicadas?

¿Qué tiempo hace? ¿Qué ropa van a llevar? ¿Qué deportes van a practicar?

1. Sevilla
2. Valladolid
3. Oslo
4. Roma
5. Berlín

Temperaturas extremas

En Madrid: máxima, 28 grados; mínima, 11.
En la Península: máxima, 34 grados en Sevilla y Córdoba; mínima, 7 grados en León, Valladolid, Soria, Salamanca y Ávila.

En Europa:
Oslo: 10–24
Estocolmo: 14–19
Londres: 16–24
Amsterdam: 15–20
Berna: 6–18

Bruselas: 14–19
Copenhague: 13–21
París: 12–22
Berlín: 11–17
Hamburgo: 13–19
Bonn: 9–19
Roma: 14–24

D. **¿Qué va a hacer?** You decide to take one day off from work/school to relax and do whatever you want—within your financial limits. What will you do if your free day falls on a day with the following weather conditions? The example describes **el día ideal** of the woman shown in the cartoon on the next page.

Es el 12 de octubre. Llueve todo el día. Es un día muy feo, pero no importa. No voy a salir de casa en todo el día. Prefiero descansar. No salgo de mi cama. Voy a tomar café y leer el periódico. También hablo por teléfono con mis amigas. ¡Es un día maravilloso! No tengo que trabajar, no tengo que preparar la comida, no tengo que hacer las labores aburridas de la casa. Así estoy muy, muy contenta.

—*Te digo*°, *Mabel, que es necesario un día como este para saber*° *apreciar la vida.*

Te... *I tell you / to know how to*

1. Es el 12 de octubre.   Llueve todo el día.
2. Es el 15 de mayo.   Hace sol; hace un tiempo maravilloso.   Hace 25 grados (*77°F*).
3. Es el 24 de diciembre.   Hace frío y mucho viento.   Nieva, pero las calles (*streets*) y carreteras (*highways*) están en buenas condiciones.

A propósito...

The following greetings (**saludos**) and closings (**despedidas**) are used in writing to friends.

Saludos:	**Estimado/a amigo/a**	*Dear (Esteemed) friend*
	Querido/a Víctor/Victoria	*Dear Victor/Victoria*
Despedidas:	**Con mucho cariño**	*With much affection*
	Tu amigo/a	*Your friend*
	Abrazos	*Hugs*

Holiday greetings include:

Feliz Navidad y Próspero Año Nuevo	*Merry Christmas and Happy (Prosperous) New Year*
Con los mejores deseos para Navidad y Año Nuevo	*With best wishes for Christmas and the New Year*
Felices Pascuas	*Merry Christmas*

E.   **Muy estimada amiga...**   The following letter was sent from Spain as a thank-you note for a Christmas gift.   Using it as a model, write a thank-you letter to a friend.   Be sure to comment on the weather and include appropriate wishes for the New Year.

Santander, 16 de enero

Muy estimada amiga:

Le mando° un recuerdo muy cariñoso y le° deseo mucha felicidad en este Año Nuevo.

También le mando mis más° sinceras gracias por el regalo maravilloso de Navidad, que es la cinta° *cassette* con su música preciosa de *jazz*. Recuerdo° con mucho afecto° aquellas conversaciones del verano pasado sobre° esta música.

En la televisión estos días ponen escenas de varias ciudades de Norteamérica que pasan un frío muy intenso. Aquí en el Norte de España no estamos pasando mucho frío —las temperaturas más bajas son de 6 ó 7 grados sobre° cero.

Deseándole muchas felicidades en este año, le mando un saludo muy cariñoso.

Mercedes

le... I send you / you

most

tape / I remember
affection / about

above

Lectura cultural: La geografía y el clima de Sud América

¿Prefiere Ud. un lugar donde hay muchos cambios° de estaciones o desea Ud. vivir donde hay pocos cambios? En Suramérica se puede escoger° entre lo mejor de ambos mundos°.

La presencia de los Andes y del ecuador crea° un clima ideal y sin cambios en muchas partes del continente. Si Ud. vive en Venezuela,

changes
choose
lo... the best of both worlds
creates

© Freda Leinwand/Monkmeyer Press Photo

Alain Keler/EPA, Inc.

Colombia, Ecuador, Perú o partes de Chile, puede gozar de° una gran   **gozar..** *enjoy*
variedad de climas y de regiones distintas: la costa y el mar, la selva° y el   *jungle*
calor, las montañas altas y la nieve. Y claro está que la manera de vivir de
la gente° y aun° su personalidad cambian según° el clima. Se cree que los   *people / even /* **cambian...**
costeños —la gente de la costa— por lo general son gente muy alegre que   *change according to*
prefiere pasar sus días en la calle o en la playa tomando refrescos y con-
versando con los amigos. Los habitantes de las ciudades altas de las
montañas, en cambio°, se consideran más reservadas y algo ensimis-   **en...** *on the other hand*
mados°. Allí el clima depende de la altura y cuanto más alto°, más frío   **algo..** *somewhat*
hace.   *introverted /* **cuanto...**
                                                                                 the higher
   Más al sur° en Chile y la Argentina existen las cuatro estaciones, pero   *south*
como° están en el hemisferio sur, las estaciones ocurren en meses dife-   *since*
rentes de las estaciones del hemisferio norte. Por eso, cuando los habitantes de Nueva York llevan abrigo y están luchando° con el frío y la nieve,   *fighting*
los rioplatenses° están en bikini en las deliciosas playas del Mar de Plata.   *people from the River*
                                                                                 Plate region

Comprensión

Check your comprehension of the reading selection by completing the following
sentences:

1. Con respecto al clima, en Sudamérica hay _____.
2. Las distintas regiones que existen en el noroeste (*northwest*) del continente
   sudamericano son _____.

3. Además de (*besides*) afectar la manera de vivir, el clima _____.
4. Se cree que los costeños son _____.
5. Se cree que la gente de las montañas es _____.
6. En Chile y la Argentina las cuatro estaciones ocurren en diferentes meses que en los Estados Unidos porque _____.
7. La gente de Buenos Aires está de vacaciones en la playa cuando los neoyorquinos _____.

Ejercicios escritos

A. Write a brief paragraph introducing a Latin American to the geography and climate of the United States. You may want to give an overview, or you may prefer to describe the area in which you live. Some of the following questions may help you to organize your ideas.

1. ¿Hay mucha variedad geográfica en los Estados Unidos?
2. ¿Cuáles son algunos diferentes fenómenos geográficos de los Estados Unidos? ¿Dónde están situados? En su opinión, ¿uno de estos fenómenos es más interesante (hermoso [*beautiful*], importante) que los otros? ¿Cuál es? ¿Por qué?
3. ¿Cómo es el clima de los Estados Unidos? ¿Hay mucha variedad?
4. ¿Qué tiempo hace en su estado? ¿Cuándo ocurren las diferentes estaciones?
5. ¿Cómo afectan las estaciones la vida en las diferentes regiones del país?
6. ¿Prefiere Ud. vivir en su propio (*own*) estado o en otra parte del país? ¿Por qué?

B. Write a brief paragraph about your favorite season by completing the following sentences. Describe your attitudes and activities during this season, as well as the weather.

Yo prefiero _____ porque _____. Durante esta estación _____.

capítulo 6 En un restaurante español

Carlos Hernandez/EPA, Inc.

OBJETIVOS

In this chapter you will learn vocabulary and expressions you can use in a restaurant.

You will also learn about the following aspects of Spanish grammar:

26. indefinite and negative words (*some, any, none, never,* and so on), including the "double negative," which is frequently used in Spanish
27. the present tense of the irregular verbs **decir** (*to tell, to say*), **oir** (*to hear*), **traer** (*to bring*), and **ver** (*to see*)
28. the *personal* **a,** used when the direct object of a verb is a person
29. direct object pronouns (*him, her, me,* and so on)
30. the two Spanish verbs that mean *to know*—**saber** and **conocer**—as well as when to use each

Un paso más includes activities related to foods and restaurants, and a reading about Mexican food.

VOCABULARIO: PREPARACIÓN

La comida

Otras frases útiles

el/la camarero/a	waiter, waitress	**estar a dieta**	to be on a diet
la cena	supper, dinner	**¿nos sentamos?**	shall we sit
cenar	to eat supper, dinner		down?
la cuenta	check, bill	**el plato**	"special" of the
la especialidad de la casa	specialty of the house	**del día**	day
		recomendar (ie)	to recommend

A. *Llene los espacios en blanco con las palabras apropiadas.*

1. El _____ es una sopa española.
2. El _____ y la _____ son bebidas alcohólicas.
3. El _____ es un ingrediente de la paella.
4. El _____ es un tipo de carne.
5. La _____ _____ _____ _____ es el mejor (*best*) plato de un restaurante.
6. La _____ es un plato típico de España; tiene muchos ingredientes.
7. Dos ingredientes de una ensalada pueden ser el _____ y la _____.
8. Antes de almorzar o cenar, se comen unos _____.
9. Se come mucha _____ en verano—bananas, naranjas, etcétera.
10. El viernes por la noche, vamos a preparar una _____ especial para el cumpleaños de Celia. De postre, vamos a tener un _____.
11. En una cena elegante se toman unos entremeses, sopa, una _____, postre y un vino excelente.
12. Después de cenar, se pide la _____.

B. *What might you say in each of the following situations?   Match each situation with the appropriate comments.*

1. Ud. entra en un restaurante con un amigo. Hay una mesa libre (*free*).
2. Su amigo no come nada (*anything*).
3. Ud. es *barman* y un cliente pide vino.
4. Ud. es camarera en un restaurante. Un cliente desea una comida barata.
5. Ud. es camarero. Un cliente pide un *sándwich*.
6. Ud. sale con Enriqueta esta tarde.
7. La camarera pregunta qué desea Ud. de postre.

a. —¿Dónde vamos a cenar?
b. —¿Nos sentamos?
c. —¿Qué desea, señor? ¿Vino tinto o vino blanco?
d. —¿Puedo recomendar el plato del día?
e. —Un flan, por favor.
f. —¿Estás a dieta?
g. —¿De queso o de jamón?

C. *¿Qué palabras asocia Ud. con las palabras siguientes?*

1. beber 2. bistec 3. una hamburguesa 4. cenar 5. el/la camarero/a

D. *¿Qué va Ud. a pedir en las situaciones siguientes?*

1. Es hora de cenar y Ud. está en un restaurante. También está a dieta.
2. Es el cumpleaños de su novio/a (esposo/a).
3. Ud. está en la cafetería de la universidad con unos amigos. Es hora de almorzar.
4. Ud. no puede volver a casa porque tiene que estudiar para un examen. Ud. entra en McDonald's.

Acabar de + Infinitive
Acabo de pedir la cena.   I've just ordered supper.
Acaban de almorzar.   They've just had lunch.

Acabar de + *infinitive* corresponds to the English expression *to have just done something*.

E. *Ud. está en los lugares siguientes. ¿Qué acaba de pedir?*

1. un restaurante elegante
2. un restaurante español
3. un restaurante mexicano
4. la cafetería de la universidad

PRONUNCIACIÓN: R and RR

Spanish has two *r* sounds, one of which is called a *flap*, the other a *trill*. The rapid pronunciation of *tt* and *dd* in the English words *Betty* and *ladder* produces a sound similar to the Spanish flap *r*. Although English has no trill, when people imitate a motor, they are producing the Spanish trill, which is a rapid series of flaps.

The trilled **r** is written **rr** between vowels **(carro, correcto)** and **r** at the beginning of a word **(rico, rosa)**. Any other **r** is pronounced as a flap. Be careful to distinguish between the flap **r** and the trilled **r.** A mispronunciation will often change the meaning of a word—for example, **pero** (*but*)/**perro** (*dog*).

PRÁCTICA

A. Inglés: potter   ladder   cotter   meter   total   motor
   Español: para   claro   cara   mire   toro   moro

B. 1. rico 2. ropa 3. roca 4. Roberto 5. Ramírez 6. rebelde 7. reportero
    8. real 9. corro 10. carro 11. corral 12. barra

C. 1. coro/corro 2. coral/corral 3. pero/perro 4. vara/barra 5. ahora/ahorra
    6. caro/carro 7. cero/cerro

D. 1. el nombre correcto 2. un corral grande 3. una norteamericana 4. Puerto
    Rico 5. rosas amarillas 6. un libro negro y rojo 7. una camarera rica
    8. Enrique y Carlos 9. El perro está en el corral. 10. Estos errores son raros.
    11. Deseo un carro caro. 12. Pedro quiere ir.

MINIDIÁLOGOS Y GRAMÁTICA

26. INDEFINITE AND NEGATIVE WORDS

Doña Pilar está de visita.

MARCOS: Doña Pilar, ¿toma Ud. *algo* con nosotros?

PILAR: No, gracias. *Nunca* ceno, pero ya que Uds. van a cenar, yo...

MARCOS: ¿Un poco de pescado, quizá? ¿*Algo* de postre? Si Ud. quiere, *también* tenemos...

ANITA: ¡Marcos, por favor! Pilar *no* quiere tomar *nada*. *No* estás sirviendo en tu restaurante. ¡Estás en tu casa!

1. ¿*Todos están en casa de doña Pilar o en casa de Marcos y Anita?*
2. ¿*Qué hora es, aproximadamente? ¿Qué van a hacer Marcos y Anita?*
3. ¿*Qué va a tomar doña Pilar? ¿Por qué?*
4. ¿*Qué quiere hacer Marcos? ¿Por qué? ¿Está confundido* (confused) *Marcos?*

algo	something	**nada**	nothing, not anything
alguien	someone, anyone	**nadie**	no one, nobody, not anybody
algún (alguno/a/os/as)	some, any	**ningún** (ninguno/a)	no, none, not any
siempre	always	**nunca, jamás**	never
también	also	**tampoco**	neither, not either

Double Negative

When a negative word comes *after* the main verb, Spanish requires that another negative word—usually **no**—be placed before the verb. When a negative word precedes the verb, **no** is not required.

¿**No** estudia **nadie?** ¿**Nadie** estudia?	*Isn't anyone studying?*
No estás en clase **nunca.** **Nunca** estás en clase.	*You're never in class.*
No hablan árabe **tampoco.** **Tampoco** hablan árabe.	*They don't speak Arabic, either.*

Doña Pilar is visiting. MARCOS: Doña Pilar, will you have something to eat/drink with us? PILAR: No, thanks. I never eat supper, but since you are going to have dinner, I . . . MARCOS: A little bit of fish, perhaps? Some fruit? If you want, we also have . . . ANITA: Marcos, please! Pilar doesn't want to eat anything. You're not serving in your restaurant. You're in your (own) home!

Alguno and Ninguno

The adjectives **alguno** and **ninguno** shorten to **algún** and **ningún** respectively before a masculine singular noun, just as **uno** shortens to **un**. The plural forms **ningunos** and **ningunas** are rarely used.

¿Tiene Ud. **algunos** amigos mexicanos?   *Do you have any Mexican friends?*

No, no tengo **ningún** amigo mexicano.   *No, I don't have any Mexican friends.*

PRÁCTICA

A. Answer these questions by following the example and cues given.

1. ¿Hay **algo** en la pizarra? (palabras)
   ¿en la mesa? (periódico)
   ¿en la calle? (carro)
   ¿en la montaña? (pueblo)

Sí, hay **algo** en la pizarra. Hay unas **palabras** en la pizarra.

No, no hay **nada** en la pizarra.

2. ¿Hay **alguien** en la clase? (estudiantes)
   ¿en el parque? (amigos)
   ¿en el restaurante? (unos clientes)
   ¿en la estación? (unos pasajeros)

Sí, hay **alguien** en la clase. Hay unos **estudiantes.**

No, no hay **nadie** en la clase.

3. ¿Hay **algunos** libros en la silla?
   ¿en el suelo (*floor*)?
   ¿en el cuarto?
   ¿en la oficina?

Sí, hay **algunos** libros en la silla.

No, no hay **ningún** libro en la silla.

B. *Exprese negativamente, usando el negativo doble.*

1. Hay algo en el suelo.
2. Hay algunos platos interesantes en el menú.
3. Yo voy también.
4. Siempre cenamos a las diez.
5. Hacemos algo.
6. Habla con alguien.
7. Elena siempre prepara la lección.
8. Raúl duerme allí también.

C. *Dé Ud. frases nuevas según las indicaciones.*

1. —¿Qué pregunta Ud. cuando entra en la casa el día de su cumpleaños?
   —¿Hay alguna *carta* para mí? (*regalo, flores, plato especial, telegramas*)
2. —Es casi imposible ser perfecto, ¿verdad?
   —Sí, ninguna *idea* es perfecta. (*hermano, amiga, plan* [m.], *familia*)

D. *¿Cómo se dice en español?*

1. Is there anything for me?
2. There's someone in the car.
3. No one thinks that.
4. They also serve dinner there.
5. There's no one at home.
6. Marcos doesn't understand this sentence, either.
7. You never study with Carmen.
8. We don't want to order anything.
9. There's no restaurant in that town.
10. No one is as tired as I am.

CONVERSACIÓN

A. *Rosa es una persona muy positiva, pero su hermano Demetrio es negativo. Siempre
tiene ideas muy negativas. Aquí hay unas frases que expresan las ideas de Rosa.
¿Cómo puede reaccionar Demetrio?*

1. Tengo hambre; quiero comer algo.
2. Alguien puede hacer un pastel para la fiesta.
3. Siempre salgo con mis amigos.
4. Hay algo interesante en la televisión.
5. Hay algunos estudiantes excelentes en mi clase de sicología.
6. Hay algunos estudiantes más listos que yo.

B. *Preguntas*

1. ¿Vamos a vivir en la luna algún día? ¿y en los otros planetas? ¿Dónde
   va Ud. a vivir algún día?

2. ¿Hay algo más importante que el dinero? ¿que la amistad? ¿que el amor? ¿algo tan importante como la clase de español?
3. ¿Algunos de sus amigos son de habla española? ¿De dónde son?
4. En la clase, ¿hay alguien más inteligente que el/la profesor(a)? ¿más estudioso/a que Ud.? ¿más rico/a que Ud.?
5. ¿Hay algo en la mesa en este momento? ¿en el suelo? ¿en su silla?

27. PRESENT TENSE OF *DECIR, OIR, TRAER,* AND *VER*

DECIR: *to say, tell*		OIR: *to hear*		TRAER: *to bring*		VER: *to see*	
digo	decimos	oigo	oímos	traigo	traemos	veo	vemos
dices	decís	oyes	oís	traes	traéis	ves	veis
dice	dicen	oye	oyen	trae	traen	ve	ven
	diciendo		oyendo		trayendo		viendo

Decir: ¿Qué **dice** Ud.?   *What are you saying?*
Los profesores siempre **dicen** la   *Professors always tell the truth.*
verdad.

¡OJO! Do not confuse **decir** (*to say* or *to tell*) with **hablar** (*to speak*). In Spain and some parts of Latin America, the command form of **decir**— **Diga**—is used to answer the phone.

Oir: No **oigo** bien.   *I can't hear well.*
Esa canción ya no se **oye**   *You don't hear that song much*
mucho.   *any more.*

English uses *listen* or *hey* to attract someone's attention. In Spanish the command forms of **oir** are used: **oye (tú), oiga (Ud.), oigan (Uds.).**

Oye, Juan, ¿vas a la fiesta?   *Hey, Juan, are you going to the party?*

PRÁCTICA

A. Dé Ud. frases nuevas según las indicaciones.

1. —En diciembre, antes de la Navidad, todos dicen la verdad. ¿Quién dice la verdad?
   —*Cristina* dice la verdad. (*tú, los niños, yo, Ud., la nieta, vosotros*)
2. —Durante la cena, ¿quién trae la sopa?
   —*Ernesto* trae la sopa. (*nosotros, Eduardo, yo, Uds., tú, vosotros*)

3. —En el club, es difícil oir la música porque hay mucho ruido (*noise*).
   ¿Quién no oye bien?
   —*Los señores* no oyen bien la música. (*Juan y yo, tú, Uds., yo, la camarera, vosotros*)

4. —En el restaurante no se ve bien porque hay poca luz (*light*). ¿Quién no ve bien el menú?
   —*Ud.* no ve bien el menú. (*yo, nosotros, Andrés, los clientes, tú, vosotros*)

B. *Form complete sentences by using one word or phrase from each column.*

Juan y yo			la entrada
tú			un programa de televisión
la camarera		decir	las respuestas (*answers*)
yo		traer	canciones mexicanas
el hombre viejo	(no)	oir	la verdad
———		ver	el vino
			la especialidad de la casa
			bien
			———

CONVERSACIÓN

A. *Se usa la expresión* **¿Cómo se dice?** *cuando se quiere aprender una palabra nueva. Repase Ud. (review) el vocabulario nuevo de esta lección, preguntando a sus compañeros,* **¿Cómo se dice** ——— **en inglés?** *o* **¿Cómo se dice** ——— **en español?**

B. *Los estudiantes van a hacer una comida (meal) todos juntos (together) en la clase. Pregunte Ud. a varios de sus compañeros,* **Oye, ¿qué vas a traer?**

C. *Muchas personas ven la televisión o van al cine con frecuencia. Pregunte Ud. a otros estudiantes de la clase,* **¿Qué programa ves con frecuencia y por qué? ¿Qué película(s) nueva(s) quieres ver y por qué?**

28. PERSONAL *A*

Esperando a un amigo
GRACIELA: ¿No vamos a esperar *a Miguel* para pedir?
CARLOS: ¿*A Miguel*? ¿Por qué? Siempre llega tan tarde.
GRACIELA: Bueno... si llega tan tarde como siempre, ¡puede pagar la cuenta!

Waiting for a friend GRACIELA: Aren't we going to wait for Miguel to (before we) order? CARLOS: For Miguel? Why? He always arrives so late. GRACIELA: Well . . . if he arrives as late as usual, he can pay the check!

© Katherine A. Lambert 1980

1. *¿Dónde están Graciela y Carlos?*
2. *¿A quién esperan?*
3. *¿Qué va a hacer Miguel si llega tarde?*

In English and in Spanish, the *direct object* (**complemento directo**) of a sentence answers the question *what?* or *whom?* in relation to the subject and verb.

Ann is preparing dinner.}   Ann is preparing *what?* } *dinner*
What is Ann preparing?

They can't hear the baby. }   They can't hear *whom?* } *the baby*
Whom can't they hear?

Indicate the direct objects in the following sentences:

1. I don't see Betty and Mary here.
2. Give the bone to the dog.
3. No tenemos dinero.
4. ¿Por qué no pones los entremeses en la mesa?

In Spanish, the word **a** is inserted between the verb and the direct object of a sentence when the direct object refers to a specific person or persons.* This **a** has no equivalent in English.

	Buscamos **a sus padres.**	*We're looking for their parents.*
but	Buscamos **nuestro coche.**	*We're looking for our car.*
	Van a visitar **al profesor.**	*They're going to visit the professor.*
but	Van a visitar **el museo.**	*They're going to visit the museum.*

The personal **a** is used before **alguien/nadie** and **quién** when these words function as direct objects.

| ¿Vas a invitar **a alguien?** | *Are you going to invite someone?* |
| **¿A quién** llamas? | *Whom are you calling?* |

¡OJO!   Remember that the verbs **esperar** (*to wait for*), **escuchar** (*to listen to*), **mirar** (*to look at*), and **buscar** (*to look for*) include the sense of the English prepositions *for, to,* and *at.* These verbs take direct objects in Spanish (not prepositional phrases as in English).

| Estoy buscando **mi carro.** | *I'm looking for my car.* |
| Estoy buscando **a mi hijo.** | *I'm looking for my son.* |

PRÁCTICA

A. *Dé Ud. frases nuevas según las indicaciones.*

1. —¿A quién o qué ve Ud. (*do you see*) en este momento?
   —Veo *el texto.* (*el/la profesor[a], la pizarra, los estudiantes, la mesa, mi amigo/a, la puerta*)
2. —¿A quién o qué busca Ud. en este momento?
   —Estoy buscando *a mi abuelo.* (*mi libro, Felipe, la cuenta, el amigo de Tomás, alguien, el menú*)

B. *¿Cómo se dice en español?*

1. We're going to call Michael.
2. They're inviting Ann.
3. I'm not looking at anyone.
4. I'm going to listen to José Feliciano.
5. Whom are you waiting for?
6. Estela has four cousins.

*The personal **a** is not usually used with **tener: No tenemos hijos.**

CONVERSACIÓN

A. *Este sábado Ud. va a dar una fiesta y puede invitar a cualquier* (any) *persona famosa.*
    ¿A quién quiere invitar?

Quiero invitar a _____ porque _____.

B. *Se necesitan personas para hacer varios trabajos.   ¿A quién puede Ud. recomendar?*

Puedo recomendar a _____ para presidente porque _____.

¿Para camarerola?   ¿para abogadola?   ¿para médicola?   ¿para _____?

C. *¿A quién va a llamar Ud. esta noche?   ¿Por qué?*

Voy a llamar a _____ porque _____.

29. DIRECT OBJECT PRONOUNS

Tell what Mary is looking at in each picture. Follow the models given.

María está mirando **al niño.** →
  María **lo** está mirando.
También María está mirando _____.

María está mirando **la flor.** →
  María **la** está mirando.
También María está mirando _____.

María está mirando **a los señores.** →
  María **los** está mirando.
También María está mirando _____.

María está mirando **las montañas.** →
  María **las** está mirando.
También María está mirando _____.

DIRECT OBJECT PRONOUNS			
me	*me*	**nos**	*us*
te	*you* (fam. sing.)	**os**	*you* (fam. pl.)
lo*	*you* (form.), *him, it* (m.)	**los**	*you* (form. pl.), *them* (m., m. + f.)
la	*you* (form.), *her, it* (f.)	**las**	*you* (form. pl.), *them* (f.)

Like direct object nouns, *direct object pronouns* **(pronombres del complemento directo)** answer the questions *what?* or *whom?* in relation to the subject and verb. Direct object pronouns are placed before a conjugated verb and after the word **no** when it appears.

Ellos **me** ayudan.	*They're helping me.*
Diego **no lo** necesita.	*Diego doesn't need it.*
¿Dónde están la revista y el periódico? **Los** necesito ahora.	*Where are the magazine and the newspaper? I need them now.*

The direct object pronouns may be attached to an infinitive or a present participle.

Las tengo que leer. ⎫ Tengo que leer**las.** ⎭	*I have to read them.*
¿**Nos** están buscando? ⎫ ¿Están buscándo**nos?** ⎭	*Are you looking for us?*

When a pronoun object is attached to a present participle, a written accent is needed on the stressed vowel: **buscándonos.**

The direct object pronoun **lo** can refer to actions, situations, or ideas in general. When used in this way, **lo** expresses English *it* or *that.*

Lo comprende muy bien.	*He understands it (that) very well.*
No **lo** creo.	*I don't believe it (that).*

PRÁCTICA

A. Dé Ud. frases nuevas según las indicaciones.

1. —¿Qué necesita Ud. ahora? ¿el bolígrafo?
   —*El bolígrafo,* no. No lo necesito ahora. (*¿el menú?   ¿los platos?   ¿la maleta?   ¿el carro?   ¿las cuentas?   ¿los lápices?*)
2. —¿Qué tienen Uds. que preparar para mañana? ¿el ejercicio?
   —*¿El ejercicio?* Sí, tenemos que prepararlo para mañana. (*¿la sopa?   ¿los postres?   ¿la lección?   ¿el flan?   ¿las patatas?   ¿la cena?*)

*In Spain and in other parts of the Spanish-speaking world, **le** is frequently used instead of **lo** for the direct object pronoun *him*. This usage will not be practiced in *Puntos de partida.*

3. —Uds. están en un restaurante. ¿Qué están pidiendo? ¿cerveza?
   —¿Cerveza? Sí, estamos pidiéndola ahora. (¿queso? ¿carne? ¿té?
   ¿entremeses? ¿fruta? ¿vino?)

B. *Cambie: los complementos directos → pronombres.*

1. El camarero pone los vasos en la mesa.
2. Mis hijos están usando el carro ahora.
3. Voy a leer esa novela esta noche.
4. ¿Por qué no pagas tú la cuenta?
5. ¿El dinero? No tengo el dinero.
6. Necesitamos dos pasteles para la fiesta.
7. Estoy escribiendo las oraciones.
8. Los niños están abriendo los libros.

C. *Your roommate (**compañero/a de cuarto**) is constantly suggesting things for you to do, but you've always just finished doing them. How will you respond to each of the following suggestions? Follow the model.*

MODELO   COMPAÑERO/A: ¿Por qué no escribes la composición para la clase de español?
UD.:   *¡Porque **acabo de** escribirla!*

1. ¿Por qué no estudias la lección ahora?
2. ¿Por qué no visitas el museo conmigo?
3. ¿Por qué no aprendes el vocabulario nuevo?
4. ¿Por qué no compras el periódico de hoy?
5. ¿Por qué no pagas la matrícula?
6. ¿Por qué no me ayudas más?

D. *Ud. y sus amigos están muy negativos hoy. ¿Cómo van a responder a las preguntas siguientes?*

MODELO   ¿Creen Uds. eso? → *¡No, no **lo** creemos!*

1. ¿Prefieren Uds. eso?
2. ¿Comprenden Uds. eso?
3. ¿Desean Uds. eso?
4. ¿Piensan Uds. eso?

CONVERSACIÓN

Preguntas

1. ¿Quién lo/la mira a Ud. en este momento? ¿el/la profesor(a)? **(Sí, me mira.)** ¿los otros estudiantes? ¿el/la presidente/a de la universidad? ¿sus padres? ¿su compañero/a de cuarto? ¿_____?

2. Todos necesitamos la ayuda de nuestros parientes y amigos.   ¿Quién los/las
   ayuda a Uds.?   ¿sus padres?   (**Sí, nos ayudan.**)   ¿sus amigos?   ¿sus compañeros
   de cuarto?   ¿sus profesores?   ¿sus consejeros?   ¿_____?

30. *SABER* VERSUS *CONOCER*

Simone Oudot/EPA, Inc.

Delante de un restaurante

AMALIA: ¿Dónde vamos a almorzar?

ERNESTO: (*Entrando en el restaurante.*)   ¿Por qué no aquí mismo?

AMALIA: *¿Conoces* este restaurante?

ERNESTO: Sí, lo *conozco* y *sé* que es excelente.

AMALIA: ¿Y cómo *sabes* que es tan bueno?

ERNESTO: *Conozco* muy bien a la dueña.   ¡Es mi tía!   ¿Nos sentamos?

1. *¿Qué hora es, aproximadamente?*
2. *¿Conoce Ernesto el restaurante?*
3. *¿Cuál es su opinión del restaurante?*
4. *¿Cómo sabe Ernesto que el restaurante es muy bueno?*
5. *¿Por qué conoce a la dueña del restaurante?*

In front of a restaurant   AMALIA: Where are we going to have lunch?   ERNESTO: (*Entering the
restaurant.*)   Why not right here?   AMALIA: Do you know (are you familiar with) this restaurant?
ERNESTO: Yes, I know it, and I know that it's excellent.   AMALIA: And how do you know that
it's so good?   ERNESTO: I know the owner very well.   She's my aunt!   Shall we sit down?

SABER: to know		CONOCER: to know	
sé	sabemos	conozco	conocemos
sabes	sabéis	conoces	conocéis
sabe	saben	conoce	conocen

Saber means *to know facts or pieces of information.* When followed by an infinitive, **saber** means *to know how to do something.*

No **saben** el teléfono de Alejandro.   *They don't know Alejandro's phone number.*

¿**Saben** Uds. dónde vive Carmela?   *Do you know where Carmela lives?*

¿**Sabes** tocar el piano?   *Do you know how to play the piano?*

Conocer means *to know or to be acquainted (familiar) with a person, place, or thing.* It can also mean *to meet.*

No **conocen** a la nueva estudiante todavía.   *They don't know the new student yet.*

¿**Conocen** Uds. el restaurante mexicano en la calle Goya?   *Are you familiar with the Mexican restaurant on Goya Street?*

¿Quieren **conocer** a aquel joven?   *Do you want to meet that young man?*

PRÁCTICA

A. Dé Ud. frases nuevas según las indicaciones.

1. —Sus amigos van a dar una fiesta. ¿Quién sabe cuándo es?
   —*Tú* sabes cuándo es la fiesta. (*ellos, yo, Elvira, Ud., Ana y tú, vosotros*)
2. —¿Quién conoce a los padres de Graciela?
   —*Nosotros* conocemos a sus padres. (*yo, Uds., Juan y yo, tú, Raúl y Mario, vosotros*)

B. Describe what these well-known people know how to do.

José Feliciano		jugar al béisbol
Mikhail Baryshnikov		tocar el piano
Pete Rose		cantar en español
Liberace	sabe	escribir novelas
James Michener		leer rápidamente
Evelyn Wood		bailar

C. *Can you match these famous couples?*

Adán		Marta
Archie Bunker		Cleopatra
Romeo		Eva
Rhett Butler	conoce a	Julieta
Antonio		Scarlett O'Hara
Jorge Washington		Edith

D. *Form complete sentences by using one word or phrase from each column.*

yo			cuando es el examen final
los estudiantes			al nuevo novio de Marta
tú			el nombre (*name*) de aquel profesor
el/la profesor(a)	(no)	conocer	jugar al tenis
Uds.		saber	al rey de España
_____			todos los verbos nuevos
			Bolivia
			donde sirven una paella magnífica
			_____

CONVERSACIÓN

A. *Ud. es el/la presidente/a de los Estados Unidos y puede invitar a cualquier (any) persona a la Casa Blanca. ¿A quién quiere Ud. conocer?*

Quiero conocer a _____ porque _____.

B. *Ud. ya conoce a los otros estudiantes de la clase y sabe mucho de ellos. Describa Ud. a varios de sus compañeros de clase.*

Conozco a _____. Sé que él/ella _____.

DIÁLOGO: El placer° de comer en un restaurante español   *pleasure*

Ana María, de Madrid
Manuel (Manolo), de Sevilla, amigo de Ana María
Camarero

A. *Por teléfono*

ANA MARÍA:	¡Diga! No lo oigo bien. ¿Qué dice? Más alto°, por favor.	**Más...** *louder*
MANUEL:	¿Está° la señorita Ana María Hernández?	*Is . . . home?*
ANA MARÍA:	¡Manolo! ¿Eres tú? ¿No conoces mi voz°? ¿Qué te trae por acá°?	*voice* / *here*

MANUEL: ¡Anamari! Perdón, chica, no te oigo bien. Estoy de vacaciones, ¿sabes? Si no tienes ningún compromiso° esta noche, ¿por qué no cenamos juntos° en El Toledano? Tú conoces el lugar, ¿verdad?

ANA MARÍA: ¡Estupendo, chico! Lo conozco pero no muy bien. No estoy haciendo nada ahora y tampoco tengo compromiso para esta noche.

commitment, engage-
ment/together

MANUEL: Pues te invito. Cenamos y oímos a don Paco y su trío. Paso por ti° a las nueve y media, ¿vale°?

Paso... *I'll come by for you / OK?*

ANA MARÍA: De acuerdo. Hasta luego.

B. *En El Toledano*

MANUEL: ¿Nos sentamos? Creo que desde° aquí se ve y se oye bien.

from

ANA MARÍA: Perfecto. Aquí viene el camarero. ¿Por qué no pides tú la cena ya que° conoces este restaurante?

ya... *since*

CAMARERO: Buenas noches, señores. ¿Qué desean de aperitivo?

MANUEL: Para la señorita un vermú°; para mí un jerez°. Los trae con jamón, queso y anchoas°, por favor. ¿Y qué recomienda Ud. de comida?

vermouth / sherry
anchovies

CAMARERO: El solomillo a la parrilla° es la especialidad de la casa. También el bacalao°: lo preparamos a la vizcaína°. Como plato del día hay paella...

solomillo... *grilled filet mignon*
codfish / **a...** *Biscayan style*

MANUEL: Bueno. De sopa, el gazpacho. De plato fuerte°, el solomillo con patatas y guisantes°. Ensalada de lechuga y tomate. Y de postre, flan. Vino tinto y, al final, dos cafés.

plato... *main dish*
peas

ANA MARÍA: Manolo, basta ya. ¡Estoy a dieta y he merendado más de la cuenta°!

he... *I snacked more than I should have*

MANUEL: Chica, ¿qué importa? Luego vamos a bailar.

Comprensión

¿Cierto o falso? Corrija las oraciones falsas.

A. 1. Ana María y Manolo no son amigos.
   2. Tienen que hablar más alto —no se oye bien.
   3. Ana María tiene otro compromiso; no puede salir con Manolo.
   4. Ana María conoce bien El Toledano.
   5. Durante la cena van a escuchar música.

B. 1. Manolo y Ana María encuentran (*find*) una mesa muy buena.
   2. No toman bebidas alcohólicas.
   3. El camarero recomienda varios platos.
   4. El plato del día es el bacalao a la vizcaína.
   5. Manolo tiene miedo de comer demasiado (*too much*).

Comentario cultural

Hispanic eating habits are quite different from those in the United States. Not only is the food itself somewhat different, but there are some differences in the meal schedule.

There are three fundamental meals: **el desayuno** (*breakfast*), **la comida/el almuerzo** (*midday meal*), and **la cena** (*supper*). Breakfast, which is eaten around seven or eight o'clock, is a very simple meal—frugal by most U.S. standards. **Café con leche** or **chocolate** (*hot chocolate*) with a plain or sweet roll or toast; that is all. The **café con leche** is mostly heated milk with a small amount of very strong coffee to add flavor and color.

The main meal of the day, **la comida/el almuerzo,** is frequently eaten as late as two P.M., and it is a much heartier meal than the average U.S. lunch. It might consist of soup, a meat or fish dish with vegetables and potatoes or rice, a green salad, and then dessert (often fruit or cheese). Coffee is usually served after the meal.

The evening meal, **la cena,** is somewhat lighter than the noon meal. It is rarely eaten before eight o'clock, and in Spain is commonly served as late as ten or eleven P.M. Because the evening meal is served at such a late hour, it is customary to eat a light snack or **merienda** about 5 or 6 P.M. The **merienda** might consist of a sandwich or another light snack with **café con leche** or **chocolate.** Similarly, a light snack is often eaten in the morning between breakfast and the midday meal.

Whether eaten at home or in a restaurant, a Spanish meal is an event given great care and attention. The result is an adventure long remembered.

¡Buen provecho! *Enjoy your meal!*

Study Hint: Practicing Spanish Outside of Class

The few hours you spend in class each week are not enough time for practicing Spanish. But once you have done your homework and gone to the language lab (if one is available to you), how else can you practice your Spanish outside of class?

1. Practice "talking to yourself" in Spanish as you walk across campus, wait for a bus, and so on. Have an imaginary conversation with someone you know, or simply practice describing what you see or what you are thinking about at a given moment. Write notes to yourself in Spanish.

2. Hold a conversation hour—perhaps on a regular basis—with other students of Spanish. Or make regular phone calls to practice Spanish with other students in your class. It is difficult to communicate on the phone, since you do not have gestures and facial expres-sions to rely on, but such practice is an excellent way to improve your skill.

3. See Spanish-language movies when they are shown on campus or in local movie theaters. Check local bookstores, libraries, and record stores for Spanish-language newspapers, magazines, and music. Read the radio and television listings. Are there any Spanish-language programs or any stations that broadcast partially or exclusively in Spanish?

4. Practice speaking Spanish with a native speaker—either a Hispanic American or a foreign student. Is there an international students' organization on campus? An authentic Hispanic restaurant in your town? Spanish speakers employed in stores where you shop? Try out a few phrases—no matter how simple—every chance you get. Every bit of practice will enhance your ability to speak Spanish.

UN POCO DE TODO

A. Form complete sentences based on the words given, in the order given. Conjugate the verbs, and add other words if necessary.

1. profesor Cortina / conocer / ninguno / chica / clase
2. yo / conocer / ninguno / francés
3. camarero / estar / traer / lo
4. ¿ / Hay / alguien / patio / ? / — / yo / oir / nadie
5. ¿ / decir / Ud. / nada, / Sra. Medina / ?
6. ¿ / teléfono / de / profesor? / yo / no / lo / saber

B. *Rearrange the following words to form complete sentences. Do not add any words.*

1. estudiante / diciendo / la / está / lo
2. ¿ / no / Ud. / nada / por qué / dice / ?
3. en / pizarra / vemos / ninguna / frase / no / la
4. ¿ / si / mi / ellos / sabes / a / amiga / conocen / ?
5. veo / en / los / este / no / momento
6. señor / no / oir / la / Gómez / señorita / al / puede / Padilla

C. *Working with two other students, ask and answer questions according to the model.*

MODELO   BLANCA: *¿Ves al profesor?*
          EDUARDO: No, no *lo* veo. / Sí, *lo* veo.
          BENI: Yo no *lo* veo tampoco. / Yo también *lo* veo.

1. ¿Ves a _____?
2. ¿Conoces al presidente de los Estados Unidos?
3. ¿Sabes todas las respuestas para el examen de hoy?
4. ¿Me oyes bien?
5. ¿Ves las sillas?
6. ¿Traes a tus padres a la universidad?
7. ¿Sabes la lección?

D. *Hablando con otros dos estudiantes, ¿pueden contestar las preguntas siguientes? Uno debe preguntar, otro debe responder afirmativamente y el último (last one) debe contestar negativamente.*

Pueden hablar de la clase y de los estudiantes:
1. ¿Ves algo en la pizarra?
2. ¿Traes algunos libros a la clase?
3. ¿Ves a alguien en la clase?
4. ¿Sabes algo de la historia de Puerto Rico?
5. ¿Sabes algo de la comida de Sudamérica?

Pueden hablar de sus amigos:
6. ¿Conoces a alguien de la Argentina?
7. ¿Conoces a alguien de Cuba?
8. ¿Conoces a algunos españoles?
9. ¿Tienes algunos amigos de habla española?

E. *Todos nuestros amigos son diferentes.   Tienen características especiales que los hacen únicos.   De sus amigos/as,*

1. ¿quién conoce a mucha gente (*people*) latina?
2. ¿quién sabe hablar muy bien el español?
3. ¿quién no estudia nunca?
4. ¿quién nunca tiene ganas de trabajar mucho?
5. ¿quién siempre trae mucho dinero a la clase?
6. ¿quién dice que es un Don Juan?
7. ¿quién conoce a una persona famosa?

VOCABULARIO

VERBOS

acabar de (+ *inf.*) to have just (*done something*)
ayudar to help
cenar to have supper
conocer (*irreg.*) to know, be acquainted with
decir (i, i) to say, tell
esperar to wait (for); to expect
invitar to invite
llamar to call
oír to hear
pasar (por) to pass (by); to come by (for someone)
preparar to prepare
recomendar (ie) to recommend
saber (*irreg.*) to know; to know how
tocar to play
traer to bring
usar to use
ver to see

SUSTANTIVOS

el bistec steak
la cafetería cafeteria
la carne meat
la cena supper

la cuenta check, bill
la ensalada salad
la entrada entrée, main course
los entremeses hors d'oeuvres
la especialidad de la casa specialty of the house
el flan custard
la flor flower
la fruta fruit
el gazpacho tomato soup (served chilled)
el jamón ham
la lección lesson
la lechuga lettuce
el menú menu
la novela novel
la paella paella (dish made with rice, shellfish, often chicken, and flavored with saffron)
el pastel cake; pastry
el pescado fish
la pizarra blackboard
el plato dish
el plato del día "special" of the day
el pollo chicken
el postre dessert
el queso cheese
la respuesta answer

la silla chair
la sopa soup
el suelo floor
el té tea
el teléfono telephone; telephone number
el tomate tomato
la verdad truth
el vino blanco white wine
el vino tinto red wine

ADJETIVOS

algún (alguno/a/os/as) some, any
ningún (ninguno/a) no, none, not any

PALABRAS Y EXPRESIONES ÚTILES

a dieta (*with* **estar**) on a diet
algo something
alguien someone, anyone
antes de before
basta enough, that's enough
jamás never
nada nothing, not anything
nadie no one, nobody, not anybody
¿nos sentamos? shall we sit down?
tampoco neither, not either

Un paso más 6

Actividades

© Barbara Alper/Stock, Boston

A. **El menú, por favor.** Using the menu on the next page to help you, answer the following questions that a waiter/waitress would ask. Try to answer each question in several different ways.

MODELO   ¿Qué desea Ud. de postre? → —*Para mí, la fruta.*
                                       —*Me trae un helado, por favor.*
                                       —*Favor de traerme un helado.*
                                       —*¿Todavía hay flan?*
                                       —*¿Qué tal los pasteles?*
                                       —*No deseo nada, gracias.*

1. ¿Qué desean Uds. de antojitos (*hors d'oeuvres*)?
2. ¿Va a tomar sopa?
3. ¿Qué desea Ud. de plato fuerte?
4. ¿Y para beber?
5. ¿Qué quiere de postre?
6. ¿Prefiere Ud. té o café?

B. **Gustos y preferencias.** Survey some of the members of your class to determine their tastes and preferences in food. Tabulate the responses to find the most/least popular foods, restaurants, and so on.

1. ¿Prefieres cenar en casa, en un restaurante o en la cafetería de estudiantes?
2. ¿Hay días cuando no cenas?
3. ¿Prefieres comer una hamburguesa o un bistec con papas fritas?
4. ¿Prefieres comer en McDonald's (o en otro restaurante donde se sirve la comida rápidamente) o en un restaurante de lujo (*deluxe*)?
5. ¿Qué comes —y dónde— cuando tienes mucha prisa?
6. ¿Qué comes —y dónde— cuando tienes mucho dinero?
7. ¿Qué plato(s) comes con frecuencia? ¿Qué platos(s) no comes nunca? ¿Qué platos(s) comes solamente en casa de tus padres?
8. ¿Qué bebida(s) prefieres?
9. Cuando tienes hambre a las tres de la tarde, ¿qué prefieres comer? ¿Un yogurt? ¿galletas (*cookies*) y leche? ¿zanahorias (*carrots*)? ¿un jugo de tomate? ¿chocolate? ¿un *sándwich* con una cerveza? ¿un pastel con un vaso de leche? ¿otra cosa?
10. ¿Qué comes cuando tienes hambre a las once de la noche?

—*¿Sopa fría?   Parece que está aún bastante templada°...*   **bastante...** *rather warm (lukewarm)*

C.   **¿Sopa fría?**   This cartoon elaborates a theme typically found in "restaurant jokes."   Working with one or more students, write a short dialog that presents some problem related to meals; it may take place either in a restaurant or at home.   Work up to the "critical moment," ending your dialog as soon as you have presented a problem to be resolved.   Present your dialog to the other students in your class, who should then suggest as many solutions to the problem as they can.   For the problem shown in the cartoon they might suggest:

—Los clientes pueden ir a otro restaurante.
—El camarero debe traer otro plato de sopa.
—Deben pedir otro plato, y no deben pagar la sopa.
—Los clientes pueden hablar con el dueño del restaurante.

You may base your skit on one of the following problems or on one of your own creation.

En un restaurante

1. Hay una mosca (*fly*) en mi sopa.
2. El camarero trae la cuenta; los clientes no pueden pagar.
3. Un violinista da un concierto al lado de la mesa de los clientes.   Ellos quieren hablar; no quieren oir música.   Además, el violinista toca muy mal.

En casa

4. El niño no come sus verduras (*vegetables*) pero sí pide postre.
5. El/la hijo/a de la familia invita a unos amigos a comer. No hay bastante (*enough*) comida.

A propósito...

Here are some useful expressions related to eating:

Buen provecho.	*Enjoy your meal. Eat hearty.*
Me muero de hambre.	*I'm starving. (I'm dying of hunger.)*
¡A comer!	*Let's eat! Everybody to the table!*
¿Vamos a tomar algo?	*Shall we get something to eat/drink?*
¿Me trae un café, por favor?	*Please bring me some coffee.*

Hispanics traditionally linger longer over meals—talking with friends and family—than do Americans, and waiters will not usually bring the bill until asked to do so. Use the following expressions to get your waiter's attention and to ask for the check.

Psst.	Used to get a waiter's/waitress' at-
Oiga.	tention. While not considered im-
Camarero/señorita, por favor.	polite, **psst** is not used in formal settings.
La cuenta, por favor.	*The check/bill, please.*

D. **¿Qué va a decir?** Much of life centers around meals and eating. What will you say in each of the following situations? Consult the expressions in **A propósito.**

1. Nos sentamos a la mesa. Antes de empezar a comer, Ud. nos dice _____
2. Ud. tiene mucha sed y quiere ir a un bar. Habla con su amigo y dice _____

3. Ud. acaba de preparar la comida y llama a todos los miembros de la familia. Ud. dice _____
4. Ud. acaba de volver a casa después de un partido (*match*) de tenis y tiene un hambre feroz. Ud. exclama ¡_____!
5. Acabamos de comer en un buen restaurante. Tomamos un café y hablamos un rato (*a while*). Queremos salir, pero primero tenemos que pagar. Ud. llama al camarero y dice _____
6. Estamos sentados (*seated*) a la mesa y todos tenemos mucha hambre. Los camareros están trabajando mucho y no nos ven. Para llamar la atención de uno de ellos, Ud. dice _____

Lectura cultural: La comida mexicana

David Powers/Stock, Boston

Hoy en día la comida mexicana es muy popular en los Estados Unidos. En todas las ciudades grandes hay restaurantes que la sirven. Algunos de estos lugares ofrecen auténtica comida mexicana, mientras° otros ofrecen adaptaciones americanizadas.

    La base de la comida mexicana es la tortilla. Es un tipo de pan que se hace por lo general con maíz°. Se usa la tortilla para hacer varios otros

while

corn

platos. Por ejemplo, la enchilada es una mezcla° de carne picada° bien condimentada° y envuelta° en una tortilla arrollada°. Se sirve con una salsa de ají°.

mixture / chopped
seasoned / wrapped / rolled
salsa... *chili sauce*

Quizá el plato mexicano que se conoce mejor en los Estados Unidos es el taco. Consiste en una tortilla llena° de carne picada, lechuga, tomate y queso. Se cubre° a menudo° con una salsa picante°. Y hablando de platos famosos, ¡cuidado con los "burritos"! No es comida mexicana auténtica. Son muy buenos, pero son una invención de origen tejano.

full
Se.. *it is covered / a ... frequently / spicy (hot)*

Comprensión

Check your understanding of the reading selection by matching the sentence fragments to form complete sentences.

1. La popularidad de la comida mexicana en los Estados Unidos es evidente
2. Algunos restaurantes mexicanos
3. La tortilla
4. La carne picada
5. Se usa la salsa de ají
6. El taco
7. Los tejanos

a. es probablemente el plato mexicano más famoso en los Estados Unidos.
b. se usa en el taco y en la enchilada.
c. porque hay muchos restaurantes que la sirven.
d. ofrecen platos americanizados.
e. es la parte esencial de la comida mexicana.
f. para hacer la enchilada.
g. son responsables de (*for*) la invención del burrito.

Ejercicios escritos

A. Create your own composition about eating and drinking habits in the United States by completing the sentences of the following paragraph.

En los Estados Unidos la gente no da gran importancia a las comidas. La vida americana es tan rápida que _____. Muchas veces el padre o la madre _____ y no puede _____. También los niños _____. Por eso cada miembro de la familia americana _____.

B. Write a brief paragraph about your eating preferences or those of your family. Use the following questions as a guide in developing your paragraph.

1. ¿Cuántas veces comen al día? ¿A qué horas?
2. ¿Comen juntos?
3. ¿Quién(es) prepara(n) la comida?
4. ¿Qué prepara(n)? ¿Es excelente la comida? ¿buena? ¿mala? ¿regular?
5. ¿Qué comida prefieren cuando comen en un restaurante? ¿comida china? ¿comida mexicana? ¿comida italiana? ¿hamburguesas?
6. ¿En qué restaurantes comen?
7. ¿Comen allí con frecuencia? ¿Cuántas veces al año? ¿Cuándo van a volver?

capítulo 7 En el aeropuerto

Simone Oudot/EPA, Inc.

OBJETIVOS

In this chapter you will learn vocabulary and expressions related to travel in general, and to travel by plane in particular.

You will also learn about the following aspects of Spanish grammar:

31. how to express to or for whom something is done, using the indirect object pronouns (*to him, for me,* and so on),
32. how to express the idea of "liking" using the verb **gustar** with an indirect object

33. how to form adverbs from many adjectives by using the suffix **-mente**, the Spanish equivalent of the English suffix *-ly*
34. how to give commands to persons whom you address as **Ud.** or **Uds.**
35. numbers over 100

Un paso más includes activities related to travel and getting along in Spanish abroad, and a reading about important and interesting places to visit in Latin America.

VOCABULARIO: PREPARACIÓN

En el aeropuerto: ¡Buen viaje!

el avión	plane	**el/la pasajero/a**	passenger
el asiento	seat	**la azafata**	female flight attendant
el vuelo	flight		
la demora	delay	**el camarero**	male flight attendant
el boleto	ticket	**la sala de espera**	waiting room
el pasaje	passage, ticket	**la sección de (no) fumar**	(no) smoking section
primera clase	first class		
clase turística	economy class	**guardar (un puesto)**	to save (a place)
anunciar	to announce	**hacer cola**	to wait in line
bajar (de)	to get down (from); to get off (of)	**hacer escalas**	to have stopovers
		hacer la(s) maleta(s)	to pack one's suitcase(s)
desayunar	to eat breakfast		
estar atrasado/a	to be late		
facturar el equipaje	to check the baggage	**subir (a)**	to go up; to get on (a plane)
fumar	to smoke	**volar (ue)**	to fly

A. *¿Cuántas cosas y acciones puede Ud. identificar o describir en este dibujo?*

B. *Ud. va a hacer un viaje en avión. El vuelo sale a las ocho de la mañana. Usando las letras **a** a **i**, indique Ud. en qué orden va a hacer las cosas siguientes.*

___ 1. Subo al avión.
___ 2. Desayuno y hago las maletas.
___ 3. Espero el vuelo en la sala de espera.
___ 4. Hago cola para comprar el pasaje y facturar el equipaje.

—— 5. Llego al aeropuerto a tiempo (*on time*) y bajo del taxi.
—— 6. Se anuncia el vuelo.
—— 7. Guardo un puesto para otro pasajero.
—— 8. Estoy atrasado/a. Salgo para el aeropuerto en un taxi.
—— 9. La azafata me indica el asiento.

C. *¿Qué va Ud. a hacer en estas situaciones?*

1. Ud. no tiene mucho dinero. ¿Qué clase de pasaje va a comprar?
   a. clase turística b. primera clase c. un pasaje en la sección de fumar
2. Ud. quiere pedir dos pasajes —uno para Ud., el otro para su amigo/a.
   Él/ella tiene alergia a los cigarrillos (*cigarettes*). ¿Qué pide Ud.?
   a. Dos boletos, sección de fumar, por favor. b. Dos pasajes, sin escala,
   por favor. c. Dos asientos, sección de no fumar, por favor.
3. Ud. es una persona muy nerviosa y tiene miedo de volar. Necesita ir desde
   Nueva York a Madrid. ¿Qué pide Ud.?
   a. un vuelo con muchas escalas b. un vuelo sin escalas c. un boleto de
   tren
4. Ud. tiene muchas maletas. Pesan (*they weigh*) mucho y Ud. no quiere
   llevarlas. ¿Qué hace Ud.?
   a. Compro boletos. b. Guardo un asiento. c. Facturo el equipaje.
5. Su amigo/a va a llegar al aeropuerto antes que Ud. Ud. quiere hablar con
   él/ella durante el vuelo. ¿Qué va a decir a su amigo/a?
   a. ¿Me facturas el equipaje? b. ¿Me guardas un asiento? c. ¡Buen viaje!
6. Su vuelo está atrasado, pero Ud. está tranquilo/a. ¿Qué dice Ud.?
   a. Azafata, insisto en hablar con el capitán. b. Una demora más... no
   importa. c. Si no salimos dentro de (*within*) diez minutos, bajo del avión.

D. *Opiniones. ¿Está Ud. de acuerdo con las siguientes oraciones? ¿Sí o no?*

Peter Menzel/Stock, Boston

1. Es peligroso (*dangerous*) volar.
2. Las colas en el aeropuerto siempre son largas.
3. Prefiero la sección de fumar.
4. Siempre pido asientos de primera clase.
5. La primera clase es más tranquila que la clase turística.
6. Es divertido (*fun, enjoyable*) viajar con niños.
7. Prefiero los vuelos con muchas escalas.
8. Las demoras no me importan.
9. Prefiero volar por la noche.

PRONUNCIACIÓN: S, Z, Ce, and Ci

Spanish **s** and **z** are usually pronounced like the [s] in English *class, Sue*. The letter **c** before **e** and **i** also produces an [s] sound: **cine, once.*** Except in a few words borrowed from other languages **(zigzag),** the letter **z** never occurs before an **e** or **i** in Spanish. For this reason, spelling changes sometimes occur: **lápiz → lápices; vez → veces.**

PRÁCTICA

1. asiento desea desierto discusión pasión pase hasta
   Buenas tardes, señora. ¿Es jueves o viernes? Siempre insisten.
2. jerez azafata conozco zona zapatos quizás ¡zas!
   un lápiz y una tiza (*chalk*) ¿Hay gazpacho?
3. elección César emigración ciencias
   Es el doce de marzo.

MINIDIÁLOGOS Y GRAMÁTICA

31. INDIRECT OBJECT PRONOUNS

En la sala de espera del aeropuerto

HIJO: Mamá, tengo hambre. *¿Me* das un chocolate?

MAMÁ: No, hijo. No *te* voy a dar un chocolate. Acabas de comer.

HIJO: Mamá, quiero leer. *¿Me* compras un librito?

MAMÁ: No *te* voy a comprar más libros. Ya tienes tres.

HIJO: Mamá...

MAMÁ: No, hijo. Te quiero mucho, pero no *te* voy a comprar nada más.

HIJO: Pero mamá...

*In many parts of Spain, the letter **z,** as well as **c** before **e** and **i,** is pronounced like *th* in English *thin.*

MAMÁ: ¡Que no!
HIJO: Pero mamá, ¿no ves? Ese señor acaba de robar*te* la maleta.

1. *¿Quién tiene hambre?*
2. *¿La mamá le da un chocolate a su hijo?*
3. *¿Le compra un librito a (for) su hijo?*
4. *¿La mamá le compra algo más a su hijo?*
5. *¿Escucha a su hijo?*
6. *¿Quién acaba de robar la maleta?*

me	*to, for me*	**nos**	*to, for us*
te	*to, for you* (fam. sing.)	**os**	*to, for you* (fam. pl.)
le	*to, for you* (form.), *him,*	**les**	*to, for you* (form. pl.), *them*
	her, it		(m.) (m. + f.)

As you have seen, direct object nouns and pronouns answer the questions
what? or *whom? Indirect object* nouns and pronouns usually answer the
questions *to whom?* or *for whom?* in relation to the verb. The word *to* is
frequently omitted in English.

Indicate the direct and indirect objects in these sentences:

1. I'm giving her the present tomorrow.
2. Could you tell me the answer now?
3. El profesor nos va a dar un examen.
4. ¿No me compras el librito ahora?

   Like direct object pronouns, *indirect object pronouns* (**pronombres del
complemento indirecto)** are placed before a conjugated verb and after the
word **no** if it appears in the sentence. Indirect object pronouns may be
attached to a gerund—with the addition of an accent mark—or to an
infinitive.

Están facturándo**me** el equipaje. ⎫
Me están facturando el equipaje. ⎬   *They're checking my bags for me.*
                                      ⎭

Voy a guardar**te** el asiento. ⎫
Te voy a guardar el asiento. ⎬   *I'll save your seat for you.*
                                 ⎭

In the airport waiting room SON: Mom, I'm hungry. Will you give me a piece of chocolate? MOM: No,
son. I will *not* give you a piece of chocolate. You just ate. SON: Mom, I want to read. Will you buy me
a little book? MOM: I'm not going to buy you any more books. You already have three. SON: Mom . . .
MOM: No, son. I love you a lot, but I'm not going to buy you anything else. SON: But mom . . .
MOM: (I said) No! SON: But mom, don't you see? That man just stole your suitcase.

Since **le** and **les** have several different equivalents, their meaning is often clarified or emphasized with the preposition **a** and the pronoun objects of prepositions.

Voy a mandar**le** un telegrama **a Ud.** **(a él, a ella).**	*I'm going to send you (him, her) a telegram.*
Estoy haciéndo**les** un regalo **a Uds.** **(a ellos, a ellas).**	*I'm making you (them) a present.*

When there is a noun indirect object in a sentence, the indirect object pronoun is frequently used in addition. This construction is very common in Spanish.

Vamos a decir**le** la verdad **a Juan.**	*Let's tell Juan the truth.*
¿Les guardo los asientos **a Jorge y Marta?**	*Should I save the seats for Jorge and Marta?*

PRÁCTICA

A. *Substitute the phrases in parentheses for the words in italics, and make other necessary changes.*

    1. —Ud. está de vacaciones. ¿A quién escribe tarjetas postales (*postcards*)?
       —Les escribo una tarjeta postal *a mis padres.* (*a ti, a Ud., a Ángel, a Uds., a Alicia, a vosotros*)
    2. —Ud. tiene que comprar los boletos de avión para unos amigos que viajan con Ud. ¿A quién (*for whom*) le está comprando el boleto ahora?
       —Ahora estoy comprándole el boleto *a Jorge.* (*a Sergio, a ti, a Estela, a Uds., a Marta y Rosa, a vosotros*)

B. *Hoy es el cumpleaños de Marcos. ¿Quién le da a Marcos el libro? ¿el regalo grande? ¿el radio portátil? ¿la camisa? ¿Qué les dice Marcos a todos? ¿Ud. le da algún regalo a Marcos? ¿Por qué no? ¿No lo conoce Ud.? Y a Ud., ¿qué le van a dar sus amigos este año el día de su cumpleaños?*

C. *Hoy es el aniversario de los Sres. González. ¿Quién les da el regalo pequeño? ¿el televisor? ¿los boletos para un viaje a Puerto Vallarta? ¿la pintura bonita? ¿Qué les da Ud. a sus padres para su aniversario?*

D. *Ud. y su amigo/a están en el aeropuerto. Su amigo/a necesita mucha ayuda y Ud. quiere ayudarlo/la. Con otro estudiante, practique este diálogo y sus variaciones.*

MODELO　　comprar el boleto → AMIGO/A:　¿Me puedes *comprar el boleto?*
　　　　　　　　　　　　　　　　UD.:　　Sí, te *compro el boleto.*

1. guardar (*to watch*) el equipaje
2. facturar el equipaje
3. guardar el puesto en la cola
4. guardar el asiento
5. buscar el pasaporte
6. ayudar con las maletas

CONVERSACIÓN

A. *Using the model sentence given below, tell whom you would like to write to about the following problems.*

MODELO　　Quiero escribirle a _____ para decirle que _____ es un problema serio.

Problemas	**Personas**
1. la contaminación del aire	el presidente de los Estados Unidos
2. la matrícula	el presidente de Aerolíneas Iberia
3. el precio de un pasaje a Madrid	el/la dueño/a de la librería
4. el precio de la gasolina	el/la rector(a) (*president*) de la uni-
5. el precio de los libros	versidad
6. _____	_____

B. *Complete las oraciones en una forma lógica.*

1. Mi novio/a siempre me manda _____.
2. Mis padres me pagan _____.
3. Quiero darle a _____ un(a) _____ porque _____.
4. ¿Deben los hombres abrirles la puerta a _____?
5. En casa les sirvo _____ a mis amigos.
6. Para el cumpleaños de mi mejor amigo/a, voy a hacerle _____.
7. En _____, mi restaurante favorito, les recomiendo a Uds. el/la _____.
8. En el avión, la azafata y el camarero nos sirven _____.

32. GUSTAR

Lo malo de volar

RÓMULO: Cuando vuelo, me *gusta* estar en el aeropuerto con mucha anticipación. Pero ¿cómo se llega sin carro?

GRACIELA: Bueno, es más fácil y más barato tomar el autobús. El 92 te lleva directamente al aeropuerto.

RÓMULO: Pero sabes que a mí no me *gusta* nada viajar en autobús. Siempre hay tanta gente...

GRACIELA: Es curioso, ¿no? Parece que la cosa más difícil no es llegar a Cancún —¡es llegar al aeropuerto!

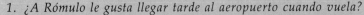

1. *¿A Rómulo le gusta llegar tarde al aeropuerto cuando vuela?*
2. *¿Tienen carro Rómulo y Graciela?*
3. *Sin carro, ¿cómo se llega al aeropuerto?*
4. *¿A Rómulo le gusta viajar en autobús? ¿Por qué (no)?*
5. *Según Graciela, ¿cuál es la parte más difícil del viaje?*

SPANISH	LITERAL EQUIVALENT	ENGLISH
Me gusta la playa.	The beach is pleasing to me.	*I like the beach.*
No le gustan sus cursos.	His courses are not pleasing to him.	*He doesn't like his courses.*
Nos gusta volar.	Flying is pleasing to us.	*We like to fly.*

The verb **gustar** is used to express likes and dislikes, but **gustar** does not literally mean *to like*. **Gustar** means *to be pleasing* (to someone).

Gustar is always used with indirect object pronouns: someone or something is pleasing *to* someone else. It is most commonly used in the third person singular or plural **(gusta/gustan),** and must agree with its subject, which is the person or thing liked, *not* the person whose likes are being described. Note that an infinitive (**volar** in the final sentence above) is viewed as a singular subject in Spanish.

A mí me gustan los tacos.   *I like tacos.*
¿**A ellos les** gusta leer?   *Do they like to read?*

As in the preceding sentences, **a mí** (**a ti, a Ud.,** and so on) may be used in addition to the indirect object pronouns for clarification or emphasis.

The bad thing about flying RÓMULO: When I fly, I like to be at the airport with a lot of time to spare. But without a car how do you get there? GRACIELA: Well, it's easiest and cheapest to take the bus. The (number) 92 takes you directly to the airport. RÓMULO: But you know that I really don't like to travel by bus. There are always so many people . . . GRACIELA: It's funny, isn't it? It seems the most difficult thing isn't getting to Cancún (*resort area in Mexico*)—it's getting to the airport!

The indirect object *pronoun* must be used with **gustar** even when an indirect object *noun* is expressed.   A common word order is as follows:

(**A** + pronoun/noun)	indirect object pronoun	**gustar** subject
(A Juan)	le	gusta esquiar.
(A ellas)	les	gustan las fiestas.

However, word order of sentences with **gustar** is flexible:

Le gusta esquiar a Juan. ⎫
Le gusta a Juan esquiar. ⎬   *Juan likes to ski.*
A Juan le gusta esquiar. ⎭

PRÁCTICA

A. *Tell whether or not you like each of these things.*

MODELO   ¿El café? → (No) **Me gusta** el café.
¿Los pasteles? → (No) **Me gustan** los pasteles.

1. ¿El vino?
2. ¿El español?
3. ¿Esta universidad?
4. ¿El invierno?
5. ¿La gramática?
6. ¿Hacer cola?

7. ¿Los entremeses? (dishes / dinner)
8. ¿Los fines de semana?
9. ¿Las clases este semestre?
10. ¿Los exámenes?
11. ¿Las flores?
12. ¿Los vuelos con muchas escalas? (flights / stops)

B. *Dé Ud. frases nuevas según las indicaciones.*

1. —Ud. es muy simpático/a —¡le gusta casi todo! ¿Qué le gusta?
   —(No) Me gusta *la primavera.* (*el otoño, los médicos, volar, las discotecas, los animales, fumar*)
2. —A todos nos gustan las vacaciones, ¿verdad? ¿A quién le gustan?
   —*A nosotros* nos gustan las vacaciones. (*a mí, a Rico, a ellas, a ti, a Uds., a vosotros*)

C. *¿Cómo se dice en español? Pida Ud. (order) una pizza para su familia. Todos tienen gustos diferentes.*

My father likes anchovies **(las anchoas)**, but he doesn't like sausage **(el chorizo)**. My mother likes sausage, but she doesn't like cheese a lot. My brothers like cheese, but they don't like mushrooms **(los hongos)**. I like everything **(todo)!**

CONVERSACIÓN

A. *¿Qué le gusta más a Ud.? ¿y por qué?*

1. ¿el color rojo, azul o verde? Me gusta más el _____.
2. ¿el verano, el otoño, el invierno o la primavera?
3. ¿jugar al tenis o esquiar?
4. ¿viajar en clase turística o en primera clase?
5. ¿dar regalos o recibirlos?
6. ¿el vino o la Coca-Cola?
7. ¿las fiestas formales o las fiestas informales?
8. ¿el café con azúcar o sin azúcar?
9. ¿los programas de televisión o las películas?
10. ¿manejar *(to drive)* o volar?

B. *Complete las oraciones en una forma lógica.*

1. A mí me gusta(n) _____.
2. A mi padre (hermano, tío) le gusta(n) _____.
3. A mi madre (hermana, tía) le gusta(n) _____.
4. Al/A la profesor(a) le gusta(n) _____.
5. A los estudiantes de la clase les gusta(n) _____.

33. ADVERBS

You already know some of the most common Spanish *adverbs* **(adverbios): bien, mal, mejor, peor, mucho, poco, más, menos, muy, pronto, a tiempo, tarde, temprano, siempre, nunca.**   The form of adverbs is invariable.

Adverbs that end in *-ly* in English usually end in **-mente** in Spanish. The suffix **-mente** is added to the feminine singular form of adjectives. Adverbs ending in **-mente** have two stresses: one on the adjective stem and the other on **-mente**. The stress on the adjective stem is the stronger of the two.

Adjective	Adverb	English
rápido	**rápidamente**	*rapidly*
fácil	**fácilmente**	*easily*
valiente	**valientemente**	*bravely*

In Spanish, adverbs modifying a verb are placed as close to the verb as possible. When they modify adjectives or adverbs, they are placed directly before them.

Hablan **estupendamente** el español.   *They speak Spanish marvelously.*
Ese libro es **poco** interesante.*   *That book is not very interesting.*
Vamos a llegar **muy tarde.**   *We're going to arrive very late.*

PRÁCTICA

A. Cambie: adjetivos → adverbios.

1. práctico   2. especial   3. alegre   4. estupendo   5. perfecto   6. triste
7. final   8. típico   9. personal

B. Complete Ud. estas oraciones con adverbios basados en los adjetivos siguientes.

directo   posible   puntual
inmediato   rápido   tranquilo
paciente   fácil   total

1. La familia está esperando _____ en la cola.
2. Hay examen mañana y tengo que empezar a estudiar _____.
3. Se vive _____ en aquel pueblo en la montaña.
4. ¿Las enchiladas? Se preparan _____.
5. ¿El hombre va a vivir en la luna algún día? Mi hermana contesta, «_____.»
6. ¿Qué pasa? Estoy _____ confundido.
7. Un vuelo que hace escalas no va _____ a su destino.

CONVERSACIÓN

Complete las oraciones en una forma lógica.

1. Yo _____ rápidamente, pero no _____ rápidamente.
2. Yo siempre _____ tranquilamente.
3. Es necesario llegar a clase _____.
4. Mi mejor amigo/a _____ más fácilmente que yo.
5. Yo _____ mejor que mis padres.
6. Yo _____ peor que mi amigo/a _____.
7. Yo _____ más que el/la profesor(a).

*Note that the Spanish equivalent of *not very* + *adjective* is **poco** + *adjective.*

34. FORMAL COMMANDS

En el avión

AZAFATA: *Pase Ud.*, señor. Bienvenido a bordo.

PASAJERO: Gracias. Éste es mi asiento, ¿verdad?

AZAFATA: Sí, es el 24A. *Tome* asiento y *no olvide* el cinturón de seguridad.

PASAJERO: ¿Puedo fumar?

AZAFATA: Ésta es la sección de fumar, pero *no fume Ud.* ahora, por favor. Vamos a despegar pronto para Quito.

PASAJERO: ¿Para Quito? Pero... el vuelo 112 (ciento doce) va a Cuzco.

AZAFATA: Sí, señor, pero éste es el vuelo 102 (ciento dos). *¡Baje Ud.* ahora mismo —todavía hay tiempo!

1. ¿Quién dice «Pase Ud., señor»?
2. ¿El pasajero encuentra bien su asiento? ¿Cuál es?
3. ¿Por qué no debe fumar ahora el pasajero?
4. ¿Cuál es el error del pasajero?
5. ¿Qué debe hacer el pasajero?

Commands (imperatives) are verb forms used to tell someone to do something. In this section you will learn the *formal commands* (**mandatos formales**), that is, the commands used with people whom you address as **Ud.** or **Uds.**

Formation of Formal Commands

Regular verbs　　　　Stem	Singular	Plural	English equivalent
hablar: hablø → habl-	Hable (Ud.)	Hablen (Uds.)	*Speak*
comer: comø → com- escribir: escribø → escrib-	Coma (Ud.) Escriba (Ud.)	Coman (Uds.) Escriban (Uds.)	*Eat* *Write*

A. **Ud./Uds.** commands are formed by dropping the final **-o** from the first person singular of the present tense and adding **-e/-en** for **-ar** verbs and **-a/-an** for **-er** and **-ir** verbs. Using **Ud.** or **Uds.** after the command forms makes the command somewhat more formal or more polite.

On the plane FLIGHT ATTENDANT: Come in, sir. Welcome aboard. PASSENGER: Thank you. This is my seat, isn't it? FLIGHT ATTENDANT: Yes, it's (number) 24A. Take your seat and don't forget the seatbelt. PASSENGER: May I smoke? FLIGHT ATTENDANT: This is the smoking section, but don't smoke now, please. We're going to take off for Quito right away. PASSENGER: For Quito? But . . . flight 112 goes to Cuzco. FLIGHT ATTENDANT: Yes, sir, but this is flight 102. Get off right now—there's still time!

B. Formal commands of stem-changing verbs will show the stem change, since these commands are based on the **yo** form.

Piense Ud.   Vuelva Ud.   Pida Ud.

C. Verbs ending in **-car, -gar,** and **-zar** require a spelling change in the command form in order to preserve the **-c-, -g-,** and **-z-** sounds.

buscar: bus**que** Ud.   pagar: pa**gue** Ud.   empezar: empie**ce** Ud.

D. Remember that some verbs have irregular **yo** forms.   The **Ud./Uds.** commands for these verbs will reflect the irregularity.

conocer:	conozcø → **conozca Ud.**	salir:	salgø → **salga Ud.**
decir:	digø → **diga Ud.**	tener:	tengø → **tenga Ud.**
hacer:	hagø → **haga Ud.**	traer:	traigø → **traiga Ud.**
oir:	oigø → **oiga Ud.**	venir:	vengø → **venga Ud.**
poner:	pongø → **ponga Ud.**	ver:	veø → **vea Ud.**

E. A few verbs have irregular **Ud./Uds.** commands:

dar: **dé Ud.**   saber: **sepa Ud.**
estar: **esté Ud.**   ser: **sea Ud.**
ir: **vaya Ud.**

[Práctica A]

Position of Object Pronouns with Formal Commands

Direct and indirect object pronouns follow affirmative commands and are attached to them.   In order to maintain the original stress of the verb form, an accent mark is added to the stressed vowel if the original command has two or more syllables.

Léalo Ud.   *Read it.*
Búsquele el bolígrafo.   *Look for the pen for him.*

Direct and indirect object pronouns precede negative commands.

No lo lea Ud.   *Don't read it.*
No le busque el bolígrafo. *Don't look for the pen for him.*

[Práctica B, C, D, E, F]

PRÁCTICA

A. Dé Ud. mandatos formales basados en las indicaciones.

1. You're a doctor. One of your patients isn't taking very good care of himself. What should he *not* do?
   —Sr. Casiano, no *coma tanto.* *(trabajar tanto, cenar demasiado, fumar, beber tanto, volver tarde a casa, almorzar tan fuerte, jugar al fútbol todos los días, salir tanto por la noche, ir a las discotecas, ser tan impaciente)*
2. You're the instructor for the day. What commands will you give to the class?
   —*Hablen **Uds.** español. (llegar a tiempo, leer la lección, escribir una composición, abrir los libros, pensar en español, estar en clase mañana, _____)*

B. Cambie: mandato afirmativo → mandato negativo
      mandato negativo → mandato afirmativo

1. ¿El cigarrillo? No lo fume Ud.
2. ¿El equipaje? Factúrenlo Uds. aquí.
3. ¿Eso? No lo crean Uds.
4. ¿Las canciones? No las toque Ud.
5. ¿Eso? Olvídenlo Uds.

C. Give affirmative commands to Mr. López based on the following situations. Change direct object nouns to pronouns.

MODELO   El Sr. López no está guardando su equipaje. → *Sr. López, guárdelo Ud.*

1. No lleva su pasaporte a la oficina de emigración.
2. Nunca pide paella.
3. No pone su dinero en el banco.
4. No factura su equipaje.
5. No empieza la lección.

D. Give negative commands to Mr. and Mrs. Corral based on the following situations. Change direct object nouns to pronouns.

MODELO   Los Sres. Corral miran la televisión. → *Sres. Corral, no la miren Uds.*

1. Recomiendan ese restaurante.
2. Abren su tienda muy tarde.
3. Piden el bacalao.
4. Pagan la cuenta.
5. Traen vino.

E. Give a singular command (affirmative or negative, as appropriate) in response to
    each exclamation.

MODELO   ¡Qué canción más bonita!   (What a pretty song!)   (tocar) → Tóquela.

1. ¡Qué canción más fea!   (tocar)
2. ¡Qué vestido más elegante!   (comprar)
3. ¡Qué abrigo más caro!   (comprar)
4. ¡Qué novela más interesante!   (leer)
5. ¡Qué libro más aburrido!   (leer)
6. ¡Qué pintura más estupenda!   (ver)

F. ¿Cómo se dice en español?

1. Pack your bags.   2. Go to the airport.   3. Don't be **(llegar)** late.   4. Buy
your ticket.   5. Check your bags.   6. Wait in line.   7. Give your ticket to the
steward.   8. Get on the plane.

CONVERSACIÓN

You are a clerk at an airport ticket counter **(el mostrador)** and someone asks you how
to get to **Sala de espera.** Give him or her directions in Spanish. Here are some phrases
to help you.

ir: Vaya Ud. go   **seguir (i, i): Siga Ud.** continue
doblar: Doble Ud. turn   **pasar: Pase Ud. por** pass through/by

todo derecho straight ahead   **a la izquierda**   to the left
a la derecha to the right   **el pasillo**   the hall, corridor

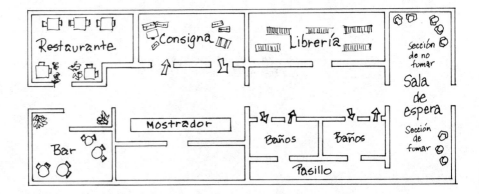

If you are at: tell someone how to get to:

1. la sala de espera   el bar
2. la consigna (baggage claim area)   la sala de espera
3. el restaurante   los baños/los servicios (restrooms)

35. NUMBERS OVER 100

100	cien(to)	700	setecientos/as
101	ciento uno/una	800	ochocientos/as
200	doscientos/as	900	novecientos/as
300	trescientos/as	1.000	mil
400	cuatrocientos/as	2.000	dos mil
500	quinientos/as	1.000.000	un millón
600	seiscientos/as	2.000.000	dos millones

A. The number **ciento** shortens to **cien** before a noun and before **mil** or **millón: cien casas, cien mil, cien millones. Ciento** is used before numbers smaller than 100.

> 145   **ciento cuarenta y cinco**
> 2.159 **dos mil ciento cincuenta y nueve**

B. When the numbers 200 through 900 modify a noun, they must agree in gender.

> 637   seiscien**tos** treinta y siete
> 400 chicas   cuatrocien**tas chicas**
> 202 casas   doscien**tas** dos **casas**

C. The number **mil** means *one thousand* or *a thousand.*

> **mil** dólares   *one/a thousand dollars*

D. **Mil** does not have a plural form in counting, but **millón** does. When used with a noun, **millón (dos millones,** and so on), must be followed by **de.** In numerals, Spanish often uses a period where English uses a comma and vice-versa.

> 1.899   **mil** ochocientos noventa y nueve
> 3.000 habitantes **tres mil** habitantes
> 14.000.000 **de** habitantes **catorce millones de** habitantes

E. In Spanish, **mil...** is always used to express the year.

> 1981   **mil novecientos ochenta y uno**   *nineteen eighty-one*

PRÁCTICA

A. Practique los números.

1. 930 años
2. 7.354 personas
3. 100 países
4. 5.710 habitantes

5. 240 universidades
6. 670 pasajes
7. 2.486 mujeres
8. $1.000

9. 528 boletos
10. 863 pesetas
11. 101 niñas
12. $1.000.000,00

B. Lea los años siguientes en español.   ¿A qué descripción corresponden?

1. 1492
2. 1776
3. 1865
4. 1945
5. 1963
6. 1984
7. 2001

a. el fin de la guerra (*war*) civil norteamericana
b. una película muy famosa
c. la novela de George Orwell
d. Tomás Jefferson escribe la Declaración de la Independencia de los Estados Unidos.
e. Cristóbal Colón descubre América.
f. el año de la bomba atómica
g. el asesinato del presidente Kennedy

CONVERSACIÓN

Ud. es el alcalde/la alcadesa (mayor) *de una ciudad.   Tiene unos 20 millones de dólares. ¿Cómo quiere Ud. gastar* (to spend) *el dinero?*

Quiero gastar _____ para *los parques.*   (*las escuelas, la gente pobre, las calles y plazas públicas, los hospitales, los viejos, la policía,* _____)

DIÁLOGO: Un viaje en avión

Francisca y Rosalba, dos estudiantes mexicanas, desean hacer un viaje a Buenos Aires.

A. *En la agencia de viajes*

FRANCISCA: Me gusta viajar con gente alegre, ¿sabes? La clase turística es más divertida. ¿Qué te parece?°

¿**Qué...** What do you think?

ROSALBA: Eso digo yo. La primera clase es demasiado seria y tranquila.

EMPLEADO: Pues para el vuelo 257 a Buenos Aires todavía hay dos pasajes en clase turística. ¿Los quieren?

FRANCISCA: Sí, sí. Dénos los boletos. ¿A qué hora tenemos que estar en el aeropuerto?

EMPLEADO: El vuelo sale a las ocho de la mañana. Deben estar allí puntualmente a las siete. Se sirve el desayuno en el avión.

B. *En el aeropuerto*

FRANCISCA: Los otros pasajeros ya están subiendo al avión. Estamos atrasadas y todavía tenemos que facturar el equipaje.

ROSALBA: Yo tomo las dos maletas. Tú puedes guardarnos el puesto en la cola.

FRANCISCA: Está bien. Te espero allí.

C. *Un poco más tarde*

EMPLEADA: Los boletos y los pasaportes, por favor.

ROSALBA: Tómelos. Y dígame, por favor, de aquí, ¿adónde vamos?

EMPLEADA: A la oficina de emigración. Sigan todo derecho por la sala de espera y doblen a la izquierda. Luego pasen por la puerta número cuatro, ¿eh?

ROSALBA: Bien. ¿Volamos directamente a Buenos Aires?

EMPLEADA: Sí. No hay escalas. ¿Quieren asientos en la sección de fumar?

ROSALBA: Nosotras no fumamos, pero eso no importa.

EMPLEADA: Pues entonces°, las pongo en la cola° del avión con aquel grupo estudiantil que regresa a la Universidad de Buenos Aires. ¡Buen viaje!   *then / tail*

Comprensión

¿Cierto o falso?   Corrija las oraciones falsas.

A. 1. A Francisca le gusta viajar en clase turística.
2. Rosalba prefiere la primera clase.
3. El empleado puede venderles dos pasajes en clase turística.
4. Francisca y Rosalba no los quieren.
5. Tienen que estar en el aeropuerto una hora antes de la salida (*departure*) de su vuelo.

B. 1. Francisca y Rosalba llegan temprano al aeropuerto.
2. Francisca factura las dos maletas.
3. Francisca espera a Rosalba en la cola.

C. 1. Una azafata les pide los boletos y los pasaportes.
2. Tienen un vuelo directo a Buenos Aires.
3. Piden asientos en la sección de no fumar.
4. Van a estar con un grupo de personas viejas.

Comentario cultural

Except for a wide belt along the southern and eastern portion of the continent, surface travel in South America is difficult and time-consuming. Much of the remaining area is covered by dense tropical forest and by the Andes, a high range

of mountains that extends from the Caribbean coast in the north to Tierra del
Fuego in the extreme south.   Today the airplane is the most common way to
travel any distance in South America, and frequently it is the only way to get
from one place to another.

Throughout Spanish America, **boleto** is the word used for a ticket for travel.
Billete is the term preferred in Spain.   **Entrada** and **localidad** are used to refer to
theater or movie tickets.

UN POCO DE TODO

A. *Cambie por el plural.*

1. No sea Ud. demasiado serio.
2. No le haga eso.
3. ¿Le gusta todo eso?
4. No me diga Ud. las respuestas.
5. No me gusta nunca jugar al tenis.

Cambie por el singular.

6. No nos gustan estos asientos.
7. No les den Uds. tanta comida a los niños.
8. ¿Les gustan a Uds. aquellas clases?
9. Tráiganles los discos a ellos.
10. Nos gusta comer tranquilamente.

B. *Rearrange the words given to form complete sentences.   Do not add any words.*

1. vino / no / al / sirva / le / Ud. / niño
2. en / me / la / palabras / página / lea / las / Ud. / 542
3. Vicente / a / llegar / le / clase / gusta / puntualmente / a
4. rápidamente / lo / mí / hagan / para / Uds.
5. ¿ / ? / gusta / no / te / verdad / eso / ti / a

C. *Using commands based on the information in parentheses, give advice to the
following persons:*

1. El hijo de la Sra. Cruz está enfermo.
   Sra. Cruz, _____   (preparar sopa)
2. Los estudiantes del Profesor Fernández no estudian bastante.
   Profesor Fernández, _____   (dar más exámenes)
3. Los hijos de los Sres. Fuentes necesitan un pasaje en el vuelo 774.
   Sres. Fuentes, _____   (comprar boletos)

4. Francisco quiere entrar en la clase y la profesora está cerca de la puerta.
   Profesora, _____   (abrir la puerta)
5. En el aeropuerto Rosario necesita las maletas y el señor las tiene.
   Señor, _____   (traer las maletas)
6. El niño está triste. Sus amigas Carlota y Carmen tocan muy bien la guitarra y cantan.
   Carlota y Carmen, _____   (tocar y cantar una canción)

D. *React to each situation by answering the following questions:* **¿Le gusta a Ud.?** **¿No le gusta?** **¿Por qué?**

1. Su profesor(a) de español habla español rápidamente.
2. Su compañero/a de cuarto siempre llega a casa muy tarde.
3. Su amigo/a le llama frecuentemente a la una de la mañana.
4. Su compañero/a de cuarto fuma constantemente.
5. Su familia siempre va de vacaciones a las montañas.
6. Su compañero/a de cuarto siempre está contento/a por la mañana y siempre quiere hablar.

E. *Complete las oraciones en una forma lógica.*

1. Voy a decirle a _____ que (no) me gusta cuando _____.
2. Profesor(a), (no) _____ Ud. _____, por favor.
3. (No) Quiero decirles a mis padres que yo (no) _____.
4. Me gusta _____ rápidamente.

VOCABULARIO

VERBOS
anunciar to announce
bajar (de) to get down (from); to get off (of)
desayunar to eat breakfast
doblar to turn
facturar to check (*baggage*)
fumar to smoke
guardar to save (*a place*)
gustar to be pleasing
importar to be important
mandar to send
olvidar to forget
parecer to seem
pasar to happen
seguir (i, i) to continue; to follow

subir (a) to go up; to get on
volar (ue) to fly

SUSTANTIVOS
el **aeropuerto** airport
la **agencia** agency
el **asiento** seat
el **avión** plane
la **azafata** female flight attendant
el **boleto** ticket
el **camarero** male flight attendant
la **canción** song
la **demora** delay
el **equipaje** baggage, luggage
la **gente** people
el **pasaje** passage, ticket

el/la **pasajero/a** passenger
el **pasaporte** passport
la **película** movie
el **puesto** place (*in line, etc.*)
la **sala de espera** waiting room
el **vuelo** flight

ADJETIVOS
atrasado/a (with estar) late
directo/a direct
divertido/a amusing, funny, pleasant
rápido/a fast, rapid
serio/a serious
tranquilo/a calm, tranquil

PALABRAS Y EXPRESIONES ÚTILES

a tiempo on time
la clase turística tourist class
demasiado too, too much
derecho straight ahead

hacer
  cola to wait in line
  escalas to have stopovers
  las maletas to pack one's
    suitcases
la primera clase first class
la sección de (no) fumar (no)
  smoking section

todavía still, yet
vacaciones
  estar de vacaciones to be on
    vacation
  ir de vacaciones to go on
    vacation

Un paso más 7

Actividades

A. **En la agencia de viajes.** Haga el papel (*play the role*) de agente de viajes que habla con su cliente. Pueden utilizar algunas de las preguntas que siguen. Ud. debe hacer unas sugerencias (*suggestions*) a su cliente. Los viajes salen de Madrid y los precios se dan en pesetas españolas.

Agente:

1. ¿Quiere Ud. visitar un lugar en nuestro país o prefiere viajar al extranjero (*abroad*)?
2. ¿Prefiere Ud. viajar solo/a o con un grupo?
3. ¿Le gusta más viajar en avión, en barco o en tren?
4. ¿Quiere viajar en chárter? Es más barato que un vuelo normal.
5. ¿Prefiere Ud. un hotel de lujo (*deluxe*), de primera clase o de segunda?
6. ¿Qué le gusta más—pasar todo el tiempo en un lugar o visitar varios lugares?
7. Entonces, ¿por qué no va Ud. a _____? Le va a gustar porque _____.

IBERIA
LÍNEAS AÉREAS INTERNACIONALES DE ESPAÑA

	Días	Al contado° desde	Al mes° desde
Nueva York	12	50.550	2.022
Miami-Disneyworld	12	71.650	2.866
Canadá-EE.UU.	12	91.200	3.648
Costa Oeste	14	105.750	4.230
Cuba-Méjico	16	104.000	4.160
París	4	12.575	503
Roma	4	14.925	597
Lóndres	4	13.955	558
Grecia	7	29.475	1.179
Viena	4	19.800	792
África del Sur	12	99.990	3.996
Circuito Marruecos	8	28.225	1.129
Canarias	8	12.990	520
Baleares	8	8.205	328

al contado *cash*
al mes *monthly*

Cliente:

1. Me gustan las *zonas tropicales*. ¿Qué me recomienda Ud.?
2. ¿Cuánto cuesta *un pasaje* (*el viaje*)?
3. ¿No puede Ud. recomendar *algo más barato* (*un lugar más interesante*)?
4. ¿Hay *muchas discotecas* (*buenos teatros, playas hermosas, museos interesantes*)?
5. ¿Aceptan Uds. Visa/Master Card?

A propósito...

Communicating with a minimum of words. In class you are frequently asked to use complete sentences. But when you speak Spanish outside of the classroom, you don't always speak in complete sentences—sometimes because you do not know or cannot remember how to say something. And when you try to say a long sentence, such as *"Would you be so kind as to tell me how I can get to the train station?"* it is easy to get tongue-tied, to omit something, or to mispronounce a word. When this happens, the listener often has trouble understanding. A shorter, more direct phrase or sentence often yields more effective results. A simple **perdón** or **por favor** followed by **¿la estación de trenes?** is both adequate and polite.

To accomplish something more complicated, such as buying two first-class tickets on Tuesday's 10:50 A.M. train for Guanajuato, you might begin by saying **"Dos boletos para Guanajuato, por favor."** After that, you can add other information, often in response to the questions that the ticket agent will ask you. By breaking the message down into manageable bits of information, you simplify the communication process for both parties.

B. **Por favor.** How would you go about getting the following information? Using the suggestions in **A propósito,** prepare a series of short statements and questions that will help you get all the information you need.

> MODELO   You need to buy two first-class tickets on Tuesday's 10:50 A.M. train for Guanajuato. → *Dos boletos para Guanajuato, por favor. Para el martes, el tren de las 10:50. De primera clase, por favor.*

1. You need to buy two second-class train tickets for today's 2:50 P.M. train for Barcelona.
2. You are at the train station and need to find out how to get to the university—which you understand is quite some distance away—by 10:00 A.M.
3. You want to find out from your travel agent what you need to do before taking your first trip abroad. In what order should things be done?
4. The flight that you are on is arriving late, and you will probably miss your connecting flight to Mexico City. You want to explain your situation to the flight attendant and to find out how you can get to Mexico City by 7:00 this evening.
5. You are talking to a travel agent and want to fly from Santiago, Chile, to Quito, Ecuador. You are traveling with two friends who prefer to travel first class, and you need to arrive in Quito by Saturday afternoon.

C. **Necesito comprar...** Imagine that you need to buy the following items but do not know—or have forgotten—the words in Spanish. Try to get your idea across to the clerk by paraphrasing, using synonyms, telling what the item is like, what it is used for, what it is made of, and so on.

MODELO   a suitcase → *Necesito comprar algo para mi viaje. Lo uso para llevar mi ropa y mis otras cosas. Cuando tengo demasiada ropa y demasiadas cosas, otra persona me ayuda a cerrarlo.*

1. a bird cage
2. a small transistor radio
3. a bread box
4. a hammock

5. a notebook
6. carrots
7. a wallet
8. a pair of boots

D. **¿Dónde está mi maleta?** You arrive at your destination, but your luggage does not. When you go to the baggage claim area, you are required to fill out a form. With a classmate take the roles of **agente** and **pasajero/a**. The **agente** will ask the questions on page 208 in order to fill out the form. The words at the bottom of the form will help you describe your suitcase.

IBERIA
LÍNEAS AÉREAS DE ESPAÑA S.A

PARTE DE IRREGULARIDAD DE EQUIPAJE
PROPERTY IRREGULARITY REPORT   **P. I. R.**

Apellido(s) del Pasajero *Passenger's name*		Inicial(es) del Nombre *Initial(s)*

Itinerario del pasajero según su cupón *Passenger's itinerary as per passenger coupon*	Compañia *Airline* N.º de Vuelo *Flight N.* Mes *Month* Día *Day* De A *From To*	

| Etiqueta de equipaje n.º de serie *Baggage Tag-Serial N.* | Compañia *Airline*   4 últimos dígitos *Last 4 digits* | |

| Tipo de equipaje y Código de Colores *Baggage Type and Colour Codes* | Tipo *Type*   Color *Colour* | Tipo *Type*   Color *Colour* | Tipo *Type*   Color *Colour* |

| Contenido (Cualquiera de los artículos más corrientes indicados en el reverso) *Contents (Any of the distinct items listed overleaf)* | |

| Instrucciones para la entrega local *Local delivery instructions* | Peso total del equipaje facturado *Total weight of checked baggage* |

| Título del pasajero *Passenger's title* | Correspondencia con el pasajero *Correspondence with the passenger*   Idiomas: Español Inglés Otro *Languages: Spanish English Other* | Llaves adjuntas al PIR-*Keys attached to PIR* ☐ Llaves no adjuntas al PIR-*Keys not attached to PIR* ☐ |

| Dirección permanente del pasajero y n.º de teléfono *Passenger's permanent address and telephone n°* | Direccion temporal y n.º de teléfono. A partir de/hasta *Temporary address telephone n°. Date from/to* |

| Fecha-*Date* | Firma del empleado autorizado por la Compañia *Company official's signature* | Este informe no supone ninguna aceptación de responsabilidad por parte de IBERIA. *This report does not involve any acknowledgement of liability for IBERIA.* | Firma del pasajero *Passenger's signature* |

EQUIPAJE
Baggage

Color: Use el siguiente Código de colores.
Colour: Use following colour codes.

ALU	Plateado (*Aluminum, Silver*).
BLU	Azul (*Blue*).
BLK	Negro (*Black*).
BRN	Marrón, Tostado, del Cervato, Bronce, Cobre, Óxido de hierro, Rojo oscuro (*Brown, Tan, Fawn, Bronze, Copper, Rust, Oxblood*).
CLR	Claro, Traslúcido, Opaco, Plástico (*Clear, Translucent, Opaque, Plastic*).
CRM	Beige, Crema, Marfil, Ante (*Beige, Cream, Ivory, Buff*).
GRN	Verde (*Green, Olive*).
GRY	Gris (*Grey*).
PLD	Cuadros escoceses, Ajedrezado, Jaspeado (*Plaid, Checked, Tweed*).
RED	Rojo, Castaño, Rosa (*Red, Maroon, Pink*).
STR	Listado (*Striped*).
TPY	Tapizado, Floreado, Moteado (*Tapestry, Floral, Spotted*).
WHT	Blanco (*White*).
YLW	Amarillo, Naranja (*Yellow, Orange*).

Material: Para describir la clase de material, utilice una de las siguientes palabras:
Material: For the description of the material, use one of the following.

CUERO	—	*LEATHER*
FIBRA	—	*FIBRE*
METAL	—	*METAL*
PLÁSTICO	—	*PLASTIC*
MADERA	—	*WOOD*
LONA	—	*CANVAS*
CARTÓN	—	*CARDBOARD*

Agente:
1. ¿Cuál es su apellido, por favor? ¿y sus iniciales?
2. ¿De dónde salió (*took off*) su vuelo? ¿Cuál es el número de su vuelo?
3. ¿Cuál es el número de la etiqueta (*tag*) de su maleta?
4. ¿De qué material es? ¿de qué color?
5. ¿Cuál es el contenido de su maleta?
6. ¿Cuál es su dirección (*address*) permanente? ¿y su teléfono?
7. ¿Cuál es su dirección temporal aquí? ¿y el nombre de su hotel? ¿hasta qué fecha?

E. **Situaciones inesperadas.** Unexpected situations frequently occur when you are traveling. With a classmate choose one of the following situations—or invent your own—and create the conversation that might take place. How will the situation be resolved?

```
ZVIACO
TARJETA DE EMBARQUE
BOARDING PASS


NOMBRE _____
NAME

VUELO _____
FLIGHT

DESTINO _____
DESTINATION

FECHA _____
DATE
```

1. **Personajes:** Pasajero y azafata/camarero
   Situación: El pasajero no puede encontrar su tarjeta de embarque. La azafata/el camarero no le permite subir al avión.
2. **Personajes:** Dos pasajeros y un camarero/una azafata
   Situación: Uno de los pasajeros habla y habla y habla. El otro pasajero prefiere leer, escribir cartas y dormir.
3. **Personajes:** Dos pasajeros
   Situación: Uno de los pasajeros quiere ir a Cuba y por eso piensa secuestrar (*hijack*) el avión. Tiene pistola.
4. **Personajes:** Pasajero y agente de la línea aérea
   Situación: El pasajero quiere comprar un boleto de primera clase. El boleto cuesta noventa y nueve dólares, pero el pasajero tiene sólo noventa y ocho. Sin embargo el pasajero insiste.
5. **Personajes:** Pasajero y azafata/camarero
   Situación: Al pasajero no le gusta la comida que le sirven en el vuelo.

–Odia° el sol, odia la arena, odia el agua,
pero odia más quedarse° en casa.

odia *she hates*
quedarse *to stay, remain*

F. **¿Qué le gusta? ¿Qué odia?**   Almost every situation has aspects that one likes and dislikes, even hates.   One person has the following reactions to a number of situations.   Are the statements true for you?   If not, change them to make them true.

MODELO   *En la playa:* Me gusta *el agua* pero odio *el sol.*
   → Me gusta *el sol* pero odio *el agua.*
   → Me gusta *nadar* pero odio *la arena.*

1. *En el avión:* Me gusta volar pero odio la comida.
2. *En una fiesta:* Me gusta la gente pero odio el ruido.
3. *En la discoteca:* Me gusta la música pero no me gusta nada bailar.
4. *En la biblioteca:* Me gusta estudiar allí pero odio a los estudiantes que hablan constantemente.
5. *En el carro:* Me gusta manejar (*to drive*) pero no me gusta el tráfico.
6. *En clase:* Me gusta contestar preguntas orales pero no me gusta nada escribir los ejercicios.
7. *En el hospital:* Me gusta recibir flores y tarjetas pero odio las inyecciones.
8. *En la cafetería:* Me gusta comer con mis amigos pero odio la comida.
9. *En el parque:* Me gustan las flores pero odio los insectos y los animales.
10. *En un almacén grande:* Me gustan los precios bajos pero odio el gentío (*crowds*).

Lectura cultural: Las maravillas° del mundo hispánico: Latinoamérica

marvels

Teotihuacán (1)*.   Cerca de la ciudad de México, Teotihuacán es una de las grandes ciudades precolombinas°.   Fue° una ciudad ceremonial de los aztecas.   Se encuentran en ella las grandes pirámides del Sol y de la Luna. Otro edificio importante es el Templo de Quetzalcóatl, así nombrado° por las esculturas° de la serpiente emplumada° que decoran su fachada°.

pre-Columbian / it was

named
sculptures / plumed / facade

El Canal de Panamá (2).   El Canal de Panamá, construido a lo largo de° siete años a un costo de 366.000.000,00 de dólares y terminado en 1914, es el enlace° más importante entre el Océano Atlántico y el Pacífico.   El Canal mide° ochenta kilómetros (cincuenta millas) y tiene seis esclusas°, tres a cada lado del istmo que cruza.

a lo largo de *over*
link
measures / locks

Machu-Picchu (3).   Situada en las grandes alturas° de los Andes, a unas ochenta kilómetros de la ciudad de Cuzco, Machu-Picchu es conocida° como la capital escondida° de los incas.   Construida de grandes bloques de piedra°, la ciudad es uno de los ejemplos más importantes de la arquitectura incaica.   Fue un refugio y ciudad de vacaciones para los reyes incaicos.

heights
known
hidden
stone

La Catedral de Sal (4).   Al noroeste de la ciudad de Bogotá, capital de Colombia, está la ciudad de Zipaquirá, pueblo conocido por sus minas de sal.   En las afueras° del pueblo, donde antes había° una de las minas más

outskirts / there was

*Numbers refer to photos on page 210.

Jerry Frank/DPI

1.

3.
Peter Buckley

4.
Courtesy, Colombia Information Service

J. P. Laffont/Sygma

2.

grandes, se encuentra ahora una fantástica catedral bajo tierra°. Para   **bajo...** *underground*
entrar uno pasa por un gran túnel que lo lleva a una nave principal enorme.
(*Esta lectura continúa en el capítulo 8.*)

Comprensión

¿Cierto o falso? Corrija las oraciones falsas.

Teotihuacán:
1. Es la capital política de los aztecas.
2. Es famosa por sus grandes pirámides.
3. Tiene un templo dedicado a la serpiente emplumada.

El Canal de Panamá:
1. El costo de su construcción fue (*was*) enorme.
2. Tiene seis esclusas al lado atlántico.
3. Cruza cincuenta millas de territorio centroamericano.

Machu-Picchu:
1. Es una representación de la arquitectura de los incas.
2. Es de madera principalmente.
3. Es la ciudad ceremonial de los incas.

La Catedral de Sal
1. Está en la plaza central de Zipaquirá.
2. Es un túnel bajo tierra.
3. Tiene una nave grande.

Ejercicios escritos

A. Complete the following sentences with a description of each **"maravilla norteamericana."**

    1. El Gran Cañón: _____
    2. El Puente "Golden Gate": _____
    3. La ciudad de Nueva York: _____
    4. Las montañas "Rockies": _____
    5. La montaña Rushmore: _____

B. Write a brief paragraph about a place of interest that you have visited or about an interesting place where you live. Use the following questions as a guide in developing your paragraph.

    1. ¿Cuál es el nombre del lugar?
    2. ¿Dónde está situado el lugar?
    3. ¿Por qué es importante el lugar?
    4. ¿Puede Ud. describirlo?
    5. ¿Por qué le gusta a Ud.?

capítulo 8 En casa

© Owen Franken 1975/Stock, Boston

OBJETIVOS

In this chapter you will learn vocabulary and expressions related to everyday household activities and personal appearance.

You will also learn about the following aspects of Spanish grammar:

36. reflexive pronouns (*myself, yourself, themselves,* and so on) and how to use them

37. how to use reflexive pronouns to express reciprocal actions: *they looked at each other, we love each other*

38. how to talk about actions in the past using regular verbs in the preterite (one of the

Spanish past tenses), plus **dar, hacer, ir,** and **ser,** which are irregular in the preterite

39. how to use direct and indirect object pronouns when they occur together in the same sentence

40. verbs that require a preposition or **que** before an infinitive: **empiezo a leer, tengo que estudiar**

Un paso más includes activities related to advertisements, making excuses, and courtesy in everyday situations, as well as a reading about places of interest in Spain.

VOCABULARIO: PREPARACIÓN

La vida doméstica

Los quehaceres (tasks) domésticos

hacer la cama	to make the bed
lavar (las ventanas, los platos)	to wash (the windows, dishes)
limpiar la casa entera	to clean the whole house
poner la mesa	to set the table
preparar la comida/ cocinar	to prepare food/ to cook
sacar la basura	to take out the trash
sacudir los muebles	to dust the furniture

Las máquinas domésticas

el (aire) acondicionador	air conditioner
la cafetera	coffee pot
la estufa	stove
la lavadora	washer
el refrigerador	refrigerator
la secadora	dryer

aspiadora   — vacum chaner

A. *¿Es Ud. buena ama de casa* (housekeeper)? *¿Con qué frecuencia hace Ud. los siguientes quehaceres? Si Ud. vive en una residencia estudiantil, imagínese que vive en una casa o un apartamento.*

0 = nunca   1 = a veces   2 = frecuentemente   3 = todos los días

___ 1. Lavo las ventanas.
___ 2. Hago las camas.
___ 3. Pongo la mesa.
___ 4. Preparo la comida.

___ 5. Sacudo los muebles.
___ 6. Lavo los platos.
___ 7. Limpio la casa entera.
___ 8. Saco la basura.

☐ TOTAL

Interpretaciones

0–6   puntos: ¡Cuidado (*careful*)! Ud. estudia demasiado. Por favor, ¡limpie su casa!

7–12 puntos: Ud. puede vivir en su casa, pero no debe invitar a otras personas si no la limpia bien primero.

13–18 puntos: Su casa, aunque (*although*) no está perfecta, está limpia. Es un buen modelo para todos.

19–24 puntos: ¡Ud. es una maravilla y tiene una casa muy, muy limpia! Pero, ¿pasa Ud. todo el día limpiando la casa?

B. *Ud. y su amigo/a van a tener invitados* (guests), *pero Uds. tienen sólo dos horas para limpiar la casa y prepararlo todo. ¿Qué trabajos hace Ud.? ¿su amigo/a? ¿Qué trabajos no va a hacer nadie?*

lavar los platos y vasos
sacudir los muebles
limpiar el baño (*bathroom*)
poner la mesa
sacar la basura de la cocina (*kitchen*)

limpiar la estufa
cocinar
hacer las camas
poner los discos en el estéreo
sacar unas botellas de vino

C. *Familias de palabras. Dé Ud. el verbo que corresponde al sustantivo* (noun) *indicado en cada oración.*

MODELO   **PREPARA**ción → *PREPARAr*

1. La SECAdora sirve para _____ la ropa o el pelo (*hair*).
2. Es necesario _____ la comida en un REFRIGERAdor.
3. En la COCINA se puede _____.
4. La LAVAdora sirve para _____ ropa.
5. El ACONDICIONAdor sirve para _____ el aire.

Más verbos útiles

acostar (ue)	to put to bed	**levantar**	to lift, raise
afeitar	to shave	**quitar**	to remove, take away
bañar	to bathe	**sentar (ie)**	to seat, to lead to
despertar (ie)	to wake		a seat
divertir (ie, i)	to amuse, entertain	**vestir (i, i)**	to dress

---

C. *Complete las frases en una forma lógica, usando estas palabras o cualquier* (any) *otra.*

la televisión / el ruido / una película buena / el sol / la clase de español / mi compañero/a / el despertador (*alarm clock*)

la enfermera (*nurse*) / el camarero / el barbero / el dueño / el padre / la esposa / un estudiante

1. _____ me despierta.
2. _____ me divierte.
3. _____ baña al bebé.
4. _____ nos sienta en el restaurante.
5. _____ nos afeita en la barbería.
6. _____ acuesta a los niños en el hospital.
7. _____ quita los platos después de la comida.
8. _____ viste a los niños.
9. _____ levanta la mano (*hand*).

PRONUNCIACIÓN: More on Stress and the Written Accent

Some English words are distinguished from each other solely by the position of stress: *objéct* (*to express disagreement*), *óbject* (*thing*); *súspect* (*one who is suspected*), *suspéct* (*to be suspicious*).   The same is true in Spanish: **tomas** (*you take*), **Tomás** (*Thomas*).   Because many past-tense verb forms are accented on the last syllable, it is important to pay special attention to stress: **hable** (*speak*) versus **hablé** (*I spoke*); **hablo** (*I speak*) versus **habló** (*he spoke*).

Remember that when a word does not carry a written accent, (1) it is stressed on the next-to-last syllable if it ends in a vowel, **-n,** or **-s,** and (2) it is stressed on the last syllable if it ends in a consonant other than **-n** or **-s.** If the pronunciation of a word does not conform to these rules, the word must have a written accent mark on the stressed syllable.   Note the effect of the addition of an object pronoun to a verb form or of an ending to nouns and adjectives: **usando → usándolo; ambición → ambiciones; francés → franceses.**

PRÁCTICA

A. *Pronounce the following groups of words.   Stress is the only difference in pronunciation.*

1. tomas, Tomás   esta, está   papa, papá   halla, allá
2. hablo, habló   trabajo, trabajó   estudio, estudió   llego, llegó
3. baile, bailé   termine, terminé   cante, canté   compre, compré
4. cálculo, calculo, calculó   intérprete, interprete, interpreté

B. *Explain why accents are needed or not needed on the following words.*

1. joven, jóvenes   5. nación, naciones
2. francés, franceses   6. dando, dándonos, dándonoslo
3. orden, órdenes   7. diga, dígame, dígamelo
4. examen, exámenes   8. hagan, háganlos, háganselos

MINIDIÁLOGOS Y GRAMÁTICA

36. REFLEXIVE PRONOUNS

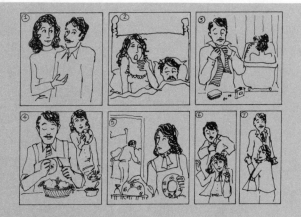

Un día típico

1. *Me llamo* Alicia; mi esposo *se llama* Miguel.   2. *Me despierto* y *me levanto* temprano, a las seis.   Él también *se levanta* temprano.   3. *Nos bañamos* y *nos vestimos.*   4. Luego yo pongo la mesa y él prepara el desayuno.   5. Después él hace las camas y yo lavo los platos.   6. ¡Por fin!   Estamos listos para salir para la oficina.   7. Pero... un momentito. ¡Es sábado!   ¿Es demasiado tarde para *acostarnos* otra vez?

1. *¿Cómo se llaman los esposos?*
2. *¿Se levantan tarde los dos, generalmente?*
3. *¿Se bañan por la mañana o por la noche?*
4. *¿Cuáles son los quehaceres domésticos de Alicia?   ¿y de Miguel?*
5. *¿Cuál es su error?*
6. *¿Van a acostarse otra vez?*

A typical day 1. My name is Alicia; my husband's name is Miguel. 2. I wake up and get up early, at six. He also gets up early. 3. We bathe and get dressed. 4. Then I set the table, and he makes breakfast. 5. Next he makes the beds, and I wash the dishes. 6. Finally! We're ready to leave for the office. 7. But . . . just a minute. It's Saturday! Is it too late to go back to bed?

BAÑARSE: *to take a bath*		
(yo)	**me** baño	*I'm taking a bath*
(tú)	**te** bañas	*you're taking a bath*
(Ud.) (él) (ella)	**se** baña	*you're taking a bath* *he's taking a bath* *she's taking a bath*
(nosotros)	**nos** bañamos	*we're taking baths*
(vosotros)	**os** bañáis	*you're taking baths*
(Uds.) (ellos) (ellas)	**se** bañan	*you're taking baths* *they're taking baths* *they're taking baths*

In English and in Spanish, *reflexive pronouns* (**pronombres reflexivos**) refer to the subject of the sentence. English reflexives end in *-self/-selves: myself, yourself,* and so on. The Spanish reflexive pronouns are **me, te,** and **se** in the singular; **nos, os,** and **se** in the plural.

Spanish frequently uses reflexive pronouns with verbs to express ideas that are not reflexive or are not expressed reflexively in English: *I'm taking a bath* → **me baño** (literally, *I'm bathing myself*).

The pronoun **se** at the end of an infinitive indicates that the verb is used reflexively. When the verb is conjugated, the reflexive pronoun that corresponds to the subject must be used: (*yo*) *me* **baño**, (*tú*) *te* **bañas**, and so on.

The following Spanish verbs that you have already used nonreflexively are also frequently used with reflexive pronouns.* Many of them are stem-changing.

acostarse (ue)	to go to bed	**lavarse**	to wash oneself,
afeitarse	to shave		get washed
bañarse	to take a bath	**levantarse**	to get up; to stand up
despertarse (ie)	to wake up	**llamarse**	to be named, called
divertirse (ie, i)	to have a good	**ponerse**	to put on (clothing)
	time, enjoy	**quitarse**	to take off (clothing)
	oneself	**sentarse (ie)**	to sit down
dormirse (ue, u)	to fall asleep	**vestirse (i, i)**	to get dressed

¡OJO!   After **ponerse** and **quitarse,** the definite article—not the possessive—is used with articles of clothing.

Se pone **el** abrigo.   *He's putting on his coat.*
Se quitan **el** sombrero.   *They're taking off their hats.*

*Compare: **Juan se lava.** / **Juan lava la ropa.** (**Juan la lava.**)

Placement of Reflexive Pronouns

Like direct and indirect object pronouns, reflexive pronouns are placed before a conjugated verb but after the word **no** in a negative sentence: **No se bañan.** They may either precede the conjugated verb or be attached to an infinitive or gerund.

Me tengo que levantar temprano. ⎫
Tengo que levantar**me** temprano ⎬ *I have to get up early.*

¿**Te** estás divirtiendo? ⎫
¿Estás divirtiéndo**te**? ⎬ *Are you having a good time?*

¡OJO!   Regardless of its position, the reflexive pronoun corresponds to the subject of the sentence.

Reflexive pronouns are attached to affirmative commands, but they precede the verb in negative commands. When a reflexive and a direct object pronoun are used together, the reflexive comes first.

Quít**ese** el suéter.	*Take off your sweater.*
Quíte**selo** Ud.	*Take it off.*
No **se** ponga esa blusa.	*Don't put on that blouse.*
No **se la** ponga Ud.	*Don't put it on.*

PRÁCTICA

A. Dé Ud. frases nuevas según las indicaciones.

1. —¿Quién se quita el suéter cuando hace calor?
   —*Ellos* se quitan el suéter. (*yo, Carolina, nosotras, tú, todos los estudiantes, vosotros*)
2. —¿Quién se acuesta temprano por lo general?
   —*Él* se acuesta temprano. (*tú, nosotros, Arturo, yo, Evangelina y Nati, vosotras*)
3. —¿Quién se baña y se viste temprano?
   —*Roberto* se baña y se viste temprano. (*ellos, yo, nosotros, tú, Ana María, vosotros*)

B. Complete las oraciones, usando la forma correcta de los verbos a la derecha.

1. Cuando hace frío, yo _____ una chaqueta.	lavarse
2. Nosotros _____ muy temprano, a las seis de la mañana.	sentarse
3. Carlos siempre _____ en una fiesta.	despertarse
4. En la escuela primaria los niños _____ en el suelo.	ponerse
5. Si hace calor, yo _____ el abrigo.	quitarse
6. Voy a _____ antes de acostarme.	divertirse

C. *Ud. es un(a) consejero/a.   Dé Ud. consejos a un(a) estudiante que es muy perezoso/a
y que no estudia mucho.   Déle mandatos basados en estos verbos.*

MODELO   afeitarse → *Aféitese.*

1. despertarse más temprano
2. levantarse más temprano
3. no acostarse tan tarde
4. vestirse mejor
5. no divertirse tanto
6. quitarse esa ropa sucia y ponerse ropa limpia
7. bañarse más

D. *Ud. está en el hospital y es necesario quitarse la ropa.   Pregunte Ud. al/a la
enfermero/a, —¿Me quito los zapatos?* Él/ella contesta, —Sí, quíteselos, por
favor.*

1. los pantalones
2. la camisa/la blusa
3. el suéter
4. los calcetines/las medias
5. toda la ropa

E. *¿Cómo se dice en español?*   (Some of the verbs require the reflexive construction;
others do not.)

1. I'm going to go to bed later.
2. I'm going to put my son to bed later.
3. Wake up now!
4. Wake your wife now!
5. His name is Agustín.
6. He calls his parents.
7. They're putting on their shoes.
8. They're putting the coffee pot on the stove.

CONVERSACIÓN

A. *Preguntas*

1. ¿Prefiere Ud. bañarse por la mañana o por la noche?
2. ¿Dónde le gusta a Ud. sentarse para leer, en un sofá o en la cama?
3. ¿Le gusta a Ud. vestirse elegante o informalmente?
4. ¿A qué hora tiene Ud. que levantarse todos los días?   ¿Y a qué hora se
   acuesta?
5. ¿Ud. se duerme fácilmente o con dificultad?   ¿Qué hace cuando no puede
   dormirse?
6. ¿Se afeita Ud. todos los días?

*Note that Spanish uses the simple present to express English questions that begin with *Shall I (we,*
and so on).

B. *Using the following verbs as a guide, ask another student what he/she does during a typical day. Note the answers; then tell the class about his/her day.*

MODELO   despertarse → *¿Se despierta Ud. temprano? ¿tarde? ¿fácilmente?*
¿A qué hora se despierta Ud.?

1. despertarse
2. levantarse
3. bañarse
4. afeitarse
5. vestirse
6. desayunar
7. salir para la universidad

8. asistir a clases
9. almorzar
10. divertirse
11. volver a casa
12. cenar
13. lavar los platos
14. limpiar la cocina

15. sacar la basura
16. sentarse para ver la televisión
17. quitarse la ropa
18. acostarse
19. dormirse
20. dormir_____ horas

37. RECIPROCAL ACTIONS WITH REFLEXIVE PRONOUNS

Nos queremos

Se miran

The plural reflexive pronouns, **nos, os,** and **se,** can be used to express *reciprocal actions* **(acciones recíprocas).** Reciprocal actions are usually expressed in English with *each other* or *one another.*

Nos queremos.	*We love each other.*
¿Os ayudáis?	*Do you help one another?*
Se miran.	*They're looking at each other.*

PRÁCTICA

Exprese como acciones recíprocas.

1. Estela me mira a mí. Yo miro a Estela.
2. Eduardo habla con Pepita. Pepita habla con Eduardo.
3. El padre necesita a su hijo. El hijo necesita a su padre.
4. Tomás me conoce a mí. Yo conozco a Tomás.
5. Tú escribes a Luisa. Luisa te escribe a ti.
6. La profesora escucha a los estudiantes. Los estudiantes escuchan a la profesora.
7. Ud. quiere a su esposo. Su esposo la quiere también a Ud.

CONVERSACIÓN

Describa Ud. la triste historia de amor de Orlando y Patricia. Use Ud. estos verbos:

verse en clase / mirarse / hablarse mucho / llamarse por teléfono constantemente / mandarse regalos / escribirse durante las vacaciones / quererse mucho / ayudarse con los problemas / casarse / no llevarse (*get along with*) bien / separarse / divorciarse

38. PRETERITE OF REGULAR VERBS AND OF *DAR, HACER, IR,* AND *SER*

Un problema con la agencia de empleos

SRA. GÓMEZ: ¡La criada que Uds. me *mandaron* ayer *fue* un desastre!

SR. PARDO: ¿Cómo que *fue* un desastre? ¿Qué *hizo*?

SRA. GÓMEZ: Pues no *hizo* nada. *Pasó* todo el día en mi casa, pero no *lavó* los platos, no *sacó* la basura, ni *sacudió* los muebles. Luego cuando *salió* de mi casa a las tres, me *dio* las buenas tardes como si nada.

SR. PARDO: Pero, señora, cada persona tiene sus más y sus menos. Por lo menos esta criada *fue* mejor que la otra que le mandamos anteayer —que ni *llegó*.

---

1. *De las dos personas que hablan en el diálogo, ¿quién es el ama de casa?*
2. *¿Quién es el dueño de la agencia?*
3. *¿Por qué fue un desastre la criada de ayer, según* (according to) *la Sra. Gómez?*
4. *Según el Sr. Pardo, ¿cuál de las dos criadas fue peor? ¿Por qué?*

A problem with the employment agency GÓMEZ: The maid you sent me yesterday was a disaster! PARDO: What do you mean, a disaster? What did she do? GÓMEZ: Well, she didn't do anything. She spent all day at the house, but she didn't wash the dishes, take out the trash, or dust the furniture. Then, when she left the house at three, she said, "Good afternoon" as if nothing were wrong. PARDO: But, madam, everyone has his or her good and bad points. At least this maid was better than the other one we sent you the day before yesterday—who didn't even arrive.

Spanish has two simple past tenses (tenses formed without an auxiliary or "helping" verb): the preterite and the imperfect.* The *preterite* (**pretérito**) has several equivalents in English. For example, **hablé** can mean *I spoke* or *I did speak.* The preterite is used to report finished, completed actions or states of being in the past. If the action or state of being is viewed as completed—no matter how long it lasted or took to complete—it will be expressed with the preterite.

Preterite of Regular Verbs

HABLAR		COMER		VIVIR	
hablé	*I spoke (did speak)*	comí	*I ate (did eat)*	viví	*I lived (did live)*
hablaste	*you spoke*	comiste	*you ate*	viviste	*you lived*
habló	*you/he/she spoke*	comió	*you/he/she ate*	vivió	*you/he/she lived*
hablamos	*we spoke*	comimos	*we ate*	vivimos	*we lived*
hablasteis	*you spoke*	comisteis	*you ate*	vivisteis	*you lived*
hablaron	*you/they spoke*	comieron	*you/they ate*	vivieron	*you/they lived*

Note the accent marks on the first- and third-person singular of the preterite tense. These accent marks are dropped in the conjugation of **ver: vi, vio.**

Verbs that end in **-car, -gar,** and **-zar** show a spelling change in the first-person singular of the preterite.

> buscar: busqué, buscaste,...
> pagar: pagué, pagaste,...
> empezar: empecé, empezaste,...†

As in the present participle, an unstressed **-i-** between two vowels becomes **-y-.**

> creer: creyó creyeron
> leer: leyó   leyeron

---

*The forms of the preterite are presented in this section and in Chapters 12 and 13; the imperfect is presented in Chapter 13.

†**-Ar** and **-er** stem-changing verbs show no stem change in the preterite: **desperté, volví. -Ir** stem-changing verbs do show a change. You will practice the preterite of most stem-changing verbs in Chapter 12.

Irregular Preterite Forms

DAR		HACER		IR and SER	
di	dimos	hice	hicimos	fui	fuimos
diste	disteis	hiciste	hicisteis	fuiste	fuisteis
dio	dieron	hizo	hicieron	fue	fueron

The preterite endings for **dar** are the same as those used for regular **-er/-ir** verbs in the preterite except that the accent marks are dropped. The third-person singular of **hacer**—**hizo**—is spelled with a **z** to keep the [s] sound of the infinitive. **Ser** and **ir** have identical forms in the preterite. Context will make the meaning clear.

Fui al centro anoche.   *I went downtown last night.*
Fui profesora.   *I was a professor.*

PRÁCTICA

A. *Dé Ud. frases nuevas según las indicaciones.*

1. —Hay examen en clase hoy. Por eso todos estudiaron anoche. ¿Quién estudió hasta muy tarde?
   —Anoche *Pepe* estudió hasta muy tarde. *(yo, Uds., tú, Graciela, nosotros, vosotros)*

2. —Con frecuencia se escriben cartas a los amigos que están en otras ciudades. ¿Quién escribió una carta ayer?
   —*Tú* (no) escribiste una carta ayer. *(Rosendo, yo, nosotras, ellas, Uds., vosotros)*

3. —Anoche, en casa de Julio, todos bailaron y bebieron demasiado. ¿Quiénes bailaron y bebieron demasiado en la fiesta?
   —*Carmen y Adolfo* bailaron y bebieron demasiado. *(yo, José, nosotros, tú, Uds., vosotros)*

4. —Es buena idea practicar el español en el laboratorio de lenguas. ¿Quién fue al laboratorio la semana pasada?
   —*Julio* (no) fue al laboratorio la semana pasada. *(yo, Paula, tú, nosotros, Estela y Clara, vosotras)*

5. —Esta mañana, ¿quién hizo la cama antes de salir de casa?
   —*Ana* (no) hizo la cama antes de salir. *(yo, nosotros, Uds., tú, Adolfo, vosotros)*

B. *¿Qué hicieron ayer? Dé oraciones completas, usando los verbos en el pretérito.*

1. **Julián:** hacer cola para comprar una entrada de cine / comprarla por fin / entrar en el cine / ver la película / gustarle mucho / regresar a casa tarde
2. **yo:** llegar a la universidad temprano / asistir a las clases / ir a la cafetería / almorzar / estudiar en la biblioteca

C. *Cambie los verbos al pretérito.*

1. *Regreso* tarde a casa. Mi compañero *prepara* la cena y *cenamos* juntos (*together*). Luego *empiezo* a estudiar, pero mi compañero *sale* con unos amigos a ver una película.
2. *Paso* un semestre estudiando en México. Mis padres me *pagan* el vuelo y *trabajo* para ganar (*to earn*) el dinero para la matrícula y los otros gastos (*expenses*). En México *vivo* con una encantadora familia mexicana y *aprendo* mucho. *Voy* a muchos lugares interesantes. Mis amigos me *escriben* muchas cartas.
3. ¡La fiesta de cumpleaños de la Sra. Sandoval *es* un desastre! Alicia le *hace* un pastel pero no lo *come* nadie. Y a la señora no le *gustan* los regalos que le *dan*. Todos *salen* descontentos.

D. *¿Qué hicieron estas personas ayer?   ¿Qué piensa Ud.?*

Julia Child	hablar mucho en clase
el/la profesor(a)	leer las noticias (*news*)
Andy Williams	cantar
Walter Cronkite	cocinar
los estudiantes	enseñar
el presidente	sentar a los clientes
la camarera	dar un discurso (*speech*)

CONVERSACIÓN

A. *Preguntas*

1. ¿Qué comió Ud. anoche? ¿y dónde?
2. ¿Quién llegó tarde a clase hoy?
3. ¿Alguien le mandó flores a Ud. el año pasado?
4. ¿Cuándo decidió estudiar Ud. el español?
5. ¿Cuánto pagó Ud. por su libro de español?
6. ¿Qué hizo Ud. ayer? ¿Adónde fue? ¿Y anteayer?
7. ¿Qué le dio Ud. a su mejor amigo/a para su cumpleaños el año pasado?
8. ¿Qué le dio a Ud. su amigo/a?
9. ¿Los abuelos de Ud. fueron latinos?   ¿europeos?   ¿norteamericanos? ¿orientales? ¿africanos?

B. *Complete las oraciones en una forma lógica.*

1. El año pasado yo leí _____.   Mi amigo/a leyó _____.
2. Ayer ayudé a _____.
3. Anoche volví a casa a _____.
4. El año pasado, mis amigos me invitaron a _____.
5. Ayer yo llamé a _____ por teléfono. _____ me llamó a mí.
6. Una vez salí con _____.
7. Una vez fui a _____. Fue un viaje _____.

39. DOUBLE OBJECT PRONOUNS

¿Por qué no **nos lo** dices?   *Why don't you tell it to us?*
Acaba de dár**melas.**   *He's just given them to me.*
Me lo está sirviendo ahora.   *She's serving it to me now.*
Págue**melo.** (No **me lo** pague.)   *Pay it for me. (Don't pay it for me.)*

When both an indirect and a direct object pronoun are used in a sentence, the indirect object pronoun precedes the direct: **ID.** Note that nothing separates the two pronouns. The position of double object pronouns with respect to the verb is the same as that of single object pronouns.

[Práctica A, B]

When both the indirect and the direct object pronouns begin with the letter **l,** the indirect object pronoun always changes to **se.** (In this construction **se** is not reflexive in meaning.) The direct object pronoun does not change.

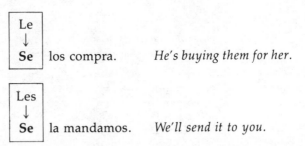

Since **se** stands for **le** (*to/for you* [sing.], *him, her*) and **les** (*to/for you* [pl.], *them*), it is often necessary to clarify its meaning by using **a** plus the pronoun objects of prepositions.

Se las doy **(a Ud., a él, a ella).**   *I'll give it to (you, him, her).*
Se lo escribo **(a Uds., a ellos, a**   *I'll write it to (you, them).*
ellas).

[Práctica C, D, E]

PRÁCTICA

A. *Dé Ud. frases nuevas según las indicaciones.*

    1. —Ud. todavía tiene hambre. ¿Qué va a comer?
       —¿Hay más *ensalada?* Me la pasas, por favor. *(pan, tomates, tortillas, vino, fruta, jamón)*
    2. —La casa de su amigo/a es un desastre. Dígale a su amigo/a que le va a ayudar.
       —¿*El carro?* Te lo lavo mañana. (*¿las ventanas? ¿el refrigerador? ¿los platos? ¿la ropa?*)

B. *Match the situations on the left with the statements or questions on the right.*

    1. Acabamos de recibir una carta de Jorge.
    2. ¿Pero no sabe Ud. la respuesta?
    3. Acabo de escribir una canción.
    4. Ud. tiene las manos muy llenas (*your hands full*). ¿Le abro la puerta?
    5. No comprendo los verbos reflexivos.
    6. La cafetera está muy sucia. Ya que estás lavando los platos, ¿me la lavas?
    7. Hace un calor de mil demonios. Si quieres, pongo el acondicionador.

    a. Claro que te la lavo.
    b. No. Dígamela, por favor.
    c. Sí, ábramela, por favor.
    d. ¿Te los explico?
    e. ¿Me la lees?
    f. ¿Por qué no nos la cantas?
    g. Sí. ¿Por qué no me lo pones, por favor?

C. *Answer the questions, basing your answers on what you observe happening in the drawings. Use double object pronouns.*

    1. ¿El empleado le vende el carro a María? (→ *No, no se lo vende a ella.*) ¿a los Sres. Benítez? ¿a Esteban?

    2. ¿El camarero le sirve una cerveza a Carlos? ¿a los hermanos? ¿a Emilia?

3. ¿Ramiro le manda flores a Tomás?   4. ¿Carmen les recomienda los tacos
   ¿a los Sres. Padilla? ¿a Carmen?   a Raúl y Celia? ¿a Estela? ¿a
                                            Lucas?

D. *Tell your friend Fausto that what you are doing is not for him but for someone
   else.*

   MODELO   ¿Las flores? No te *las* mando a ti. *Se las mando a Margarita.*

   1. ¿El poema? No te _____ escribo a ti. (a mis padres)
   2. ¿Las respuestas? No te _____ pido a ti. (al profesor)
   3. ¿El dinero? No te _____ doy a ti. (a Pepe)
   4. ¿Los libros? No te _____ compro a ti. (a mi hermana menor)
   5. ¿La sopa? No te _____ sirvo a ti. (a mis primos)

E. *Change the direct object nouns to pronouns and make other necessary changes.*

   1. Acaban de decirme la verdad.
   2. No me lea Ud. los anuncios (*ads*).
   3. No tienen que pagarnos la cena.
   4. Estoy guardándole el equipaje.
   5. Cómprele Ud. los pasajes.
   6. ¿Me quieres sacudir los muebles?
   7. La camarera les sirve las Coca-Colas.
   8. Le recomiendo la clase turística, señor.

CONVERSACIÓN

*Ud. acaba de comprar las siguientes cosas para unos amigos y parientes: un libro, dos
maletas, un televisor, una cafetera, unas flores, un estéreo y _____.*

El dependiente le pregunta:
   —Y *el libro*, ¿se *lo* mandamos a Ud.?
Y Ud. contesta, dando el nombre de un amigo o un pariente:
   —No, mánde*selo a mi primo Jaime*, por favor.

40. USE OF THE INFINITIVE AS A VERB COMPLEMENT

Michael D. Sullivan

El placer de vivir en una residencia

ROSALÍA: (*Entrando en el cuarto de Carmen.*) ¿Qué haces?

CARMEN: *Trato de estudiar,* pero no *puedo concentrarme.* Hay tanto ruido por aquí. ¿No lo oyes? Abajo en la cafetería están lavando los platos y ahora *empiezan a pasar* la aspiradora en el pasillo.

(*Se oyen unos gritos desde el pasillo. Entra Marta.*)

MARTA: ¿No saben la noticia? Ana *acaba de ser* aceptada en la Facultad de Derecho.

CARMEN: ¡Qué bien! Pero sin un poco de silencio por aquí, ¡yo ni *voy a poder terminar* el semestre!

---

1. *¿Quién acaba de entrar en el cuarto de Carmen?*
2. *¿Qué trata de hacer Carmen? ¿Puede hacerlo?*
3. *¿Qué ruidos se oyen?*
4. *¿Qué noticia trae Marta?*
5. *¿Cómo reacciona Carmen? ¿Por qué?*

A. When two verbs occur in series, the second verb is usually in the infinitive form. In Spanish some verbs require the use of a word (usually a preposition) before the infinitive.

B. Many verbs require no preposition before an infinitive.

The pleasure of dormitory living ROSALÍA: (*Entering Carmen's room.*) What are you doing? CARMEN: I'm trying to study, but I can't concentrate. There's so much noise around here. Don't you hear it? In the cafeteria below they're washing dishes, and now they're starting to vacuum the hall. (*Some shouts are heard from the hallway. Marta enters the room.*) MARTA: Don't you know the news? Ann was just accepted in law school. CARMEN: Great! But without a little bit of quiet around here, I won't even be able to finish the semester!

Prefieren poner la mesa.   *They prefer to set the table.*

deber	**pensar (ie)** (*to intend*)
decidir	**poder (ue)**
desear	**preferir (ie)**
esperar	**querer (ie)**
necesitar	**saber**

C. Some verbs require **a** before an infinitive.

La profesora nos **enseña a bailar.**   *The professor is teaching us to dance.*

aprender a	invitar a
ayudar a	ir a
empezar (ie) a	venir (ie) a
enseñar a	

D. Other verbs require **de** before an infinitive.

Siempre **tratamos de llegar** en punto.   *We always try to arrive on time.*

acabar de	tratar de

E. One frequently used verb requires **en** before an infinitive.

Insisten en venir esta noche.   *They insist on coming over tonight.*

insistir en

F. Two verbs require **que** before an infinitive.

Hay que sacar la basura.   *It's necessary to take out the garbage.*

hay que	tener que

PRÁCTICA

A. Complete las oraciones según las indicaciones.

1. Me gusta cuando mis amigos me invitan a _____ (jugar al volibol, comer, salir con ellos, visitarlos, bailar)
2. Mis profesores me ayudan a _____ (aprender el idioma español, comprender el mundo [*world*] moderno, descubrir nuevas ideas, hacer buenas preguntas, expresar mejor mis ideas)
3. En esta clase hay que _____ (estudiar mucho, conjugar muchos verbos, estar alerta siempre, escuchar bien, saber el vocabulario)

B. *Form complete sentences by using one word or phrase from each column, if necessary. Remember to conjugate the first verb.*

			cocinar
			anunciar su noviazgo
			fumar
el camarero	insistir	en	volar a Acapulco
yo	empezar	de	preguntarnos algo
tú	acabar	a	buscar los platos
nosotras	desear	que	creerlo
Jorge y Lupe	venir		pensar en español
_____	tener		poner la secadora
			limpiar la casa entera
			_____

CONVERSACIÓN

*Complete each of the following sentences in several different ways, using an infinitive or an infinitive phrase each time. Use **a, de, en,** or **que** where necessary.*

1. Mi profesor(a) de español me enseña _____.
2. En esta clase preferimos _____.
3. En clase hay _____.
4. En esta clase aprendo _____.
5. Mañana tengo _____.
6. Siempre trato _____ pero no puedo.
7. Acabo _____.
8. Esta noche, pienso _____.

DIÁLOGO: Los anuncios

Hay anuncios por todas partes del mundo y los hay° de todos tipos. Algunos aparecieron primero en los Estados Unidos, pero ahora son internacionales:

los... *there are some* *(ads)*

Beba Coca-Cola, deliciosa y refrescante.

Algunos nos prometen° un futuro mejor: *promise*

¡Juan Fernández se ganó° un millón de   **se...** *won*
pesos en la lotería nacional!

Y algunos son oficiales, como este anuncio «anti-moscas°» de una   *flies*
campaña publicitaria que hizo el Ministerio de Salud° Pública de un   *health*
país latinoamericano:

Mate° una y cuente° mil.   *kill / count*

Un estadounidense que viaja por Latinoamérica o España puede tener
la impresión de que cada hombre se afeita con Gillette y que todos se
bañan y se lavan los dientes° con productos norteamericanos.   *teeth*

¿No estás contento de usar Dial?
La nueva sonrisa° Colgate   *smile*

Por otro lado, el hispano que viene a hacer turismo en los Estados
Unidos va a poder comprarse en muchos lugares algunos de sus productos favoritos, especialmente las bebidas alcohólicas, como Dos
Equis, San Miguel y Dry Sack.
    Los anuncios de todas partes del mundo tienen el mismo propósito° *purpose*
y con frecuencia usan las mismas técnicas, las mismas frases y...
parece que° las mismas personas hermosas°. Nos dicen: «¡Use...!   **parece...** *it seems (as*
¡Cómprelo! ¡Dígaselo a sus amigos!»   *if they use)/ beautiful*

Piense Ud. en un producto que compró la semana pasada. ¿Dónde lo compró y cuánto le costó? ¿Cuántas veces lo usó? ¿Qué le gustó o no le gustó del producto? ¿Puede Ud. darles a sus compañeros de clase una recomendación sobre° el producto? «¡Compren _____! ¡Se   *about* lo recomiendo a Uds. porque _____!»

¿Sus compañeros van a seguir la recomendación de Ud.? ¿O saben el refrán que dice: «No hay cosa más barata que las buenas palabras»?

Comprensión

Conteste en oraciones completas.

1. ¿Cómo es la Coca-Cola, según el anuncio?
2. ¿Cuánto ganó Juan Fernández en la lotería?
3. ¿Cómo es que uno puede contar mil cuando mata una mosca? ¿Las moscas se reproducen mucho?
4. Aquí tiene Ud. el resto del anuncio para Dial: «¿No quisieras que todos lo usaran?» ¿Qué significa en inglés?
5. ¿Tiene Ud. una sonrisa Colgate? ¿un bronceado Coppertone?
6. ¿Sabe Ud. qué son Dos Equis, San Miguel y Dry Sack? ¿Le gustan a Ud.?
7. ¿Cuál es el equivalente en inglés del refrán «No hay cosa más barata que las buenas palabras»?
8. ¿Cuál es anuncio favorito de Ud.? Trate de expresarlo en español.

Comentario cultural

Although products such as automobiles, computer systems, machine tools, and jet transports compose a large part of U.S. exports to Hispanic countries, the products of everyday life—toothpaste, suntan lotion, detergents, and so on—are also important items in U.S. trade with Latin America and Spain. The English names of products—often pronounced as if they were Spanish words—are frequently maintained abroad, and the advertising slogans that accompany them are often direct translations of the English ad into Spanish.

At times, however, linguistic factors have to be taken into account. The name of the popular U.S. car the Nova was jokingly distorted into **No va** in some Latin countries. Since **no va** (*it doesn't go/run*) is hardly an appropriate name for an automobile, the name of that particular model was changed to **Caribe.**

In Latin America and Spain there is a lot of advertising for the lottery **(la lotería),** an institution of long standing in Hispanic countries. Run by the state, the lottery supplements the tax revenues of the country, and the income it generates is used primarily to support public and charitable works.

The same lottery number usually has ten or twenty tickets. The player may buy the entire sheet of tickets **(el billete entero/el número entero)** or only a portion of the sheet **(un décimo/un vigésimo).** If the number comes up in the drawing **(el sorteo),** the player shares in the winnings according to the portion of the number purchased. There are many winning combinations, and it is everyone's hope to win **el premio gordo** (*the grand* ["fat"] *prize*).

UN POCO DE TODO

A. *Cambie por el plural.*

1. No sé cómo se llama ella. ¿Me la presentas?
2. Ud. viene a leérmela, ¿verdad?
3. Ud. se despertó a las seis, ¿no? Pues, acuéstese temprano esta noche.
4. Todavía estoy tratando de comprender el diálogo. No me lo explicó bien el tutor.
5. No se levante a las siete si no tiene que estar allí hasta las once.

B. *Form complete sentences based on the words given, in the order given. Conjugate the verbs in the preterite, and add other words if necessary.*

1. ¿ / cafetera / ? / yo / se la / dar / mi / padres
2. Pablo / Claudia / se / conocer / Buenos Aires / pero / él / nunca / la / invitar / salir
3. Carlos / empezar / vestirse / ocho
4. yo / tratar / explicar / se lo / ellos / pero / no / me / escuchar
5. Pedro / afeitarse / bañarse / y / acostarse

C. *Match the **anuncios** given on the left with the corresponding product or type of product on the right.*

1. Yo encontré ayuda rápidamente en las páginas amarillas.
2. Una nueva forma de sentarse y dormirse.
3. Póngalo en su vaso favorito.
4. ¡Qué bien se duerme con _____!
5. ¿Busca Ud. un clima perfecto? Se lo da _____.
6. Acaba de morir (*to die*) un niño.
7. Se llevará (*you'll get*) una sorpresa: ¡el precio!

a. UNICEF
b. sillas cómodas para el patio
c. la guía telefónica
d. un acondicionador
e. pastillas (*pills*) para dormir
f. un radio muy barato
g. un jerez

D. *A Ud. lo/la invitan a aparecer en un anuncio para la televisión. Otro/a estudiante, haciendo el papel (role) de entrevistador(a), va a hacerle a Ud. las preguntas siguientes. Uds. pueden hablar de un carro, una aspiradora, una lavadora, una secadora, una cafetera o de cualquier otro producto.*

1. ¿Dónde compró Ud. este/a _____? ¿Cuándo lo/la compró?
2. ¿Cuánto pagó Ud. por él/ella?
3. ¿Quién se lo/la recomendó?
4. ¿Puede Ud. recomendárselo/la a nuestros televidentes (*viewers*)?
5. ¿Qué le gusta más de este producto?
6. ¿Lo/la va a comprar otra vez? ¿Por qué?

E. *Complete las oraciones en una forma lógica.*

1. _____ y yo nos queremos mucho. El/ella me ayuda a _____.
2. Generalmente, me levanto a _____ pero hoy me levanté a _____.
3. A veces me despierto a _____ pero hoy me desperté a _____.
4. Me divierto más cuando mis amigos me invitan a _____.
5. Esta noche, _____ viene(n) a mi casa a _____. Luego vamos a _____.
6. Me gusta mi _____. Me lo/la dio mi _____.
7. Ayer compré _____.
8. El año pasado compré _____ y se lo/la di a _____.

VOCABULARIO

VERBOS

acostar (ue) to put to bed
  acostarse to go to bed
afeitar to shave
  afeitarse to shave (oneself)
aparecer to appear
bañar to bathe
  bañarse to take a bath
casarse to get married
cocinar to cook
costar (ue) to cost
decidir to decide
descubrir to discover
despertar (ie) to wake
  despertarse to wake up
divertir (i, i) to amuse, entertain
  divertirse to have a good time,
    enjoy oneself
dormirse (ue, u) to fall asleep
explicar to explain
expresar to express
hay que it is necessary
lavar to wash
  lavarse to wash oneself, get
  washed
levantar to lift, raise
  levantarse to get up; to stand up
limpiar to clean
llamarse to be named, called
morir (ue, u) to die

pasar to spend (*time*)
ponerse to put on (*clothing*)
querer (ie) to love
quitar to remove, take away
  quitarse to take off (*clothing*)
sacar to take out, remove
sacudir to dust
sentar (ie) to seat, to lead to a seat
  sentarse to sit down
tratar de to try to
vestir (i, i) to dress
  vestirse to get dressed

SUSTANTIVOS

el **acondicionador** air conditioner
el **anuncio** ad; announcement
la **aspiradora** sweeper
la **basura** garbage
la **cafetera** coffee pot
la **cama** bed
el/la **criado/a** servant
el/la **enfermero/a** nurse
el/la **estadounidense** person from
  the United States
la **estufa** stove
el/la **hispano/a** Hispanic person
la **lavadora** washer
la **máquina** machine
los **muebles** furniture

el **mundo** world
el **producto** product
el **quehacer** task, chore
el **refrigerador** refrigerator
la **residencia estudiantil**
  dormitory
el **ruido** noise
la **secadora** dryer
la **ventana** window
la **vez** time, occasion

ADJETIVOS

cada each, every
cualquier any
doméstico/a domestic
entero/a whole, entire
mismo/a same
pasado/a past, last (*in time*)

PALABRAS Y EXPRESIONES ÚTILES

anoche last night
anteayer the day before yesterday
ayer yesterday
hacer la cama to make the bed
otra vez again
poner la mesa to set the table
según according to
ya que since

Un paso más 8

Actividades

A. **¿Qué pasa?** Describe what is happening in the cartoon. Use short, simple sentences, but be as creative as possible.

—*¿Tú crees que cada vez que nos encontramos tenemos que saludarnos dándonos la mano?*

Palabras útiles

el pulpo	*octopus*
el pez (*pl.* **peces**)	*fish*
encontrarse (ue)	*to meet*
saludar(se)	*to greet* (*each other*)
darse la mano	*to shake hands*

Preguntas útiles
1. ¿Quiénes se encuentran? ¿Dónde se encuentran?
2. ¿Cómo se saludan?
3. ¿Son amigos? ¿Cómo se sabe?
4. Si los pulpos continúan la conversación, ¿qué van a decir? ¿Cómo se va a terminar la conversación?

B. **¿Por qué no sacudió Ud. los muebles?** The housekeeper in the cartoon on page 236 will have to explain why she did not dust the furniture. An able excuse-maker, she could point out all the other tasks that she *did* complete during the day. She could also indicate the many unexpected complications that kept her from dusting.

—¡*Ah, pues... Naturalmente, si le pasa usted el dedo!*°...   **le...** *you run your finger over it*

MODELO   ¿Por qué no sacudió Ud. los muebles?
  → No fue posible, señora, pero sí hice muchas otras cosas: hice todas las camas, lavé las ventanas, saqué la basura, preparé la cena y...
  → No lo hice hoy, señora, porque —como Ud. sabe— llegó inesperadamente (*unexpectedly*) su hermana con sus diez niños. Les preparé la comida, los llevé al museo de arte moderno, fui al mercado a comprar más carne y tuve que (*I had to*)...

Following the model of the housekeeper's excuses, give the most elaborate excuses that you can in response to the following questions.

1. ¿Por qué llegó Ud. tarde a la oficina?
2. ¿Por qué no terminó Ud. los ejercicios de hoy?
3. ¿Por qué no me escribiste la semana pasada?
4. ¿Por qué no le ayudaste a tu amigo/a a pintar su apartamento ayer?
5. ¿Por qué no comiste nada esta mañana?
6. ¿Por qué no fuiste a la fiesta?

C. **¡Cómprelo hoy!**   The following phrases are typical of those found in popular advertising.

Frases útiles

Cómprelo hoy.
Descubra algo nuevo.
Vea nuestro _____.
Disfrute de (*enjoy*) _____.
Para ser elegante lleve/use _____.
Es un símbolo de distinción.
Nuestro _____ **se hace «como Dios manda».**

Estamos orgullosos (*proud*) **de presentarles nuestro** _____.
Es económico/moderno/cómodo _____.
Es la solución de todos sus problemas.
Es ideal para _____.
¡Un gran éxito (*success*)!
La técnica más avanzada.
La técnica del futuro, la tradición del pasado.

Using some of the preceding phrases, write an ad that will convince your classmates to buy a product—one of the following items or another of your own choosing. The product can be real or imaginary.

un perfume   un café especial   una bebida o una comida
un perro   ropa de París   un lavaplatos (*dishwasher*)
una planta carnívora un coche italiano   un televisor (*television set*)
aspirinas   un reloj   un detergente líquido

D. **Hora de comer.** Explain the story depicted in the cartoon. Tell who the people are, what happened, and what is going to happen. Use the questions below as a guide.

—*Ahora no me podrás° negar que te levantas por la noche a saquear° el refrigerador.*

won't be able to
to plunder, raid

1. ¿Qué hora es?
2. ¿Quién se levantó primero? ¿Quién se despertó después?
3. ¿Quién está sacando una foto?
4. ¿El esposo comió mucho para la cena? ¿Qué está sacando del refrigerador?
5. ¿Va a comer algo la esposa?
6. ¿A qué hora van a acostarse otra vez?

A propósito...

The following phrases are useful for communicating about basic everyday matters while living with a Spanish-speaking family. They should help you to be a polite guest, to fit into the family schedule, to offer and ask for help and information.

¿A qué hora se cena?   *What time do you eat?*

Salgo ahora pero vuelvo a las dos.	I'm going out now but I'll be back at two.
Voy a cenar fuera esta noche.	I'm going to eat out tonight.
¿Cómo te/le puedo ayudar?	How can I help you?
(¿Pongo la mesa? ¿Saco la basura?)	(Shall I set the table? Shall I take out the garbage?)
Voy de compras. ¿Necesita(s) algo?	I'm going shopping. Do you need anything?
¿Me puede(s) prestar (enseñar, decir) _____?	Can you lend (show, tell) me _____?
No quiero molestarte/lo/la, pero _____.	I don't want to bother you, but _____.
¿Dónde puedo comprar _____?	Where can I buy _____?
Me falta* jabón (papel higiénico).	I need soap (toilet paper).
Me faltan* toallas.	I need towels.
¿Está libre el baño?	Is the bathroom free? (Is anybody in the bathroom? Does anyone else want to use the bathroom?)
Quisiera lavarme el pelo. ¿Hay agua caliente?	I would like to wash my hair. Is there any hot water?
¿Se puede usar el teléfono (mirar la televisión) ahora?	Is it okay to use the phone (watch television) now?

E. **En familia.** Referring to the phrases in **A propósito,** give as many different questions or statements as possible about each of the following situations.

MODELO   Ud. acaba de llegar a México sin tener alojamiento (*lodging*). La universidad le da una lista de familias que ofrecen alojamiento a estudiantes extranjeros. Ud. va a la casa de una de ellas. ¿Qué les pregunta?

—*¿La habitación es para una persona o para dos?*
—*¿Cuánto es?*
—*¿Se incluyen las comidas?*
—*¿Hay niños en la familia?*
—*Tengo un radio. (Toco la guitarra.) ¿Les va a molestar* (bother)?

1. Ud. vive ya con una familia mexicana, pero acaba de llegar y todavía no sabe mucho de la familia, de su rutina, sus costumbres, sus gustos (*likes*). ¿Qué necesita Ud. saber para hacerse parte de la familia? ¿Qué pregunta?

---

*The use of the verb **faltar** (*to be lacking*) is similar to that of **gustar.** It takes an indirect object, and the subject usually follows the verb.

Me falta un libro.   *I need a book. (A book is lacking to me.)*
Me faltan diez dólares.   *I need ten dollars. (Ten dollars are lacking to me.)*

2. Ud. es como parte de la familia ya. Por eso Ud. quiere ayudarles a todos los miembros de la familia. ¿Qué va a decir para ofrecer su ayuda?
3. Ud. también necesita pedirles ayuda a los miembros de la familia cuando no sabe algo o cuando necesita algo. ¿Qué les puede preguntar?

Lectura cultural: Las maravillas del mundo hispánico: España

La Alhambra (1): La Alhambra, en Granada, no es sólo una de las maravillas del mundo hispánico; es también una de las maravillas del mundo. Construida por los árabes a lo largo de° un siglo (1248–1348), consiste en varios edificios: la ciudadela°, el palacio de los reyes, los cuartos de los miembros de la corte. Es el ejemplo más importante de la arquitectura morisca° en España.

Toledo (2): Esta ciudad, situada a las orillas° del río Tajo, es un monu-

a... *during*

citadel

Moorish

banks

1.

Owen Franken/Stock, Boston

2.

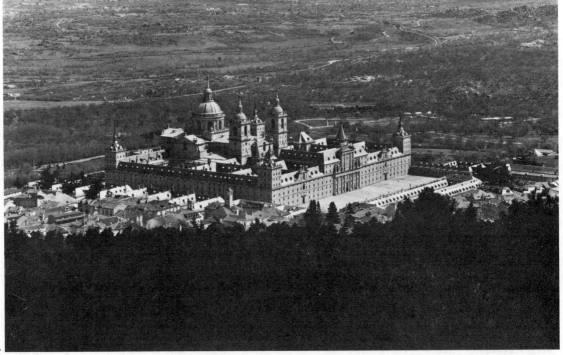

3.

mento nacional de España. En ella se conservan raros ejemplos de la arquitectura gótica°, en especial la catedral. Además, se encuentran en la   *Gothic*
ciudad muchas de las pinturas del famoso pintor El Greco (1542–1614),
quien inmortalizó la ciudad en uno de sus cuadros° más famosos, *Vista*°   *paintings / view*
de Toledo.

   El Escorial (3): El Monasterio de San Lorenzo de El Escorial es un gran
edificio severo y frío. El emperador Felipe II (1556–1598) lo mandó cons-   **lo...** *ordered it built*
truir° de granito de la Sierra de Guadarrama, cerca de Madrid. Ademas   **panteón,** *mausoleum /*
de su panteón°, donde están enterrados° muchos de los reyes españoles, el   *buried*
edificio contiene una biblioteca, un museo de arte y el monasterio-
colegio de frailes agustinos°.   **frailes...** *Augustinian*
                                                                               monks

Comprensión

Check your comprehension of the reading selection by indicating which of the
statements are true and which are false.

La Alhambra: a. Es de la época de los árabes en España.
                  b. Es un edificio moderno.
                  c. Es una de las maravillas del mundo.

Toledo: a. Tiene una catedral gótica muy importante en España.
                  b. Se ve en una pintura famosa de Picasso.
                  c. Hay muchas pinturas de El Greco en Toledo.

El Escorial: a. Contiene los restos (*remains*) de algunos reyes españoles.
                  b. Es una de las contribuciones a la cultura española del Rey
                     Felipe II.
                  c. Tiene un museo de arte y un monasterio-colegio.

Ejercicios escritos

A. Write two **¿cierto/falso?** sentences about each of the following American cities.
    Your classmates should indicate whether they are **cierto** or **falso.** Sub-
    stitute other places if you prefer.

    1. Nueva York
    2. Chicago
    3. Miami
    4. San Francisco

B. Prepare a brief written report **(informe)** on one of the places discussed in
    the **Lectura cultural** in **Un paso más... siete** or **ocho.** Give information
    beyond that provided in the text. Use simple sentence structures, and try
    to use the dictionary as little as possible. Include information on at least
    one of the following aspects of the place you choose to write about: (1) its
    historical background, (2) its artistic interest, (3) advice to tourists who
    might visit the place, (4) contemporary issues related to the place, (5) aspects
    of pre-Columbian Indian culture or civilization related to it.

capítulo 9 El trabajo

Andrew Sacks/EPA, Inc.

OBJETIVOS

In this chapter you will learn vocabulary and expressions related to the professions and business.

You will also learn about the following aspects of Spanish grammar:

41. the concept and forms of the subjunctive mood (until now you have studied the indicative mood) and the use of the subjunctive after **ojalá** (*I wish*)

42. how to use the subjunctive after expressions of willing: *I want you to . . .*

43. how to use the **nosotros** form of the subjunctive to express *Let's* (*eat, dance,* and so on)

44. how to use **de** plus a *noun* as an adjective to describe another noun: **el libro de matemáticas** (*the math book*), **una casa de adobe** (*an adobe house*)

Un paso más includes activities related to jobs and professions, and a reading about Hispanic cinema.

VOCABULARIO: PREPARACIÓN

En la oficina: jefes y empleados			
el/la empleado/a	employee	quitar	to take out,
el/la director(a)	manager,		withhold
	director	el aumento	raise, increase
el/la jefe/a	boss	el cheque	check
cambiar (de puesto)	to change	los impuestos	taxes
	(jobs)	el negocio	business
dar consejos	to give advice	la oficina	office
despedir (i, i)	to fire	el puesto	job, position
funcionar	to function	el sueldo	salary
ganar	to earn; to win	el trabajo	job, work

A. *¿Qué consejos —serios o cómicos— da Ud. para resolver cada problema a la izquierda?*

1. Su jefe es muy antipático.
2. Los empleados llegan tarde todos los días.
3. Ud. gana un sueldo muy bajo.
4. Un empleado habla mucho por teléfono con sus amigos.
5. El viernes, quince minutos antes de la hora de cerrar, la jefa le da a Ud. un trabajo muy largo y complicado que necesita el lunes.
6. Le quitan muchos impuestos del cheque.
7. Dos empleados no se llevan (*get along*) bien.

a. No trabaje Ud. Así (*thus*) no tiene que pagar nada al estado.
b. Cuando Ud. ve que llama a alguien, déle otra cosa que hacer e* indique que no debe hablar con sus amigos durante las horas de oficina.
c. Hable con los dos, déles consejos y trate de resolver las diferencias. Si esto no da resultado, despida a uno de ellos.
d. Dígale que Ud. tiene que salir de la ciudad este fin de semana y que no vuelve hasta muy tarde el domingo.
e. Por cada minuto de retraso (*tardiness*), quíteles un dólar de su cheque.
f. Dígale al director que Ud. necesita ganar más dinero y pídale un aumento.
g. Cambie de puesto, porque los jefes no cambian nunca.

*Y (*and*) becomes e before a word that begins with i or hi: Isabel y Fernando, but Fernando e Isabel; hijos y padres, but padres e hijos.

B. *¿La directora o el empleado? ¿Quién lo dijo?* (Who said it?)

1. Le di un buen consejo, pero no me escuchó.
2. Este negocio no funciona bien.
3. Creo que hay un error en el cheque —me quitaron demasiado para los impuestos federales.
4. La despedí y salió furiosa.
5. Cambié de trabajo porque me gusta la responsabilidad de ser jefa.
6. Creo que los jefes ganan mucho más que nosotros.

Profesiones y oficios°   *trades*

el/la abogado/a	lawyer	**el/la obrero/a**	worker,
el/la comerciante	merchant		laborer
el/la enfermero/a	nurse	**el/la plomero/a**	plumber
el hombre/la mujer de negocios	business man/ woman	**el/la siquiatra**	psychiatrist

---

C. *¿Qué profesión/oficio corresponde a cada descripción? ¿Cuáles son las ventajas* (advantages) *y desventajas* (disadvantages) *de cada trabajo?*

un(a) empleado/a   un(a) abogado/a   un(a) mujer/hombre de negocios
un(a) obrero/a   un(a) comerciante   un(a) plomero/a
un(a) enfermero/a   un(a) director(a)   un(a) siquiatra

1. Recibe muchas invitaciones para comer en los buenos restaurantes. Es muy susceptible a los ataques al corazón (*heart*). Viaja mucho.
2. Compra y vende cosas. Pone anuncios de sus productos en la televisión, en los periódicos, etcétera. Está contento/a cuando los empleados venden mucho.
3. Tiene que leer mucho. Tiene un puesto de mucho prestigio. A veces no sabe si su cliente es inocente o no.
4. Puede dar mandatos a los empleados y los despide cuando es necesario. Gana más que sus empleados. Tiene un trabajo más interesante que ellos.
5. No tiene tanta responsabilidad como un jefe, ni tiene que tomar tantas decisiones. Le pagan menos que al jefe.
6. A veces tiene que trabajar en lugares muy sucios. Gana un buen sueldo. Tiene que ir a las casas de sus clientes.
7. Tiene que trabajar sólo ocho horas —normalmente no lleva el trabajo a casa. Su trabajo puede resultar monótono.
8. Escucha a otras personas todo el día. Sabe los secretos de sus clientes y les ayuda a resolver sus problemas.
9. Trabaja en un hospital. Sus clientes están enfermos, generalmente, y tiene mucha responsabilidad con respecto a la salud de ellos.

D. *¿Qué profesiones asocia Ud. con estas frases?*

actor/actriz	*barman*	dentista	policía
ama de casa	camarero/a	enfermero/a	político/a
artista	capitán	médico/a	presidente/a
azafata/camarero	consejero/a	pintor(a)	profesor(a)
barbero	cura/pastor/rabino	poeta/poetisa	secretario/a

1. intelectual   2. aburrido/a   3. sensible (*sensitive*)   4. mucho dinero
5. mucho poder (*power*)   6. mucha responsabilidad   7. mucho prestigio
8. mucha prisa   9. mucho peligro (*danger*)

E. *¿Qué profesión le interesa más a Ud.? Explique por qué, dando las ventajas y desventajas como las ve Ud.*

PRONUNCIACIÓN: Ñ, Y, and LL

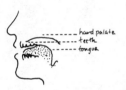

hard palate
teeth
tongue

The three consonants **ñ, y,** and **ll** are called *palatals* because they are produced with the middle of the tongue against the hard palate.

Ñ The **ñ** resembles the [ny] sound of English *canyon, union*, but it is a single sound, not an [n] followed by a [y].

Y and LL In Spanish the **y** at the beginning of a syllable (**yo, papaya**) resembles English *y* (*yoyo, papaya*) except that the tongue is closer to the palate. The result is a sound with some palatal friction, in between English *y* and the *zh* sound of *measure*. When the speaker is emphatic, **y** at the beginning of a word has even more friction, sounding like the *j* in English *Joe:* —**¿Quién va?** —**¡Yo!** When Spanish speakers learn English, this habit often carries over into their English, with *yes* sounding like *Jess.*

In most parts of the Spanish-speaking world, **ll** is pronounced exactly like **y,*** which means that pronunciation alone will not tell you whether a word is spelled with **y** or **ll.** Even Hispanics sometimes have trouble spelling words with these two letters, and it is not uncommon to see misspellings such as **llo** for **yo,** and **me yamo** for **me llamo.**

PRÁCTICA

A. 1. cana/caña   3. mono/moño   5. sonar/soñar   7. tino/tiño
    2. pena/peña   4. una/uña   6. lena/leña   8. cena/seña

B. compañero año señora baño cañón español pequeña niño

C. llamo lleva llueve llegar yate ya yanqui yoga

*In many areas of Spain, **ll** is an [l] sound made with the middle of the tongue against the palate. This resembles the [ly] sound of English *million*, but is one sound, not an [l] plus a [y].

D. ellas tortilla aquellos calle silla ayuda haya proyecto mayo reyes oye

E. 1. El señor Muñoz es de España y enseña español.
   2. Vaya Ud. a la casa de Yolanda Carrillo en la calle Sevilla.
   3. ¿Llueve o no llueve allá en Yucatán?
   4. El niño ñoño (*whining*) está triste porque la niña le robó el yoyo.

MINIDIÁLOGOS Y GRAMÁTICA

41. PRESENT SUBJUNCTIVE: INTRODUCTION, FORMATION, USE WITH *OJALÁ*

El viernes, por la tarde

JEFE: Tenemos que trabajar el sábado, señores, y tal vez el domingo. *Quiero* que el inventario *esté* listo el lunes.

EMPLEADO: ¿Ud. *quiere* que *lleguemos* a las ocho, como siempre?

JEFE: No, una hora más temprano. Y si quieren comer, *recomiendo* que *traigan* algo de casa. No va a haber tiempo para salir.

EMPLEADO: ¡Ay! Mis planes para el fin de semana... *Ojalá* que Ud. *cambie* de idea.

JEFE: Yo no. *Ojalá* que Ud. *cambie* de planes, señor, o...

1. ¿Quién quière que todos trabajen el fin de semana?
2. ¿Por qué tienen que trabajar?
3. ¿Qué otras recomendaciones tiene el jefe?
4. ¿Al empleado le gusta la idea del trabajo extra?
5. ¿Qué puede pasar si el empleado no cambia de planes?

Friday afternoon BOSS: We'll have to work on Saturday, people, and maybe on Sunday. I want the inventory to be ready on Monday. EMPLOYEE: Do you want us to be here at eight, as usual? BOSS: No, an hour earlier. And if you want to eat, I recommend that you bring something from home. There won't be any time to go out. EMPLOYEE: Oh, my plans for the weekend! I hope you change your mind. BOSS: Not me. I hope you change your plans, sir, or . . .

In addition to showing person and tense, all conjugated verbs in English and Spanish show mood: indicative or subjunctive. You have already studied present and preterite forms of the *indicative* (**indicativo**). In both English and Spanish the indicative is used to state facts and to ask questions. It is the mood used to express real-world actions or states of being:

   A. She's writing the letter.
   B. We are there already!
   C. He is late.

In contrast to the indicative, the *subjunctive* (**subjuntivo**) is used to express a conceptualized action or state, one that exists in the mind of the speaker rather than in the real world. The English subjunctive is italicized in the following sentences:

   A. I recommend that she *write* the letter immediately.
   B. I wish (that) we *were* there already!
   C. It's possible (that) he *may be* late.

In sentence A, the English subjunctive follows an expression of willing; in sentence B, it follows an expression of emotion; in sentence C, it follows an expression of uncertainty. Each sentence has two clauses: an independent clause with a conjugated verb and subject that can stand alone (*I recommend, I wish, It's possible*) and a dependent (subordinate) clause that cannot stand alone (*that she write, that we were there, that he may be late*). The subjunctive is used in the dependent clause.

Indicate the independent and dependent clauses in the following sentences:

   1. I don't think (that) they're very nice.
   2. We feel (that) you really shouldn't go.
   3. He suggests (that) we be there on time.
   4. We don't believe (that) she's capable of that.

To summarize:

Independent Clause		Dependent Clause
indicative (expression of willing, emotion or uncertainty)	(that)	subjunctive

In English, when the indicative verb in the independent clause contains an expression of (1) willing, (2) emotion, or (3) uncertainty, the subjunctive may occur in the dependent clause.*

---

*The subjunctive has decreased in modern English usage, and many native speakers of English no longer use it.

Forms and Meanings of the Present Subjunctive

PRESENT SUBJUNCTIVE OF REGULAR VERBS		
HABLAR: hablø → habl-	COMER: comø → com-	VIVIR: vivø → viv-
hable hablemos hables habléis hable hablen	coma comamos comas comáis coma coman	viva vivamos vivas viváis viva vivan

Like the present indicative, the Spanish present subjunctive has several English equivalents. For example, **hable** can mean *I speak, I am speaking, I do speak,* or *I may speak.* The present subjunctive can also be used to refer to the future: *I will speak.* Ultimately, the English equivalent of the Spanish present subjunctive depends on the context in which it occurs.

In Spanish the subjunctive mood is indicated by personal endings that are added to the first-person singular of the present indicative minus its **-o** ending. **-Ar** verbs add endings with **e**; **-er/-ir** verbs add endings with **a**. Since the present subjunctive of Spanish verbs is formed in the same way as the **Ud.** and **Uds.** commands (**hable Ud., coma Ud., vivan Uds.**), irregularities found in the formal commands also occur in the present subjunctive.

Present subjunctive of verbs with spelling changes:
-car: c → **qu** buscar: bus**que**, bus**que**s,...
-gar: g → **gu** pagar: pa**gue**, pa**gue**s,...
-zar: z → **c**   empezar: empie**ce**, empie**ce**s,...

Present subjunctive of stem-changing verbs:

-Ar and **-er** stem-changing verbs follow the stem-changing pattern of the present indicative.

pensar (ie):   p**ie**nse, p**ie**nses, p**ie**nse, pensemos, penséis, p**ie**nsen
poder (ue):   p**ue**da, p**ue**das, p**ue**da, podamos, podáis, p**ue**dan

-Ir stem-changing verbs show the first stem change in four forms and the second stem change in the **nosotros** and **vosotros** forms.

dormirse (ue, u):   me d**ue**rma, te d**ue**rmas, se d**ue**rma, nos d**u**rmamos, os d**u**rmáis, se d**ue**rman
preferir (ie, i):   pref**ie**ra, pref**ie**ras, pref**ie**ra, pref**i**ramos, pref**i**ráis, pref**ie**ran

Other **-ir** stem-changing verbs include **(des)pedir (i, i), divertirse (ie, i), morir (ue, u), seguir (i, i), servir (i, i),** and **vestirse (i, i).**

Present subjunctive of verbs with irregular indicative **yo** *form:*

conocer: **conozca, conozcas, conozca, conozcamos, conozcáis, conozcan**

decir:	**diga**	poner:	**ponga**	traer:	**traiga**
hacer:	**haga**	salir:	**salga**	venir:	**venga**
oir:	**oiga**	tener:	**tenga**	ver:	**vea**

Irregular present subjunctive forms:

dar:	**dé, des, dé, demos, deis, den**
estar:	**esté, estés, esté, estemos, estéis, estén**
haber (hay):	**haya**
ir:	**vaya, vayas, vaya, vayamos, vayáis, vayan**
saber:	**sepa, sepas, sepa, sepamos, sepáis, sepan**
ser:	**sea, seas, sea, seamos, seáis, sean**

Present Subjunctive with *Ojalá*

Independent Clause		Dependent Clause
ojalá	**que**	<u>subjunctive</u>

Ojalá (que) vengan a la fiesta.   *I hope (that) they'll come to the party.*
Ojalá (que) podamos terminar tem-   *I hope (that) we can finish early.*
prano.

Ojalá is one way of saying *I wish* or *I hope* in Spanish. It is not a verb form like others you have learned, and it is never conjugated or used with **no.** It comes from an Arabic word that means *may Allah grant,* but it does not have religious connotations in modern usage.

Ojalá is followed by the subjunctive in the dependent clause. In informal speech it is possible to omit the word **que;** however, **ojalá que** is more frequently used in writing.

PRÁCTICA

A. Dé el presente de subjuntivo.

1. yo: bailar cenar mirar llegar buscar quitar
2. tú: aprender escribir leer asistir responder sacudir
3. Ud.: empezar pensar volar jugar sentarse despertarse
4. nosotros: pedir servir preferir morir divertirse despedir
5. Uds.: esperar deber bañarse decidir almorzar cambiar
6. yo: conocer hacer poner traer saber decir
7. ella: ser dar venir ir oir salir

B. *Dé el presente de subjuntivo.*

1. despertarse: Ana nosotros yo ellos vosotros
2. dormir: nosotros tú Paco y yo Uds. vosotros
3. poder: Ud. Emanuel nosotros yo vosotros

C. *Dé Ud. frases nuevas según las indicaciones.*

1. —¿Qué desea Ud. para el futuro?
   —Ojalá que yo _____ (*pasar las vacaciones en México, tener buenas notas* (grades) *este semestre, conocer al presidente algún día, encontrar un buen trabajo, ganar un buen sueldo algún día*)
2. —¿Qué desean Uds. para el resto del semestre?
   —¡Ojalá que (nosotros) _____! (*hablar mejor el español, no tener muchos exámenes, contestar bien todas las preguntas en el examen final, aprender a expresarnos mejor, no tener que escribir más composiciones*)

CONVERSACIÓN

A. *Complete las oraciones en una forma lógica.*

1. Ojalá que yo _____.
2. Ojalá que mis padres _____.
3. Ojalá que mi mejor amigo/a _____.
4. Ojalá que el/la profesor(a) _____.
5. Ojalá que (no) haya _____.

B. *¿Qué desean estas personas? Exprese Ud. los deseos de ellos, usando frases con* **ojalá que.**

1. 2. 3. 4.

1. una jefa (Ojalá que los empleados _____)
2. un secretario (Ojalá que el director _____)
3. un comerciante
4. el presidente

C. *Ud. tiene tres deseos. Puede desear cualquier cosa para cualquier persona. ¿Qué va a desear? Empiece sus deseos con* **ojalá que.**

42. USE OF THE SUBJUNCTIVE AFTER EXPRESSIONS OF WILLING

¿Quieres que lo haga ahora o mañana?

Independent clause		Dependent clause
indicative (expression of willing)	**que**	subjunctive

El director **quiere** que los empleados **lleguen** a tiempo.	*The manager wants the employees to arrive on time.*
¿**Prefieres** tú que (yo) **haga** un flan o un pastel?	*Do you prefer me to make (that I make) a flan or a cake?*

Expressions of willing are those in which speakers express their will, desire, permission, or preference that someone else do something: *I want you to come, I suggest that you be there on time, We'll allow you to do it.* English usually uses the infinitive after such expressions. In Spanish, expressions of willing, however strong or weak, are followed by the subjunctive mood in the dependent clause.

Verbs of willing include **decir, desear, insistir (en), mandar** (*to order* or *to send*), **pedir (i, i), permitir** (*to permit*), **preferir (ie, i), prohibir** (*to prohibit* or *forbid*), **querer (ie),** and **recomendar (ie).** Because it is impossible to give a complete list of all Spanish verbs of willing, remember that verbs that convey the sense of willing—not just certain verbs—are followed by the subjunctive.

¡OJO! The subjunctive is used in the dependent clause after **decir** when **decir** conveys an order. The subjunctive is not used when **decir** conveys information. Compare:

Carolina dice que **son** simpáticos.	*Carolina says (that) they're nice.*

but

Carolina nos dice que **lleguemos** a las siete en punto.	*Carolina says (that) we should arrive at seven sharp.*

Many verbs of willing are frequently used with indirect object pronouns.

Nos dicen		*They tell us to*	
Nos piden	} que **vengamos**	*They ask us to*	} *come.*
Nos recomiendan		*They recommend that we*	

The indirect object indicates the subject of the dependent clause, as in the sentences above: **nos → vengamos.**

Remember to use the infinitive—not the subjunctive—after verbs of willing when there is no change of subject.

No change of subject:	**Desean cenar** ahora.	*They want to have dinner now.*
Change of subject:	**Desean** que **Luisa y yo cenemos** ahora.	*They want Luisa and me to have dinner now.*

PRÁCTICA

A. *Dé Ud. frases nuevas según las indicaciones.*

1. —¿Se puede fumar en clase?
   —No, *el/la profesor(a)* no quiere que fumemos en clase. (*yo, nosotros, tú, los estudiantes, Lupe, vosotros*)
2. —¿Qué le piden a Ud. sus amigos?
   —Mis amigos me piden que _____. (*sentarme con ellos en la cafetería, salir con ellos, explicarles la gramática, ir al cine, no tomar tanto*)
3. —¿Quién tiene que trabajar el sábado?
   —La directora le recomienda a *Pascual* que trabaje el sábado. (*ti, Mariana, Uds., Ud., todos, vosotros*)

B. *Complete las oraciones, usando el subjuntivo de los verbos indicados.*

1. No me gusta *pagar* los impuestos, pero el estado manda que los _____.
2. Quiero *manejar* (*to drive*) todos los días, pero el gobierno (*government*) prefiere que no _____.
3. El jefe no quiere *despedir* al Sr. Yáñez, pero el dueño quiere que el jefe lo _____.
4. El abuelo está enfermo y el niño quiere *verlo*, pero sus padres no permiten que el niño lo _____.
5. Ayer *me levanté* tarde. Hoy mi esposo/a (padre, madre, compañero/a de cuarto) insiste en que yo _____.
6. El semestre pasado *tomé* ocho cursos, pero este semestre el consejero no permite que _____.
7. Amanda no le *dio* el regalo a su primo. Ahora su madre insiste en que Amanda se lo _____.

C. *Form complete sentences, using one word or phrase from each column. Be sure to have a change of subject and to use the appropriate conjugated verb form:* **indicative + que + subjunctive.**

				darle los cheques ahora
				darle la cuenta ahora
				estudiar más
yo			mis amigos	limpiar las mesas
el dueño del			tú	darme una fiesta
restaurante	desear		el camarero	venir con nosotros
nosotros	prohibir	que	la jefa	servir la comida
los empleados	recomendar		yo	dormir más
tú			los clientes	quitarnos menos
_____			el gobierno	impuestos
				darle un aumento
				de sueldo
				_____

D. *¿Cómo se dice en español? ¿Qué quiere la directora que Ud. haga?*

I want you to do the inventory. I insist that it be ready by tomorrow, and if you can't have it done by then **(para entonces),** I want you to work this weekend.

CONVERSACIÓN

A. *¿Qué quieren estas personas?*

1. El empleado _____.   2. El sargento _____.   3. La madre _____.

B. *¿Qué quiere Ud. que estas personas hagan? Use Ud. los verbos a la derecha o cualquier otro.*

MODELO   la criada → *Yo quiero que la criada limpie la casa.*

1. la siquiatra   decirme si el doctor está ocupado
2. el plomero   escuchar mis problemas
3. el comerciante   terminar la construcción de la casa pronto
4. la abogada   venir pronto —hay mucha agua en el suelo del cuarto
5. el enfermero   de baño
6. la criada   bajar sus precios
7. el obrero   lavar la ropa
                      darme consejos legales

C. Complete las oraciones en una forma lógica.

1. Yo siempre deseo que mis (amigos, padres) _____.
2. Mis (amigos, padres) siempre quieren que yo _____.
3. Insisto en que _____.
4. En esta clase, prefiero que _____.
5. Todos mis profesores me piden que _____.
6. Voy a escribirle a mi amigo/a en _____ para decirle que _____.
7. Anoche estudié desde las siete hasta las doce. Esta noche prefiero _____.
8. El gobierno manda que nosotros _____ y eso (no) me gusta.
9. (No) Deseo _____.

43. *NOSOTROS* COMMANDS

Una celebración oficial

EMPLEADA A: ¡Ya lo tengo! *Comprémosle* un reloj.

EMPLEADA B: No... *Mandémosle* una figurita para su oficina.

EMPLEADA C: Por favor, ¡*pongámonos* de acuerdo!

EMPLEADA D: (*Que acaba de entrar.*) Tanto ruido... ¿qué están pla-
              neando? ¿una fiesta para la jubilación de doña Aurora?

EMPLEADA A: ¡Qué va! ¡Es una fiesta para doña Amalia, que por fin
              la va a reemplazar!

---

1. *¿Qué planean las empleadas?   ¿Es una ocasión alegre o triste?*
2. *¿Cuáles son los regalos que se mencionan?*
3. *¿Se ponen de acuerdo rápidamente las empleadas?*
4. *¿Para quién es la fiesta?*
5. *¿Quién reemplaza a quién?*

An official celebration EMPLOYEE A: I've got it! Let's buy her a watch. EMPLOYEE B: No . . . Let's send
her a figurine for her office. EMPLOYEE C: Please, let's agree (get together) on this! EMPLOYEE D: (*Who
has just come in.*) So much noise . . . What are you planning? A party for doña Aurora's retirement?
EMPLOYEE A: Are you kidding? It's a party for doña Amalia, who's finally going to replace her!

Let's (*eat, dance,* and so on) can be expressed with **vamos a** + *infinitive* in Spanish. It can also be expressed with the **nosotros** form of the present subjunctive:

Vamos a comer ahora.	*Let's eat now.*	**Comamos** ahora.
Vamos a pedir.	*Let's order.*	**Pidamos.**
¡Vamos a brindar!	*Let's toast!*	**¡Brindemos!**

¡OJO! **Vayamos** (present subjunctive of **ir**) is rarely used as an affirmative command. The present indicative is normally used instead.

¡Vamos!   *Let's go!*

but

No vayamos.   *Let's not go.*

Direct and indirect object pronouns are attached to affirmative **nosotros** commands, but precede negative commands.

Comprémoslo pronto.   *Let's buy it soon.*
No se lo compremos hasta la fiesta.   *Let's not buy it for her until the party.*

When either **nos** (reflexive pronoun) or **se** (as in **se lo, se la,** and so on) is attached to the affirmative **nosotros** command, the final **-s** of the subjunctive form is dropped.

Acosté**monos.**   *Let's go to bed.*
Hagá**moselo** a ellos.   *Let's do it for them.*

but

No nos acostemos.   *Let's not go to bed.*
No se lo hagamos a ellos.   *Let's not do it for them.*

PRÁCTICA

A. *Conteste afirmativamente, usando mandatos* (**nosotros**).

1. ¿Vamos a esperar?
2. ¿Vamos a bailar?
3. ¿Vamos a comer ahora?
4. ¿Vamos a leer?
5. ¿Vamos a salir?
6. ¿Vamos a divertirnos?
7. ¿Vamos a acostarnos temprano?
8. ¿Vamos a levantarnos tarde mañana?

B. *Conteste según el modelo, usando pronombres.*

MODELO   ¿Tomamos café? → *Sí, tomémoslo.*
                    → *No, no lo tomemos todavía.*

1. ¿Invitamos a César?
2. ¿Le escribimos una carta a Matilde?
3. ¿Vendemos el carro a esa señora?
4. ¿Lo decimos a nuestros amigos?
5. ¿Ayudamos a Guadalupe?
6. ¿Nos ponemos el sombrero?
7. ¿Sacudimos los muebles?
8. ¿Nos quitamos el abrigo ahora?

CONVERSACIÓN

*¿Qué dicen estas personas?   Use mandatos con **nosotros.***

1. los marineros de Cristóbal Colón   brindar
2. Neil Armstrong   regresar a España
3. el dueño de la cafetería   ser buenos
4. los niños, antes de la Navidad   ir a la luna
5. un siquiatra   hablan de los sueños (*dreams*)
6. los invitados en una boda   vender más hamburguesas

44. *DE* PLUS A NOUN

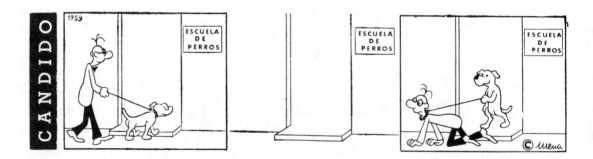

In English a noun can modify another noun in order to express the material of which something is made or the nature of a place or thing: *a **gold** watch, the **language** lab, a **summer** day.* In Spanish this structure is expressed by using the preposition **de: un reloj *de* oro, el laboratorio *de* lenguas, un día *de* verano.**

PRÁCTICA

A. *¿De qué material pueden ser estas cosas?*

una casa		adobe	plástico
una mesa		metal	diamantes
un plato	de	porcelana	cristal
un vaso		madera	plata (*silver*)
un anillo (*ring*)		oro	aluminio
una estatua			
una cadena (*chain*)			

B. *¿Qué encontramos en la universidad?*

el laboratorio		lenguas	física
un texto		francés	antropología
la clase	de	sicología	matemáticas
un(a) profesor(a)		química	inglés

C. *¿Cómo se dice en español?*

1. my Spanish book
2. a fall day
3. our science teacher
4. her telephone number

CONVERSACIÓN

A. *Describa Ud. estas cosas.*

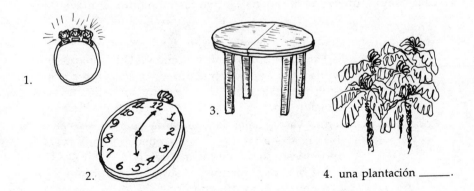

1.

2.

3.

4. una plantación _____.

B. *Imagínese que Ud. puede comprarle cualquier cosa a un(a) amigo/a. Describa Ud. los objetos que va a comprar.*

A _____ le voy a comprar un _____ de _____.

DIÁLOGO: Juntos para el futuro

© Elizabeth Hamlin 1978/Stock, Boston

Gerardo, estudiante de último° año de Derecho° y empleado de una   *last / law*
gran cadena de tiendas
Don Ramón, dueño de la cadena de tiendas y hombre ya mayor

A. En la oficina

DON RAMÓN: Estoy muy contento con tu trabajo, Gerardo.

GERARDO: Es Ud. muy amable, don Ramón. Ud. siempre me
ayuda y así aprendo mucho. Quiero que sepa que
estoy muy agradecido°. Pero mi ambición es ser   *grateful*
abogado y por eso ayer decidí dejar° mi puesto aquí.   *to leave*

DON RAMÓN: Pero, ¿vas a dejar la compañía cuando se van a
abrir dos tiendas más? ¿No puedes seguir trabajando y estudiando al mismo tiempo?

GERARDO: Imposible, don Ramón. Estoy en mi último año
y tengo muy poco tiempo libre°.   *free*

DON RAMÓN: Bueno, de acuerdo, hijo. Ojalá que te gradúes
pronto y bien. Es más°, quiero que sepas que tienes   **Es...** *what's more*
toda mi cooperación.

GERARDO: Mil gracias, don Ramón. Ojalá que comprenda mi
situación.

B. *Unas horas más tarde*

DON RAMÓN: Oye, Gerardo, tengo una idea. Esta mañana te di consejos. En el futuro, quiero que tú me des consejos a mí; consejos legales, ¿sabes?

GERARDO: Su confianza me honra. ¿En qué quiere que le dé consejos?

DON RAMÓN: Depende de tu especialización.

GERARDO: Si Dios quiere, me voy a especializar en derecho mercantil.

DON RAMÓN: ¡Muy bien, muchacho! Pues desde ahora pongamos de acuerdo nuestros planes. Tú vas a estudiar y terminar bien tu carrera° con tu especialización.   *course of studies*

GERARDO: ¿Y usted?

DON RAMÓN: Mientras tanto°, yo voy a continuar extendiendo la compañía por todas las capitales de provincia.   **Mientras...** *meanwhile*

GERARDO: Pero no quiero ser comerciante.

DON RAMÓN: Vamos poco a poco°, Gerardo. Primero quiero que tú te gradúes; también, que centralicemos los departamentos legales de la compañía...   **poco...** *little by little*

GERARDO: Es una buena idea, económica y eficiente.

DON RAMÓN: Hay más. Yo quiero que tú seas el director general de ese departamento central.

GERARDO: Ya veo, don Ramón, cuáles son sus planes. Estoy muy agradecido.

DON RAMÓN: Pues, ¡brindemos por mi futuro abogado!

GERARDO: ¡Brindemos por la compañía y por Ud., mi primer cliente!

Comprensión

¿Cierto o falso? Corrija las oraciones falsas.

A. 1. Gerardo estudia para comerciante.
2. Gerardo es un buen empleado.
3. A Gerardo le gusta su trabajo.
4. Gerardo va a dejar sus estudios porque su trabajo es más importante.
5. Don Ramón comprende la situación de Gerardo y quiere que se gradúe sin problemas.

B. 1. Gerardo le pide consejos a don Ramón.
2. Gerardo quiere especializarse en derecho civil.
3. Don Ramón quiere que los dos trabajen juntos en el futuro.
4. Don Ramón piensa centralizar los servicios legales de su compañía con un nuevo director general.
5. A Gerardo no le gusta mucho el plan de don Ramón.

Comentario cultural

Like the successful entrepreneur everywhere, don Ramón is interested in expanding and improving the efficiency of his enterprise. Gerardo—typical of the ambitious young man—is working and at the same time studying to complete an education that will enable him to improve his economic and social status. Don Ramón's fatherly attitude toward his employee is very normal in Hispanic culture.

The difference in status between don Ramón and Gerardo is shown linguistically by the fact that Gerardo always addresses his employer formally, using **Ud.** In fact, it would probably be a breach of etiquette for Gerardo to address don Ramón informally. On the other hand, don Ramón always addresses Gerardo informally, with **tú.** Indeed, Gerardo might feel somewhat uncomfortable if don Ramón were to address him with **Ud.** But once Gerardo graduates and becomes a professional, the relationship may become one in which they address each other as **tú.**

The dialog in this chapter would most likely take place between two men. However, more and more Hispanic women are entering the work force. In metropolitan areas, women of the lower classes have always worked out of necessity. Tradition, however, expected women—particularly middle-class and upper-class women—to stay at home and attend to the needs of the family. This tradition is gradually changing, and the percentage of women in the work force in Spanish America and Spain has increased rapidly in recent years. Increasing numbers of women are completing college, and many more are working in industry and entering the professions—law, medicine, and so on. A majority, however, continue to be employed in auxiliary occupations.

UN POCO DE TODO

A. *Form complete sentences based on the words given, in the order given. Conjugate the verbs, and add other words if necessary. // indicates the break between two sentences.*

1. yo / prohibir / que / Uds. / comprar / aquel / anillo / plata
2. ojalá / Lauro / venir / programa / música / argentina
3. Felipa / preferir / que / no / la / llamar / Carlos // llamar / la / nosotros
4. nosotros / insistir / que / tú / no / dejar / universidad // nosotros / querer / tú / graduarse / primero
5. yo / recomendar / que / Roberto / trabajar // divertirse / nosotros

B. *¿Cómo se dice en español?*

1. I don't want Mary to write the letter. I prefer that John do it.
2. We're going to ask them to come. I hope they do (come)!
3. So **(entonces)** you recommend that we visit Taxco? Let's go!
4. I hope it's not too **(demasiado)** late. Let's leave now.

5. I hope that Ana makes the dessert. But if she doesn't, let's make it together.
6. Why do you want us to go by bus? Let's fly.

C. *Working with another student, discuss the suggested situations, according to the
model.*

MODELO   Antonia / ayudar a Carmen en la tienda →
    ABEL: Quiero que *Antonia ayude a Carmen en la tienda.*
    JUANA: Ojalá que *la ayude.*
    ABEL: Y si no *la ayuda, ayudémosla* nosotros.
    JUANA: De acuerdo.

1. Federico / preparar una paella
2. la criada / limpiar el baño esta semana
3. los niños / cantar en la fiesta
4. Marcos / escribir un poema para el cumpleaños de Andrea
5. los señores Santana / invitar a nuestro amigo Ramón a la cena
6. Arturo / decirles la verdad a sus padres

D. *Make recommendations based on the following situations. Use the verbs suggested
on the right or any others you can think of.*

1. Ud. es ama de casa; la criada viene hoy. ¿Qué quiere Ud. que haga?
—Quiero que Ud. _____.

lavar la cafetera y los platos que están
   en la cocina
limpiar los muebles
sacar los vasos de cristal
prepararlo todo para una cena especial

2. Ud. es director(a) de una oficina. Hoy un nuevo empleado viene a la oficina por primera vez. ¿Qué consejos le va a dar Ud.?
—Recomiendo que Ud. _____.
—Ojalá que nosotros _____.

trabajar todos juntos aquí
llegar a la hora en punto
no dejar para mañana el trabajo de hoy
siempre estar de acuerdo con el jefe

3. Ud. es consejero/a universitario/a. Hoy tiene que hablar con un nuevo estudiante que quiere especializarse en español. ¿Qué le va a recomendar Ud.?
—Recomiendo que Ud. _____.

visitar el laboratorio de lenguas con frecuencia
conocer a todos los profesores del
   departamento
comprar un buen diccionario de
   español
hablar con unos estudiantes que están
   en su último año

E. *Working in groups, make a list of five things you would like someone else to do.
Then present each request to someone in the class, who must either do it, promise
to do it, or give a good excuse for not doing it.*

MODELO   *Queremos que Roberto nos traiga café mañana.* →
ROBERTO: —No les voy a traer café porque no tengo dinero.

VOCABULARIO

VERBOS
brindar   to toast (*with drink*)
cambiar (de)   to change
dejar   to leave (behind)
despedir (i, i)   to fire
encontrar (ue)   to find
especializarse   to major (*in an academic area*)
funcionar   to function
ganar   to earn; to win
graduarse   to graduate
mandar   to order
permitir   to permit, allow
prohibir   to prohibit, forbid
quitar   to take out, withhold
resolver (ue)   to solve, resolve

SUSTANTIVOS
el **anillo**   ring
el **aumento**   raise, increase
la **cadena**   chain
el/la **cliente**   client

el/la **comerciante**   merchant
la **compañía**   company
el **cheque**   check
el **deseo**   desire, wish
el/la **director(a)**   manager, director
el/la **dueño/a**   owner
el **gobierno**   government
el **hombre de negocios**   business man
el **impuesto**   tax
el/la **jefe/a**   boss
el **laboratorio**   lab, laboratory
la **madera**   wood
la **mujer de negocios**   business woman
el **negocio**   business
la **nota**   grade (*in a class*)
el/la **obrero/a**   worker, laborer
el **oficio**   trade
el **oro**   gold
la **plata**   silver
el/la **plomero/a**   plumber

el **puesto**   job
el **reloj**   watch, clock
el **semestre**   semester
el/la **siquiatra**   psychiatrist
el **sueldo**   salary

ADJETIVOS
juntos/as   together
último/a   last

PALABRAS Y EXPRESIONES ÚTILES
a veces   at times
así   so, thus, that way
desde   from
estar listo/a (para)   to be ready (to)
ojalá (que)...   I hope that . . .
ponerse de acuerdo   to reach an agreement, get together (*on an issue*)
por fin   finally

Un paso más 9

Actividades

A. **De ventajas y desventajas.** Todos los trabajos tienen sus ventajas y sus desventajas. Esta lista indica las perspectivas con respecto al número de puestos en los Estados Unidos y salario para personas aptas que aspiran a ciertas profesiones. Imagínese que Ud. trabaja en los puestos de la lista. ¿Qué le gusta de su trabajo? ¿Qué no le gusta? Considere el salario, las horas, los colegas, las condiciones de trabajo, etcétera.

PROFESIONES CON FUTURO					
Profesión (número de empleados)	Crecimiento° estimado de empleos hasta 1985	Perspectivas para aspirantes° aptos	Salario inicial típico	Salario típico de profesionales establecidos	*growth* *candidates*
Médicos (400.000)	37,8%	Excelentes	$17.000	$62.000	
Dentistas (130.000)	20,8%	Excelentes	$25.500	$47.000	
Veterinarios (30.500)	27,0%	Excelentes	$19.000	$39.000	
Analistas de sistemas (160.000)	32,9%	Excelentes	$19.000	$28.000	
Ingenieros (1.133.000)	32,0%	Buenas	$19.500	$34.000	
Geólogos (34.000)	38,1%	Buenas	$18.000	$31.000	
Administradores de personal° (335.000)	34,9%	Buenas	$18.000	$26.500 (Continúa...)	*personnel*

...Y CON PROBLEMAS

Abogados (460.000)	25,0%	Malas	$15.000	$29.000	
Profesores universitarios (593.000)	2,9%	Malas	$15.000	$29.000	
Biólogos (101.000)	29,3%	Malas	$14.500	$25.000	
Reporteros de diarios° (40.500)	13,9%	Malas	$13.000	$24.000	newspapers
Bibliotecarios° (128.000)	13,3%	Malas	$14.000	$20.000	librarians
Guardabosques° (25.000)	15,7%	Malas	$12.500	$20.000	forest rangers
Maestros° (2.475.000)	0,3%	Malas	$13.000	$16.000	teachers

MODELO   Administrador de personal →
Me gusta ayudar a otros a encontrar puestos.
Me gusta resolver los problemas entre los empleados.
Me gusta el salario.

No me gusta tener que despedir a los empleados.
No me gusta trabajar tantas horas.

B. **Recomendaciones.** Ud. es miembro de los grupos siguientes y quiere pedir (recomendar, etcétera) muchas cosas —el número máximo posible— a las personas indicadas. ¿Qué va a decir? Use los siguientes verbos:

pedir que	**insistir en que**	**preferir que**
recomendar que	**prohibir que**	**querer que**

1. un grupo de empleados, todos miembros de un sindicato (*union*) / a sus jefes
2. un grupo de prisioneros / al jefe de la prisión
3. un grupo de niños mimados (*spoiled*) / a sus padres
4. un grupo de viejos militantes (como las "Panteras Grises") / al gobierno
5. los padres / a un hijo de dieciséis años
6. los ciudadanos (*citizens*) de los Estados Unidos / al presidente
7. la consejera / a un grupo de estudiantes nuevos
8. _____ / a _____

A propósito...

In English we frequently use vocalized pauses ("uh," "um") and filler words ("well now," "okay," "let's see") when we don't quite know what to say or when we are looking for the right words. When you need a few seconds to collect your thoughts in Spanish, use one of the following expressions:

este	*uh, um*	**bien**	*well, OK*
pues	*well*	**a ver**	*let's see*
bueno	*well, OK*	**ahora bien**	*well now*

When you want to avoid taking a position on an issue, perhaps to avoid an argument, use one of these phrases:

En mi opinión...	*In my opinion . . .*	**Puede ser.**	*That might be.*
Depende.	*It depends.*	**Posiblemente.**	*Possibly.*
No sé.	*I don't know.*	**A veces.**	*At times.*
Tal vez.	*Perhaps.*	**¿Ud. cree?**	
Es posible.	*It's possible.*	**¿Tú crees?**	*Do you think so?*

C. **¿Cómo responde Ud.?** Un(a) amigo/a o un miembro de la familia pregunta o declara las siguientes opiniones. Ud. no está de acuerdo, pero no quiere ofender a la otra persona. ¿Cómo va a responder? Use algunas de las frases que aparecen en **A propósito.**

MODELO   Jorge trabaja mucho y debe recibir un aumento de salario. →
Puede ser, pero hay otros empleados que trabajan más que él y por eso ellos van a recibir el aumento.

Pues no sé. Me dicen que es un hombre muy simpático, pero, ¿de veras (really) *trabaja bien?*

1. El señor Gutiérrez es muy amable, ¿no?
2. El Rancho es un restaurante excelente.
3. Un novio/una novia es una limitación.
4. Las personas de los Estados Unidos son los únicos (*only*) americanos.
5. Limpiar la casa es muy divertido (*fun*).
6. Aquí tengo un libro muy interesante. ¿No quieres leer los artículos que tiene?

—*Lamento decirle que no podemos aceptar «depende» como parte del juramento°.*   oath

D. **¿Qué hacemos?** Give as many suggestions as possible for things that you might want to do in each of the following places.

MODELO   Estamos en la biblioteca. → *Estudiemos.*
                                            Busquemos el libro que tenemos que leer
                                            para la clase de historia.
                                            Durmamos.

1. Estamos en una discoteca.
2. Estamos en la oficina hablando y el jefe nos mira.
3. Estamos en la ciudad de Nueva York (Washington, D.C., San Francisco, etcétera).
4. Estamos en la sala de espera del aeropuerto.
5. Estamos en un restaurante mexicano.
6. Estamos en un museo de arte.
7. Estamos en un parque.
8. Estamos en España (México, la Argentina, etcétera).

E. **Buscando empleo.** Estos anuncios aparecieron en *ABC*, un diario (*newspaper*) de Madrid. En los dos anuncios se busca secretaria bilingüe, pero los puestos no son idénticos. Analice Ud. los aspectos siguientes de los dos puestos: salario, horario (*work schedule*), lenguas, habilidades (*skills*), nacionalidad. Después, prepare su propio (*own*) anuncio para otro puesto —médico/a, plomero/a, profesor(a), etcétera. Use frases cortas como las frases de los dos anuncios. Incluya muchos datos (*facts*) sobre los requisitos y las ventajas del puesto.

SECRETARIA BILINGÜE
español-inglés, para director general

SE REQUIERE:
- Dominio total del inglés y taquigrafía° en ambos idiomas.   *shorthand*
- Nacionalidad española.

SE OFRECE:
- Zona de trabajo en Generalísimo.
- Horario de 9 a 17,30 y 5 meses de 8,30 a 14,30.
- Salario: 700.000–800.000 ptas.° año.   *pesetas*
- Incorporación inmediata.

Interesadas llamar al Teléfono 261 43 92

COMPAÑÍA INTERNACIONAL
Busca
SECRETARIA
BILINGÜE

OFRECEMOS:
- Un trabajo interesante y variado.
- Un sueldo atractivo.
- Un excelente ambiente de trabajo.
- Jornada de trabajo° de lunes a viernes.   *jornada...work schedule*
- Zona Generalísimo.

SE REQUIERE:
- Dominio del idioma inglés hablado y escrito.
- Nacionalidad española o permiso de trabajo-residencia.
- Una experiencia de dos años.
- Mecanografía° perfecta.   *typing*

Interesadas enviar° urgentemente «curriculum   *send*
vitae» a: **Oficina de Empleo INEM. General
Pardiñas, 5. Madrid-1**, indicando en el sobre°   *envelope*
la Ref.° M-889.294   *referencia*

Study Hint: Reading

You will be able to read complex selections more easily and minimize the time you spend looking up words if you follow these suggestions:

1. Look at the title, the photographs or drawings, and the comprehension questions that accompany the reading *before* you read. This will give you a general idea about the kinds of information to expect.

2. Plan to "read" each reading several times. First, try to grasp general concepts rather than details. Don't look up every unfamiliar word during this reading. You will be able to guess the meaning of many new words from context the second time around.

3. Look for cognates—they are similar to their English equivalents in spelling and meaning. Here are some of the cognates that appear in the **Lectura cultural** in this chapter. What do they mean? Verbs: **apreciar, abandonar, documentar, disputar.** Nouns: **orientación, técnicas, frustraciones, obstáculos, burocracia, reforma.** Adjs.: **rutinarios, agraria.**

4. Be flexible when you give English equivalents to Spanish words, especially in the case of prepositions and phrases that might be idioms. If the standard or most frequent meaning of a word doesn't fit the context, try an alternate meaning.

5. If you "trip"—you thought you understood everything, but all of a sudden something doesn't make sense—go back and reread the entire paragraph or section. Isolate the subject, verb, and object of each sentence. Pay particular attention to verb endings and to pronouns in order to make certain that you know who is saying or doing what to whom.

6. *Now* look up any words that you cannot guess from context.

7. After you have gone through a paragraph once, go back and reread it quickly. And after going through the whole reading in this way, reread it all several times to develop reading fluency and to reinforce new vocabulary, structures, and information.

Lectura cultural: Hablemos de películas

Para muchos de nosotros el cine es un escape. Permite que salgamos de nuestros mundos rutinarios y que entremos en mundos diferentes. Los hispanos, como los norteamericanos, saben apreciar este nuevo arte del siglo° XX, y en muchos de los países hispánicos se producen películas de alta calidad°.

century
alta... *high quality*

Sin duda, muchos norteamericanos están familiarizados con las películas de Luis Buñuel, el gran director español que nos dio películas famosísimas como *Tristana* y *Viridiana*. Pero desgraciadamente muy pocos americanos han tenido° la ocasión de apreciar películas menos conocidas como *Los Tarantos*, una versión gitana° de *Romeo y Julieta*, dirigida° por Rovira-Beleta. En esta película, el director coloca° la acción en Barcelona y allí, Rafael Taranto, joven de una familia pobre, se enamora de° Juana Zoronga, hija de una familia rica. La película sigue la obra° de Shakespeare, pero el director coloca la acción en lugares reales, y las emociones se expresan mediante° el baile flamenco de los gitanos.

han... *have had*
gypsy / directed
places
se... *falls in love with*
work

through, via

Hoy día en Hispanoamérica se producen películas en casi todos los países, en especial en la Argentina, México, Perú, Bolivia y Cuba. Las

Peter Menzel/Stock, Boston

películas de mayor calidad de esos países llevan una orientación socio-política.   Los directores desean que el público piense en los problemas que confrontan diariamente los hispanoamericanos.   Dentro de este tipo de película se encuentran:

Lucía (Cuba, 1969): presenta el papel° de la mujer en la historia cubana   *role*

Don Segundo Sombra (Argentina, 1969): documenta la vida en las pampas durante los primeros años del siglo XX

Yawar Mallku (Bolivia, 1969): estudia los problemas socio-políticos del indio boliviano

De todas las películas hispanoamericanas, *La muralla° verde* (Perú, 1970)   *wall* tiene una verdadera reputación internacional.   En esta película, usando las técnicas más modernas, el director Robles Godoy presenta las frustraciones de una familia joven (padre, madre e hijo) que decide abandonar la ciudad para ir a vivir en la selva°.   Venciendo° muchos obstáculos, se   *jungle / overcoming* establecen idílicamente en la selva.   Pero su felicidad es destruida°   *destroyed* cuando una culebra venenosa muerde° al hijo y cuando la burocracia de la   **culebra...** *poisonous* Comisión de Reforma Agraria disputa su título a la tierra.   *snake bites*

Comprensión

Check your understanding of the reading selection by answering the following questions:

1. ¿Qué representa el cine para mucha gente?
2. ¿Quiénes son dos directores españoles?
3. ¿Qué interés puede tener *Los Tarantos* para un público de habla española?
4. En general, ¿cómo es el cine hispanoamericano?
5. ¿Qué interés puede tener una película como *Lucía*?
6. ¿Por qué es importante la película *La muralla verde*? ¿Cuál es el tema de esta película?

Ejercicios escritos

A. Escriba un párrafo sobre su película favorita. Las preguntas siguientes pueden ayudarle a organizar sus ideas.

   1. ¿Cuál es el título de su película favorita?
   2. ¿Quién es el/la director(a)?
   3. ¿Quiénes son los actores/las actrices?
   4. ¿Quiénes son los protagonistas (*main characters*)?
   5. ¿Cuál es el tema?

B. ¿Quién es su actor/actriz favorito/a? Descríbalo/la, pero no indique su nombre. Lea su descripción y pídales a sus compañeros de clase que adivinen (*guess*) quién es.

   1. ¿Cómo es? (alto, bajo / joven, viejo / rubio, moreno / etcétera)
   2. ¿En qué película (o programa de televisión) trabaja?
   3. ¿Hace papeles cómicos? ¿dramáticos?

capítulo 10 El coche

Jerry Frank/DPI

OBJETIVOS

In this chapter you will learn vocabulary and expressions related to cars and driving.

You will also learn to use the subjunctive in the following situations:

45. after expressions of emotion (*I'm glad that* _____)
46. after expressions of doubt (*I don't think that* _____)
47. after many impersonal expressions (*It's necessary that* _____)
48. after **tal vez** and **quizá(s),** both of which mean *perhaps*

Un paso más includes activities related to forms of transportation, road signs in Spanish-speaking countries, and cars in general. It also includes a reading about the kinds of transportation available in the Hispanic world.

VOCABULARIO: PREPARACIÓN

Los automóviles

el aceite	oil	**arrancar**	to start
la batería	battery	**arreglar**	to fix, repair
el camino	street, road	**contener** (like	to contain, hold
la carretera	highway	**tener)**	
la esquina	corner (of	**doblar**	to turn
	a street)	**estacionar(se)**	to park
la estación de gaso-	gas station	**gastar (mucha**	to use (a lot of
lina/la gasolinera		**gasolina)**	gas)
los frenos	brakes	**llenar (el**	to fill (the tank)
la gasolina	gasoline	**tanque)**	
la licencia (de	(driver's)	**manejar**	to drive
manejar)	license	**parar**	to stop
la llanta	tire	**seguir (todo**	to keep on going;
una llanta desinflada	a flat tire	**derecho)**	to go (straight ahead)

A. Describa Ud. las cosas y acciones que se ven en el dibujo.

B. **Definiciones.** *Match the description with the appropriate item.*

1. Se pone en el tanque.
2. Se llenan de aire.
3. Lubrica el motor.
4. Es necesaria para arrancar el carro.
5. Cuando se llega a una esquina hay que hacer esto o seguir todo derecho.
6. No contiene aire y por eso hay que cambiarla.
7. Es un camino público, ancho (*wide*) y espacioso.
8. Se usan para parar el coche.
9. El policía nos la pide cuando nos para en el camino.
10. Allí se vende gasolina y se arreglan los carros.
11. Gasta pocos litros de gasolina.

a. los frenos
b. doblar
c. la carretera
d. la batería
e. la gasolinera
f. una llanta desinflada
g. la gasolina
h. las llantas
i. el aceite
j. un carro económico
k. la licencia

C. *De estas frases, ¿cuáles describen la forma de manejar de Ud.?*

1. Prefiero manejar por las carreteras —no me gustan los caminos municipales porque tienen muchos semáforos (*traffic lights*).
2. Con frecuencia dejo mi licencia en casa cuando voy a manejar.
3. Acelero (*I speed up*) cuando doblo una esquina.
4. Cuando no sé cómo llegar a mi destino, sigo todo derecho.
5. Nunca manejo después de beber.
6. Siempre observo el límite de velocidad.
7. Nunca estaciono el coche donde dice «Prohibido estacionarse».

© Katherine A. Lambert

Comprando un carro			
la agencia (de automóviles)	(car) dealership	**firmar**	to sign
		funcionar	to run, work (machines)
la ganga	bargain		
el pago inicial	down payment	**pagar a plazos**	to pay for in
el/la vendedor(a)	salesperson		installments

D. *¿Desea Ud. un coche nuevo? Llene los espacios con palabras de **Comprando un carro.***

Si Ud. quiere comprar un carro nuevo, va a tener que visitar una _____.   Allí hay muchos modelos nuevos.   Para comprar un coche, tiene que hablar con el _____.   Si Ud. busca un coche muy barato, o sea (*that is*), una _____, tiene que ir a muchas agencias.   Después de examinar muchos coches, por fin decide comprar uno. Ud. habla con el vendedor y le pregunta si es posible manejar el coche, para ver cómo es. Cuando regresa Ud., le da al vendedor un cheque —es el _____. Como Ud. no tiene todo el dinero, el vendedor le da un plan para _____. Ud. _____ los papeles necesarios y va a celebrar. ¡Felicitaciones y...buena suerte! Ojalá que el carro _____ bien.

E. *Su viejo carro no arrancó esta mañana y en el garaje dicen que no lo pueden arreglar. Es hora de comprar un carro nuevo pero ¿qué tipo de carro desea Ud.?*

Yo deseo un carro _____.

1. grande / económico
2. con una transmisión de cambios (*manual shift*) / con una transmisión automática
3. con llantas convencionales / con llantas radiales
4. con aire acondicionado / sin aire acondicionado
5. con radio AM / con radio AM/FM / sin radio
6. con frenos regulares / con frenos de disco

PRONUNCIACIÓN: More on Linking

When you say an English sentence, such as *They don't like to wash windows*, you link the words together with no breaks between them. Natural pauses tend to occur just at phrase and sentence breaks, not between all words. The Spanish speaker links the words of a sentence together in the same way. Because the Spanish language is still new to you, however, you may tend to pause slightly between words. To overcome this tendency, practice pronouncing whole phrases and sentences as a single connected sequence: **Nolesgustalavarlasventanas.**

In English, adjacent vowels at word breaks are often separated by a slight "pop" or catch in the voice called a *glottal stop* (phonetic symbol [ʔ]): *theʔapple, toʔunderstand*. The glottal stop is never used in Spanish. Be especially careful to link adjacent vowels in Spanish: **para usted, la casa entera.** Adjacent like vowels become one in rapid Spanish: **mi hijo** → [mixo], **qué es** → [kes].

PRÁCTICA

1. el abuelo el hijo el autobús el elefante el otoño
2. los Andes los errores los habitantes las azafatas las ideas
3. es Andrés es increíble es ella son interesantes somos americanos
4. con Adela con Eduardo con Inés con ellas mis hermanos tus animales
5. de usted para ella se habla no estudian lo usan me invitaron
6. mi hijo me escucha la arregló la abuela lo oyó

7. Aquí hay ocho estudiantes.
8. Tiene un hijo y una hija.
9. ¿A qué hora es la ópera?
10. Viven así en el Ecuador.
11. ¿Qué es esto?

MINIDIÁLOGOS Y GRAMÁTICA

---

45. USE OF SUBJUNCTIVE AFTER EXPRESSIONS OF EMOTION

© Bob Combs 1975/Rapho/Photo Researchers, Inc.

Un futuro peatón

ANITA: ¿Qué tal el tráfico en la carretera esta mañana?

CARLOS: Un desastre, un verdadero desastre. Pasé dos horas al volante, un policía me puso una multa porque no paré en un semáforo en rojo, y ahora *tengo miedo* de que no *esté* totalmente bien la transmisión.

ANITA: ¡Chico, con todos los problemas que tienes para llegar por la mañana, *me sorprende* que no *vengas* a vivir en la oficina!

---

1. *Para Carlos, ¿es fácil llegar a la oficina?*
2. *¿Qué le pasó a Carlos esta mañana?*
3. *¿De qué tiene miedo Carlos?*
4. *¿Dónde vive Carlos ahora? ¿cerca de la oficina?*
5. *¿Dónde recomienda Anita que viva Carlos? ¿Por qué?*

A future pedestrian ANITA: How was the highway traffic this morning? CARLOS: Terrible, just terrible. I spent two hours at the wheel, a policeman gave me a ticket (fine) because I didn't stop at a red light, and now I'm afraid that the transmission isn't quite right. ANITA: Boy, with all of the problems you have getting here in the morning, I'm surprised that you don't come to live at the office.

Independent Clause		Dependent Clause
<u> indicative </u> (expression of emotion)	**que**	<u> subjunctive </u>

Esperamos que Ud. **pueda** asistir.   *We hope (that) you'll be able to come.*
Tengo miedo (de) que el abuelo   *I'm afraid (that) my grandfather is*
esté muy enfermo.   *very ill.*

Expressions of emotion are those in which speakers express their feelings:
I'm glad you're here; We hope they can come. Such expressions of emotion
are followed by the subjunctive mood in the dependent clause in Spanish.

Expressions of emotion include **alegrarse (de)** *(to be happy about),*
esperar, gustar, sentir (ie, i) *(to regret or feel sorry),* **me** *(te, le, and so on),*
sorprende *(it is surprising to me [you, him]),* **temer** *(to fear),* and **tener
miedo (de).** Since not all expressions of emotion are given here, remember that any expression of emotion—not just certain verbs—is followed
by the subjunctive.

Remember to use the infinitive—not the subjunctive—after expressions
of emotion when there is no change of subject.

      Siento **estar** tan cansado.   *I'm sorry to be so tired.*
but
      Siento que **estés** tan cansado.   *I'm sorry (that) you're so tired.*

PRÁCTICA

A. Dé Ud. frases nuevas según las indicaciones.

1. —¿Cuáles son algunas de las cosas que le gustan a Ud.?
   —Me gusta que _____. *(estar contentos mis amigos, funcionar bien mi coche,
   venir muchos a mis fiestas, divertirse mis amigos en mi casa, estar bien mis
   padres)*
2. —Todos tenemos miedo de algo. ¿De qué tiene miedo Ud.?
   —Tengo miedo de que _____. *(haber mucho tráfico en la carretera mañana,
   no venir nadie a mi fiesta, tener una llanta desinflada el carro, costar demasiado
   arreglar mi carro, haber un examen mañana, pasarles algo a mis maletas, haber
   una crisis internacional)*
3. —A Uds. les sorprende que el español sea tan fácil, ¿verdad? ¿A quién
   le sorprende?
   —A Juan le sorprende que el español sea tan fácil. *(mí, todos los estudiantes,
   ti, nosotros, Armando, vosotros)*

*B. Complete las frases con la forma apropiada del verbo indicado. Use el subjuntivo
si es necesario.*

1. Dicen en la agencia que mi carro nuevo *es* económico, pero temo que el carro no _____.
2. Los empleados dicen que van a *llegar* al trabajo más temprano. Espero que _____.
3. El jefe *está* enfermo. Siento que el jefe _____.
4. El profesor dice que va a *haber* un examen y que los exámenes *son* necesarios. Los estudiantes sienten que _____.
5. Nos gustan las clases, pero nos divertimos más cuando *hay* vacaciones. Nos alegramos de que _____ vacaciones en verano.
6. El policía me dice que no me *va* a poner una multa. Me alegro de que _____.

C. *Form complete sentences by using one word or phrase from each column. Use the appropriate form of the verb: indicative in the main clause, subjunctive in the dependent clause.*

yo			tu carro viejo	(no) ser de plata
el mecánico	sentir		la agencia de	(no) ser una ganga
tú	temer	que	automóviles	poder pagar a plazos
la vendedora	alegrarse (de)		el mecánico	el carro
_____			mi nuevo carro	tener que cambiar
			nosotros	las llantas
			el anillo	(no) arrancar
				(no) tener todavía los nuevos modelos
				tener que arreglar la transmisión
				gastar tanta gasolina
				_____

D. *¿Cómo se dice en español?*

I'm sorry your daughter is sick, and I hope that the doctor can help her quickly. I'm glad that your son is feeling better.

CONVERSACIÓN

A. *¿Qué piensan estas personas? Conteste las preguntas según los dibujos.*

1. ¿Qué siente Jorge?   2. ¿Qué espera Fausto?   3. ¿Qué teme Mariana?

B. *Ud. es mecánico/a y encuentra muchos problemas con el coche de un cliente. ¿Cuáles son? Ud. y el cliente pueden hablar de los frenos de disco, la transmisión, el aire acondicionado, las llantas, la batería, el radiador, el aceite, etcétera. Use estas palabras como guía.*

Temo que
Recomiendo que
Me sorprende que

su _____ estar roto
no funcionar bien _____
poner un(a) _____ nuevo/a
arreglar _____
ir a costarle _____
no hay _____ en _____

_____

C. *Complete las oraciones en una forma lógica.*

1. Espero que mi mejor amigo/a _____.
2. Espero _____ mañana.
3. Me alegro de que mis padres _____.
4. Me sorprende que en esta clase _____.
5. Siento que _____.
6. Tengo miedo de que el/la profesor(a) _____.
7. Me gusta que mi novio/a (esposo/a) _____.
8. Me gusta _____.

46. USE OF SUBJUNCTIVE AFTER EXPRESSIONS OF DOUBT

Independent Clause		Dependent Clause
indicative (expression of doubt)	**que**	subjunctive

No creo que **sean** estudiantes.   *I don't believe they're students.*
No están seguros de que Roberto   *They're not sure that Roberto is right.*
tenga razón.

Expressions of doubt are those in which speakers express uncertainty or denial: *I doubt he's right; We're not sure that they're Puerto Ricans.* Such expressions of doubt, however strong or weak, are followed by the subjunctive in the dependent clause in Spanish.

Expressions of doubt include **no creer, dudar** (*to doubt*), **no estar seguro,** and **negar (ie)** (*to deny*). Not all Spanish expressions of doubt are given here. Remember that any expression of doubt is followed by the subjunctive in the dependent clause.

When there is no subject change, Spanish uses either the subjunctive or the infinitive after expressions of doubt.

> Dudo que **tenga** el dinero.
> Dudo **tener** el dinero.   *I doubt that I have the money.*

Indicative Versus Subjunctive

No creer, dudar, no estar seguro, and **negar** are followed by the subjunctive. However, **creer, no dudar, estar seguro,** and **no negar** are usually followed by the indicative, since they do not express doubt, denial, or negation.

No niego que **es** simpático.	*I don't deny that he's nice.*

but

Niego que **sea** simpático.	*I deny that he's a nice person.*

Estamos seguros que el examen **es** hoy.	*We're sure the exam is today.*

but

No estamos seguros que el examen **sea** hoy.	*We're not sure that the exam is today.*

Creo que **son** ricos.	*I believe they're rich.*

but

No creo que **sean** ricos.	*I don't believe they're rich.*

In questions with **creer,** the use of the indicative or the subjunctive in the dependent clause reflects the opinion of the person asking the question.

Indicative:	¿Crees que los Ramírez **son** ricos?	*Do you think the Ramirezes are rich?* (The speaker believes they are.)
Subjunctive:	¿Crees que los Ramírez **sean** ricos?	*Do you think the Ramirezes are rich?* (The speaker doubts that they are rich or does not know whether they are.)

PRÁCTICA

A. *Dé Ud. frases nuevas según las indicaciones.*

1. —Se necesita un mecánico. ¿Hay un buen mecánico en la clase?
   —Dudo que *Luis* sea un buen mecánico. (*tú, el/la profesor(a), ellos, nosotros, Ud., vosotros*)
2. —¿Por qué no funciona bien el carro? ¿Es la transmisión?
   —No, *no creo* que sea la transmisión. (*creo, dudo, estoy segura/o, niego, no dudo, no estoy segura/o*)

B. *Form complete sentences by using one word or phrase from each column. Make any necessary changes in the dependent clause.*

(No) Creo		es buena idea manejar sin licencia
(No) Dudo		es bueno manejar a 55 millas por hora
(No) Niego	que	es necesario tener un carro con aire acondicionado
(No) Estoy segura/o		el español es más fácil que el inglés

todos los vendedores de autos usados son deshonestos

los carros modernos son maravillas de economía

los casados están más contentos que los solteros

los hombres siempre deben pagarlo todo en una cita

las mujeres no son buenas para estacionar el carro

hay vida en los otros planetas

es necesario leer un contrato antes de firmarlo

C. *¿Cómo se dice en español? ¿Qué va a pasar en clase mañana?*

There's an exam, but I'm not sure that it's tomorrow. I doubt that the subjunctive is **(entrar)** on the test, and I don't think there will be commands. Do you think it will be easy?

CONVERSACIÓN

A. *¿Cómo van a contestar estas personas las preguntas? ¿Y cómo contesta Ud.?*

1. ¿El carro es económico?   2. ¿El niño tiene catorce años?

3. ¿El hombre puede volar?   4. ¿Cuatro y cuatro son nueve?

B. *Escriba Ud. dos frases controversistas* (controversial) *y pregúnteles a los otros miembros de la clase su opinión sobre ellas. ¿Cuántos están de acuerdo con las opiniones expresadas en las frases y cuántos no?*

MODELOS   *Creo que el aborto debe ser legal.*
             No creo que se deba fumar marihuana.

C. *Complete Ud. las oraciones en una forma lógica.*

1. Mis amigos (no) creen que _____.
2. Yo (no) dudo que _____.
3. (No) Estoy seguro/a que _____.
4. Yo (no) creo que _____.
5. (No) Niego que _____.

47. USE OF SUBJUNCTIVE AFTER IMPERSONAL EXPRESSIONS

¿Por qué no anda el carro?
ESPOSA: Querido, el carro no arranca.
ESPOSO: *Es probable* que *sea* la batería.
ESPOSA: No puede ser. Es nueva.
ESPOSO: Entonces, *es posible* que *haya* un problema con la transmisión.
         Ayer me dio la impresión de que...
ESPOSA: No querido, nada de eso. Es que ayer nos olvidamos de
         llenar el tanque.

1. *¿Qué problema tiene la esposa con el carro?*
2. *¿Qué explicaciones da el esposo?*
3. *¿Cuál es la verdadera causa del problema?*

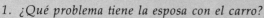

Why won't the car run? WIFE: Dear, the car won't start. HUSBAND: It's probably (probable that it is) the battery. WIFE: That can't be. It's new. HUSBAND: Then it's possible that there's a problem with the transmission. Yesterday I had the feeling that . . . WIFE: No, dear, nothing like that. The fact is that yesterday we forgot to fill the tank.

A. Impersonal expressions are followed by the infinitive when no other subject is expressed: **Es necesario estudiar.**
B. Where there is a specific subject in the dependent clause, impersonal expressions of willing, emotion, and doubt—like other verbs that express those concepts—are followed by the subjunctive.

Independent Clause		Dependent Clause
indicative (impersonal expression of willing, emotion, or doubt)	que	subjunctive

Es necesario que Álvaro **estudie** más. — *It's necessary for Álvaro to study more (that he study more).*
Es terrible que **haya** tantos crímenes. — *It's terrible that there is so much crime.*

C. Impersonal expressions of **willing** include **es necesario, es importante, es urgente, es preferible,** and **es preciso** (*necessary*).
D. Impersonal expressions of **emotion** include **es terrible, es ridículo, es mejor/bueno/malo, es increíble, es extraño** (*strange*), **qué extraño, es lástima** (*shame*), and **qué lástima** (*what a shame*).
E. Impersonal expressions of **doubt** include **es posible, es imposible, es probable, es improbable, no es verdad, no es cierto** (*certain*), and **no es seguro.**
F. Impersonal expressions that express certainty are not followed by the subjunctive. These include **es verdad, es seguro, es cierto, es evidente,** and **no hay duda.**

Es verdad que **maneja** bien. — *It's true (that) she drives well.*
No hay duda que el coche **es** una ganga. — *There's no doubt (that) the car is a bargain.*

PRÁCTICA

A. *Dé Ud. frases nuevas según las indicaciones.*

1. —El carro del profesor Corrales es viejo y él gasta mucho dinero en gasolina y reparaciones (*repairs*).
   —Sí, es *necesario* que compre otro carro. (*mejor, cierto, posible, seguro, probable*)
2. —Hay muchas cosas que hacer para la fiesta. ¿Qué hay que hacer?
   —Es preciso que alguien _____. (*comprar la cerveza, limpiar el apartamento, buscar unos discos, invitar a los amigos, traer la comida*)

B. *Form new sentences by using one word or phrase from each column. Choose the correct verb forms from those in italics.*

Es importante
Es terrible
Es imposible   que
Es verdad

Ernesto *trabaja/trabaje* tanto
cuesta/cueste mucho llenar el tanque de un carro
encontramos/encontremos una ganga en la agencia
el español se *habla/hable* mucho en el mundo de hoy
nos *levantamos/levantemos* temprano mañana
el carro *funciona/funcione* sin transmisión
vamos/vayamos a la Argentina el año que viene
hay/haya guerras (*wars*) en el mundo
Juan *sale/salga* todas las noches, que no *estudia/
      estudie* nunca y que *recibe/reciba* buenas notas
seguimos/sigamos todo derecho

CONVERSACIÓN

A. *Algunos creen que las frases siguientes describen el mundo de hoy. ¿Qué cree Ud.? Reaccione Ud. a estas frases, empezando con una de estas expresiones:*

Es bueno/malo que _____   Es extraño que _____
Es lástima que _____   (No) Es verdad que _____
Es increíble que _____   No hay duda que _____
Es terrible que _____

1. Los niños ven la televisión seis horas al día.
2. Hay mucha pobreza (*poverty*) en el mundo.
3. En los Estados Unidos, gastamos mucha energía.
4. Hay mucho sexo y violencia en la televisión y en las películas.
5. Se come poco y mal en muchas partes del mundo.
6. Los niños de habla española reciben una buena educación en los Estados Unidos.
7. Hay mucho interés en la exploración del espacio.
8. El fumar (*smoking*) no es malo para la salud (*health*).

Indique Ud. soluciones para algunos de los problemas. Empiece las soluciones con

Es urgente que _____   Es necesario que _____
Es preferible que _____   Es importante que _____

B. *Complete las oraciones en una forma lógica.*

1. Es lástima que _____.
2. Es ridículo que _____.
3. Es evidente que _____.
4. Es improbable que _____.
5. No es seguro que _____.
6. Es preciso que _____.

48. USE OF SUBJUNCTIVE AFTER *TAL VEZ* AND *QUIZÁ(S)*

Tal vez le cueste a Ud. menos comprar un carro nuevo.

If the speaker wishes to imply doubt or uncertainty, he or she uses **tal vez** and **quizá/quizás** (*perhaps, maybe*), followed by the subjunctive, in a single-clause sentence.

Tal vez esté en casa ya.	*Maybe she's already home.*
Quizá(s) sean cubanos.	*Perhaps they're Cuban.*

When **tal vez** or **quizá/quizás** follows the verb, the indicative is normally used.

Es la batería, **quizá.**	*It's the battery, maybe.*

PRÁCTICA

*Make the following sentences reflect doubt or uncertainty by beginning each with **tal vez** or **quizá(s)** and changing the verb to the subjunctive.*

1. Eso se anuncia en la radio.
2. Volvemos mañana.
3. Estela está viajando con su madre.
4. Se prohíbe estacionarse en aquella calle.
5. Los visitamos en verano.
6. Hace calor esta tarde.
7. Es mayor que su hermano.
8. No hay gasolina en el tanque.
9. Toman aquel camino.
10. Se dobla en esa esquina.

CONVERSACIÓN

A. *¿Cómo se ganan la vida* (earn their living) *estas personas? ¿Cuál es su profesión?*

   1. Con frecuencia la ropa de este hombre está sucia al final del día. Pasa el día llenando y arreglando cosas. No debe fumar cuando trabaja porque es peligroso (*dangerous*). Tal vez _____.
   2. Estas dos personas llevan uniforme y gorra (*cap*) cuando trabajan. Su trabajo es muy importante y peligroso. Trabajan con el público y tienen que volar mucho. Trabajan juntos pero no están juntos siempre en el trabajo. Tal vez _____.

   Describa Ud. otra profesión, usando los párrafos anteriores como modelo, y presente su descripción a la clase.

B. *Diga Ud. tres cosas que va a hacer mañana... quizá. Use Ud. su imaginación —no tiene que decir la verdad. Empiece Ud. cada frase con **tal vez.***

DIÁLOGO: Un carro nuevo... ¿una compra esencial?

José Luis (Pepe) y Ángela, recién casados°   recién... *newlyweds*
Don Gregorio, el padre de Ángela, hombre de buena posición
económica

A. *En el coche*

DON GREGORIO: Miren, allí en la esquina está la agencia de que les
               hablé.

JOSÉ LUIS: ¿Todavía insiste Ud. en que cambiemos el auto-
               móvil?

ÁNGELA: Papá, compramos éste el año pasado y todavía
               funciona bien.

DON GREGORIO: Pero, Pepe, no creo que un vendedor como tú deba
               manejar un trasto antiguo° de tiempos de la   trasto... *old clunker*
               Segunda Guerra Mundial°. ¿Qué van a pensar tus   Segunda... *Second*
               clientes? Si quieres dar una buena impresión en   *World War*
               el mundo de los negocios...

B. *En la agencia de automóviles*

VENDEDOR: Buenas tardes, señores. ¿En qué puedo servirles?

JOSÉ LUIS: Buscamos un coche económico, de seis cilindros...

ÁNGELA: Pero es probable que no lo compremos ahora.

VENDEDOR: ¡Quién piensa en eso! No hay ninguna obliga-
               ción... Antes que nada°, vean Uds. uno de los   Antes... *first of all*
               nuevos modelos. Líneas modernas, frenos de
               disco, transmisión automática, radio, calefacción
               y aire acondicionado, todo incluido en el precio.
               ¡Una ganga!

ÁNGELA: No diga más. ¡Toda una maravilla de belleza° y de   *beauty*
               funcionamiento°! Pero dudo que sea una ganga.   *performance*

JOSÉ LUIS: No sé. Déjeme pensar... Tal vez podamos dar
               nuestro coche viejo como pago inicial y luego
               pagamos a plazos la diferencia.

VENDEDOR: No veo por qué no. Primero tasamos° el coche de   *we'll appraise*
               ustedes y luego arreglamos cuentas°. ¿En qué   *terms*
               banco tienen su cuenta°?   *account*

DON GREGORIO: Mire Ud., no hablemos de cuentas. Yo le ayudo a
               pagar.

C. *En la estación de gasolina, unos meses más tarde*

JOSÉ LUIS: Lléneme el tanque, por favor.

EMPLEADO: ¿Quiere que le revise° las llantas y el aceite?   *check*

JOSÉ LUIS: Sí, por favor, y el agua de la batería y del radiador.

ÁNGELA:	Temo que estemos gastando mucha gasolina, ¿no, Pepe?	
JOSÉ LUIS:	Yo lo calculé la semana pasada y estoy seguro que en la carretera no llegamos a los diez kilómetros por litro° que nos prometió el vendedor. Y temo que en la ciudad gaste aún más°.	**diez...** *10 kilometers per liter (22.6 miles per gallon)* **aún...** *even more*
EMPLEADO:	Fueron diez litros y medio de gasolina, señor... seiscientos pesos justos°.	*exactly*
JOSÉ LUIS:	¡Válgame Dios!° Con estos precios, necesito clientes —¡pronto!	**¡Válgame...!** *For heaven's sake!*

Comprensión

¿Cierto o falso?   Corrija las oraciones falsas.

A. 1. Don Gregorio no quiere que José Luis compre un automóvil nuevo.
   2. El coche de José Luis y Ángela está en muy malas condiciones.
   3. Según don Gregorio, José Luis debe manejar un coche nuevo para impresionar a sus clientes.
   4. Don Gregorio no trata de influir en la decisión de José Luis y Ángela.

B. 1. Ángela piensa comprar un coche hoy.
   2. Según el vendedor, no importa que no compren nada.
   3. Ángela cree todo lo que (*what*) dice el vendedor.
   4. Después de hablar con el vendedor, parece que a José Luis le gusta la idea de comprar un coche nuevo.
   5. Don Gregorio les va a ayudar en la compra del automóvil.

C. 1. El coche nuevo es una verdadera ganga.
   2. Gasta mucha gasolina.
   3. La gasolina es muy barata.

Comentario cultural

As in many societies, in Hispanic culture outward appearance is important, particularly among the middle class.   When don Gregorio says, —¿**Qué van a pensar tus clientes?** he is expressing in a different way the phrase that most Hispanics have very likely heard many times—¿**Qué dirán?** (*What will they say?*), commonly referred to as **el qué dirán.**   Although individualism is very much a part of the Hispanic character, what others think is also important, and one often feels obliged to do what society expects, given one's age, position, and status.

As is the case in the dialog, it is common for a son-in-law to get along well with, and accept advice from, his wife's parents.   He has been a visitor in her home many times during their courtship; on the other hand, she may not be very familiar with his home or family.   For economic reasons urban newlyweds often have to postpone having an apartment or condominium of their own.   In that situation they most frequently live with the parents of the bride, a custom described in the saying: **Tu hijo se casa y pierdes** (*you lose*) **tu hijo; tu hija se casa y ganas otro.**

UN POCO DE TODO

A. *Form complete sentences based on the words given, in the order given. Conjugate the verbs, and add other words if necessary.*

   1. nosotros / esperar / que / Julio / firmar / pero / tal vez / no / querer
   2. ellos / negar / que / Adolfo / ser / bueno / mecánico
   3. tal vez / ser / batería / —yo no / estar / seguro
   4. agente / ir / alegrarse / que / nosotros / darle / pago inicial / hoy
   5. ser / evidente / que / Ud. / no / creer / que yo / ser / bueno / estudiante

B. *¿Cómo se dice en español?*

   1. We're sorry you can't be there. Perhaps you'll come next year.
   2. I doubt that it's necessary to work so much **(tanto).**
   3. I'm surprised it's so sunny now. But it's possible it will rain later.
   4. It's true that the highway is better, but that road is more interesting.
   5. We're sure they know her, but we doubt that they know her mother.

C. *Working with another student, ask and answer questions according to the model.*

   MODELO   preparar la cena →

       JUAN: ¿Es posible que Eloisa *prepare la cena?*
       SILVIA: Bueno, no creo que *la prepare.*
       JUAN: Quizá *la prepare* su hermano.

   1. comprar aquel carro tan barato
   2. poder arreglar el radiador
   3. visitar a Ramiro en el hospital
   4. tocar el piano en la fiesta
   5. conocer a los padres de Evita
   6. saber el número de teléfono de Mateo

D. *Make at least five statements about yourself or about your family. At least one of the five should be false. The class will react to your statements, beginning their reactions with phrases such as*

   Es probable que _____   **Dudo que** _____
   Me alegro de que _____   **Es posible que** _____ **pero yo no lo**
   Me sorprende que _____ **pero lo creo.**   **creo.**
   Es imposible que _____

E. *Adopt the identity of each of the following persons and describe two things about which they might be either happy or concerned. Begin your statements with phrases such as* me alegro de que, temo que, no creo que, *and* espero que.

1. una persona de noventa años
2. un(a) turista hispano/a en los Estados Unidos
3. un(a) turista norteamericano/a en Latinoamérica
4. un(a) policía

VOCABULARIO

VERBOS

alegrarse (de) to be happy (about)
arrancar to start (*with cars*)
arreglar to fix, repair
contener (ie) to contain, hold
describir to describe
dudar to doubt
estacionar(se) to park
firmar to sign
funcionar to run, work (*with machines*)
gastar to use, expend
haber *infinitive form of* **hay** (there is/are)
llenar to fill
manejar to drive
negar (ie) to deny
parar to stop
prometer to promise
sentir (ie, i) to regret, to feel sorry
sorprender to be surprising
temer to fear

SUSTANTIVOS

el **aceite** oil
el **automóvil** car, automobile
la **batería** battery
el **camino** street, road
la **carretera** highway
la **compra** purchase
la **esquina** corner (*of a street*)
la **estación de gasolina** gas station
los **frenos** brakes
la **ganga** bargain
la **gasolina** gasoline
la **gasolinera** gas station
la **licencia** license
el **litro** liter
la **llanta** tire
una **llanta desinflada** a flat tire
la **maravilla** wonder, marvel
el/la **mecánico** mechanic
la **multa** fine, ticket
el **pago inicial** down payment
el **semáforo** stop light
el **tanque** tank
el **tráfico** traffic
el/la **vendedor(a)** sales person

ADJETIVOS

cierto/a certain
económico/a economical
extraño/a strange
increíble incredible
preciso/a necessary
preferible preferable
ridículo/a ridiculous
seguro/a sure
urgente urgent
verdadero/a true, real

PALABRAS Y EXPRESIONES ÚTILES

a plazos on installments
es lástima it's a shame
no hay duda there's no doubt
prohibido estacionarse no parking
qué lástima what a shame
quizá, quizás perhaps
tal vez perhaps
todo derecho straight ahead

Un paso más 10

Actividades

A. **De vacaciones.** Cuando menos se espera, las cosas no van bien —sobre todo cuando se trata de coches (*where cars are concerned*). La escena de este dibujo no es una excepción. Describa la situación. ¿Quiénes son estas personas? ¿Por qué tienen que empujar (*to push*) el coche? ¿Adónde van? ¿De dónde vienen? ¿Qué cae (*is falling*) del coche? ¿Van a llegar a la estación de gasolina? ¿Van a hacer autostop (*to hitchhike*)? ¿Cómo va a terminar el episodio?

B. **Los carros.** Use the following questions to interview another student about cars and transportation in general. Without using notes, tell the class what you have learned.

1. ¿Tienes coche? ¿Tiene coche tu família?

Si responde que sí a la pregunta 1:

2. ¿De qué año es? ¿De qué color? ¿Qué modelo?
3. ¿Cómo es el coche? ¿Es grande o pequeño? ¿Funciona bien o tiene muchos problemas mecánicos?
4. ¿Funciona bien la calefacción en invierno? ¿Tiene aire acondicionado?
5. ¿Gasta mucha gasolina? ¿Cuántas millas por galón? ¿Es económico el carro?
6. ¿Lavas el coche con frecuencia?
7. ¿Te gusta el coche? ¿Tiene nombre? ¿Cómo se llama?

Si responde que no a la pregunta 1:

2. ¿Quieres tener coche o prefieres usar el transporte público?
3. Si compras un coche, ¿vas a comprar un coche grande o un coche pequeño?
4. ¿Cómo es tu coche ideal?
5. Generalmente, ¿prefieres tomar el autobús, tomar un taxi o caminar (*to walk*)?
6. Cuando haces un viaje largo, ¿prefieres viajar por avión, por tren, en bus o en coche de un(a) amigo/a? ¿Por qué?
7. En tu opinión, ¿cuáles son las ventajas de tener un coche? ¿las desventajas?

Yo quería° ir a su oficina a pagar la tasa de estacionamiento°, pero no pude° hacerlo porque no encontré sitio para estacionar.

wanted
tasa...parking fee
no... I couldn't

C. **Escenas.** Working with another student, create a short dialog about one of the following situations or about one of your own invention.

1. Dos personas viajan juntas en coche en una parte de la ciudad que no conocen bien. Una persona cree que deben doblar a la derecha para llegar a la casa de sus amigos; la otra persona cree que deben doblar a la izquierda.

2. Una persona maneja muy rápido (100 kilómetros por hora) y pasa el límite de velocidad (80 kilómetros por hora). El/la policía la para y quiere ponerle una multa.

3. A las doce de la noche, en un camino aislado, se le acaba la gasolina (*you run out of gas*). Otro coche para y el conductor (*driver*) le pregunta a Ud. si necesita algo. Ud. le pide que le lleve a su casa en la próxima (*next*) ciudad. Su casa está hacia (*toward*) el norte y la otra persona viaja hacia el sur.

D. **¡Una ganga!** Imagínese que Ud. es vendedor(a). Descríbales a sus clientes la cosa que Ud. quiere venderles. Indique su condición, sus cualidades especiales y su precio. Sus clientes van a decidir si es una verdadera ganga o no.

MODELO   un coche viejo → *Este coche está en muy buenas condiciones, aunque es del año 1960. Sólo tiene unas noventa mil millas, nada más. Es de un color precioso, ¿verdad? Tampoco gasta mucha gasolina —alcanza (it gets) unas siete millas por galón. Señores, ¡es una ganga! ¿El precio? Sólo cinco mil dólares.*

Algunas posibilidades
1. un libro antiguo
2. un par de zapatos
3. una máquina de escribir eléctrica (*electric typewriter*)
4. todos los discos de _____
5. una fotografía de _____
6. un animal
7. una bicicleta nueva de diez velocidades

A propósito...

On the next page are a few of the road signs you will see when driving in Spanish-speaking countries.

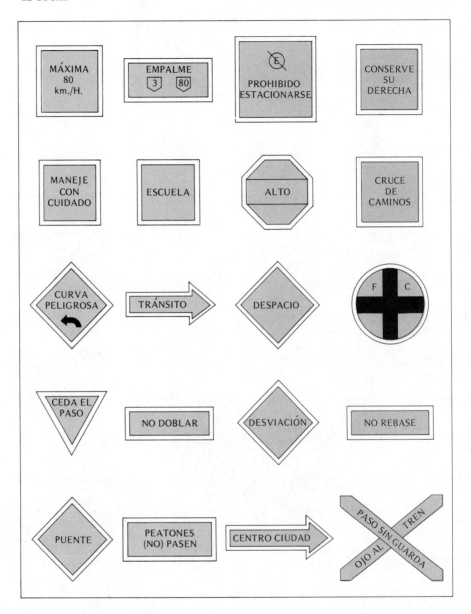

E. **En camino.** Match the following English traffic signs with their Spanish equivalents in **A propósito.**

1. Speed Limit 50 MPH 2. Drive carefully 3. Dangerous curve 4. Yield (right of way) 5. Bridge 6. No turns 7. Downtown 8. Unguarded crossing. Pay attention to train. 9. Detour (**vía** = *way*) 10. Slow. School Zone 11. Keep to the right 12. Railroad Crossing 13. No passing 14. (Don't) Walk 15. One-way street 16. Stop 17. Junction Routes 3 and 80 18. No parking 19. Slow 20. Intersection

F. **Los anuncios.** Find the Spanish equivalents of the following words and phrases in the ads below.

Avis

1. first-class 2. to rent 3. to be left (over) 4. a smile 5. to wait on you
6. efficiency 7. effort 8. lips 9. leader 10. We try harder.

Seat

11. best-selling 12. built, manufactured 13. maneuverability 14. turn radius 15. (gas) consumption 16. expenses 17. upkeep, maintenance 18. family budget 19. upholsteries 20. trunk

Avis: primera clase.
En unos minutos, le alquilamos un coche y nos sobra tiempo para dedicarle una sonrisa.

Usted no tiene tiempo que perder.
Y a nosotros nos bastan unos minutos; no necesitamos más tiempo para atenderle con la mayor eficacia y cordialidad, para alquilarle un coche nuevo.
Y esto en todas las oficinas de AVIS, porque el esfuerzo por prestarle a usted un servicio de "primera clase" es el denominador común de los miles de personas que AVIS tiene distribuidas por todo el país. Y todas, por supuesto, siempre con la mejor sonrisa en los labios.

AVIS

Nuestra fuerza es nuestro esfuerzo.

Sólo el líder puede sonreír así. En cualquier punto del país.

Nos esforzamos más.

¿Por qué el SEAT 127 es el coche más vendido?

SEAT-127

1.000.000 de coches fabricados en España,
4.000.000 en el mundo.

Por sus prestaciones: (velocidad: 145°Km/h., reprise: 0-100 en 15,7"*, maniobrabilidad perfecta: 9,6 m. diámetro de giro) que permiten un óptimo disfrute del mismo.

Por su economía: (bajo consumo: 6,25 a 100 Km/h., 1,94 pesetas Km. con gasolina normal: versiones para gasolina normal o súper, menores gastos de mantenimiento) para respetar su presupuesto familiar.

Por su amplia gama: (con dos, tres y cuatro puertas, diversidad de colores y tapizados, y **dos niveles de motorización**) que le permiten elegir lo que usted necesita.

Por su confort: (mayor capacidad: 80% de espacio útil, con 365 dm³ de maletero, ampliables a 1.070 dm³) para comodidad de los cinco pasajeros y todo su equipaje.

Pero el 127 ofrece otras muchas ventajas. Pregunte a quien lo usa.

SEAT 127

SEAT

Lectura cultural: Aventuras de transporte

Si Ud. quiere hacer una excursión por el mundo hispánico, no hay duda de que va a tener a su servicio todos los medios° posibles de transporte: avión, tren, autobús, taxi particular o colectivo°, y metro. Además es muy posible que su viaje sea uno de los más interesantes de su vida; primero por el paisaje° y segundo por el propio° medio de transporte.

means
taxi... *private or shared taxi*
landscape / actual

Si Ud. necesita transporte en una ciudad como Madrid, México o Buenos Aires, puede tomar el metro. En estas mismas ciudades y también en todas las otras, el autobús o un taxi le pueden llevar a cualquier parte. Pero tenga cuidado con los taxistas: como los taxistas de toda ciudad grande, muchos creen que son conductores de las 500 Millas de Indianapolis... y que su taxi es el único vehículo que ocupa la calle.

Una manera muy agradable de viajar de una parte de la ciudad a otra en muchos de los países hispanos es el colectivo. Es, en realidad, un taxi, pero se cobra° un precio fijo y se venden hasta cinco asientos. Así que Ud. viaja con cuatro compañeros que siguen la misma ruta.

se... *they charge*

Hablando de compañeros de ruta... si quiere conocer los pueblitos del campo°, tal vez tenga Ud. que viajar en los pequeños autobuses campesinos°. Es posible que una señora suba al autobús con varios gallos y gallinas en una bolsa° y que deje caer° la bolsa sobre los pies° de Ud. Pero no es nada. Un quiquiriquí° durante un viaje por los Andes puede ser muy agradable.

countryside
rural
gallos... *roosters and hens in a bag* / **deje**... *she drops / feet*
cock-a-doodle-doo

No queremos dar la impresión de que los medios de transporte del mundo hispánico son atrasados°, ni mucho menos°. Hay una gran variedad de vehículos. Además, los trenes españoles son bastante buenos, y todos los países tienen sus líneas aéreas. De hecho, Avianca —la línea colombiana— fue la primera línea aérea comercial establecida en el hemisferio occidental. También las aerolíneas Mexicana, Iberia (España) y Lacsa (Costa Rica), entre otras, todas ofrecen servicio excelente por todas partes de Hispanoamérica y también tienen rutas hasta los Estados Unidos y Europa.

backward / ni... *not at all*

Comprensión

¿Cierto o falso? Corrija las oraciones falsas.

1. Es dudoso que haya muchos medios de transporte en el mundo hispánico.
2. Un viaje en el mundo hispánico puede ser muy divertido.
3. En ciudades como Buenos Aires, México y Madrid se puede viajar sólo en autobús.
4. Por lo general, los taxistas hispánicos manejan con mucho cuidado.
5. Un colectivo es un taxi donde hay hasta cinco pasajeros.
6. Un viaje en un autobús campesino puede ser muy interesante porque algunos campesinos viajan con animales.

7. Avianca es la más nueva de todas las líneas aéreas del hemisferio occidental.

8. Lacsa e Iberia tienen rutas solamente entre España y Chile.

Ejercicios escritos

A. Write a paragraph about an imaginary **aventura** related to one of the means of transportation mentioned in the reading. Use as many of the words listed below as possible.

excursión	tener cuidado	vehículo
medio de transporte	destinación	manejar
aventura	viajar	viaje

B. Think about a past, present, or future mode of transportation and describe it in several sentences. Present your description to the class. Can your classmates guess what you are describing?

capítulo 11 En busca de un puesto

© Joan Menschenfreund

OBJETIVOS

In this chapter you will learn vocabulary and expressions related to education and to job hunting.

You will also learn about the following aspects of Spanish grammar:

49. how to give commands to persons whom you address as **tú**
50. how to express superlatives, such as *the most intelligent* (**el/la más inteligente**) and *the best* (**el/la mejor**), as well as the Spanish equivalent of such English phrases as *super/extremely/ very, very intelligent* (**inteligentísimo/a**)

51. the uses of the preposition **por** (*by, through, during,* and so on)
52. how to express such phrases as *the red one, the new ones* with the definite article and an adjective: **el/la rojo/a, los/las nuevos/as**

Un paso más includes activities dealing with interviews and application forms, and with situations in which you don't understand what someone says to you in Spanish. The reading discusses the educational system of Hispanic countries.

VOCABULARIO: PREPARACIÓN

Las entrevistas°   interviews

el apellido	last name	**caer (caigo)**	to fall
el/la aspirante	applicant	**caer bien/mal**	to make a
el/la ciudadano/a	citizen		good/bad
el colegio	elementary or		impression
	secondary school	**dejar**	to quit; to
	(¡**OJO**! not		leave
	college)		behind
la dirección	address	**escribir a**	to type
el nombre	(first) name	**máquina**	
la solicitud	application form	**graduarse**	to graduate
		nacer (nazco)	to be born
		llenar	to fill out
			(*a form*)
		renunciar (a)	to resign
			(from)

Solicitud de empleo   Madrid/México, D.F./Nueva York
Hermanos Alfonso
Importación/exportación

apellido(s)	nombre	fecha
Doe	*Jane*	*el 28 de febrero de 1981*

dirección		ciudad
Avenida de la Moncloa, 89		*Madrid*

nacimiento: día - mes - año	ciudad	provincia
3 - 2 - 1958	*Nueva York*	*Nueva York - USA*

¿Es Ud. ciudadano español? sí _____ no _✓___

Si no, nacionalidad _U S A_

EDUCACIÓN   fechas

colegio/universidad	dirección	de	a	títulos obtenidos
Colegio público no. 1894	*Nueva York*	*1972*	*1976*	*graduada*
City College of New York	*Nueva York*	*1976*	*1980*	*B.B.A. (licencia en comercio)*

EXPERIENCIA (los tres últimos puestos)			fechas		por qué dejó ese
nombre de la compañía	dirección	puesto	de	a	trabajo
"Peking" (Restaurante chino)	Nueva York	cocinera	6-1976	9-1976	me matriculé en CCNY
City College of New York	Nueva York	asistente de laboratorio	9-1977	6-1980	me gradué
Freeman Exports	Nueva York	agente	7-1980	12-1980	para venir a España

Idiomas:
inglés, español, un poco de francés

¿Qué puesto pide Ud. en esta compañía? ____asistente del director____

¿Por qué desea Ud. este trabajo? ____salí licenciada en comercio____
y tengo 6 meses de experiencia en una compañía de
exportación.

A. Conteste las siguientes preguntas sobre la solicitud.

1. ¿Cuál es el apellido de la aspirante? ¿y su nombre?
2. ¿Cuándo llenó la aspirante la solicitud?
3. ¿Cuál es su dirección? ¿De qué país es ciudadana?
4. ¿Cuándo nació y dónde?
5. ¿Cuándo se graduó la aspirante del colegio? ¿de la universidad?
6. ¿Qué idiomas habla?
7. ¿Por qué renunció la señorita a sus tres últimos puestos?
8. ¿Qué puesto espera obtener ahora? ¿Por qué?
9. ¿Qué preparación tiene para ese puesto?

B. De la oraciones siguientes, ¿cuáles describen las experiencias y las opiniones de Ud.?
Cambie las oraciones que no lo/la describen.

1. Renuncié a mi último trabajo.
2. Me gusta llenar solicitudes.
3. Creo que las personas nacen para ciertos trabajos.
4. Cuando tengo una entrevista llevo ropa conservadora para caerle bien al entrevistador.
5. Creo que mis estudios en la universidad me preparan para un buen trabajo.
6. Durante una entrevista estoy muy tranquilo/a.
7. Mi trabajo ideal es un trabajo donde puedo estar sentado/a (*seated*) todo el día.
8. Después de graduarme espero pasar a una «escuela graduada».
9. Es necesario que los estudiantes aprendan a escribir a máquina.

Adjetivos ordinales

primer(o)	first	**quinto**	fifth	**noveno**	ninth
segundo	second	**sexto**	sixth	**décimo**	tenth
tercer(o)	third	**séptimo**	seventh		
cuarto	fourth	**octavo**	eighth		

Ordinal numbers are adjectives and must agree in number and gender with the nouns they modify. Ordinals usually precede the noun: **la cuarta lección, el octavo ejercicio.** The most commonly used ordinals in Spanish are **primer(o)** through **décimo.** Above *tenth,* the cardinal numbers are normally used: **Alfonso XIII (trece).**

Like **bueno,** the ordinals **primero** and **tercero** shorten to **primer** and **tercer,** respectively, before masculine singular nouns: **el primer niño, el tercer mes.** Ordinal numbers are frequently abbreviated with superscript letters that show the adjective ending: **las 1as lecciones, el 1er grado, el 5° estudiante.**

C. *Diga Ud. los nombres de los días de la semana y de los meses del año, indicando su posición.*

    MODELO   *El lunes es el primer día de la semana,... Enero es el primer mes del año.*

D. *¿En qué grado están estos niños?*

1. Manuel — 5°
2. Teresa — 3er
3. Eduardo — 7°
4. Jesús — 1er
5. Pablo — 10°
6. Evangelina — 2°

E. *Conteste las preguntas según el dibujo.*

1. ¿Quién es la décima persona? ¿la quinta? ¿la tercera? ¿la novena? ¿la segunda?
2. ¿En qué posición está Ángela? ¿Cecilia? ¿Juan? ¿Simón? ¿Linda?

PRONUNCIACIÓN: X, M, and N

X   The letter **x** is usually pronounced as [ks], as in English.   Before a consonant, however, the [k] is often dropped and the resulting sound is simply an [s] sound, as in **texto** and **extranjero.**

M and **N**   Spanish **m** and **n** are usually pronounced as in English. However, before **p, b/v,** and **m,** the letter **n** is pronounced [m]; before the sounds [k] and [g], and the spellings **j** and **ge/gi,** it has an [ng] sound, as in the English word *sing.*

PRÁCTICA

1. [ks] laxo   sexo   axial   existen   examen
2. [s] explique   extraordinario   sexto   extremo   extraterrestre
3. [m] convence   un beso   un peso   con Manuel   con Pablo   con Verónica   con Bárbara   en Perú   en Venezuela   en Bolivia   en México   son buenos
4. [ng] en casa   en Castilla   un genio   son generosos   son curiosos   son jóvenes   en Colombia   en Japón   en Quito   en Granada   con Carlos   con Juan   con Gregorio

MINIDIÁLOGOS Y GRAMÁTICA

49. *TÚ* COMMANDS

En la escuela primaria: frases útiles para la maestra
—Maritere, *toma* tu leche; *no tomes* la leche de Carlos.
—Cristina, *escribe* las oraciones en la pizarra; *no escribas* en la pared.
—Joaquín, *escucha; no hables* tanto.
—Esteban, *siéntate* en tu silla; *no te sientes* en el suelo.
—Silvia, *quítate* el abrigo; *no te quites* el suéter.
—Graciela, *dale* el cuaderno a Ernesto; *no se lo des* a Joaquín.
—Mario, *ponte* el abrigo; *no olvides* tus libros.
—Ramón, *ten* cuidado; *no corras, no te caigas.*
—Juana, *no hagas* eso; *tráeme* el papel.

In grade school: useful phrases for the teacher.   Maritere, drink your milk; don't drink Carlos' milk.
Cristina, write the sentences on the board; don't write on the wall.   *Joaquín,* listen; don't talk so much.
Esteban, sit in your chair; don't sit on the floor.   *Silvia,* take off your coat; don't take off your sweater.
Graciela, give the notebook to Ernesto; don't give it to Joaquín.   *Mario,* put on your coat; don't forget
your books.   *Ramón,* be careful; don't run, don't fall.   *Juana,* don't do that; bring me the paper.

1. ¿Qué dice la maestra cuando Maritere no toma su leche? ¿cuando alguien debe escribir en la pizarra? ¿no escucha? ¿no se sienta en la silla? ¿no se quita el abrigo? ¿no le da el cuaderno a Ernesto? ¿no se pone el abrigo? ¿no tiene cuidado? ¿no trae el papel?
2. ¿Por qué da la maestra los mandatos negativos? Por ejemplo, ¿por qué dice la maestra «no tomes la leche de Carlos»?
   → *Porque Maritere tomó la leche de Carlos.*
   →*Porque no está tomando su propia* (own) *leche.*

Informal commands (**mandatos informales**) are used with persons whom you address as **tú**.

Negative **Tú** Commands

-AR VERBS		-ER/-IR VERBS	
No hables.	*Don't speak.*	**No comas.**	*Don't eat.*
No cantes.	*Don't sing.*	**No escribas.**	*Don't write.*
No juegues.	*Don't play.*	**No pidas.**	*Don't order.*

Like **Ud.** commands (section 34), the negative **tú** commands are expressed with the present subjunctive: **no hable Ud., no hables tú.** The pronoun **tú** is used only for emphasis.

No cantes **tú** tan fuerte.   *Don't you sing so loudly.*

Object pronouns—direct, indirect, reflexive—precede negative **tú** commands, as with negative **Ud.** commands.

No lo mires.   *Don't look at him.*
No les escribas.   *Don't write to them.*
No te levantes.   *Don't get up.*

[Práctica A, B]

Affirmative **Tú** Commands

-AR VERBS		-ER/-IR VERBS	
Habla.	*Speak.*	**Come.**	*Eat.*
Canta.	*Sing.*	**Escribe.**	*Write.*
Juega.	*Play.*	**Pide.**	*Order.*

As opposed to the other command forms you have already learned, most affirmative **tú** commands are identical to the third-person singular of the present *indicative*.

The following verbs have irregular affirmative **tú** command forms:

decir:	**di**	poner:	**pon**	tener:	**ten**
hacer:	**haz**	salir:	**sal**	venir:	**ven**
ir:	**ve**	ser:	**sé**		

¡OJO! The affirmative **tú** commands for **ir** and **ver** are identical: **ve.** Context will clarify meaning.

¡**Ve** esa película!	*See that movie!*
Ve a casa ahora mismo.	*Go home right now.*

As in affirmative **Ud.** commands, object and reflexive pronouns follow affirmative **tú** commands and are attached to them. Accent marks are necessary except when a single pronoun is added to a one-syllable command.

Dile la verdad.	*Tell him the truth.*
Tócala, por favor.	*Play it, please.*
Póntelos.	*Put them on.*

[Práctica C, D, E]

PRÁCTICA

A. Cambie los mandatos formales (Ud.) por mandatos informales (tú).

1. No gaste Ud. tanto.
2. No despierte Ud. al niño.
3. No lo cierre Ud., por favor.
4. No lo limpie Ud.
5. No le arregle Ud. el carro hoy.
6. No escriba Ud. la carta a máquina.
7. No corra Ud. tanto.
8. No venga Ud. tan tarde.
9. No lo lea Ud., por favor.
10. No haga Ud. tanto ruido, por favor.

B. Dé Ud. mandatos informales para continuar estos comentarios que Ud. hace a unos miembros de su familia. Siga el modelo.

MODELO　*Hablaste tanto ayer.* → *No hables tanto, por favor.*
　　　　　Dejaste tu ropa en el suelo ayer. → *No la dejes en el suelo, por favor.*

1. *Dejaste* tus libros en el suelo también.
2. Ayer *regresaste* tarde a casa.
3. No quiero que *lleves* mi ropa.

4. No me gusta que *juegues* y *corras* en la calle.
5. No es necesario que *vayas* al parque todos los días.
6. No es bueno que *mires* la televisión constantemente.
7. Siempre le *dices* mentiras (*lies*) a papá.
8. Siempre *te olvidas* de sacar la basura.
9. ¿Por qué *doblas* en esta esquina?
10. *Eres* tan mala.

C. *Cambie los mandatos formales (Ud.) por mandatos informales (tú).*

1. Llene Ud. la solicitud.
2. ¡Niéguelo Ud.!
3. Contéstele Ud. inmediatamente al aspirante.
4. Pregúntele Ud. su apellido.
5. Almuerce Ud. allí.
6. Apréndala Ud. bien.
7. Salga Ud. de aquí.
8. Sírvale Ud. el vino.
9. Vaya Ud. al colegio.
10. Venga Ud. al aeropuerto.

D. *Dé Ud. mandatos informales afirmativos para continuar estos comentarios a unos miembros de su familia.*

1. No le *escribiste* a Santiago.
2. No me *ayudas* nunca.
3. No *tienes* paciencia.
4. Insisto en que *desayunes*.
5. Nunca me *escuchas*.
6. Es terrible que nunca *termines* tus proyectos.
7. Nunca *dices* la verdad.
8. Ayer no *hiciste* ensalada.
9. Nunca *pones* la mesa.
10. Quiero que *seas* buena.

E. *Dé Ud. mandatos informales según el modelo.*

MODELO   Carlos escribe la carta con *lápiz*. (*bolígrafo*) →
               Carlos, escríbela con bolígrafo; no la escribas con lápiz.

1. Anita habla *inglés* en la entrevista. (*español*)
2. Gilberto lee *un periódico*. (*una novela*)
3. Nati pregunta a *Carmen* la dirección. (*Lorenzo*)
4. Santiago bebe *el café*. (*una limonada*)
5. Maricarmen nos está comprando *tres* boletos. (*cuatro*)
6. Mariela baila *el tango*. (*el chachachá*)
7. Dolores trae *cerveza*. (*vino*)
8. Silvia estaciona el carro *en el estacionamiento* (*parking lot*). (*en la calle Bolívar*)

CONVERSACIÓN

A. *Su amigo/a tiene una entrevista para un trabajo que le interesa mucho y quiere caerle bien al entrevistador. Déle Ud. consejos sobre la entrevista en forma de mandatos informales.*

MODELO   *Llega a la hora en punto.*

B. *Dé Ud. diez mandatos informales para ser un(a) esposo/a feliz (happy) o para ser el compañero/a de cuarto perfecto/a.*

Study Hint: Listening

When you are listening to someone speaking Spanish, try to pick out cognates and to guess the meaning of unfamiliar words from context, just as you do when you are reading (**Study Hint,** page 267). The following suggestions will also help you to understand more of what you hear in Spanish.

1. Remember that it is not necessary to understand every word in order to get the "gist" of the conversation. You may feel uncomfortable if you cannot understand absolutely everything, but chances are good that you will still be able to handle the conversational situation.
2. Watch the speaker's facial expressions and gestures—they will give you a general idea about what he or she is saying. For example, if there is a pause and the speaker is looking at you expectantly, it is reasonable to guess that he or she has just asked you a question.
3. Use brief pauses in the conversation to "digest" the words that you have just heard.
4. The more familiar you are with the vocabulary being used, the easier it will be to understand what you are hearing. Listen for familiar words—and be flexible: they may appear with a different meaning in a new context. Listen also for specific clues, such as

a. the gender of nouns and adjectives: Is the speaker talking about **un chico alto** or **una chica alta?** Here you have three chances —with the article, the noun itself, and the adjective—to catch the gender of the person being described.
b. verb endings: Who did what to whom? If you hear **habló,** for example, you know that the speaker is not talking about him or herself, since the **-ó** ending signals a third person.
c. object pronouns: The sentence **La vi en el restaurante** can only refer to a woman or to a feminine noun.
d. intonation: Did you hear a question or a statement?

Above all, if you really have not understood what someone said to you, react, ask questions, admit that you haven't understood, and ask him or her to repeat. You will find some phrases to help you do this politely in the **A propósito** section on page 319.

50. SUPERLATIVES AND ABSOLUTE SUPERLATIVES

Superlatives

David es **el** estudiante **más inteligente de** la clase.

Son **los mejores** doctores **de** aquel hospital.

David is the smartest student in the class.

They're the best doctors at that hospital.

The *superlative* (**superlativo**) is formed in English by adding *-est* to adjectives or by using expressions such as *the most, the least,* and so on, with the adjective. In Spanish, this concept is expressed in the same way as the comparative and is always accompanied by the definite article. In this construction **mejor** and **peor** tend to precede the noun; other adjectives follow. *In* or *at* is expressed with **de**.

[Práctica A]

Absolute Superlatives

—¡*Perezosísimo!*

Esos ejercicios son **facilísimos.**

Esa mujer es **inteligentísima.**

Those exercises are very, very easy.

That woman is extremely intelligent.

When **ísimo/-a/-os/-as** is used with an adjective, the idea *extremely* (*exceptionally, very, very, super*) is added to the quality described. This form is called the *absolute superlative* (**superlativo absoluto**). If the adjective ends in a consonant, **-ísimo** is added to the singular form. If the adjective ends in a vowel, the final vowel is dropped before adding **-ísimo: perezosø → perezosísimo.** Any accents on the adjective stem are dropped when **-ísimo** is added: **difícil → dificilísimo.**

Spelling changes occur when the final consonant of an adjective is **c, g,** or **z: rico → riquísimo; largo → larguísimo; feliz → felicísimo.**

[Práctica B, C]

PRÁCTICA

A. *Cambie por el superlativo según el modelo.*

> MODELO   Carlota es una estudiante muy inteligente.   (la clase) →
> Carlota es *la* estudiante *más inteligente de la clase.*

1. Olga y Paula son empleadas muy trabajadoras.   (la oficina)
2. Es una plaza muy pequeña.   (la ciudad)
3. El Brasil es un país muy grande.   (Suramérica)
4. La Sra. Gómez es una aspirante muy buena.   (la lista)
5. La lección once es una lección muy importante.   (el texto)
6. ¡Es una clase mala!   (la universidad)

B. *Dé el superlativo absoluto.*

1. importante	3. alto	5. especial	7. perfecto
2. difícil	4. pobre	6. fácil	8. atrasado

C. *Complete las oraciones, usando el superlativo absoluto de uno de estos adjetivos—* *o cualquier otro.*

famoso	grande	divertido	contaminado	_____
cansado	rico	pesado (*boring*)	interesante	

1. Mis mejores amigos vienen a cenar esta noche, y es necesario que la cena esté _____.
2. Nueva York es una ciudad _____.
3. No hay muchas personas _____ en la clase.
4. Cuando trabajo mucho, estoy _____ después.
5. No me gusta que la clase sea/esté _____.
6. Una persona _____ me cae bien.
7. Una persona _____ me cae mal.

CONVERSACIÓN

A. *Usando oraciones completas, dé Ud. el nombre de*

1. el/la mejor estudiante de la clase
2. la persona más pobre de su familia
3. el/la profesor(a) más paciente de la universidad
4. la persona más guapa del mundo
5. una persona riquísima

6. un(a) profesor(a) buenísimo/a
7. un carro baratísimo
8. un carro rapidísimo
9. una persona simpatiquísima

B. *Usando oraciones completas, dé Ud. el nombre de*

1. el mejor restaurante de la ciudad y el peor
2. la mejor clase de la universidad y la peor
3. un plato riquísimo
4. un programa de televisión interesantísimo
5. la mejor carretera de la ciudad y el peor camino

51. USES OF *POR*

Una conversación *por* teléfono

ÁLVARO: Así que *por* la mañana te entrevistaron durante cuatro horas. *Por* la tarde hablaste con el jefe. Les caíste bien a todos y no te dieron el puesto. No comprendo por qué.

BERNARDO: *Por* el accidente.

ÁLVARO: ¡*Por* Dios! ¿Qué accidente?

BERNARDO: El choque con el carro del presidente de la compañía.

1. *¿Los dos amigos hablan cara (face) a cara?*
2. *¿A quién entrevistaron por la mañana?*
3. *¿Qué pasó por la tarde?*
4. *¿Por qué no le dieron el puesto a Bernardo?*
5. *¿Qué tipo de accidente tuvo (did he have)?*

The preposition **por** has the following English equivalents:

1. BY, BY MEANS OF

Vamos **por avión (tren, barco,** etcétera).	*We're going by plane (train, ship, and and so on).*
Le voy a hablar **por teléfono.**	*I'll talk to him by phone.*
¿Por qué no pasan **por la casa** esta noche?	*Why don't you come by the house tonight?*

A telephone conversation ÁLVARO: So in the morning they interviewed you for four hours. In the afternoon you talked with the boss. Everybody liked you, and they didn't give you the job. I don't understand why. BERNARDO: Because of the accident. ÁLVARO: Good heavens! What accident? BERNARDO: The crash with the company president's car.

2. THROUGH, ALONG

¿No quieres caminar **por el parque?**	*Don't you want to walk through the park?*
Recomiendan que caminemos **por la playa.**	*They suggest that we walk along the beach.*

3. DURING, IN (the morning, afternoon, and so on)

Por la mañana jugamos al tenis.	*We play tennis in the morning.*

4. BECAUSE OF

Estoy nervioso **por la entrevista.**	*I'm nervous because of the interview.*

5. FOR, when *for* means
   a. IN EXCHANGE FOR

¿Cuánto me das **por este sombrero?**	*How much will you give me for this hat?*
Gracias por el regalo.	*Thanks for the gift.*

   b. FOR THE SAKE OF, ON BEHALF OF

Lo voy a hacer **por ti.**	*I'm going to do it for you (for your sake).*

   c. IN ORDER TO GET, IN SEARCH OF

Van **por el médico.**	*They're going for (going to get) the doctor.*

   d. FOR A PERIOD OF TIME

Elena manejó **(por)** tres horas esta tarde.	*Elena drove for three hours this afternoon.*

Many native speakers of Spanish do not use **por** in this and similar sentences; **tres horas** implies *for three hours.*

Por is also used in a number of fixed expressions.

por Dios	*for heaven's sake*	**por lo general**	*generally, in general*
por ejemplo	*for example*	**por lo menos**	*at least*
por eso	*that's why*	**por primera/**	*for the first/last time*
por favor	*please*	**última vez**	
por fin	*finally*	**por si acaso**	*just in case*

PRÁCTICA

A. *Conteste Ud. en frases completas, usando* **por** *y las expresiones entre paréntesis.*

1. ¿Cómo quiere Ud. ir a Europa? (barco)
2. ¿Cómo habla Ud. con sus amigos en otros países? (teléfono)
3. ¿Por dónde le gusta a Ud. caminar? (universidad)
4. ¿Cuándo le gusta a Ud. estudiar? (la tarde)
5. ¿Por qué está Ud. tan nervioso/a? (el examen)
6. ¿Cuánto tiempo estudia Ud. todos los días? (tres horas)
7. ¿Cuánto pagó Ud. por el coche? ($2.000)
8. ¿Por quién se sacrifican (*make sacrifices*) los padres? (los niños)
9. ¿Por quién habla el secretario de estado? (el presidente)
10. ¿Por qué volvió Ud. a la tienda? (vino)

B. *Match the statements in the left-hand column with the responses on the right.*

1. Acabo de jugar al basquetbol por dos horas.
2. Pero nunca están en casa por la tarde.
3. Tengo que salir inmediatamente.
4. Siento llegar tan tarde.
5. No puedo tomar el examen por muchas razones.
6. Juan acaba de tener un accidente horrible.
7. Pero, papá, quiero ir.

a. Te digo que no, por última vez.
b. Pero por fin estás aquí.
c. ¡Por Dios! ¿Qué le pasó?
d. ¿No vas a tomar nada? ¿por lo menos un *sándwich?*
e. ¿Por ejemplo?
f. Ah, por eso estás tan cansado.
g. ¿Por qué no los llamamos, por si acaso…?

CONVERSACIÓN

A. *Preguntas*

1. En esta ciudad, ¿es agradable caminar por los parques públicos? ¿por el centro?
2. ¿Cómo se llega de Washington a California por carro? **(Hay que pasar por _____)** ¿de los Estados Unidos a Guatemala? ¿del Canadá a México?
3. Generalmente, ¿qué hace Ud. por la mañana? ¿por la tarde? ¿por la noche?
4. ¿Por qué quiere Ud. viajar a Acapulco? ¿por el sol? ¿a España? ¿a California? ¿a Nueva York?
5. ¿Adónde se va por gasolina? ¿por ropa? ¿por comestibles (*food*)?
6. ¿Quiénes se sacrifican por Ud.? ¿sus padres? ¿Ud. se sacrifica por alguien?
7. ¿Cuándo salió Ud. por primera vez con un(a) chico/a?

B. *Complete las oraciones en una forma lógica.*

1. Es más fácil ir a México por _____.
2. Casi nunca veo a _____ pero hablo con él/ella por teléfono.

3. (No) Es probable que _____ pase(n) por mi casa esta noche.
4. Para llegar a la universidad, paso por _____.
5. En este momento, estoy alegre (triste, nervioso/a) por/porque _____.
6. _____ no está en clase hoy por/porque _____.
7. Los días de clase no veo la televisión por _____.
8. Es una tontería pagar _____ por un carro (una casa, un vestido).

52. NOMINALIZATION OF ADJECTIVES

Prefiero este vestido caro pero
debo comprar el barato.

Me gustan los platos panameños y **los mexicanos.**	*I like Panamanian dishes and Mexican ones.*
Quiero comprar esta blusa verde y **aquella blanca.**	*I want to buy this green blouse and that white one.*

English frequently uses the word *one* or *ones* (*the blue sweater and the green one*) to avoid the repetition of a noun. Spanish avoids such repetition by nominalizing adjectives (using them as nouns). This procedure involves dropping the nouns they modify, while retaining the article or demonstrative adjective. Both the *nominalized adjectives* (**adjetivo sustantivado**) and the article or demonstrative must agree with the noun to which they refer.

aquel carro **blanco**	→ **aquel blanco**	*that white one* (car)
los hombres **ricos**	→ **los ricos**	*the rich, the rich ones (men)*
la hermana **más simpática**	→ **la más simpática**	*the nicest one* (sister)
una mujer **joven**	→ **una joven**	*a young person, a young woman*

PRÁCTICA

A. *Dé Ud. frases nuevas que se refieren a las palabras indicadas.*

—¿Qué *abrigo* vas a comprar?
—Pues... me gusta más el rojo. (*blusa, pantalones, camisas, sombrero, falda, calcetines*)

B. *Complete the following sentences by selecting the item you want to buy.* Use *nominalized adjectives.*

1. Tenemos un diccionario barato y otro diccionario caro.

Debo comprar el _____.

2. Tenemos unas plantas grandes y aquellas plantas más pequeñas.

Prefiero las _____.

3. Tenemos una refrigeradora verde y otra amarilla.

Voy a compar la _____.

4. Tenemos esta guitarra española y esa mexicana.

Me gusta más la _____.

5. Tenemos unos televisores americanos y esos japoneses.

Me da el _____, por favor.

CONVERSACIÓN

A. *Conteste Ud., expresando sus gustos y preferencias.* Use *adjetivos sustantivados.*

1. ¿Prefiere Ud. los perros grandes o los pequeños?
2. ¿Prefiere Ud. los gatos siameses o los persas?
3. ¿los restaurantes mexicanos o los italianos?
4. ¿la comida norteamericana o la extranjera?
5. ¿las clases fáciles o las difíciles?
6. ¿los coches americanos o los extranjeros? ¿los japoneses o los italianos?
7. ¿la música clásica o la popular?
8. ¿las películas dramáticas o las cómicas?

B. *En su clase de español, ¿quién es el/la más cómico/a? ¿el/la más guapo/a? ¿el/la más simpático/a? ¿el/la más inteligente? el/la más trabajador(a)?*

DIÁLOGO: Quien tiene padrino se bautiza—una sátira[1]

Miguel Ángel Inclán y de la Torre, hombre de unos treinta años
Don Antonio, padre de Miguel Ángel
Empleado de la Dirección° de Personal de un ministerio del gobierno   (director's) office

A. *En casa de los Inclán*

DON ANTONIO: Ven, Miguel Ángel, y siéntate aquí conmigo.

MIGUEL ÁNGEL: Muy bien, papá. ¿De qué se trata?°   ¿**De**... *What's it about?*

DON ANTONIO: De tu mesada°, hijo. Con fecha de hoy°, te la   *monthly allowance/***con**...
                       corto°, ¿comprendes? Miguel Ángel, eres un   *as of today*
                       Inclán. Sé fuerte, haz algo con tu vida. Ve a   **te**... *I'm going to stop it*
                       buscar trabaja—¡mañana!

B. *En la oficina de la Dirección de Personal*

EMPLEADO: Pero, hombre, ¿todavía no ha llenado° las solici-   **no**... *haven't you filled*
                     tudes?   *out*

MIGUEL ÁNGEL: La azul, sí, pero no entendí° algunas preguntas de   **no**... *I didn't understand*
                       la amarilla.

EMPLEADO: A ver°; démela y se la escribo a máquina. Dígame   **A**... *let's see*
                     primero su nombre y apellidos.

MIGUEL ÁNGEL: Me llamo Miguel Ángel Inclán y de la Torre.

EMPLEADO: ¿Es Ud. de los Inclán de la provincia de Manga-
                     nillas?

MIGUEL ÁNGEL: Sí. Mi padre fue gobernador de la provincia por
                       treinta años.

EMPLEADO: ¡Ah! Siéntese, don Miguel. ¿Dónde y cuándo nació
                     Ud.?

MIGUEL ÁNGEL: Nací en la capital de Manganillas el 2 de marzo de
                       1949. Todos los Inclán nacimos allí.

EMPLEADO: ¿Dónde estudió Ud.?

MIGUEL ÁNGEL: Aprendí las primeras letras en la Academia Francesa, la primaria más exclusiva de la provincia. Después pasé a la secundaria de Manganillas, pero decidí no estudiar más y no me gradué.

EMPLEADO: Hummm... ¿Renunció Ud., don Miguel, o lo despidieron° de su último trabajo?

lo... did they fire you

MIGUEL ÁNGEL: Pues en realidad nunca he trabajado°. El trabajo me cae pesadísimo. Pero dice mi padre que ya es hora de hacer algo...

nunca... I've never worked

EMPLEADO: Comprendo... muy bien... muy bien. Voy a hablar de su caso con la Dra. González Esquivel, directora del Departamento de Personal. Vuelva Ud. mañana por la mañana, por favor.

C. *A la mañana siguiente*

EMPLEADO: ¡Mi enhorabuena°, don Miguel! Con fecha de ayer, día primero de julio, el Excelentísimo Sr. Ministro lo nombró a usted director de personal.

congratulations

MIGUEL ÁNGEL: ¡¿A mí?! ¿Y qué pasó con la Dra. González Esquivel?

EMPLEADO: La despidieron por recomendar que lo mandaran a Ud. a paseo°.[2]

lo... they send you on your way

Comprensión

Conteste en oraciones completas.

A. 1. ¿Cuál es el tema de la conversación entre Miguel Ángel y su padre?
   2. ¿Qué quiere don Antonio que haga su hijo?

B. 1. ¿Cuál es la primera pregunta del empleado? ¿Por qué pregunta eso?
   2. ¿Cuántas solicitudes tiene que llenar Miguel Ángel? ¿Tiene algún problema?
   3. ¿De dónde es Miguel Ángel?
   4. ¿Cuál fue el trabajo de don Antonio durante treinta años?
   5. ¿Cuándo nació Miguel Ángel? ¿Cuántos años tiene?
   6. ¿Dónde empezó a estudiar? ¿Se graduó de la secundaria? ¿Por qué (no)?
   7. ¿A Miguel Ángel le gusta trabajar? ¿Por qué busca trabajo?
   8. ¿Por qué va a hablar el empleado con la Dra. González Esquivel?

C. 1. ¿Quién es el nuevo director de personal? ¿Por qué?
   2. ¿Qué le pasó a la Dra. González Esquivel?

Comentario cultural

1. The Spanish word **padrino** describes several kinds of relationships. A **padrino de bautizo** holds the infant at a baptism, and a **padrino de boda** assists the bride and groom during the marriage ceremony. The **padrino**'s subsequent

role is that of sponsor and protector, a person whom the child or married couple can count on in time of need.

In a more general sense, the term **padrino** is applied to anyone who acts as the sponsor and protector of another. Because of his status and connections, the **padrino** in this dialog, the **ministro,** is able to cut through bureaucratic red tape and convince others to perform favors for his **ahijado** (*godchild*). This system is expressed in the Spanish saying **Quien tiene padrino se bautiza.** Just as an infant needs a sponsor in order to be baptized as a Catholic, one also needs a sponsor or patron in order to advance professionally or simply to get things done.

2. Although one's ability and education are frequently the basis for advancement, the patronage system continues to play an important role in Hispanic life. The dialog satirizes the traditional system that judges a person by his or her family background and influence rather than by ability. Note the change in the clerk's attitude when he learns **"don"** Miguel's name and family background. And when Dr. González attempts to evaluate the applicant only in terms of his abilities and experience, she is dismissed.

UN POCO DE TODO

A. *Form complete sentences based on the words given in the order given. Use* tú *commands where appropriate and the superlative form of the italicized adjectives. Add other words if necessary.* / / *indicates the break between two sentences.*

1. no / comprar / primero / carro / que / (tú) ver / / Comprar / mejor
2. primero / película / de / aquel / actriz / ser / *bueno* / pero / segundo / ser / *malo*
3. Raquel, / doblar / en segundo / esquina / / No / doblar / en / primero
4. decirme / tu / apellidos / / No / decirme / tu / nombre
5. vender / tu / casa / *grande* / y / comprar / ese / *pequeño*

B. *Rearrange the words given to form complete sentences.*

1. lección / la / lee / quinta / pero / sexta / no / la / leas
2. por / gusta / experiencia / el / más / aspirante / me / su / último
3. mañana / llené / por / solicitud / la / una / larguísima
4. me / el / cayó / primer / pesadísimo / aspirante
5. preséntame / altísimo / a / panameño / ese

C. *Working with another student, ask and answer questions according to the model.*

MODELO   leer / lección / difícil →
          RAFAEL: ¿Leíste la primera *lección?*
          CARMEN: Sí, y también *leí* la segunda.

RAFAEL: Fueron *dificilísimas*, ¿no?
CARMEN: La primera no fue tan *difícil* como la segunda.

1. escribir / ejercicio / complicado
2. renunciar / tu puesto / pesado
3. prepararse / para clase / aburrido
4. aprender / diálogo / largo
5. hablar con / aspirante / listo

D. *Dé Ud. mandatos informales según el modelo.*

MODELO   Genaro está leyendo la segunda lección. (difícil, 1ª) →
          Genaro, no leas la segunda lección; es dificilísima. Lee la primera.

1. Jacinto siempre estudia por la noche. (malo para la salud, la tarde)
2. Carlota piensa ir a Europa por barco. (caro, avión)
3. Pedro piensa tomar el autobús. (pesado, tren)
4. Consuelo está comprando la blusa amarilla. (feo, azul)
5. Anamari está llenando la solicitud blanca. (viejo, nuevo)
6. El niño está jugando en la calle. (peligroso, parque)

E. *Complete las oraciones en una forma lógica.*

1. En el _____ año de la secundaria, estudié _____ y me gustó muchísimo.
2. Durante el _____ año de la secundaria, viajé a _____. Fue una ciudad/un país _____-ísimo/a.
3. Mi primer(a) amigo/a se llamó _____. Fue un(a) chico/a _____-ísimo/a.
4. No corras en la calle _____ —es la peor calle de la ciudad. Corre en _____ —es la mejor.
5. Toma _____, es la mejor clase de esta universidad. No tomes _____. Es _____.
6. Pon _____ (*nombre de programa*) en la televisión esta noche —es un programa estupendo. Pero no pongas _____. Es aburridísimo.

VOCABULARIO

VERBOS

caer (caigo) to fall
caer bien/mal to make a good/bad impression
caminar to walk
correr to run
dejar to quit; to leave (behind)
entrevistar to interview
escribir a máquina to type
llenar to fill out (*a form*)
nacer (nazco) to be born
renunciar (a) to resign (from)

SUSTANTIVOS

el apellido last name
el/la aspirante candidate, applicant
el barco boat, ship
el centro center; downtown
el/la ciudadano/a citizen
el colegio elementary or secondary school
la dirección address; director's office
la entrevista interview
el idioma language

la leche milk
el miembro member
el nombre (first) name
el padrino patron; godfather
el perro dog
la pregunta question
la solicitud application form

ADJETIVOS

agradable agreeable, pleasant
cuarto/a fourth
décimo/a tenth

feliz happy
fuerte strong; loud
Japonés, Japonesa Japanese
mejor best
nervioso/a nervous
noveno/a ninth
octavo/a eighth
peor worst
pesado/a boring
primero/a first

quinto/a fifth
segundo/a second
séptimo/a seventh
sexto/a sixth
tercero/a third

PALABRAS Y EXPRESIONES ÚTILES
durante during; for (*a period of time*)
por Dios for heaven's sake

por ejemplo for example
por lo general generally, in general
por lo menos at least
por primera/última vez for the first/last time
por si acaso just in case
sobre about; above; on
tener cuidado to be careful

Un paso más 11

Actividades

SOLICITUD DE EMPLEO

apellido(s)	nombre	fecha
dirección: número calle ciudad		estado país
nacimiento: día - mes - año ciudad país		
¿Es Ud. ciudadano americano? sí _____ no _____ Si no, nacionalidad: _____		número de seguro social
EDUCACIÓN fechas colegio/universidad dirección de a títulos obtenidos		

EXPERIENCIA (los tres últimos puestos)   fechas   por qué dejó
nombre de la compañía   dirección   puesto   de   a   ese trabajo

Idiomas:

¿Qué puesto pide Ud. en esta compañía? _____

¿Por qué desea Ud. este trabajo? _____

A. **En el Departamento de Personal.** Ud. está en la oficina tejana (*Texan*) de una compañía mexicana y busca un puesto—por ejemplo, abogado/a, director(a) de ventas (*sales*), enfermero/a, secretario/a. Con otro/a estudiante, haga los papeles (*play the roles*) de aspirante y de empleado/a del Departamento de Personal. El/la empleado/a debe hacerle preguntas al/a la aspirante y llenar la solicitud de empleo.

B. **Una entrevista con el/la director(a) de personal.** Una semana después de llenar la solicitud, Ud. vuelve a la misma compañía para entrevistarse con el/la director(a) de personal. Durante la entrevista las dos personas van a hacer preguntas—las siguientes o varias otras que Uds. preparan.

Preguntas que hace el/la director(a)
1. ¿Qué experiencia tiene Ud.? ¿Dónde y qué estudió?
2. ¿Por qué quiere trabajar en nuestra compañía?
3. ¿Por qué dejó su último puesto? (¿Por qué quiere dejarlo?) ¿Le gustó? (¿Le gusta?)
4. ¿Cuáles son sus puntos fuertes (*strengths*)? ¿sus puntos débiles (*weaknesses*)?
5. ¿Qué sabe Ud. de nuestra compañía? ¿Qué desea saber de ella?
6. ???

Preguntas que hace el/la aspirante
1. ¿Cuántos empleados hay en la compañía?
2. ¿Cuáles son las responsabilidades del puesto? ¿el sueldo?
3. ¿Cuáles son las horas de trabajo?
4. ¿Existe la posibilidad de subir en la compañía?
5. Si deseo estudiar más, ¿la compañía va a pagar mis estudios?
6. ???

C. **¿Dónde se oye?** In which of these places would the following commands be appropriate? After you have matched the items given, create as many different **tú** or **Ud.** commands as possible for each location.

en una fiesta familiar	en casa
en una fiesta universitaria	en la cafetería universitaria
en el camino/la carretera	en el aeropuerto
en la agencia de automóviles	en el avión
en una tienda de ropa	en el Departamento de Personal
en un almacén	en Alaska, un día de invierno

1. Cómpralo—es una ganga.
2. Pregúntaselo a tu abuelo. Él debe saberlo, hijo, yo no.
3. Maneja con cuidado.
4. No comas eso. Te vas a enfermar.
5. Sube al avión. Va a salir dentro de cinco minutos.
6. No bebas tanta cerveza.
7. Vuelve mañana, Ana, para la entrevista.
8. No regatees—aquí no se puede.
9. Compra ese suéter azul, que es mucho más bonito que los otros.
10. Lava los platos y saca la basura.
11. Guárdame un asiento, por favor.
12. Ponte el abrigo y las botas.

A propósito...

In English, when you don't understand what someone says, it is appropriate to ask *"What?"* For this reason, it seems natural to ask *"¿Qué?"* in Spanish, but the word **qué** is seldom used in this way. If you want a speaker to repeat what he or she said, use one of these expressions:

¿Cómo?	*What? How's that*
Mande. (México)	*again?*
¿Qué (me) dice(s)?	*What did you say?*
Perdón, no entendí bien.	*Excuse me, I didn't understand.*
¿Puede(s) hablar más despacio, por favor?	*Could you speak more slowly, please?*

If you understand most of what is said but miss a single important word or phrase, you can repeat what you *did* understand, leaving it to the speaker to fill in the part you missed: **¿El autobús para León sale a...?** **¿Quieres que yo...?** Or, you can simply use an interrogative such as **¿cuántos? ¿cuál(es)? ¿quién(es)? ¿dónde?** or **¿cuándo?** to elicit the missing information.

D. **¿Cómo?** You hear the following sentence fragments. How can you get the entire message in each situation? Give as many different responses as possible to each fragment, using the expressions in the **A propósito** section.

1. Cuesta... pesos el kilo.
2. Primero vaya Ud. a la calle Princesa, después... y por fin doble a la derecha.
3. ...no tienen que tomar el examen final.
4. ...mi tío.
5. Es necesario que tú... hoy.
6. El tren para Madrid sale a las...
7. Siento decirte que tu amigo...
8. ¡...me lo contó ayer! ¡Qué horror!

E. **El mejor de los mejores.** Your friend Julio perceives everything in terms of extremes—the best, the worst, the biggest. How will he describe each of the following discoveries and experiences? Use the present tense in order to make your description more vivid.

Como siempre dice la maestra, de los peores estudiantes de química, soy el mejor.

MODELO   su nuevo coche →
    Acabo de comprar un coche nuevo que me gusta muchísimo. Es lindísimo, ¿sabes? También es el más económico de todos los nuevos modelos. El precio es bajísimo y gasta poquísima gasolina. Es el mejor coche del mundo. Ven a verlo.

1. su viaje a un lugar maravilloso (por ejemplo, San Francisco, México, Cape Cod, la Florida, Outer Banks)
2. su nuevo/a jefe/a

     3. el nuevo disco de _____
     4. su mejor amigo/a
     5. una película nueva
     6. su perro/gato

Lectura cultural: La educación en los países hispanos

Por lo general, el sistema de educación de los países hispanos es mucho más tradicional o clásico que el de° los Estados Unidos. Tomemos como ejemplo el caso de Jairo, un ingeniero° colombiano que acaba de recibir su título de la Universidad Nacional.

     Jairo entró en la escuela primaria a los seis años de edad. Asistió a una escuela particular° para varones° y dirigida° por padres jesuitas. Después de terminar los seis años de primaria, entró en otra escuela particular para hacer los seis años de colegio, o escuela secundaria. En este colegio,

el... that of

engineer

private / males / directed

Jairo siguió° once cursos al año; estos cursos incluyeron ciencias, mate-   *took*
máticas, religión, filosofía, dibujo°, inglés, francés, latín, literatura y   *drawing*
economía.   Cuando decidió continuar sus estudios al nivel° universitario,   *level*
Jairo empezó a estudiar en la Universidad Nacional, porque la matrícula
era° más barata que la de las universidades particulares.   *was*

Este programa educativo de Jairo es un ejemplo de la educación que
reciben muchos de los estudiantes hispanos.   Por lo general, el sistema
hispano requiere que el estudiante —y en especial el colegial°— siga un   *student at a* **colegio**
programa mucho más rígido que el de las escuelas secundarias de los
Estados Unidos; hay menos cursos «electivos».   Por sus esfuerzos° el   *efforts*
estudiante recibe el título de Bachiller, después de aprobar° los exámenes   *passing*
de bachillerato.   Ya, en la universidad, se estudia para una profesión
determinada en una de las facultades° profesionales, como Ingeniería,   *schools (divisions of a*
Medicina o Derecho°.   También hay muchos estudiantes que asisten a   *university)*
clases en la Facultad de Filosofía y Letras°.   En ella se amplían° los estudios   *law*
generales humanísticos sin especialización.   El concepto de *major* no existe   **Filosofía...** *liberal arts /*
tal como en° los Estados Unidos.   *se... are broadened*
    tal... *exactly as in*

Comprensión

Conteste en oraciones completas.

1. ¿Cómo es el sistema de educación de los países hispanos?
2. ¿A qué tipo de escuela primaria asistió Jairo?
3. En Colombia, ¿cuántos años se pasan en la primaria? ¿en la secundaria?
4. ¿Qué es un colegio?
5. ¿Qué cursos tienen que seguir los estudiantes de colegio?
6. ¿Qué título recibe el estudiante hispano cuando termina el colegio?
7. ¿En qué (how) es diferente el sistema universitario hispano del sistema universitario de los Estados Unidos?

Ejercicios escritos

A. Complete the following paragraph about your chosen career.

Yo estudio para ser _____ porque _____. Después de graduarme, quiero _____. En esta profesión se puede _____.

B. A Hispanic friend has asked you the following questions about the educational system in the United States. Answer his/her questions in a brief paragraph, using these questions as a guide.

1. ¿A qué edad empezaste la escuela primaria? ¿Qué es eso de *kindergarten*?
2. En los Estados Unidos, ¿cuántos años se asiste a la primaria? ¿a la secundaria?
3. ¿Cuántas materias se estudian cada año en la secundaria? ¿Cuáles son las materias que se estudian cada año? ¿Qué materias hiciste tú?
4. ¿Qué materia te gustó más? ¿Por qué?
5. ¿Hay algunas actividades en la escuela secundaria? ¿En cuáles participaste tú?
6. ¿Son difíciles las materias de la secundaria? ¿de la universidad?
7. ¿Es difícil que le acepten a uno/a en la universidad? ¿Cuánto hay que pagar de (*in*) matrícula?
8. ¿Cuántas horas de clase tienes en una semana? ¿Cuántas horas más estudias en casa o en la biblioteca?
9. ¿Los estudios universitarios son mucho más difíciles que los de la secundaria?

capítulo 12 El bautizo

Henri Cartier-Bresson/Magnum

OBJETIVOS

In this chapter you will learn more words to describe emotions and behavior, and you will learn vocabulary and expressions related to several religious and folk customs of the Hispanic world.

You will also learn about the following aspects of Spanish grammar:

53. verbs that have irregular preterite tense forms

54. ways of expressing smallness and affection by using diminutives: **casita** *small house*, **librito** *little book*, **Juanita** *Janie*
55. when to use the preposition **para** (*for*) as well as when to use **para** in contrast with **por**

Un paso más includes activities related to telling jokes and keeping conversations going, and a reading about the regions of Spain.

VOCABULARIO: PREPARACIÓN

El comportamiento° y las emociones			behavior
enojado/a	angry	**portarse**	to behave
enojarse	to get angry	**recordar (ue)**	to remember
faltar	to be absent, missing, lacking	**reírse (i, i)**	to laugh
		sentirse (ie, i)	to feel
llorar	to cry	**sonreír (i, i)**	to smile

A. *Describa Ud. el comportamiento de esta persona. Luego diga Ud. cómo se siente.*

1.   2.   3.   4.

La señorita (se) está _____.
Se siente _____.

B. *De los miembros de su clase de español,*

1. ¿quién falta a clase con frecuencia? ¿quién nunca falta?
2. ¿quién nunca recuerda los verbos?
3. ¿quién se porta de una forma cómica?
4. ¿quién se enoja fácilmente?
5. ¿quién se ríe con frecuencia? ¿quién sonríe mucho?
6. ¿quién tiene una sonrisa bonita? ¿y una risa cómica?

To become (get)

¿Por qué **te pones** tan furioso?	Why are you getting (becoming) so angry?
Vamos a **ponernos** muy sucios.	We're going to get (become) very dirty.
Se hizo ⎫ directora de la com- **Llegó a ser** ⎭ pañía.	She became director of the company.
Quiere ⎰ **hacerse** ⎱ rico. ⎱ **llegar a ser** ⎰	He wants to become rich.

Ponerse + adjective is used to indicate physical, mental, or emotional changes. **Hacerse** and **llegar a ser** + noun indicate a change as the result of a series of events or as the result of effort. They are also frequently used with the adjective **rico**.

C. *¿Qué ambiciones tiene Ud.?   Complete las oraciones en una forma lógica.*

Yo quiero hacerme _____ algún día.
No quiero nunca llegar a ser _____.

D. *¿Cómo se pone Ud. en estas situaciones?   Complete Ud. la frase con los adjetivos siguientes.*

serio/a   triste
nervioso/a   furioso/a
alegre

1. Cuando hay un examen me pongo _____. 2. Cuando tengo que estudiar me pongo _____. 3. Cuando un amigo está enfermo me pongo _____. 4. Cuando mis amigos me invitan a salir con ellos me pongo _____. 5. Cuando termino un examen difícil me pongo _____. 6. Cuando termino un examen fácil me pongo _____. 7. Cuando no recuerdo algo durante un examen me pongo _____. 8. Cuando alguien llora me pongo _____. 9. Cuando alguien se porta de una forma descortés me pongo _____.

El nacimiento° y el bautizo°			birth / baptism
el bebé	baby	**bautizar**	to baptize
la niña	female child, girl	**pesar**	to weigh
el varón	male child, boy	**regalar**	to give (as a gift)
¡felicidades!	congratulations!		

The terms **varón/niño** and **niña** are used to refer only to persons.   The words **macho** and **hembra** are used to indicate gender with animals.

E. *Complete Ud. estos diálogos sobre el nacimiento de un bebé.*

1. —¿Cuánto _____ el niño cuando nació?
   —Tres kilos.
2. —¡_____! Ahora son abuelos.
   —Por fin, y nos sentimos muy orgullosos (*proud*).

3. —María, ¿qué le _____ a tu nieto? ¿un juguete (toy)?
   —No, un par de botitas (booties).
4. —¿Quieres un _____ o una niña?
   —Yo, una niña, porque ya tengo tres varones en casa.
5. —¿Quién le compró al _____ esas botitas?
   —Su abuela se las regaló.
6. —¿Cuándo la van a _____?
   —Mañana. ¿Vas a asistir a la ceremonia?

PRONUNCIACIÓN: I and U with Other Vowels

When unstressed **u** and **i** occur next to another vowel, they always form diphthongs. For this reason, the words **bueno** and **siete** have two syllables each; the **u** and the **i** form diphthongs with the following vowel and are pronounced [w] and [y] respectively: [bwe-no], [sye-te].

When **u** and **i** have written accent marks, they do not form diphthongs. Thus, **dios** has one syllable, while **días** has two syllables; **continuo** has three syllables, and **continúo** has four.

Unaccented **i** represents [y] in the participle ending **-iendo** and the preterite endings **-ió** and **-ieron: comiendo, comió, comieron.** When the verb stem ends in a vowel, the **i** changes to **y: oyendo, oyó, oyeron; leyendo, leyó, leyeron; cayendo, cayó, cayeron.** Verbs with stems ending in a vowel will also have written accents in the first- and second-persons plural of the preterite to show that the **i** does not form a diphthong: **oímos, oíste; leímos, leíste; caímos, caíste.**

PRÁCTICA

A. ai/aí   uo/úo   ia/ía   au/aú
   ue/úe   ie/íe   io/ío   ua/úa

B. viaje experiencia historia bien tierra
   radio idioma ciudad traigo aire
   seis veinte treinta oigo ciudadano ruido

C. Guadalajara suave puedo fueron antiguo
   cuota causa bautizo Europa europeo

D. país paraíso oímos sociología energía leíste
   período reíste ríe gradúa continúe acentúo

MINIDIÁLOGOS Y GRAMÁTICA

53. IRREGULAR PRETERITES

Prognóstico de un nombre

FÉLIX: ¿Por qué faltaste al bautizo de la nieta de don Pepe ayer?

BEGOÑA: *Quise* ir pero no *pude* por el trabajo. ¿Qué tal *estuvo*?

FÉLIX: La fiesta *estuvo* estupenda. ¡Cuánta gente! ¡Y qué divertido todo!

BEGOÑA: ¿Qué nombre le *pusieron* a la niña?

FÉLIX: Arántzazu Gazteizgogeascoa. Son vascos, sabes.

BEGOÑA: ¡Por Dios! Con un nombre así, tiene que hacerse oculista. ¡No hay más remedio!

1. *¿Por qué faltó Begoña al bautizo?*
2. *¿Qué tal estuvo la fiesta?*
3. *¿Qué nombre le pusieron a la niña?*
4. *¿Por qué es probable que la niña llegue a ser oculista?*

You have already learned the irregular preterite forms of **dar, hacer, ir,** and **ser.** The following verbs are also irregular in the preterite. Note that the first- and third-person singular endings, which are the only irregular ones, are unstressed, in contrast to the stressed endings of regular preterite forms.

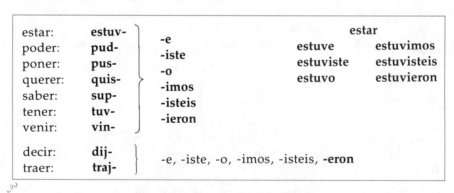

estar:	estuv-			estar	
poder:	pud-	-e		estuve	estuvimos
poner:	pus-	-iste		estuviste	estuvisteis
querer:	quis-	-o		estuvo	estuvieron
saber:	sup-	-imos			
tener:	tuv-	-isteis			
venir:	vin-	-ieron			
decir:	dij-	-e, -iste, -o, -imos, -isteis, **-eron**			
traer:	traj-				

When the verb stem ends in **-j-,** as in **decir** and **traer,** the **-i-** of the third-person plural ending is omitted: **dijeron, trajeron.**

Prognosis for a name FÉLIX: Why weren't you at the baptism of don Pepe's granddaughter yesterday? BEGOÑA: I tried to go, but I couldn't because of work. How was it? FÉLIX: The party was marvelous. So many people! And what fun! BEGOÑA: What name did they give the child? FÉLIX: Arántzazu Gazteizgogeascoa. They're Basques, you know. BEGOÑA: Heavens! With a name like that, she has to be an eye doctor. She has no choice!

The preterite of **hay (haber)** is **hubo** (*there was/were*).

Several of these Spanish verbs have an English equivalent in the preterite tense that is different from that of the infinitive.

saber:	Lo sé.	*I know it.*
	Lo **supe** ayer.	*I found it out (learned it) yesterday.*
conocer:	La conozco.	*I know her.*
	La **conocí** ayer.	*I met her yesterday.*
querer:	Quiero hacerlo.	*I want to do it.*
	Quise hacerlo ayer.	*I tried to do it yesterday.*
	No quise hacerlo.	*I refused to do it.*
poder:	Puedo leerlo.	*I can (am able to) read it.*
	Pude leerlo.	*I could (and did) read it.*
	No pude leerlo.	*I couldn't (did not) read it.*

PRÁCTICA

A. *Dé Ud. frases nuevas según las indicaciones.*

1. —¿Quién tuvo una entrevista ayer?
    —*Amanda* (no) tuvo una entrevista ayer. (*Raúl, yo, nosotros, tú, nadie, vosotros*)
2. —¿Quién estuvo en España el verano pasado?
    —*Xavier* (no) estuvo en España el verano pasado. (*yo, nosotros, Soledad, tú, Carlos y Fidelia, vosotras*)
3. —Muchos se enojaron por el tráfico ayer. ¿Quién se puso furioso?
    —*Yo* me puse furioso. (*Silvia, mi esposo/a, Uds., nosotros, tú, vosotros*)
4. —Anoche, ¿quién quiso dormir y no pudo?
    —Anoche *Alfredo* quiso dormir pero no pudo. (*yo, ellos, Eloísa, tú, Ud., vosotras*)
5. —Después del último examen en esta clase, ¿quién dijo que fue difícil?
    —*Alicia* dijo que fue difícil. (*tú, el/la profesor[a], Ud., nosotros, todos los estudiantes, vosotros*)
6. —Muchos amigos no vinieron a la última fiesta de Ud. por el examen al (*on the*) día siguiente. ¿Quién no vino?
    —No vino *Pablo*. (*Ud., nosotros, Uds., tú, Rosalba, vosotros*)

B. *Describa Ud. estos hechos* (events) *históricos, usando una palabra o frase de cada columna. Use el pretérito de los verbos.*

en 1969 los estadounidenses	traer	un hombre en la luna
Adán y Eva	saber	en Valley Forge con sus soldados
Jorge Washington	conocer	«que coman (*let them eat*) pasteles»
los europeos	decir	que las serpeintes son malas
Stanley	estar	a Livingston en África
María Antonieta	poner	el caballo (*horse*) al Nuevo Mundo

C. *Cambie por el pretérito.*

1. El nieto de Ana *viene* a visitarnos. El niño se *porta* muy bien. *Está* en casa una hora; luego *dice* adiós y se *va.*
2. Los Sres. Torres *hacen* la cena y *ponen* la mesa a las seis. Luego *tienen* que lavar los platos. No *pueden* salir hasta las ocho.
3. *Quiero* estudiar pero no *puedo* porque mi amigo Octavio *viene* a casa con un amigo ecuatoriano. *Tengo* que ver las fotos que *traen.*

CONVERSACIÓN

A. *Conteste Ud. en frases completas.*

1. ¿En qué mes conoció Ud. al/a la profesor(a) de español por primera vez? ¿Tuvo Ud. que hablar español el primer día?
2. En la clase de español, ¿hubo examen ayer? ¿Qué dijo Ud. cuando supo la nota del último examen? ¿Pudo Ud. hacer los ejercicios de esta lección? ¿Fue difícil aprender el pretérito?
3. ¿Alguien vino tarde a clase hoy? ¿Dónde puso sus libros cuando entró en la clase?
4. ¿Dónde estuvo Ud. el pasado fin de semana? ¿Dónde estuvo el verano pasado?
5. ¿Qué hizo Ud. anoche? ¿Qué quiso hacer ayer?
6. ¿Alguien le hizo a Ud. una fiesta de cumpleaños este año? ¿Qué le trajeron sus amigos? ¿Qué le regalaron sus padres? ¿Alguien le hizo un pastel?

B. *Complete las oraciones en una forma lógica.*

1. La semana pasada, hubo examen en la clase de _____. Fue _____.
2. Ayer/la semana pasada supe que _____.
3. El año pasado conocí a _____. Me cayó bien/mal.
4. Ayer/la semana pasada me puse furioso/a porque tuve que _____.
5. Una vez no quise _____.

54. DIMINUTIVES

mesa

mesita

Carmen

Carmencita

Diminutive forms of nouns denote small size or affection. In English, some nouns, especially proper names, form the diminutive by adding a suffix: *John → Johnny; Mom → Mommy, drop → droplet.* Usually, however, diminutives are formed in English by using an adjective with the noun: *a little table, a cute little youngster.*

In Spanish, *diminutives* (**diminutivos**) are usually formed by adding suffixes to nouns.

1. mesa → **mesita**   hermano → **hermanito**   papel → **papelito**

The suffix **-ito (-a/ -os/ -as)** is added to nouns that end in **o, a,** or **l.** Final **o/a** is dropped before the suffix is added. When **c, g,** or **z** precede **-ito,** there is a spelling change in the diminutive form: **chica → chiquita; lago** (*lake*) **→ laguito; taza → tacita.**

2. varón → **varoncito**   pobre → **pobrecito**   madre → **madrecita**

The suffix **-cito (-a/ -os/ -as)** is added to nouns that end in **e** or in a consonant other than **l.**

The form of diminutives is very flexible in Spanish. For this reason, you will sometimes hear diminutives that do not follow these rules exactly: **pueblo → pueblecito** or **pueblito.**

PRÁCTICA

A. Dé Ud. el diminutivo.

1. libro	5. hombre	9. chico
2. ángel	6. lago	10. perro
3. autor	7. bota	
4. joven	8. varón	

B. The following persons have named their children after themselves. Tell what they call their children by giving the diminutive form of each name.

1. Carmen	4. Rafael	7. Ana
2. Juana	5. Álvaro	8. Lola
3. Xavier	6. Sara	

CONVERSACIÓN

A. Rosario cumplió nueve años ayer y todos le regalaron algo. Describa Ud. los regalos con el diminutivo.

MODELO   el abuelo / libro → *El abuelo le regaló un librito a Rosario.*

1. el abuelo / tren

2. la abuela / una muñeca (*doll*)
3. el tío Genaro / ropa para la muñeca
4. la tía Julia / una mesa, sillas, platos y tazas
5. la mamá / un avión
6. el papá / pantalones (pantalon-)
7. el hermanito / zapatos
8. su amigo Daniel / una araña (*spider*) de plástico

B. *¿Cómo reaccionó Rosario cuando recibió cada regalo?*

Rosario $\left\{ \begin{array}{l} \text{sonrió (smiled)} \\ \text{se rió (laughed)} \\ \text{lloró} \end{array} \right\}$ cuando ＿＿＿ le dio ＿＿＿.

55. USES OF *PARA,* AND *PARA* VERSUS *POR*

La política de un expolítico

ADELA: Lincoln lo expresó muy bien en su discurso —¿no lo recuer-
das?— «...que el gobierno del pueblo, *por* el pueblo, *para*
el pueblo no desaparezca de la tierra».

BENITO: (*levantándose, enojado*) Pues *para* mí un gobierno del, *por*
y *para* el pueblo no existe todavía.

ADELA: Pero si el pueblo va a gobernarse, es necesario educarlo *para*
gobernar. ¿Por qué crees que...? (*Se va Benito.*) ¡Ay, qué
pesado! Últimamente se enoja cada vez que se habla de
política.

CARLOS: Lógico. No te olvides de que lo botaron en las últimas
elecciones.

1. *¿Quién es Benito? ¿De qué hablan los amigos?*
2. *¿De qué tipo de gobierno habló Lincoln?*
3. *¿Está Benito de acuerdo con Lincoln? ¿Cómo reacciona?*
4. *¿Adela cree que es necesario educar al pueblo? ¿Para qué?*
5. *¿Por qué se enoja Benito cuando se habla de política?*

Para

The preposition **para** has many English equivalents, including *for*. Under-
lying all of them is reference to a goal or a destination.

The politics of an ex-politician ADELA: Lincoln said it very well in his speech—Don't you remember
it?—"that government of the people, by the people, for the people shall not perish from the earth."
BENITO: (*getting up, angry*) Well, as far as I'm concerned a government of, by, and for the people
doesn't exist yet. ADELA: But if the people are going to govern themselves, you have to teach them
to govern. Why do you think that . . . ? (*Benito leaves.*) What a pain! Lately he gets mad every time
anyone talks politics. CARLOS: Of course. Don't forget that they threw him out (of office) in the last
elections.

1. IN ORDER TO + *infinitive*

Se quedaron en Andorra **para esquiar.**
They stayed in Andorra to (in order to) ski.

Sólo regresaron **para cenar.**
They only came back to have dinner.

Ramón estudia **para (ser) abogado.**
Ramon is studying to be a lawyer.

2. FOR when *for* means
   a. DESTINED FOR, TO BE GIVEN TO

Le regalé un libro **para su hijo.**
I gave him a book for his son.

Todo esto es **para ti.**
All of this is for you.

   b. FOR (BY) A SPECIFIED FUTURE TIME

Para mañana estudien Uds. la página 72.
For tomorrow, study page 72.

Lo tengo que terminar **para la semana que viene.**
I have to finish it by next week.

   c. TOWARD, IN THE DIRECTION OF

Salieron **para Acapulco** ayer.
They left for Acapulco yesterday.

   d. TO BE USED FOR

Es un vaso **para agua.**
It's a water glass (a glass for water).

¡OJO! Compare: Es un vaso **de agua.**
It's a glass (full) of water.

   e. COMPARED WITH OTHERS, IN RELATION TO OTHERS

Para mí el español es fácil.
For me Spanish is easy.

Para (ser) extranjera habla muy bien el inglés.
She speaks English very well for a foreigner.

   f. IN THE EMPLOY OF

Trabajan **para ese hotel.**
They work for that hotel.

[Práctica A, B]

Para versus Por

Sometimes either **por** or **para** can be used in a given sentence, but there will always be a difference in meaning depending on which one is used. Compare the following pairs of sentences:

Vamos **para** las montañas.	*Let's head toward the mountains.*
Vamos **por** las montañas.	*Let's go through the mountains.*
Déle el dinero **para** el carro.	*Give her the money for* (so that she can buy) *the car.*
Déle el dinero **por** el carro.	*Give her the money* (*in exchange*) *for the car.* (Buy the car from her.)
Es alto **para** su edad.	*He's tall for his age* (compared to others of his same age).
Es alto **por** su edad.	*He's tall because of his age.* (He's no longer a child.)

[Práctica C]

PRÁCTICA

A. *Dé Ud. frases nuevas según las indicaciones.*

1. —¿Para qué están Uds. en esta clase?
   —(No) Estamos aquí para _____. (*aprender español, divertirnos, conversar, escuchar*)
2. —En el restaurante Ud. tiene que pedir porque nadie más habla español. ¿Qué va a pedir?
   —Para mi *padre, la paella.* (*madre / pescado, hermanito / bistec, abuela / paella, mí / pollo*)
3. —¿Para dónde salieron estas personas?
   —*Ponce de León* salió para *la Florida.* (*Colón / la India, los astronautas / la luna, Lewis y Clark / el oeste, Hernán Cortés / México*)

B. *Conteste Ud. negativamente en frases completas, usando las expresiones entre paréntesis.*

1. Para mañana, ¿hay que leer el capítulo 14? (el diálogo 12)
2. ¿Esa camisa es para hombre? (mujer)
3. Para niño, Juanito pronuncia muy mal, ¿verdad? (bien)
4. Para la semana que viene, ¿tenemos que aprender el subjuntivo? (el pretérito)
5. ¿No trabajó Ud. para el señor Medina el año pasado? (la señora Hernández)
6. Para Ud., el español es muy difícil, ¿verdad? (fácil)

C. *Llene Ud. los espacios con **por** o **para**.*

1. Salieron _____ el Perú ayer. Van _____ avión.
2. Hoy _____ la tarde, vamos a prepararnos _____ el examen.
3. Le pagué veinte dólares _____ esta blusa _____ Clara.
4. Vaya Ud. a la tienda _____ cerveza _____ la fiesta.

5. Sé que tienes mucho que hacer _____ el bautizo mañana. ¿Te puedo traer algo _____ la fiesta después?
6. Buscamos un regalo de boda _____ nuestra nieta. ¿No tienen Uds. unos vasos de cristal _____ vino?
7. Graciela quiere estudiar _____ (ser) doctora. _____ eso trabaja _____ un médico _____ la mañana; tiene clases _____ la tarde.
8. _____ la nieve (snow) no vamos.

CONVERSACIÓN

A. Describa los dibujos, usando **por** o **para**.

1. 2. 3. 4. 5.

B. Complete las oraciones en una forma lógica.

1. Para mañana tengo que _____.
2. Esta noche voy a _____ para _____.
3. Quiero comprar algo especial para _____.
4. Este fin de semana salgo para _____.
5. Para mí es fácil/difícil _____.
6. Mi _____ trabaja para _____.
7. Estudio para (ser) _____.

DIÁLOGO: Un nuevo miembro de la familia

José Pelayo (Pepito), el bebé
Inés, la madre
Agustín, hermano de Inés y tío del bebé
Julián, íntimo amigo de la familia
los abuelos, españoles que ahora viven en México

A. Hablando del nacimiento
JULIÁN: Llamé a tu casa y me dijeron que tu hermana ya dio a luz°.   dio... gave birth

AGUSTÍN: Sí, esta mañana. Inés está muy bien y todos estamos contentísimos.

JULIÁN: Por fin, ¿qué tuvo, varón o niña?

AGUSTÍN: Un varoncito hermosísimo. Pesó cuatro kilos. Vamos a bautizarlo el domingo a las dos de la tarde. Luego hay una fiesta en casa. No dejes de° asistir, ¿eh?[1]   **No**... be sure you

B. *El domingo, en casa de la familia*

ABUELA: ¡Qué bueno que llegaste para la fiesta, Julián! Te extrañamos° en la iglesia, pues para nosotros tú eres como de la familia.   we missed

JULIÁN: Lo siento, señora. No pude venir antes. ¿Qué tal fue el bautizo?

ABUELA: Magnífico. ¡Cuánta gente, Julián, y qué ruido!

JULIÁN: Cuénteme del nietecito. ¿Se puso pesado° durante la ceremonia?   **Se**... did he act up

ABUELA: ¡Qué va! El gordito° se portó increíblemente bien. No lloró nada. ¡Es un angelito! Vamos a verlo, ¿quieres?   chubby little fellow

(*Van a ver al bebito.*)

JULIÁN: ¿Qué nombre le pusieron?

ABUELA: Le pusimos José Pelayo. José por su padre, como es el primer varón. Además, nació el 19 de marzo[2].

JULIÁN: ¿Y Pelayo? ¿Por qué?

ABUELA: Por su abuelo que es de Asturias.³ Llegó a México muy joven, después de la Guerra Civil⁴, y se hizo ciudadano mexicano, pero todavía es más asturiano que Pelayo.

JULIÁN: (*al niño*) Pues mucho gusto en conocerte, Pepito. (*a la abuela*) El chamaquito está muy elegante para ser un recién nacido°.   recién... *newborn*

ABUELA: Gracias, Julián. Yo le hice las botitas azules y el padrino le regaló la medalla de oro de nuestra patrona la Virgen de Guadalupe⁵.

C. *Más tarde*

JULIÁN: Felicidades, señor abuelo. Debe estar Ud. contento con el nieto, ¿verdad?

ABUELO: Su nacimiento me hizo muy feliz. Pero, el bautizo, no. Faltó algo... la sidra°. No hay bautizo asturiano   *hard cider* sin sidra.

JULIÁN: Pero no estamos en Asturias, ni es español el chamaco.

ABUELO: Pero estamos en mi casa, ¡caramba!, y mi nieto tiene sangre° asturiana. ¿No conoces la tradición?   *blood*

INÉS: Perdonen que los interrumpa, pero, ¿puedo saber quién puso sidra en el biberón° de Pepito?   *baby bottle*

ABUELO: La tradición, mujer, la tradición.

Comprensión

Conteste en oraciones completas.

A. 1. ¿Quién acaba de dar a luz? ¿Es varón o niña el bebé?
    2. Para un recién nacido, ¿es muy grande?
    3. ¿Qué va a hacer la familia el domingo después del bautizo?

B. 1. ¿Quién no pudo asistir al bautizo?
    2. ¿Por qué lo extrañaron todos?
    3. ¿Por qué dice la abuela que el niño es un angelito?
    4. ¿Qué nombre le pusieron?
    5. ¿Por qué le pusieron José? ¿y Pelayo?
    6. ¿Quién le regaló las botitas? ¿y la medalla?

C. 1. ¿Por qué está contento el abuelo?
    2. Según el abuelo, ¿qué falta?
    3. ¿De dónde es el abuelo? ¿Dónde vive ahora?
    4. ¿Quién puso sidra en el biberón de Pepito?

Comentario cultural

1. In a Hispanic family, a christening is always an important event. After the baptismal ceremony at the church, there is usually a party at home for friends and family.

2. **Pepito** is the diminutive form of **Pepe,** the nickname for **José** (*Joseph*). **Pepito,** named for his father, was born on March 19, St. Joseph's Day on the Catholic calendar. March 19, then, is not only **Pepito's** birthday; it is also his saint's day or name day. In Spain and Spanish America one traditionally celebrates one's saint's day, the day on the Catholic calendar that corresponds to the saint for whom one is named.

3. In Spain, people often identify more strongly with the province in which they were born and raised than with Spain as a nation. Each of the fourteen regions of Spain has its own history and personal and linguistic characteristics.

   Asturias is a small region on the north coast of Spain. There, in the year A.D. 718, a band of Christians led by don Pelayo defeated the invading Moorish armies at the Battle of Covadonga, thus preventing Islam from completely overtaking the Iberian Peninsula. Later, don Pelayo was elected king of Asturias. Pelayo is now regarded as a national hero in Spain, and the heir to the Spanish throne holds the honorary title prince of Asturias.

   Pepito's grandfather still has strong feelings for Asturias, even though he is now a citizen of Mexico, and he is proud that his Mexican-born grandson will have the name *Pelayo.*

4. The Spanish Civil War was a bitter conflict between Republicans and Nationalists that lasted for three years (1936–1939). It is estimated that as many as 1 million people died as a result of the war. Thousands of refugees fled from Spain, many going to Mexico and other countries of North and South America.

5. In some Hispanic countries, certain saints' days are national holidays. The Virgin of Guadalupe, the patron saint of Mexico, is commemorated on Decem-

Marilu Pease/Monkmeyer Press Photo

ber 12, a national holiday in Mexico and one that is celebrated by many Mexicans and Mexican-Americans living in the United States.

UN POCO DE TODO

A. *Cambie por el pretérito. Dé el diminutivo de las palabras indicadas.*

1. ¿Por qué te pones tan triste, mi *amor?*
2. *Rosa* llega a ser enfermera.
3. Se hace maestra en un *pueblo* de asturianos.
4. Tiene un *niño* gordo.
5. Se enoja porque no hay sidra en el bautizo.

B. *Form complete sentences based on the words given, in the order given. Conjugate the verbs in the preterite, and give the diminutive form of the italicized words. Add other words if necessary.*

1. Ana / me / regalar / *medalla* / oro
2. ¿ / tu / amigo / venir / a / fiesta / con / su / *hermanas* / ?
3. *chamaca* / decir / palabras / en español / para / abuelo
4. marido / le / traer / su mujer / *reloj* / oro / para / su / cumpleaños
5. cuando / prima / hacerse / rico / comprar / *casa* de / verano / para / familia

C. *Working with another student, ask and answer questions according to the model.*

MODELO   prima / dos días / figurita / casa →
ÁBEL: La semana pasada vino a vernos mi *prima.*
ANA: ¿Qué tal su visita?
ÁBEL: Fue muy agradable. Se quedó *dos días.*
ANA: ¿Cuándo se fue entonces?
ÁBEL: Ayer, y cuando salió, le regalamos una *figurita* para su *casa.*

1. hermanos / cinco días / perrito / hijo
2. nietas / dos semanas / libros / biblioteca
3. abuelos / una semana / una foto de toda la familia / álbum
4. nuestro amigo Julio / seis días / radio / cumpleaños

D. *Explique la situación que resulta en estas preguntas. Después, conteste las preguntas.*

MODELO   ¿Por qué quiere hacerse presidente?
→ **Situación:** *Entrevista con un reportero del periódico estudiantil*
→ **Respuesta:** *Porque el presidente actual* (current) *no es bueno.*

1. ¿Por qué vino Ud. a verme?
2. ¿Qué quieres que te traiga este año?
3. ¿Por qué te pusiste tan contento/a?
4. ¿Por qué quiere hacerse presidente?
5. ¿Por qué no quiso hacerlo?
6. ¿Por qué estás llorando? Fue una tacita, nada más.

E. *Indique su reacción ante* (in) *estas situaciones, completando una de las oraciones.*

Me sentí _____.   Me reí mucho/un poco _____.
Me puse _____.   Empecé a llorar _____.
Sonreí mucho/un poco _____.

Situaciones
1. No pude recordar las formas del pretérito en el examen.
2. Estudié ocho horas sin aprender bien todo para el examen de _____.
3. Salí para las montañas por la mañana, pero por el tráfico no llegué hasta muy tarde.
4. Unos amigos pasaron por la casa anoche para verme. Fue una sorpresa.
5. Fui a ver una nueva película de Woody Allen.

VOCABULARIO

VERBOS
bautizar to baptize
contar (ue) to tell about
dar a luz to give birth
enojarse to get angry
existir to exist
extrañar to miss (*the presence of someone or something*)
faltar to be absent, missing, lacking
hacerse to become
irse to leave, go away
llegar a ser to become
llorar to cry
pesar to weigh
ponerse to become, get
portarse to behave
quedarse to stay, remain

recordar (ue) to remember
regalar to give (as a gift)
reírse (i, i) to laugh
sentirse (ie, i) to feel
sonreír (i, i) to smile

SUSTANTIVOS
el **bautizo** baptism
el **bebé** baby
el **comportamiento** behavior
el/la **chamaco/a** child (*Mexican*)
la **emoción** emotion
la **forma** form; manner
la **foto** photo
el **lago** lake
la **luna** moon
la **medalla** medal, medallion
el **nacimiento** birth

la **política** politics
la **taza** cup
el **varón** male child, boy

ADJETIVOS
asturiano/a Asturian
enojado/a angry
furioso/a furious
gordo/a fat, plump
hermoso/a beautiful

PALABRAS Y EXPRESIONES ÚTILES
felicidades congratulations
hasta until
no hay más remedio nothing can be done about it

Un paso más 12

Actividades

A. **Reacciones.** Imagínese que ocurrieron las siguientes situaciones en algún momento en el pasado. ¿Cómo reaccionó Ud.? ¿Sonrió? ¿Lloró? ¿Se rió? ¿Se enojó? ¿Se puso triste, contento/a, furioso/a? ¿Qué hizo?

MODELO   Su compañero de cuarto hizo mucho ruido anoche. ¿Cómo reaccionó Ud.?
→ Me enojé.
→ Me puse furioso/a.
→ Salí de casa y fui a la biblioteca a estudiar.
→ Hablé con él.

Situaciones
1. Una amiga le regaló un libro interesante a Ud.
2. El profesor le dijo que no hay clase mañana.
3. Ud. rompió las gafas (*broke your eyeglasses*).
4. Su hermano perdió las llaves (*lost the keys*) de su coche.

5. Su mejor amigo le llamó a las seis de la mañana el día de su cumpleaños.
6. Nevó anoche.
7. Unos amigos le invitaron a una fiesta formal.
Ahora, usando las formas del pretérito, invente otras situaciones y pídales a sus compañeros de clase que le indiquen sus reacciones. Use la siguiente lista de verbos para preparar las situaciones.

hacer	venir	fumar	perder	estar
decir	poner(se)	graduarse	vender	levantarse
traer	salir	olvidar(se)	romper	leer
ir	ayudar	cancelar	beber	abrir

B. **Sin palabras.** The type of cartoon that has no caption in English is usually labeled **Sin palabras** in Spanish. On the next page are several cartoons that were originally **Sin palabras.** Match each of them with one of the captions on that page, or make up your own captions.

SIN PALABRAS

1.

2.

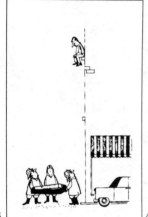

3.

4.

5.

Captions

1. ¿No quieres un cafecito, querido?
2. Mamá, te cogí (*I picked*) una florecita.
3. Lo hago sólo para estar segurísimo. Siento cierta responsabilidad en estas cosas, ¿sabe?
4. Saltar (*to jump*) o no saltar. Ésa es la pregunta.
5. ¿Es necesario que lo «lleven» al hospital?

C. **Chistes.** In all countries there are jokes about children and families.

JAIMITO: Abuelita, ¿quién trajo a Pepito?
ABUELITA: Una cigüeña (*stork*) lo trajo.
JAIMITO: ¿Y por qué no lo trajo directamente a la casa en vez de dejarlo en el hospital?

—Lo siento, la señora no está en casa.

ROSITA: Abuelito, ¿de dónde vienen los niños?
ABUELITO: De París, guapa, de París.
ROSITA: Y si yo vine de París, ¿cómo es que no hablo francés?

Write in simple Spanish an English joke that does not involve a play on words. If you need to use a dictionary, follow the suggestions in the **Study Hint** on page 143. Practice reading your joke aloud; then present it to the class.

A propósito...

Carrying on a conversation in a second language requires effort. When you are speaking to someone in Spanish, you may be making such an effort to understand everything or to formulate even simple answers that you forget to say the things that you would automatically say in English.

A conversation is somewhat like a tennis game—it is important to keep the ball moving. But to keep a conversation going, you need to do more than just answer the other person's questions mechanically. If you volunteer a comment or ask a question in return, you not only provide more information but let the other person know that you are interested in continuing the conversation. For example, in answer to the question **¿Juegas al béisbol?**, the words **Sí** or **Sí, juego al béisbol** do little more than hit the ball back. They are factually and grammatically correct, but since they provide no more new information, they return the burden of carrying the conversation to the other person. Answers such as **Sí, soy el pícher** or **Sí, ¿a ti te gusta también? ¿Quieres jugar con nosotros el domingo?** or **No, pero juego al tenis** demonstrate your willingness to keep on talking.

D. **No te pares allí.** With another student ask and answer the following questions. After answering the questions with a minimal amount of information, volunteer an additional comment or ask your partner a follow-up question. Using the suggestions in the **A propósito** section, keep each conversation going for a minimum of three or four exchanges before going on to the next question.

1. ¿A ti te gusta bailar el chachachá?
2. ¿Conoces la ciudad de Nueva York?
3. ¿Dónde vive tu familia?
4. ¿Tienes coche?
5. ¿Por qué estudias español?
6. ¿Cuál es tu programa de televisión favorito?
7. ¿Quieres viajar por México?
8. ¿Qué hiciste el verano pasado?

E. **Entrevistas.** Many U.S. families have special traditions that come from their ethnic or cultural heritage. Other family customs originate in special events that have meaning only to individual families. Explain some of your family traditions to the class by answering the following questions:

1. ¿De dónde viene su familia?
2. ¿Se habla otra lengua en casa? ¿Cuál?
3. ¿Un miembro de su familia nació en otro país? ¿Cuál?
4. ¿Cuáles son las fiestas que se celebran en su familia con reuniones (*gatherings*) familiares o con costumbres (*customs*) especiales? ¿la Navidad? ¿la Pascua (*Passover*)? ¿la Pascua florida (*Easter*)? ¿el Día de Gracias? ¿el 4 de julio? ¿el cumpleaños de alguien?
5. ¿Cómo se celebra esta fiesta? ¿Hay comida especial? ¿Quiénes vienen a casa? ¿Van Uds. a casa de otro pariente?

Lectura cultural: Las regiones de España

España y Portugal son los dos países que se encuentran en la Península Ibérica. Los Pirineos separan a España del resto de Europa.

En la Edad Media°, España fue un territorio dividido en varios reinos° pequeños. La nación que se conoce hoy día como España es, en realidad,

Edad... *Middle Ages / kingdoms*

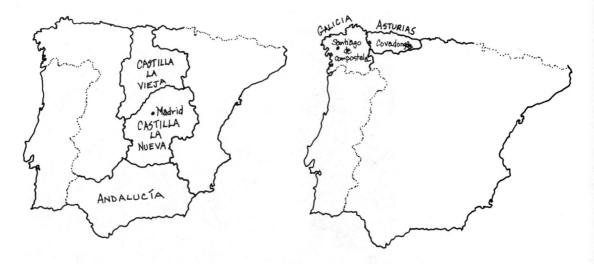

el conjunto° de estos reinos antiguos (hoy, regiones) que se unieron   *totality*
políticamente, poco a poco, a lo largo de la historia española.

Las regiones más famosas de España son Castilla la Vieja, Castilla la
Nueva y Andalucía. Castilla la Nueva está situada en la parte central del
país y allí se encuentra Madrid, la capital. Esta región dio origen a la
lengua castellana° y llegó a dominar políticamente al país. Andalucía,   *Spanish*
en el sur de la península, es la región que recibió más influencia de la
cultura árabe durante la dominación mora° (desde 711 hasta 1492).   *Moorish*
También esta región es famosísima por sus gitanos° y la música flamenca.   *gypsies*

Las regiones de Galicia, Asturias, las Provincias Vascongadas y Cataluña
están en el norte de España. Galicia fue durante la época medieval el
destino de muchas peregrinaciones° religiosas. Según la tradición, el   *pilgrimages*
apóstol Santiago°, el santo patrón de España, estaba enterrado° allí en la   *St. James / estaba... was buried*
ciudad de Santiago de Compostela (1).

Para los españoles, Asturias, la región más montañosa del norte, es
importantísima. Ahí°, en la famosa cueva° de Covadonga, el héroe Pelayo   *there / cave*
empezó en 718 la Reconquista, la guerra para expulsar a los árabes.

Las Provincias Vascongadas son tres. Están cerca de los Pirineos y
tienen límite° con la región vasca de Francia. Muchos vascos° se con-   *borders / Basque people*
sideran una raza y una cultura aparte. Por esta razón, existen por toda la
región sentimientos y actividades separatistas (2), las cuales° se están   *las... which*
infiltrando ahora en las regiones vascas de Francia.

Como las Vascongadas, Cataluña (capital: Barcelona) es una región de
sentimientos separatistas. Cataluña es la región más industrializada de
España. Al sur de Cataluña está Valencia, la huerta° de España. Las   *garden*
huertas de naranjas, limones, arroz° y melones reciben su agua por sis-   *rice*
temas de irrigación que construyeron los árabes durante su ocupación de
la península.

Las otras regiones son León en el noroeste, Navarra y Aragón en el
norte, Murcia en el sureste y Extremadura en el oeste. Esta última región

1.

2.

3.

fue muy importante en la historia de Hispanoamérica: ahí nacieron Cortés, Pizarro (3), De Soto y Balboa, hombres que participaron en el descubrimiento y la conquista de las Américas.

Además de estas regiones, son parte de España las Islas Baleares (Mallorca, Menorca, Ibiza) en el Mediterráneo y las Islas Canarias en el Atlántico.

La diversidad lingüística y cultural de todas estas regiones le da a España una gran atracción turística, pero también le proporciona° al país   *gives* problemas internos políticos que todavía tienen que resolverse.

Comprensión

Check your understanding of the reading by completing the sentence fragments in the left-hand column with phrases from the right-hand column.

1. En la Edad Media, España
2. La lengua castellana
3. Durante la Edad Media muchas personas viajaron a Galicia
4. La primera batalla (*battle*) de la Reconquista
5. El propósito (*purpose*) de la Reconquista
6. Los árabes estuvieron
7. Se cultivan frutas cítricas
8. Algunos de los primeros hombres que llegaron al Nuevo Mundo
9. La patria de los vascos
10. La diversidad regional española

a. ocurrió en Asturias.
b. contribuye a sus atracciones para los extranjeros pero causa algunos problemas políticos.
c. para visitar la tumba del apóstol Santiago.
d. en Valencia.
e. nació en Castilla.
f. consistió en varios reinos independientes.
g. en la Península Ibérica durante casi ochocientos años.
h. fueron de Extremadura.
i. tiene una historia de sentimientos separatistas.
j. fue retomar territorios perdidos (*lost*) a manos de los árabes.

Ejercicios escritos

A. Identifique estas regiones con una frase que las caracterice.

1. Andalucía   4. Castilla la Nueva
2. Cataluña   5. Galicia
3. Extremadura

B. Write a brief paragraph about the state in which you live or the state of your family origins.

Yo vivo en/Yo soy de _____. Este estado es famoso por _____. Su clima es _____. Durante la época colonial de los Estados Unidos, esta región _____. Ahora es _____. Para mí esta región es _____ porque _____.

capítulo 13 ¡Huy! ¡perdón!

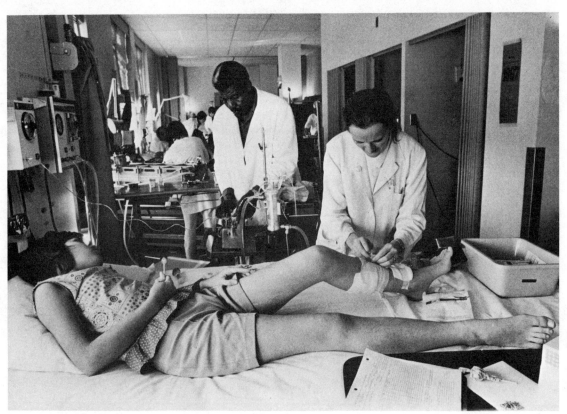

© Phiz Mezey/DPI

OBJETIVOS

In this chapter you will learn vocabulary and expressions for coping with everyday problems.

You will also learn about the following aspects of Spanish grammar:

56. the preterite forms of stem-changing verbs
57. how to use the reflexive pronoun **se** to describe unplanned events: **se me rompió la taza** (*the cup broke on me*)

58. how to form and use another past tense in Spanish, the imperfect

Un paso más includes activities related to days when everything goes wrong, as well as to nostalgia for the past and to differences between the past and the present. There is also a reading about the history of the Spanish monarchy, including present-day developments.

VOCABULARIO: PREPARACIÓN

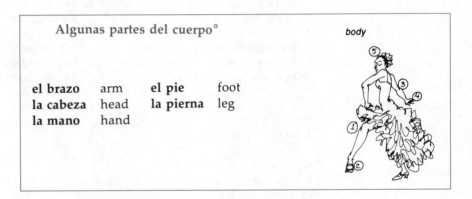

Me levanté con el pie izquierdo°			**Me...** *I got up on the wrong side of the bed*
la aspirina	aspirin	**equivocarse**	to be wrong, make a mistake
el despertador	alarm clock		
la llave	key	**hacerse daño**	to hurt oneself
distraído/a	absent-minded	**olvidarse (de)**	to forget
acordarse (ue) de	to remember	**pegar**	to hit, strike
		perder (ie)	to lose
apagar	to turn off	**romper**	to break
cambiar de lugar	to move (something)	**¡Qué mala suerte!**	What bad luck!
despedirse (i, i) (de)	to say good-bye (to)	**Fue sin querer.**	It was unintentional. I (he . . .) didn't mean to do it.
doler (ue)	to hurt		
Me duele la cabeza.	I have a headache.		

Algunas partes del cuerpo°				*body*
el brazo	arm	**el pie**	foot	
la cabeza	head	**la pierna**	leg	
la mano	hand			

A. Busque el comentario que mejor describe cada dibujo y complételo.

1. —¿Qué pasó aquí?
   —Ernesto _____ al otro señor sin querer.

2. —¡Qué hombre más _____! ¡Ojalá que no se caiga!

3. —¡Ay, no! Yo dejé las _____ dentro del carro.

4. —Pobre Armando. Le duele mucho el _____.

—¿Cómo se hizo _____?

5. —Doctor, me _____ mucho la cabeza.

—Tómese dos _____ y llámeme por la mañana.

B. *¿Qué verbos asocia Ud. con estas palabras?*

adiós   el brazo   la luz
la pierna   la aspirina   los pies
la mano   la cabeza   el accidente

Aquí hay unas posibilidades: despedirse, doler, apagar, caminar, levantar, correr, preguntar, pegar, escribir, pensar, tomar, caerse, hacerse daño, poner

C. *Match each response from column B with the appropriate statement from column A.*

1. Anoche no me acordé de poner (*to set*) el despertador.

2. ¡Ay! ¡Me pegaste!

3. Nunca miro por donde camino. Esta mañana me caí otra vez.

4. Lo siento, señores, pero ésta no es la casa de Lola Pérez.

5. No cambié de lugar el coche y el policía me puso una multa.

6. Anoche en casa de unos amigos rompí su lámpara favorita.

a. ¿Vas a comprarles otra?

b. Perdón, señora. Nos equivocamos de casa.

c. ¿Otra vez? ¡Qué distraído eres! ¿Te hiciste daño?

d. Huy, perdón. Fue sin querer.

e. ¿Te olvidaste otra vez? ¿A qué hora llegaste al trabajo?

f. ¡Qué mala suerte! ¿Cuánto tienes que pagar?

D. *¿Se levanta Ud. con el pie izquierdo? Indique la frecuencia de cada situación en la vida de Ud. ¿Es correcta la interpretación?*

1 = con frecuencia   2 = algunas veces   3 = nunca

_____ 1. Rompo objetos en casa y en el trabajo/la universidad.

_____ 2. No me acuerdo de llevar las cosas necesarias al trabajo/a clase.

_____ 3. Me equivoco en los pequeños detalles (*details*) de la vida.

_____ 4. Cuando me despido de un amigo, digo «Buenas tardes»... a las ocho de la mañana.

_____ 5. Me equivoco en asuntos (*matters*) importantes.

_____ 6. Cuando oigo el despertador, lo apago y me duermo otra vez.

_____ 7. Cierro el carro con las llaves adentro.

_____ 8. Pierdo objetos como las llaves, mis cuadernos, mi cartera.

☐ Total

Interpretaciones

8–12 ¡Quédese en cama y no salga de casa!

13–19 Ud. no es perfecto/a, pero lleva una vida típica.

20–24 Ud. es una persona ideal... pero... ¡qué vida más aburrida!

E.　*¿De cuántas maneras diferentes puede Ud. reaccionar en cada situación? Describa sus reacciones.*

1. Son las seis de la mañana. Ud. oye el despertador, pero todavía tiene sueño.
2. Al hablar (*when speaking*) con una persona que Ud. no conoce muy bien, se equivoca Ud. de nombre. (Por ejemplo, le dice Ud. «José» a Julián.)
3. A Ud. le duele muchísimo la cabeza.
4. Ud. quiere despedirse, pero la persona con quien está hablando quiere hablar más.
5. En clase, al hacer (*while doing*) un ejercicio con un compañero, Ud. no se acuerda de una palabra muy importante.
6. Ud. pierde su cartera y con ella todo su dinero y el pasaporte. Va a la estación de policía.
7. El vecino siempre deja su carro delante del garaje de Ud. y Ud. no puede sacar su carro.

PRONUNCIACIÓN: Rhythm and Intonation

When read aloud, the English proverb *A bird in the hand is worth two in the bush* and its Spanish equivalent **Más vale pájaro en mano que cien volando** illustrate important differences between Spanish and English: rhythm and intonation **(ritmo y entonación).**

　In English the stressed syllables (*bird, hand, two, bush*) are drawn out or prolonged, and the unstressed syllables are shortened and almost swallowed.

A b i r d in the h a n d is worth t w o in the b u s h.

This pattern dominates English, giving it a very distinctive "da-DUM-di-DUM" *rhythm.* In Spanish, however, all syllables—stressed and unstressed alike—tend to be of equal length. Each syllable receives one beat, giving Spanish a staccato "DOT-DOT-DOT" rhythm.

Más va- le pá- ja- ro en ma- no que cien vo- lan- do.

Stressed syllables are somewhat louder than unstressed syllables, but they are not much longer.

　English and Spanish also differ in *intonation* (the rise and fall in pitch

of the voice). In general, the voice of a person speaking Spanish does
not rise and fall as often as does that of the English speaker, nor is the
Spanish range of pitches so great.

A bird in the hand is worth two in the bush.

Más vale pájaro en mano que cien volando.

PRÁCTICA

A. 1. Veo el rojo pero no veo el azul. 2. Trabajó en la universidad. 3. Nació
    el cuatro de enero de 1961. 4. El primer mes del año es enero. 5. No olvides
    el diccionario. 6. Acabo de comprarte una blusa blanca. 7. Se cayó el libro
    de geografía.
B. 1. Tal vez no pueda venir mañana. 2. Quiero que me ayudes con esto.
    3. Se come bien en ese café. 4. Es necesario que terminemos la lección.
    5. Usted no me hizo la mesita que pedí. 6. Le pusieron el nombre de su tío.
    7. El niño no lloró durante el bautizo.

MINIDIÁLOGOS Y GRAMÁTICA

56. PRETERITE OF STEM-CHANGING VERBS

¿Está mejor el paciente?
JAIME: ¡Ay, pobre Pablito! Menos mal que no *se murió.*
RODOLFO: ¿Quién es Pa...?
JAIME: Se enfermó ayer y no pudo dormir anoche. Por fin *se durmió*
           esta mañana. Esta tarde *se despertó* a las cuatro y estuvo
           mejor.
RODOLFO: Pero, ¿quién...?
JAIME: *Pidió* agua y comida y se las dio mi hermana.
RODOLFO: Hombre, por favor, ¿quién es Pablito? ¿tu hermano?
JAIME: ¡Qué va, hombre! Es nuestro pájaro.

1. *¿Quién se enfermó ayer?*
2. *¿Pudo dormir anoche Pablito?*
3. *¿Cómo se sintió Pablito cuando se despertó? ¿Qué pidió?*
4. *¿Quién le dio a Pablito agua y comida?*
5. *¿Quién es Pablito?*

Is the patient any better? JAIME: Oh, poor Pablito! Boy, I'm glad he didn't die. RODOLFO: Who
is Pa—? JAIME: He took sick yesterday and couldn't sleep last night. Finally he fell asleep this
morning. This afternoon he woke up at four and was better. RODOLFO: But who—? JAIME: He
asked for water and food, and my sister gave them to him. RODOLFO: For heaven's sake, please,
who is Pablito? Your brother? JAIME: Oh, no! He's our bird.

-Ar and **-er** stem-changing verbs have no stem change in the preterite.

ACORDAR (UE)		PERDER (IE)	
acordé	acordamos	perdí	perdimos
acordaste	acordasteis	perdiste	perdisteis
acordó	acordaron	perdió	perdieron

-Ir stem-changing verbs have a stem change in the preterite but only in the third-person singular and plural, where the stem vowels **e** and **o** change to **i** and **u** respectively.   This is the same change that occurs in the present participle of **-ir** stem-changing verbs.

PEDIR (I, I)		DORMIR (UE, U)	
pedí	pedimos	dormí	dormimos
pediste	pedisteis	dormiste	dormisteis
pidió	pidieron	durmió	durmieron

-Ir stem-changing verbs include:

despedir(se) (i, i)	reír(se) (i, i)*
divertir(se) (ie, i)	seguir (i, i)
dormir(se) (ue, u)	sentir(se) (ie, i)
morir(se) (ue, u)	servir (i, i)
pedir (i, i)	sonreír (i, i)*
preferir (ie, i)	vestir(se) (i, i)

PRÁCTICA

A. Dé Ud. frases nuevas según las indicaciones.

1. —Todos se olvidaron del cumpleaños de su amiga Gloria. ¿Quién no se acordó?
   —*Yo* no me acordé de su cumpleaños. (*tú, Raúl, nosotros, Ud., ellos, vosotros*)
2. —La lección de matemáticas fue dificilísima y nadie pudo terminarla. ¿Quién perdió la paciencia por fin?
   —*Elena* perdió la paciencia. (*todos, tú, Horacio y Estela, yo, Ud., vosotros*)
3. —Muchos de Uds. fueron a comer en un restaurante mexicano. ¿Qué pidieron allí?
   —*Rita* pidió enchiladas. (*yo, Jacinto, tú, nosotros, Uds., vosotros*)
4. —Algo muy cómico pasó ayer. ¿Quién se rió mucho?
   —*Ada* se rió. (*nosotros, yo, Esteban, tú, todos, vosotros*)

*Note the simplification: **ri-ió → rió; ri-ieron → rieron; son-ri-ió → sonrió; son-ri-ieron → sonrieron.**

5. —¿Quién durmió mal anoche y se levantó con el pie izquierdo?
   —*Rafael* durmió mal. (*yo, todos, tú, Irma, Uds., vosotros*)

B. *Form complete sentences by using one word or phrase from each column. Use preterite forms of the verbs.*

		muchos cursos el semestre
la primavera pasada	llover	pasado
Romeo	acordarse de	en Acapulco
la Segunda Guerra Mundial	divertirse	en 1939
Rip Van Winkle	dormir	por Julieta
los turistas	morir	muchos años
los estudiantes	empezar	todo el vocabulario en el
	seguir	último examen
		mucho

C. *Cambie por el pretérito.*

1. Juan se *sienta* en un restaurante. *Pide* una cerveza. El camarero no se *acuerda* de su pedido (*order*) y le *sirve* una Coca-Cola.
2. Rosa se *acuesta* temprano y *apaga* las luces. *Duerme* bien y se *despierta* temprano, a las siete. Se *viste* y *sale* para la universidad.
3. Yo me *visto, voy* a una fiesta, me *divierto* mucho y *vuelvo* tarde a casa. Mi compañero de cuarto *decide* quedarse en casa y se *divierte* poco. *Pierde* una fiesta excelente y lo *siente* mucho.

CONVERSACIÓN

A. *Use Ud. estos verbos en el presente para describir un día típico en la vida de Domingo Meléndez. Luego diga lo que (what) Ud. hizo ayer, usando el pretérito. ¡Ojo! Hay verbos de todos tipos en la lista: regulares (sección 38), irregulares (sección 53) y verbos que cambian el radical (sección 56). Haga un repaso (review) del pretérito antes de empezar este ejercicio.*

despertarse	divertirse con los amigos	no poder estudiar
apagar el despertador	estudiar en la biblioteca	mirar la televisión
levantarse	volver a casa	decir buenas noches
bañarse	preparar la cena	a _____
vestirse	poner la mesa	quitarse la ropa
desayunar	cenar	acostarse
ir a la universidad	lavar los platos	leer un poco
asistir a clases	quedarse en casa toda la	poner el despertador
almorzar	noche	dormirse pronto

B. *Preguntas*

1. ¿Dónde almorzó Ud. ayer? ¿Quién le sirvió a Ud. la comida? ¿Ud. le sirvió la comida a alguien ayer? La última vez que Ud. fue a un restaurante, ¿qué pidió?

2. ¿A qué hora se acostó Ud. anoche? ¿Cuántas horas durmió? ¿Durmió bien? ¿Se sintió descansado/a (*rested*) cuando se despertó? ¿Cómo se vistió Ud. ayer, elegante o informalmente? ¿Se levantó con el pie izquierdo?
3. ¿Sonrió Ud. ayer? ¿Se divirtió mucho con sus amigos? ¿Se rió mucho?
4. ¿Qué personas famosas murieron el siglo (*century*) pasado?

57. REFLEXIVE FOR UNPLANNED OCCURRENCES

Se me cayó el vaso.
I dropped the glass. (The glass fell from my hands.)

A Mario se le perdieron los libros.
Mario lost his books. (Mario's books were lost to him.).

Unplanned or unintentional events (*I dropped, we lost, you forgot*) are frequently expressed with a reflexive construction that uses **se** and the third person of the verb. Note that this construction is the same as the passive reflexive (section 11) except that the occurrence is viewed as happening *to* someone—the unwitting performer of the action. Thus the performer is indicated by an indirect object pronoun, often clarified by **a** + a noun or pronoun at the beginning of the sentence. In such sentences the subject (the thing that is dropped, broken, forgotten) usually follows the verb.

(**A** + noun or pronoun)	**Se**	Indirect object pronoun	Verb	Subject
(A mí)	Se	me	cayó	el vaso.
A Mario	se	le	perdieron	los libros.

The verb agrees with the grammatical subject of the Spanish sentence **(el vaso, los libros),** not with the indirect object pronoun. **No** immediately precedes **se: A Mario** *no se* **le perdieron los libros.**

As with **gustar,** the clarification of the indirect object pronoun is optional. But the indirect object pronoun itself is always necessary whether or not the performer is named: *A la mujer* se *le* **rompió el plato.**

Verbs frequently used in this construction include:

acabar	to finish; to run out of	**perder (ie)**	to lose
caer	to fall	**quedar**	to remain
olvidar	to forget	**romper**	to break

PRÁCTICA

A. *Dé Ud. frases nuevas según las indicaciones.*

1. —¿A quiénes se les olvidó el libro de texto hoy?
   —A *Pablo* se le olvidó el libro. (*mí, nosotros, Inés, ti, Héctor y Ramiro, vosotros*)
2. —María es una persona muy distraída.   ¿Qué cosas se le olvidaron hoy?
   —A María se le olvidó *el libro.* (*tomar el desayuno, las llaves, estudiar para el examen, los cheques, venir a clase*)
3. —Sus amigos esperan que Ud. lleve los vasos y el champán a una fiesta, pero Ud. llega sin nada.   Explíqueselo a sus amigos.

   —Se me _____ los vasos.   (*olvidar, romper, caer, quedar en*
   —Se me _____ el champán.   *casa, acabar*)
   —Se les _____ el champán en la tienda.

B. *Restate the following sentences, using the reflexive for unplanned occurrences.*

   MODELO   Marcial olvidó los discos. → *A Marcial se le olvidaron* **los discos.**
               Juan dejó las llaves en casa. (quedar) → *A Juan se le quedaron*
                                                           las llaves en casa.

1. Jorge rompió los vasos.
2. Roberto y Jacinta se olvidaron de cambiar el carro de lugar.
3. Olvidé tomar las aspirinas.
4. Dejamos los boletos en casa. (quedar)
5. Perdí las llaves.
6. Ayer rompí varias cosas.
7. No pudieron servir más pan (*bread*). (acabar)

CONVERSACIÓN

A. *¿Qué les pasó a estas personas?*

1.

2.

3.

4.

B. *Complete las oraciones en una forma lógica.*

   1. Una vez se me cayó/cayeron _____.
   2. Es posible que se me olvide(n) _____, pero nunca se me olvida(n) _____.
   3. En la fiesta esta noche, ojalá no se nos acabe(n) _____.
   4. Una vez a mi amigo/a se le rompió/rompieron _____ y se enojó.
   5. Hoy se me quedó/quedaron _____ en casa.
   6. El año pasado se me perdió/perdieron _____.

58. IMPERFECT OF REGULAR AND IRREGULAR VERBS

© Rick Winsor 1978/Woodfin Camp & Assoc.

La nostalgia

MATILDE: ...y todos los hijos *eran* chiquitos. *Entraban* y *salían* de casa como locos. ¡Qué ruido *había* siempre! ¿Te acuerdas?

ARMANDO: Sí, sí, sí, aquéllos *eran* otros tiempos.

MATILDE: Y luego en verano *íbamos* siempre a la playa con todos los tíos y tus padres y dos criados y los amigos de los niños. *Teníamos* aquella casita tan linda... ¡Casi la puedo ver! ¿No la ves?

ARMANDO: Sí, sí, sí, aquéllos *eran* otros tiempos.

MATILDE: Dime una cosa, Armando. De verdad, ¿qué prefieres, aquella época o estos tiempos más tranquilos?

ARMANDO: Sí, sí, sí, aquéllos *eran* otros tiempos.

MATILDE: Ay, querido, parece que las cosas nunca cambian. ¡Tampoco me *escuchabas* en aquel entonces!

Nostalgia MATILDE: . . . and all the kids were little. They went in and out of the house like mad. There was always so much noise! Remember? ARMANDO: Yes, yes, yes, those were different times. MATILDE: And then in the summer we would go to the beach with all the uncles and aunts and your parents and two servants and the kids' friends. We used to have that pretty little house . . . I can almost see it! Don't you see it? ARMANDO: Yes, yes, yes, those were different times. MATILDE: Tell me something, Armando. Honestly, which do you prefer—those times or these more peaceful times? ARMANDO: Yes, yes, yes, those were different times. MATILDE: Well, dear, I guess things never change. You never used to listen to me back then, either!

1. *¿Qué hacían los niños de Matilde y Armando?*
2. *¿Su casa estaba muy tranquila?*
3. *¿Adónde iban siempre en verano? ¿Iban solos?*
4. *¿Qué pregunta Matilde a Armando? ¿Cómo responde?*
5. *¿Armando escucha bien a Matilde? Y antes, ¿la escuchaba?*

The *imperfect* **(imperfecto)** is another past tense in Spanish. In contrast to the preterite, which views actions or states of being as finished or completed, the imperfect tense views past actions or states of being as habitual or as "in progress." The imperfect is also used for description.

The imperfect has several English equivalents. For example, **hablaba,** the first-person singular of **hablar,** can mean *I spoke, I was speaking, I used to speak,* or *I would speak* (when *would* implies a repeated action). Most of these English equivalents indicate that the action was still in progress or was habitual, except *I spoke,* which can correspond to either the preterite or the imperfect.

Forms of the Imperfect

HABLAR		COMER		VIVIR	
hablaba	hablábamos	comía	comíamos	vivía	vivíamos
hablabas	hablabais	comías	comíais	vivías	vivíais
hablaba	hablaban	comía	comían	vivía	vivían

Stem-changing verbs do not show a change in the imperfect because their stem is unstressed: **almorzaba, perdía, pedía.** The imperfect of **hay** is **había** (*there was, there were, there used to be*).

Only three verbs are irregular in the imperfect: **ir, ser,** and **ver.**

IR		SER		VER	
iba	íbamos	era	éramos	veía	veíamos
ibas	ibais	eras	erais	veías	veíais
iba	iban	era	eran	veía	veían

Uses of the Imperfect

The imperfect is used

1. to describe REPEATED HABITUAL ACTIONS in the past

Siempre **nos quedábamos** en aquel hotel.	We always stayed (used to stay, would stay) at that hotel.
Todos los veranos **iban** a la costa.	Every summer they went (used to go, would go) to the coast.

2. to describe an ACTION THAT WAS IN PROGRESS

Pedía la cena.	She was ordering dinner.
Buscaba el carro.	He was looking for the car.

3. to describe two SIMULTANEOUS ACTIONS IN PROGRESS, with **mientras**

Tú **leías mientras** Juan **escribía** la carta.	You were reading while John was writing the letter.

4. to describe PHYSICAL, MENTAL, OR EMOTIONAL STATES in the past

Tenía dieciocho años.	She was eighteen years old.
Estaban muy distraídos.	They were very distracted.
La **quería** muchísimo.	He loved her a lot.

5. to tell TIME in the past

Era la una.	It was one o'clock.
Eran las dos.	It was two o'clock.

¡OJO! Just as in the present, the singular form of the verb **ser** is used with one o'clock, the plural form from two o'clock on.

6. to form the PAST PROGRESSIVE: imperfect of **estar** + *present participle**

Estábamos cenando a las diez.	We were having dinner at ten.
¿No **estabas estudiando**?	Weren't you studying?

---

*A progressive tense can also be formed with the preterite of **estar**: *Estuvieron* **cenando** hasta las doce. The progressive with the preterite of **estar**, however, is relatively infrequent, and it will not be practiced in *Puntos de partida*.

PRÁCTICA

A. Dé Ud. frases nuevas según las indicaciones.

1. —¿Quién cantaba y jugaba mucho en la escuela primaria?
   —*Tina* cantaba y jugaba mucho en la primaria. (*yo, Uds., tú, nosotros, Demetrio, vosotros*)
2. —¿Y quién bebía leche y dormía la siesta?
   —*Tina* bebía leche y dormía la siesta. (*todos los niños, tú, nosotros, Alicia, yo, vosotros*)
3. —Anoche, ¿qué estaba haciendo Ud. a las doce?
   —Anoche, yo (no) estaba _____. (*leer, mirar la televisión, escribir, llorar, comer, apagar las luces*)
4. —¿Quién veía un programa interesante a las nueve anoche?
   —*Ramiro* veía un programa interesante. (*tú, yo, Uds., Pablo, ella, vosotros*)
5. —Anoche, ¿quién iba a acostarse a las doce porque era tan tarde?
   —*Uds.* iban a acostarse a las doce. (*tú, yo, nosotros, Pablo, ella, vosotros*)

B. ¿Cómo eran o qué hacían estas personas?

O. J. Simpson	ser	fútbol
todos los niños	cantar	música popular
Elvis Presley	tocar	Santa Claus
Elizabeth Taylor	estudiar	mucho/poco
Burt Bacharach	jugar al	el piano
Chris Evert-Lloyd	creer en	tenis
yo	acostarse	temprano
_____	_____	guapo/a
		_____

C. Cambie por el imperfecto.

1. Olga *va* a la universidad todos los días. Siempre *asiste* a sus clases. *Pregunta* mucho porque *es* inteligente. Sus profesores *están* muy contentos con ella.
2. Yo *trabajo* para el gobierno. Mi jefe, que se *llama* Angel, nos *hace* trabajar mucho. Siempre *almorzamos* juntos en el mismo restaurante y a veces *jugamos* al basquetbol por la tarde.
3. *Vivo* en Sacramento. Siempre *llueve* mucho en invierno y en primavera, pero me *gusta* mucho el clima. Además (*besides*), las montañas *están* cerca y *puedo* esquiar.

D. ¿Cómo se dice en español? Describa una noche tranquila en casa.

It was eight o'clock, and I was reading while my friend was writing checks. There was little noise, and it was snowing outside (**afuera**). We weren't expecting (**esperar**) anyone, and we thought that it was going to be a quiet evening.

CONVERSACIÓN

A. *Using the following questions as a guide, interview another student about his/her childhood. Then report the information to the class.*

1. ¿Dónde vivías y con quién? ¿Tenías un apodo (*nickname*)?
2. ¿Cómo se llamaba tu escuela primaria? ¿y tu maestro/a en el primer grado?
3. ¿Cuál era tu materia favorita? ¿Por qué?
4. ¿Cómo se llamaba tu mejor amigo/a? ¿Dónde vivía? ¿Siempre se llevaban bien (*did you get along*)?
5. ¿Perdías o rompías muchas cosas? ¿Eras un(a) niño/a distraído/a?
6. ¿Practicabas algunos deportes? (**Sí, jugaba** _____.)
7. ¿Tenías un perrito? ¿un gato (*cat*)? ¿Cómo se llamaba?

B. *Describa Ud. la casa o el apartamento en que vivía de niño/a. ¿Cómo era el cuarto de Ud.?*

C. *Complete las oraciones en una forma lógica.*

1. En otra época siempre me gustaba _____. No me gustaba nada _____.
2. Anoche a las diez, yo estaba _____.
3. Y esta mañana a las ocho, yo estaba _____.
4. Anoche mientras yo _____, mi compañero/a (esposo/a, etcétera) _____.
5. Siempre leía _____.
6. En otra época siempre veía _____ en la televisión, pero ahora no lo **ponen**.

DIÁLOGO: Fue sin querer

El marido°[1], empleado de oficina, torpe° y distraído   *husband / clumsy*
La esposa, ama de casa, torpe y distraída

ÉL: ¿Sabes lo que° me pasó anoche? Se me olvidó poner el des-   *lo... what*
pertador. Dormí como los angelitos, pero hoy, cuando me
desperté, ya era tardísimo. Ni pude bañarme ni desayunar
antes de salir para la oficina.

ELLA: Sí, te oí salir con mucha prisa... pero no importaba, mi vida.
De todos modos° no había desayuno. El pan estaba viejo° y   *De... anyway / stale*
se nos acabó la leche anoche. No me acordé de ir al mercado
ayer.[2] Pero, dime, ¿llegaste tarde a la oficina?

ÉL: Hice lo que pude, pero ¡qué va! Salí a toda prisa en el carro.
Me vio un policía, me paró y me puso una multa de cincuenta
pesos. Llegué tardísimo.

ELLA: ¡Qué mala suerte! ¿Desayunaste, por fin?

ÉL: Ni agua. Yo estaba tan nervioso que dejé el carro en un espacio marcado «prohibido estacionarse». Luego me di cuenta°, volví para cambiarlo de lugar y tuve que romper la ventanilla° porque, cuando cerré el carro, se me quedaron las llaves adentro.

me... *I realized*
(car) window

ELLA: ¡Ay, mi vida! Creo que te levantaste hoy con el pie izquierdo.

ÉL: Yo creo que sí. Me dolía la cabeza, me sentía mal... A las once y media tomé dos de esas aspirinas que me diste ayer para llevar a la oficina. Pero fue peor. Creí que iba a dormirme sobre el escritorio°.

desk

ELLA: ¡Ay! Olvidé decirte que me equivoqué. Te di pastillas° para dormir.

pills

ÉL: ¿Cómo pudiste pensar que era lo mismo una aspirina que° una pastilla para dormir? Pero, mujer, un día me vas a matar...

era... *an aspirin was the same thing as*

ELLA: Fue sin querer, mi vida. ¿Me perdonas?

ÉL: Cómo no, mi amor. Pero no creo que el presidente de la compañía me perdone...

ELLA: ¿Por qué tiene que perdonarte? ¿Hiciste algo malo?

ÉL: Una tontería. Tenía sueño por las pastillas, él tenía prisa y... se me fueron dos ceros más en° un cheque. Vino en persona a mi escritorio. ¡Estaba enojadísimo! Yo me puse de pie° inmediatamente... y... se me cayó la taza de café sobre el balance general° que estaba preparando. Me miró —estaba furiosísimo. Creí que iba a pegarme. «¡Lo siento muchísimo, viejo», le dije, «fue sin querer, créemelo».

se... *two extra zeros got on*
Yo... *I stood up*
balance... *balance sheet*

ELLA: ¿Y qué te dijo entonces?

ÉL: Me despidió por torpe, maleducado y confianzudo°.[3]

forward, overly familiar

Comprensión

Conteste en oraciones completas.

1. ¿Qué se le olvidó al marido?
2. ¿Durmió bien? ¿Cuándo se levantó?

3. ¿Qué no hizo antes de salir para la oficina?
4. ¿Qué se le olvidó a la esposa ayer?
5. ¿Dónde dejó el coche el marido?   ¿Qué otro problema hubo con el auto?
6. ¿Qué tomó cuando le dolía la cabeza?   ¿Y qué pasó como resultado?
7. ¿En qué se equivocó la esposa?
8. ¿En qué se equivocó el esposo cuando escribió un cheque?   ¿Por qué se equivocó?
9. ¿Cómo reaccionó el jefe?
10. ¿Qué le dijo el marido al jefe?   ¿Le llamó de **tú** o de **Ud.**?
11. ¿Por qué lo despidió el jefe?

Comentario cultural

1. This dialog uses many of the Spanish words that refer to spouses or to friends. **Esposa, mujer,** and **señora** all can mean *wife.* **Mujer** is the least formal of these terms, and **señora** is the most formal.   The words **marido** and **esposo** are synonyms in all situations.   The word **hombre,** however, can never mean *husband.*

   The words **viejo** and **vieja** can also be used to refer affectionately to one's spouse, with no connotation of age.   They are also terms of endearment used among friends.   **Mi vida** is also a term of endearment.

2. Since the homemaker in the dialog forgot to go shopping the day before, it is quite possible that there is little food in the kitchen.   Many items of food— bread, meat, milk, eggs, and so on—are purchased fresh daily in Hispanic countries.   Although most city kitchens now have refrigerators, they are not likely to be so large as those found in many U.S. homes, for electricity and appliances are very expensive.   Convenience foods—powdered beans in Mexico, packaged soups in Spain, for example—have only recently begun to have an impact on the Hispanic marketplace.

3. The husband in the dialog would not have been dismissed for being late to work.   He might have been dismissed for making the error on the check.   But his real mistake was being overly familiar (**confianzudo**) with his boss, addressing him as **tú** (**créemelo**), as if they were equals.   The husband's use of **viejo** was also offensive, since it implied a familiarity and camaraderie that was not acceptable to his superior.   Such camaraderie, however, might have been the rule in another office.

   The husband's boss also used the term **maleducado** to refer to his employee. **Maleducado** implies *ill-mannered, rude, poorly brought-up.*   In contrast, to be described as **educado** is to be considered *well-mannered, polite, cultured.*   The ideal expressed by the term **educado** is moderation in dress, behavior, and speech, as well as propriety and politeness, no matter what the provocation.

UN POCO DE TODO

A. *Change the verbs and pronouns from the first person to the third person wherever possible and make any other necessary changes.*

1. Me divertí mucho porque la película era muy cómica.
2. Dormimos hasta muy tarde porque estábamos muy cansados.
3. ¡Casi nos morimos de hambre! No había nada de comida.
4. Me perdí en el centro cuando buscaba su casa.
5. Pedí paella porque mi amigo me dijo que estaba buena.

B. *Form complete sentences based on the words given in the order given. Give the
   preterite form of the first verb and the imperfect of the others. Add other words
   if necessary.*

   1. ella / servir / cena / temprano / porque / todos / tener / hambre
   2. nosotros / apagar / luces / porque / tener / sueño / y / querer / dormir
   3. Lorenzo / despedirse / temprano / porque / tener / que / levantarse / siete
   4. nosotros / no / ir / montañas / esta mañana / porque / nevar / mucho
   5. hombre / reírse / mucho / aunque / estar / triste

C. *Working with another student, ask and answer questions based on the model.
   Ask the question in the preterite and answer it in the imperfect.*

   MODELO   por qué / pedir Ud. / tanto / restaurante →
               ¿Por qué pidió Ud. tanto en el restaurante?
               tener / hambre → *Tenía hambre.*

   Preguntas: pretérito   **Respuestas: imperfecto**
   1. por qué / quedarse tú / en casa   1. saber / que / no / ir / gustar /
                                                 aquella / película
   2. por qué / dormir ellos / tanto   2. tener / mucho sueño
   3. por qué / olvidar Uds. / regalos de /   3. estar / distraído / por / examen
      primitos
   4. por qué / reírse tú / tanto   4. Horacio / portarse / como un loco
   5. por qué / se te / caer / vaso   5. pensar / otra cosa
   6. por qué / equivocarse Ud. / tanto /   6. no / saber / bien / fórmulas
      en / detalles / de / examen

D. *Complete the following sentences, using a verb in the imperfect to describe the
   feelings, condition, or emotions of the person named.*

   1. A Cristina se le olvidaron los libros hoy porque _____.
   2. Ayer Roberto no se despertó temprano porque _____.
   3. Cuando se le murió la abuela, Leopoldo _____.
   4. Cuando se despidió de su novio, Ángela _____.
   5. Anoche Gregorio volvió temprano a casa porque _____.
   6. Cuando se le rompió el reloj que le dieron sus padres, Angelito _____.

E. *Complete estas oraciones, usando un verbo en el pretérito para describir una acción.*

   1. La semana pasada, yo estaba muy preocupado/a. Por eso yo (no) _____.
   2. Era tarde y tenía que estudiar más todavía. Por eso yo _____.

3. Eran las cuatro de la mañana cuando mi amigo/a _____.
4. Yo manejaba a setenta millas por hora. Por eso el policía _____.
5. El carro estaba en un lugar marcado «prohibido estacionar». Por eso yo lo _____.
6. Me dolían los pies. Por eso yo _____.
7. Todos tenían mucha sed. Por eso yo les _____.

VOCABULARIO

VERBOS
acabar to finish, to run out of
acordarse (ue) de to remember
apagar to turn off
cambiar de lugar to move (*something*)
despedirse (i, i) (de) to say good-bye (to)
doler (ue) to hurt
equivocarse to be wrong, make a mistake
hacerse daño to hurt oneself
olvidarse (de) to forget
pegar to hit, strike
perdonar to pardon, forgive
perder (ie) to lose
quedar to remain, be left
romper to break

SUSTANTIVOS
la aspirina aspirin
el brazo arm
la cabeza head
el cuerpo body
el despertador alarm clock
la época era, time (*period*)
la luz light
la llave key
el/la maestro/a teacher
la mano hand
el marido husband
la paciencia patience
el pájaro bird
el pan bread
la pastilla pill
el pie foot
la pierna leg

la prisa haste, hurry

ADJETIVOS
distraído/a absent-minded
loco/a crazy
torpe clumsy

PALABRAS Y EXPRESIONES ÚTILES
fue sin querer it was unintentional
levantarse con el pie izquierdo to get up on the wrong side of the bed
lo que what, that which
mientras while
qué mala suerte what bad luck

Un paso más 13

Actividades

A mí... nada me sale a derechas°

sale... *turns out right*

A. **Me levanté con el pie izquierdo.** Hay días en que nada sale a derechas, como dice el paracaidista (*parachutist*) del dibujo. Usando las siguientes preguntas como guía, describa Ud. un día en la vida de una persona que se levantó con el pie izquierdo. Puede describir un día en su propia (*own*) vida o en la vida de otra persona—un(a) amigo/a, un hombre/una mujer de negocios, una ama de casa, el presidente, etcétera.

1. ¿A qué hora se despertó? ¿Se levantó inmediatamente? ¿Se sentía bien?
2. ¿Tuvo tiempo para comer y vestirse bien? ¿Le faltaba algo? ¿Qué no podía encontrar?
3. ¿Había problemas con los otros miembros de la familia? ¿con el coche?
4. ¿Qué tiempo hacía? ¿Llovía? ¿Nevaba?
5. ¿Dónde estaba por la mañana? ¿por la tarde? ¿Qué le pasó en cada lugar?
6. ¿Se le perdió algo?
7. ¿Había problemas con los amigos (el jefe, los empleados, los niños)?
8. ¿Recordó todo lo que tenía que hacer ese día? ¿Se le olvidó algo?

   9. ¿Cuál fue el último problema del día?   ¿Cómo se sentía?
  10. ¿A qué hora se acostó por fin?

B. **Los tiempos cambian.**   Muchas cosas y costumbres actuales (*current customs*)
   son diferentes de las del pasado.   Las oraciones siguientes describen algunos
   aspectos de la vida de hoy.   Después de leer cada oración, escriba Ud. otra,
   describiendo cómo eran las cosas antes, en otra época.   Use el imperfecto para
   hacer los contrastes.

   MODELO   Ahora casi todos los bebés nacen en el hospital. →
               Antes casi todos los bebés nacían en casa.

   1. Ahora muchas personas viven en apartamentos.
   2. Se come con frecuencia en un restaurante.
   3. Muchísimas mujeres trabajan fuera de casa.
   4. Muchas personas van al cine y miran la televisión.
   5. Ahora las mujeres —no sólo los hombres— llevan
      pantalones.
   6. Ahora hay enfermeros y maestros —no sólo
      enfermeras y maestras.
   7. Ahora tenemos coches pequeños que gastan poca
      gasolina.
   8. Ahora usamos más máquinas y por eso hacemos
      menos trabajo físico.
   9. Ahora las familias son más pequeñas.
  10. _____

Ayer

Hoy

A propósito...

Familiarity with the following expressions can help smooth over
embarrassing moments. Use the expressions given below on the left
when you need to apologize to someone.   You can follow these phrases
by a brief explanation of what caused the problem.   To accept someone
else's apology graciously, use one of the expressions on the right.

Perdón, me equivoqué.	**Está bien.**	*It's all right.*
Perdón, es que...	**No se preocupe.**	
¿Me perdona(s)?	**No te preocupes.**	*Don't worry.*
Lo siento mucho.	**No importa.**	*It doesn't matter.*
¡Cuánto lo siento!	**Tranquilo/a.**	*Don't worry. Be calm.*
Me equivoqué de...		
Fue sin querer.		
Lo hice sin querer.		

C. **¡Ay, perdón!** With another student, practice making and accepting apologies. Offer your apology in as many different ways as possible and give a brief explanation for your behavior.

1. Ud. llega tarde a su clase de español. Es la tercera vez esta semana.
2. Ud. pisa (*step on*) a una viejecita en el autobús.
3. Ud. no pudo prepararle el desayuno a su compañero/a (esposo/a, hermano/a).
4. Ud. quería llamar a su amiga Paquita; su número de teléfono es el 2-44-66-78. Ud. marcó (*dialed*) el 2-44-66-88.
5. Se le cayó un plato de sopa encima de otra persona.
6. Se le olvidó el cumpleaños de alguien.
7. Ud. dijo que iba a llamar a su tío/a, pero se le olvidó.

D. **La nostalgia.** Think of something pleasant from your past—a special person, place, moment, or thing—and use one of the following sets of questions to describe it.

Una persona especial
1. ¿Cómo se llamaba?
2. ¿Cómo era —su aspecto físico, su personalidad?
3. ¿Dónde vivía? ¿Dónde trabajaba/estudiaba?
4. ¿Ud. lo/la conocía bien?
5. ¿Por qué le gustaba a Ud. esta persona?

Un lugar favorito
1. ¿Cuál era su lugar favorito?
2. ¿Dónde estaba?
3. ¿Iba Ud. allí con frecuencia? ¿Iba solo/a o con otra persona?
4. ¿Qué hacía allí?
5. ¿Cómo era el lugar?

Un momento agradable del pasado
1. ¿Cuántos años tenía Ud.?
2. ¿Dónde estaba? ¿Con quién(es) estaba?
3. ¿Qué hacía Ud.?
4. ¿Qué tiempo hacía?
5. ¿Cómo se sentía?

Una cosa del pasado
1. ¿Qué cosa era?
2. ¿Cómo era la cosa? ¿Era grande o pequeña? ¿nueva o vieja?
3. ¿De qué color era?
4. ¿Dónde estaba?
5. ¿Qué hacía Ud. con la cosa?
6. ¿Por qué le gustaba a Ud.?

E. **Refranes.**　Proverbs often focus on extremes—the very good and the very bad aspects of life, the positive and the negative.　Tell why you agree or disagree with one of the following proverbs, or tell about an incident from your own life that illustrates it.

1. Después de la tempestad (*storm*) viene la calma.
2. Con amor y aguardiente (*brandy*), nada se siente.
3. Cada día que amanece (*dawns*), el número de tontos crece (*grows*).
4. Quien (*he/she who*) nunca subió no puede caer.
5. Poco a poco se va lejos.

Lectura cultural: La monarquía española

La historia de la monarquía española cuenta entre sus episodios algunos de los éxitos° y algunos de los fracasos° más notables de todas las monarquías europeas.

Los Reyes Católicos.　La monarquía empezó con los Reyes Católicos, Fernando de Aragón (1479–1516) e Isabel de Castilla (1474–1504).　Estos dos monarcas lograron° la unificación política y religiosa de España.　También fue Isabel quien le dio a Cristóbal Colón la ayuda financiera que él necesitaba para su viaje de descubrimiento al Nuevo Mundo.

Los Hapsburgos.　Cuando murió en 1516, Fernando dejó su corona a su nieto Carlos, quien también heredó el trono del Imperio Romano de su padre, Felipe I, de la casa alemana de los Hapsburgos.　Así Carlos llegó a ser Carlos V de Alemania y Carlos I de España, el rey más poderoso de Europa.　Entre sus dominios contó territorios de España, Alemania, Austria, Italia y los Países Bajos°.　Se continuaron durante su reinado las exploraciones en el Nuevo Mundo, y España estaba en el apogeo° de su poder.　Pero los problemas internos, y también las constantes guerras en el extranjero°, le costaron a España bastante dinero y muchas vidas.

Otro rey hapsburgo de gran importancia fue Felipe II (1556–1598).　Estableció la capital permanente en Madrid y también hizo construir° el gran palacio de El Escorial.　Felipe II ocupó el trono español durante las grandes disputas en Europa entre los católicos y los protestantes.　Poco

successes / failures

achieved

Países... *Netherlands, Flanders*
height

en... *abroad*

hizo... *had built*

a poco España iba perdiendo° dinero y fuerzas militares.   Al fin, con la
derrota° de la Armada Invencible por Inglaterra en 1588, se veía el final de
la grandeza imperial española.

*Iba... continued to
   lose*
defeat

Los Borbones.   Esta casa francesa ganó control de la monarquía española
en 1700.   El mejor rey de los Borbones fue Carlos III (1759–1788).   Bajo
su dirección la política española era progresista y reformista.   Se nacio-
nalizó la instrucción y se estableció el servicio de correos°.   También se
llevaron a cabo° proyectos de industrialización y de cultura.

mail

se... were accomplished

El siglo XIX fue de grandes trastornos° políticos, entre ellos el intento
de fundar una república (1873–1874).   A finales del siglo, España cayó al
punto más bajo de su decadencia política al perder la guerra con los
Estados Unidos en 1898 y con ella las Islas Filipinas, Puerto Rico y Cuba
—casi todo el resto de sus dominios extrapeninsulares.

upheavals

En el siglo XX hubo un segundo intento de fundar una república (1931).
Luego, después de tres años de sangrienta° guerra civil (1936–1939), el
dictador Francisco Franco, el «Generalísimo», ganó el control en 1939.

bloody

La monarquía actual.   El monarca actual de España es el rey don Juan
Carlos I, quien subió al trono en España después de la muerte de Franco
en 1975.   Mucha gente creía que el nuevo rey iba a seguir la política
conservadora establecida por Franco durante su régimen (1939–1975).   Sin
embargo, Juan Carlos está haciendo cambios de espíritu liberal y
democrático en España.

UPI

Europa Press-Sepa Press/EPA, Inc.

Comprensión

Conteste en oraciones completas.

1. ¿Qué importancia tuvo el reinado de Fernando e Isabel en la historia española?
2. ¿Cuáles fueron los dos títulos reales del nieto del rey católico Fernando? ¿De quiénes heredó los títulos?
3. ¿Cómo era la situación política de España durante el reinado de Carlos V?
4. ¿Qué monumento hizo construir Felipe II?
5. ¿Qué acontecimiento (*event*) de gran importancia ocurrió en 1588?
6. ¿Qué avances se hicieron en España durante el reinado de Carlos III?
7. ¿Qué conflicto tuvo España con los Estados Unidos en el siglo XIX?
8. ¿En qué año empezó la guerra civil?
9. ¿Quién fue Francisco Franco?
10. Describa el gobierno actual de España.

Ejercicios escritos

A. Write a brief description of an outstanding president of the United States. Use the following phrases as a guide in writing your description.

1. su nombre y las fechas de su presidencia
2. sus contribuciones a los Estados Unidos y al mundo
3. los problemas de su presidencia

B. Read a recent newspaper or magazine article on Juan Carlos and write five sentences in Spanish, giving information that you learned from your reading.

capítulo 14 La salud

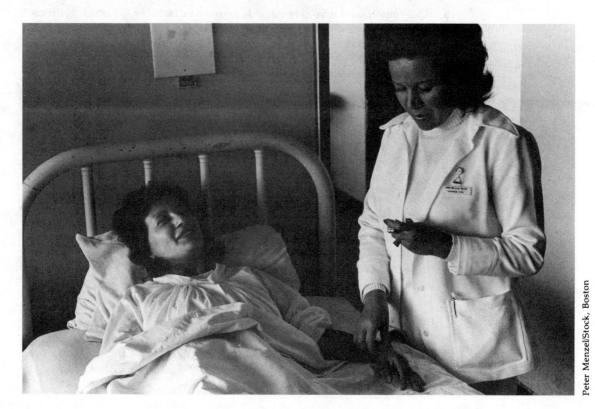

Peter Menzel/Stock, Boston

OBJETIVOS

In this chapter you will learn vocabulary and expressions related to aspects of health, physical fitness, and illness.

You will also learn about the following aspects of Spanish:

59. how to determine when to use the preterite or the imperfect

60. when to use and when to omit the definite articles (**el, la, los, las**)

61. how to express ideas such as *the bad part* (**lo malo**), *the important thing* (**lo importante**) using **lo** plus an adjective

Un paso más includes activities related to health and medical situations, and a reading about the origin and development of the Spanish language.

VOCABULARIO: PREPARACIÓN

Más partes del cuerpo		La salud° y el bienestar°		*health / wellbeing*
la boca	mouth	**comer bien**	to eat well	
el corazón	heart	**cuidarse**	to take care of oneself	
el estómago	stomach	**dormir lo suficiente**	to sleep enough	
la garganta	throat	**hacer ejercicio**	to exercise, get exercise	
la nariz	nose			
el ojo	eye	**llevar una vida tranquila (sana)**	to lead a calm (healthy) life	
los pulmones	lungs	**practicar deportes**	to participate in sports	

A. *¿Cómo se llaman estas partes del cuerpo?*

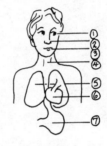

B. *¿Qué hacen estas personas?*

1.

2.

3.

4.

En el consultorio° del médico			office
el/la paciente	patient	**enfermarse**	to get sick
el/la enfermero/a	nurse	**resfriarse**	to get/catch a cold
congestionado/a	congested	**respirar**	to breathe
mareado/a	nauseated	**sacar la lengua**	to stick out your
el jarabe	(cough) syrup		tongue
la receta	prescription	**tener dolor (de)**	to have a pain (in)
el resfriado	cold	**tener fiebre**	to have a fever
la tos	cough	**tomarle la**	to take someone's
		temperatura	temperature
		toser	to cough

C. *Describa Ud. la situación de estas personas. ¿Dónde están y con quiénes?   ¿Qué síntomas tienen?   ¿Qué les recomienda Ud.?*

Anamari está muy bien
   de salud.
Nunca le duele(n) _____.
Nunca tiene _____.
Siempre _____.

Martín tiene resfriado.
Le duele(n) _____.
Tiene _____.
Debe _____.

Inés tiene apendicitis.
Le duele(n) _____.
Tiene _____.
Debe _____.

D. *¿Describen a Ud. las siguientes oraciones?*

1. En la sala de espera de un médico, si la persona sentada a mi lado empieza a toser, me cambio de lugar.
2. Me pongo nervioso/a en el consultorio del médico.
3. Cuando tengo resfriado, nunca tomo pastillas ni antibióticos ni jarabes.
4. Estoy de acuerdo con esta frase: Mente sana en cuerpo sano.
5. Me da más miedo ir al consultorio del dentista que ir al consultorio del médico.
6. Si no corro (hago ejercicio o yoga) casi todos los días, empiezo a sentirme nervioso/a.

E. *Estudio de palabras.* *Complete las siguientes frases con una palabra de la misma familia de la palabra en letras cursivas.*

1. Si me *resfrío,* tengo _____.
2. La *respiración* ocurre cuando alguien _____.
3. Si me _____, estoy *enfermo/a;* un(a) _____ me toma la temperatura.
4. Cuando alguien *tose,* se oye una _____.
5. Si me *duele* el estómago tengo un _____ de estómago.

F. *¿Qué partes del cuerpo asocia Ud. con las siguientes palabras?*

1. un ataque   2. la digestión   3. comer   4. respirar   5. congestionado
6. ver

G. *Ud. no se siente bien y va al consultorio del médico.* *Complete el diálogo entre Ud. y el médico.*

PACIENTE: Buenas tardes, doctor.
DOCTOR: Buenas tardes. ¿Qué le pasa? ¿Qué tiene?
PACIENTE: Es que me _____ muy mal. Me _____ la cabeza y tengo una _____ muy alta.
DOCTOR: Entonces, ¿tiene resfriado?
PACIENTE: Bueno, Ud. es el médico.
DOCTOR: ¿Se tomó la temperatura antes de venir?
PACIENTE: No, pero la _____ me la tomó y tuve 38,5.
DOCTOR: ¿Tiene dolor de estómago? ¿Se siente _____?
PACIENTE: No, pero respiro sólo con dificultad; estoy muy _____. Yo toso tanto que me duelen también los _____. Es que me duele el _____ entero.
DOCTOR: Vamos a ver. Abra Ud. la _____, por favor, y saque la lengua. Humm... tiene la _____ bastante (*rather*) inflamada. Ahora la respiración... _____ Ud. profundamente... Me parece que está bien. ¿Tiene alergia a los antibióticos?
PACIENTE: No, no creo.
DOCTOR: Bueno, aquí tiene Ud. una _____. Vaya a la farmacia y compre este _____ para la tos. Tómeselo cuatro veces al día. Para la fiebre, tome un par de _____ cada cuatro horas y este _____ para combatir la infección. Si todavía se siente mal la semana que viene, venga a verme otra vez. Y cuídese, ¿eh?
PACIENTE: Muchas gracias, doctor. Adiós.

98.6

96   98   100   2   4   6

37,0.

PRONUNCIACIÓN: More Cognate Practice

Most Spanish cognates differ in both spelling and pronunciation from their English equivalents. However, it is possible to predict the spelling of many Spanish words from the English. For example, English often spells one sound with a double letter where the Spanish cognate uses only one:

addition / **adición**	*mission* / **misión**	*attest* / **atestar**
apparatus / **aparato**	*illicit* / **ilícito**	*comment* / **comentar**

Note also the Spanish spelling of **Misisipí, Pensilvania, Calcuta, Rusia,** and **Caribe.** The only double consonants found in Spanish cognates are **rr, cc,** and **nn. Rr (error, corrupto)** represents a trill, as distinguished from the flap **r. Cc** occurs only before **e** or **i,** where it represents two sounds [ks],* as in **acceso, acción.** Spanish words ending in **-cción** often correspond to English words ending in *-ction.* **Nn** occurs only when the first **n** is part of a prefix: **necesario → innecesario. Ll** appears only when it represents the **y** sound in Spanish: *valley* / **valle.**

Additional guidelines for the spelling of Spanish cognates include:

English *ph* =	Spanish **f: teléfono**
English *th* =	Spanish **t: teatro**
English *ch* =	{ Spanish **c** (before **a, o, u**): **carácter**
	Spanish **qu** (before **e, i**): **parroquial**
initial English *ps* =	Spanish **s: sicología**

PRÁCTICA

Fill in the blanks with the proper Spanish spelling. Listen carefully as your instructor pronounces the Spanish cognates.

1. attention / a___ención
2. ammonia / a___oníaco
3. theology / ___eología
4. opposition / o___osición
5. pseudo- / ___eudo-
6. correct / co___ecto
7. photography / ___otogra___ía
8. innumerable / i___umerable
9. exaggerate / exa___erar
10. classify / cla___ificar
11. chaos / ___aos
12. phosphate / ___os___ato
13. physical / ___ísico
14. theory / ___eoría

15. progress / progre___o
16. architect / ar___itecto
17. annual / a___ual
18. chlorophyll / ___loro___i___a
19. affirm / a___irmar
20. collection / co___e___ión
21. pathetic / pa___ético
22. archangel / ar___ángel
23. chemical / ___ímico
24. accident / a___idente
25. alliance / a___ianza
26. photosynthesis / ___otosín___esis
27. psychologist / ___i___ólogo
28. atheism / a___eísmo

*In many parts of Spain, cc is pronounced as [k] followed by a *th* sound [θ]: **acción** [ak-θyón].

Study Hint: False Cognates

Not all Spanish and English cognates are identical in meaning. Here are a few important "traps" to be aware of: **sano** is *healthy;* **renta,** *income;* **pariente,** *relative;* **gracioso,** *funny;* **actual,** *current, up-to-date;* **fábrica,** *factory;* **colegio,** *elementary or secondary school;* **una molestia,** *a bother;* **sopa,** *soup;* **ropa,** *clothing;* **real,** *real or royal;* **sensible,** *sensitive;* **éxito,** *success;* and **constipado** means *suffering from a head cold.* These words are *false,* or misleading, *cognates* **(amigos falsos).**

Occasionally such words can lead to communication problems. The American tourist who, feeling embarrassed, describes him or herself as **embarazado/a** may find people chuckling at the remark, since **embarazada** means not *embarrassed* but *pregnant.*

> ¿SABES LO QUE TE DIGO? QUE NO ME DA LA REAL GANA°.

no... *I really don't feel like it*

MINIDIÁLOGOS Y GRAMÁTICA

59. PRETERITE VERSUS IMPERFECT

No es para tanto...

CARMEN: Yo no *sabía* lo que *tenía*, pero la doctora lo *diagnosticó* en seguida.

PILAR: ¿Y qué te *dijo* que *tenías?*

CARMEN: Pues... que tengo insomnio... y que tengo los ojos muy irritados... y que de todos modos todavía tengo que tomar el examen de filosofía el viernes.

It's not that serious . . . CARMEN: I didn't know what I had, but the doctor diagnosed it immediately. PILAR: And what did she say you had? CARMEN: Well . . . that I have insomnia . . . and that my eyes are very irritated . . . and that in any case I still have to take the philosophy exam on Friday.

1. *¿Quién acaba de consultar con la médica?*
2. *¿La doctora pudo diagnosticar la enfermedad?*
3. *¿Qué dijo la doctora que tenía Carmen?*

Summary of the Preterite and the Imperfect

A. When speaking about the past in English, you choose which past-tense forms to use in a given context: *I wrote letters, I did write letters, I was writing letters, I used to write letters,* and so on.   Usually only one or two of these options will convey exactly the idea you want to express. Similarly, in some Spanish sentences either the preterite or the imperfect can be used, but the meaning of the sentence will be different. The choice between the preterite and imperfect depends on the speaker's perspective: how does he/she view the action or state of being?

B. The PRETERITE is used to report *completed actions or states of being* in the past, no matter how long they lasted or took to complete; if the action or state is viewed as finished or over, the preterite is used.   The IMPERFECT is used, however, if the *ongoing or habitual nature* of the action is stressed, with no reference to its termination.

Escribí las cartas.	*I wrote (did write) the letters.*
Escribía las cartas cuando...	*I was writing the letters when . . .*
Carlos **fue** estudiante.	*Carlos was a student* (and no longer is).
Carlos **era** estudiante.	*Carlos was (used to be) a student.* (Charles may or may not still be a student.)
Anita **estuvo** nerviosa.	*Anita was nervous* (and no longer is).
Anita **estaba** nerviosa.	*Anita was (used to be) nervous.* (Anita may or may not still be nervous.)

C. *A series of actions that takes place in sequence* will be expressed in the PRETERITE (unless it refers to habitual actions).

Me **levanté,** me **vestí** y **desayuné.**	*I got up, got dressed, and ate breakfast.*

Simultaneous actions or states in progress are expressed with the IMPERFECT, usually with the word **mientras**.   The IMPERFECT is also used to express most *descriptions; physical, mental, and emotional states;* and *the hour.*

Escribía las cartas **mientras** Ana **leía**.	*I was writing letters while Ann was reading.*
Estaban cansados.	*They were tired.*
Eran las ocho.	*It was eight o'clock.*

D. Certain words and expressions are associated with the preterite, others with the imperfect.

Words associated with the preterite:	ayer, anteayer, anoche
	una vez (*once*), dos veces (*twice*), etcétera
	el año pasado, el lunes pasado, etcétera
	de repente (*suddenly*)
Words associated with the imperfect:	todos los días, todos los lunes, etcétera
	siempre, frecuentemente
	mientras
	de niño/a (*as a child*), de joven
	English *was* _____-*ing, were* _____-*ing*
	English *used to, would* (when *would* implies *used to*)

The words do not automatically cue either tense, however. The most important consideration is the meaning that the speaker wishes to convey.

Ayer cenamos temprano.	*Yesterday we had dinner early.*
Ayer cenábamos cuando Juan llamó.	*Yesterday we were having dinner when Juan called.*
De niño jugaba al fútbol.	*He played football as a child.*
De niño empezó a jugar al fútbol.	*He began to play football as a child.*

E. Remember the special English equivalents of the preterite forms of **saber, conocer, poder,** and **querer: supe** (*I found out*), **conocí** (*I met*), **pude** (*I could and did*), **no pude** (*I failed*), **quise** (*I tried*), **no quise** (*I refused*).

[Práctica A, B]

F. The preterite and the imperfect frequently occur in the same sentence.

Miguel **estudiaba** cuando **sonó** el teléfono.	*Miguel was studying when the phone rang.*
Olivia **comió** tanto porque **tenía** mucha hambre.	*Olivia ate so much because she was very hungry.*

In the first sentence the imperfect tells what was happening when another action—conveyed by the preterite—broke the continuity of the ongoing activity. In the second sentence the preterite reports the action that took place because of a condition, described by the imperfect.

G. The preterite and imperfect are also used together in the narration of an event. The preterite advances the action while the imperfect sets the stage, describes the conditions that caused the action, or emphasizes the continuing nature of a particular action.

[Práctica C, D, E]

PRÁCTICA

A. *The following sentences are given out of context. Give the preterite or the imperfect of the verbs in parentheses, basing your decision on the clues in the sentences.*

1. De niños, Jorge y yo _____ en Río Lindo.   (vivir)
2. Yo _____ un antibiótico anoche.   (tomar)
3. Nosotros siempre _____ en el Hotel Fénix.   (quedarse)
4. El año pasado ellos _____ durante sus vacaciones.   (enfermarse)
5. _____ las once de la noche.   (ser)
6. La tía Anita _____ ayer.   (resfriarse)
7. El paciente _____ muy congestionado.   (estar)
8. ¿No lo _____ tú una vez en Chile?   (ver)
9. El niño _____ mientras la doctora le _____.   (toser / hablar)
10. ¡De repente, _____ las luces!   (apagarse)
11. El médico me _____ la temperatura, me _____ la garganta y me _____ un jarabe.   (tomar / examinar / dar)
12. Todos los lunes Antonio _____ en aquella farmacia.   (trabajar)

B. *¿Cómo se dice en español?*

1. I couldn't read Spanish in grade school.
2. When I met them, I already knew their son.
3. They tried to do it but couldn't.
4. He knew how to play the piano when he was five.
5. She had to study but didn't want to.
6. When did you find that out?

C. *Explain the reasons for the use of the preterite or the imperfect for each verb in the following paragraph:*

Hacía mucho frío. Ester cerró con cuidado todas las ventanas y puertas, pero todavía tenía frío. Se preparó una taza de té y se puso otro suéter, pero todavía temblaba de frío. Eran las once de la noche cuando sonó el teléfono. Era su esposo. Entre otras cosas, dijo que hacía mucho frío afuera. Ester ya lo sabía.

Which Spanish past tense should be used to express each verb in the following paragraph? Explain why in each case.

We were walking down Fifth Street when we saw him. He looked very tired and his clothes were very dirty. He asked us for money. We gave him all the money that we had because he was an old friend.

D. *Read the following paragraph at least once to familiarize yourself with the sequence of events in it. Then read it again, giving the proper form of the verbs in parentheses in the preterite or the imperfect, according to the needs of each sentence and the context of the paragraph as a whole.*

Rubén _____ estudiando cuando Soledad _____ en el
　　　　　(estar)　　　　　　　　　　　　　　　　　　(entrar)
cuarto. Le _____ a Rubén si _____ ir al cine con ella. Rubén
　　　　　(preguntar)　　　　　　　(querer)
_____ que sí porque se _____ un poco aburrido con sus estudios.
　(decir)　　　　　　　　　　　(sentir)
Los dos _____ para el cine en seguida. _____ una película
　　　　　(salir)　　　　　　　　　　　　　　　　　(ver)
cómica y _____ mucho. Luego, ya que _____ frío, _____
　　　　　(reírse)　　　　　　　　　　　　(hacer)　　　　　(entrar)
en El Gato Negro y _____ un chocolate. _____ las dos de la
　　　　　　　　　　(tomar)　　　　　　　　　　　(ser)
mañana cuando por fin _____ a casa. Soledad _____ inmediata-
　　　　　　　　　　　(regresar)　　　　　　　　　(acostarse)
mente porque _____ cansada, pero Rubén _____ a estudiar
　　　　　　　(estar)　　　　　　　　　　　　(empezar)
otra vez.

Answer the following questions based on the paragraph about Rubén and Soledad. ¡Ojo! A question is not always answered in the same tense as that in which it is asked.

1. ¿Qué hacía Rubén cuando Soledad entró?
2. ¿Qué le preguntó Soledad a Rubén?
3. ¿Por qué dijo Rubén que sí?
4. ¿Les gustó la película? ¿Por qué?
5. ¿Por qué tomaron un chocolate?
6. ¿Regresaron a casa a las tres?
7. ¿Qué hicieron cuando llegaron a casa?

E. *Read the following paragraphs once for meaning. Then read them again, giving the proper form of the verbs in parentheses in the present, preterite, or imperfect.*

Durante mi segundo año en la universidad, yo _____ a Roberto en una
　　　　　　　　　　　　　　　　　　　　　(conocer)
clase. Pronto nos _____ muy buenos amigos. Roberto _____
　　　　　　　　(hacer)　　　　　　　　　　　　　　　　　(ser)

una persona muy generosa que _____ una fiesta en su apartamento
                                    (dar)
todos los viernes. Todos nuestros amigos _____. _____
                                              (venir)   (haber)
muchas bebidas y comida, y todo el mundo _____ y _____
                                              (cantar)   (bailar)
hasta muy tarde.

Una noche algunos de los vecinos (*neighbors*) de Roberto _____ a la
                                                              (llamar)
policía y _____ que nosotros _____ demasiado ruido.
              (decir)   (hacer)
_____ un policía al apartamento y le _____ a Roberto que la
    (venir)   (decir)
fiesta _____ demasiado ruidosa. Nosotros no _____ aguar (*to*
          (estar)   (querer)
spoil) la fiesta, pero ¿qué _____ hacer? Todos nos _____, aunque
                                  (poder)   (despedir)
_____ solamente las once de la noche.
    (ser)
Aquella noche Roberto _____ algo importantísimo. Ahora cuando
                          (aprender)
_____ una fiesta, siempre _____ a sus vecinos.
    (tener)   (invitar)

CONVERSACIÓN

A. *Dé Ud. sus impresiones del primer día de la clase de español. Use estas preguntas como guía.*

1. ¿A qué hora llegó Ud. a la universidad? ¿Por qué llegó tan tarde/temprano?
2. ¿A qué hora era la clase y dónde era (*was it taking place*)?
3. ¿Vino Ud. a clase con alguien?
4. ¿Qué hizo Ud. después de entrar en la sala de clase? ¿Qué hacía el/la profesor(a)?
5. ¿A quién conoció Ud. aquel día? ¿Ya conocía a unos miembros de la clase? ¿A quiénes?
6. ¿Aprendió Ud. muchas palabras y expresiones nuevas durante la clase? ¿Ya lo sabía todo?
7. ¿Le cayó bien o mal el/la profesor(a)? ¿Por qué? ¿Cómo era?
8. ¿Les dio tarea (*homework*) el/la profesor(a)? ¿Pudo Ud. hacerla fácilmente?
9. ¿Cuánto tiempo estudió Ud. español antes de la próxima clase?

B. *Describa Ud. las acciones que se ven en los dibujos. Use dos verbos en cada descripción, uno en el imperfecto, el otro en el pretérito. ¿Qué hicieron estas personas después?*

1.   2.   3.

C. *Describa Ud. su última enfermedad. Use estas preguntas como guía.*

1. ¿Cuándo empezó Ud. a sentirse mal? ¿Dónde estaba Ud.? ¿Qué hacía?
2. ¿Cuáles eran sus síntomas? ¿Cómo se sentía? ¿Estaba mareado/a? ¿congestionado/a? ¿Le dolía alguna parte del cuerpo?
3. ¿Qué hizo? ¿Regresó a casa? ¿Se desvistió (*did you get undressed*)? ¿Tosía mucho? ¿Se acostó?
4. ¿Fue al consultorio del médico? ¿Lo/la examinó? ¿Cuál fue su diagnóstico?
5. ¿Le dio una receta el médico? ¿Llevó Ud. la receta a la farmacia? ¿Cuánto le costó la medicina?
6. ¿Cuándo se sintió bien por fin?

Study Hint: Writing

You can develop a more mature writing style in Spanish by using transition words to link shorter sentences. Follow these suggestions:

1. Write a first draft of your composition, trying to express your ideas in short, simple sentences. Be sure that each sentence contains at least a subject and a verb.
2. Analyze your sentences to determine which ones have a logical relationship and can be linked together. Choose transition words that show these relationships.
3. Rewrite the composition, adding the transition words and making changes, if necessary. For example, if you link the following sentences together with **cuando,** the word **ella** will not be necessary.

Vimos a Jacinta. Ella estaba en la cafetería. →

Cuando vimos a Jacinta, estaba en la cafetería.

Remember to use words with which you are familiar because you have used them before, and avoid using the dictionary too much (**Study Hint,** page 143).

Transition Words

además	*besides*	**pero**	*but*
así	*thus, so*	**por ejemplo**	*for example*
cuando	*when*	**por eso**	*therefore, for that reason*
de vez en cuando	*from time to time*	**por fin**	*at last, finally*
en cambio	*on the other hand*	**pues**	*well; since*
luego	*then, next*	**sin embargo**	*nevertheless*
mientras	*while*	**también**	*also*

60. SUMMARY OF THE USE AND OMISSION OF THE DEFINITE ARTICLE

¡Me robaron la bolsa donde tenía la cartera!

In Spanish, as in English, the definite article is used to point out or indicate a specific noun: *El* **libro está en** *la* **mesa.** The use of the definite article in Spanish differs from English usage in the following ways:

A. The definite article is generally repeated before each noun in a series.

> **El** libro, **el** bolígrafo y **el** cuaderno están en la mesa.
>
> *The book, pen, and notebook are on the table.*

B. The definite article is used before a title (except **don** and **doña**) when you are talking *about* a person: **el Sr. Romero, la profesora Burgos.** The article is not used when you are talking directly *to* the person.

> **La Dra.** López va a estar en el consultorio a las nueve.
>
> *Dr. López will be in the office at nine.*
>
> *but*
>
> **Dra.** López, ¿cuándo va a estar en el consultorio mañana?
>
> *Dr. López, when are you going to be in your office tomorrow?*

C. The definite article is used to express *on* with the days of the week.

> **El lunes** vamos al centro.
> La farmacia está cerrada **los miércoles.**
>
> *On Monday we're going downtown.*
> *The pharmacy is closed on Wednesdays.*

D. The definite article—not the possessive adjective—is used before articles of clothing or parts of the body when context makes meaning clear.

> Me puse **el** sombrero.
> Puse **el** sombrero en la mesa cuando entré.
>
> *I put on my hat.*
> *I put my hat on the table when I I came in.*
>
> *but*
>
> ¿Dónde pusiste **mi** sombrero?
>
> *Where did you put my hat?*
>
> Tiene **el** pelo largo.
> Me duele **la** garganta.
>
> *He has long hair.   (His hair is long.)*
> *My throat hurts me.*
>
> *but*
>
> Estas botas son demasiado pequeñas para **mis** pies.
>
> *These boots are too small for my feet.*

E. The definite article appears before abstract nouns and before nouns used in a general (or generic) sense.

La vida es breve.	*Life is short.*
La salud es importante.	*Health is important.*
Nos gustan **las flores.**	*We like flowers* (in general).

F. The definite article is used with the names of languages. except when they immediately follow **de, en,** and **hablar.** The article is often omitted after **escribir, aprender, leer, estudiar,** and **enseñar.**

El francés es una lengua bonita.	*French is a pretty language.*
Hablan bien **el español.**	*They speak Spanish well.*
but	
Hablan español.	*They speak Spanish.*

G. The definite article has traditionally been used with the names of certain countries. However, many native speakers of Spanish no longer observe this rule.

la Argentina	**los Estados Unidos**	**el Perú**
el Brasil	**la India**	**la República Dominicana**
el Canadá	**el Japón**	**El Salvador**
el Ecuador	**el Paraguay**	**el Uruguay**

PRÁCTICA

A. Dé Ud. frases nuevas según las indicaciones.

1. —¿Quiénes vinieron a celebrar el cumpleaños de Dolores?
   —Vinieron los *abuelos,* los *primos* y los *tíos.* (*primos, tío, abuela; padres, abuelos, otros parientes; primos, hermanas, esposos de ellas*)
2. —¿Cuándo está en el consultorio el doctor? ¿los lunes?
   —Sí, el doctor está los *lunes.* (*miércoles, viernes, sábados, martes, jueves*)
3. —¿Hacía mucho frío esta mañana?
   —Sí, y me puse el *suéter* porque hacía tanto frío. (*abrigo, sombrero, botas, calcetines*)
4. —¿Qué tiene el paciente? Está muy mal, ¿no?
   —Sí, le duele la *garganta.* (*estómago, pulmones, cabeza, ojos, nariz*)
5. —Su amiga Antonia es una verdadera experta en lenguas extranjeras. ¿Habla español?
   —Sí, Antonia habla muy bien el *español.* Tomó muchos cursos de español en la secundaria. (*francés, inglés, japonés, chino,' ruso, portugués*)
6. —¿Son latinoamericanos estos países? ¿(el) Perú?
   --—Sí, (el) *Perú* es un país latinoamericano. (*Argentina, Japón, Brasil, Francia, Paraguay, México, Ecuador, Canadá, Colombia, Estados Unidos*)

B. *Describe Dr. García, using the following words and phrases to give information about him:* **buen médico, cubano, cincuenta y siete años, una familia grande, español, la Habana.**

   MODELO   *El Dr. García es un buen médico.*

   Now ask Dr. García questions that would elicit the information given above.

   MODELO   *Dr. García, ¿es Ud. un buen médico?*

C. *Describa Ud. algunos de sus valores* (values).

   (No) Creo que _____ es/sea importante.   dinero / amistad / amor / salud / matrimonio / educación / libertad

D. *¿Cómo se dice en español?   Use el imperfecto y el pretérito.*

   Mr. Radillo met **(buscar)** us at the station on Sunday. We put our suitcases, presents, and coats in his car and walked to a restaurant. Argentine food is excellent, and I ordered in Spanish. I didn't need help from anyone. I think we're going to like life in Argentina.

CONVERSACIÓN

A. *Using last names and the titles* **Sr., Srta., Sra.,** *or* **profesor(a),** *tell something about several people in your Spanish class or about several famous persons.*

   MODELO   El profesor _____ va a México en verano todos los años.

B. *Complete las oraciones en una forma lógica.*

   1. En cuanto a la comida (*as far as food is concerned*), me gusta(n) _____, pero no me gusta(n) _____.
   2. Creo que _____ es una de las cosas más importantes en la vida.
   3. Algún día quiero viajar a _____.
   4. _____ es una lengua bonita, pero prefiero _____.
   5. De niño/a, tenía mucha dificultad en ponerme _____.
   6. Los lunes yo siempre _____.
   7. El domingo pasado yo _____.
   8. En este momento (no) me duele(n) _____.

C. *Preguntas*

   1. ¿Se habla español en España?   ¿y en (el) Uruguay?   ¿en (el) Brasil?
   2. ¿Hay algo más importante que las notas en la vida de un estudiante?   ¿qué?

3. ¿Qué piensa Ud. hacer el sábado?

4. ¿Tiene Ud. el pelo largo? ¿los pies grandes? ¿los ojos azules?

5. ¿Cuáles son los síntomas de una persona que tiene resfriado? ¿Cómo tiene la temperatura? ¿Qué le duele? ¿Pierde el apetito?

61. NOMINALIZATION: *LO* + ADJECTIVE

¿Qué te dije?

ISABEL: ¿Qué más te dijo el doctor?

BEATRIZ: Que *lo más importante* es quedarme en cama y descansar.

ISABEL: ¿No te dije *lo mismo* yo? —¡y sin cobrar!

1. *¿Quién está enferma?*
2. *¿Qué es lo más importante, según el doctor?*
3. *¿Quién dijo exactamente lo mismo?*

Spanish adjectives can be nominalized with an article or with a demonstrative adjective: **el rojo, aquella española** (section 52). They can also be nominalized by using the masculine singular form with **lo**. Adjectives nominalized with **lo** describe general qualities or characteristics that are usually expressed in English by the words *part* or *thing*. They do not refer to any one noun in particular.

lo cómico	*the funny thing (part)*
lo bueno/malo	*the good/bad thing (part)*
lo más importante	*the most important thing (part)*
lo mejor	*the best thing (part)*
lo mismo	*the same thing (part)*

PRÁCTICA

A. *Cambie, usando lo + adjetivo.*

MODELO   importante → lo importante

1. divertido   4. curioso
2. peor   5. necesario
3. interesante   6. bueno

What did I tell you? ISABEL: What else did the doctor say? BEATRIZ: That the most important thing is to stay in bed and rest. ISABEL: Didn't I tell you the same thing? And without charging!

B. *Exprese sus ideas sobre lo más importante de la vida.*

Lo más importante de la vida (no) es/son* _____. las clases / la libertad / las vacaciones / la salud / los amigos / la familia / _____

C. *¿Cómo se dice en español?*

1. the good news
2. the important part
3. the worst thing
4. what's sad is . . .

CONVERSACIÓN

A. *Complete las oraciones en una forma lógica.*

1. Lo mejor/peor de esta clase es/son _____.
2. Cuando alguien está enfermo, lo peor es/son _____.
3. Durante mis últimas vacaciones lo más interesante fue/fueron _____.
4. Lo malo/bueno de la vida de un estudiante es/son _____.
5. Lo bueno de la vida en general es/son _____.

B. *Give "good news" and "bad news" for each of the following situations.*

MODELO   en el restaurante →
          Lo bueno es que la comida es excelente.
          Lo malo son los precios.

1. en la gasolinera
2. en la oficina de la profesora
3. en el aeropuerto
4. en el consultorio del médico
5. en casa
6. en el trabajo

DIÁLOGO: En el consultorio de la médica.[1]

Tomás Hernández Rodríguez, esudiante universitario
Enfermera
Dra. Ruiz Sánchez, especialista en medicina general

A. *El paciente habla con la enfermera*
  ENFERMERA: ¿Tiene Ud. cita con la doctora Ruiz Sánchez?   Pues siéntese, por favor.   ¿Cómo se llama?

*Use **es** before a singular noun and **son** before a plural.   The verb **ser** anticipates the noun that follows.

TOMÁS: Me llamo Tomás Hernández Rodríguez.

ENFERMERA: ¿De qué se trata?

TOMÁS: Pues anteayer me sentía perfectamente bien. Corrí cinco kilómetros, jugué al fútbol[2], nadé° y fui a una fiesta. Había una comida deliciosa —comí y bebí de todo.   *I swam*

ENFERMERA: ¿Cuándo empezó a sentirse mal?

TOMÁS: A la mañana siguiente tuve fiebre. Tosía mucho y me dolía todo el cuerpo. Hoy me siento peor y lo malo es que tengo examen de literatura. No sé nada porque anoche no pude estudiar.

ENFERMERA: ¿Tiene otros síntomas?

TOMÁS: No, gracias a Dios.

ENFERMERA: Dígame su edad, su peso° y su estatura°, por favor.   *weight / height*

TOMÁS: Tengo veintiún años, mido° un metro ochenta y cinco y peso ochenta kilos[3].   *I am (measure)*

ENFERMERA: Muy bien. Ahora, voy a tomarle la temperatura… Humm… tiene Ud. fiebre: treinta y ocho grados[4]. Súbase la manga° derecha, que le voy a tomar la presión°.   **Súbase…** *roll up your sleeve* / *blood pressure*

TOMÁS: ¿Todo esto para un resfriado?

ENFERMERA: Es rutinario. Ahora pase Ud. al consultorio de la doctora.

B. En el consultorio de la Dra. Ruiz Sánchez

DOCTORA: Siéntese. Saque la lengua. Abra bien la boca y diga: «Aaaaa… aaa…» La garganta está un poco inflamada. Ahora respire profundamente. Diga: «treinta y tres». Bien. Ud. no tiene nada serio en los pulmones.

TOMÁS: Pero de noche toso mucho, doctora. Ya tosía cuando me resfrié.

DOCTORA: Es que fuma demasiado. Ahora calle° mientras le ausculto° el corazón. Humm… ¿hace Ud. muchos ejercicios físicos?   *be quiet* / *I listen to (medical)*

TOMÁS: Fui campeón° de natación° en el colegio. Todavía hago mucho ejercicio y practico varios deportes.   *champion / swimming*

DOCTORA: Como consecuencia Ud. tiene corazón de atleta, es decir, lo tiene más fuerte que lo normal. En general, Ud. está en muy buen estado físico.

TOMÁS: ¿Y para este resfriado?

DOCTORA: Pues, unas aspirinas y… paciencia. Para su salud en general, deje de° fumar. Y para sus exámenes, ¡no los deje para el último momento! No es necesaria otra receta.   **deje…** *stop*

Comprensión

Conteste en oraciones completas.

A. 1. ¿Quién está enfermo?
    2. ¿Se sentía mal anteayer?
    3. ¿Estuvo muy activo anteayer? ¿Adónde fue?
    4. ¿Qué síntoma tenía ayer?
    5. ¿Cómo está hoy?
    6. ¿Por qué no pudo estudiar para su examen?
    7. ¿Tiene otros síntomas?
    8. ¿Cuántos años tiene? ¿Es alto?
    9. ¿Quién le toma la temperatura y la presión?

B. 1. ¿Qué tiene que hacer el paciente cuando abre la boca? ¿cuando respira?
    2. ¿Tiene pulmonía (*pneumonia*)?
    3. ¿Por qué tose tanto?
    4. ¿Era buen atleta? ¿Es muy deportista ahora?
    5. ¿Cómo es el corazón de Tomás?
    6. ¿Qué medicina le recomienda la doctora para el resfriado?
    7. ¿Qué otros consejos le da la doctora? **(Debe _____.)**

Comentario cultural

1. The term **médico/a** is used to refer to a medical doctor, whose title in direct address is **doctor(a).** Many Hispanic doctors complete residencies and advanced studies at medical centers in the United States and Europe. The number of doctors in relation to the population varies greatly from country to country, and in some Latin American countries the health needs of the people cannot be adequately met. The 1977 *United Nations Statistical Yearbook* showed 1 doctor for every 911 persons in Uruguay, and 1 for every 4,330 in Guatemala. The ratio in the United States is 1 to 622, although this varies from region to region.

   Many U.S. prescription drugs are sold over the counter in Hispanic **farmacias.** For this reason, many people just explain their symptoms to the pharmacist **(farmacéutico/a),** who then prescribes a drug for them. The **farmacéutico** is usually well trained and up to date in pharmacology.

   Medical services are also performed by **practicantes,** persons with three years of medical training who are licensed to treat the sick, give injections, and perform very minor surgery. There are also **curanderos** and **curanderas** (*healers*), who may recommend an herb or herb tea, or perform some magical cure. Many babies are delivered by midwives, **parteras,** rather than by doctors.

2. **El fútbol** (*soccer*) is the favorite spectator and participation sport in Hispanic countries. Children begin developing soccer skills at an early age by kicking a ball in neighborhood streets, at school, and in the parks and fields. Many continue to play as teen-agers and adults. The loyalty and enthusiasm of the fans for the home team in local matches is as intense as it is for the national squad in international playoffs. The game called football in the United States is referred to in Hispanic countries as **fútbol (norte)americano.**

Carl Frank/Photo Researchers, Inc.

3. A meter equals 39.37 inches, and a kilo equals 2.2 pounds. Tom is therefore 6 feet, 3/4 inches (1.85 meters) tall and weighs 176 pounds (80 kilos).

4. On the Fahrenheit scale, Tom has a temperature of 100.4 degrees (38 degrees Centigrade). To convert centigrade to Fahrenheit, use the formula $F = 9/5C + 32$.

UN POCO DE TODO

A. *Cambie por el pasado (pretérito o imperfecto) según el contexto.*

1. Rómulo toma el jarabe. Dice que no le gusta el sabor (*taste*).
2. Me explican que lo mejor es quedarme en cama.
3. Lo peor es que me resfrío durante mis vacaciones.
4. Ellos se quitan el abrigo porque tienen calor.
5. Los martes y jueves lo más interesante es la clase de portugués.

B. *Form complete sentences based on the words given in the order given. Use preterite or imperfect forms, as appropriate. Add other words if necessary.*

1. Dr. Matamoros / le / dar / niño / antibiótico / porque / tener / fiebre / alto
2. atleta / decir / que / fundamental / ser / hacer / ejercicio

3. ser / cuatro / mañana / cuando / por fin / niño / enfermo / empezar / respirar / sin dificultad
4. cuando / nosotros / ser / niños / pensar / que / mejor / de / escuela / ser / vacaciones
5. el lunes / yo / ir / centro / con / Sra. Medina / aunque (*although*) / yo / no / querer / comprar / nada

C. *Working with another student, ask and answer questions based on the following model. Use preterite or imperfect forms as indicated.*

MODELO   verano pasado / ir al Japón / vivir allí mi hermana →
      DIANA: Para ti, ¿qué fue lo más interesante del *verano pasado?*
      SARA: *Fui al Japón.*
      DIANA: ¿Por qué *fuiste allí?*
      SARA: Porque *mi hermana vivía allí.*

1. cumpleaños / comer en El Toledano / querer comer comida española
2. niñez (*childhood*) / vivir en el Perú / trabajar mi padre allí
3. vacaciones / ir a esquiar en las montañas / querer descansar y divertirse
4. escuela secundaria / estudiar español / hablar español en casa mis abuelos
5. fiesta / bailar la noche entera / tener ganas de bailar

D. *Use the following pairs of questions to interview another student about his/her childhood and about specific events in the past.*

1. ¿Dónde vivías cuando tenías _____ años? / ¿Dónde viviste en 1970?
2. ¿A qué escuela asistías? / ¿Asististe a esta universidad el año pasado?
3. ¿Qué lenguas estudiabas? / ¿Estudiaste latín en la secundaria?
4. ¿Qué hacías cuando te enfermabas? / ¿Cuántas veces te resfriaste el año pasado?
5. ¿Qué películas te gustaban más? / ¿Te gustó la última película que viste?
6. ¿Qué era lo más importante de tu vida? / ¿Qué cosa importante te pasó el año pasado?
7. ¿Qué hacías durante los veranos? / ¿Qué hiciste el verano pasado?

E. *Complete las oraciones en una forma lógica.*

1. Lo primero que me quité anoche fue/fueron _____.
2. Lo más interesante del/de la profesor(a) _____ es/son _____.
3. Anoche tenía (me sentía) _____. Por eso yo _____.
4. Anoche me dolía _____. Por eso yo _____.
5. Lo peor de un resfriado es/son _____.

VOCABULARIO

VERBOS

cuidarse   to take care of oneself
enfermarse   to get sick
examinar   to examine
hacer ejercicio   to exercise, get
  exercise
llevar una vida...   to lead a . . . life
practicar   to participate in (*sports*);
  to practice
resfriarse   to get/catch a cold
respirar   to breathe
sacar   to stick out (*a tongue*)
sonar   to ring
toser   to cough

SUSTANTIVOS

el **antibiótico**   antibiotic
el **bienestar**   wellbeing
la **boca**   mouth
el **consultorio**   office
el **corazón**   heart

el **deporte**   sport
la **dificultad**   difficulty
el **dolor**   pain
la **enfermedad**   illness
el **estómago**   stomach
el **estudio**   study; *pl.* studies,
  school work
la **farmacia**   drugstore, pharmacy
la **fiebre**   fever
la **garganta**   throat
el **jarabe**   (cough) syrup
la **lengua**   tongue
la **medicina**   medicine
el/la **médico/a**   doctor
la **nariz**   nose
el **ojo**   eye
el/la **paciente**   patient
el **pelo**   hair
los **pulmones**   lungs
la **receta**   prescription
el **resfriado**   cold

la **salud**   health
el **síntoma**   symptom
la **temperatura**   temperature
la **tos**   cough

ADJETIVOS

congestionado/a   congested
mareado/a   nauseated
sano/a   healthy

PALABRAS Y EXPRESIONES ÚTILES

de joven/niño/a   as a youth/child
de repente   suddenly
en seguida   immediately
lo suficiente   enough
profundamente   deeply
tener dolor de   to have a pain in
una vez   once

Un paso más 14

Actividades

A. **¿Te importa tu salud?** What steps do you take to stay healthy? Working with another student, ask and answer the following questions:

1. ¿Cuántas horas duermes cada noche? ¿Duermes bien?
2. ¿Comes bien? ¿Comes muchos dulces (*sweets*)? ¿mucha proteína? ¿mucha ensalada? ¿muchas legumbres (*vegetables*)? ¿mucha fruta?
3. ¿Comes comidas «instantáneas» o prefieres comidas «naturales»?
4. ¿Tomas mucho café, mucho té o mucha Coca-Cola? ¿bebidas alcohólicas?
5. ¿Fumas? ¿mucho o poco? ¿Quieres dejar de fumar? ¿Cuándo fumas?
6. ¿Consultas a tu médico por lo menos una vez al año?
7. ¿Sigues las recomendaciones de tu médico?
8. Cuando necesitas tomar medicina, ¿sigues las instrucciones?
9. ¿Llevas una vida de mucha tensión? ¿Tienes muchas responsabilidades?
10. ¿Tienes tiempo para pensar, meditar o simplemente descansar?
11. ¿Caminas mucho o siempre vas en coche (tomas el autobús, etcétera)?
12. ¿Haces mucho ejercicio? ¿Corres? ¿Practicas algún deporte?
13. ¿Llevas una vida sana?

A propósito…

It is important to be able to communicate accurately when you are in need of medical or dental attention. English-speaking doctors and dentists are available in most large cities in Spanish-speaking countries. But if you do need to speak Spanish with medical personnel, the following words and phrases will be useful.

¿Cuánto tiempo hace que Ud. está enfermo/a?	*How long have you been ill?*
Hace (dos días) que estoy enfermo/a.	*I've been sick for (two days).*
¿Cuándo se enfermó?	*When did you get sick?*
¿Padece de algo más?	*Is anything else wrong?*
Sí, padezco de _____.	*Yes, I'm also suffering from _____.*
¿Ha tenido Ud. _____?	*Have you had _____?*
Sí, he tenido/No, no he tenido _____.	*Yes, I've had/No, I haven't had _____.*
¿Toma Ud. alguna medicina?	*Are you taking any medicine?*
Vamos a sacar los rayos equis/las radiografías.	*We're going to take X-rays.*
Voy a ponerle una inyección.	*I'm going to give you a shot.*
Tenemos que sacerle el diente (la muela).	*We have to pull the tooth (molar).*

Remember that any temperature above 37 degrees Centigrade (98.6 degrees Farenheit) constitutes a fever.

B. **En el consultorio.** Este paciente está muy enfermo. Usando algunas de las frases de **A propósito,** describa Ud. lo que pasa en el dibujo.

C. **Dramas médicos.** Con otro/a estudiante, haga los papeles de paciente y doctor(a), dentista o enfermero/a en una de las siguientes situaciones:

1. En la sala de urgencia (*emergency*). Una señora mayor habla con un médico. Ella sigue repitiendo: «¡Ay, Dios! Me voy a morir» y no quiere decir otra cosa.
2. En la sala de urgencia. Un niño de seis años se cayó de un árbol. Se rompió el brazo y le duele muchísimo. Está gritando (*screaming*) como loco.
3. En el consultorio del dentista. A un señor de cuarenta años le duele mucho una muela. Es cobarde (*coward*) y no quiere que se la saque.
4. En el hospital. La paciente tuvo un ataque de apendicitis y la van a operar. Habla con la enfermera.
5. En el consultorio de la médica. El paciente es hipocondríaco y quiere que la médica lo opere. Hablan los dos.

—¿*Pero cómo quiere que le opere si no tiene usted nada?*
—*Mejor, doctor. Así la operación le va a ser más fácil.*

D. **Análisis de un anuncio.**   The following article was written in response to a
Spanish billboard ad for small cigars **(puros)** with the brand name **Chicos.**
The advertising slogan **"Chicos ¿fumáis chicos?"** contains a play on words
using two different meanings of the word **chicos:** *young people* and *small.*

The author of the article has strong feelings about the message the ad contains.   Read the article several times to get a clear idea of the author's opinions.
Then match the following Spanish words and phrases with their English
equivalents and answer the questions that follow.

"Brevería" ilustrada

UN ANUNCIO NOCIVO

«"Chicos", ¿fumáis "chicos"?» Pocas veces tres palabras, barajando el doble sentido
de su sinonimia, encerrarán un mensaje tan deletéreo como el que ofrecemos a la
consideración de nuestros lectores y, por supuesto, de sus autores, sobre un producto tan diametralmente opuesto a la salud física y moral de los «chicos», como el
tabaco. En este caso elaborado en su forma más agresiva: el puro. La restricción en la
divulgación del alcohol y del tabaco es una norma unánimemente aceptada en los
países de mayor escrupulosidad sanitaria y, por su desarrollo social, de mayor experiencia democrática y de ejercicio de las libertades privadas. Norma que informa la
ética publicitaria, también vigente en España, y que aquí se rompe, precisamente en
perjuicio de sus más escogidos destinatarios: los «chicos», es decir, los adolescentes.
En el aluvión de impresiones de todo orden que hieren su sensibilidad, abriéndoles
apetitos estragantes, tenemos que dejar hoy triste constancia de este anuncio.

---

1. nocivo
2. barajando su doble sentido
3. mensaje tan deletéreo
4. por supuesto
5. la divulgación del alcohol y del tabaco
6. unánimemente
7. escrupulosidad sanitaria
8. vigente en
9. en perjuicio de
10. en el aluvión de
11. hieren su sensibilidad
12. apetitos estragantes
13. triste constancia

a. unanimously
b. in force, prevailing in
c. sad evidence, proof, certainty
d. deleterious, poisonous message
e. depraved, corrupt appetites
f. in the flood (torrent) of
g. harm, hurt their sensitivity
h. making drugs and alcohol available to the public
i. naturally, of course
j. noxious, hurtful
k. scrupulous care with respect to
   matters of health
l. entangling its double meaning
m. to the detriment or harm of

Preguntas

1. ¿Qué palabra emplea el anuncio con doble sentido (*meaning*)?
2. ¿A quiénes se dirige (*is directed*) el anuncio?
3. ¿En qué país apareció (*appeared*) este anuncio?
4. Según el autor del artículo, ¿cómo es el anuncio?
5. ¿Apoya (*supports*) el autor la restricción en la divulgación del alcohol y del tabaco?
6. ¿Este anuncio es típico de los anuncios que se ven hoy en los Estados Unidos?
7. ¿Está Ud. de acuerdo con las opiniones del autor? ¿Por qué sí o por qué no?

E. **Más refranes.** Many proverbs and sayings refer to health, medicine, and doctors. Comment briefly on one of the following proverbs, explaining what it means, telling why you agree or disagree with it, and giving an illustration of it, if possible.

1. Músculos de Sansón (*Sampson*) con cerebro de mosquito.
2. Si quieres vivir sano, acuéstate y levántate temprano.
3. Para enfermedad de años, no hay medicina.
4. De médico, poeta y loco, todos tenemos un poco.
5. La salud no se compra, no tiene precio.

Lectura cultural: La lengua española

Para las personas que viven en esta edad del *jet*, es de mucha importancia saber más de una lengua. En el caso de los que viven en la América del Norte, tal vez la segunda lengua deba ser el español. La lengua española es la lengua nacional de México, de casi todos los países de Centroamérica y de Suramérica (menos el Brasil) y de varias de las repúblicas del Caribe. Además, su uso en los Estados Unidos está aumentando° en todas partes del país.　　*increasing*

Como las otras lenguas románicas° —el francés, el italiano, el portugués y el rumano° —el español tuvo sus orígenes en el latín, lengua que se extendió por todas las regiones del Mediterráneo durante la época del Imperio Romano. De los dialectos de cada región resultaron las lenguas modernas.　　*romance* / *Rumanian*

Cuando España era todavía una región de reinos independientes durante la Edad Media, se hablaban en la Península Ibérica varios dialectos, tales como el gallego, el catalán, el aragonés, el leonés y el castellano (lengua del reino de Castilla). Cuando Castilla llegó a ser la región más poderosa° y los reinos formaron la nación española, el castellano naturalmente llegó a ser la lengua nacional. Mientras los árabes ocupaban la Península　　*powerful*

Gallego-portugués		Catalán	
Leonés		Vascuence	
Aragonés		Castellano	

Ibérica (711–1492), entraron en la lengua unas cuatro mil palabras de origen
árabe: ajedrez°, álgebra, alcohol, aceite°.   *chess / oil*

Los conquistadores que llegaron al Nuevo Mundo llevaron la lengua castellana a las Américas. Esto resultó en el reemplazo° de gran parte de las   *replacement*
lenguas indígenas° por el castellano. Sin embargo, aquellas lenguas tam-   *native (Indian)*
bién, como el árabe, contribuyeron al español algunas palabras nuevas:
patata, maíz, chocolate, aguacate°, canoa, huracán, tomate.   *avocado*

Lo interesante del castellano actual° es la unidad estructural y gramatical   *present-day*
del idioma en las muchas regiones del mundo donde se habla. Aunque
hay algunas diferencias de vocabulario y de entonación de región en
región, una persona de habla española puede entender y hacerse entender
en cualquier lugar donde se habla la bella y rica lengua castellana.

Comprensión

Complete las oraciones en una forma lógica.

1. El español es importante en el hemisferio occidental porque _____.
2. Las lenguas románicas aparecieron cuando _____.

3. El gallego, el catalán, el aragonés, el leonés y el castellano eran _____.
4. Las lenguas románicas nacieron cuando _____.
5. El castellano llegó a ser la lengua más importante de la Península Ibérica cuando_____.
6. El vocabulario del español recibió nuevas palabras cuando _____ y _____.
7. El castellano actual puede usarse en muchas regiones distintas porque _____.

Ejercicios escritos

A. Using the general knowledge you already have, write a brief paragraph about the use of Spanish in the United States. Use the following questions as a guide in organizing your paragraph.

1. ¿Dónde se habla el español en los Estados Unidos?
2. ¿Quiénes lo hablan?
3. ¿Por qué es importante saber el español?
4. ¿Por qué está aumentando su uso?
5. ¿En qué profesiones puede ser muy útil?
6. ¿Cómo puede ayudarle a Ud. en su futuro?

B. Write a brief history of your study of Spanish, using the following phrases as a guide.

1. empezar a estudiarlo cuando tenía _____ años
2. decidir estudiarlo porque _____
3. el primer día de clase
4. unos días después
5. ahora

capítulo 15 El dinero

© Joel Gordon 1980

OBJETIVOS

In this chapter you will learn vocabulary and expressions related to money and to personal finances.

You will also learn about the following aspects of Spanish grammar:

62. how to form and use the future verb forms: *I will (go, dance)*
63. the use of the future verb forms to express

conjecture and probability in Spanish
64. how to use the conditional verb forms, the equivalent of English *would be* in *She told me that she would be there.*

Un paso más includes activities related to money, credit cards, and foreign currency, and a reading about the economic status of Latin America.

VOCABULARIO: PREPARACIÓN

<table>
<tr><td colspan="4" align="center">Una cuestión de dinero</td></tr>
<tr><td>el alquiler</td><td>rent</td><td>cobrar</td><td>to cash (a check); to charge (someone for an item or service)</td></tr>
<tr><td>el banco</td><td>bank</td><td></td><td></td></tr>
<tr><td>la cuenta corriente</td><td>checking account</td><td></td><td></td></tr>
<tr><td>la cuenta de ahorros</td><td>savings account</td><td>dejar de + infinitive</td><td>to stop (doing something)</td></tr>
<tr><td>el cheque</td><td>(bank) check</td><td>economizar</td><td>to economize</td></tr>
<tr><td>la factura</td><td>bill</td><td>gastar</td><td>to spend (money)</td></tr>
<tr><td>los gastos</td><td>expenses</td><td>mudarse</td><td>to move (from one residence to another)</td></tr>
<tr><td>el presupuesto</td><td>budget</td><td></td><td></td></tr>
<tr><td>la tarjeta de crédito</td><td>credit card</td><td></td><td></td></tr>
<tr><td></td><td></td><td>pagar al contado/ con cheque</td><td>to pay cash/ by check</td></tr>
<tr><td>ahorrar</td><td>to save (money)</td><td>quejarse</td><td>to complain</td></tr>
<tr><td>aumentar</td><td>to increase</td><td></td><td></td></tr>
<tr><td>cargar (a la cuenta de uno)</td><td>to charge (to someone's account)</td><td></td><td></td></tr>
</table>

A. *¿Cómo pagan estas personas?*

1.   2.   3.

B. *¿Qué va a hacer Ud. en las siguientes situaciones?*

1. Los gastos mensuales (*monthly*) de Ud. están aumentando y Ud. necesita dos trabajos. ¿Cuál va a ser su segundo empleo?
   a. camarero/a   b. *barman*   c. dependiente/a   d. detective   e. otra cosa
2. Ud. no tiene suficiente dinero para mantener su presupuesto actual (*current*); tiene que economizar. ¿Qué deja Ud. de comer, de tomar o de usar?
   a. bebidas alcohólicas   b. carne   c. cigarrillos   d. gasolina   e. otra cosa

3. Ud. es el/la presidente/a.   ¿Qué hace para combatir la inflación?
   a. Prohibo más aumentos de precios.
   b. Prohibo aumentos de sueldos.
   c. Pongo un límite a las ganancias (*earnings*) de las compañías.
   d. No hago nada.
   e. otra cosa
4. El/la dueño/a de su apartamento le aumenta el alquiler un 50 por ciento.
   ¿Cómo reacciona Ud.?
   a. Decido comprar una casa.
   b. Me mudo a otro apartamento.
   c. Me quejo pero pago el aumento.
   d. Pago el aumento pero dejo de mantener el apartamento.
   e. otra cosa
5. Ud. tiene que economizar con respecto a la comida.   ¿Qué va a hacer?
   a. Me hago vegetariano/a.
   b. Me invito a comer en casa de los amigos.
   c. Dejo de comer dos días a la semana.
   d. Me hago miembro de una cooperativa.
   e. otra cosa

C. *De estas frases, ¿cuáles describen la situación económica de Ud.?*

1. Es imposible ahorrar dinero.
2. Uso mis tarjetas de crédito demasiado; por eso tengo muchas facturas que pagar.
3. Es mejor pagar al contado que cargarlo todo a la cuenta.
4. Necesito dos empleos para poder pagar todas mis facturas.
5. Si mi producto favorito sube un 50 por ciento de precio, dejo de comprarlo.
6. Si el dependiente de una tienda me cobra demasiado, me quejo en seguida.
7. Si no tengo dinero a fines del mes, saco dinero de mi cuenta de ahorros.
8. Mi cuenta corriente siempre tiene mucho dinero a fines del mes.

D. *Indique una respuesta para cada pregunta.*

1. ¿Cómo prefiere Ud. pagar?
2. ¿Hay algún problema?

3. Me da su pasaporte, por favor. Necesito verlo para poder cobrar su cheque.
4. ¿Quiere usar su tarjeta de crédito?
5. ¿Va a depositar este cheque en su cuenta corriente o en su cuenta de ahorros?
6. ¿Adónde quiere Ud. que mandemos la factura?

a. En la cuenta de ahorros, por favor.
b. Me la manda a la oficina, por favor.
c. No, prefiero pagar al contado.
d. Sí, señorita, Ud. me cobró demasiado por el jarabe.
e. Aquí lo tiene Ud.
f. Cárguelo a mi cuenta, por favor.

PRONUNCIACIÓN: Intonation and Punctuation

In Spanish and English the voice rises at the end of *yes/no* questions and falls at the end of information questions. The voice falls at the end of exclamations, also.

¿Fuiste tú? (*Did you go?*)   **¿Adónde fuiste?** (*Where did you go?*)

¡Que va! (*Good grief!*)

Spanish uses punctuation marks to signal the beginning and end of exclamations and questions. When just one part of a sentence is an exclamation or question, only that part is enclosed by the appropriate punctuation marks.

¿Dónde está la casa de Miguel?   (The whole sentence is a question.)
Su casa está allí, ¿no?   (Just the **no** is a question.)
Yo estudié la lección, ¿y tú?   (Just **y tú** is a question.)
¡Voy a salir esta noche!   (The whole sentence is an exclamation.)
Pero mi hijito, ¡no puedes!   (Just **no puedes** is an exclamation.)

In a series of words joined by a conjunction, English tends to use commas after all of them: *A, B, and C.* Spanish usually omits the comma before the conjunction: *A, B y C.* Intonation also differs in this construction. In English the voice often rises in pitch on each item in the series, falling only on the last one. In Spanish, however, the pitch tends to rise just on the next-to-last item. For example:

↗ ⌒ ↗ ⌒   ⌒ ⌒ ⌒ ⌒

one, two, three, four   uno, dos, tres, cuatro

PRÁCTICA

Punctuate the following sentences. Then pronounce them, paying particular attention to intonation.

1. Cuál es tu profesora   Cómo se llama ella
2. Uno dos tres cuatro   Caramba   él compró cuatro trajes
3. Qué ejercicio más fácil
4. Fue Juan al mercado
5. Dónde estuviste ayer
6. Ja ja   Tú no hablas en serio   verdad
7. Quiénes vienen   Luisa María y Juan

MINIDIÁLOGOS Y GRAMÁTICA

---

62. FUTURE VERB FORMS

¡Hay que reducir los gastos! ¿Qué vamos a hacer?

MADRE:	*Tomaré* el autobús en vez de usar el carro.
ANDRÉS:	*Comeremos* más ensalada y menos carne y postres.
PADRE:	Los niños no *irán* al cine con tanta frecuencia.
JULIETA:	*Dejaré* de fumar.
MADRE:	Los niños *gastarán* menos en dulces.
PADRE:	No *cargaré* nada a nuestras cuentas. Lo *pagaré* todo al contado.
JULIETA:	*Bajaremos* el gas.
GABRIELA:	Y yo me *iré* a vivir con los abuelos. Allí *habrá* de todo como siempre, ¿verdad?

---

1. *¿Quién dejará de usar el carro? ¿de fumar?*
2. *¿Qué comerá la familia? ¿Qué no comerá?*
3. *¿Cómo gastará menos dinero el padre? ¿y los niños?*
4. *¿Adónde irá a vivir Gabriela? ¿Por qué?*

It's necessary to cut down on expenses! What are we going to do? MOTHER: I'll take the bus instead of using the car. ANDRÉS: We'll eat more salad and less meat and desserts. FATHER: The kids won't go to the movies so much. JULIETA: I'll stop smoking. MOTHER: The kids will spend less on candy. FATHER: I won't charge anything. I'll pay for everything in cash. JULIETA: We'll turn down the heat. GABRIELA: And I'll go to live with our grandparents. There they'll have (*there will be*) everything as usual, right?

HABLAR		COMER		VIVIR	
hablaré	hablaremos	comeré	comeremos	viviré	viviremos
hablarás	hablaréis	comerás	comeréis	vivirás	viviréis
hablará	hablarán	comerá	comerán	vivirá	vivirán

Future actions or states of being can be expressed with the **ir** + **a** + *infinitive* construction or with the future. In English the future is formed with the auxiliary verbs *will* or *shall: I will/shall speak.* The *future* (**futuro**) of most Spanish verbs is formed by adding the future endings to the infinitive: **-é, -ás, -á, -emos, -éis, -án.** No auxiliary verbs are needed.

The following verbs add the future endings to irregular stems.

decir:	**dir-**		decir	
hacer:	**har-**	**-é**	**diré**	**diremos**
poder:	**podr-**	**-ás**	**dirás**	**diréis**
poner:	**pondr-**	**-á**	**dirá**	**dirán**
querer:	**querr-**	**-emos**		
saber:	**sabr-**	**-éis**		
salir:	**saldr-**	**-án**		
tener:	**tendr-**			
venir:	**vendr-**			

The future of **hay** is **habrá** (*there will be*).

Remember that present tense forms can be used to express the immediate future. Compare:

Llegaré a tiempo. — *I'll arrive on time.*
Llego a las ocho mañana. ¿Vienes a buscarme? — *I arrive at eight tomorrow. Will you pick me up?*
No creo que Pepe **llegue** a tiempo. — *I don't think Pepe will arrive on time.*

¡OJO! When English *will* refers not to future time but to the willingness of someone to do something, Spanish uses a form of the verb **querer,** not the future.

¿**Quieres** cerrar la puerta, por favor? — *Will you please close the door?*

PRÁCTICA

A. Dé Ud. frases nuevas según las indicaciones.

1. —En el viaje que Uds. van a hacer a México, todos hablarán español, ¿verdad?
   —Sí, *Juan* hablará español. (*yo, Uds., nosotros, el/la profesor[a], tú, vosotros*)

2. —¿Quién insistirá en levantarse temprano para verlo todo?
   —*Estela* insistirá en levantarse temprano. (*tú, Elena y Miguel, yo, nosotros, Ud., vosotros*)

3. —¿Quién se levantará temprano para verlo todo?
   —*Estela* se levantará temprano. (*el/la profesor[a], yo, nosotros, tú, Uds., vosotros*)

B. *Ud. es astrólogo/a, y puede predecir* (predict) *el futuro. ¿Qué predicciones puede Ud. formar usando una palabra o frase —en su forma correcta— de cada columna? Use el futuro de los verbos.*

			pagar todas las facturas algún día
			casarse, mudarse a _____, retirarse
yo	(no)	querer	un aumento de salario por fin
el/la profesor(a)		tener	en un país hispano, en _____
mis amigos		poder	casado/a, soltero/a, rico/a, famoso/a
_____		ser	ahorrar dinero para comprar _____
		vivir	muchos/pocos/ningún hijo(s)
			médico/a, abogado/a, _____
			_____

C. *Ud. quiere imitar todas las acciones de su amigo Gregorio. Cuando Gregorio dice que va a hacer algo, diga Ud. que lo hará también, usando el futuro.*

MODELO   Gregorio va a gastar menos este mes. → *Yo también gastaré menos.*

1. Gregorio va a mudarse de apartamento.
2. Va a hacer un presupuesto y lo va a seguir.
3. Va a saber todas las respuestas en el próximo examen.
4. Va a salir para la playa este fin de semana.
5. Va a ir a la fiesta esta noche.
6. Va a decirle a Graciela que vaya a la fiesta también.
7. Va a casarse algún día.
8. Va a poner todo su dinero en una cuenta de ahorros.

D. *¿Cómo se dice en español? Un grupo de turistas está en una tienda en Guatemala. Usando el futuro, explique cómo pagarán sus compras.*

Mr. Adams says (that) he will pay in cash. Mrs. Walsh will use her credit card. Ms. Smith says that she will have to cash a check at (**en**) the bank. Mr. Collins says that the shop will have to send the bill to his home.

CONVERSACIÓN

Haga una descripción del mundo del año 2500, completando estas frases:

1. (No) Habrá _____. (pobreza [*poverty*], guerras, igualdad [*equality*] para todos, un gobierno mundial, gasolina, otros tipos de energía, _____)

2. La gente (no) vivirá en _____.
　　　　　　　　 tendrá _____.
　　　　　　　　 se quejará de _____.
　　　　　　　　 hablará _____.
　　　　　　　　 comerá _____.
3. Nosotros (no) viajaremos a/en _____.
　　　　　　　　 usaremos más/menos _____.
　　　　　　　　 podremos _____.
　　　　　　　　 comeremos _____.

¿Está Ud. de acuerdo con las predicciones de sus compañeros de clase?　Exprese su opinión, completando estas frases:

Estoy de acuerdo en que _____ en el futuro.
No creo que _____ en el futuro.　(¡OJO!　subjuntivo)

63. FUTURE OF PROBABILITY

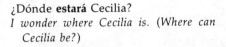

¿Dónde **estará** Cecilia?
I wonder where Cecilia is. (Where can Cecilia be?)

Cecilia **estará** en la carretera.
Cecilia is probably (must be) on the highway.　(I bet Cecilia is on the highway.)

In addition to indicating future actions, the future often expresses probability or conjecture in the present.　This construction is called the *future of probability* **(futuro de probabilidad).**　English *probably, I guess, I bet,* and *I wonder* are not directly expressed in Spanish; their sense is contained in the future form of the verb used.

PRÁCTICA

A. *¿Cómo se dice en español?   Use el futuro de probabilidad.*

    1. It's probably four o'clock.
    2. He probably is a patient.
    3. They must know the answer.
    4. She must be in Phoenix.
    5. They probably have a lot of children.
    6. I wonder where she lives.
    7. I wonder how old he is.
    8. I wonder who has the credit cards.

B. *Cambie por el futuro para expresar probabilidad o conjetura.*

    1. La doctora le da un antibiótico.
    2. Cobran mucho en aquella tienda.
    3. ¿Cuánto es el alquiler?
    4. Hay un 10 por ciento de descuento.
    5. Tiene resfriado.
    6. Salen mañana.
    7. ¿Cuántos grados de fiebre tiene?
    8. No vienen esta tarde.
    9. ¿Está enfermo?

CONVERSACIÓN

A. *Describa Ud. a estas personas.   ¿Quiénes serán?   ¿Dónde estarán?*

B. *Using the future of probability, speculate about the life of a member of your class or of a well-known person.   Use these questions as a guide.*

    1. ¿Dónde vivirá?
    2. ¿Cuántos años tendrá?
    3. ¿Estará casado/a?   ¿Tendrá hijos?
    4. ¿Cuánto ganará?
    5. ¿Ahorrará mucho dinero?

64. CONDITIONAL VERB FORMS

Un viaje ideal
Necesito salir... creo que me *gustaría* ir a Puerto Rico... no *haría* nada de trabajo... *podría* nadar... *tomaría* el sol... *visitaría* a mis amigos los señores Casiano... *comería* platos exóticos... *podría* usar mi tarjeta de crédito, como dice el anuncio —pero al fin y al cabo lo *tendría* que pagar todo.

1. *A la mujer, ¿adónde le gustaría ir?*
2. *¿Qué haría en Puerto Rico?*
3. *¿Cómo pagaría las vacaciones?*

HABLAR		COMER		VIVIR	
hablaría	hablaríamos	comería	comeríamos	viviría	viviríamos
hablarías	hablaríais	comerías	comeríais	vivirías	viviríais
hablaría	hablarían	comería	comerían	viviría	vivirían

Conditional actions or states of being are expressed with the conditional. In English the conditional uses the auxiliary verb *would: I would speak.* The Spanish *conditional* (**condicional**) is formed by adding the conditional endings to the infinitive: **-ía, -ías, -ía, -íamos, -íais, -ían.** No auxiliary verb is needed.

 Verbs that form the future on an irregular stem use the same stem to form the conditional.

				decir	
decir:	**dir-**				
hacer:	**har-**			diría	diríamos
poder:	**podr-**	-ía		dirías	diríais
poner:	**pondr-**	-ías		diría	dirían
querer:	**querr-**	-ía			
saber:	**sabr-**	-íamos			
salir:	**saldr-**	-íais			
tener:	**tendr-**	-ían			
venir:	**vendr-**				

The conditional of **hay** is **habría** (*there would be*).

An ideal trip I need to get away . . . I think I'd like to go to Puerto Rico . . . I wouldn't do any work . . . I could swim . . . I would sunbathe . . . I would visit my friends Mr. and Mrs. Casiano . . . I would eat exotic food . . . I could use my credit card, as the ad says—but in the end I would have to pay for it all.

Uses of the Conditional

The conditional expresses what you would do in a particular situation, given a particular set of circumstances.

¿Hablarías francés en México?	*Would you speak French in Mexico?*
No, **hablaría** español.	*No, I would speak Spanish.*

The conditional tense is also used in English and Spanish to make a request sound softer, more polite.

¿Querrías almorzar con nosotros?	*Would you like to have lunch with us?*
Sí, **querría** pero no puedo.	*I would like to but I can't.*
Deberías estudiar más.	*You really ought to study more.* (It would be a good idea for you to study more.)

¡OJO! When *would* implies *used to* in English, Spanish uses the imperfect.

Íbamos a la playa todos los veranos.	*We would go to the beach every summer.*

The conditional is often used in Spanish to express probability or conjecture about past events or states of being, just as the future is used to indicate probability or conjecture about the present. This use of the conditional is called the **condicional de probabilidad.**

¿Dónde **estaría** Cecilia?	*I wonder where Cecilia was.* (Where could Cecilia have been?)
Cecilia **estaría** en la carretera.	*Cecilia was probably on the highway.*

[Práctica D]

PRÁCTICA

A. Dé Ud. frases nuevas según las indicaciones.

1. —¿Adónde irían Uds. para sus vacaciones?
   —Cristina (no) iría a la playa. (*yo, Ud., tú, Uds., nosotros, vosotras*)
2. —Hay que ahorrar energía. ¿Quién dijo que lo haría?
   —Juan dijo que lo haría. (*tú, Armando, yo, Uds., nosotros, vosotros*)
3. —El Sr. Cortina dijo que nunca viviríamos en la luna. ¿Quién no estaría de acuerdo con él?
   —Anita (no) estaría de acuerdo con él. (*los astronautas, nosotras, yo, Ud., tú, vosotros*)

B. *Cambie por el condicional.*

1. Salimos pronto.
2. Digo que sí.
3. Lo saben los señores Santos.
4. ¿Puedes hacerlo?
5. No tengo tiempo.
6. No te quejas, ¿verdad?
7. Uds. deben ahorrar más.

C. *¿Cómo se dice en español? Invite Ud. a un amigo a cenar.*

Would you like to have dinner with us tonight? I know you would enjoy
yourself and that you would meet some interesting people.

*Ahora, siguiendo la forma de esta invitación, invite a un(a) compañero/a de clase a
hacer algo con Ud.*

D. *Lea el párrafo siguiente.*

Había una mujer detrás de un mostrador (*counter*). Vino un hombre con una
maleta. El hombre parecía nervioso y la maleta parecía pesar mucho. El
hombre habló con la mujer y luego sacó dinero de su cartera. Se lo dio a la
mujer, quien le dio un papelito. El hombre le dio a la mujer la maleta y fue
a sentarse. Parecía muy agitado. Escuchaba los anuncios que se oían
periódicamente mientras escribía rápidamente una tarjeta postal (*postcard*).

*¿Qué pasaría aquí? Conteste, usando el condicional de probabilidad. Si quiere,
puede inventar más detalles.*

1. ¿Dónde estarían el hombre y la mujer?
2. ¿Quién sería la mujer? ¿y el hombre?
3. ¿Por qué estaría nervioso el hombre?
4. ¿Qué tendría el hombre en la maleta?
5. ¿Qué preguntaría el hombre a la mujer?

6. ¿Por qué le daría dinero a la mujer?
7. ¿Qué le daría la mujer al hombre?
8. ¿Por qué le daría el hombre la maleta a la mujer?
9. ¿Qué serían los anuncios?
10. ¿A quién le escribiría el hombre?

CONVERSACIÓN

A. *Explique Ud. por qué no va a hacer estas cosas:*

1. Pagaría el alquiler, pero _____.
2. Economizaría más, pero _____.
3. Me mudaría de apartamento, pero _____.
4. Tomaría francés el semestre que viene, pero _____.

B. *Preguntas*

1. ¿Qué le gustaría a Ud. comer esta noche?
2. ¿Qué lengua hablaría una persona de Pekín? ¿de Moscú? ¿del Canadá? ¿de Lisboa? ¿de Guadalajara?
3. ¿Qué haría Ud. para obtener mucho dinero? ¿y para gastar mucho dinero?
4. ¿Cuánto dinero necesitaría Ud. para pagar todas sus facturas?
5. ¿Dónde le gustaría a Ud. vivir? ¿Por qué?
6. ¿Votaría Ud. por Walter Cronkite para presidente? ¿por Barbara Walters? ¿Por qué?
7. ¿Qué persona famosa le gustaría ser? ¿Por qué?
8. ¿Qué tipo de persona sería Abrahán Lincoln? ¿Florence Nightingale? ¿Hernán Cortés? ¿Cristóbal Colón? ¿la reina Isabel?
9. ¿Dónde estaría su profesor(a) de español a las once anoche?

DIÁLOGO: El pluriempleo°   *moonlighting*

Eva, estudiante hispanoamericana
Ramón (Raymond), estudiante de los Estados Unidos en un país hispano

RAMÓN: Hay algo que todavía no comprendo de la economía latina.
EVA: ¿Qué es?
RAMÓN: ¿Cómo podrá existir el pluriempleo aquí donde hay tantas personas que no pueden encontrar ni° un trabajo?   *even*
EVA: Te parecerá imposible, pero así es en casi todos nuestros países. Para la persona que tiene dos trabajos es una oportunidad estupenda para aumentar las ganancias. Pero para

la persona que no puede encontrar ni un puesto, es otra desigualdad° del sistema económico. *inequality*

RAMÓN: Yo, en los Estados Unidos, viviré más o menos bien con un puesto. Seré profesor, me casaré y buscaré una casa.

EVA: Aquí probablemente no sería así. Para vivir bien tendrías que ser un profesor eminente o... de familia rica. De lo contrario°, vivirías estrechamente° y tu mujer tendría que trabajar por necesidad, no por gusto. *De... if that were not the case / barely making ends meet*

RAMÓN: Los sueldos aquí serán pequeños, ¿no?

EVA: Sí, sobre todo al principio° de la carrera. Además, la competencia° para los puestos es mucha. *al... at the beginning* *competition*

RAMÓN: Es decir° que aquí yo sería profesor por vocación y otra cosa por necesidad. *Es... that means*

EVA: Exacto.

RAMÓN: ¿Y esto pasa en todas las clases sociales?

EVA: Más o menos, pero sobre todo en la clase baja y la clase media°. *middle*

RAMÓN: El pluriempleo no es parte de la idea que tenemos los americanos de los latinos.

EVA: Pues... no somos perezosos como nos pinta el estereotipo del cacto, el burrito y el indio durmiendo la siesta. Pero más que nada, el pluriempleo existe porque a todos —blancos, negros, indios y mestizos— no nos pagan los sueldos que merece° nuestro trabajo. *deserves*

RAMÓN: En fin°, la ambición personal y la necesidad económica producen el pluriempleo. *En... in short*

EVA: Correcto, amigo. Por eso tengo dos empleos y una esperanza°: la esperanza de poder dedicarme a un solo trabajo en el futuro. *hope*

Comprensión

Conteste en oraciones completas.

1. ¿Qué no comprende Ramón?
2. ¿Qué es el pluriempleo?
3. ¿Todos lo consideran una ventaja (*advantage*)?
4. Según Ramón, ¿cómo será su vida en los Estados Unidos?
5. ¿Cómo sería su vida de profesor en Hispanoamérica?
6. ¿Ganaría mucho dinero en Hispanoamérica? ¿Qué otra desventaja habría?
7. ¿Por qué tendría Ramón dos empleos en Hispanoamérica?
8. ¿Por qué hay mucho pluriempleo en Hispanoamérica?
9. ¿En qué clases sociales se encuentra?
10. ¿Cuál es la esperanza de Eva?

Comentario cultural

Pluriempleo (*moonlighting*), or holding down more than one job, is a common feature of the economy of Hispanic countries. Wage scales, modest in comparison to the high cost of basic necessities, force people in all types of employment, including white-collar professions, to hold a second job. Approximately one-third of the labor force has more than one job. The postman may also work at a restaurant, a utility company employee may work as a porter or tend bar, a beginning attorney or doctor may also teach. The second job is often the only way some families can finance a television set or a car. For others, it is the only way to survive economically.

UN POCO DE TODO

A. *Cambie por el condicional.*

1. Gastarán mucho, no ahorrarán y nunca pagarán sus facturas.
2. Habrá gente de todos los países en el banco.
3. ¿Tendrá una cuenta corriente o una cuenta de ahorros?
4. ¿Qué harán con el dinero?
5. Dejaré de usar mi tarjeta de crédito.

B. *¿Qué dijeron estas personas?*

MODELO   CARLOS Y PEPE: Viviremos en San Francisco. →
           Carlos y Pepe dijeron que vivirían en San Francisco.

1. ALICIA: Hará calor mañana.
2. TOMÁS Y ANA: Nos mudaremos para reducir nuestros gastos.
3. UD. Y SUS PADRES: Estaremos allí a las ocho en punto.
4. EL EMPLEADO: Lo cargaré a la cuenta de la Sra. Pérez.
5. LOS SRES. DELGADO: Será necesario abrir otra cuenta.

C. *Working with another student, ask and answer questions according to the model.*

MODELO   llegar el trece de junio / tres →
           ELVIRA: *Llegaré el trece de junio.*
           PABLO: ¿No dijiste que *llegarías el tres?*
           ELVIRA: ¡Que no! Dije que *llegaría el trece.* Entendiste mal.

1. estar en el bar a las dos / doce
2. estudiar con Juan / Juana
3. ir de vacaciones en julio / junio
4. verte en casa / en clase
5. comprar la blusa rosada / roja

D. *Su amiga Ángela tiene los siguientes problemas y preguntas. Déle consejos, según el modelo.*

MODELO   ÁNGELA: Tengo mucha sed. →
           UD.:   *Yo tomaría una Coca-Cola.*

1. Necesito más dinero. No podré pagar mis cuentas este mes.
2. Estoy locamente enamorada de Jaime.
3. No me gusta la clase de italiano.
4. ¿Dónde estará Carmen? No la encuentro.
5. No sé qué película ponen en el cine Apolo.
6. Mi jefe se queja de mi trabajo.

E. *Complete las oraciones en una forma lógica.*

1. Algún día seré _____. No me gustaría ser _____.
2. Este verano iré a _____. No me gustaría ir a _____.
3. El año que viene, viviré en/con _____. No me gustaría vivir en/con _____.
4. Esta noche yo _____. No me gustaría _____.
5. Este año voy a ganar _____ dólares. Me gustaría ganar _____.

VOCABULARIO

VERBOS

ahorrar to save (*money*)
aumentar to increase
cargar to charge (*to an account*)
cobrar to cash (*a check*); to charge
 (*someone for an item or service*)
dejar de + *inf.* to stop (*doing
 something*)
economizar to economize
entender (ie) to understand
gastar to spend (*money*)
mudarse to move (*from one
 residence to another*)
nadar to swim
quejarse to complain
reducir (reduzco) to reduce, cut
 down

SUSTANTIVOS

el **alquiler** rent
el **banco** bank
la **cuenta** account
la **cuenta corriente** checking
 account
la **cuenta de ahorros** savings
 account
la **cuestión** question, matter
la **energía** energy
la **esperanza** hope
el **estereotipo** stereotype
la **factura** bill
el **futuro** future
las **ganancias** earnings
los **gastos** expenses
la **guerra** war
la **igualdad** equality
la **necesidad** necessity, need

el **pluriempleo** moonlighting
el **presupuesto** budget
la **tarjeta de crédito** credit card
la **ventaja** advantage

ADJETIVOS

actual current, up-to-date
próximo/a next

PALABRAS Y EXPRESIONES ÚTILES

a fines de at the end of
además besides, in addition
al contado cash
con cheque by check
en vez de instead of
por ciento percent
sobre todo above all, especially
solamente only

Un paso más 15

Actividades

—*Quizá si dejo° el café y tú te vas a trabajar en bicicleta...*

I stop drinking

A. **Para conseguir más dinero.** What can you do to get extra cash or to save money? Some possibilities are shown in the cartoon and in the following drawings. What are the advantages and disadvantages of each plan?

MODELO   dejar el café →
Si dejo el café, estaré menos nervioso/a, pero será más difícil despertarme por la mañana.

1. pedirles dinero a mis amigos

2. cometer un robo
3. alquilar (*to rent out*) un cuarto de
   mi casa a otras personas
4. _____

B. **El presupuesto.** Imagínese que Ud. gana ochocientos dólares (otra cantidad, si prefiere) al mes. ¿Cuánto dinero piensa Ud. gastar en cada categoría de este presupuesto? Trate de ser realista. Si no quiere gastar nada, ponga un cero. Después, conteste las preguntas.

 1. Ropa   _____
 2. Casa (alquiler, hipoteca [*mortgage*])   _____
 3. Gas, luz, agua, teléfono   _____
 4. Comida   _____
 5. Diversiones (cine, fiestas, restaurantes, etcétera)   _____
 6. Gastos médicos   _____
 7. Seguros (*insurance*) (automóvil, casa, etcétera)   _____
 8. Automóvil (préstamos, reparaciones, gasolina, aceite, etcétera) _____
 9. Educación (matrícula, libros, etcétera)   _____
10. Impuestos   _____
11. Ahorros   _____
12. Miscelánea: _____   _____

                                                      TOTAL: _____

Preguntas
1. ¿Cuánto gastaría Ud. en cada categoría?
2. ¿Gastaría más en la ropa o en las diversiones? ¿en la comida o en el gas,

© Joel Gordon 1980

etcétera? ¿en los gastos médicos o en los seguros? ¿en el automóvil o en la educación?

3. ¿Gastaría más en el alquiler (la hipoteca) o en los impuestos?
4. ¿Ahorraría Ud. mucho dinero? ¿Sería fácil o difícil? Explique.
5. Imagínese que alguien le da cien dólares y Ud. puede hacer cualquier cosa con ese dinero. ¿Qué haría con el dinero? ¿Lo ahorraría? ¿Compraría algo? ¿Pagaría sus facturas? Explique.
6. Para economizar, ¿qué haría? ¿Podría gastar menos en las diversiones? ¿Cargaría más a sus cuentas para pagar más tarde? Comente.

A propósito...

Using foreign currency when traveling outside of the United States can be confusing. Often tourists have no concrete sense of what foreign currency is worth or how much they are paying for an item or a service, even though they know the current conversion factor used to exchange money at the bank.

Here are the exchange rates **(cambios)** for the currencies of several Spanish-speaking countries. These rates of exchange fluctuate; they may be different by the time you read this.

México: 1 peso = $.05 U.S.A.
(approximately 20 pesos = $1.00; 200 pesos = $10.00)
España: 1 peseta = $.015 U.S.A.
(approximately 70 ptas. = $1.00; 700 ptas. = $10.00)
Colombia: 1 peso = $.025 U.S.A.
(approximately 40 pesos = $1.00; 400 pesos = $10.00)

Familiarize yourself with these exchange rates by determining the following equivalents.

¿Cuánto valen?

1. 350 ptas.	a. $24.50	b. $5.00
2. 1.000 ptas.	a. $14.00	b. $7.00
3. 14.000 ptas.	a. $20.00	b. $200.00
4. 2.000 pesos (Méx.)	a. $200.00	b. $100.00
5. 50 pesos (Méx.)	a. $2.50	b. $5.00
6. 750 pesos (Méx.)	a. $37.50	b. $50.00
7. 100 pesos (Col.)	a. $2.50	b. $5.10
8. 3.000 pesos (Col.)	a. $7.50	b. $75.00

C. **¿Una ganga?** Are the following people getting a bargain, or are they paying an exorbitant price by U.S. standards? Refer to the rates of exchange in the **A propósito** section, if necessary.

1. Los señores Wilson van a Bogotá, donde tienen una habitación (*room*) en el Hotel Ritz. Pagan ochocientos pesos al día.

2. Mary Drummond va a México y encuentra una habitación en un hostal de estudiantes. Paga cuarenta pesos al día. Está incluido el desayuno.

3. Bob Walters vive en Madrid. Allí en una tienda de lujo paga cinco mil pesetas por una cartera de cuero (*leather*) para su padre.

4. Jane Black cena en un restaurante español. Cena muy bien, aunque el restaurante no es de lujo. Le cobran ciento cincuenta pesetas.

5. Wayne Curtis toma un taxi en Guadalajara, México. Hace un viaje de unos cuarenta kilómetros y paga sesenta pesos.

6. Eric Burlingame va a Colombia. Allí compra un suéter por seiscientos cincuenta pesos colombianos.

7. Los señores Walsh van a ver la Pirámide del Sol en México. En una pequeña tienda compran un libro sobre las civilizaciones precolombinas. Es un libro grande y elegante, con muchas fotografías en colores. Pagan cien pesos mexicanos.

D. **¡Cómo sube la vida!** The cost of living continues to rise, and inflation is a concern in many parts of the world. The drawing below indicates some of the price increases that occurred in Spain over a ten-year period (from 1969 to 1979). Look at the drawing and match the following Spanish phrases with the appropriate Spanish synonym or description. Then answer the questions that follow.

1. diario
2. "Ducados"
3. piso
4. 20 pulgadas (pulg.)
5. cine de estreno
6. *La guerra de las galaxias*
7. litro

a. casa o apartamento
b. nombre de una película famosa de 1978
c. periódico
d. una marca de cigarrillos
e. una medida: equivale a 50,80 centímetros
f. la presentación de una película por primera vez
g. una medida: equivale a 1,1 *quarts*

Preguntas

1. ¿Cuáles son las tres cosas que sufrieron el mayor aumento de precio en España en este período?
2. ¿Cuáles son las tres cosas sufrieron el menor aumento?
3. Supongamos que setenta pesetas equivalen a un dólar (U.S.A.). ¿Qué cosas tienen más o menos el mismo precio en los Estados Unidos y en España? ¿Cuáles son más baratas aquí? ¿Cuáles son más caras?
4. En los Estados Unidos, ¿qué cosas sufren los mayores aumentos de precio actualmente?

E. **Estereotipos.** Stereotypic ideas about individuals from a particular national or ethnic background are extremely common. There may be a grain of truth in some stereotypic images, but most are inaccurate. As Eva points out in the dialog (page 415), "No somos perezosos como nos pinta el estereotipo del cacto, el burrito y el indio durmiendo la siesta."

What do people in other countries think of us? Describe what you think a non-American's stereotypic idea of a North American (U.S.A.) might be like. What part of the stereotype is fairly accurate, even though it is an overgeneralization? What part of it is inaccurate?

—*Ha ganado° el primer premio en el baile de disfraces°.*   **Ha...** *he won / costumes*

Lectura cultural: El futuro económico de Hispanoamérica —comentarios especulativos

Por lo general, cuando hablamos del sistema económico de los países hispanoamericanos, pensamos en economías de un solo producto —el café colombiano o la banana de las repúblicas centroamericanas. Esta imagen viene en gran parte de la historia de la explotación por los intereses internacionales de los productos latinos más deseables y valiosos°.

valuable

Esta explotación empezó con la Conquista, época en que España sacaba oro y plata de los territorios americanos. Después de ganar la independencia de España en el siglo XIX, las nuevas naciones hispanoamericanas —políticamente débiles°— llegaron a ser un lugar de explotación económica para los países industriales europeos y para los Estados Unidos. Los casos clásicos son la explotación extensa del cobre° chileno, del petróleo venezolano y de la fruta centroamericana.

weak

copper

Actualmente los hispanoamericanos parecen tener una clara conciencia° de ese pasado de explotación por extranjeros e insisten más en el derecho de tener voz en su propio destino económico. Por lo tanto, ya no es ridículo hacer la siguiente pregunta: ¿formarán algún día los países de Hispanoamérica una de las regiones más económicamente importantes del mundo? Cuando se considera la gran cantidad de recursos° naturales que quedan por desarrollarse° en Hispanoamérica, es muy fácil responder que sí.

awareness

resources

quedan... *remain to be developed*

Para realizar° tal° desarrollo económico, sin embargo, habrá que resolver los muchos problemas internos que son, en gran parte, el resultado de una historia de poca gente con mucha riqueza y mucha gente que no tiene nada. El reciente descubrimiento del petróleo en México es sólo un ejemplo de la riqueza natural que tiene Hispanoamérica. Existen también grandes depósitos de petróleo en Venezuela y la Argentina. Sin duda, esta riqueza hispanoamericana tendrá muchísimo valor en esta edad de crisis de energía.

to bring about / such a

Además del petróleo, las tierras hispanoamericanas contienen grandes depósitos de cobre, plata, hierro°, plomo°, estaño° y tungsteno; todos son productos que necesitará el mundo aun más industrializado del futuro.

iron / lead / tin

Serán importantes también las industrias agrícolas y pesqueras° de Hispanoamérica. Con sus vastos territorios cultivables y con la pesca —en especial a lo largo de la costa del Pacífico—las naciones hispanoamericanos, con el desarrollo apropiado, podrían producir comida para su propio consumo y para la exportación.

fishing

Comprensión

Conteste en oraciones completas.

1. ¿Cuál es la imagen tradicional de la economía hispanoamericana?
2. ¿A qué se debe esa imagen?
3. ¿Cuándo y cómo empezó la explotación de los recursos naturales de Hispanoamérica?
4. ¿Qué les pasó económicamente a las naciones hispanoamericanas después de ganar la independencia de España?
5. ¿Por qué es posible pensar que Hispanoamérica será una región de gran importancia económica?
6. ¿Qué será necesario hacer para realizar el desarrollo económico de Hispanoamérica?
7. ¿Por qué son de importancia los depósitos de petróleo en Hispanoamérica?
8. ¿Cuáles son algunos otros recursos naturales de Hispanoamérica?
9. ¿Por qué tendrán importancia en el futuro las industrias agrícolas y pesqueras de Hispanoamérica?

Ejercicios escritos

A. ¿Cuántos productos importados usa Ud.? ¿De qué países son? ¿Le gustaría usar más? ¿menos? Complete Ud. estas oraciones.

Uso ____ de ____. Me gustaría poder comprar en los Estados Unidos ____ de ____. No usaría ____ de ____.

B. Escriba un párrafo sobre uno de los temas siguientes.

1. ¿Cómo serán nuestras casas en el año 2000?
2. ¿Cómo serán nuestros coches en el año 2000?
3. ¿Cómo será la situación política y económica de los Estados Unidos en el año 2000?
4. ¿Cómo serán nuestras ciudades en el año 2000?

capítulo 16 La ciudad y el campo

Peter Menzel/Stock, Boston

OBJETIVOS

In this chapter you will learn vocabulary and expressions related to city and country living.

You will also learn about the following aspects of Spanish grammar:

65. how to form the past participle and how to use it as an adjective: **un libro usado,** (*a used book*), **la puerta cerrada** (*the closed door*), **los ejercicios escritos** (*the written exercises*)

66. how to form the present perfect tense with the auxiliary verb **haber** and the past participle: **he estudiado / aprendido / vivido** (*I have studied / learned / lived*)

67. how to form and use the past perfect tense: **había trabajado** (*I had worked*)

Un paso más includes activities related to camping, the environment and conservation, and expressing yourself politely, as well as a reading about urbanization in Latin America.

VOCABULARIO: PREPARACIÓN

¿La ciudad o el campo?

bello/a	beautiful	**encantar**	to enchant
denso/a	dense	**me encanta**	I like very much
puro/a	pure	**madrugar**	to get up early
		montar a caballo	to ride horseback
		recorrer	to pass through; to cover (*territory, miles, and so on*)
la autopista	freeway	**los servicios**	financial
el/la campe-	farm	**financieros**	(legal/public)
sino/a	worker	**(legales/públicos)**	services
el crimen	crime	**la soledad**	solitude
la finca	farm	**los transportes**	(*means of*)
la naturaleza	nature		transportation
la población	population	**la vaca**	cow
el ranchero	rancher	**el/la vaquero/a**	cowhand
el ritmo	(fast) pace		
(acelerado)	of life,		
de la vida	living		

A. *De las siguientes frases, ¿cuáles corresponden al campo? ¿a la ciudad?*

1. El aire es más puro y hay menos contaminación.
2. La naturaleza se ve más bella.
3. El ritmo de la vida es más acelerado.
4. Hay menos autopistas y menos tráfico.
5. Los crímenes son más frecuentes.
6. Los servicios financieros y legales son más asequibles (*available*).
7. Hay pocos transportes públicos.
8. La población es menos densa.

B. *¿Cierto o falso?*

1. Es posible encontrar vacas y caballos en una finca.
2. Hay muchas autopistas en una finca.
3. Un vaquero trabaja en un rancho.
4. Es improbable que un vaquero sepa montar a caballo.
5. Los campesinos se acuestan temprano y madrugan.
6. La única manera de recorrer largas distancias en la ciudad es en coche.
7. Un ranchero es un campesino.

C. *Dé Ud. una definición de estas palabras.*

> MODELO   ranchero → *Es el dueño de un rancho.*

1. autopista	3. crimen	5. naturaleza	7. soledad
2. campesino	4. finca	6. población	8. vaquero

D. *Pancho cree que la vida del campo es ideal. No puede ver ni una sola ventaja de vivir en la ciudad. Gabriela, la amiga de Pancho, es una mujer muy cosmopolita. Le encanta la ciudad y no puede decir nada bueno de la vida del campo. ¿Quién dijo las siguientes frases? ¿Qué desventaja podría citar la otra persona en cada caso?*

1. No hay buenos servicios públicos.
2. Hay más actividades culturales —el teatro, la música sinfónica y los museos.
3. Es posible encontrar soledad y tranquilidad allí.
4. No me gusta levantarme temprano; allí hay que madrugar para terminar el trabajo.
5. Me encanta recorrer la ciudad de noche en una autopista.
6. Necesito vivir en contacto con la naturaleza.
7. Cuando la nieve cubre (*covers*) las calles, las ciudades están paralizadas.

E. *Sounds made by animals are often but not always represented in similar ways in Spanish and in English. Match the following animals with the written representation of the sound they make.*

MUUU
AHIIIII
GUAU GUAU
MIAU
CUA CUA
PÍO PÍO
CLOC CLOC
QUI-QUI-RI-QUÍ
GRRR

vaca   caballo   pajarito   perro

gato   león   pato

gallina   gallo

Ways of Expressing the Word *Time*

hora:	specific hour or time of day	
	¿Qué **hora** es?	What time is it?
	Es **hora** de comer.	It's time to eat.
un rato:	a short period of time	
	Hablamos **un rato.**	We spoke (for) a time (a little while).
	¿Vas a pasar por casa **un ratito** esta tarde?	Will you stop by the house for a short time (a few minutes) this afternoon?
vez:	time, occasion	
	una vez, dos veces, muchas veces, pocas veces	once, twice (two times), many times (often), infrequently
	a veces	at times
	otra vez	another time (again)
tiempo:	*time* in a general or abstract sense	
	El tiempo vuela.	Time flies.
	¿Tienes **tiempo** de/para ayudarme?	Do you have time to help me?

F. *Llene el espacio con la palabra apropiada para expresar la palabra* time.

1. ¡Por Dios, Anita! Come más rápido. Ya es _____ de salir.
2. Perdone, señorita, pero ¿podría Ud. repetir el número una _____ más?
3. Si tienes _____, podríamos tomar un café y hablar un _____.
4. ¿Otra _____? ¿Cuántas _____ tengo que decirte que no hagas eso?
5. Bebí un vaso de leche y después de leer un _____ me acosté.
6. Muchos mexicanos preguntan: «¿Qué horas son?» pero los españoles generalmente preguntan: «¿Qué _____ es?»
7. Me gustaría acompañarte, pero no tengo _____.

G. *Pregúntele a otro/a estudiante.*

1. ¿A qué hora vas a despertarte mañana?
2. ¿Qué haces cuando es hora de estudiar?

3. ¿Qué haces cuando tienes un rato libre?
4. Si un amigo o una amiga va a llegar tarde, ¿estás dispuesto/a (*willing*) a esperar un rato?
5. En un mes, ¿cuántas veces faltas a tus clases?
6. ¿Faltas a veces cuando no estás enfermo/a?
7. ¿Qué es más importante, el tiempo o el dinero?
8. ¿Siempre tienes tiempo de divertirte con los amigos?

MINIDIÁLOGOS Y GRAMÁTICA

65. PAST PARTICIPLE USED AS ADJECTIVE

Unos refranes y dichos españoles

1. En boca *cerrada* no entran moscas.
2. *Aburrido* como una ostra.
3. Cuando está *abierto* el cajón, el más *honrado* es ladrón.

1. *A veces, ¿es mejor no decir nada?*
2. *¿Cómo es el ritmo de la vida de las ostras?*
3. *¿Cometen todos los crímenes las personas deshonestas?*

Forms of the Past Participle

HABLAR	COMER	VIVIR
hablado (*spoken*)	comido (*eaten*)	vivido (*lived*)

A few Spanish proverbs and sayings 1. Into a closed mouth no flies enter. 2. Bored as an oyster.
3. When the drawer is open, the most honest (person) is (can become) a thief.

The past participle of most English verbs ends in -*ed*—for example, *to walk* → *walked; to close* → *closed.* However, many English past participles are irregular: *to sing* → *sung; to write* → *written.* In Spanish the *past participle* (**participio pasivo**) is formed by adding **-ado** to the stem of **-ar** verbs, and **-ido** to the stem of **-er** and **-ir** verbs. An accent mark is used on the past participle of **-er/-ir** verbs with stems ending in **-a, -e,** or **-o:**

caído   creído   leído   oído   (son)reído   traído

The following Spanish verbs have irregular past participles.

abrir:	**abierto**	morir:	**muerto**
decir:	**dicho**	poner:	**puesto**
cubrir:	**cubierto**	resolver:	**resuelto**
describir:	**descrito**	romper:	**roto**
descubrir:	**descubierto**	ver:	**visto**
escribir:	**escrito**	volver:	**vuelto**
hacer:	**hecho**		

The Past Participle Used as an Adjective

In both English and Spanish the past participle can be used as an adjective to modify a noun. Like other Spanish adjectives, the past participle must agree in number and gender with the noun modified.

Tengo una bolsa **hecha** en El Salvador.	*I have a purse made in El Salvador.*
El español es una de las lenguas **habladas** en los Estados Unidos.	*Spanish is one of the languages spoken in the United States.*

The past participle is frequently used with **estar** to describe conditions that are the result of a previous action.

La puerta **está abierta.**	*The door is open.*
Todos los lápices **estaban rotos.**	*All the pencils were broken.*

¡OJO! English past participles often have the same form as the past tense: *I closed the book. The thief stood behind the closed door.* The Spanish past participle is never identical in form or use to a past tense. Compare:

Cerré la puerta.	*I closed the door.*
Ahora la puerta está **cerrada.**	*Now the door is closed.*

PRÁCTICA

A. *Dé Ud. frases nuevas según las indicaciones.   Use el participio pasivo de los verbos.*

1. —Eugenio, su amigo español, dejó muchos recuerdos de su visita a los Estados Unidos.   ¿Qué tiene Ud. en casa que le recuerde su visita?
   —Aquí tengo un libro _____ por Eugenio. (*usar, mandar, recomendar, pagar, comprar, leer, traer*)
2. —¿Qué objetos tiene Ud. de Latinoamérica?
   —Tengo *una bolsa* hecha en el Ecuador. (*un vestido, una figurita, unos vasos, unas florecitas de papel*)

B. *Describa Ud. las condiciones en las situaciones siguientes, siguiendo el modelo.*

MODELO   La nieve va a *cubrir* la *tierra.* →
          La tierra no está cubierta de nieve todavía.

1. Natalia tiene que *escribir* una *carta.*
2. Los Sres. García tienen que *abrir* la *tienda.*
3. *David y Marta* van a *casarse* mañana.
4. Pablo tiene que *cerrar* la *ventana.*
5. Los turistas tienen que *facturar* el *equipaje.*
6. Delia tiene que *poner* la *mesa.*

C. *¿Cómo se dice en español?*

1. money saved 2. a signed check 3. the paid bills 4. the lost luggage
5. a repeated phrase 6. the fired employee 7. dead flies

CONVERSACIÓN

A. *Describa Ud. estos dibujos.*

1.

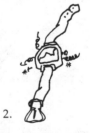

2.

3.

B. *Preguntas*

1. ¿Tiene Ud. algo hecho en Francia? ¿en un país latinoamericano? ¿en España?
2. ¿Sabe Ud. el nombre de un libro escrito por un autor latinoamericano? ¿por un autor español?

3. En casa de Ud., ¿algo está roto?

4. En su casa, ¿el televisor está puesto constantemente? ¿el estéreo? ¿el radio?

5. ¿El Nuevo Mundo ya estaba descubierto en 1700? ¿La penicilina ya estaba descubierta en 1960?

C. *Dé Ud. el nombre de:*

1. algo contaminado
2. una persona bien/mal organizada
3. una persona cansada
4. un edificio bien/mal construido
5. un grupo explotado
6. algo que puede estar cerrado o abierto
7. un curso acelerado
8. un servicio necesitado por muchas personas
9. un tipo de transporte usado por muchas personas
10. algo deseado por muchas personas

66. PRESENT PERFECT TENSE

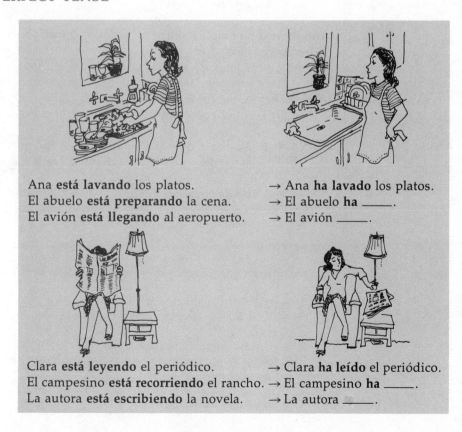

Ana **está lavando** los platos.   → Ana **ha lavado** los platos.
El abuelo **está preparando** la cena.   → El abuelo **ha** _____.
El avión **está llegando** al aeropuerto. → El avión _____.

Clara **está leyendo** el periódico.   → Clara **ha leído** el periódico.
El campesino **está recorriendo** el rancho. → El campesino **ha** _____.
La autora **está escribiendo** la novela.   → La autora _____.

FORMS OF THE PRESENT PERFECT			
he hablado	*I have spoken*	**hemos** hablado	*we have spoken*
has hablado	*you have spoken*	**habéis** hablado	*you (pl.) have spoken*
ha hablado	*you have spoken,*	**han** hablado	*you (pl.) have spoken,*
	he/she has spoken		*they have spoken*

In English the present perfect is a compound tense consisting of a present tense form of the verb *to have* plus the past participle: *I have written, you have spoken,* and so on.

In the Spanish present perfect **(presente perfecto)** the past participle is used with present tense forms of **haber,** the equivalent of English *to have* in this construction. **Haber,** an auxiliary verb, is not interchangeable with **tener.**

In general, the use of the Spanish present perfect parallels that of the English present perfect.

No **hemos estado** aquí antes.   *We haven't been here before.*
Me he divertido mucho.   *I've had a very good time.*
Ya **le han escrito** la carta.   *They've already written her the letter.*

The masculine singular form of the past participle is always used with **haber,** regardless of the gender or number of the subject. The past participle always appears immediately after the appropriate form of **haber** and is never separated from it. Object pronouns and **no** are always placed directly before the form of **haber.**

The present perfect of **hay** is **ha habido** (*there has/have been*).

¡OJO!   Acabar + de + the *infinitive*—not the present perfect tense— is used to state that something *has just* occurred.

Acabo de cobrar el cheque.   *I've just cashed the check.*

PRÁCTICA

A. *Dé Ud. frases nuevas según las indicaciones. Use el participio pasivo de los verbos.*

1. —¿Se ha preparado Ud. para la clase hoy?
   —Sí, he *leído* la lección. (*escribir, empezar, estudiar, comprender, aprender, olvidar*)
2. —¿Quién más se ha preparado muy bien?
   —José se ha preparado muy bien. (*tú, el/la profesor[a], los estudiantes, Luis, Carmen y Pilar, vosotros*)
3. —Son las ocho de la mañana, pero Lidia ha hecho muchas cosas ya. ¿Qué ha hecho esta mañana?

—Esta mañana Lidia ha *madrugado*. (*levantarse, bañarse, vestirse, desayunar, correr, leer, reír*)

4. —Muchos fueron al campo para sus vacaciones. ¿Quién no ha vuelto todavía?

—*Tomás* no ha vuelto todavía. (*yo, ellos, Carlos, nosotros, tú, vosotros*)

B. *Ud. y su amigo/a visitan un rancho. Es el segundo día de su visita. ¿Qué han hecho Uds.? Dé frases basadas en estas palabras:*

1. recorrer el rancho entero　2. ver las vacas y los toros　3. montar a caballo
4. hablar con los campesinos

C. *Margarita lo/la llama a Ud. por teléfono. Quiere saber lo que Ud. está haciendo. Con otro/a estudiante, forme y conteste preguntas, según el modelo.*

MODELO　　cenar →
　　　　　MARGARITA:　Estarás *cenando*, ¿no?
　　　　　UD.:　　　　No, ya he *cenado*.

1. cocinar　2. descansar　3. lavar los platos　4. leer el periódico　5. poner la mesa

Ahora Margarita tiene unos recados (messages).

MODELO　　llamarlo →
　　　　　MARGARITA:　Jorge dice que *lo llames*.
　　　　　UD.:　　　　Pero ya *lo he llamado*.

6. mandarle una invitación a Pablo　7. hablar con Concepción　8. pasar por casa　9. ver ___(película)___　10. escribir la composición esta tarde

D. *¿Cómo se dice en español? ¿Qué ha hecho Ud. en clase esta semana?*

There has been a lot of work in class. I still have three exercises to (**que**) write for tomorrow. I've just done the first one, but I haven't finished the second and third.

CONVERSACIÓN

A. *¿Qué han hecho estas personas?*

1.　　　　　2.　　　　　3.

B. *Complete las oraciones en una forma lógica.*

1. Quiero/tengo que _____ pero no he _____ todavía.
2. Esta mañana, ya he _____. Todavía no he _____.
3. Este año, mis padres han _____.
4. En clase este semestre, hemos _____ algunas veces.
5. Hoy he _____ un rato.
6. Nunca he _____.
7. Me han dicho que _____, pero no es verdad.
8. Me han dicho que _____ y es verdad, aunque parezca (*it may seem to be*) mentira.

67. PAST PERFECT TENSE

Cambio de paso

RAFAEL: Antes de mudarme al campo, yo siempre *había usado* el carro para ir a todas partes. Nunca *había tenido* tiempo de apreciar la naturaleza. Y nunca *había madrugado* tanto.

LINDA: Pues, antes de mudarme a la ciudad, yo siempre *había vivido* en una finca. Nunca *había visto* tantas autopistas en un solo lugar. Y nunca *había tenido* la oportunidad de visitar museos ni de ver obras de teatro y películas con tanta frecuencia.

RAFAEL: Es verdad que la ciudad tiene muchas ventajas, pero yo me siento más a gusto ahora.

LINDA: Y yo estoy a gusto precisamente en la ciudad que tú has dejado. Como dicen, ¡no hay nada escrito sobre gustos!

1. *¿Quién no había vivido antes en la ciudad?*
2. *¿Quién no había apreciado las flores y las montañas?*
3. *¿Quién había tenido menos oportunidades culturales antes?*
4. *¿Quién no se había levantado temprano con frecuencia?*
5. *¿Quién no había visto tantas autopistas en un solo lugar?*
6. *¿Quién había manejado mucho?*
7. *¿Dónde se siente más a gusto Linda?   ¿y Rafael?*

Change of pace RAFAEL: Before I moved to the country, I had always used the car to go everywhere. I had never had time to appreciate nature. And I had never gotten up early so often. LINDA: Well, before I moved to the city, I had always lived on a farm. I had never seen so many freeways in one place. And I had never had the chance to visit museums or see plays and movies so frequently. RAFAEL: It's true that the city has a lot of advantages, but I'm more comfortable now. LINDA: And I'm at home precisely in the city that you left. As they say, there's no accounting for tastes!

FORMS OF THE PAST PERFECT			
había hablado	*I had spoken*	**habíamos** hablado	*we had spoken*
habías hablado	*you had spoken*	**habíais** hablado	*you (pl.) had spoken*
había hablado	*you had spoken, he/she had spoken*	**habían** hablado	*you (pl.) had spoken, they had spoken*

The English past perfect consists of the past tense of *to have* plus the past participle: *I had written, you had written,* and so on.

In Spanish the past perfect (**pluscuamperfecto**) is formed with the imperfect of **haber** plus the past participle.

Ya **había cenado** cuando llegó Juan. *I had already eaten dinner when Juan arrived.*

Habíamos visto aquella película antes de 1950. *We had seen that movie before 1950.*

The past perfect tense is used to emphasize the fact that an action (**Ya había cenado, Habíamos visto**) took place before another action, event, or moment in the past (**llegó Juan, 1950**).

PRÁCTICA

A. *Dé Ud. frases nuevas según las indicaciones.*

1. —¿Quién había estudiado el español antes del semestre pasado (*last semester*)?
   —*Carmen* (no) había estudiado el español antes del semestre pasado. (*tú, yo, Armando, nosotros, Ud., vosotros*)

2. —¿Qué cosas no habían hecho Uds. antes del año pasado?
   —Antes del año pasado, no habíamos _____. (*asistir a la universidad, montar a caballo, visitar Patagonia, viajar a Moscú, comer flan, conocer a Rita Moreno*)

3. —Jaimito es un niño acusón (*tattle-tale*). Siempre le dice a su madre las cosas que ha hecho —y que no ha hecho— su hermana mayor. ¿Qué le dijo a su madre ayer?
   —Jaimito le dijo que su hermana *había dicho una mentira*. (*mirar la televisión toda la tarde, perder sus libros, romper un vaso, faltar a clase, comer todo el pastel*)

B. *Working with another student, ask and answer questions according to the model.*

MODELO   leer la lección para mañana →
UD.:   Ayer, cuando llamaste, no tuve tiempo para hablar
              contigo. Lo siento.
COMPAÑERO: Estabas *leyendo la lección para hoy,* ¿no?
UD.:   No, ya *la* había *leído.*

1. escuchar las noticias (*news*)
2. bañarse
3. preparar la cena
4. hacer las maletas
5. mirar ____(programa de televisión)____

CONVERSACIÓN

A. *Describa Ud. su juventud* (youth). *Antes de tener dieciocho años, ¿qué había hecho? ¿Qué no había hecho?*

B. *Complete las oraciones en una forma lógica.*

1. Antes de 1492 Cristóbal Colón no _____.
2. Antes de 1938 la Segunda Guerra Mundial no _____.
3. Antes de 1500 Shakespeare no _____.
4. Antes de 1950 mis padres (no) _____.
5. Antes de 1975 yo (no) _____.

DIÁLOGO: Otra faceta del campo

Epifanio, un hispanoamericano en su país
Pedro (Peter), un estadounidense en el país de Epifanio

EPIFANIO: Mamá nos ha invitado a pasar el fin de semana en su finca[1].
PEDRO: ¡Qué bien! Estoy loco por ir al campo. ¿Naciste allí?
EPIFANIO: Sí, viví allí en la finca hasta hace unos años°, pero dice   **hace...** *a few years ago*
            mamá que le han hecho arreglos° a la casa y que ha cambiado   *repairs*
            mucho.
PEDRO: ¿Qué preparativos tenemos que hacer para el viaje? ¿Iremos
            en automóvil o en tren?
EPIFANIO: En coche, pero no te preocupes°, ya tengo el carro preparado   **no...** *don't worry*
            para el viaje.
PEDRO: ¿A qué hora vamos a estar allí?
EPIFANIO: Saldremos a las seis de la mañana. A las ocho, si hace buen
            tiempo, estaremos a mitad de camino°.   **a...** *half-way there*
PEDRO: Entonces llegamos a las diez.

EPIFANIO: ¡Ojalá! La segunda mitad del viaje no es por autopistas ni por carreteras. Es por caminos rurales que están en muy malas condiciones.

PEDRO: No importa. Me encanta el campo.

EPIFANIO: A mí siempre me han encantado las fincas también —pero sólo para los fines de semana. Prefiero la ciudad con sus servicios públicos bien organizados y sus oportunidades de trabajo.

PEDRO: Y el aire contaminado, el ritmo acelerado de la vida, las viviendas amontonadas°, los crímenes...

viviendas... houses crowded one on top of another

EPIFANIO: Es verdad. Ya me lo había dicho mi madre cuando dejé la finca. La gente campesina es más sana y su vida es más sencilla°. Pero... no sé cómo es en tu país, Pedro, pero aquí, la ciudad siempre ha explotado al campo y a los campesinos².

simple

PEDRO: ¿Cómo es eso?

EPIFANIO: Pues, los intermediarios° se han enriquecido° con nuestro trabajo. Siempre nos han dado precios de hambre° por nuestras cosechas°. Cuando murió papá, decidí venir a la capital para educarme y poder ayudar a mamá y a mis hermanos. Y hasta ahora en todo me ha ido muy bien.

intermediaries (profi-teers) / gotten rich de... too low (unfair) harvests

PEDRO: Espero que siempre sea así. Ahora pensemos en el fin de semana. Ya son las diez de la noche y mañana tenemos que madrugar.

EPIFANIO: No te preocupes. ¿Para qué crees que tenemos el desper-tador?

Comprensión

Conteste en oraciones completas.

1. ¿Por qué van al campo Pedro y Epifanio? ¿Cómo van?
2. ¿A Pedro le gusta el campo?
3. ¿Por qué tienen que madrugar?
4. ¿Cómo son los caminos cerca de la finca?
5. ¿A quién le gustan las fincas? ¿A quién le gustan menos?
6. Según Epifanio, ¿cuáles son las ventajas de vivir en la ciudad?
7. Según Pedro, ¿cuáles son las desventajas de la ciudad?
8. Según la madre de Epifanio, ¿cuáles son las ventajas de la vida campesina?
9. Según Epifanio, ¿cómo explota la ciudad al campo?
10. ¿Por qué vino Epifanio a la ciudad?
11. ¿Se despertarán a tiempo mañana Pedro y Epifanio?

Comentario cultural

1. **Finca** is the general term meaning *farm*. It may be a large or a small land holding. **Rancho** means *ranch* or *farm;* in Mexico, **un rancho** is a small farm. A large rural land holding is called **una hacienda** in Mexico, **un hato** in

Venezuela, **una estancia** in Uruguay and Argentina, and **un fundo** in Chile. Cattle raising is an important industry in many countries of Latin America. The people who tend the large herds are called **vaqueros** in Mexico, **llaneros** in Venezuela, **gauchos** in Argentina, and **huasos** in Chile.

Many Spanish words used in connection with cattle raising have become common terms in English, some with little or no change: **rancho,** *ranch;* **corral,** *corral;* **mesteño,** *mustang;* **la reata,** *lariat;* **pinto,** *pinto;* **rodeo,** *rodeo.*

2. In Spain and Latin America, agriculture is a profitable enterprise for large land-owners and for the professionals who manage the estates on their behalf. For the owner of a small farm, however, farming is often a marginal operation at best, demanding long hours of hard work. For the tenant farmer, farming is even less rewarding. Remote areas still lack roads and schools, and life in general is not easy.

As a result, many **campesinos** opt for the uncertainties of the city, hoping to find employment for themselves and a better education and future for their children. The migration of people into urban centers has accelerated during the past decades, creating large concentrations of population around cities such as Buenos Aires, Lima, and Mexico City in Latin America, and Madrid, Barcelona, Valencia, and Bilbao in Spain. This migration has placed a great strain on housing and public services in the cities, and many migrants are forced to live in makeshift dwellings on the outskirts of the large cities.

EL ÚLTIMO EMIGRANTE—Bueno, en este pueblo, al menos, ya se ha resuelto el problema del campo.

UN POCO DE TODO

A. *Form complete sentences based on the words given in the order given. Use the present perfect form of the first verb and the past perfect of the second. Two slashes (//) indicate the break between sentences.*

1. yo / madrugar / este / mañana // (yo) nunca / levantarse / tan temprano / antes
2. ellos / depositar / todo / dinero / banco // nunca / depositar / tanto / antes
3. hoy / Juan / faltar / clase / primero / vez // nunca / faltar / antes
4. nosotros / reírse / tanto / en aquel / película // nunca / reírse / tanto / en una película / antes
5. tú / pedir / pollo // antes / siempre / pedir / bistec

B. *Rearrange the words given to form complete sentences. Do not add any words. A double slash indicates the break between sentences.*

1. vivido / construidas / siempre / en / hemos / bien / casas
2. José Feliciano / oído / escrita / nunca / canción / por / he / una
3. ¿ / flan / gustado / te / el / ha / ? // ¿ / comido / nunca / lo / antes / habías / ?
4. mañana / habían / tienda / abierta / por / dicho / me / estaba / la / que la
5. entero / nunca / recorrido / antes / rancho / había / el // he / hoy / hecho / lo // encantado / me / todo / ha

C. *Working with another student, ask and answer questions according to the model.*

MODELO   escribir la carta →
   PAULA: *¿Ya está escrita la carta?*
   MIGUEL: No, no *la* he *escrito* todavía.
   PAULA: Ah, creía que ya *la* habías *escrito.*

1. hacer las maletas
2. pagar las facturas
3. preparar la paella para la cena
4. facturar el equipaje
5. abrir la cuenta en el Banco Nacional
6. sacudir los muebles

D. *Using the following phrases as a guide, interview another student according to the model.*

MODELO   participar en fútbol americano →
   ¿Has participado en fútbol americano este año?
   Y *antes de este año, ¿habías participado en fútbol americano?*

1. recorrer unos países latinoamericanos
2. montar a caballo
3. viajar a España
4. hablar con una persona de otro planeta
5. ahorrar mucho dinero

E. *Complete las oraciones en una forma lógica.*

1. He comparado un(a) _____ hecho/a en _____.
2. Este año he _____, pero antes de 1975 nunca había _____.
3. Nunca he estado en una ciudad tan contaminada (bien organizada, mal organizada) como _____.
4. Nunca he leído un libro escrito en/por _____.
5. Nunca he conocido a una persona nacida en _____.

VOCABULARIO

VERBOS

cubrir to cover
encantar to enchant
explotar to exploit
madrugar to get up early
montar a caballo to ride horseback
preocuparse to worry
recorrer to pass through; to cover
  (*territory, miles and so on*)
repetir (i, i) to repeat

SUSTANTIVOS

el **aire** air
la **autopista** freeway
el/la **autor(a)** author, writer
el **caballo** horse
el/la **campesino/a** farm worker
el **campo** country; field
el **crimen** crime
la **finca** farm
el **gusto** taste; preference; pleasure
la **mentira** lie
la **mosca** fly
la **naturaleza** nature
la **nieve** snow
la **oportunidad** opportunity
la **población** population
el **ranchero** rancher
el **rancho** ranch
el **rato** short period of time
el **ritmo** rhythm
el **servicio** service
la **soledad** solitude
la **tranquilidad** peace, tranquility
el **transporte** means of
  transportation
la **vaca** cow
el/la **vaquero/a** cowhand

ADJETIVOS

acelerado/a fast, accelerated
bello/a beautiful
construido/a constructed
contaminado/a contaminated,
  polluted
denso/a dense
financiero/a financial
legal legal
organizado/a organized
público/a public
puro/a pure

PALABRAS Y EXPRESIONES ÚTILES

a gusto comfortable, at home
dos veces twice
muchas veces frequently, a lot
pocas veces infrequently

Un paso más 16

Actividades

—*Desde que° en los sitios solitarios se encuentra uno a tanta gente, se pasa mucho mejor.*

Desde... *since*

A. **¡Ah, la naturaleza!** Este dibujo presenta una escena casi universal en el mundo de hoy. Muchas personas quieren escaparse de la ciudad para disfrutar de la naturaleza. Por eso hacen *camping* o se mudan al campo. ¿A Ud. le gusta la vida del campo? ¿Cómo reacciona a las siguientes frases?

0 = máximo desacuerdo   1 = desacuerdo   2 = acuerdo   3 = máximo acuerdo

___ 1. Me gusta hacer *camping*.
___ 2. Vivo en el campo o pienso vivir allí en el futuro inmediato.
___ 3. Haría cualquier cosa para escaparme del aire contaminado de la ciudad.
___ 4. Prefiero la tranquilidad del campo al ritmo acelerado de la vida de la ciudad.
___ 5. Estoy dispuesto/a a manejar cinco horas para pasar otras ocho horas de tranquilidad en el campo.
___ 6. La vida de un campesino es mejor que la vida de una persona que vive en una metrópoli grande.
___ 7. Cuando salgo de vacaciones, es más probable que vaya a las montañas, a la playa o a un rancho que a una ciudad grande como Nueva York.
___ 8. Estoy dispuesto/a a ganar menos dinero para poder vivir en el campo.

☐ TOTAL

Interpretaciones

0–9   ¡Ojalá que Ud. viva en la ciudad. De lo contrario, lo estará pasando mal, ¿no?

10–14 Ud. sufre de una doble personalidad. Si tiene el dinero, cómprese dos casas—una en el centro de la ciudad, la otra en el campo.

15–24 Si Ud. no vive en el campo, cómprese un perrito, tres gatos y veintidós plantas. Así, si Ud. no puede ir al campo, puede crear su propio ambiente campestre (*country environment*) en la ciudad.

hubiéramos... *we had gone*

B. **Hagamos** *camping.* Ud. va a hacer *camping* con un(a) amigo/a este fin de semana. Ud. hace *camping* con mucha frecuencia, pero la otra persona no lo ha hecho nunca. ¿Qué le va a decir Ud. a su amigo/a sobre los problemas y dudas siguientes? ¿Qué consejos le va a dar?

MODELO   He visto un oso. → *¡Corre!*

1. ¡Nos hemos perdido!
2. No tenemos fósforos.
3. ¡Ay, Dios! Ha llovido y todas nuestras cosas en la tienda están mojadas.

el oso

los fósforos

la tienda

4. Me ha picado un mosquito.
5. ¿Oíste ese ruido?
6. Quiero bañarme. ¿Dónde está el cuarto de baño?
7. Me caí al río y estoy mojadísimo/a.
8. Tengo miedo. Me han dicho que hay muchas serpientes en este parque.
9. ¡Mira! He encontrado una planta verde de tres hojas. Es muy bonita, pero ahora me empiezan a picar (*itch*) las manos.

estar mojado/a

Picar

A propósito...

Más sobre la cortesía. When you are searching for words to express the exact nature of a problem or situation, it is possible to sound abrupt or impolite, even though that is not your intention. The use of phrases such as **por favor, perdón,** and **con permiso** will show that you want to be polite, even when you may not be able to express yourself as precisely or as eloquently as a native speaker of Spanish.

Other phrases that will help you to communicate respect and politeness include:

Quisiera hablar con el Sr. Jiménez.	*I would like to talk to Mr. Jimenez.*
Me gustaría comprar una blusa azul.	*I would like to buy a blue blouse.*
Me trae otro café, **si fuera tan amable.**	*Bring me another cup of coffee, if you would be so kind.*
Es Ud. muy amable.	*You are very kind.*
Mil gracias. Ud. me ha ayudado muchísimo.	*Thanks a million (a thousand thanks). You have helped me a lot.*
Ha sido un placer hablar con Ud.	*It has been a pleasure to talk with you.*

Both **quisiera** and **me gustaría** (*I would like*) are more polite than **quiero** (*I want*). This usage parallels that of English.

C. **¿Qué decimos?** What would you say to try to be especially polite in each of the following situations? How would you thank the person for helping you?

1. You need to return an article of clothing to a department store because it is the wrong size. You want the clerk to help you select the right size.
2. You know that you need to catch the number 17 bus to get to the **Museo de Arte,** but you don't know where to catch it. You ask a police officer on the street corner.
3. You have lost the key to your hotel room and need to tell the clerk. You also need to get another key.
4. The waiter has just brought you a cup of coffee. You ordered tea.
5. Something is wrong with your car. You want the mechanic to fix it as soon and as cheaply as possible.
6. You have gone to the doctor with a routine ailment. After he or she has examined you and you have received a prescription, you discover that you have left your money and checkbook at home and cannot pay at this moment.

D. **Los recursos naturales y el futuro.** Most people are concerned about the future of our natural resources, but not everyone agrees on what is the best way to protect both our resources and the environment. Do you agree or disagree with the following statements? Be prepared to defend your opinions.

Vocabulario útil

conservar	to conserve, save
contaminar (el aire)	to pollute (the air)
la energía	energy
el medio ambiente	environment
el petróleo	petroleum
proteger (protejo)	to protect
los recursos naturales	natural resources

1. Para conservar energía debemos bajar la calefacción en invierno y usar menos el aire acondicionado en verano.
2. Es mejor calentar la casa con una estufa de leña (*wood stove*) que con gas o electricidad.
3. Debemos proteger nuestras «zonas verdes» y establecer más parques públicos para las futuras generaciones.
4. Es más importante conservar los recursos naturales que proteger el medio ambiente.
5. Para gastar menos gasolina, debemos tomar el autobús, caminar más y formar *car pools.*
6. No debemos importar petróleo de otros países.
7. El gobierno debe ponerles multas muy fuertes a las compañías y a los individuos que contaminan el aire.
8. Debemos adoptar una manera de vivir más sencilla.

E. **Una noche misteriosa.** Imagínese que Ud. está haciendo *camping* con un grupo de amigos. Alguien pregunta: «¿Por qué no contamos un cuento (*story*) de misterio?» ¿Cómo es el cuento que se va a contar? Para empezar, puede usar una de las situaciones siguientes. Luego, use las preguntas para continuar su cuento.

Una noche de invierno dos jóvenes entraron en una casa abandonada, una casa que estaba en una zona aislada en las afueras (*outskirts*) de la ciudad. Los jóvenes estaban hablando de _____ cuando de repente...

Una noche de verano un grupo de jóvenes fue al Parque Transilvania porque se decía que estaba muy bonito de noche. Habían caminado mucho cuando...

1. ¿Quiénes son los personajes (*characters*) del cuento? ¿Dónde estaban?
2. ¿Qué hora era?
3. ¿Qué tiempo hacía?
4. ¿Qué hacían los personajes?
5. ¿Qué oyeron?
6. ¿Cómo se sintieron?
7. ¿Qué hicieron?
8. ¿Qué pasó después?
9. ¿Y después?
10. ¿Cómo terminó su aventura?

Lectura cultural: La urbanización hispanoamericana

Las últimas estrellas° de la noche apenas° habían desaparecido cuando el Sr. Raquejo, su esposa y los seis hijos se despidieron de su casita de campo y de los vecinos° para empezar el largo viaje a la capital. Habían oído que la ciudad les podría ofrecer una nueva vida, que había trabajo y la oportunidad de vivir en una casa decente, de ganar un buen sueldo y de darles a los niños una educación buena. Aunque el campo les había ofrecido el aire fresco y la tranquilidad de la naturaleza, también les había dado trabajo duro° sin mucho pago. Ya era hora de cambiar de vida, de mudarse a la capital para mejorar° sus condiciones de vida.

Aunque hay otros factores que han contribuido al crecimiento° rapidísimo de las ciudades hispanoamericanas, esta llegada° de los campesinos a la ciudad es uno de los problemas urbanos más graves que tiene Hispanoamérica. Los campesinos no encuentran, desgraciadamente°, «El Dorado»; al contrario, tienen que enfrentarse al° desempleo, a la falta de vivienda adecuada para los pobres y a la miseria. No tienen la educación necesaria para obtener buenos puestos y, por eso, viven en los barrios° pobres. Allí, muchos cocinan y duermen todos juntos en viviendas de un solo cuarto. Para ganar dinero, el señor vende cigarrillos en las calles, la señora lava ropa y los niños —quienes raras veces asisten a la escuela— limpian zapatos en el centro comercial de la ciudad.

stars / scarcely

neighbors

hard

to improve

growth
arrival

unfortunately
enfrentarse a *to confront*

neighborhoods

Existe al lado de tal pobreza el lujo y la grandeza que siempre han caracterizado a ciertos sectores de Hispanoamérica. Desde la ciudad de México hasta Buenos Aires hay ciudades de rascacielos° modernos, *skyscrapers* elegantes palacios y suntuosas iglesias. En las afueras° hay casas modernas *outskirts* y elegantes con todas las últimas comodidades°. Grandes sistemas de *conveniences* autopistas conectan los varios sectores de las ciudades que, como toda ciudad moderna, sufren problemas de contaminación del aire y de tráfico incontrolable.

Según los demógrafos, varias de las ciudades de Hispanoamérica estarán entre las diez ciudades más grandes del mundo en el año 2000. La ciudad de México, con una población metropolitana actual de más de catorce millones de habitantes, es ahora la tercera ciudad del mundo. Igualmente, ciudades como Caracas, Bogotá, Lima, Santiago y Buenos Aires siguen creciendo° de una manera extraordinaria. Como los otros países del *growing*

Nicholas Sapieha/Stock, Boston

mundo, las naciones hispanoamericanas tendrán que esforzarse para hacer de estas metrópolis gigantescas lugares apropiados para la vida sana y moderna.

Comprensión

Conteste en oraciones completas.

1. ¿Por qué va la familia Raquejo a la ciudad?
2. ¿Qué les había dado la vida del campo a los señores Raquejo?
3. ¿Por qué están creciendo las ciudades hispanoamericanas tan rápidamente?
4. ¿Cómo son las condiciones de vivienda de los pobres en las ciudades hispanoamericanas?
5. ¿Cómo se gana la vida una familia pobre?
6. ¿En qué consisten los contrastes de las ciudades hispanoamericanas?
7. En cuanto a población, ¿cómo se comparan las ciudades hispanoamericanas con otras ciudades grandes del mundo?
8. ¿Qué importancia tiene la Ciudad de México?
9. ¿Qué problema general tienen las ciudades hispanoamericanas?

Ejercicios escritos

A. Describe the largest city with which you are familiar. Include the following items in your description:

1. dónde está
2. su importancia nacional e internacional
3. población: tamaño (*size*), grupos étnicos o culturales
4. lugares de interés
5. industrias
6. política

B. Escriba un párrafo sobre uno de estos temas:

1. Las ventajas de vivir en la ciudad
2. Las ventajas de vivir en el campo

capítulo 17 Se alquilan apartamentos

Peter Menzel/Stock, Boston

OBJETIVOS

In this chapter you will learn vocabulary and expressions related to housing—the rooms of a house or apartment, furniture, household expenses, and so on.

You will also learn about the following aspects of Spanish grammar:

68. how to form and use the present perfect subjunctive: **haya estudiado, hayas estudiado,** and so on.

69. how to use the subjunctive to refer to persons

or things that do not or may not exist: **no hay nadie en la clase que hable chino** (*there is no one in the class who speaks Chinese*)

70. the use of the subjunctive after conjunctions such as **para que** (*so that*) and **antes (de) que** (*before*)

Un paso más includes activities related to the place where you live and to moving, and a reading about what houses and apartments are like in the Hispanic world.

VOCABULARIO: PREPARACIÓN

	¿Dónde vive Ud.?	¿Dónde quiere vivir?	
alquilar	to rent	las escaleras	stairs
		el garaje	garage
el primer piso	second floor	el gas	gas; heat
	(*first floor up*)	el/la inquilino/a	renter, tenant
		la luz	light, electricity
el ascensor	elevator	la piscina	swimming pool
el centro	downtown	el/la portero/a	building
la dirección	address		manager;
el/la dueño/a	owner, landlord,		doorman
	landlady	el/la vecino/a	neighbor
		la vista	view

A. *¿Qué preferiría Ud.?*

1. ¿vivir en una casa o vivir en una casa de apartamentos?
2. ¿vivir en el centro o en los suburbios? ¿o tal vez en el campo?
3. ¿alquilar una casa/un apartamento o comprar una casa?
4. ¿vivir en una casa de apartamentos con ascensor o con escaleras?
5. ¿vivir en el primer piso o en un piso más alto?
6. ¿pagar el gas y la luz —o pagar un alquiler más alto con el gas y la luz incluidos?
7. ¿ser el dueño del apartamento o ser el inquilino?
8. ¿quejarse al portero de algo o arreglarlo Ud. mismo/a (*yourself*)?
9. ¿tener un garaje o una piscina?
10. ¿un apartamento pequeño con una vista magnífica o un apartamento más grande sin vista?
11. ¿un apartamento pequeño con una dirección elegante o un apartamento grande con una dirección más modesta?
12. ¿conocer muy bien a los vecinos o mantenerse a distancia?

B. *Dé Ud. una definición de estas palabras.*

1. inquilino   2. ascensor   3. centro   4. garaje   5. portero   6. vecino

Los cuartos y las otras partes de una casa			
la alcoba	bedroom	la entrada	entry way
el balcón	balcony	el patio	patio; yard
el baño	bathroom	la sala	living room
la cocina	kitchen	la terraza	terrace
el comedor	dining room		

C. *¿Cuál es la función de los cuartos de una casa o de un apartamento?*

MODELO   la alcoba → Allí se duerme.
                        Uno se acuesta en la alcoba.

D. *Ud. es corredor(a) de casas* (real estate agent). *Descríbales la siguiente casa a sus clientes, inventando los detalles necesarios.*

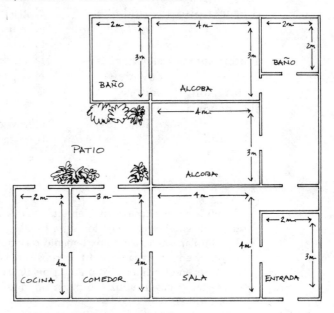

¿Dónde se encuentra la casa? ¿Cuántos cuartos tiene? ¿Cuáles son? ¿Cómo son? ¿Cuánto cuesta la casa? ¿Tiene alguna desventaja? ¿Por qué deben comprarla sus clientes?

1 metro = 39.37 inches
Mide _____ por _____. *It measures _____ by _____.*
La alcoba mide _____ por _____. *The bedroom measures _____ by _____.*

E. *Ud. tiene los siguientes muebles. Usando el plan, decida cómo va a amueblar* (to furnish) *la casa.*

una cama grande
una cama pequeña

dos estantes
dos escritorios

dos cómodas

dos sillones
un sofá

el estante

el sillón

la cómoda

una mesa con cuatro sillas de plástico
una mesa con seis sillas de madera fina
cuatro mesitas
cuatro lámparas
tres alfombras

la alfombra

F. *¿Qué muebles le faltan todavía a Ud. para tener la casa bien amueblada?*

   ¿un estéreo? ¿un televisor? ¿dos televisores? ¿una «cama de agua»?

G. *¿Qué muebles asocia Ud. con estas palabras?*

   1. estudiar 2. ropa 3. sentarse 4. libros 5. luz 6. comida 7. suelo
   8. _____.

MINIDIÁLOGOS Y GRAMÁTICA

---

68. PRESENT PERFECT SUBJUNCTIVE

Una cuestión de perspectiva

El dueño	El inquilino
No creo que *hayan construido* mejor casa de apartamentos en toda la ciudad.	Me voy a mudar de aquí. Han construido unos apartamentos elegantes en la avenida Goya —y con piscina.
Espero que ya *haya mandado* el alquiler, pero lo dudo. Siempre lo manda con un retraso de cinco días.	El dueño dirá otra vez que no ha recibido mi cheque. Pero nunca he faltado.
Es probable que *haya destruido* la casa entera. Por eso me preocupo tanto.	Es probable que nunca arregle ese agujero que hicieron los primeros inquilinos.

A question of perspective

The owner	The tenant
I don't think they've built a better apartment house in the whole city.	I'm going to move. They've built some elegant apartments on Goya Avenue—and with a pool.
I hope he's already sent the rent, but I doubt it. He's always five days late.	The owner will say again that he hasn't gotten my check. But I've never missed.
He's probably (It's probable that he has) destroyed the whole house. That's why I worry so much.	He'll probably never (It's probable that he'll never) fix that hole that the original tenants made.

¿Quién cree...
1. *que esta casa de apartamentos es ideal?*
2. *que es importante tener piscina?*
3. *que el otro es impaciente?*
4. *que el otro no es muy puntual?*
5. *que el otro no se preocupa por la condición del apartamento?*
6. *que el otro no respeta la propiedad* (property) *de otros?*

FORMS OF THE PRESENT PERFECT SUBJUNCTIVE	
haya hablado	**hayamos** hablado
hayas hablado	**hayáis** hablado
haya hablado	**hayan** hablado

The present perfect subjunctive **(perfecto del subjuntivo)** is formed with the present subjunctive of **haber** plus the past participle. It is used to express *I have spoken (written,* and so on) when the subjunctive is required. Although its most frequent equivalent is *I have + past participle*, its exact equivalent in English depends on the context in which it occurs.

Es posible que lo **haya hecho.**	*It's possible (that) he may have done (he did) it.*
Me alegro de que **hayas venido.**	*I'm glad (that) you have come (you came).*
Es bueno que lo **hayan construido.**	*It's good that they built (have built) it.*

Note that the English equivalent of the present perfect subjunctive can be expressed as a simple or as a compound tense: *did/have done; come/have come; built/have built.*

PRÁCTICA

A. Dé Ud. frases nuevas segun las indicaciones.

1. —Todos quieren mudarse. ¿Quién ha encontrado ya un apartamento?
   —Es posible que *Lucía* haya encontrado un apartamento. *(tú, Uds., Roberto y Hernando, nosotros, yo, vosotros)*
2. —Esta mañana, el agua del apartamento de arriba *(above you)* empezó a entrar en el baño de Ud. ¿Ha hecho el dueño los arreglos necesarios?
   —Espero que ya haya *venido a examinarlo. (ver el agua, descubrir el problema, llamar al plomero, hacer los arreglos)*

B. Conteste, empezando las respuestas con las palabras entre paréntesis.

1. ¿Ha alquilado Armando un apartamento con vista? (Dudo que _____.)
2. ¿Han vendido esa alfombra tan elegante? (Tal vez _____.)

3. ¿Uds. se han mudado al cuarto piso? (Sí, y me alegro mucho de que _____.)
4. ¿Ellos han pagado el gas y la luz este mes? (No creo que _____.)
5. ¿Los vecinos se han sentado a comer ya? (Sí, es probable que _____.)
6. ¿Han subido en ascensor o por las escaleras? (Es probable que _____.)
7. ¿Han alquilado un carro o una motocicleta? (Espero que _____.)
8. ¿Ya hemos perdido (*missed*) el vuelo? (Sí, es probable que _____.)
9. ¿No sabes? Se ha muerto el portero. (Siento que _____.)
10. Julián ha puesto el carro en el garaje, ¿no? (No, no creo que _____.)

C. *¿Cómo se dice en español?*

I'm glad that he has returned from his year in Uruguay, and I hope that he has brought us a souvenir. I don't think that he's found an apartment yet.

CONVERSACIÓN

A. *Lupe ha ganado cien mil dólares en la lotería y ha ido de compras. ¿Qué cree Ud. que ha comprado?*

1. Es probable que Lupe haya comprado _____. (*una casa grande, una casa en_____, una casa de _____, una casa con_____*)
2. No creo que Lupe haya comprado _____. (*una casa pequeña, una casa en_____, una casa de _____, una casa con _____*)

B. *Complete las oraciones en una forma lógica.*

1. Yo siento que mis padres hayan _____.
2. Mis padres sienten que yo haya _____.
3. Es probable que mi amigo/a _____ ya haya _____, pero no sé.
4. Es posible que mi amigo/a _____ ya haya _____, pero lo dudo.
5. Es bueno que hayamos _____ este año.
6. Es malo que hayamos _____ este año.

69. SUBJUNCTIVE AFTER NONEXISTENT AND INDEFINITE ANTECEDENTS

Aquí hay unas personas que **hablan** español y que **son** de Latinoamérica.
No hay nadie aquí que **hable** inglés, que **sea** de los Estados Unidos, que _____. (*llamarse Smith, ser rubio, vivir en Kansas, tener parientes en Cincinnati*)

Los Sres. Alonso **tienen una casa** que **es** bonita y que **está** en el centro.

Los Sres. Alonso **buscan una casa** que **sea** más grande, que **esté** en el campo, que _____. (*no costar mucho, tener un patio enorme, tener una terraza, ser elegante*)

In English and in Spanish an adjective clause is a dependent clause that modifies a noun or a pronoun: *I have a car **that gets good gas mileage;** I need a house **that is closer to the city.*** The noun or pronoun that precedes the adjective clause and is modified by it is called the *antecedent* (**antecedente**) of the clause.

In Spanish, when the antecedent of an adjective clause refers to someone (something, a place, and so on) that does not exist, the subjunctive must be used in the adjective clause.

EXISTENT ANTECEDENT: **Hay algo** aquí que me **interesa.** *There is something here that interests me.*

NONEXISTENT ANTECEDENT: **No hay nada** aquí que me **interese.** *There is nothing here that interests me.*

Similarly, when the existence of the antecedent is indefinite or uncertain, the subjunctive is used.

DEFINITE ANTECEDENT: **Tenemos un portero** que lo **arregla** todo. *We have a manager who fixes everything.*

INDEFINITE ANTECEDENT: **Necesitamos un portero** que lo **arregle** todo. *We need a manager who will (can) fix everything.*

The personal **a** is not used with direct object nouns that refer to hypothetical persons. Compare:

Busco **un señor** que lo **sepa.** *I'm looking for a man who knows that.*
Busco **al señor** que lo **sabe.** *I'm looking for the man who knows that.*

Even though the subjunctive is used in a question that contains an indefinite antecedent, when the answer confirms the existence of the antecedent, the indicative is used in the answer.

—**¿Hay algo** aquí que te **guste?** *Is there something here that you like?*
—**Sí, hay algo** que me **gusta.** *Yes, there is something that I like.*

PRÁCTICA

A. *Dé Ud. frases nuevas según las indicaciones.*

1. —Ud. quiere mudarse. ¿Qué tipo de apartamento va a buscar?
   —Voy a buscar un apartamento que _____. *(tener tres alcobas, tener una vista magnífica, estar en el centro, tener un garaje amplio, ser cómodo, tener por lo menos dos baños)*
2. —¿Cuáles son algunas de las habilidades que los miembros de la clase de Ud. no tienen?
   —No hay nadie en clase que _____. *(ser actor/actriz, hablar chino, saber tocar la viola, coleccionar insectos, saber preparar comida turca, montar a caballo muy bien)*

B. *Cambie según las indicaciones.*

MODELO   Hay *alguien* que lo sabe. *(nadie)* →
             No hay *nadie* que lo *sepa*.

1. Buscamos *al secretario* que sabe escribir a máquina en español. *(un secretario)*
2. Hay *algo* aquí que me gusta. *(nada)*
3. Quieren bailar con *la señora* que sabe bailar el tango. *(alguien)*
4. *Busco* un dentista que no cobre mucho. *(he encontrado)*
5. Hay *alguien* que puede hacerlo. *(nadie)*
6. Aquí hay *algunos* vecinos que se quejan mucho. *(ningún —¡OJO! singular)*
7. *Necesitamos* un sillón que sea un poco más grande. *(aquí tenemos)*
8. Hay *algo* de su personalidad que me encanta. *(nada)*

C. *¿Cómo se dice en español?*

1. I have a doctor who speaks Spanish.
2. We need a doctor who speaks Spanish.
3. I know someone who plays tennis well.
4. I don't know anyone who plays football well.
5. Is there someone here who can fix it?
6. There is no one here who can fix it.

CONVERSACIÓN

A. *¿Qué dicen o piensan estas personas?*

1. No hay nadie que _____.

2. Armando quiere un coche
   que _____.

3. En esta clase no hay nadie
   que _____.

B. *Preguntas*

1. ¿Hay alguien que lo/la quiera a Ud. tanto como sus padres?
2. ¿Hay algo que le interese a Ud. más que la clase de español?
3. ¿Busca Ud. una especialización (*major*) que sea interesante y útil?
4. Para el semestre que viene, ¿quiere Ud. una clase que empiece a las ocho de la mañana?

C. *Complete las oraciones en una forma lógica.*

1. Tengo un carro que es _____.
2. Necesito un carro que _____.
3. Tengo un apartamento que está _____.
4. Busco un apartamento que _____.
5. En mi familia hay alguien que _____, pero no hay nadie que _____.
6. En clase hay algo que _____, pero no hay nada que _____.
7. En clase hay alguien que _____, pero no hay nadie que _____.

70. SUBJUNCTIVE AFTER CERTAIN CONJUNCTIONS

¿Otra vez?

JUAN: Pongamos el sillón aquí *para que esté* cerca del televisor.

ADA: Ahí no, *a menos que se cambien* de lugar el estante y el escritorio.

ROBERTO: (Poniendo el sillón en el centro de la sala.) ¡No! Aquí se va a quedar el sillón —¡*para que* yo no lo *tenga* que levantar otra vez!

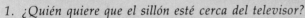

1. ¿Quién quiere que el sillón esté cerca del televisor?
2. Para que el sillón esté allí, ¿qué muebles tienen que cambiarse de lugar?
3. ¿Dónde quiere poner el sillón Roberto? ¿Por qué?

Again? JUAN: Let's put the armchair here so that it's close to the television set. ADA: Not there, unless the bookcase and desk are moved. ROBERTO: (putting the armchair in the middle of the living room) No! The armchair is going to stay here—so that I don't have to lift it again!

In Spanish the subjunctive always occurs in dependent clauses introduced by these *conjunctions* (**conjunciones**):

a menos que	*unless*	**en caso de que**	*in case*
antes (de) que	*before*	**para que**	*so that*
con tal que	*provided*	**sin que**	*without*

Voy **con tal que** ellos me **acompañen.**	*I'm going provided that they go with me.*
En caso de que llegue Juan, dile que he salido.	*In case Juan arrives, tell him that I've gone out.*

Note that these conjunctions introduce dependent clauses in which the events have not yet materialized; the events are conceptualized, not real world. When there is no change of subject in the dependent clause, Spanish more frequently uses the prepositions **antes de, para,** and **sin** plus an infinitive, instead of the corresponding conjunctions plus the subjunctive. Compare:

PREPOSITION:	Estoy aquí **para aprender.**	*I'm here to (in order to) learn.*
CONJUNCTION:	Estoy aquí **para que Uds. aprendan.**	*I'm here so that you will learn.*
PREPOSITION:	Voy a comer **antes de salir.**	*I'm going to eat before leaving.*
CONJUNCTION:	Voy a comer **antes (de) que salgamos.**	*I'm going to eat before we leave.*

PRÁCTICA

A. *Dé Ud. frases nuevas según las indicaciones.*

1. —Ud. espera una llamada (*call*) muy importante de su amigo Luis, ¿verdad?
   —Sí, es verdad. No salgo esta tarde _____ llame Luis. (*a menos que, antes de que, en caso de que, sin que*)
2. —Ud. acaba de comprar una casa nueva. ¿Invita a todos sus amigos a pasar por casa?
   —Sí, quiero que vengan todos para que (ellos) _____. (*nadar en la nueva piscina, divertirse, ver la casa, conversar, celebrar conmigo*)

B. *Use la conjunción entre paréntesis para unir las dos oraciones. Haga todos los cambios necesarios.*

1. Vamos a las montañas. Llueve. (a menos que)
2. Voy al centro. Tú me acompañas. (con tal que)

3. Dígale a Jaime que he salido. (Jaime) Regresa. (en caso de que)
4. Los padres trabajan tanto. Sus hijos viven cómodamente. (para que)
5. Alquilemos aquella casa. Otra persona la alquila. (antes de que)
6. No me caso contigo. Vendes tu motocicleta. (a menos que)
7. Voy a alquilar el apartamento. Tiene dos alcobas. (con tal que)
8. Compre Ud. pan ahora. No tienen pan en la otra tienda. (en caso de que)
9. Les doy tanta tarea (*homework*). Uds. aprenden. (para que)
10. Ojalá que lleguemos a la casa pronto. Nieva. (antes de que)

C. *¿Cómo se dice en español?*

1. We go there to have fun.
2. We go there so that the kids can have fun.
3. They're going to swim before cleaning (they clean) the garage.
4. They're going to swim before we clean the garage.
5. Don't leave without talking to her.
6. Don't leave without her talking to you.

CONVERSACIÓN

A. *Complete las oraciones en una forma lógica.*

1. Voy a graduarme en _____ a menos que _____.
2. Este verano voy a _____ a menos que _____.
3. Voy a seguir estudiando español el semestre que viene con tal que _____.
4. Voy a seguir viviendo en esta ciudad con tal que _____.
5. En caso de que me llame el presidente, dígale que _____.
6. En caso de que llueva mucho, (no) voy a _____.
7. Asisto a la universidad para/para que _____.
8. Nunca estudio sin/sin que _____.
9. Siempre me baño antes de/antes de que _____.

B. *Los Sres. Cortina quieren alquilar un apartamento, pero no quieren pagar el alquiler alto que les pide el dueño. Al dueño de la casa de apartamentos le caen muy bien los Sres. Cortina, pero no quiere bajar el alquiler. ¿Podrán ponerse de acuerdo los Sres. Cortina y el dueño? Use estas frases como una guía en la conversación sobre el apartamento.*

LOS SRES. CORTINA: No alquilamos el apartamento a menos que _____.
EL DUEÑO: Bajo el alquiler con tal que _____.
LOS SRES. CORTINA: Alquilamos el apartamento con tal que _____.
EL DUENO: No puedo bajar el alquiler a menos que _____.

DIÁLOGO: Una nueva dirección

Maricarmen, mujer joven y práctica
Ramón, esposo de Maricarmen
Ana María, amiga de Maricarmen
Portero

A. *En casa*

ANA MARÍA: Me parece imposible, Maricarmen, que Ramón y tú hayan vivido en el centro de la ciudad durante tres años. ¡Qué ruido! ¡Qué falta° de panorama!   *lack*

MARICARMEN: Es verdad, pero es barato y desde aquí llegamos más rápidamente al trabajo.   Ahora la cosa es distinta. Yo me he matriculado en los cursos nocturnos° y   *night* necesitamos un apartamento que esté más cerca de la universidad.

ANA MARÍA: Pues mira, cerca de nuestra casa hay un edificio recién construido —tal vez haya algún apartamento allí.

MARICARMEN: Con tal que no sea excesivamente caro, no nos importaría pagar un poco más.   ¿Me acompañarías a verlo, Anamari?

ANA MARÍA: Con mucho gusto.   ¿Por qué no vamos esta tarde?

B. *En busca de° otro apartamento*   **En...** *in search of*

MARICARMEN: ¿Es Ud. el portero?

PORTERO: Para servirla a Ud., señora.

MARICARMEN: Pues a nosotras nos interesaría ver un apartamento que tenga dos alcobas y vista al exterior.

PORTERO: De momento° hay dos: uno en el primer piso y otro   **De...** *right now* igual en el quinto, que es mucho más barato.

ANA MARÍA: No sé... a menos que haya ascensor...

PORTERO: No hay, señora, por eso el apartamento del quinto es más económico.   Pero, en cambio°, desde su terraza   **en...** *on the other hand* se ve toda la ciudad.   Es una vista magnífica.

MARICARMEN: Yo no conozco a nadie a quien le guste subir hasta el quinto piso a pie —sobre todo después de trabajar mañana y tarde y estudiar de noche.

ANA MARÍA: Pues veamos el apartamento del primer piso.

PORTERO: En seguida.   (*En el apartamento.*)   Observen Uds. que tiene dos baños, sala grande, comedor separado y armarios° amplísimos.   *closets*

MARICARMEN: Sí, sí, se ve muy bonito todo.   ¿Cuáles son las condiciones del contrato?

© Peter Menzel

PORTERO: El alquiler, cuatrocientos veinticinco pesos. Mes
adelantado° y un mes de garantía°. La luz y el gas,
los pagará el inquilino.

*in advance / de... as a
security deposit*

C. *Otra vez en casa*

RAMÓN: Es posible que yo no haya oído bien, pero ¿de dónde
diablos vamos a sacar ciento veinticinco pesos más
y un mes de garantía?

MARICARMEN: Cálmate, querido, que te pones feo cuando te
enojas. Mira, mi hermana viene a estudiar a la
universidad y no tiene con quién vivir todavía.
Pues... ella puede quedarse con nosotros y ayudar
un poco con el alquiler...

RAMÓN: ¡Y así matamos dos pájaros de un tiro°!

shot

MARICARMEN: Exacto. ¿Qué te parece?

RAMÓN: ¡Trato hecho!°

¡Trato... It's a deal!

Comprensión

A. 1. ¿Qué no puede creer Ana María? ¿Por qué?
   2. ¿Por qué han vivido Maricarmen y Ramón en el centro de la ciudad hasta
      ahora?
   3. ¿Por qué quieren mudarse?
   4. ¿Cuándo van a ver los apartamentos recién construidos?

B. 1. ¿Qué tipo de apartamento desea ver Maricarmen?
   2. ¿Cuál es la diferencia entre los dos apartamentos?

    3. ¿Es una diferencia importante? ¿Por qué?
    4. ¿Cómo es el apartamento del primer piso?
    5. ¿Cuáles son las condiciones del contrato?
    6. ¿Quién paga la luz y el gas?

C. 1. ¿Por qué está Ramón un poco enojado?
    2. ¿Cuál es el plan de Maricarmen?
    3. ¿Cómo van a matar dos pájaros de un tiro?
    4. ¿Qué piensa Ramón de este plan?

Comentario cultural

In Hispanic cities, most city dwellers still reside in apartments; many of these, like condominiums, are owned, not rented. Modern apartments in Hispanic countries are comparable in design and conveniences to the most modern ones found in the United States. But not all apartments are as spacious as the one Maricarmen and Ramón have rented. There is a great variety of apartments, ranging from the very small to the luxurious. Many older apartments are quite spacious and elegant, with balconies, shuttered windows (usually without screens) and attractive grillwork.

    Built-in closets are a standard feature of only the most modern Hispanic apartments. The word **armario,** although used in the dialog to refer to a built-in closet, generally designates the piece of furniture that is used instead of walk-in closets. It is a large, moveable closet in which clothing is hung and stored; it may also contain a chest of drawers.

    Most apartment buildings in Hispanic countries have an apartment on the ground floor for the family of the **portero** or **portera,** the building manager, who plays a somewhat greater role in the lives of the tenants than does his or her counterpart in the United States. The **portero/a** takes care of the building and the grounds or sidewalk, deals with persons who have business in the building (the mail carrier, delivery persons, and so on), and in general is responsible for knowing when the tenants are in or out, in residence or away.

UN POCO DE TODO

    A. *Substitute the words in parentheses for those in italics and make any other necessary changes.*

      1. *Tengo* un secretario que ha vivido en Venezuela. (busco)
      2. Aquí *hay alguien* que ha visto la nueva casa de Carmen. (no hay nadie)
      3. El trato está hecho *si* el dueño ha firmado el contrato. (con tal que)
      4. No lo alquilamos *si no* han instalado el ascensor. (sin que)
      5. *Si* lo han terminado, pueden irse. (con tal que)

B. *Rearrange the words given to form complete sentences. Do not add any words.*

1. empieces / te lo / no / explicado / antes de que / hayamos
2. tenga / ninguna / no / que / tienda / hay / estante / el
3. llame Ud. / en caso de que / más / haya / tarde / vuelto
4. ¿ / plástico / tenga / de / mesa / prefieres / de / madera / una / que / o / sillas / sillas / ?
5. lámpara / no / a menos que / puerta / apagado / la / la / cierres / hayas

C. *Working with another student, ask and answer questions according to the model.*

MODELO   casa / tener cuatro alcobas / tener cada hijo su propia alcoba →
       ADELA: Buscamos una *casa* que *tenga cuatro alcobas.*
       PABLO: ¿Para qué?
       ADELA: Para que *cada hijo tenga su propia alcoba.*

1. casa / tener piscina / aprender a nadar los niños
2. casa de apartamentos / tener ascensor / no tener que subir las escaleras el abuelo
3. apartamento / tener un garaje doble / no tener que dejar el carro en la calle Ramón
4. apartamento / estar cerca del centro / llegar más rápido al trabajo Elena
5. casa / estar cerca de la universidad / no tener que usar el carro tanto Catalina

D. *Es muy importante que un aspirante tenga las habilidades y la experiencia necesarias para el puesto que solicita. ¿Qué experiencia deben tener los aspirantes siguientes?*

1. Se necesita piloto que haya _____.
            que sepa/pueda _____.
2. Se busca profesor(a) de español que haya _____.
               que sepa/pueda _____.
3. Se busca compañero/a de cuarto que pueda _____.
               que sea _____.

E. *Complete las oraciones en una forma lógica.*

1. Quiero un esposo/a que haya _____.
2. No me caso antes de/antes de que _____.
3. Busco un apartamento que tenga _____.
4. En esta clase no hay ningún estudiante que haya _____.
5. Nunca he conocido a nadie que haya _____.
6. Siempre he querido conocer a alguien que haya _____.

VOCABULARIO

VERBOS
acompañar to accompany, go with
alquilar to rent
construir (construyo) to build, construct
interesar to interest, be interesting
medir (i, i) to measure

SUSTANTIVOS
la **alcoba** bedroom
la **alfombra** rug
el **ascensor** elevator
el **balcón** balcony
el **baño** bathroom
la **casa de apartamentos** apartment house
la **cocina** kitchen
el **comedor** dining room
la **cómoda** bureau, chest of drawers

el/la **dueño/a** landlord, landlady
la **entrada** entry way
las **escaleras** stairs
el **escritorio** desk
el **estante** bookcase
el **garaje** garage
el **gas** gas; heat
el/la **inquilino/a** renter, tenant
la **lámpara** lamp
la **luz** light, electricity
la **mesita** end table
el **patio** patio; yard
la **piscina** swimming pool
el **piso** floor, story (*of a building*)
el/la **portero/a** building manager; doorman
la **sala** living room
el **sillón** armchair
el **sofá** sofa
el **televisor** television set

la **terraza** terrace
el/la **vecino/a** neighbor
la **vista** view

ADJETIVOS
amplio/a ample, large, spacious
cómodo/a comfortable

PALABRAS Y EXPRESIONES ÚTILES
a menos que unless
antes (de) que before
con tal que provided that
en caso de que in case
para que so that
primer piso second floor (*first floor up*)
recién + *adj.* recently + *adj.*
sin que without

Un paso más 17

Actividades

—¿Te has suscrito° tú a una revista° de decoración?

subscribed / magazine

A. **Una casa sin muebles.** Invente un cuento que explique el dibujo. Use estas preguntas como guía.

1. ¿Quiénes son estos señores? ¿Dónde viven?
2. ¿Cuánto tiempo han vivido allí? ¿Dónde vivían antes?
3. ¿Por qué se ha suscrito la señora a una revista de decoración?
4. ¿Qué muebles necesitan?
5. ¿Por qué no tienen muebles?
6. ¿Es probable que tengan muebles en el futuro inmediato? Explique.
7. Si estos señores le piden a Ud. que les dé consejos para la decoración de su casa, ¿qué les aconseja Ud.? ¿Deben comprar muebles nuevos o muebles usados? ¿antigüedades (*antiques*)? ¿Qué colores deben emplear? ¿Cuáles son las primeras cosas que ellos deben hacer o comprar para decorar la sala? ¿las últimas?

A propósito...

In Spanish-speaking countries the phrase **primer piso** does not generally indicate the first floor of a building, as it does in the United States. Rather, the **primer piso** is the first floor up. The ground, or first, floor is usually called **la planta baja,** the second floor **el primer piso,** the third floor **el segundo piso,** and so on.

B. **¿En qué piso...?** ¿A qué piso subiría Ud. en cada caso?

1. ¿En qué piso vive la familia García?
2. ¿A qué piso necesita Ud. subir si quiere decorar la sala?
3. ¿En qué piso está el consultorio del médico? ¿del dentista?
4. ¿Dónde se encuentra una compañía de mudanzas (*moving*)?
5. Si su auto no funciona bien y necesita alquilar otro, ¿a qué piso debe subir?
6. Si Ud. quiere comprar una blusa para su hermana, ¿a qué piso sube?
7. ¿En qué piso viven sus amigos italianos?
8. Si Ud. busca algo interesante para leer durante sus vacaciones, ¿a qué piso sube?
9. Si ha tenido un accidente de coche, ¿a qué piso debe subir?

TODO LO QUE USTED NECESITA...

una localización ÚNICA
APARTAMENTOS
EL MONTE

- En lo mejor de la ciudad
- Todo cerca: centros comerciales, universidad, escuelas
- Vigilancia 24 horas

- Piscina, áreas verdes y recreativas
- Estacionamiento
- Acceso inmediato a avenidas y autopistas
- Modernos apartamentos de 1, 2, 3, alcobas
- Sala-comedor con terraza
- Cocina totalmente amueblada
- Profusión de armarios

VISÍTENLOS DIRECTAMENTE

C. **Entrevista: casa y mudanzas.** Use the following questions to interview another student. Without using notes, report as much information to the class as you can.

1. ¿Prefieres vivir en una casa o en un apartamento? ¿Por qué?
2. ¿Cómo es la casa (el apartamento, el cuarto) en que vives ahora?
3. ¿Tienes muchos muebles? ¿Cómo son? ¿Te gustan las antigüedades?
4. ¿Cómo es tu casa/apartamento ideal?
5. ¿Te gustaría vivir en los Apartamentos El Monte? ¿Por qué (no)?
6. Si tienes que mudarte a una casa de apartamentos muy alta, ¿en qué piso prefieres vivir —la planta baja, el primer piso o el piso más alto? ¿Por qué?
7. ¿Te mudas con frecuencia? ¿Por qué?
8. ¿Qué te gusta menos —quedarte en una casa que no te gusta o mudarte? Explica.

D. **Haga su mudanza más fácil.** Moving is not quite as exhausting when you are organized. Study the ad and find the Spanish equivalent of these words and phrases.

1. exhausting
2. in advance
3. cut out and save (*command*)
4. to make easier
5. moving, the move
6. arrangements
7. safe-deposit box
8. notify (*command*)
9. change of address
10. Social Security
11. family members
12. insurance companies

¿Es Ud. una persona muy organizada —o espera hasta el último momento para hacerlo todo? Imagínese que Ud. va a mudarse pronto. ¿Cómo contestaría las siguientes preguntas?

Una semana (un mes) antes de mudarme
Un día o dos antes
El día de la mudanza
Unos días después de mudarme
¡Nunca!

1. ¿Prepararía Ud. una lista para organizarse? ¿Cuándo la prepararía?
2. ¿Llamaría a una compañía de mudanzas o alquilaría un camión (*truck*)? ¿Cuándo lo haría?
3. ¿Les pediría ayuda a otras personas? ¿a quiénes? ¿Qué harían ellos?
4. ¿Cuándo buscaría las cajas de empacar? ¿Dónde las buscaría? ¿Cuándo empacaría los platos y las otras cosas de la cocina?
5. ¿Compraría cortinas (*curtains*) nuevas? ¿alfombras? ¿muebles? ¿Cuándo?
6. ¿Qué otras cosas haría antes de mudarse? ¿Qué tendría que hacer después de mudarse?
7. ¿Cuándo notificaría a la oficina de correos (*post office*) de su cambio de dirección? ¿Cuándo mandaría la nueva dirección y el número de teléfono a sus amigos y a sus familiares?

E. **Más refranes.** There are many Spanish proverbs and expressions that begin with **No hay.** What is the English equivalent of these?

1. No hay monte tan alto que un asno cargado de (*loaded with*) oro no lo suba.
2. No hay mal que cien años dure (*lasts*).
3. No hay mal que por bien (*for a good purpose*) no venga.
4. No hay peros que valgan.
5. No hay mucho que no se acabe, ni poco que no se alcance (*reach, attain*).
6. No hay regla sin excepción.
7. No hay peor sordo (*deaf person*) que el que no quiere oir.
8. No hay mejor espejo (*mirror*) que el amigo viejo.
9. No hay renta (*income*) más segura y cierta que dejar de gastar lo que se puede excusar (*to do without*).

Now invent some **refranes** of your own that use the same structure.

10. No hay clase (universidad, profesor) que _____.
11. No hay amigo (hombre, mujer, niño) que _____.
12. No hay mentira (problema, dolor) que _____.

13. No hay compañero de cuarto (vecino, dueño, ladrón) tan malo (pobre, rico, inteligente, corrupto) que _____.
14. No hay _____.

Lectura cultural: La vivienda hispánica

La variedad de viviendas en el mundo hispánico se debe en gran parte a su diversidad climática y cultural.

Tanto en España como en Hispanoamérica ha habido en años recientes un desarrollo° tremendo en la construcción de casas de apartamentos y de casas, especialmente en las ciudades. Los edificios nuevos tienden a ser ultramodernos y, por lo tanto°, han cambiado bastante la apariencia de las ciudades hispánicas. En la construcción de casas hay una tendencia a algunos elementos de diseño° tradicional, tales como el patio —de influencias romana y árabe— y las ventanas con rejas°. El patio ya no está necesariamente en el centro de la casa, pero todavía está presente, detrás de la casa o a un lado, y siempre rodeado de un muro° para que la familia goce° de su vida privada. Las ventanas con rejas, que fueron una vez el lugar adonde podía asomarse° una novia para hablar con su novio, tienen ahora una función decorativa y práctica, la de proteger° la casa contra intrusos. En algunas casas nuevas se encuentra también un pequeño apartamento, el cual se alquila para que la familia tenga ayuda financiera con que pagar la nueva casa.

En el campo hay aun más° variedad. Tal vez la vivienda campestre° más conocida fuera del mundo hispánico sea la hacienda. Es un tipo de vivienda lujosa que tiene su origen en el cortijo° de España. Se encuentra en Hispanoamérica en la estancia argentina y el rancho mexicano. Por lo general, la hacienda consiste en una gran casa donde viven los dueños de la tierra, los establos para los caballos, los corrales para el ganado° y algunos edificios menores donde viven los trabajadores.

Una forma más modesta de vivienda de campo en España es la barraca valenciana. Se encuentra en las zonas de regadío° de Valencia y se caracteriza por un techo puntiagudo y pajizo°.

En Hispanoamérica, donde hay muchos extremos de clima, los campesinos de las zonas tropicales de Centroamérica y de las Antillas viven en bohíos, pequeñas casas construidas por lo general de madera y con techos de paja°. Troncos de árboles sirven de pies para la casa y sostienen° el suelo a una altura sobre la tierra. En las zonas montañosas de las Américas se ven casitas de adobe y algunas más nuevas, de ladrillos°, construidas por los campesinos mismos.

Por lo general, la vivienda hispánica refleja lo viejo y lo moderno,

development

por... thus

design

grillwork

rodeado... surrounded by a wall / can enjoy

appear, peek out

protecting

aun... even more / country

country home, farm

cattle

irrigation

techo... pointed, thatched roof

straw / hold up

brick

y también lo lujoso y lo humilde, lo puramente bello y lo puramente
práctico.

Comprensión

Complete las siguientes oraciones.

1. La variedad de viviendas del mundo hispánico viene de _____.
2. En las ciudades hispánicas ha habido recientemente _____.
3. Los apartamentos nuevos se caracterizan por _____.
4. El cambio de apariencia de las ciudades hispánicas es un resultado de _____.
5. El patio y las ventanas con rejas son elementos _____.
6. Actualmente las rejas y el patio sirven para _____.
7. En el pasado las ventanas con rejas _____.
8. El cortijo español, la estancia argentina y el rancho mexicano son _____.
9. La barraca valenciana puede identificarse por _____.
10. Los bohíos se distinguen de las casas de las zonas montañosas por _____.

Ejercicios escritos

A. Complete las oraciones en una forma lógica.

1. (No) Me gustaría vivir en una hacienda porque _____.
2. (No) Me gustaría vivir en un bohío porque _____.

B. Complete el párrafo siguiente, describiendo la casa de sus sueños.

Quiero una casa que tenga _____. En esta casa yo podría _____. Quiero que
la casa esté en la ciudad/en el campo porque _____.

capítulo 18 De viaje

© Bernard Pierre Wolf 1978/Photo Researchers, Inc.

OBJETIVOS

In this chapter you will learn more vocabulary and expressions related to travel—train travel, going through customs, and making arrangements at a hotel.

You will also learn about the following aspects of Spanish grammar:

71. how to use **aunque** (*although*) with the subjunctive and with the indicative
72. when to use the subjunctive and when to use the indicative after conjunctions of time, such

as **cuando** (*when*) and **en cuanto** (*as soon as*)

73. how to express possession, using the stressed possessive adjectives—**unas maletas mías** (*some suitcases of mine*)—and possessive pronouns—**las mías** (*mine*)

Un paso más includes activities related to aspects of international travel and a reading about two important Hispanic museums: el Museo del Prado in Madrid and el Museo Nacional de Antropología in Mexico City.

VOCABULARIO: PREPARACIÓN

En la aduana°			customs
el/la inspec-tor(a) (de aduanas)	(customs) inspector	pagar los derechos/ una multa	to pay customs duty/a fine
la nacionalidad	nationality	registrar	to search,
el pasaporte	passport		examine
el/la viajero/a	traveler	viajar en el extranjero/ir al extranjero	to travel abroad, to go abroad
cruzar la frontera	to cross the border		
declarar (algo)	to declare (something)		

A. *Llene los espacios para describir lo que ocurre cuando pasamos por la aduana.*

Cuando cruzamos una _____, es necesario pasar por la _____. Primero el _____ nos pide el _____ y pregunta cuánto tiempo vamos a estar en el país. A veces pregunta también: «¿De qué _____ es Ud.?» También pregunta si tenemos algo que (*to*) _____. Por ejemplo, la aduana norteamericana no permite más de trescientos dólares de compras hechas en el _____. Si llevamos más de eso, tendremos que pagar unos _____. Después de varias preguntas, el inspector _____ las maletas. Si llevamos algo ilegal, el inspector toma el objeto y nos pone una _____ o llama a la policía.

B. *Cuando los viajeros contestan así, ¿cuál ha sido la pregunta del inspector de aduanas?*

1. Soy española, de Toledo.
2. No sabía yo que era ilegal traer fruta fresca.
3. Solamente estos libros y estos cigarrillos para uso personal.
4. Espere Ud. un momento. Mi esposa tiene la llave.
5. No compré esta cámara en el extranjero. La compré aquí antes de salir.

En la estación de trenes/de autobuses			
el andén	platform	la llegada	arrival
el billete (de ida)	(one-way) ticket	el maletero	porter
el billete de ida y vuelta	round-trip ticket	la salida	departure
		la taquilla	ticket office
el horario	timetable, schedule		
la litera	berth (on a train)	cambiar de (tren, autobús)	to change (trains, buses)

C. *¿Qué hace Ud.?*

1. Si tengo que cambiar de tren durante un viaje,
   a. no llevo mucho equipaje.
   b. busco un maletero en el andén para que lleve mi equipaje.
   c. facturo el equipaje y dejo que la compañía lo cambie.
2. Si tengo que hacer un largo viaje por tren, de noche, prefiero
   a. comprar un billete de primera clase.
   b. volar.
   c. comprar un billete de segunda clase con litera.
3. Cuando voy a la taquilla a comprar un billete de ida y vuelta en tren y
   encuentro que no tengo suficiente dinero para comprarlo,
   a. compro un billete de ida solamente.
   b. voy en autobús, porque es más barato.
   c. vuelvo a casa a buscar más dinero.
4. Cuando no estoy seguro/a de la hora de la salida del tren,
   a. se la pregunto a un maletero.
   b. pido un horario.
   c. vuelvo a la taquilla a preguntar.
5. La última cosa que pregunto después de comprar un billete es
   a. la hora de la salida y de la llegada.
   b. el número del andén.
   c. si hay que cambiar de autobús.

D. *Definiciones*

1. litera 2. horario 3. andén 4. taquilla 5. maletero

En el hotel o en la pensión°			boardinghouse
la ducha	shower	**con (____ días**	(____ days) in
la habitación	room	**de) anticipación**	advance
el/la huésped(a)	guest	**desocupado/a**	unoccupied,
el mozo (el	bellhop		vacant, free
botones)		**confirmar**	to confirm
la propina	tip	**reservar**	to reserve
la recepción	front desk		

E. *Describa Ud. las cosas y los cuartos que se ven en el dibujo.*

F.   ¿El Hotel Primera Clase o la Pensión Libertad?   De estas frases, ¿cuáles describen un hotel grande e internacional?   ¿una pensión pequeña y modesta?

1. Tiene todas las comodidades (*comforts*) que se encuentran en los mejores hoteles.
2. Los botones llevan el equipaje a la habitación.
3. Muchos de los huéspedes y del personal hablan solamente una lengua, el español.
4. Hay que reservar una habitación con muchos días de anticipación.
5. Los dependientes confirman la reservación del huésped.
6. Generalmente se puede llegar sin reservaciones y encontrar una habitación desocupada.
7. Hay que gastar mucho dinero en propinas.
8. Los huéspedes suben (*carry up*) su equipaje, o el dueño les ayuda a subirlo.
9. Hablan muchos idiomas en la recepción.
10. Todas las habitaciones tienen ducha y, a veces, baño completo con ducha.

MINIDIÁLOGOS Y GRAMÁTICA

71. INDICATIVE AND SUBJUNCTIVE AFTER *AUNQUE*

Antes de aterrizar

AZAFATA: Su atención, por favor, señoras y señores.   Les entregaremos ahora las planillas de inmigración y de la declaración de aduana.   Llénenlas y ténganlas a mano con sus pasaportes antes de que aterricemos.   Muchas gracias.

VIAJERA: Señorita, por favor.   ¿Es necesario que declare la cámara fotográfica y la grabadora, *aunque* no *son* para vender?

AZAFATA: Con tal que no las traiga de regalo o para comerciar, no pagará derechos.   Pero declárelas de todos modos, *aunque sean* para su uso personal.

VIAJERO: ¿Y hasta cuántas cámaras se permiten para uso personal?

AZAFATA: No sé exactamente, pero ¡creo que menos de las diez que Ud. tiene!

Before landing ATTENDANT: Your attention please, ladies and gentlemen. We will be passing out the immigration and customs-declaration forms. Fill them out and have them within easy reach, along with your passports, before we land. Thank you very much. TRAVELER: Please, Miss. Is it necessary for me to declare my camera and tape recorder even though I don't intend to sell them? ATTENDANT: Provided that you're not bringing them as a gift or for business reasons, you won't pay duty. But declare them anyway, although they may be for your personal use. TRAVELER: And (up to) how many cameras are permitted for personal use? ATTENDANT: I don't know exactly, but I think fewer than the ten that you have!

1. *¿Qué les entrega la azafata a los pasajeros?*
2. *¿Qué tienen que hacer los pasajeros?*
3. *¿Qué pregunta la viajera?*
4. *¿Cuándo pagará derechos un viajero?*
5. *¿La cámara y la grabadora de la viajera son para su uso personal? ¿y las cámaras del viajero?*

The subjunctive is used after the conjunction **aunque** (*although, even though*) to imply doubt or uncertainty. When there is no doubt or uncertainty, **aunque** is followed by the indicative. Compare

No me gusta **aunque sea** amigo de Rita.	*I don't like him although he may (might) be Rita's friend.*
No me gusta **aunque es** amigo de Rita.	*I don't like him even though (even if) he is Rita's friend.*

PRÁCTICA

A. *Dé Ud. frases nuevas según las indicaciones.*

1. —Los amigos de Ud. quieren ir a Puerto Vallarta en autobús, pero Ud. no. Si insisten, ¿qué les va a decir Ud.?
   —No voy en autobús aunque *Uds.* sigan insistiendo. (*Ramón, tú, Ud., Catalina y Juan, vosotros*)

2. —No hay habitación desocupada en la única pensión de un pueblo pequeño. Ud. insiste, pero el dueño sigue diciendo que no hay. ¿Qué le dice a Ud. el dueño?
   —No hay habitaciones, aunque Ud. _____. (*prometer pagar el doble, esperar aquí en la recepción toda la noche, insistir en quedarse aquí, darme una propina enorme, haber reservado una habitación, haber confirmado su reservación, quejarse a la policía*)

B. *Últimas palabras famosas. Complete Ud. las frases a la izquierda con las palabras a la derecha.*

1. Julieta: Aunque sea uno de los Capuletos,
2. Un estudiante: Aunque haya examen en clase mañana,
3. El agente de viajes: Aunque no se hayan confirmado las reservaciones,
4. El segundo de los tres cochinitos (*little pigs*): Aunque sea débil (*weak*) de construcción,

a. no va a encontrar la grabadora que no declaré.
b. quiero conocer a aquel joven.
c. no se preocupe Ud. Habrá habitación.
d. no te preocupes—no hay policías por aquí.
e. no importa. Los trenes nunca salen a tiempo.
f. no voy a estudiar más esta noche.

5. Una amiga: Aunque maneje a setenta millas por hora,
6. El turista que pasa por la aduana: Aunque el inspector registre muy bien mi maleta,
7. El viajero que toma el tren: Aunque no estemos en la estación a la hora de la salida que ponen en el horario,

g. voy a hacer mi casa de madera.

C. ¿Cómo se dice en español?

1. Although he's a guest
2. Although he may be a guest
3. Although we cross the border
4. Although we may cross the border
5. I won't take the train, even though I may have to go alone (a solas).

CONVERSACIÓN

A. *Su amigo/a está enamoradísimo/a de* (madly in love with) *Ud. y quiere que los dos se casen en seguida. Ud. no quiere casarse con nadie, y menos con este/a amigo/a. Explíquele su punto de vista, completando esta frase.*

—No me caso contigo aunque _____.

B. *Complete las oraciones en una forma lógica.*

1. Aunque _____ lo niegue, él/ella es _____.
2. Aunque yo _____, no importa.
3. No voy a _____ aunque _____.
4. Aunque _____, no lo/la voy a comprar.

72. SUBJUNCTIVE AND INDICATIVE AFTER CONJUNCTIONS OF TIME

—*Apenas*° *ha empezado sus estudios y ya*   scarcely
está descontento, inquieto°, *malhumorado...*   uneasy
¡Imagínate como estará cuando sea médico!

In a dependent clause after a conjunction of time, the subjunctive is used to express a future action or state of being, that is, one that is still pending or has not yet occurred. The events in the dependent clauses are conceptualized—not real-world—events. Conjunctions of time include:

cuando	*when*	**hasta que**	*until*
después (de) que	*after*	**tan pronto como**	*as soon as*
en cuanto	*as soon as*		

The indicative is used after conjunctions of time to describe a habitual action or an action in the past. Compare:

FUTURE ACTION (Subjunctive):
   Saldremos **en cuanto llegue** Felipe. — *We'll leave as soon as Felipe arrives.*
HABITUAL ACTION (Indicative):
   Siempre salimos **en cuanto llega** Felipe. — *We always leave as soon as Felipe arrives.*
PAST ACTION (Indicative):
   Anoche, salimos **en cuanto llegó** Felipe. — *Last night, we left as soon as Felipe arrived.*

The subject and verb are frequently inverted in the subordinate clause following conjunctions of time.

¡OJO! Even though it is a time conjunction, **antes de que** always requires the subjunctive (Section 70).

Note that the subjunctive is used with conjunctions of time even when there is no change of subject in the dependent clause.

Vamos a salir tan pronto como **terminemos.** — *We're going to leave as soon as we finish.*

However, when there is no change of subject in the dependent clause, the prepositions **después de** + *infinitive* and **hasta** + *infinitive* are more frequently used than the conjunctions **después de que** and **hasta que.** Compare:

Salimos después de comer. — *We're leaving after we eat (after eating).*

Salimos después de que coman ellos. — *We're leaving after they eat.*

PRÁCTICA

A. Dé Ud. frases nuevas según las indicaciones.

1. —En el avión los viajeros tienen que llenar la planilla de inmigración. ¿Cuándo la tienen que entregar?
   —Entregan las planillas _____ aterrice el avión. (*tan pronto como, cuando, después de que, en cuanto, No... hasta que*)
2. —El inspector quiere que Ud. le entregue el pasaporte. ¿Qué le dice Ud. al inspector?
   —Le entrego el pasaporte tan pronto como yo _____. (*encontrarlo, encontrar la llave de mi maleta, cerrar mi maleta, dármelo mi esposo/a, recordar dónde lo tengo*)

B. Use la conjunción entre paréntesis para unir las dos oraciones. Haga todos los cambios necesarios.

1. Voy a decidirlo. Cruzo la frontera. (cuando)
2. Juana va a mudarse. Su amiga regresa del Perú. (después de que)
3. No digas nada. Julio paga el billete. (hasta que)
4. El inspector va a registrar la maleta. Mi esposo la abre. (en cuanto)
5. Van a construir una nueva casa de apartamentos. El gobierno les da el permiso. (tan pronto como)

C. Cambie según las indicaciones.

MODELO   *Llamé* cuando llegué. (*voy a llamar*) →
            Voy a llamar cuando *llegue.*

1. Mi hijo *nació* después de que mi esposo volvió de Guatemala. (*nacerá*)
2. *Tuvimos que caminar* mucho cuando cambiamos de tren. (*vamos a caminar*)
3. En cuanto sabes la respuesta, *siempre me la dices.* (*dímela*)
4. *El año pasado llamamos* con dos días de anticipación cuando confirmamos las reservaciones. (*este año llamaremos*)
5. *Anoche compramos* el billete en cuanto se abrió la taquilla. (*hoy compraremos*)

D. ¿Cómo se dice en español?

We'll take the room without a shower until the room with the shower is free. Please notify (**avisar**) us as soon as the other guests leave. Will the bell boy help us when we change rooms?

CONVERSACIÓN

A. Describa Ud. los dibujos, completando las frases. Luego, describa Ud. su propia vida.

1. Pablo va a estudiar hasta que
   _____.
   Esta noche yo voy a estudiar hasta
   que _____.
   Siempre estudio hasta que _____.
   Anoche estudié hasta que _____.

2. Los señores Castro van a cenar tan
   pronto como _____.
   Esta noche voy a cenar tan pronto
   como _____.
   Siempre ceno tan pronto como
   _____.
   Anoche cené tan pronto como
   _____.

3. Lupe va a viajar al extranjero en cuanto _____.
   Voy a _____ en cuanto _____.
   Siempre _____ en cuanto _____.
   De niño/a _____ en cuanto _____.

B. *Preguntas*

   1. ¿Qué piensa Ud. hacer después de graduarse en la universidad?   ¿Qué le
      van a regalar sus padres/amigos cuando Ud. se gradúe?   ¿Qué recibió Ud.
      cuando se graduó en la escuela secundaria?
   2. Cuando Ud. tenga el tiempo y el dinero, ¿adónde va a ir?   ¿Adónde fue
      Ud. el año pasado cuando estaba de vacaciones?   Cuando todavía vivía
      Ud. con su familia, ¿adónde iban Uds. de vacaciones?

C. *¿Qué excusas puede Ud. ofrecer en estas situaciones?*

   Su amigo/a quiere que Ud. le ayude con sus maletas en el andén.
      Yo lo voy a hacer tan pronto como _____.
   Su amigo/a quiere que Ud. le acompañe al cine.
      Yo te acompañaré en cuanto _____.

73. STRESSED POSSESSIVE ADJECTIVES AND POSSESSIVE PRONOUNS

Un lío en la aduana
SEÑORA: Perdón, señor, pero esa maleta es *mía*.
 SEÑOR: ¿Y cómo sabe Ud. que esta maleta es *suya* y que no es *mía*?
SEÑORA: Porque *las mías* llevan mi nombre y *las suyas* no.

1. *¿De quién es la maleta?*
2. *¿Qué lleva la maleta de la señora?*

Stressed Possessive Adjectives

FORMS OF THE STRESSED POSSESSIVE ADJECTIVES			
mío/a/os/as	*my (of mine)*	**nuestro**/a/os/as	*our (of ours)*
tuyo/a/os/as	*your (of yours)*	**vuestro**/a/os/as	*your (of yours)*
suyo/a/os/as	*your (of yours), his (of his), her (of hers), its*	**suyo**/a/os/as	*your (of yours), their (of theirs)*

Stressed forms **(las formas tónicas)** of the possessive are, as the term implies, more emphatic than the unstressed forms **(las formas átonas),** discussed in Section 18. The stressed forms are used when in English you would emphasize the possessive with your voice, or when you want to express English *of mine (of yours, of his,* and so on).

Es **mi** amigo.	*He's my friend.*
Es **un** amigo **mío.**	*He's **my** friend.* *He's a friend of mine.*
Es **su** perro.	*It's her dog.*
Es **el** perro **suyo.**	*It's **her** dog.*

The stressed forms of the possessive adjective follow the noun, which must be preceded by a definite or indefinite article or by a demonstrative adjective. Like the unstressed forms of the possessive adjectives, the stressed forms agree with the noun modified in number and gender.

[Práctica A]

A hassle in customs SRA.: Pardon me, sir, but that suitcase is mine. SR.: And how do you know that this suitcase is yours and that it isn't mine? SRA.: Because mine have (carry) my name on them and yours don't.

Possessive Pronouns

Aquí está mi **maletín.** ¿Dónde está **el suyo?**	*Here is my small suitcase. Where is yours?*
Sus **literas** están preparadas; **las nuestras,** no.	*Their berths are ready; ours aren't.*
No es el **pasaporte** de Juan; es **mío.**	*It isn't Juan's passport; it's mine.*

The stressed possessive adjectives—never the unstressed possessives—can be used as possessive pronouns. **la maleta suya → la suya.** The article and the possessive form agree in gender and number with the noun to which they refer. The definite article is frequently omitted after forms of **ser: Es suya.**

[Práctica B, C, D]

PRÁCTICA

A. Dé Ud. frases nuevas según las indicaciones.

1. —Su amigo Antonio nunca arregla las cosas rotas, pero Ud., sí. ¿En qué condición están las cosas de Ud.? Su carro, por ejemplo.
   —¿El *carro* mío? Ya lo he arreglado. (*lámparas, estéreo, cámara, frenos, transmisión*)
2. —¿Ya han registrado todo el equipaje?
   —El maletín de Juan, sí, pero las maletas *mías*, no. (*de ellos, tus, nuestras, de Antonia, mis, de vosotros*)

B. Dé Ud. frases nuevas según las indicaciones.

1. —Hay una maleta abandonada en la aduana. ¿Es de Ud.?
   —No, no es *mía*. (*de Juan, de Uds., de Alicia, de Ud., de ti, de vosotros*)
2. —Ud. ha perdido varios objetos. ¿Son suyos estos objetos que tienen en la recepción? ¿El radio?
   —No, no es *mío*. *El mío* es más pequeño. (*guitarra, zapatos, llave, televisor, maletas, diamante*)

C. Complete las oraciones según el modelo.

MODELO   Voy a lavar mi carro esta tarde, pero tú _____. →
          Voy a lavar mi carro esta tarde, pero tú *no vas a lavar el tuyo.*

1. No puedo pagar mis facturas este mes, pero tú _____.
2. No han confirmado sus reservaciones, pero yo _____.
3. He dejado mi billete en casa, pero Rafael _____.
4. No puedo encontrar mi litera, pero ellos _____.
5. Podremos usar nuestro carro, pero Ud. _____.
6. Tú has declarado todas tus compras, pero nosotros _____.
7. Nosotros no perdimos nuestro tren, pero ellos _____.
8. Ya he reservado mi habitación, pero los señores Benítez _____.

D. *¿Cómo se dice en español?*

1. She's a friend of his.
2. These are *our* tickets.
3. This is my berth, not yours.
4. That isn't your seat; it's mine.
5. She has her passport, and I have mine.

CONVERSACIÓN

A. *Ask another student the following questions. He or she should answer using the stressed forms of the possessive adjective or the possessive pronoun.*

1. ¿Cuáles son más interesantes, las clases mías o las tuyas?
2. ¿Cuál es más fácil, el horario mío o el tuyo?
3. ¿Prefieres el carro mío o el tuyo?
4. ¿Cuál es más barato, el apartamento mío o el tuyo?
5. ¿Cuál es más grande, la familia mía o la tuya?

B. *Ud. es un(a) empleado/a de una compañía de autobuses. Usando el modelo, compare el servicio que ofrece su compañía con el servicio de otra compañía. Ud. puede hablar de las demoras, las líneas directas entre ciudades, los conductores (drivers), los autobuses nuevos, el servicio en general, las estaciones, los horarios.*

MODELO   *Los autobuses suyos* siempre están atrasados, pero *los nuestros* siempre llegan a la hora indicada en el horario.

C. *Piense Ud. en algo que Ud. tiene o en alguien que conoce. Luego descríbalo/la a la clase, sin mencionar su nombre. Sus compañeros tienen que decir qué/quién es.*

MODELO   La mía contiene muchas tarjetas de crédito.
La mía es de cuero (*leather*) y metal.
La mía está debajo de mi silla en este momento.

(*una bolsa*)

DIÁLOGO: Un viaje en el extranjero

A. *En la aduana*

INSPECTOR: ¿Su nacionalidad, por favor?
VIAJERA: Soy colombiana. Aquí tiene Ud. mi pasaporte.
INSPECTOR: Muchas gracias. Y esa maleta... ¿es suya?
VIAJERA: Sí, señor, es mía, pero contiene solamente objetos de uso personal. No tengo nada que declarar.[1]

Michael A. Rogers

INSPECTOR: Aunque sea así, ábrala, por favor. Es necesario que la registremos, aunque esto la demore° un poco. En cuanto yo termine, Ud. puede cerrarla y seguir hacia la salida°, con tal que no tenga que pagar derechos.

may delay

exit

VIAJERA: Muy bien, inspector.

INSPECTOR: A ver°, ropa… libros… nada de alcohol ni de cigarrillos… pues todo está bien. Puede salir ahora, señorita. Ojalá que le guste nuestro país.

A... let's see

B. *En la estación de autobuses del aeropuerto*

VIAJERA: ¿Hay autobuses para la ciudad?

MALETERO: Acaba de salir el último. Es tardísimo, ¿comprende? Algunos hoteles tienen sus propios autobuses, pero tendrá Ud. que llamar y esperar hasta que llegue.

VIAJERA: ¿Cuestan mucho?

MALETERO: No cuestan nada, es decir que son gratis con tal que Ud. se quede en uno de sus hoteles.

VIAJERA: Pero tengo una habitación reservada ya en un hotel pequeño[2] en la Calle 8 de Agosto. Será mejor que tome un taxi. Pero, ¿dónde están los taxis? No veo ninguno.

MALETERO: Muchos de los taxistas están en huelga°. Además, es muy tarde. Pero yo soy muy bueno para encontrar taxis. Espere un minuto hasta que yo le encuentre uno —a menos que decida Ud. ir a su hotel caminando.

strike

C. *El taxi llega al hotel.*

TAXISTA: Aquí es, señorita.

VIAJERA: ¡Por fin! En cuanto llegue a mi habitación, me voy a acostar. Estoy cansadísima... ¿Cuánto le debo?

TAXISTA: Son treinta y cinco pesos, señorita.[3]

VIAJERA: Tome cuarenta, pero no se vaya, por favor, hasta que yo confirme la reservación.

TAXISTA: Con tal que regrese pronto, aquí me quedo.

(Cinco minutos más tarde)

VIAJERA: Todo está bien. Tienen preparada mi habitación y parece que es un hotel con todas las comodidades.

TAXISTA: Menos mal° que Ud. hizo la reservación con anticipa-   **Menos...** *it's good*
ción porque durante el mes de agosto hay muy pocas habitaciones desocupadas.

VIAJERA: Aquí viene el mozo por mis maletas. Buenas noches y muchas gracias.

Comprensión

Conteste las preguntas en oraciones completas.

A. 1. ¿De dónde es la viajera?
    2. ¿Por qué no tiene nada que declarar?
    3. ¿Qué tiene que hacer el inspector antes de que pueda salir la señorita?
    4. ¿Necesita pagar derechos?
    5. ¿Cuáles son las últimas palabras del inspector a la viajera?

B. 1. ¿Por qué es imposible que encuentre un autobús público?
    2. ¿Cuánto cuestan los autobuses de los hoteles?
    3. ¿Por qué es difícil que ella encuentre un taxi?
    4. ¿Quién le ofrece su ayuda?

C. 1. ¿Cómo se siente la viajera?
    2. ¿Cuánto le da de propina al taxista?
    3. ¿Qué le pide al taxista?
    4. ¿Cómo es el hotel? ¿y la habitación suya?
    5. ¿Por qué es importante, según el taxista, hacer las reservaciones con anticipación?

Comentario cultural

1. Customs duty is usually not charged on items taken into a country other than one's own for personal use. However, if you plan to send gifts to friends living in another country, it is a good idea to find out if they will have to pay duty on the items you have sent. It may be quite expensive for them to pick up your "gifts"!

2. Many types of lodging are available to travelers in Hispanic countries. There are youth hotels, motels, inexpensive hotels with few conveniences, and ultra-modern hotels. In Spain, many historic buildings have been converted into elegant **paradores nacionales** (*national inns*). There guests can enjoy the illusion of living in another century—with none of the inconveniences! There are a number of modern **paradores** as well. Reasonable accommodations can also be found in the **pensiones,** small boardinghouses that rent rooms to long-term guests, as well as to tourists or travelers who plan to stay for only a few nights.

3. There are often fixed fees for traveling from one place to another by taxi. In other cases, drivers may charge by the kilometer or fraction thereof. It is best to discuss payment *before* you start your taxi ride.

UN POCO DE TODO

A. *Substitute the words in parentheses for those in italics and make any other necessary changes.*

1. *Siempre visitamos* a los abuelos cuando tenemos tiempo. (*esta semana vamos a*)
2. *Este verano* vamos a recorrer el rancho suyo tan pronto como empiece el buen tiempo. (*todos los veranos*)
3. El dependiente *va a traer* nuestra alfombra cuando te traiga la tuya. (*trajo*)
4. En cuanto *terminen* nuestro garaje, van a empezar el tuyo. (*terminaron*)
5. Aunque había una demora, nuestro autobús *llegó* a tiempo. (*va a llegar*)

B. *Form complete sentences based on the words given in the order given. Add any necessary words.*

1. aunque / tú / no / tener / nada / importante / que / decir, / llamarnos
2. nosotros / ir / mandar / cartas / en cuanto / tú / terminar / tuyo
3. nosotros / pensar / confirmar / nuestro / horario / después de / confirmar / tuyo
4. tú / no / ir / salir / con / tu / maletas / hasta que / yo / tener / mío / ¿verdad?
5. se / llegar / a / su / finca / pero / no / a / nuestro / por / autopista

C. *Working with another student, ask and answer questions according to the model.*

MODELO   lavar el carro / tener un momento libre →
       YOLANDA: ¿Te *lavamos el carro* cuando *lavemos el nuestro*?
       JOSÉ: No, gracias. Yo voy a *lavar el mío* en cuanto *tenga un momento libre.*

1. confirmar la reservación / poder llamar
2. comprar un billete / ir al banco
3. reservar una litera / abrirse la taquilla
4. entregar la planilla de inmigración / contestar la última pregunta
5. comprar un periódico / facturar el equipaje

D. *Complete las oraciones según el modelo.*

MODELO   Voy a depositar mi dinero cuando _____. →
          Voy a depositar mi dinero cuando *deposite el tuyo.*

1. El inspector va a registrar mis maletas en cuanto _____.
2. El maletero va a llevar mi equipaje al andén tan pronto como _____.
3. Vamos a comprarte un billete de ida y vuelta cuando _____.
4. Van a preparar mi habitación en cuanto _____.
5. El recepcionista va a entregarme el pasaporte tan pronto como _____.

E. *You are an employee of one of the places specified below. How many different ways can you explain the following situations to your customers, who are quite upset about the delay?*

1. *En el hotel:* —Aunque la habitación suya esté confirmada, Uds. no la pueden ocupar hasta que _____.
2. *En la estación de autobuses:* —Aunque se haya anunciado la salida para las once, el autobús suyo no puede salir hasta que _____.

VOCABULARIO

VERBOS
aterrizar to land
confirmar to confirm
cruzar to cross
declarar to declare
entregar to hand in, over
ofrecer (ofrezco) to offer
registrar to search, examine

SUSTANTIVOS
la **aduana** customs
el **andén** platform, track
el **autobús** bus
el **billete (de ida)** (one-way) ticket
el **billete de ida y vuelta** round-trip ticket
el **botones/mozo** bellhop
la **cámara** camera
la **comodidad** comfort
los **derechos** customs duty
la **ducha** shower

el **extranjero** abroad
la **frontera** border, frontier
la **grabadora** tape recorder
la **habitación** room
el **horario** schedule
el **hotel** hotel
el/la **huésped(a)** guest
la **inmigración** immigration
el/la **inspector(a)** inspector
el **inspector de aduanas** customs inspector
la **litera** berth (*on a train*)
la **llegada** arrival
el **maletero** porter
el **maletín** small suitcase
la **nacionalidad** nationality
la **pensión** boardinghouse
la **planilla** form
la **propina** tip (*to a porter, etc.*)
la **recepción** front desk
la **reservación** reservation
la **salida** departure; exit

la **taquilla** ticket office
el/la **taxista** cab driver
el **uso** use
el **viaje** trip, voyage
el/la **viajero/a** traveler

ADJETIVOS
desocupado/a unoccupied, vacant, free
propio/a (one's) own
único/a only; unique

PALABRAS Y EXPRESIONES ÚTILES
aunque although, even though
con (...días de) anticipación (...days) in advance
después (de) que after
en cuanto as soon as
hasta que until
ir al extranjero to go abroad
tan pronto como as soon as

Actividades

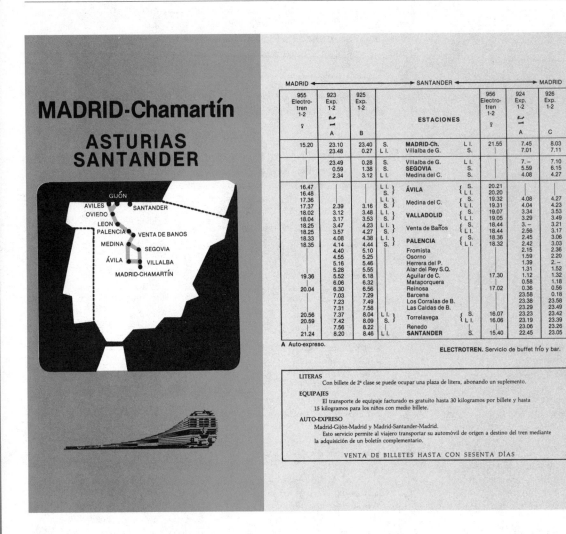

A. **¿Sabe Ud. usar un horario de tren?** Para usar un horario de tren, hay que saber que emplean el mismo sistema que usan los militares, es decir que usan un sistema de veinticuatro horas. Así no hay necesidad de decir «de la mañana (tarde/noche)». Ponen 2.20 si el tren sale a las 2.20 de la mañana y ponen 14.20 si sale a las 2.20 de la tarde, ponen 10.30 si sale a las 10.30 de la mañana y 22.30 si sale a las 10.30 de la noche.

Ahora conteste las preguntas según el horario que se da en la página 490.

1. ¿Qué es el servicio auto-expreso? ¿Qué tren debe Ud. tomar si desea transportar su coche desde Madrid a Santander?
2. ¿A qué hora sale el electrotrén de Madrid (estación de Chamartín) para Santander? ¿A qué hora llega a Santander? ¿El electrotrén para en Segovia? ¿A qué hora pasa por Reinosa?
3. Si Ud. desea viajar de Santander a Madrid de noche y con litera, ¿qué tren debe tomar? ¿A qué hora sale de Santander? ¿A qué hora llega a Madrid?
4. ¿A qué hora llega el tren-exprés 926 a Valladolid? ¿A qué hora sale?
5. ¿Cuál es el último tren de noche que sale de Segovia? ¿Este tren para en Ávila?
6. ¿Se ofrecen comidas en los electrotrenes? ¿Se ofrecen literas? ¿Por qué sí o por qué no? Si se toma el electrotrén 956 en Santander, ¿cuánto tiempo se tarda (*does it take*) en llegar a Madrid? ¿Cuánto se tarda si se toma el exprés 926? ¿Cuál es más rápido—el electrotrén o el exprés? ¿Cuál de los dos preferiría Ud.? ¿Por qué?

B. **Uno, dos, tres...** Describa Ud. lo que está pasando —y lo que va a pasar— en este dibujo. Use las preguntas como guía.

1. ¿Quién es el viajero? ¿Cómo es?
2. ¿Quiénes lo esperan?
3. ¿Cómo es el inspector?
4. ¿Qué problema va a haber?
5. ¿Cómo se resolverá el problema?
6. ¿Qué le pasará al viajero?

C. **La aduana.** As you are going through customs, the inspector asks you the following questions. Give as many appropriate responses as possible.

MODELO   INSPECTOR: Su pasaporte, por favor. →
               VIAJERO/A: Cómo no.
                           Claro.
                           Aquí tiene Ud. mi pasaporte.
                           Un minuto, por favor. Está en mi maleta.

1. ¿De qué nacionalidad es Ud.?
2. ¿Cuánto tiempo va Ud. a estar en nuestro país?
3. ¿Tiene Ud. algo que declarar? ¿licores? ¿tabaco?
4. ¿Por qué lleva Ud. tantos cigarrillos americanos?
5. ¿Cuáles son sus maletas?
6. ¿Quiere Ud. abrir sus maletas, por favor?
7. ¿Qué hay en la maleta pequeña?
8. Ud. tiene que pagar doscientos pesos de derechos.

A propósito...

The following phrases—most of which you already know—will be useful to you in arranging for lodging in a Spanish-speaking country.

Frases útiles para el hotel

un hotel de lujo	*a deluxe hotel*
un hotel de primera (segunda) clase	*a first-class (second-class) hotel*
una habitación para una persona (dos personas)	*a single (double) room*
con baño (ducha)	*with a bath (shower)*
sin baño	*without a bath*
para una noche (dos noches)	*for one night (two nights)*
¿Necesita Ud. mi pasaporte?	*Do you need my passport?*
¿Aceptan Uds. cheques de viajero (tarjetas de crédito)?	*Do you accept traveler's checks (credit cards)?*

Frases útiles para la pensión

pensión completa	*room and full board (all meals included),*
media pensión	*breakfast and one other meal included*

D. **Problemas del viajero.** With another student, act out one of the following situations. How will the situation be resolved? How does your solution compare with that of other groups?

1. **Personajes:** Viajero/a y recepcionista del hotel
   Situación: El/la viajero/a hizo una reservación, pero el/la recepcionista no la puede encontrar.
2. **Personajes:** Viajero/a y hotelero (*hotelkeeper*)
   Situación: El/la viajero/a llega al único hotel del pueblo y encuentra que la única habitación desocupada cuesta mucho más de lo que quiere pagar. Por eso quiere que el hotelero baje el precio.
3. **Personajes:** Dos amigos que viajan juntos
   Situación: Uno de ellos quiere quedarse en un hotel de lujo con toda comodidad—aire acondicionado, televisor y refrigerador en la habitación. El otro prefiere quedarse en un hotel de segunda clase y prefiere una habitación sin baño porque es más barata.
4. **Personajes:** Viajero/a y recepcionista
   Situación: El/la viajero/a está listo/a para salir y quiere pagar su cuenta pero sólo tiene cheques de viajero. El hotel no los puede aceptar. Es domingo y los bancos están cerrados.
5. **Personajes:** Viajero/a e inspector de aduana

Peter Southwick/Stock, Boston

Situación: El/la viajero/a acaba de volver del extranjero, donde compró una guitarra excelente por el equivalente de unos cincuenta dólares, pero no tiene el recibo (*receipt*). El inspector no lo cree y dice que el/la viajero/a tiene que pagar unos cincuenta dólares más de derechos.

E. **¿Cómo es nuestro hotel?** Muchos hoteles piden que sus huéspedes llenen un formulario como el siguiente, indicando lo bueno y lo malo del hotel. Piense Ud. en un hotel/motel/pensión que conoce o que otra persona le ha descrito. ¿Cómo lo/la evaluaría? ¿Se quedaría allí otra vez? ¿Por qué?

Hotel Colón

Favor de llenar, cerrar y entregar en la recepción.

Fecha _____   Habitación _____

	Excelente	Bueno	Regular	Malo
1. ¿Cómo fue atendida su reservación?				
2. ¿Cómo se efectuó su registro [*registration*]? ¿con rapidez? ¿con cortesía?				
3. ¿Cómo encontró su habitación? ¿limpia? ¿cómoda y agradable?				
4. ¿Cómo encontró nuestro restaurante? ¿la comida? ¿el servicio?				
5. ¿Cómo encontró nuestra lavandería [*laundry*]? ¿calidad? ¿rapidez de servicio? ¿cortesía del personal?				
6. ¿Qué opina Ud. de la cortesía y eficiencia del siguiente personal? ¿botones? ¿telefonistas? ¿recepcionistas? ¿camareras [*maids*]?				

¿Es esta su primera estancia [*stay*] en nuestro hotel? _____

Observaciones: _____

Lectura cultural: Dos museos hispánicos

De todos los museos del mundo hispánico, los dos más conocidos son el Museo del Prado en Madrid y el Museo Nacional de Antropología en la ciudad de México.

El Museo del Prado se reconoce como uno de los museos más importantes del mundo. Su historia está íntimamente ligada° al amor al arte de los reyes españoles. Apasionados por el arte, casi todos los reyes, desde Isabel la Católica, compraban gran número de obras° para sus colecciones privadas. Por eso, cuando se abrió el Museo del Prado en 1819, las 311 pinturas exhibidas eran de las colecciones reales. Ahora el Prado tiene una colección de más de 2.000 pinturas, 360 esculturas y 4.000 dibujos de° España, Italia, Bélgica, Holanda, Alemania, Francia y otros países.

Siendo la galería nacional de España, el Prado tiene colecciones magníficas de los grandes pintores españoles del Siglo de Oro°. Hay 35 obras de El Greco (1548–1625), quien interpretaba las escenas religiosas de una manera única. También hay 50 obras de Velázquez (1599–1660), incluso la famosísima «Las Meninas°», que está exhibida en su propia sala. De los otros grandes pintores españoles hay 40 obras de Murillo (1617–1682), pintor de escenas religiosas, y 118 de Goya (1746–1828) más° 485 dibujos de éste°. Las pinturas de Goya se caracterizan sobre todo por su visión satírica de la política y de la sociedad de su época. La exhibición de las «pinturas negras» de Goya —pinturas que presentan una visión pesimista del hombre y de la civilización en general— es una de las más impresionantes del museo.

El Museo Nacional de Antropología, situado en el Parque de Chapultepec en la ciudad de México, es tal vez el mejor lugar del mundo para conocer la América de la época precolombina°. Este museo —el edificio en sí° una obra de arte— fue inaugurado en 1964 y contiene riquezas estupendas de las antiguas civilizaciones indígenas de México y Centroamérica. Las salas de exhibiciones, organizadas según las civilizaciones, están situadas alrededor de° un enorme patio (1). Las exhibiciones incluyen de todo, desde las piedras° y fósiles de las primeras civilizaciones preclásicas (1700–200 a.C.°) hasta los tesoros° aztecas encontrados por los españoles cuando llegaron a Tenochtitlán, la capital azteca, en 1519.

Además de figuras, urnas y otros artículos de valor artístico, se encuentran en el museo esculturas de algunos de los dioses principales y magníficas reproducciones de algunos de los templos más importantes. Por ejemplo, en la Sala de Teotihuacán se ve una estatua que pesa cincuenta y siete toneladas° y que representa a Chalchuitlicue, el dios de la lluvia (2). En la Sala Azteca se encuentra el famosísimo «Calendario azteca»(3). Esta obra, además de ser calendario, es un monumento al sol, cuya° cabeza aparece en el centro del calendario.

Las obras del Museo de Antropología son de tremenda importancia

linked

works (of art)

dibujos... *sketches from*

Siglo... *Golden Age*

Ladies in Waiting

plus
the latter

pre-Columbian, before Columbus
itself

alrededor... *around*
stones
antes de Cristo / *treasures*

tons

whose

1.

2.

© Marc & Evelyne Bernheim 1980/Woodfín Camp & Assoc.

3.

para el mundo y, en particular, para los mexicanos, descendientes de estas
antiguas civilizaciones.

Comprensión

Conteste las preguntas en oraciones completas.

1. ¿Qué relación existe entre los reyes españoles y algunas de las pinturas del Museo del Prado?
2. ¿Todas las pinturas que están en el Prado son de pintores españoles?
3. ¿Quiénes son algunos de los pintores españoles cuyas obras se ven?
4. ¿Cuáles son algunas de las pinturas más importantes del Prado?
5. ¿Dónde está el Museo Nacional de Antropología?
6. ¿Qué tipo de arte se encuentra en el Museo Nacional de Antropología?
7. ¿Cómo se organizan las obras en el museo?
8. ¿Cuáles son algunas de las cosas que el visitante puede ver allí?
9. Además de ser calendario, ¿qué representa el calendario azteca?

Ejercicios escritos

A. Escriba una descripción de un museo que Ud. ha visitado. Use estas preguntas
como guía.

   1. ¿Dónde está el museo?
   2. ¿Qué tipo de museo es?
   3. ¿Cuáles son algunas de las obras o exhibiciones más famosas del museo?
   4. ¿Qué le gusta más a Ud. de este museo?
   5. Si una persona tiene sólo una hora para ver este museo, ¿qué debe ver?

B. Describa una de las obras de arte que se ven en las fotos de esta lectura.

capítulo 19 Los hispanos en los Estados Unidos

Simone Oudot/EPA, Inc.

OBJETIVOS

In this chapter you will learn vocabulary and expressions related to family origins.

You will also learn about the following aspects of Spanish grammar:

74. how to form and use the simple past subjunctive: **hablara, comiera, viviera**
75. how to express conditional situations: **Si yo fuera tú, no lo haría** (*If I were you, I wouldn't*

do it)
76. how to coordinate the subjunctive tenses you know with the indicative tense used in the independent clause

Un paso más includes activities related to major Hispanic groups and the use of Spanish in the United States, and a reading about political history and revolutionary changes in Latin America.

VOCABULARIO: PREPARACIÓN

Los inmigrantes

los bienes	possessions (property)	**bilingüe**	bilingual
		por necesidad	out of necessity
la costumbre	custom	**acostumbrarse (a)**	to get used (to)
la cultura	culture	**añorar**	to long for
el/la exiliado/a	person in exile, expatriate	**emigrar**	to emigrate
		establecerse (establezco)	to establish oneself
el idioma	language	**mantener (ie)**	to maintain,
la patria	native land, homeland	**(mantengo)**	support (*a family, and so on*)
las raíces (la raíz)	roots		
el/la refugiado/a	refugee		
la tierra natal	native land, place of birth		

A. *Escoja* (choose) *la mejor manera de completar cada oración.*

1. **Querer a su patria** significa que uno quiere a _____.
   a. su papá b. su tierra natal c. su iglesia
2. Si una persona **añora** su patria _____.
   a. no quiere verla b. desea dejarla c. desea estar allí otra vez
3. **Emigrar** significa _____.
   a. salir de su país b. llegar a otro país c. quedarse en su país
4. Un **exiliado** es una persona que ha salido de su país _____.
   a. por gusto b. porque le gusta viajar c. por razones políticas
5. **Mantener a su familia** significa _____.
   a. pagar todos los gastos de la familia b. establecer una familia c. tener una familia grande
6. Las **costumbres** de un país son _____.
   a. su ropa más típica b. los precios en el mercado c. parte de su cultura

B. *Un exiliado cubano. Escoja las mejores palabras para llenar los espacios.*

Miguel García es un médico excelente que _____ de Cuba
(estableció/emigró/añoró)
después de la revolución de Fidel Castro. Miguel quería mucho a su patria

pero no podía vivir con el nuevo sistema político. Así, salió de Cuba por

_____ y llegó con su familia a los Estados Unidos en 1963. Trajeron
(gusto/necesidad)

solamente la ropa que tenían puesta. El gobierno cubano tampoco les dejó

sacar dinero, así que (*so*) llegaron sin un centavo.

La vida empieza otra vez cuando uno es un _____ político.
(ciudadano/refugiado)

Miguel tenía sus _____ en Cuba. Cuando se estableció
(refugiados/países/raíces)

en los Estados Unidos, tuvo que experimentar (*to experience*) muchos cambios.

El _____, por ejemplo, le representó un obstáculo para Miguel.
(idiota/idioma)

Sabía bastante (*a fair amount of*) gramática inglesa, pero hablarlo con

facilidad... eso era otra cosa. También tuvo que buscar trabajo. Aunque era

médico en su país, tuvo que trabajar en una fábrica (*factory*) para poder

_____ a su mujer y a sus tres hijos. Mientras tanto (*meanwhile*),
(emigar/mantener)

hizo la residencia en medicina y se examinó (*he took exams*) en el estado de

Florida, donde vivía. Por fin consiguió (*he obtained*) un buen puesto en un

hospital de Miami.

Además, los García tuvieron que _____ a una vida y a una
(acostarse/acostumbrarse)

cultura completamente diferentes, especialmente en cuanto a las _____
(costumbres/

_____ y las comidas. Por ejemplo, en _____
costas)   los Estados Unidos/su tierra natal)

se comía (arroz) congrí, lechón asado, plátanos fritos, pasta de guayaba*, café

expreso y muchos otros platos. También adoptaron una vida _____
(monolingüe/

_____. Hablaban español en casa pero inglés en la calle.
bilingüe)

Después de muchos años de exilio, Miguel y su familia se han _____
(acostumbrado/

_____ a la vida en los Estados Unidos. Ahora son ciudadanos de este
renunciado)

país aunque _____ siempre su tierra natal.
(mantendrán/añorarán)

C. *Los chicanos son personas de descendencia mexicana o mexicano-americana que
   viven en los Estados Unidos y que consideran que los Estados Unidos es su patria.
   De las frases siguientes, dos no describen a los chicanos. ¿Cuáles son las frases
   falsas?*

   1. Los chicanos viven solamente en California y Tejas.
   2. Muchos de los chicanos del oeste son descendientes de mexicanos que se
      establecieron allí en el siglo (*century*) XIX o antes.

***arroz...** rice mixed with black beans, roast (suckling) pig, fried plantains (large, coarse bananas used
for cooking), guava paste

© Abigail Heyman/Magnum

3. Todos los chicanos con apellidos hispanos hablan el idioma español.
4. Muchos chicanos católicos tienen la costumbre de venerar a la Virgen de Guadalupe.
5. Como tienen sus raíces culturales en México, los chicanos comen muchas comidas mexicanas como pan dulce (*sweet rolls*) y chocolate, tacos y tortillas, frijoles y arroz.
6. El Cinco de Mayo es una fiesta mexicana celebrada por muchos chicanos.

Pero and *Sino*

Sino means *but* when *but* implies *but rather* or *but on the contrary*. Thus **sino** is used to contradict or give the opposite of a preceding negative.

No es **rico sino pobre.**	*He isn't rich but (rather) poor.*
No van **al cine sino a la playa.**	*They're not going to the movies but (rather) to the beach.*

When there is no contradiction, **pero** (*but, on the other hand, yet*) is used, even after a negative.

No es rico, **pero** es amable.	*He isn't rich, but he's nice.*

---

1. *Falso.* Los chicanos se han establecido en casi todas partes de los Estados Unidos. 2. *Verdad.* 3. *Falso.* Algunos chicanos son bilingües, pero otros son monolingües. No todas las personas con apellidos españoles hablan español. 4. *Verdad.* La Virgen de Guadalupe es la santa patrona de México (página 338). 5. *Verdad.* 6. *Verdad.* En México esta fiesta conmemora la batalla de Puebla, el 5 de mayo de 1863, entre los franceses que invadían el país y las fuerzas mexicanas.

D. *Llene los espacios con la palabra apropiada:* **pero** *o* **sino**.

1. La casa que me gusta no es blanca _____ amarilla.
2. No tengo bolígrafo _____ lápiz.
3. Tengo un lápiz _____ no tengo bolígrafo.
4. El idioma materno de Carlos no es el inglés _____ el español.
5. Pepe no tiene mucho dinero _____ vive bien.
6. Félix no comió allí por gusto _____ por necesidad.
7. Nuestro abogado no es simpático _____ es muy inteligente.
8. Ramón no trabaja mucho _____ gana mucho dinero.
9. Los García no querían quedarse _____ emigrar.
10. El Canadá no es su tierra natal _____ su país de exilio.

E. *Llene los espacios para formar oraciones lógicas.*

1. __(nombre)__ no es soltero/a sino _____.
2. __(nombre)__ no es antipático/a sino _____.
3. Yo no soy _____ sino _____.
4. Yo no soy de _____ sino de _____.
5. Este verano no voy a _____ sino a _____.
6. No quiero ser _____ sino _____.

MINIDIÁLOGOS Y GRAMÁTICA

74. PAST SUBJUNCTIVE

Idénticos pero diferentes

MAMÁ: A comer, todos.

RAÚL: ¡Qué bien huele!, mamá. El arroz, los frijoles, el mole... Pero, ¿dónde están las tortillas de maíz?

MAMÁ: ¿De maíz? Pediste que las *hiciera* de harina y así las hice.

RAÚL: No, mamá. Juanita las quería de harina; yo quería que las *prepararas* de maíz. Son las mejores, ¿no sabes?

MAMÁ: Ay, mi hijo... creo que en todo el mundo no hay dos gemelos que tengan gustos tan diferentes. Ándale pues, la próxima vez te las preparo de maíz.

The same but different MAMÁ: Let's eat, everybody. RAÚL: Gee, it smells good, mom. Rice, beans, the mole (turkey in chocolate-base chili sauce) . . . But where are the corn tortillas? MAMÁ: Corn? You asked me to make them from (wheat) flour, and that's what I did. RAÚL: No, mom. Juanita wanted them out of (wheat) flour; I wanted you to make them from corn. They're the best, don't you think? MAMÁ: Oh, my son . . . I think that in all the world there aren't two twins who have such different tastes. OK, I'll make them from corn the next time.

1. ¿Quién ha preparado la comida?
2. ¿Cómo quería Raúl que su mamá hiciera las tortillas?
3. ¿De qué quería Juanita que las hiciera?
4. ¿En qué son idénticos Raúl y Juanita?   ¿En qué no son idénticos?

In Spanish, although there are two simple indicative past tenses (preterite and imperfect), there is only one simple subjunctive past tense, **el imperfecto del subjuntivo** (*past subjunctive*).   Its exact English equivalent depends on the context in which it appears.

Forms of the Past Subjunctive

PAST SUBJUNCTIVE OF REGULAR VERBS*		
HABLAR: hablarǿǿ	**COMER:** comierǿǿ	**VIVIR:** vivierǿǿ
hablara habláramos	comiera comiéramos	viviera viviéramos
hablaras hablarais	comieras comierais	vivieras vivierais
hablara hablaran	comiera comieran	viviera vivieran

The past subjunctive endings **-a, -as, -a, -amos, -ais, -an** are identical for **-ar, -er,** and **-ir** verbs.   These endings are added to the third-person plural of the preterite indicative, minus its **-on** ending.   For this reason, the forms of the past subjunctive reflect the irregularities of the preterite.

Stem-changing verbs
  -Ar and **-er** verbs: no change

> **empezar (ie):** empezarǿǿ → **empezara, empezaras, empezara, empezáramos, empezarais, empezaran**
> **volver (ue):** volvierǿǿ → **volviera, volvieras, volviera, volviéramos, volvierais, volvieran**

  -Ir verbs: all persons of the past subjunctive reflect the vowel change in the third-person plural of the preterite.

> **dormir (ue, u):** durmierǿǿ → **durmiera, durmieras, durmiera, durmiéramos, durmierais, durmieran**
> **pedir (i, i):**   pidierǿǿ → **pidiera, pidieras, pidiera, pidiéramos, pidierais, pidieran**

---

*An alternate form of the past subjunctive (used primarily in Spain) ends in **-se: hablase, hablases, hablase, hablásemos, hablaseis, hablasen.** This form will not be practiced in *Puntos de partida.*

Spelling changes

i → y (caer, construir, creer, destruir, influir, leer, oir)

creer: creyer~~on~~ → **creyera, creyeras, creyera, creyéramos, creyerais, creyeran**

Verbs with irregular preterites

dar: dier~~on~~   → **diera, dieras, diera, diéramos, dierais, dieran**

decir:	dijer~~on~~ → **dijera**		**poner:**	pusier~~on~~ → **pusiera**
estar:	estuvier~~on~~ → **estuviera**		**querer:**	quisier~~on~~ → **quisiera**
haber:	hubier~~on~~ → **hubiera**		**saber:**	supier~~on~~ → **supiera**
hacer:	hicier~~on~~ → **hiciera**		**ser:**	fuer~~on~~ → **fuera**
ir:	fuer~~on~~ → **fuera**		**tener:**	tuvier~~on~~ → **tuviera**
poder:	pudier~~on~~ → **pudiera**		**venir:**	vinier~~on~~ → **viniera**

Uses of the Past Subjunctive

The past subjunctive usually has the same applications as the present subjunctive but is used for past events.

Quiero que **jueguen** por la tarde.	*I want them to play in the afternoon.*
Quería que **jugaran** por la tarde.	*I wanted them to play in the afternoon.*
Siente que no **estén** allí.	*He's sorry (that) they aren't there.*
Sintió que no **estuvieran** allí.	*He was sorry (that) they weren't there.*
Dudamos que se **equivoquen.**	*We doubt that they will make a mistake.*
Dudábamos que se **equivocaran.**	*We doubted that they would make a mistake.*

Remember that the subjunctive is used (1) after expressions of WILLING, EMOTION, and DOUBT; (2) after many IMPERSONAL EXPRESSIONS; (3) after OJALÁ (QUE); (4) after TAL VEZ/QUIZÁ(S) and AUNQUE to imply doubt or uncertainty; (5) after NONEXISTENT and INDEFINITE ANTECEDENTS; and (6) after certain CONJUNCTIONS: **a menos que, antes (de) que, con tal que, en caso de que, para que, sin que.**

¿Era necesario que **regatearas?**	*Was it necessary for you to bargain?*
Ojalá que tuvieran tiempo para ver Granada.	*I hope they had time to see Granada.*

No había nadie que **pudiera** resolverlo.	*There wasn't anyone who could (might have been able to) solve it.*
Los padres trabajaron **para que** sus hijos **asistieran** a la universidad.	*The parents worked so that their children might go to the university.*

 ¡OJO! When describing the past, the indicative forms—not the past subjunctive—are used after conjunctions of time: **cuando, después (de) que, en cuanto, hasta que, tan pronto como.**

Julio me llamó cuando llegó.	*Julius called me when he arrived.*

Deber, Poder, and Querer

The past subjunctive forms of **deber, poder,** and **querer** are used to soften a request or statement.

Debieras estudiar más.	*You really should study more.*
¿Pudieran Uds. traérmelo?	*Could you bring it for me?*
Quisiéramos hablar con Ud. en seguida.	*We would like to speak with you immediately.*

PRÁCTICA

A. Dé Ud. frases nuevas según las indicaciones.

1. —Su amigo cubano Rodolfo le contó a Ud. la historia de la inmigración de su familia a la Florida.   ¿Qué le dijo Ud.?
   —Ojalá que *todos* se acostumbraran sin problemas.   (*tú, Uds., Juan, Ángel y Ana, tus padres*)
2. —El Sr. Meléndez los invitó a Uds. a cenar en casa con su familia.   ¿Por qué?
   —El Sr. Meléndez quería que *nosotros* conociéramos algunas de las costumbres de su familia.   (*Juan, ellos, yo, todos, María*)
3. —¡Felicitaciones!   Casi estamos al final de este curso.   ¿Quién dudaba que fuera posible?
   —*Victor.* Él no creía que pudiéramos hacerlo.   (*tú, ellos, Ud., yo, nosotros, vosotros*)
4. —Cuando Ud. estudiaba en la secundaria, ¿qué le gustaba?
   —Me gustaba que nosotros _____.   (*estudiar idiomas, leer libros interesantes, ver películas en la clase de historia, hacer experimentos en la clase de física, bailar durante el almuerzo, divertirnos después de las clases*)
5. —¿Cómo era la vida de Ud. de niño/a?
   —Cuando yo era niño/a, mis padres querían que yo _____.   (*ser bueno/a, estudiar mucho, creer en Santa Claus, ponerse la ropa vieja para jugar, no jugar en las calles, no comer tantos dulces, tener amigos que se portaran bien*)

B. *Cambie según las indicaciones.*

    MODELO   *Quieren* que yo les escriba en su idioma. *(querían)* →
                        Querían que yo les *escribiera* en su idioma.

© Hella Hammid 1977/Photo Researchers, Inc.

   1. Pablo *insiste* en que yo le dé consejos. *(insistía)*
   2. *Preferimos* que digas la verdad. *(preferíamos)*
   3. Me *alegro* de que lo sepas. *(alegraba)*
   4. *Siento* que no tengas tiempo de visitar tu tierra natal. *(sentía)*
   5. *Dudamos* que emigren por necesidad. *(dudábamos)*
   6. No *creen* que te duela mucho. *(creían)*
   7. *Es* probable que un profesor chicano enseñe la clase. *(era)*
   8. No me *gusta* que duerman tanto. *(gustaba)*
   9. *Necesitan* un secretario que sea bilingüe. *(necesitaban)*
  10. No *hay* nadie que añore su patria como él. *(había)*
  11. Tal vez estén allí *hoy*. *(ayer)*
  12. Aunque tenga el dinero, no *irá*. *(iría)*

C. *Combine the following pairs of sentences, using the conjunction in parentheses.
Make any other necessary changes. ¡OJO! Remember that the past* indicative—
not the past subjunctive —is used after conjunctions of time. (Exception: **antes
de que.***)*

   1. Nunca corría allí. El perro me acompañaba. (a menos que)
   2. Me escribieron. Se establecieron. (en cuanto)

3. Me lo ofreció. Yo pude pedírselo a él. (antes de que)
4. Luis dijo que me despertaría. Yo lo desperté al día siguiente. (con tal que)
5. No pasaron a la sala de espera. El maletero facturó su equipaje. (hasta que)
6. Se casaron. Sus padres anunciaron su noviazgo. (después de que)
7. Te lo dije. Te reíste. (para que)
8. El refugiado no quería perder sus costumbres. Volvió a su patria. (en caso de que)
9. Se sorprendieron. Vieron a su hijo en aquel lugar. (cuando)
10. Nunca comían en aquel restaurante. El Sr. Gutiérrez les pagaba la cuenta. (sin que)
11. Salimos. Vinieron. (tan pronto como)
12. Les dimos una fiesta. Fueron a España. (antes de que)

D. *¿Cómo se dice en español?*

1. You really should visit the Jiménez' in El Paso.
2. Could you call me tonight?
3. I would like to see the green skirt.

CONVERSACIÓN

A. *¿Cómo completarían estas personas las frases siguientes?*

1. *Cristóbal Colón:* Casi todos dudaban que
2. *Neil Armstrong:* Yo esperaba que un día
3. *Miss Piggy:* Mis padres esperaban que un día yo
4. *Franklin Delano Roosevelt:* Yo temía que
5. *El rey Tut:* Dudaba que
6. *Marie Curie:* Pocos creían que yo

a. hubiera otra guerra mundial.
b. el mundo fuera redondo (*round*).
c. descubrieran mi tumba.
d. hiciera un descubrimiento magnífico.
e. llegara a ser una actriz famosa.
f. el hombre llegara a la luna.

B. *Preguntas*

1. ¿Insistió su profesor(a) en que Uds. estudiaran anoche? ¿Era importante que lo hicieran? ¿Era posible que no lo hicieran? ¿Por qué?
2. ¿De qué tenía Ud. miedo cuando era pequeño/a? ¿Era posible que ocurrieran cosas que Ud. temía? ¿Era probable que ocurrieran?
3. ¿Qué quería el gobierno que hicieran los ciudadanos el año pasado? ¿Quería que usaran menos gasolina? ¿que pagaran los impuestos? ¿que manejaran menos rápidamente? ¿Ud. lo hizo todo?
4. ¿Qué tipo de clase buscaba Ud. para este semestre? ¿clases que fueran fáciles? ¿interesantes? ¿Las encontró Ud.?

75. CONDITIONAL SENTENCES

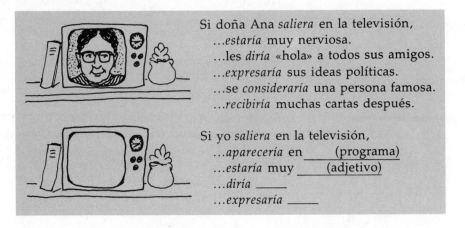

Si doña Ana *saliera* en la televisión,
...*estaría* muy nerviosa.
...les *diría* «hola» a todos sus amigos.
...*expresaría* sus ideas políticas.
...se *consideraría* una persona famosa.
...*recibiría* muchas cartas después.

Si yo *saliera* en la televisión,
...*aparecería* en _____ (programa)
...*estaría* muy _____ (adjetivo)
...*diría* _____
...*expresaría* _____

Dependent Clause: *Si* Clause	Independent Clause
Si <u>imperfect subjunctive</u>,	<u>conditional</u>

When a clause introduced by **si** (*if*) expresses a supposition, a hypothetical situation, or a contrary-to-fact situation, **si** is always followed by the past subjunctive. In such sentences, the verb in the independent clause is usually in the conditional, since the sentence expresses what one *would do or say* if the **si** clause were true.

Si yo **fuera** tú, no **haría** eso.	*If I were you, I wouldn't do that.**
Si se levantaran más temprano, **podrían** llegar a tiempo.	*If they got up earlier, they would be able to arrive on time.*
Iría a las montañas **si tuviera** tiempo.	*He would go to the mountains if he had the time.*

When the **si** clause is in the present tense, the present indicative is used—not the present subjunctive.

Si tiene tiempo, **irá** a las montañas.	*If he has time, he'll go to the moun-tains.*

If doña Ana appeared on television, . . . she would be very nervous. . . . she would say ''hello'' to all of her friends. . . . she would express her political views. . . . she would consider herself a famous person. . . . she would receive a lot of letters later. If I appeared on television, . . . I would appear on _____. . . . I would be very _____. . . . I would say _____. . . . I would express _____.

*English speakers frequently use the subjunctive after *if* (*If I were you* . . .) in conditional sentences, but this usage, like the use of the subjunctive in general, is inconsistent in contemporary English speech.

Como si (*as if, as though*) is always followed by the past subjunctive because it always indicates a condition contrary to fact.

Connie habla **como si fuera** española.	*Connie speaks as though she were Spanish.*

PRÁCTICA

A. *Dé frases nuevas según las indicaciones.*

1. —Su amigo Pablo necesita consejos. ¿Qué le dice Ud.?
   —Si yo _____, no lo haría. (*ser tú, estar allí, tener ese problema, tener que decidir, vivir allí*)
2. —¿Qué harían Uds. si estuvieran de vacaciones ahora?
   —Si estuviéramos de vacaciones, nosotros _____. (*tomar el sol en la playa, no tener que estudiar, poder pasarlo bien, no venir a clase, estar en un café, mandar unas tarjetas postales*)
3. —Su amiga Carlota es muy orgullosa (*proud*). ¿Cómo habla ella?
   —Carlota habla como si (ella) _____. (*ser rica, siempre tener razón, ser un experto en todo, saberlo todo*)

B. *Complete las oraciones en una forma lógica.*

1. Si necesitara comprar comida, iría a _____.
2. Si necesitara un libro, lo compraría en _____.
3. Si tuviera que emigrar, iría a _____.
4. Si tuviera sed, tomaría _____.
5. Si yo _____, comería un *sándwich*.
6. Si quisiera ir a _____, iría en avión.
7. Si quisiera tomar _____, esperaría en la estación.
8. Si _____ un libro, lo buscaría en la biblioteca.

C. *Exprese según el modelo.*

MODELO   Si tengo tiempo, iré. → *Si tuviera tiempo, iría.*

1. Llegaremos más rápidamente si doblas en esta esquina.
2. Si te equivocas, perderás todo el dinero.
3. Si no ganan, se enojarán.
4. No te lo perdonaré si me interrumpes.
5. Si te estacionas aquí, no tendremos que cruzar la calle.
6. Dejará de fumar si se enferma.

D. *¿Qué haría Ud. en estas situaciones? Explique su respuesta.*

1. Los señores Medina están durmiendo. De repente se oye un ruido. Un hombre con máscara y guantes (*gloves*) entra silenciosamente en la alcoba. **Si yo fuera _____.**

2. Celia está estudiando para un examen muy importante. Su compañero de cuarto se pone enfermo y lo tienen que llevar al hospital. No puede seguir estudiando para el examen y, a la mañana siguiente, no está lista para tomar el examen. **Si yo fuera** _____.

3. Los padres de Ana no quieren que se case con su novio Antonio, que vive en otro estado. Un día, Ana recibe una carta de Antonio, la lee y de repente sale de la casa. Deja la carta, abierta, en la mesa. **Si yo fuera** _____.

CONVERSACIÓN

Complete las oraciones en una forma lógica.

1. Si yo fuera presidente, yo _____.
2. Si yo estuviera en _____, _____.
3. Si tuviera un millón de dólares, _____.
4. Si yo pudiera _____, _____.
5. Si yo fuera _____, _____.
6. Si _____, (no) me casaría con él/ella.
7. Si _____, estaría contentísimo/a.
8. Si _____, estaría enojadísimo/a.

76. SEQUENCE OF TENSES WITH THE SUBJUNCTIVE

Un partido de béisbol

ALBERTO: ¿Trajiste el bate y la pelota?

EDUARDO: ¿Yo? Yo no. Alguien le *dijo* a Margarita que los *trajera* ella.

MARGARITA: A mí no. Me *pidieron* que yo *hiciera* el arroz. *Es* probable que los *traiga* Roberto.

ALBERTO: *Dudo* que se lo *hayamos pedido* a Roberto. Él trae la cerveza. Además, a él no le gusta nada el béisbol. ¿Qué hacemos?

MARGARITA: Mira, a mí no me importa volver a casa a buscarlos —*con tal que* no *coman* Uds. *antes de que* yo *vuelva.*

ALBERTO: Bueno, por lo menos te podemos prometer que sin ti no vamos a empezar el partido.

A baseball game ALBERTO: Did you bring the bat and ball? EDUARDO: Me? I didn't. Someone told Margarita to bring them. MARGARITA: Not me. They told me to bring the rice. Roberto is probably bringing them. ALBERTO: I doubt that we asked Roberto. He's bringing the beer. Besides, he doesn't like baseball. What'll we do? MARGARITA: Look, I don't mind going back home to get them—provided that you don't eat until I get back. ALBERTO: Well, at least we can promise you that we're not going to start the game without you.

Constantine Manos/Magnum

1. *¿Quién trajo el bate y la pelota?*
2. *¿Alguien le dijo a Margarita que los trajera?*
3. *¿Qué le pidieron a Margarita que hiciera?*
4. *¿Es probable que Roberto traiga el bate y la pelota?   ¿Por qué no?*
5. *¿Quién está dispuesto a volver a casa?*
6. *¿Qué teme Margarita?*
7. *¿Qué le promete Alberto?*

When the subjunctive is required in a subordinate clause, the subjunctive tenses appear with the indicative tenses in the following combinations:

INDEPENDENT (INDICATIVE) CLAUSE	DEPENDENT (SUBJUNCTIVE) CLAUSE
present present perfect command future	present subjunctive, present perfect subjunctive, past subjunctive, or past perfect subjunctive*
imperfect preterite past perfect conditional	past subjunctive or past perfect subjunctive

*The *past perfect subjunctive* (**pluscuamperfecto del subjuntivo**) is formed with the past subjunctive of **haber** plus the past participle: **hubiera hablado (ido, hecho), hubieras hablado (ido, hecho)** and so on. It is the equivalent of English *had spoken* (*gone, done*). The past perfect subjunctive forms of **haber** are **hubiera, hubieras, hubiera, hubiéramos, hubierais, hubieran.** The use of the past perfect subjunctive will not be stressed in *Puntos de partida.*

When the verb in the independent clause is a *present, future,* or *command* form, *any of the subjunctive tenses* can occur.

Me alegro de que
- **estés** aquí ahora.
- **hayas estado** aquí hoy.
- **estuvieras** allí anoche.

I'm glad that
- *you are here now.*
- *you have been here today.*
- *you were there last night.*

Busque un agente que
- **hable** español.
- **haya vivido** en México.
- **trabajara** antes en el extranjero.

Look for an agent who
- *speaks Spanish.*
- *has lived in México.*
- *worked abroad before.*

When the verb in the independent clause is a *past* or *conditional* form, either the *past subjunctive* or the *past perfect subjunctive* is used in the dependent clause; *past requires past.*

Me alegraba de que
- **estuvieras** allí.
- **hubieras estado** allí.

I was glad that
- *you were there.*
- *you had been there.*

Quería que nos **quedáramos.**   *He wanted us to stay. (He wanted that we stay.)*

Esperaba que **viniéramos.**   *She hoped (that) we would come.*

PRÁCTICA

A. *Dé Ud. frases nuevas según las indicaciones.*

1. Carmen *no permitía* que sus niños jugaran en la calle. (*no permite, no permitirá, no permitió, nunca ha permitido*)
2. *Es* necesario que se acostumbren a la vida aquí. (*era, será, fue, sería, ha sido*)
3. *Esperaban* que saliera el vuelo. (*esperan, esperarán, esperaron*)

B. *Llene los espacios con una forma correcta del verbo indicado.*

1. *añorar:*   Es probable que ellos _____ su patria.
                Era probable que ellos _____ su patria.
2. *aprender:* Él estudiará el idioma hasta que lo _____ bien.
                Él estudió el idioma hasta que lo _____ bien. (¡OJO!)
3. *conocer:*   Van a visitar su pueblo natal en México para que los hijos _____ sus raíces.
                El verano pasado visitaron su pueblo natal en México para que los hijos _____ sus raíces.
4. *ser:*   En toda la compañía no hay ni un empleado que _____ extranjero.

En toda la compañía no había ni un empleado que _____ extranjero.

5. *acostumbrarse:* No es fácil que tú _____ a la nueva cultura.

No sería fácil que tú _____ a la nueva cultura.

C. ¿Cómo se dice en español?

We are sorry that they had to leave all of their belongings behind. We insist that they accept **(aceptar)** our help. It will be easy for them **(que ellos)** to support themselves just as soon as they have found employment.

D. *Llene los espacios con la forma apropiada del verbo—indicativo o subjuntivo.*

Ayer, Carmen _____ tarde a la oficina, a las nueve y veinticuatro.
      (llegar)

_____ sin que su jefe la _____. A las seis de la tarde, mientras
   (entrar)   (ver)

ella se _____ para salir, le _____ el jefe que se _____ para que
      (preparar)   (pedir)   (quedar)

los dos _____ un proyecto importante. Era una lástima que Carmen
        (terminar)

_____ que quedarse hasta tan tarde ayer. Ojalá que mañana _____
   (tener)   (poder)

salir temprano.

CONVERSACIÓN

A. *Describa este dibujo, completando estas frases y añadiendo* (adding) *otras.*

John se encontraba _____. No hablaba _____ y no había nadie que _____. Esperaba que _____ pero dudaba que _____. Era lástima que _____. Ojalá que _____.

B. *Complete las oraciones en una forma lógica.*

1. En la secundaria yo siempre quería que mis amigos _____. Ahora quiero que mis amigos _____.

2. ¡Qué malo que mi amigo/a __(nombre)__ (no) haya _____!

3. Antes me gustaba que mis profesores _____. Ahora prefiero que _____.

4. En el año 1900 no había nadie que pudiera _____. Ahora no hay nadie que _____.

DIÁLOGO: Un *picnic* en el parque

A. *En casa de una familia puertorriqueña*[1] *de Nueva York. Es domingo por la mañana.*

ABUELA: ¿Te gustaría que comiéramos hoy en el Parque Central?

ABUELO: Ay, ¿qué más quisiera yo°? Había pensado en sugerir esto, pero no te dije nada.   **quisiera...** *could I possibly want*

ABUELA: Tal vez pudiéramos llamar a los hijos para que vengan ellos también. ¿Qué te parece?

ABUELO: Sí, diles que no vengan solos, sino con los nietos... podemos invitar a todos los familiares°. Un *picnic* como hacíamos antes.   *relatives*

ABUELA: Eso, sí —¡como si estuviéramos otra vez en Puerto Rico!

B. *Hablan por teléfono.*

HIJA: ¿Quieres que traiga algo, mamá?

ABUELA: No te preocupes, mujer. Estoy preparando comida para todos y espero que en una hora todo esté listo.

HIJA: Mira, tengo aquí en casa unos pastelillos[2] y un postre. Si quieres, los llevo.

ABUELA: ¿Pastelillos de carne? ¡Cómo me gustan! Claro que quiero que los traigas.

HIJA: Ni de carne ni de queso, mamá, sino de guayaba[3].

ABUELA: ¡Todavía mejor! Estos son los más ricos de todos.

C. *Más tarde. Toda la familia en el Parque Central.*

NIETA: Abuelito, ¿qué te gusta más: vivir en Nueva York o vivir en Puerto Rico?

ABUELO: Pues, entre Borinquen y la Babel de Hierro[4], preferimos vivir en nuestra tierra natal.

NIETA: Entonces°, ¿por qué estamos aquí?   *then*

ABUELO: Porque perdí mi finca, hija, y entre la falta de trabajo allí y la posibilidad de un trabajo bien pagado aquí, tu abuela y yo optamos por emigrar.

NIETA: Pero en los Estados Unidos no somos inmigrantes sino ciudadanos americanos.

ABUELO: No es que seamos inmigrantes sino que somos de otra cultura, de otra región geográfica, de otra lengua. Mira, tú has nacido aquí; para ti es diferente. Para nosotros, Puerto Rico es nuestra patria. La isla es muy pequeña; tiene sus riquezas°, pero son insuficientes para la población.   *riches*

NIETA: ¿Por eso han salido tantos puertorriqueños de su tierra?

ABUELO: Algunos sí. No han salido por gusto sino por necesidad.

NIETA: ¿Qué será de Puerto Rico en el futuro, abuelito? ¿Crees que algún día será un estado de la Unión?

ABUELO: No sé, hijita, pero siempre será nuestra patria.

Comprensión

Conteste las preguntas en oraciones completas.

A. 1. ¿Qué sugiere la abuela?
    2. ¿En qué había pensado el abuelo?
    3. ¿A quiénes van a invitar?
    4. ¿Dónde hacían antes este tipo de *picnic* familiar?

B. 1. ¿Qué va a llevar la hija? ¿Quién va a llevar el resto de la comida?
    2. ¿Qué tipo de pastelillos le gustan más a la abuela?

C. 1. ¿Qué otro nombre le da el abuelo a Puerto Rico? ¿a Nueva York?
    2. De los dos lugares, ¿cuál les gusta más a los abuelos?
    3. ¿Por qué viven, entonces, en Nueva York?
    4. ¿Qué sentimientos tiene el abuelo hacia Puerto Rico?
    5. ¿Por qué son diferentes los sentimientos del abuelo y los de la nieta?
    6. ¿Por qué han salido muchos puertorriqueños de la isla?
    7. ¿Añora el abuelo Puerto Rico? ¿Cómo se sabe eso?

Comentario cultural

1. Puerto Rico was a colony of Spain for over four hundred years. In 1898, at the end of the Spanish American War, the island became a territory of the United States. Puerto Ricans were granted full United States citizenship in 1917, and in 1952 Puerto Rico became a self-governing commonwealth associated with the United States. In 1967 the people of Puerto Rico reaffirmed their commonwealth status. A sizeable number of Puerto Ricans favor statehood or independence, however, and the question is still an important issue in island politics.

   Puerto Rico is one of the most densely populated areas of the world. Thousands of Puerto Ricans have emigrated to the mainland, settling primarily in the industrial cities of the east, where they have had a major impact on population and culture. For example, approximately 15 percent of the population of New York City is of Puerto Rican origin. Often the first members of a family to migrate to the mainland lack education and specialized training and must therefore work as unskilled laborers. Their hope is that their children and grandchildren, with better education and training, will be able to move upward.

   Puerto Ricans who migrate to the mainland bring with them their language and their traditional cultural patterns and values. Of primary importance is the solidarity of the family. Family members tend to live close to one another and visit regularly.

2. **Pastelillos** are small turnovers, or pastries, filled with meat, cheese, or fruit.

3. **Guayaba** (*guava*) is a tropical fruit of the West Indies. It is used in making preserves, jellies, and **pastelillos.**

4. **Borinquen** refers to Puerto Rico, and **borinqueños** are Puerto Ricans. The words are derived from **Boriquén,** the native name for the island when Columbus arrived in 1493. **Babel de Hierro** (*Babel of Iron*) refers to New York City.

UN POCO DE TODO

A. *Cambie por el pasado.*

1. Si se establece pronto, estará contento.
2. Siguen negando que sean los ladrones.
3. No creo que lo conozcas tú.
4. Es muy probable que ya te extrañen.
5. Siento que no puedan mantenerse fácilmente.

B. *Choose the verb that best completes the following sentences.*

1. Tomás está trabajando en el patio. Dígale que _____ a la casa en seguida. Tiene una llamada urgente.
   a. volviera b. vuelva c. haya vuelto
2. Teníamos que encontrar la dirección de Luisa. Preguntamos por todas partes, pero no había nadie que la _____.
   a. sepa b. haya sabido c. supiera

3. ¿El inventario? Lo estarán preparando ahora para que yo lo _____ mañana.
   a. haya visto b. vea c. viera
4. Mi hermano arreglaría el coche si no _____ bien.
   a. funcionara b. funcione c. haya funcionado
5. Es lástima que tengan que esperar tanto para emigrar. Ojalá que _____ pronto.
   a. emigraran b. emigren c. hayan emigrado
6. ¿Ya lo sabes? Es imposible que ya te lo _____.
   a. digan b. hayan dicho c. se digan

C. *What is, or was, your reaction to the following situations?* *Begin your sentences with* **Yo prefiero que** *or* **Yo quería que,** *according to the tense of the sentence. Use the information given in parentheses.*

1. Anoche mi amigo y yo fuimos a ver una película italiana. (latina)
2. Susana quiere que vayamos al campo. Pedro insiste en que vayamos a las montañas. (playa)
3. Nosotros emigramos por fin en el año 1977. (más temprano)
4. La tía Elena insiste en que vayamos en carro. Los niños quieren volar. (en autobús)
5. El verano pasado, mi amigo y yo alquilamos una casa vieja y en malas condiciones. (nueva, con todas las comodidades)
6. Nuestros niños son monolingües. (bilingües)

D. *Describe the experiences and feelings of someone who has recently come to this country by completing the following sentences.*

1. Antes de llegar, Antonio temía que _____.
   Antes de emigrar, Antonio esperaba que _____.
   Si no emigrara, Antonio _____.

   - no poder encontrar trabajo él y su esposa
   - no acostumbrarse todos fácilmente a la nueva cultura
   - no aprender sus hijos el idioma
   - tener ellos que dejarlo todo
   - encontrar la familia una vida mejor
   - haber más libertad política aquí
   - quedarse en su tierra natal
   - no tener que establecerse en otro país

2. Ahora se alegra de que _____.
   Ahora insiste en que _____.

   - haber emigrado todos
   - hablar los dos idiomas sus hijos
   - mantenerse en casa las costumbres viejas
   - estar contentos todos en el nuevo país
   - mantener contacto con los parientes en la tierra natal
   - conocer los hijos sus raíces

VOCABULARIO

VERBOS

acostumbrarse (a)   to get used (to)
añorar   to long for
considerar   to consider, think
emigrar   to emigrate
escoger (escojo)   to choose, select
establecerse   to establish oneself
mantener (ie) (mantengo)   to maintain, support (*a family, and so on*)
ocurrir   to happen, occur
significar   to mean
sugerir (ie, i)   to suggest

SUSTANTIVOS

el **arroz**   rice
los **bienes**   possessions (*property*)
el **cambio**   change

la **costumbre**   custom
el/la **cubano/a**   Cuban
la **cultura**   culture
el/la **chicano/a**   Chicano
el/la **exiliado/a**   person in exile, expatriate
el **exilio**   exile
la **falta**   lack
los **frijoles**   beans
la **guayaba**   guava
el/la **inmigrante**   immigrant
la **isla**   island
el/la **ladrón/ladrona**   thief
el/la **mexicano-americano/a**   Mexican-American
el **partido**   game (*in sports*)
el **pastelillo**   small turnover, pastry
la **patria**   native land, homeland

el/la **puertorriqueño/a**   Puerto Rican
la **raíz** (*pl.* **raíces**)   root
el/la **refugiado/a**   refugee
la **tierra natal**   native land, place of birth

ADJETIVOS

bilingüe   bilingual
monolingüe   monolingual
natal   native, of birth
político/a   political

PALABRAS Y EXPRESIONES ÚTILES

como si   as if, as though
por gusto   willingly
por necesidad   out of necessity
sino   but (rather)

Un paso más 19

Actividades

A. **Las raíces de la familia.** Los Estados Unidos se considera el crisol (*melting pot*) de las razas y muchas familias americanas tienen historias muy interesantes. Hoy día muchas personas hacen investigaciones para aprender más de la historia de sus antepasados (*ancestors*). ¿Qué piensa Ud. de este fenómeno? ¿Qué sabe Ud. de sus antepasados?

1. En su opinión, ¿es importante saber la historia de su familia? ¿Por qué sí o por qué no?
2. ¿Ha estudiado Ud. la historia de su propia familia? ¿Sabe mucho de ella?
3. ¿Dónde nacieron sus padres? ¿sus abuelos? ¿sus bisabuelos (*great grandparents*)?
4. ¿Cuándo vinieron a los Estados Unidos sus antepasados? ¿Sabe Ud. algo de su vida durante los primeros años en este país? Comente.

5. ¿Hay en su familia alguna comida típica que represente su herencia (*heritage*) cultural? ¿Cómo se llama? ¿Sabe Ud. prepararla?

6. ¿Hay costumbres o tradiciones familiares que se derivan de su herencia cultural? ¿celebraciones familiares o religiosas?

7. ¿Hay artículos—fotografías, ropa, artículos decorativos, por ejemplo—que recuerdan (*bring to mind*) la historia cultural de su familia? ¿De quién(es) son estos artículos? ¿Qué importancia tienen?

8. ¿Ha visitado Ud. la tierra natal de sus antepasados o quiere visitarla en el futuro? Comente.

B. «**Balota de Votante Ausente.**» En muchas partes de los Estados Unidos se encuentran documentos bilingües y a veces hasta trilingües. La siguiente solicitud para «balota de votante ausente» está escrita en inglés y en español. Busque las respuestas a las siguientes preguntas. Los números entre paréntesis indican la sección de la solicitud donde se encuentran las palabras necesarias. ¡OJO! Note que hay varios anglicismos: balota, aplicación, registrar, área postal.

1. ¿Qué significa **elección** (2)? ¿**electoral** (6)? ¿Cuál es la diferencia entre las dos palabras?

APPLICATION FOR ABSENT VOTER'S BALLOT
APLICACIÓN PARA BALOTA DE VOTANTE AUSENTE

	FOR REGISTRAR'S USE ONLY
	SOLAMENTE PARA USO DEL REGISTRAR

1. PRINTED NAME
LETRAS DE IMPRENTA Application MUST ALSO BE SIGNED BELOW BY APPLICANT. Signature will be compared with affidavit on file in this office.

2. ELECTION DATE _____

I hereby apply for an Absent Voter's Ballot for the election indicated above.
I expect to be absent from my election precinct on the day of the election or unable to vote therein by reason of physical disability or other reason provided by law.

Por la presente solicito una balota de Votante Ausente para la elección indicada arriba. Espero estar ausente de mi precinto electoral en el día de la elección o no poder votar allí física u otra razón prevista por la ley.

Prec. No. _____
Pol. Affil. _____
Ballot No. _____
Ballot Mailed _____
Ballot Returned _____
Aff. Record _____
Inspector's Notice _____
Signature and Registration
Verified as Correct:

_____   _____
Date   Deputy Registrar

3. BALLOT TO BE MAILED TO ME AT:
ENVÍEME LA BALOTA A:

6. ☐ I prefer election materials in English
☐ *Prefiero materiales electorales en español*

_____ Zip Code
Área Postal _____

DATE:
FECHA: _____

5. _____

Address of Applicant
Dirección del solicitante

4. _____
SIGNATURE OF APPLICANT IN FULL
FIRMA COMPLETA DEL SOLICITANTE

IF YOU HAVE MOVED
Complete this section if you have moved and now reside at an address other than that shown on your affidavit of registration.

I moved on _____ 19_____.

My residence address is _____

_____ Zip Code _____

NOTE: A voter moving within 29 days prior to this election may obtain an absentee ballot..A voter moving more than 29 days prior to this election and who did not re-register prior to the registration closing date for this election is not eligible to vote.

7.   *SI USTED SE HA CAMBIADO*
Complete esta sección si usted se ha cambiado y reside ahora en otra direcci. distinta a la que aparece en su declaración jurada de registro.

Me cambié el _____ *de 19_____*

Mi dirección es _____

_____ *Área Postal* _____

NOTA: Un votante que se cambia dentro de los 29 días anteriores a esta elección puede obtener balota ausente. Un votante que se cambia antes de los 29 días anteriores de la elección y que no se registro antes de la fecha final para registrarse de esta elección no puede votar.

8. MAIL TO: ABSENT VOTING SECTION
ENVIAR A: **REGISTRAR OF VOTERS OFFICE**

APPLICATION MUST BE RECEIVED IN REGISTRAR'S OFFICE
BY 5:00 P.M., TUESDAY, _____
7 DAYS BEFORE ELECTION DAY.

9. *LA SOLICITUD DEBE RECIBIRSE EN LA OFICINA DEL REGISTRAR ANTES DE LAS CINCO EN PUNTO DE LA TARDE. MARTES,*
_____ *EL SÉPTIMO DÍA ANTERIOR AL DÍA DE LA ELECCIÓN.*

DO NOT WRITE IN THIS AREA

2. ¿Qué significa **solicitar** (2)?   ¿**solicitud** (9)?   ¿**solicitante** (4)?

3. La frase **por la presente** (2) se refiere a una solicitud.   ¿Qué significa esta frase?

4. ¿Cómo se dice *to vote* (2)?   ¿*voter* (2)?

5. ¿Cómo se dice *foreseen* o *provided for* (2)?

6. **Esperar** puede significar *to hope*.   ¿Qué más puede significar (2)?

7. Encuentre un sinónimo de **mande** (imperativo) (3).

8. ¿Qué significa **firma** (4)?

9. Encuentre un sinónimo de **vive** (7).

10. Encuentre un sinónimo de **diferente** (7).

C. **¿Sabía Ud.?**   ¿Qué sabe Ud. de los grupos étnicos de los Estados Unidos? Tome el siguiente *test*.   Las respuestas se encuentran después del *test*.

1. Según en censo de 1970 casi _____ de americanos—o sus padres—nacieron en otro país.

    a. dos millones   b. catorce millones   c. treinta y cuatro millones

2. De las personas que han emigrado a los Estados Unidos, _____ son hispanos.

    a. el 60 por ciento   b. el 15 por ciento   c. el 5 por ciento

3. Hay más de _____ de hispanos en los Estados Unidos.

    a. 50 millones   b. 12 millones   c. 35 millones

4. De los hispanos que viven en los Estados Unidos, el _____ por ciento son puertorriqueños, el _____ por ciento son mexicano-americanos y el _____ por ciento son cubanos.

    a. 15, 60, 6   b. 30, 40, 10   c. 50, 25, 25

5. En San Antonio, Tejas, más del _____ de la población es de linaje (*ancestry*) mexicano.

    a. 20 por ciento   b. 35 por ciento   c. 50 por ciento

6. En Nueva Orleans hay más de _____ hispanos, muchos de ellos de Centro América.

    a. 10 mil   b. 100 mil   c. 500 mil

7. En Hartford, Connecticut, el _____ por ciento de los estudiantes son hispanos; la mayoría son de familias puertorriqueñas o cubanas.

    a. 6   b. 15   c. 34

1. c 2. b 3. b 4. a 5. c 6. b 7. c

A propósito...

Like English, Spanish has many different dialects.   Here are a few expressions that you are likely to hear if you listen carefully to the speech of Hispanics in the United States.   Although these expressions are typical of the following groups, they are not limited to them.

Expresiones mexicanas

Ándale.	*Está bien. OK*	**prieto/a**	*moreno/a, negro/a*
Ven pa'cá.	*Ven aquí/acá.*	**güero/a**	*rubio/a*
¡Qué chulo!	*¡Qué lindo/bonito/ precioso!*	**la pachanga**	*la fiesta*

Expresiones puertorriqueñas

¡Chévere!	*¡Magnífico! ¡Estupendo!*
¿Tienes chavos?	*¿Tienes dinero?*
un(a) jíbaro/a	*un(a) campesino/a (puertorriqueño/a)*

Expresiones cubanas

la guagua *el autobús*	**Es un pollo.** *Es una chica bonita.*

In many words and expressions, the *s* sound is pronounced as a sound similar to English *h:* **adióh** = *adiós;* **máh** = *más;* **loh libroh** = *los libros.*

Anglicismos

Because **hispanos** who live in the United States come into constant contact with the English language, it is natural that they borrow words from English and adapt them to the norms of Spanish pronunciation and grammar.   English has done the same with many Spanish words: *vamoose* = **vamos;** *alligator* = **el lagarto** (*the lizard*).   Here are some words that some Spanish speakers have borrowed from English.   Say these words aloud.   What English verbs do they sound like?

chequear   espeliar   flonquear   wachar

D. **¿Comprende Ud.?** ¿Sabe Ud. comunicarse con algunos hispanos que viven en los Estados Unidos? Si oye las expresiones en la columna A, ¿cómo va a contestar?

A	B
1. Acabo de perder la guagua.	a. No, gracias. Ya he comido mucho.
2. Ven pa'cá, amigo.	b. No, conozco a un Pablo, pero es güero.
3. ¿Tienes chavos?	
4. ¿Conoces a Teresita?	c. ¡Chévere! ¿Me prestará cien?
5. ¿No quiereh máh?	d. No te preocupes. Vendrá otra dentro de diez minutos.
6. Esta noche voy a una pachanga en casa de Mario.	e. Sí, señor. ¡Es un pollo!
7. ¿Conoces a Pablo Cervantes? Es prieto.	f. ¿Por qué? ¿Qué quieres que haga?
8. Aquí viene la señora Reyes con su niño.	g. ¡No! ¡Jíbaro soy y jíbaro seré!
9. Mi mamá acaba de ganar mil dólares en la lotería.	h. Yo no. Mañana nos pagarán.
10. ¿No quieres venir a vivir a la ciudad?	i. ¡Qué chulo! ¿Cómo se llama el chamaco?
	j. Ándale... pues yo te acompaño si quieres.

E. **Si el mundo fuera diferente...**   Adaptarse a un nuevo país o a nuevas circun-
stancias es difícil, pero también es una aventura interesante.   ¿Qué ocurriría
si el mundo fuera diferente?

MODELO   Si yo fuera la última persona en el mundo
→ tendría que aprender a hacer muchas cosas.
sería la persona más importante —y más ignorante— del mundo.
me adaptaría fácilmente/difícilmente.
los animales y yo nos haríamos buenos amigos.

1. Si yo pudiera tener solamente un(a) amigo/a, _____.
2. Si yo tuviera que pasar un año en una isla desierta, _____.
3. Si yo fuera (nombre de otra persona), _____.
4. Si el presiden*te* fuera presiden*ta*, _____.
5. Si yo viviera en otro país, _____.
6. Si fuera el año 2080, _____.
7. Si yo tuviera que pasar el resto de mi vida en una prisión, _____.
8. Si yo pudiera pedir y recibir cualquier cosa —pero solamente una cosa—,
_____.
9. Si yo fuera la persona más poderosa (*powerful*) del mundo, _____.
10. Si fuera el año 1776, _____.
11. Si los estudiantes fueran profesores y los profesores fueran estudiantes,
_____.

Lectura cultural: La revolución hispanoamericana

Desde la primera gran revolución del siglo XX, la de México (que empezó
en 1910), hasta las luchas° recientes en Nicaragua, el siglo XX en Hispano-   *fighting*
américa ha sido una era de esfuerzos para lograr° profundos cambios   *to gain*
políticos, económicos y sociales.   Algunas manifestaciones de estos

© Elliott Erwitt 1968/Magnum

esfuerzos son los movimientos indigenistas° en países como Perú, Bolivia
y Ecuador; la guerra de guerrillas° en Venezuela, Colombia, Guatemala
y Nicaragua; y las revoluciones que han ocurrido en México, Chile y
Cuba.

*supporting the interests
of the Indian*
guerra... *guerrilla
warfare*

En algunos países, la lucha por lograr el poder político y económico ha
visto la participación activa de los guerrilleros. Uno de ellos, Ernesto
«Che» Guevara de la Argentina, se dedicó a la guerra de guerrillas en todo
el continente, en especial en Guatemala, Cuba y Bolivia, y aun en África.
Su teoría de la guerra de guerrillas ayudó a las fuerzas° de Fidel Castro
en la revolución cubana. Se cree que Guevara fue muerto° en Bolivia
mientras trataba de llevar hasta allá su movimiento guerrillero.

forces

killed

Otro guerrillero fue el padre Camilo Torres, cura izquierdista que ganó
un gran número de seguidores entre la gente urbana de Colombia.
Predicaba la reforma social con mucha emoción y religiosidad. Por fin
el padre dejó la iglesia y se unió definitivamente con los guerrilleros.
Fue muerto por las fuerzas armadas en 1965.

De todas las revoluciones latinoamericanas, la revolución mexicana ha
producido, quizá, los cambios más profundos. No ha resuelto todos
los problemas de México, pero ha tenido mucho efecto sobre el nacionalismo y el orgullo° que ahora sienten los mexicanos. Esta revolución,
que derrocó° al gobierno dictatorial de Porfirio Díaz, resultó en la na-
cionalización de la tierra mexicana, programas de reforma agraria (redis-
tribución de la tierra) y una constitución democrática y permanente para
los ciudadanos mexicanos.

pride

defeated

El caso de Cuba es bastante diferente porque la revolución resultó en un gobierno comunista, encabezado° por Fidel Castro. Al derrocar al   *headed* dictator Fulgencia Batista en 1959, Castro se declaró comunista. Propuso un programa que le diera a Cuba la igualdad social, el desarrollo° econó-   *development* mico y la independencia política. Desde 1959, con la ayuda de Rusia, Cuba ha seguido ese programa.

Lo importante de todos estos movimientos revolucionarios es que, en la mayor parte de los casos, los líderes cuentan con la colaboración de la gente campesina y de los infortunados de las áreas urbanas para implementar sus programas revolucionarios.

Comprensión

¿Cierto o falso? Corrija las oraciones falsas.

1. Che Guevara y Camilo Torres eran curas que practicaban la guerra de guerrillas en África.
2. Guevara participó en la revolución mexicana.
3. Muchos colombianos urbanos estaban de acuerdo con la filosofía política de Camilo Torres.
4. Las fuerzas armadas colombianas mataron a Camilo Torres porque él era demasiado religioso.
5. La revolución mexicana ha resuelto todos los problemas de México.
6. El nacionalismo y el orgullo de los mexicanos se deben en parte a la revolución.
7. Las revoluciones en México y Cuba derrocaron a gobiernos dictatoriales.
8. Cuba ha seguido el programa de Castro con la ayuda de España.
9. Los movimientos revolucionarios dependen en gran parte de la colaboración de los campesinos y de la gente urbana pobre.

Ejercicios escritos

A. ¿Qué piensa Ud. de las revoluciones? Exprese sus opiniones en el siguiente párrafo.

Las revoluciones son _____. Ocurren en los países del Tercer Mundo porque _____. (No) Podrían ocurrir en un país como los Estados Unidos porque _____. Las revoluciones (no) tienen que ser violentas porque _____. Si hubiera una revolución en nuestro país, yo (no) participaría activamente porque _____.

B. Escriba Ud. una carta al editor de un periódico o una revista, apoyando (*supporting*) o criticando uno de los siguientes temas:

1. el establecimiento de relaciones diplomáticas con Cuba
2. las relaciones diplomáticas entre los Estados Unidos y la China
3. el reconocimiento formal del idioma español como segunda lengua de los Estados Unidos
4. _____

capítulo 20 En el extranjero

Owen Franken/Stock, Boston

OBJETIVOS

This chapter includes vocabulary and expressions that will be useful in many everyday activities— at the post office and the drugstore, in the subway, and so on. This final section also includes activities related to slang used by Spanish-speaking students in various parts of the world, and provides a guide for tourists who visit the city of Madrid.

EN EL EXTRANJERO: PALABRAS ÚTILES

Los lugares		Las cosas	
el café	café	**el champú**	shampoo
el correo	post office	**el jabón**	soap
la estación del metro	metro (subway) stop	**la pasta dental**	toothpaste
la farmacia	pharmacy, drug-store	**la tarjeta postal**	postcard
la papelería	stationary store	**los fósforos**	matches
la parada del autobús	bus stop	**el papel para cartas**	stationery
la pastelería	pastry shop	**el paquete**	package
el quiosco	kiosk (*small outdoor stand where a variety of items are sold*)	**la revista**	magazine
		el sello	stamp
		el sobre	envelope
		el batido	drink similar to a milkshake
la tabacalera	tobacco stand/shop	**una copa/un trago**	(*alcoholic*) drink
		el pastelito	small pastry

Even though the place names in the preceding list are given as equivalents, the actual places may be very different in another country. The following letter will show you one aspect of "culture shock" as it was experienced by an American university student.

Barcelona

Querido Joe:

¡Cuánto siento que no hayas podido venir con nosotros en este viaje a España! Para que sigas practicando el español, te escribo en este idioma.

Quiero contarte el *shock* cultural que estoy pasando. Por ejemplo, en los EE.UU* siempre compro el champú en el supermercado. Pero esta mañana tuve que ir a una farmacia para comprarla. Aprendí que allí sólo venden medicinas y productos de higiene —jabón, pasta dental, champú, etcétera. No venden la variedad de cosas —dulces, tarjetas postales, etcétera— que se venden en las farmacias de los EE.UU.

Después necesitaba sellos para mandar unas cartas y le pregunté a un señor que esperaba en la parada del autobús dónde estaba el correo para poder comprarlos. Me dijo que no tenía que ir hasta el correo porque los sellos también se venden en las tabacaleras. Como había una tabacalera enfrente, entré. Allí no sólo vendían fósforos, cigarrillos y puros (*cigars*) sino también sellos, sobres y tarjetas postales.

*EE.UU. is one way to abbreviate **Estados Unidos**. E.U. and USA are also used.

Cary Wolinsky/Stock, Boston

También quería comprar una revista y no tuve que ir lejos porque en la misma calle había un quiosco. Aquí hay muchas de estas tiendecitas donde se venden cosas como periódicos, libros, revistas, etcétera. Claro que también se pueden comprar estas cosas y más —lápices, papel para cartas, etcétera— en las papelerías.

Bueno, Joe, después de hacer todas estas compras, estaba muy cansado. Como era la una de la tarde, empezaron a cerrar todas las tiendas. Así, tomé el metro y volví a la pensión. Aquí estoy, descansando un rato antes de la comida.

Pues, eso es todo por el momento. Te escribo otra vez la semana que viene.

Tu amigo,

David

PRÁCTICA

A. *Conteste según la carta.*

1. ¿Dónde se compra el champú? ¿el jabón?
2. ¿Cuál es la diferencia entre una farmacia de los Estados Unidos y una farmacia de España?
3. ¿Dónde se pueden comprar sellos en España? (Mencione dos lugares.)
4. Si se necesitan cigarrillos o fósforos, ¿adónde se va?
5. ¿Qué es un quiosco? ¿Qué cosas se venden allí?
6. ¿Qué venden en una papelería?

B. ¿Cierto o falso? Corrija las oraciones falsas.

1. Se pueden comprar batidos y pastelitos en una pastelería.
2. Si yo quisiera tomar una copa, iría a un quiosco.
3. Se va a un quiosco para mandar paquetes.
4. Es más rápido ir a pie que tomar el metro.
5. Se va a un café a comprar champú.
6. Si yo necesitara pasta dental, iría al correo.
7. Se pueden comprar fósforos en una tabacalera.
8. Un batido se hace con vino.

A propósito...

The following phrases are part of the **argot estudiantil** (*student slang*) used by Hispanic students. Since slang words vary from country to country and even from city to city, the best way to keep up to date about current slang is to talk to Spanish-speaking friends in your area, whether you live in the United States or are studying abroad.

Es un(a) *empollón(a)*.	*He/she's a grind (is always studying).* (**empollar** = *to brood, hatch; to study hard*)
Esta profesora es un *hueso*.	*This professor is very demanding.* (**hueso** = *bone*)
Esta clase es un *rollo*.	*This class is a "pain."* (**rollo** = *roller*)
Juanito *hizo novillos* **ayer**.	*Johnny played hookey yesterday.* (**novillo** = *young bull;* **hacer novillos** = *to play bullfighter*)

Voy a *fumarme* **una clase esta tarde.**	*I'm going to cut class this afternoon.*

Here are some additional phrases related to university life:

Me han concedido una *beca*.	*I have won ("they" have given me) a scholarship.*
Me han *suspendido/aprobado* **en matemáticas.**	*I've failed/passed ("they" have failed/passed me) in math.*
Tengo un buen *expediente*.	*I have a good grade report.*

PRÁCTICA

La vida universitaria. Comente Ud. la vida de los estudiantes universitarios en los Estados Unidos.

1. ¿Hay muchos empollones en la universidad de Ud.? ¿Los conoce? ¿Es Ud. uno de ellos? Describa la vida de un empollón.
2. ¿Alguno de sus profesores es un hueso? ¿Por qué cree Ud. eso? ¿Cómo reacciona Ud. frente a los huesos?
3. ¿Qué puede hacer un estudiante cuando le suspenden en un curso? En la opinión de Ud., ¿qué debe hacer? ¿Por qué?
4. ¿Qué ventajas hay en tener un buen expediente? ¿Hay desventajas?
5. Algunos estudiantes se fuman las clases con bastante frecuencia. ¿Por qué? ¿Lo hace Ud. de vez en cuando? Comente.
6. ¿Alguna de sus clases es un rollo? ¿Cuál? Comente.
7. ¿Qué tipo de becas hay? ¿Tiene Ud. una beca para completar sus estudios universitarios?
8. Describa la vida de **Pepita Perfecta**, una estudiante ideal, o de **Pepita Perezosa**, la peor estudiante del mundo.

PREPARACIONES PARA UN AÑO EN EL EXTRANJERO

If you are planning a trip abroad, it is a good idea to find out as much as possible about the country and city where you will be staying. What is the weather like? What things can you buy there? What special accommodations are there for students?

The following reading is a letter written in response to a letter of inquiry from an American student who is planning to spend a year studying in Madrid.

Madrid, 4 de julio

Querida Patti,

Me alegro muchísimo de que vengas a pasar el año entero aquí en Madrid. Hace mucho tiempo que no nos vemos° y estaré contentísima de verte de nuevo° —esta vez en mi país. Me hiciste muchas preguntas y quiero contestarlas todas para que no tengas muchas sorpresas cuando llegues.

Primero, el alojamiento°. Podrías vivir en un colegio mayor°, pero yo, por mi parte, prefiero una pensión¹. Si te interesa, puedes quedarte en la misma donde yo vivo. La gente y la señora son muy amables y la pensión está muy bien situada en la Moncloa —la zona estudiantil— muy cerca de la Ciudad Universitaria². En un sitio° estupendo, con restaurantes y bares divertidísimos por todas partes —y también hay

Hace... *we haven't seen each other for a long time*
de... *again*

lodging / **colegio ...** *dormitory*

place

pastelerías excelentes; te lo digo porque te conozco y sé lo golosa que eres°. Y desde allí se llega fácilmente al centro, porque está situada entre la boca° del metro y las paradas de los autobuses.

lo... *what a sweet tooth you have*
entrance

Hablando de comida, debo decirte que las tres comidas están incluidas en el precio de la habitación. La comida es casera°, pero riquísima. Seguro que te gustaría. Sin embargo, si algún día te apeteciera° una hamburguesa y un batido, podrías ir —¿adónde crees?— ¡pues al Burger King de la calle Princesa, que está muy cerca!

home cooked
te... *you felt like (eating)*

Con respecto a tu segunda pregunta —qué debes traer y qué no debes traer— te voy a dar algunos consejos. Recuerda que no vas a estar en la Costa del Sol sino en Madrid y si no traes ropa de invierno, te vas a congelar°. El clima aquí va de un extremo al otro y empieza a hacer frío en el mes de octubre. Se dice que en Madrid hay nueve meses de invierno y tres de infierno... y por algo lo dirán°.

to freeze

por... *they must have a reason for saying it*

En cuanto a las otras cosas que piensas traer, yo te aconsejaría que no trajeras ningún aparato eléctrico, porque la corriente aquí es diferente de la de los EE.UU. Todas las cosas que vas a necesitar las puedes comprar cuando llegues. Hay muchas tiendas —papelerías, tabacaleras, librerías, farmacias y más— cerca de la pensión, y también hay quioscos donde puedes comprar el último número de *Time* si te cansas° del español.

te... *you grow tired*

También hiciste varias preguntas sobre tus cursos. De verdad no sé mucho de los cursos que vas a tomar. Tu plan de estudios ha sido preparado por el Instituto de Cultura Hispánica[3] para estudiantes norteamericanos. Es probable que tengas clases por la mañana y, quizá, también por la tarde, como las tienen muchos de los otros programas

para extranjeros.   Lo que sí sé° es que el Instituto de Cultura Hispánica   Lo... *What I do know*
queda muy cerca de la Moncloa y podrás ir caminando a tus clases y
volver a comer al mediodía° sin problema.   *mid-day*

Me dijiste que llegas por la mañana el día 20 de agosto. Si hay cambio
de vuelo, no dejes de avisarme, pues pienso ir a buscarte en el aeropuerto. Y por ahora nada más. Si tienes cualquier otra pregunta,
no dejes de escribirme. Esperando verte muy pronto, recibe un saludo
muy afectuoso de

tu amiga

Pilar

Comentario cultural

1. Hispanic students must make individual arrangements for accommodations,
   since most Spanish and Latin American universities do not provide living
   quarters, cafeterias or restaurants for students. Some students rent rooms and
   eat at nearby restaurants. Others live in **pensiones,** where the cost of the room
   includes meals and limited maid service. The **colegios mayores** mentioned in
   the dialog are similar to United States dormitories, but they are often privately
   owned and operated.
2. **La Moncloa** is the district of Madrid where the University of Madrid is located.
   The campus itself is called **la Ciudad Universitaria.**

   Hispanic universities are divided into schools **(facultades);** for example, **la
   Facultad de Derecho,** *School of Law;* **la Facultad de Medicina,** *Medicine;* **la
   Facultad de Ingeniería,** *Engineering;* **la Facultad de Filosofía y Letras,** *Humanities*
   (*Liberal Arts*). Often the divisions of a university are located in buildings found
   in different parts of the city. The University of Madrid, with its large, parklike
   campus, is an exception.
3. The Instituto de Cultura Hispánica, located on the edge of the Ciudad Universitaria, is an independent state institution that oversees Spain's cultural rela-
   tions with all other Spanish-speaking countries. The Instituto sponsors
   cultural events and also organizes programs for foreign students **(cursos para
   extranjeros).** Many foreign university programs hold their classes in its
   facilities.

¿Qué necesita Ud. saber? *Siguiendo el modelo de la carta de Pilar, escriba una de las
siguientes cartas:*

1. Ud. es un(a) estudiante latinoamericano/a que viene a los Estados Unidos
   por primera vez a pasar un año, como mínimo. Escriba una carta a la familia
   con la cual (*with which*) va a vivir. Preséntese y pida informes sobre el país
   —el clima, las costumbres, etcétera —y sobre la familia. ¿Qué debe traer?
   ¿Qué no debe traer? ¿Qué debe saber del lugar donde va a vivir? ¿de los estudiantes de su universidad?
2. Ud. es miembro de la familia con la cual un(a) estudiante extranjero/a va a
   pasar un año. Escríbale, dándole los informes que pueda necesitar.

3. Ud. es un(a) estudiante norteamericano/a que va a pasar el próximo año académico en Latinoamérica o en España. Escriba una carta a un amigo que está estudiando allí este año. Pídale informes sobre el país y sobre la vida de un estudiante —en total, todo lo que Ud. necesita saber para prepararse para el año.

UNA GUÍA DE MADRID

¿Qué haría Ud. si tuviera la oportunidad de pasar un año como estudiante en Madrid? Seguramente no pasaría todo el tiempo en las clases ni en la Ciudad Universitaria. Una parte importante de su educación consistiría en conocer a España y, en especial, a la gran ciudad de Madrid. La guía que sigue le va a explicar algunas actividades de interés.

COMPRAS. Si a Ud. le gusta buscar gangas, vaya al Rastro —el gran mercado al aire libre— donde se puede comprar todo tipo de artículos interesantes y, a menudo°, de poco uso. ¿Busca Ud. algo más elegante? Las tiendas de la Calle Serrano ofrecen artículos de alta calidad° y de precios igualmente altos. Si a Ud. le interesan las cosas viejas, la Calle del Prado está llena de tiendas que se dedican exclusivamente a la venta° de antigüedades.

a... *frequently*

de... *high quality*

sale

© Peter Menzel

Robert Rapelye/EPA, Inc.

RESTAURANTES Y VIDA NOCTURNA.   Claro está que en Madrid hay muchos restaurantes excelentes que ofrecen lo mejor de la comida castellana° y española: paella valenciana, bacalao a la vizcaína, fabada° asturiana, cochinillo° a la segoviana y gazpacho.   Y para la persona de gustos internacionales, Madrid tiene restaurantes que ofrecen comida de todas partes del mundo.

of the region of Castille / stew of ham, beans, pigs' ears, black sausage, bacon roast suckling pig

¿Le gusta tomar un aperitivo antes de almorzar o cenar?   Vaya a uno de los numerosos cafés y bares que están cerca de la Plaza Mayor, el centro de la ciudad antigua.   Ahí uno puede tomar una copa —por lo general, un vino seco o un jerez— y probar° las distintas tapas° que se ofrecen en cada lugar.   Después de la cena, diviértase en uno de los clubes de flamenco o en una discoteca donde puede bailar a los ritmos internacionales más recientes.

to taste, try / hors d'oeuvres

PARQUES.   Madrid es una ciudad de parques extensos y los domingos por la tarde los madrileños suelen° descansar paseando° en uno de ellos. El más famoso es el Parque del Buen Retiro.   Allí las estatuas de los reyes, héroes, poetas y patriotas de España se ven entre los árboles y hay un lago donde se pueden alquilar botes de remos°.

usually; tend to / strolling

botes... *rowboats*

DEPORTES.   Si a Ud. le interesan los deportes, Madrid le ofrece un poco de todo.   Hay estadios y campos deportivos, varios campos de golf y numerosas academias ecuestres y canchas de tenis.   Si a Ud. le emocionan las carreras° automovilísticas, vaya a la pista° de Jarama, donde se hacen las pruebas° para el Campeonato Mundial de automovilismo.

races / track

trials

CINE, TEATRO, MÚSICA.   El cine es una de las actividades favoritas de los madrileños.   Y en los veinte teatros de la ciudad, se representan obras clásicas y modernas del teatro español y traducciones° de obras extran-

translations

Owen Franken/Stock, Boston

jeras.   Hay conciertos sinfónicos en el Teatro Real, y en el Teatro de la
Zarzuela se representan ópera, ballet y las famosas zarzuelas españolas,
una forma de arte que es una combinación de música, baile y teatro
hablado.

Con tanta actividad es evidente que uno puede pasar muchas horas
agradables en Madrid.   Pero, ¡cuidado!   No olvide los estudios en la
universidad.

Ejercicio escrito final

Which of the preceding activities appeals to you the most?   What parts of the
Spanish-speaking world are you the most interested in visiting?   Express your
preferences by completing the following paragraphs:

1. Si yo estuviera en (Madrid, Buenos Aires, Cuernavaca,...) _____

_____ .

2. Si yo pudiera viajar a cualquier lugar del mundo, _____

_____ .

Appendix 1: Verbs

A. REGULAR VERBS: SIMPLE TENSES

Infinitive Present participle Past participle	Present	Imperfect	Preterite	Future	Conditional
			INDICATIVE		
hablar	hablo	hablaba	hablé	hablaré	hablaría
hablando	hablas	hablabas	hablaste	hablarás	hablarías
hablado	habla	hablaba	habló	hablará	hablaría
	hablamos	hablábamos	hablamos	hablaremos	hablaríamos
	habláis	hablabais	hablasteis	hablaréis	hablaríais
	hablan	hablaban	hablaron	hablarán	hablarían
comer	como	comía	comí	comeré	comería
comiendo	comes	comías	comiste	comerás	comerías
comido	come	comía	comió	comerá	comería
	comemos	comíamos	comimos	comeremos	comeríamos
	coméis	comíais	comisteis	comeréis	comeríais
	comen	comían	comieron	comerán	comerían
vivir	vivo	vivía	viví	viviré	viviría
viviendo	vives	vivías	viviste	vivirás	vivirías
vivido	vive	vivía	vivió	vivirá	viviría
	vivimos	vivíamos	vivimos	viviremos	viviríamos
	vivís	vivíais	vivisteis	viviréis	viviríais
	viven	vivían	vivieron	vivirán	vivirían

B. REGULAR VERBS: PERFECT TENSES

INDICATIVE

Present perfect		Past perfect		Preterite perfect		Future Perfect	
he		había		hube		habré	
has		habías		hubiste		habrás	
ha	hablado	había	hablado	hubo	hablado	habrá	hablado
hemos	comido	habíamos	comido	hubimos	comido	habremos	comido
habéis	vivido	habíais	vivido	hubisteis	vivido	habréis	vivido
han		habían		hubieron		habrán	

C. IRREGULAR VERBS

Infinitive Present participle Past participle	Present	Imperfect	Preterite	Future	Conditional
			INDICATIVE		
andar	ando	andaba	anduve	andaré	andaria
andando	andas	andabas	anduviste	andarás	andarías
andado	anda	andaba	anduvo	andará	andaría
	andamos	andábamos	anduvimos	andaremos	andaríamos
	andáis	andabais	anduvisteis	andaréis	andaríais
	andan	andaban	anduvieron	andarán	andarían
caer	caigo	caía	caí	caeré	caería
cayendo	caes	caías	caíste	caerás	caerías
caído	cae	caía	cayó	caerá	caería
	caemos	caíamos	caímos	caeremos	caeríamos
	caéis	caíais	caísteis	caeréis	caeríais
	caen	caían	cayeron	caerán	caerían
dar	doy	daba	di	daré	daría
dando	das	dabas	diste	darás	darías
dado	da	daba	dio	dará	daría
	damos	dábamos	dimos	daremos	daríamos
	dais	dabais	disteis	daréis	daríais
	dan	daban	dieron	darán	darían
decir	digo	decía	dije	diré	diría
diciendo	dices	decías	dijiste	dirás	dirías
dicho	dice	decía	dijo	dirá	diría
	decimos	decíamos	dijimos	diremos	diríamos
	decís	decíais	dijisteis	diréis	diríais
	dicen	decían	dijeron	dirán	dirían

─────── SUBJUNCTIVE ─────── IMPERATIVE

Present	Imperfect	
hable	hablara	habla tú,
hables	hablaras	no hables
hable	hablara	hable Ud.
hablemos	habláramos	hablemos
habléis	hablarais	hablen
hablen	hablaran	
coma	comiera	come tú,
comas	comieras	no comas
coma	comiera	coma Ud.
comamos	comiéramos	comamos
comáis	comierais	coman
coman	comieran	
viva	viviera	vive tú,
vivas	vivieras	no vivas
viva	viviera	viva Ud.
vivamos	viviéramos	vivamos
viváis	vivierais	vivan
vivan	vivieran	

─────── SUBJUNCTIVE ───────

Conditional perfect		Present perfect		Past perfect	
habría		haya		hubiera	
habrías		hayas		hubieras	
habría	hablado	haya	hablado	hubiera	hablado
habríamos	comido	hayamos	comido	hubiéramos	comido
habríais	vivido	hayáis	vivido	hubierais	vivido
habrían		hayan		hubieran	

─────── SUBJUNCTIVE ─────── IMPERATIVE

Present	Imperfect	
ande	anduviera	anda tú,
andes	anduvieras	no andes
ande	anduviera	ande Ud.
andemos	anduviéramos	andemos
andéis	anduvierais	anden
anden	anduvieran	
caiga	cayera	cae tú,
caigas	cayeras	no caigas
caiga	cayera	caiga Ud.
caigamos	cayéramos	caigamos
caigáis	cayerais	caigan
caigan	cayeran	
dé	diera	da tú,
des	dieras	no des
dé	diera	dé Ud.
demos	diéramos	demos
deis	dierais	den
den	dieran	
diga	dijera	di tú,
digas	dijeras	no digas
diga	dijera	diga Ud.
digamos	dijéramos	digamos
digáis	dijerais	digan
digan	dijeran	

C. IRREGULAR VERBS (continued)

Infinitive Present participle Past participle	INDICATIVE				
	Present	Imperfect	Preterite	Future	Conditional
estar estando estado	estoy estás está estamos estáis están	estaba estabas estaba estábamos estabais estaban	estuve estuviste estuvo estuvimos estuvisteis estuvieron	estaré estarás estará estaremos estaréis estarán	estaría estarías estaría estaríamos estaríais estarían
haber habiendo habido	he has ha hemos habéis han	había habías había habíamos habíais habían	hube hubiste hubo hubimos hubisteis hubieron	habré habrás habrá habremos habréis habrán	habría habrías habría habríamos habríais habrían
hacer haciendo hecho	hago haces hace hacemos hacéis hacen	hacía hacías hacía hacíamos hacíais hacían	hice hiciste hizo hicimos hicisteis hicieron	haré harás hará haremos haréis harán	haría harías haría haríamos haríais harían
ir yendo ido	voy vas va vamos vais van	iba ibas iba íbamos ibais iban	fui fuiste fue fuimos fuisteis fueron	iré irás irá iremos iréis irán	iría irías iría iríamos iríais irían
oir oyendo oído	oigo oyes oye oímos oís oyen	oía oías oía oíamos oíais oían	oí oíste oyó oímos oísteis oyeron	oiré oirás oirá oiremos oiréis oirán	oiría oirías oiría oiríamos oiríais oirían
poder pudiendo podido	puedo puedes puede podemos podéis pueden	podía podías podía podíamos podíais podían	pude pudiste pudo pudimos pudisteis pudieron	podré podrás podrá podremos podréis podrán	podría podrías podría podríamos podríais podrían
poner poniendo puesto	pongo pones pone ponemos ponéis ponen	ponía ponías ponía poníamos poníais ponían	puse pusiste puso pusimos pusisteis pusieron	pondré pondrás pondrá pondremos pondréis pondrán	pondría pondrías pondría pondríamos pondríais pondrían
querer queriendo querido	quiero quieres quiere queremos queréis quieren	quería querías quería queríamos queríais querían	quise quisiste quiso quisimos quisisteis quisieron	querré querrás querrá querremos querréis querrán	querría querrías querría querríamos querríais querrían
saber sabiendo sabido	sé sabes sabe sabemos sabéis saben	sabía sabías sabía sabíamos sabíais sabían	supe supiste supo supimos supisteis supieron	sabré sabrás sabrá sabremos sabréis sabrán	sabría sabrías sabría sabríamos sabríais sabrían
salir saliendo salido	salgo sales sale salimos salís salen	salía salías salía salíamos salíais salían	salí saliste salió salimos salisteis salieron	saldré saldrás saldrá saldremos saldréis saldrán	saldría saldrías saldría saldríamos saldríais saldrían

SUBJUNCTIVE		IMPERATIVE
Present	Imperfect	
esté	estuviera	está tú,
estés	estuvieras	no estés
esté	estuviera	esté Ud.
estemos	estuviéramos	estemos
estéis	estuvierais	estén
estén	estuviera	
haya	hubiera	
hayas	hubieras	
haya	hubiera	
hayamos	hubiéramos	
hayáis	hubierais	
hayan	hubieran	
haga	hiciera	haz tú,
hagas	hicieras	no hagas
haga	hiciera	haga Ud.
hagamos	hiciéramos	hagamos
hagáis	hicierais	hagan
hagan	hicieran	
vaya	fuera	ve tú,
vayas	fueras	no vayas
vaya	fuera	vaya Ud.
vayamos	fuéramos	vayamos
vayáis	fuerais	vayan
vayan	fueran	
oiga	oyera	oye tú,
oigas	oyeras	no oigas
oiga	oyera	oiga Ud.
oigamos	oyéramos	oigamos
oigáis	oyerais	oigan
oigan	oyeran	
pueda	pudiera	
puedas	pudieras	
pueda	pudiera	
podamos	pudiéramos	
podáis	pudierais	
puedan	pudieran	
ponga	pusiera	pon tú,
pongas	pusieras	no pongas
ponga	pusiera	ponga Ud.
pongamos	pusiéramos	pongamos
pongáis	pusierais	pongan
pongan	pusieran	
quiera	quisiera	quiere tú,
quieras	quisieras	no quieras
quiera	quisiera	quiera Ud.
queramos	quisiéramos	queramos
queráis	quisierais	quieran
quieran	quisieran	
sepa	supiera	sabe tú,
sepas	supieras	no sepas
sepa	supiera	sepa Ud.
sepamos	supiéramos	sepamos
sepáis	supierais	sepan
sepan	supieran	
salga	saliera	sal tú,
salgas	salieras	no salgas
salga	saliera	salga Ud.
salgamos	saliéramos	salgamos
salgáis	salierais	salgan
salgan	salieran	

C. IRREGULAR VERBS (continued)

Infinitive Present participle Past participle	INDICATIVE				
	Present	Imperfect	Preterite	Future	Conditional
ser	soy	era	fui	seré	sería
siendo	eres	eras	fuiste	serás	serías
sido	es	era	fue	será	sería
	somos	éramos	fuimos	seremos	seríamos
	sois	erais	fuisteis	seréis	seríais
	son	eran	fueron	serán	serían
tener	tengo	tenía	tuve	tendré	tendría
teniendo	tienes	tenías	tuviste	tendrás	tendrías
tenido	tiene	tenía	tuvo	tendrá	tendría
	tenemos	teníamos	tuvimos	tendremos	tendríamos
	tenéis	teníais	tuvisteis	tendréis	tendríais
	tienen	tenían	tuvieron	tendrán	tendrían
traer	traigo	traía	traje	traeré	traería
trayendo	traes	traías	trajiste	traerás	traerías
traído	trae	traía	trajo	traerá	traería
	traemos	traíamos	trajimos	traeremos	traeríamos
	traéis	traíais	trajisteis	traeréis	traeríais
	traen	traían	trajeron	traerán	traerían
venir	vengo	venía	vine	vendré	vendría
viniendo	vienes	venías	viniste	vendrás	vendrías
venido	viene	venía	vino	vendrá	vendría
	venimos	veníamos	vinimos	vendremos	vendríamos
	venís	veníais	vinisteis	vendréis	vendríais
	vienen	venían	vinieron	vendrán	vendrían
ver	veo	veía	vi	veré	vería
viendo	ves	veías	viste	verás	verías
visto	ve	veía	vio	verá	vería
	vemos	veíamos	vimos	veremos	veríamos
	veis	veíais	visteis	veréis	veríais
	ven	veían	vieron	verán	verían

D. STEM-CHANGING VERBS

Infinitive Present participle Past participle	INDICATIVE				
	Present	Imperfect	Preterite	Future	Conditional
pensar (ie)	pienso	pensaba	pensé	pensaré	pensaría
pensando	piensas	pensabas	pensaste	pensarás	pensarías
pensado	piensa	pensaba	pensó	pensará	pensaría
	pensamos	pensábamos	pensamos	pensaremos	pensaríamos
	pensáis	pensabais	pensasteis	pensaréis	pensaríais
	piensan	pensaban	pensaron	pensarán	pensarían
volver (ue)	vuelvo	volvía	volví	volveré	volvería
volviendo	vuelves	volvías	volviste	volverás	volverías
vuelto	vuelve	volvía	volvió	volverá	volvería
	volvemos	volvíamos	volvimos	volveremos	volveríamos
	volvéis	volvíais	volvisteis	volveréis	volveríais
	vuelven	volvían	volvieron	volverán	volverían
dormir (ue, u)	duermo	dormía	dormí	dormiré	dormiría
durmiendo	duermes	dormías	dormiste	dormirás	dormirías
dormido	duerme	dormía	durmió	dormirá	dormiría
	dormimos	dormíamos	dormimos	dormiremos	dormiríamos
	dormís	dormíais	dormisteis	dormiréis	dormiríais
	duermen	dormían	durmieron	dormirán	dormirían
sentir (ie, i)	siento	sentía	sentí	sentiré	sentiría
sintiendo	sientes	sentías	sentiste	sentirás	sentirías
sentido	siente	sentía	sintió	sentirá	sentiría
	sentimos	sentíamos	sentimos	sentiremos	sentiríamos
	sentís	sentíais	sentisteis	sentiréis	sentiríais
	sienten	sentían	sintieron	sentirán	sentirían

SUBJUNCTIVE		IMPERATIVE
Present	Imperfect	
sea	fuera	sé tú,
seas	fueras	no seas
sea	fuera	sea Ud.
seamos	fuéramos	seamos
seáis	fuerais	sean
sean	fueran	
tenga	tuviera	ten tú,
tengas	tuvieras	no tengas
tenga	tuviera	tenga Ud.
tengamos	tuviéramos	tengamos
tengáis	tuvierais	tengan
tengan	tuvieran	
traiga	trajera	trae tú,
traigas	trajeras	no traigas
traiga	trajera	traiga Ud.
traigamos	trajéramos	traigamos
traigáis	trajerais	traigan
traigan	trajeran	
venga	viniera	ven tú,
vengas	vinieras	no vengas
venga	viniera	venga Ud.
vengamos	viniéramos	vengamos
vengáis	vinierais	vengan
vengan	vinieran	
vea	viera	ve tú,
veas	vieras	no veas
vea	viera	vea Ud.
veamos	viéramos	veamos
veáis	vierais	vean
vean	vieran	

SUBJUNCTIVE		IMPERATIVE
Present	Imperfect	
piense	pensara	piensa tú,
pienses	pensaras	no pienses
piense	pensara	piense Ud.
pensemos	pensáramos	pensemos
penséis	pensarais	piensen
piensen	pensaran	
vuelva	volviera	vuelve tú,
vuelvas	volvieras	no vuelvas
vuelva	volviera	vuelva Ud.
volvamos	volviéramos	volvamos
volváis	volvierais	vuelvan
vuelvan	volvieran	
duerma	durmiera	duerme tú,
duermas	durmieras	no duermas
duerma	durmiera	duerma Ud.
durmamos	durmiéramos	durmamos
durmáis	durmierais	duerman
duerman	durmieran	
sienta	sintiera	siente tú,
sientas	sintieras	no sientas
sienta	sintiera	sienta Ud.
sintamos	sintiéramos	sintamos
sintáis	sintierais	sientan
sientan	sintieran	

D. STEM-CHANGING VERBS (continued)

Infinitive Present participle Past participle	INDICATIVE				
	Present	Imperfect	Preterite	Future	Conditional
pedir (i, i) pidiendo pedido	pido pides pide pedimos pedís piden	pedía pedías pedía pedíamos pedíais pedían	pedí pediste pidió pedimos pedisteis pidieron	pediré pedirás pedirá pediremos pediréis pedirán	pediría pedirías pediría pediríamos pediríais pedirían
reír (i, i) riendo reído	río ríes ríe reímos reís ríen	reía reías reía reíamos reíais reían	reí reíste rió reímos reísteis rieron	reiré reirás reirá reiremos reiréis reirán	reiría reirías reiría reiríamos reiríais reirían
seguir (i, i) siguiendo seguido	sigo sigues sigue seguimos seguís siguen	seguía seguías seguía seguíamos seguíais seguían	seguí seguiste siguió seguimos seguisteis siguieron	seguiré seguirás seguirá seguiremos seguiréis seguirán	seguiría seguirías seguiría seguiríamos seguiríais seguirían

E. VERBS WITH SPELLING CHANGES

Infinitive Present participle Past participle	INDICATIVE				
	Present	Imperfect	Preterite	Future	Conditional
sacar (qu) sacando sacado	saco sacas saca sacamos sacáis sacan	sacaba sacabas sacaba sacábamos sacabais sacaban	saqué sacaste sacó sacamos sacasteis sacaron	sacaré sacarás sacará sacaremos sacaréis sacarán	sacaría sacarías sacaría sacaríamos sacaríais sacarían
llegar (gu) llegando llegado	llego llegas llega llegamos llegáis llegan	llegaba llegabas llegaba llegábamos llegabais llegaban	llegué llegaste llegó llegamos llegasteis llegaron	llegaré llegarás llegará llegaremos llegaréis llegarán	llegaría llegarías llegaría llegaríamos llegaríais llegarían
empezar (ie) (c) empezando empezado	empiezo empiezas empieza empezamos empezáis empiezan	empezaba empezabas empezaba empezábamos empezabais empezaban	empecé empezaste empezó empezamos empezasteis empezaron	empezaré empezarás empezará empezaremos empezaréis empezarán	empezaría empezarías empezaría empezaríamos empezaríais empezarían
conocer (zc) conociendo conocido	conozco conoces conoce conocemos conocéis conocen	conocía conocías conocía conocíamos conocíais conocían	conocí conociste conoció conocimos conocisteis conocieron	conoceré conocerás conocerá conoceremos conoceréis conocerán	conocería conocerías conocería conoceríamos conoceríais conocerían
proteger (j) protegiendo protegido	protejo proteges protege protegemos protegéis protegen	protegía protegías protegía protegíamos protegíais protegían	protegí protegiste protegió protegimos protegisteis protegieron	protegeré protegerás protegerá protegeremos protegeréis protegerán	protegería protegerías protegería protegeríamos protegeríais protegerían
creer (y) creyendo creído	creo crees cree creemos creéis creen	creía creías creía creíamos creíais creían	creí creíste creyó creímos creísteis creyeron	creeré creerás creerá creeremos creeréis creerán	creería creerías creería creeríamos creeríais creerían

⎛————SUBJUNCTIVE————⎞		IMPERATIVE
Present	Imperfect	
pida	pidiera	pide tú,
pidas	pidieras	no pidas
pida	pidiera	pida Ud.
pidamos	pidiéramos	pidamos
pidáis	pidierais	pidan
pidan	pidieran	
ría	riera	ríe tú,
rías	rieras	no rías
ría	riera	ría Ud.
riamos	riéramos	riamos
riáis	rierais	rían
rían	rieran	
siga	siguiera	sigue tú,
sigas	siguieras	no sigas
siga	siguiera	siga Ud.
sigamos	siguiéramos	sigamos
sigáis	siguierais	sigan
sigan	siguieran	

⎛————SUBJUNCTIVE————⎞		IMPERATIVE
Present	Imperfect	
saque	sacara	saca tú,
saques	sacaras	no saques
saque	sacara	saque Ud.
saquemos	sacáramos	saquemos
saquéis	sacarais	saquen
saquen	sacaran	
llegue	llegara	llega tú,
llegues	llegaras	no llegues
llegue	llegara	llegue Ud.
lleguemos	llegáramos	lleguemos
lleguéis	llegarais	lleguen
lleguen	llegaran	
empiece	empezara	empieza tú,
empieces	empezaras	no empieces
empiece	empezara	empiece Ud.
empecemos	empezáramos	empecemos
empecéis	empezarais	empiecen
empiecen	empezaran	
conozca	conociera	conoce tú,
conozcas	conocieras	no conozcas
conozca	conociera	conozca Ud.
conozcamos	conociéramos	conozcamos
conozcáis	conocierais	conozcan
conozcan	conocieran	
proteja	protegiera	protege tú,
protejas	protegieras	no protejas
proteja	protegiera	proteja Ud.
protejamos	protegiéramos	protejamos
protejáis	protegierais	protejan
protejan	protegieran	
crea	creyera	cree tú,
creas	creyeras	no creas
crea	creyera	crea Ud.
creamos	creyéramos	creamos
creáis	creyerais	crean
crean	creyeran	

E. VERBS WITH SPELLING CHANGES (continued)

Infinitive Present participle Past participle	INDICATIVE				
	Present	Imperfect	Preterite	Future	Conditional
construir (y) construyendo construido	construyo construyes construye construimos construís construyen	construía construías construía construíamos construíais construían	construí construiste construyó construimos construisteis construyeron	construiré construirás construirá construiremos construiréis construirán	construiría construirías construiría construiríamos construiríais construirían
confiar confiando confiado	confío confías confía confiamos confiáis confían	confiaba confiabas confiaba confiábamos confiabais confiaban	confié confiaste confió confiamos confiasteis confiaron	confiaré confiarás confiará confiaremos confiaréis confiarán	confiaría confiarías confiaría confiaríamos confiaríais confiarían
continuar continuando continuado	continúo continúas continúa continuamos continuáis continúan	continuaba continuabas continuaba continuábamos continuabais continuaban	continué continuaste continuó continuamos continuasteis continuaron	continuaré continuarás continuará continuaremos continuaréis continuarán	continuaría continuarías continuaría continuaríamos continuaríais continuarían

── SUBJUNCTIVE ──		IMPERATIVE
Present	Imperfect	
construya	construyera	construye tú,
construyas	construyeras	no construyas
construya	construyera	construya Ud.
construyamos	construyéramos	construyamos
construyáis	construyerais	construyan
construyan	construyeran	
confíe	confiara	confía tú,
confíes	confiaras	no confíes
confíe	confiara	confíe Ud.
confiemos	confiáramos	confiemos
confiéis	confiarais	confíen
confíen	confiaran	
continúe	continuara	continúa tú,
continúes	continuaras	no continúes
continúe	continuara	continúe Ud.
continuemos	continuáramos	continuemos
continuéis	continuarais	continúen
continúen	continuaran	

Appendix 2

ANSWERS TO EXERCISES

This section gives answers to many of the exercises in the **Vocabulario: Preparación** section and to most of the **Práctica** and **Un poco de todo** exercises in the grammar sections.

ANTE TODO

SALUDOS Y EXPRESIONES DE COR-TESÍA. PRÁCTICA B. 1. Muy buenas; Buenas noches; Muy buenas, señor/señora/señorita; *and so on. There are also many possible responses to the remaining exercise items in* Práctica B. 2. Hasta luego. 3. Así así. (Muy bien.) 4. ¿Qué tal? 5. Muy bien. ¿Y usted? 6. Muy buenas. 7. De nada. 8. Adiós. 9. Me llamo _____. **CONVERSACIÓN.** 1. Con permiso. 2. Perdón. 3. Perdón. 4. Con permiso. 5. Perdón. 6. Con permiso.
EL ALFABETO ESPAÑOL. 1-c, 2-e, 3-i, 4-a, 5-f, 6-h, 7-b, 8-g, 9-d

CAPÍTULO 1

VOCABULARIO: PREPARACIÓN. EJERCICIO A. 1. C, D, A, F, E, B 2. D, F, B, E, C, A 3. B, E, D, A, C 4. D, C, A, E, B **EJERCICIO B.** 1. hombre 2. mujer 3. hombre 4. hombre **EJERCICIO D.** 1. Es para la clase de matemáticas (la clase de cálculo). 2. ...inglés. 3. ...historia. 4. ...español. 5. ...sicología. **GRAMMAR SECTION 1. PRÁCTICA A.** 1. el 2. la 3. el 4. el 5. la 6. la 7. el 8. la 9. un 10. una 11. un 12. una 13. un 14. un 15. una 16. un **PRÁCTICA B.** 1. un diccionario 2. una dependienta 3. un profesor 4. una mañana 5. un bolígrafo 6. la universidad 7. el día 8. el niño 9. la librería 10. la clase **PRÁCTICA C.** 1. las mesas 2. los libros 3. los amigos 4. las oficinas 5. unos cuadernos 6. unos lápices 7. unas extranjeras 8. unos bolígrafos 9. el profesor 10. la secretaria 11. la niña 12. una tarde 13. un lápiz 14. un papel **PRÁC-TICA D.** 1. mujer, estudiante 2. niño, profesor 3. extranjeros, amigos, estudiantes **PRÁCTICA E.** 1. los estudiantes 2. unas universidades 3. una dependienta 4. los extranjeros (*m.*) *or* las extranjeras (*f.*) 5. los secretarios 6. unas profesoras **GRAMMAR SECTION 2. PRÁCTICA A.** 1. yo 2. ellos 3. ella 4. nosotros 5. nosotras 6. él 7. ellas **PRÁCTICA B.** 1. usted (Ud.) 2. ustedes (Uds.) 3. tú

4. ustedes (vosotras *in Spain*) 5. usted (Ud.) 6. tú 7. tú (*some families use* usted) **PRÁCTICA C.** 1. ella 2. él 3. nosotros 4. ustedes (vosotros *in Spain*) 5. ellos 6. nosotras
GRAMMAR SECTION 3. PRÁCTICA A. 1. nosotros estudiamos, yo estudio, ellos estudian, Jacinto estudia, tú estudias, vosotras estudiáis 2. yo necesito, Eugenio y tú necesitan (necesitáis—*Spain*), tú necesitas, nosotras necesitamos, Ada necesita, vosotros necesitáis 3. tú tomas, Ud. toma, él toma, Uds. toman, Elena y yo tomamos, vosotras tomáis 4. nosotros bailamos y cantamos, los amigos bailan y cantan, Uds. bailan y cantan, Irene y Diego bailan y cantan, yo bailo y canto, vosotros bailáis y cantáis. **PRÁCTICA B.** 1. No necesito el dinero. 2. Ellos no cantan en clase. 3. Paula no desea tomar una cerveza. 4. Yo no trabajo todas las noches. 5. Ud. no enseña muy bien. **PRÁCTICA C.** *Forms of* desear *and* necesitar *are followed by infinitives, not by conjugated verb forms.* **PRÁCTICA D.** 1. Trabajamos en una oficina. 2. Ella enseña francés; él enseña inglés. 3. No compran el cuaderno. 4. Juan no paga los bolígrafos mañana. 5. Tú buscas la librería. 6. Él canta, pero ella trabaja.
GRAMMAR SECTION 4. PRÁCTICA A. 1. ¿Regresa Ud. a clase mañana? ¿Ud. regresa a clase mañana? 2. ¿Busca Elvira un cuaderno? ¿Elvira busca un cuaderno? 3. ¿Toma Ramón cerveza? ¿Ramón toma cerveza? 4. ¿Paga Ud. hoy? ¿Ud. paga hoy? 5. ¿Enseñan Uds. historia aquí? ¿Uds. enseñan historia aquí? 6. ¿Bailan ellos todos los días? ¿Ellos bailan todos los días? 7. ¿Trabaja ella mañana? ¿Ella trabaja mañana? **PRÁCTICA B.** 1. ¿Regresa Ud. a casa hoy? (¿Regresas a casa hoy?) 2. ¿Estudian Uds. mucho? (¿Estudiáis mucho?—*Spain*) 3. ¿Habla ella muy bien? 4. ¿Trabaja Ud. (Trabajas) aquí todos los días? 5. ¿Busca Ud. (Buscas) el diccionario? 6. ¿Necesitan Uds. (Necesitáis—*Sp.*) un lápiz?
GRAMMAR SECTION 5. PRÁCTICA A. 1. diecinueve (diez y nueve) señores 2. siete clases 3. cuatro señoras 4. catorce fiestas 5. doce amigos 6. dieciséis (diez y seis) papeles 7. treinta días 8. once lápices 9. veintiuna (veinte y una) profesoras 10. quince estudiantes **PRÁC-TICA B.** 1. Dos y tres son cinco. 2. Ocho y diecisiete (diez y siete) son veinticinco

(veinte y cinco). 3. Catorce y cuatro son dieciocho (diez y ocho). 4. Veintitrés (veinte y tres) menos trece son diez. 5. Veintinueve (veinte y nueve) menos dos son veintisiete (veinte y siete). 6. Treinta menos dieciséis (diez y seis) son catorce. 7. Trece y quince son veintiocho (veinte y ocho). 8. Once y cero son once.
UN POCO DE TODO. EJERCICIO A. 1. Ellos no desean tomar unas cervezas. 2. Uds. bailan con unos estudiantes. 3. ¿Compramos los lápices mañana? 4. ¿Por eso hablan (habláis—*Sp.*) con las dependientas? 5. ¿Hay sólo unas extranjeras en los cursos? 6. Ella no busca el dinero. 7. ¿Enseña Ud. sólo dos clases (una clase) de español? 8. Necesito un libro de texto. 9. La mujer estudia sicología. 10. ¿Paga Ud. sólo treinta pesos (un peso)? **EJER-CICIO B.** 1. Pula compran (el) papel para la clase. 2. ¿Trabaja Paco aquí en la librería todas las noches? 3. Sr. Gil, yo regreso a la universidad mañana. *Or:* El Sr. Gil y yo regresamos a la universidad mañana. 4. El extranjero no habla bien el inglés. 5. ¿Hay veintiuna (veinte y una) mujeres y sólo quince hombres? **EJERCICIO C.** Marcos busca... Toman la Coca-Cola... Desean bailar más... Marcos no desea... Por eso regresa...

CAPÍTULO 2

VOCABULARIO: PREPARACIÓN. EJER-CICIO A. 1. a. el padre; la madre b. el abuelo; la abuela c. el primo; la prima 2. a. el esposo b. el hijo; la hija c. la nieta; el nieto 3. a. la esposa b. la sobrina; el sobrino c. la hermana **EJER-CICIO B.** 1. Einstein es listo. En comparación, el chimpancé es tonto. 2. José es perezoso. Roberto es trabajador. 3. Pablo es alto. Pepe es bajo. 4. Tomás es una persona alegre. Timoteo es una persona triste. 5. El ángel es bueno y simpático. Satanás es malo y antipático. El ángel es guapo. Satanás es feo. 6. Paco Pereda es un profesor joven. Ramón Ramírez es un profesor viejo. Ramón Ramírez es casado. Paco Pereda es soltero. 7. El lápiz es nuevo. El libro es viejo. El lápiz es largo. El libro es corto. 8. La familia Pérez es una familia grande y rica. La familia Gómez es una familia pequeña y pobre.
PRONUNCIACIÓN. PRÁCTICA B. 1. examen 2. lápiz 3. necesitar 4.

perez*o*so   5. liber*t*ad   6. nación   7. herm*a*na   8. compran   9. compr*a*mos 10. h*o*mbre   11. p*e*so   12. mujer   13. matrícula   14. gener*a*l   15. plástico 16. sobr*i*nos

GRAMMAR SECTION 6. PRÁCTICA A. Yo soy estudiante. Mario y Juan son estudiantes. Uds. son estudiantes. Lilia y yo somos estudiantes. Tú eres estudiante. Vosotros sois estudiantes. **PRÁCTICA B.** 1. John Doe es de los Estados Unidos. 2. Karl Lotze es de Alemania. 3. Graziana Lazzarino es de Italia. 4. María Gómez es de México. 5. Claudette Moreau es de Francia. 6. Timothy Windsor es de Inglaterra. **PRÁCTICA C.** 1. El dinero es de papel (de metal). 2. El lápiz es de madera. 3. El libro es de papel. 4. El cuaderno es de papel. 5. El bolígrafo es de plástico (de metal). 6. La mesa es de madera. **PRÁCTICA D.** 1. La comida es para los hijos. 2. Los papeles de la matrícula son para la secretaria general. 3. El regalo es para Uds. 4. El dólar es para la sobrina. 5. La fiesta es para Evangelina. 6. La cerveza es para nosotros. **PRÁCTICA E.** 1. Sí, es importante hablar... No, no es necesario hablar... (Sí, es necesario...) No, no es posible... Sí, es necesario... 2. Sí, es posible bailar... Sí, es posible cantar... No, no es necesario pagar... No, no es necesario... **PRÁCTICA F.** *Ojo:* Carla y yo somos. **PRÁCTICA G.** 1. Carlos Miguel es doctor. Es de Cuba. Trabaja en Milwaukee ahora. 2. Maripili es extranjera. Es de Burgos. Trabaja en Miami ahora. 3. Mariela es dependienta. Es de Buenos Aires. Trabaja en Nueva York ahora. 4. Juan es artista. Es de Lima. Trabaja en Los Ángeles ahora. **GRAMMAR SECTION 7. PRÁCTICA.** 1. ¿De quién es la Coca-Cola? Es la Coca-Cola de Jesús. 2. ¿De quién es la idea? Es la idea de Paquita. 3. ¿De quién son las pesetas? Son las pesetas de Rodrigo. 4. ¿De quién es el cuaderno? Es el cuaderno de Soledad. 5. ¿De quién es la clase? Es la clase de Lorenzo. 6. ¿De quién es el cuarto? Es el cuarto de Antonia. **GRAMMAR SECTION 8. PRÁCTICA.** 1. Es el coche (la casa, el peso, el bolígrafo) del hombre. 2. Es el libro del niño (de la mujer, de los abuelos, del tío, de las amigas, del primo Juan). 3. Mañana Marcos regresa a la biblioteca (al mercado, al hotel, a la tienda, al hospital, al cuarto del abuelo, a la casa de la tía). **GRAMMAR SECTION 9. PRÁCTICA A.** 1. (No) Es una clase inteligente (interesante, importante, triste, amable, internacional, imposible). 2. Los perros (no) son leales (impacientes, inteligentes, importantes). 3. La universidad (no) es vieja (grande, pequeña, buena, mala). **PRÁCTICA B.** 1. alta, lista, trabajadora 2. viejo, grande, alto, interesante 3. viejos, religiosos, inteligentes 4. buenas **PRÁCTICA C.** Juana es casada. Es baja. Es fea. Es trabajadora. Es antipática.

PRÁCTICA D. 1. francesa 2. español (mexicano, *etc.*) 3. alemanes 4. portugués 5. italianas 6. inglés (norteamericano) **PRÁCTICA E.** 1. Necesito muchos/pocos lápices (muchas/pocas mesas, muchos/pocos cuadernos, muchas/pocas ideas, mucho/poco dinero, muchas/pocas clases). 2. Necesitamos trabajar (pagar, tomar, hablar) mucho/poco en clase. **PRÁCTICA F.** 1. libros nuevos, tres libros, libros baratos 2. una mesa baja, una mesa pequeña, una mesa larga 3. unas ciudades viejas, unas ciudades interesantes, unas ciudades grandes (unas grandes ciudades) 4. un carro pequeño, un carro francés, un carro largo 5. Por favor, deseo comprar un diccionario completo (un diccionario barato, un diccionario nuevo). 6. Unos profesores viejos (Unos profesores simpáticos, Unos profesores norteamericanos) enseñan bien. 7. Desean hablar con la hermana casada (con la otra hermana, con la hermana joven). 8. Busco una casa nueva (una casa buena *or* una buena casa, una casa blanca). **PRÁCTICA G.** 1. un buen recuerdo 2. una gran comida 3. unos buenos tíos 4. un mal hotel 5. unas malas actrices **PRÁCTICA H.** 1. ¡Es una gran idea! 2. (Él) Compra un coche/carro grande. 3. Necesitamos otro diccionario. 4. Hay unos estudiantes simpáticos (unas estudiantes simpáticas *f.*) en la clase. 5. Uds. hablan mucho. **PRÁCTICA I.** María es una buena estudiante; pues estudia mucho. Es lista y amable. Es peruana; por eso habla español. Es alta y guapa; también es muy alegre. ¡Es una persona ideal! **GRAMMAR SECTION 10. PRÁCTICA A.** 1. Es la una. 2. Son las seis. 3. Son las once. 4. Es la una y media. 5. Son las tres y cuarto (y quince). 6. Son las siete menos cuarto (menos quince). 7. Son las cuatro y cuarto (y quince). 8. Son las doce menos cuarto (menos quince). 9. Son las nueve y diez. 10. Son las diez menos diez de la noche. 11. Son las dos y veinte de la tarde. 12. Son las tres menos veinte de la tarde. 13. Son las cinco y siete de la tarde. 14. Son las once menos cinco de la noche. 15. Son las ocho de la mañana. **PRÁCTICA B.** 1. El tren llega a las dos y diecinueve de la tarde. 2. ...a las cinco y cuarto (y quince) de la tarde. 3. ...a las nueve y media de la mañana, 4. ...a las doce menos veinte de la noche. 5. ...a las dos menos uno de la mañana. 6. ...a las diez y veintidós de la noche. 7. ...a la una y siete de la tarde. 8. ...a las seis y dieciséis de la mañana. **UN POCO DE TODO. EJERCICIO A.** 1. Hay muchas ciudades interesantes en Honduras. 2. Hay veintiuna mesas largas en la cafetería. 3. Es un buen recuerdo. 4. La madre de las niñas es una doctora buena. 5. Don Carlos es un mal actor, pero es amable. 6. Yo llego a casa a las seis de la mañana. 7. Hay veinticuatro horas en un día. 8. Son los libros del

estudiante (de la estudiante). 9. Carmen regresa al mercado en la tarde. **EJERCICIO B.** 1. un abuelo 2. una prima 3. un hermano 4. un padre 5. una tía **EJERCICIO C.** 1. Guadalajara, mexicano/a, español 2. París, francés/francesa, francés 3. Roma, italiano/a, italiano 4. San Francisco, norteamericano/a, inglés 5. Madrid, español(a), español 6. Londres, inglés/inglesa, inglés 7. Berlín, alemán/alemana, alemán 8. Lima, peruano/a, español

CAPÍTULO 3

VOCABULARIO: PREPARACIÓN. EJERCICIO A. 1. El Sr. Rivera lleva zapatos (un traje, una camisa, pantalones, una chaqueta, calcetines, un abrigo). 2. La Srta. Alonso lleva un vestido (una chaqueta, zapatos, medias). 3. El estudiante lleva una camiseta (pantalones, sandalias, una chaqueta). 4. La estudiante lleva una blusa/un suéter (una falda, botas). **EJERCICIO C.** 1. almacén 2. regatear 3. comprar, precio 4. venden 5. ¿_____? 6. ¿_____? **GRAMMAR SECTION 11. PRÁCTICA A.** 1. En México se habla español. 2. ...se habla portugués. 3. ...se habla alemán. 4. ...se habla inglés. 5. ...se habla inglés (or: ...se habla español). **PRÁCTICA B.** Se viaja a México en avión (en carro, en tren, en autobús). **PRÁCTICA C.** Se necesita papel. Se necesitan lápices. Se necesita un cuaderno. Se necesita un diccionario. Se necesita un libro de texto. Se necesitan ideas buenas. **PRÁCTICA D.** 1. Se trabaja mucho. 2. Se compran camisetas en la librería. 3. No se llega tarde a la clase de español. 4. Se habla español allí. 5. Se necesitan dependientes. 6. Se estudia mucho en la universidad. **GRAMMAR SECTION 12. PRÁCTICA A.** 1. los tíos comen y beben, tú comes y bebes, Uds. comen y beben, la prima y yo comemos y bebemos, Ud. come y bebe, vosotras coméis y bebéis 2. nosotros aprendemos, yo aprendo, Ud. aprende, la estudiante francesa aprende, Uds. aprenden, vosotros aprendéis 3. papá recibe, tú recibes, nosotras recibimos, los nietos reciben, Alicia recibe, vosotros recibís 4. tú asistes, nosotros asistimos, Ud. asiste, todos los estudiantes asisten, Carlos asiste, vosotras asistís **PRÁCTICA B.** *Forms of* deber *are followed by an infinitive, not by a conjugated verb form.* **PRÁCTICA C.** 1. Sí, vivimos en Nueva York. (No, no vivimos en...) 2. No, los estudiantes no beben en clase. 3. No, no recibo siempre un suspenso en los exámenes. 4. Sí, Ud. escribe (escribes)... (No, Ud. no escribe [no escribes]...) 5. Sí, muchos mexicanos viven... 6. No, no aprendemos francés... (*or:* No, aprendemos español.) 7. No, los profesores no insisten en... 8. No, el profesor/la profesora no comprende árabe. 9. Sí, todos los niños creen en... (No, no todos los niños creen en...) **PRÁCTICA D.** 1. Venden (Se venden) muchos zapatos aquí. 2. Debo escribir la carta hoy. 3. Vivimos aquí en San Rafael. 4. (Él) Comprende italiano, ¿no?/¿verdad? 5. (Ella) No comprende francés.

GRAMMAR SECTION 13. PRÁCTICA A. 1. Pepe tiene, nosotros tenemos, Alicia y Carlos tienen, yo tengo, tú tienes, vosotras tenéis 2. yo vengo, los estudiantes vienen, tú vienes, Uds. vienen, nosotras venimos, vosotros venís 3. yo quiero... pero no puedo, ella quiere... pero no puede, nosotros queremos... pero no podemos, todos los estudiantes quieren... pero no pueden, tú quieres... pero no puedes, vosotros queréis... pero no podéis **PRÁCTICA B.** *Forms of* querer *and* poder *are followed by infinitives, not by conjugated verb forms.*

GRAMMAR SECTION 14. PRÁCTICA A. 1. Tengo sed (sueño, miedo, frío, ganas de descansar). 2. Tengo que asistir... (aprender..., leer..., estudiar..., hablar...). Tengo ganas de abrir... (vender..., vivir..., mirar..., comer...). **PRÁCTICA B.** 1. calor; frío 2. miedo 3. sueño; hambre 4. prisa 5. años 6. razón; razón 7. sed **PRÁCTICA C.** 1. Alicia tiene ganas de comprar una camiseta nueva. 2. Tenemos que estudiar para el examen. 3. ¿Tiene Ud. (Tienes) miedo de las serpientes? 4. No tengo ganas de mirar la televisión. 5. Tengo que regresar a casa ahora.

GRAMMAR SECTION 15. PRÁCTICA A. 1. Treinta y cincuenta son ochenta. 2. Cuarenta y cinco y cuarenta y cinco son noventa. 3. Treinta y dos y cincuenta y ocho son noventa. 4. Setenta y siete y veintitrés son cien. 5. Cien menos cuarenta son sesenta. 6. Noventa y nueve menos treinta y nueve son sesenta. 7. Ochenta y cuatro menos treinta y cuatro son cincuenta. 8. Setenta y ocho menos treinta y seis son cuarenta y dos. **PRÁCTICA B.** 1. sesenta y tres sombreros. 2. noventa y un pesos 3. cuarenta y cuatro calcetines 4. cien bebidas 5. setenta y seis abrigos 6. ochenta y dos ciudades 7. sesenta y una pesetas 8. treinta y nueve almacenes 9. setenta y cinco personas 10. cincuenta y siete parientes

UN POCO DE TODO. EJERCICIO A. 1. No quieren (queréis—*Sp.*) vender los abrigos del abuelo (de los abuelos), ¿verdad? 2. Se aprenden (unas) palabras importantes todos los días. 3. No deben (debéis—*Sp.*) mirar la televisión si tienen (tenéis—*Sp.*) sueño. 4. ¿Pueden Uds. aprender cien palabras en unas semanas? 5. Tenemos frío. Queremos regresar. 6. Quiero asistir a la clase. 7. ¿Por qué insiste Ud. (insistes) en llevar una maleta? ¿Qué tiene (tienes) allí? 8. Yo vengo tarde, pero se debe llegar temprano. 9. Se abre el libro en clase, ¿no? 10. Insiste en comer ahora porque tiene hambre. **EJERCICIO B.** 1. Tú siempre tienes prisa; debes descansar

más. 2. No se venden trajes y vestidos aquí, ¿verdad? 3. Ella puede entrar a las ocho porque se abre temprano. 4. Ud. comprende el español del Perú, ¿no? 5. Se vive bien en Guatemala.

EJERCICIO C. 1. Vienes al baile... estudiar... bailar... 2. Vienes al almacén... escribir... comprar... 3. Vienes al restaurante... leer... comer 4. Vienes al mercado... aprender... comprar... 5. Vienes a la clase... regresar... aprender...

CAPÍTULO 4

VOCABULARIO: PREPARACIÓN. EJERCICIO A. 1. Hoy es _____. Mañana es _____. 2. Hay siete días en una semana. 3. Tenemos clase los _____, los _____ y los _____. 4. No tenemos clase los _____. 5. Sí, estudio mucho durante el fin de semana. (No, no estudio mucho...) Sí, estudio mucho los domingos por la noche. (No, no estudio...) **EJERCICIO D.** 1. relación cariñosa entre dos novios 2. relación entre dos amigos 3. cuando se termina un matrimonio 4. relación legal entre esposos 5. preludio al matrimonio 6. pasar tiempo con el novio o un amigo

GRAMMAR SECTION 16. PRÁCTICA A. 1. Ud. da, yo doy, los abogados dan, Ud. y yo damos, la consejera da, vosotros dais 2. yo estoy, ellos están, Javier está, tú estás, Rita está, vosotras estáis 3. tú vas, Rosalba va, yo voy, nosotras vamos, Ud. va, vosotros vais 4. yo voy a asistir, todos los amigos van a asistir, nosotros vamos a asistir, tú vas a asistir, los padres de los novios van a asistir, vosotras vais a asistir **PRÁCTICA B.** *Note that the preposition* a *is used after forms of* ir *and the preposition* en *after forms of* estar. **PRÁCTICA C.** 1. Los niños van a aprender... 2. Guillermina va a tener... 3. Vamos a entrar... 4. Tú vas a vender... 5. Voy a terminar... **PRÁCTICA D.** El lunes a las diez de la noche el avión llega al aeropuerto de México. El martes vamos a visitar la catedral y las pirámides de Teotihuacán. El miércoles vamos a ir al Museo de Antropología. El jueves vamos a comprar regalos en el Mercado de la Merced y luego vamos a ir al Ballet Folklórico. El viernes regresamos a casa.

GRAMMAR SECTION 17. PRÁCTICA A. Todos están tomando (están cantando, están comiendo, están abriendo..., están hablando...). Estoy trabajando. (Estoy escribiendo..., estoy leyendo..., estoy mirando..., estoy aprendiendo...) **PRÁCTICA B.** 1. En este momento los estudiantes están leyendo mucho. 2. Ahora estás visitando la iglesia de San Pedro. 3. Ahora mismo estoy escribiendo en español. 4. En este momento estamos viajando a Acapulco. 5. Hoy están vendiendo fruta barata en el mercado.

GRAMMAR SECTION 18. PRÁCTICA A. 1. problema, dinero, amor 2. cami-

setas, novias, tazas 3. cita, suéter, carro, boda, amistad 4. trajes, limitaciones 5. camisas 6. sombrero **PRÁCTICA B.** 1. Mis hermanos son cariñosos. Mis tíos son cariñosos. Mi hija es cariñosa. Mis primos son cariñosos. Mi abuela es cariñosa. Mi esposo/a es cariñoso/a. 2. Sus zapatos son elegantes. Sus faldas son elegantes. Su abrigo es elegante. Sus bolsas son elegantes. Su ropa es elegante. 3. Nuestro/a profesor(a) es magnífico/a. Nuestros compañeros son magníficos. Nuestro español es magnífico. Nuestras ideas son magníficas. **PRÁCTICA C.** 1. sus recuerdos, los recuerdos de ella 2. su profesión, la profesión de él 3. sus ideas, las ideas de ellas 4. su cuarto, el cuarto de ella 5. sus parientes, los parientes de ellos **PRÁCTICA D.** 1. mis zapatos 2. sus parientes 3. nuestro amor 4. su razón 5. su (tu) boda 6. su novia

GRAMMAR SECTION 19. PRÁCTICA A. 1. ...¿Para la novia? —Sí, es para ella. 2. ¿Para mí? —Sí, es para Ud. (para ti). 3. ¿Para las chicas? —Sí, es para ellas. 4. ¿Para nosotros? —Sí, es para Uds. (para vosotros—*Sp.*). 5. ¿Para Uds.? —Sí, es para nosotros (nosotras *f.*). 6. ¿Para ti? —Sí, es para mí. **PRÁCTICA B.** 1. ...bailo contigo. 2. ...para ti. 3. ...contigo. 4. ...contigo. **PRÁCTICA C.** 1. Hablan de ella. 2. Estudio contigo el viernes. 3. Entre tú y yo, la fiesta es para él. 4. ¿Vienen con nosotros (nosotras *f.*)?

GRAMMAR SECTION 20. PRÁCTICA A. 1. Se necesitan estos papeles. Se necesita esta mesa. Se necesitan estos exámenes. Se necesita este diccionario. Se necesitan estos lápices. Se necesitan estos ejercicios. 2. Esa blusa es azul. Esos zapatos son azules. Esos pantalones son azules. Esa camisa es azul. Esa falda es azul. Esos calcetines son azules. **PRÁCTICA B.** 1. Aquella tienda de ropa es barata. 2. Aquellos periódicos son magníficos. 3. Aquel hotel es fenomenal. 4. Aquellos dependientes son simpáticos. 5. Aquellos precios son fijos. (*Or:* Los precios en aquellos almacenes son fijos.) **PRÁCTICA C.** 1. Éste es trigueño. 2. Ésas son argentinas. 3. Éstos son rubios. 4. Aquélla es una persona muy amable. 5. Ése es muy listo. 6. Aquéllos son para David. **PRÁCTICA D.** 1-c, 2-b, 3-d, 4-a **PRÁCTICA E.** 1. Ese traje es muy caro. 2. Esos clientes son muy pobres. 3. Necesitamos aquellos bolígrafos allí, éstos no. 4. Quiere comprar aquel hotel en las montañas. 5. Esta tienda se abre a las diez, ésa no. 6. ¿Por qué estudiamos esto?

UN POCO DE TODO. EJERCICIO A. 1. Vamos a bailar con Uds. (con vosotros/as—*Sp.*) esta noche. 2. Esos chicos están estudiando con sus primos. 3. Mis padres nunca están de acuerdo conmigo. (Nuestros...con nosotros.) 4. Los abogados están hablando con los padres de ellos. 5. Voy a estudiar esta lección con él el domingo. 6. La dama de honor está detrás de mí. 7. Doy una clase de español a su hijo. 8. Voy a vender mi libro (nuestro libro) el lunes. **EJERCICIO B.** 1. Ella está hablando conmigo en este momento. 2. Tú vas a tener hambre si no comes tu hamburguesa. 3. Esta clase se da a las tres en punto. 4. Esta tarde ellos van a regresar con nuestros tíos. 5. Esta noche mis primas van a la fiesta (a una fiesta) con nuestros abuelos. **PRÁCTICA C.** 1. ¿Quién está a tu izquierda? Ernesto está a mi izquierda. No, Carolina. Ernesto está a tu derecha. Juana está a tu izquierda. 2. ¿Quién está entre _____ y _____? Ernesto está entre _____ y _____ (entre ellos). No, Carolina. Ernesto está al lado de ellos. 3. ¿Quién está detrás de ti? Ernesto está detrás de mí. No, Carolina. Ernesto está delante de ti. Juana está detrás. 4. ¿Quién está en el centro de la clase? Ernesto está en el centro de la clase. No, Carolina. Ernesto está delante de la clase. Juana está en el centro (de la clase). 5. ¿Quién está a tu derecha? Ernesto está a mi derecha. No, Carolina. Ernesto está delante de ti. Juana está a tu derecha.

CAPÍTULO 5

VOCABULARIO: PREPARACIÓN. EJERCICIO A. ...mucho frío, mucho sol, mucho viento, muy mal tiempo, mucho calor, muy buen tiempo. **EJERCICIO B.** Hoy hace fresco (mucho frío, mucho viento). Hoy está nevando (lloviendo). Hoy hay mucha contaminación. **EJERCICIO D.** 1. el siete de marzo 2. el veinticuatro de agosto 3. el primero de diciembre 4. el cinco de junio 5. el diecinueve de se(p)tiembre 6. el treinta de mayo **EJERCICIO E.** Es viernes (lunes, sábado, martes, jueves, jueves, lunes). **EJERCICIO F.** 1. El Día de la Raza se celebra el doce de octubre. 2. El (Día del) Año Nuevo se celebra el primero de enero. 3. El Día de los Enamorados (de San Valentín) se celebra el catorce de febrero. 4. El Día de la Independencia de los Estados Unidos se celebra el cuatro de julio. 5. El Día de los Inocentes se celebra el primero de abril (el 28 de diciembre—*in the Spanish-speaking world*). **EJERCICIO G.** 1. (La fecha de) Mi cumpleaños es el _____ de _____. El cumpleaños de mi mejor amigo/a es el _____ de _____. Mañana es el _____ de _____. Hoy es el _____ de _____. 2. Los meses de otoño son se(p)tiembre, octubre y noviembre. Los meses de primavera son marzo, abril y mayo. Mi mes favorito es _____ porque _____. 3. En invierno hace (mucho) frío (hace mal tiempo, nieva, hace viento). En verano hace (mucho) calor (hace sol, hace buen tiempo). Mi estación favorita es _____ porque _____.

GRAMMAR SECTION 21. PRÁCTICA A. 1. ser 2. estar 3. ser (*to be*) or estar (*to look*) 4. estar 5. ser (*to be*) or estar

(*to look, appear*) 6. estar 7. ser 8. estar 9. ser 10. estar 11. ser 12. ser 13. estar 14. ser (*inherent characteristic*) or estar (*condition*) 15. ser (*inherent characteristic*) or estar (*condition*). **PRÁCTICA B.** 1. El vaso es de cristal (está en el apartamento, es alto, es de Pedro, es verde, está limpio, es para mí). 2. Los jóvenes están de acuerdo... (están cansados, son anglosajones, están a la derecha..., están enfermos, son simpáticos, están muy tristes hoy, son de San Francisco, son amigos..., están leyendo..., están ocupados, están en Los Ángeles, están aburridos...). **PRÁCTICA C.** 1. son 2. Estoy 3. es 4. Son 5. está 6. está 7. es 8. está 9. es 10. está(s) 11. Es 12. estoy 13. es 14. es 15. está 16. es 17. son 18. está 19. eres **PRÁCTICA D.** 1. Este libro es para Ud. (es para ti). 2. Es necesario escuchar bien. ¿Está claro? 3. Estos tacos están buenos (ricos). 4. Está(s) muy guapo/a esta noche.

GRAMMAR SECTION 22. PRÁCTICA A. 1. ¿A qué hora?, ¿Cuándo? 2. ¿Cómo? 3. ¿Quién? 4. ¿Dónde? 5. ¿Cuándo? 6. ¿Por qué? 7. ¿Quiénes? 8. ¿Cuánto? 9. ¿Cuántos? **PRÁCTICA B.** *¿Qué/¿Cuál?* 1. ¿Qué es esto? 2. ¿Cuál es la capital de California? 3. ¿Cuál es tu/su (número de) teléfono? 4. ¿Qué necesitas? 5. ¿Cuál quiere Ud. (quieres)? 6. ¿Qué es el tango? 7. ¿Qué tiempo hace en enero? *¿Quién/ ¿Quiénes/¿De quién?* 1. ¿Quién es Shirley MacLaine? 2. ¿Quiénes son las damas de honor? 3. ¿De quién es el examen? 4. ¿Quién siempre contesta todas las preguntas? *¿Dónde/¿De dónde/¿Adónde?* 1. ¿De dónde son? 2. ¿Adónde quiere Ud. (quieres) viajar? 3. ¿Adónde van los novios? 4. ¿Dónde está el cine? 5. ¿Dónde hay mucha contaminación? *¿Cuándo/¿A qué hora/¿Cuánto/a/¿Cuántos/as?* 1. ¿Cuántos dólares (Cuánto dinero) tiene Ud. (tienes)? 2. ¿A qué hora (Cuándo) llegan Uds. (llegamos)? 3. ¿Cuántos hijos tienen? 4. ¿Cuántas blusas tiene Carlota? 5. ¿Cuándo hace frío en la Argentina? 6. ¿A qué hora (Cuándo) va Ud. (vas) a escuchar ese programa?

GRAMMAR SECTION 23. PRÁCTICA A. 1. tú haces, Raúl hace, yo hago, Lilia y yo hacemos, Uds. hacen, vosotros hacéis 2. yo salgo, tú sales, nosotros salimos, el actor sale, Ud. sale, vosotros salís 3. yo pongo, Gabriela pone, tú pones, nosotros ponemos, Uds. ponen, vosotras ponéis **GRAMMAR SECTION 24. PRÁCTICA A.** 1. yo pido, nosotros pedimos, ellos piden, Lisa pide, tú pides, vosotros pedís 2. Ud. almuerza, los estudiantes almuerzan, nosotros almorzamos, tú almuerzas, yo almuerzo, vosotros almorzáis 3. Sergio prefiere, nosotros preferimos, Ana prefiere, ellas prefieren, tú prefieres, vosotras preferís 4. otros están cerrando... (pidiendo..., volviendo..., sirviendo..., jugando..., durmiendo...) **PRÁCTICA B.** 1. pensamos 2. volvemos 3. empieza 4. duerme 5. sirve 6. juega 7. cerramos

PRÁCTICA C. 1. Pienso... 2. Entro... 3. Pido... 4. Prefiero... 5. Ellos no sirven... 6. Pido... 7. El camarero sirve... 8. Como y vuelvo... 9. Duermo...

GRAMMAR SECTION 25. PRÁCTICA A. 1. Sí, la biblioteca es más alta que la tienda. 2. Sí, el museo es tan grande como el teatro. 3. Sí, la tienda es menos alta que el museo. 5. No, el teatro no es tan alto como la biblioteca. (*Or:* El teatro es menos alto que la biblioteca.) 6. No, el teatro no es menos alto que la tienda. (*Or:* El teatro es más alto que la tienda. *Or:* La tienda es menos alta que el teatro.) **PRÁCTICA B.** 1. Una limonada es más ácida que una naranjada. 2. Este periódico es más/menos interesante que ése. 3. Los tacos son más/menos deliciosos que las enchiladas. 4. Los niños son más/ menos inteligentes que sus padres. 5. El matrimonio es más/menos importante que la amistad. **PRÁCTICA C.** 1. mejor 2. peores 3. mayor 4. menor 5. más grande 6. menos grande **PRÁCTICA D.** 1. Alfredo tiene tanto dinero como Graciela. 2. Graciela tiene tanta cerveza como Alfredo. 3. Alfredo tiene tantos libros como Graciela. 4. Graciela tiene tantos bolígrafos como Alfredo. 5. Alfredo tiene más cuadernos que Graciela. 6. Graciela tiene más cartas que Alfredo. **PRÁCTICA E.** 1. Nicaragua tiene más/menos lugares interesantes que Costa Rica. 2. Hay más/ menos compañeros que compañeras en esta clase. 3. Este pueblo tiene menos habitantes que aquella ciudad. 4. Hay más/menos coches en esta calle que en aquélla. 5. Hay más/menos exámenes en la clase de español que en la clase de historia. 6. Estela bebe más/menos café que yo. 7. Aquí hace más calor en verano que en invierno.

UN POCO DE TODO. EJERCICIO A. 1. ¿Por qué piensan Uds. (pensáis—*Sp.*) que estas playas son mejores que aquéllas? 2. Siempre servimos unas naranjadas en verano. 3. Si no dormimos ocho horas, estamos cansadas todo el día. 4. ¿Cuándo hace calor en esos pueblos? 5. Mañana salimos para Panamá y pensamos volver el sábado. 6. Prefiero almorzar con Ud. (contigo) si no piensa (piensas) salir temprano. 7. Siempre almuerzo en el (un) buen restaurante que está en la Plaza de San Marcos. 8. Pongo tanto dinero en el banco como Ud. (tú). 9. ¿Con quién juego el lunes? 10. Se cierra el mercado a las nueve el miércoles (los miércoles). **EJERCICIO B.** 1. Antonia empieza a ser una estudiante excelente. 2. Yo no vuelvo a casa con tanto trabajo como Elena. 3. Esta semana yo pienso leer tantas lecciones como Estela. 4. El camarero no sirve tanta cerveza como Coca-Cola. 5. Yo hago peores tacos que mis hermanos.

CAPÍTULO 6

VOCABULARIO: PREPARACIÓN.

EJERCICIO A. 1. gazpacho 2. vino, cerveza 3. pollo 4. bistec 5. especialidad de la casa 6. paella 7. tomate, lechuga 8. entremeses 9. fruta 10. cena, pastel 11. entrada 12. cuenta **EJERCICIO B.** 1-b, 2-f, 3-c, 4-d, 5-g, 6-a, 7-e

GRAMMAR SECTION 26. PRÁCTICA A. 1. Sí, hay algo en la mesa. Hay un periódico en la mesa. No, no hay nada en la mesa. // Sí, hay algo en la calle. Hay un carro en la calle. No, no hay nada en la calle. // Sí, hay algo en la montaña. Hay un pueblo en la montaña. No, no hay nada en la montaña. 2. Sí, hay alguien en el parque. Hay unos amigos en el parque. No, no hay nadie en el parque. // Sí, hay alguien en el restaurante. Hay unos clientes en el restaurante. No, no hay nadie en el restaurante. // Sí, hay alguien en la estación. Hay unos pasajeros en la estación. No, no hay nadie en la estación. 3. Sí, hay algunos libros en el suelo. No, no hay ningún libro en el suelo. // Sí, hay algunos libros en el cuarto. No, no hay ningún libro en el cuarto. // Sí, hay algunos libros en la oficina. No, no hay ningún libro en la oficina. **PRÁCTICA B.** 1. No hay nada en el suelo. 2. No hay ningún plato interesante en el menú. 3. Yo no voy tampoco. 4. No cenamos nunca a las diez. 5. No hacemos nada. 6. No habla con nadie. 7. Elena no prepara nunca la lección. 8. Raúl no duerme allí tampoco. **PRÁCTICA C.** 1. algún regalo, algunas flores, algún plato especial, algunos telegramas 2. ningún hermano, ninguna amiga, ningún plan, ninguna familia **PRÁCTICA D.** 1. ¿Hay algo para mí? 2. Hay alguien en el coche/carro. 3. Nadie piensa/cree eso. (Or: No piensa/cree eso nadie.) 4. También sirven la cena allí. 5. No hay nadie en casa. 6. Marcos no comprende esta oración tampoco. (Or: Marcos tampoco comprende esta oración.) 7. Nunca estudias (Ud. nunca estudia) con Carmen. (Or: No estudia(s) nunca con Carmen.) 8. No queremos pedir nada. 9. No hay ningún restaurante en ese/aquel pueblo. 10. Nadie está tan cansado como yo.

GRAMMAR SECTION 27. PRÁCTICA A. 1. tú dices, los niños dicen, yo digo, Ud. dice, la nieta dice, vosotros decís 2. nosotros traemos, Eduardo trae, yo traigo, Uds. traen, tú traes, vosotros traéis 3. Juan y yo no oímos, tú no oyes, Uds. no oyen, la camarera no oye, vosotros no oís 4. yo no veo, nosotros no vemos, Andrés no ve, los clientes no ven, tú no ves, vosotros no veis

GRAMMAR SECTION 28. PRÁCTICA A. 1. Veo al profesor (a la profesora, la pizarra, a los estudiantes, la mesa, a mi amigo/a, la puerta). 2. Estoy buscando mi libro (a Felipe, la cuenta, al amigo de Tomás, a alguien, el menú). **PRÁCTICA B.** 1. Vamos a llamar a Miguel. 2. Invitan a Ana. 3. No miro (No estoy mirando) a nadie. 4. Voy a escuchar a José Feliciano.

5. ¿A quién espera Ud. (esperas)? 6. Estela tiene cuatro primos (primas f.).

GRAMMAR SECTION 29. PRÁCTICA A. 1. El menú, no. No lo... Los platos, no. No los... La maleta, no. No la... El carro, no. No lo... Las cuentas, no. No las... Los lápices, no. No los... 2. ¿La sopa? Sí, tenemos que prepararla... ¿Los postres? ...prepararlos... ¿La lección? ...prepararla... ¿El flan? ...prepararlo... ¿Las patatas? ...prepararlas... ¿La cena? ...prepararla... 3. ¿Queso? Sí, estamos pidiéndolo ahora. ¿Carne? ...pidiéndola... ¿Té? ...pidiéndolo... ¿Entremeses? ...pidiéndolos... ¿Fruta? ...pidiéndola... ¿Vino? ...pidiéndolo... **PRÁCTICA B.** 1. El camarero los pone en la mesa. 2. Mis hijos están usándolo (lo están usando) ahora. 3. Voy a leerla (La voy a leer) esta noche. 4. ¿Por qué no la pagas tú? 5. ¿El dinero? No lo tengo. 6. Los necesitamos para la fiesta. 7. Estoy escribiéndolas. (Or: Las estoy escribiendo.) 8. Los niños están abriéndolos (los están abriendo). **PRÁCTICA C.** 1. ¡Porque acabo de estudiarla! 2. ¡Porque acabo de visitarlo! 3. ¡Porque acabo de aprenderlo! 4. ¡Porque acabo de comprarlo! 5. ¡Porque acabo de pagarla! 6. ¡Porque acabo de ayudarte! **PRÁCTICA D.** 1. ¡No, no lo preferimos! 2. ¡No, no lo comprendemos! 3. ¡No, no lo deseamos! 4. ¡No, no lo pensamos!

GRAMMAR SECTION 30. PRÁCTICA A. 1. ellos saben, yo sé, Elvira sabe, Ud. sabe, Ana y tú saben (sabéis—Sp.), vosotros sabéis 2. yo conozco, Uds. conocen, Juan y yo conocemos, tú conoces, Raúl y Mario conocen, vosotros conocéis **PRÁCTICA B.** José Feliciano sabe cantar en español. Mikhail Baryshnikov sabe bailar. Pete Rose sabe jugar al béisbol. Liberace sabe tocar el piano. James Michener sabe escribir novelas. Evelyn Wood sabe leer rápidamente. **PRÁCTICA C.** Adán conoce a Eva. Archie Bunker conoce a Edith. Romeo conoce a Julieta. Rhett Butler conoce a Scarlett O'Hara. Antonio conoce a Cleopatra. Jorge Washington conoce a Marta.

UN POCO DE TODO. EJERCICIO A. 1. El profesor Cortina no conoce a ninguna chica de la clase. 2. Yo no conozco a ningún francés. 3. El camarero está trayéndolo. 4. ¿Hay alguien en el patio? —Yo no oigo a nadie. 5. ¿No dice Ud. nada, Sra. Medina? 6. ¿El teléfono del profesor? Yo no lo sé. **EJERCICIO B.** 1. La estudiante está diciéndolo (lo está diciendo). 2. ¿Por qué no dice Ud. nada? 3. No vemos ninguna frase en la pizarra. 4. ¿Sabes si ellos conocen a mi amiga? 5. No los veo en este momento. 6. La señorita Gómez (Padilla) no puede oir al señor Padilla (Gómez). **EJERCICIO C.** 1. No, no lo/la/los/las veo. / Sí, lo/la/los/las veo. Yo no lo/la/los/las veo tampoco. / Yo también lo/la/los/las veo. 2. No, no lo conozco. / Sí, lo conozco. Yo no lo conozco tampoco. / Yo también lo conozco. 3. No,

no las sé. / Sí, las sé. Yo no las sé tampoco. / Yo también las sé. 4. No, no te oigo bien. / Sí, te oigo. Yo no te oigo tampoco. / Yo también te oigo bien. 5. No, no las veo. / Sí, las veo. Yo no las veo tampoco. / Yo también las veo. 6. No, no los traigo (a la universidad). / Sí, los traigo. Yo no los traigo tampoco. / Yo también los traigo. 7. No, no la sé. / Sí, la sé. Yo no la sé tampoco. / Yo también la sé. **EJERCICIO D.** 1. Sí, veo algo... No, no veo nada... 2. Sí, traigo algunos libros... No, no traigo ningún libro... 3. Sí, veo a alguien... No, no veo a nadie... 4. Sí, sé algo de... No, no sé nada de... 5. Sí, sé algo de... No, no sé nada de... 6. Sí, conozco a alguien de... No, no conozco a nadie de... 7. Sí, conozco a alguien de... No, no conozco a nadie de... 8. Sí, conozco a algunos españoles... No, no conozco a ningún español. 9. Sí, tengo algunos amigos... No, no tengo ningún amigo...

CAPÍTULO 7

VOCABULARIO: PREPARACIÓN. EJERCICIO B. Sequence: 2, 8, 5, 4, 7, 3, 6, 1, 9. **EJERCICIO C.** 1-a, 2-c, 3-b, 4-c, 5-b, 6-b

GRAMMAR SECTION 31. PRÁCTICA A. 1. Te escribo una tarjeta postal a ti. Le escribo una tarjeta postal a Ud. Le escribo una tarjeta postal a Ángel. Les escribo una tarjeta postal a Uds. Le escribo una tarjeta postal a Alicia. Os escribo una tarjeta postal a vosotros. 2. Ahora estoy comprándole el boleto a Sergio (comprándote el boleto a ti, comprándole el boleto a Estela, comprándoles el boleto a Uds., comprándoles el boleto a Marta y Rosa, comprándoos el boleto a vosotros). **PRÁCTICA B.** Julio le da (a Marcos) el libro. Ernesto le da el regalo grande. Ana le da el radio portátil. María le de la camisa. A todos Marcos les dice "(Muchas) Gracias." No, no le doy ningún regalo (a Marcos) porque no lo conozco (porque no tengo mucho dinero, etc.). No, no lo conozco. Me van a dar _____. **PRÁCTICA C.** Pepe les da el regalo pequeño. Rodolfo les da el televisor. Irma les da los boletos para un viaje a Puerto Vallarta. Inés les da la pintura bonita. (A mis padres) les doy _____. **PRÁCTICA D.** 1. guardar el equipaje—te guardo... 2. facturar el equipaje—te facturo... 3. guardar el puesto en la cola—te guardo... 4. guardar el asiento—te guardo... 5. buscar el pasaporte—te busco... 6. ayudar con las maletas—te ayudo...

GRAMMAR SECTION 32. PRÁCTICA A. 1. (No) Me gusta el vino. 2. (No) Me gusta el español. 3. (No) Me gusta esta universidad. 4. (No) Me gusta el invierno. 5. (No) Me gusta la gramática. 6. (No) Me gusta hacer cola. 7. (No) Me gustan los entremeses. 8. (No) Me gustan los fines de semana. 9. (No) Me gustan las clases este semestre. 10. (No) Me gustan los exámenes. 11. (No) Me gustan las flores. 12. (No) Me gustan los vuelos con muchas escalas. **PRÁCTICA B.** 1. (No) Me gusta el otoño. (No) Me gustan los médicos. (No) Me gusta volar. (No) Me gustan las discotecas. (No) Me gustan los animales. (No) Me gusta fumar. 2. A mí me gustan las vacaciones. A Rico le gustan... A ellas les gustan... A ti te gustan... A Uds. les gustan... A vosotros os gustan... **PRÁCTICA C.** A mi padre le gustan las anchoas, pero no le gusta el chorizo. A mi madre le gusta el chorizo, pero no le gusta mucho el queso. A mis hermanos les gusta el queso, pero no les gustan los hongos. ¡A mí me gusta todo! **GRAMMAR SECTION 33. PRÁCTICA A.** 1. prácticamente 2. especialmente 3. alegremente 4. estupendamente 5. perfectamente 6. tristemente 7. finalmente 8. típicamente 9. personalmente **PRÁCTICA B.** 1. pacientemente (tranquilamente) 2. inmediatamente 3. tranquilamente 4. inmediatamente (rápidamente, fácilmente) 5. posiblemente 6. totalmente 7. directamente

GRAMMAR SECTION 34. PRÁCTICA A. 1. Sr. Casiano, no trabaje tanto (no cene..., no fume, no beba..., no vuelva..., no almuerce..., no juegue..., no salga..., no vaya..., no sea...). 2. Lleguen Uds...., Lean..., Escriban..., Abran..., Piensen..., Estén... **PRÁCTICA B.** 1. Fúmelo Ud. 2. No lo facturen Uds. aquí. 3. Créanlo Uds. 4. Tóquelas Ud. 5. No lo olviden Uds. **PRÁCTICA C.** 1. (Sr. López,) Llévelo (Ud.) a la oficina de emigración. 2. Pídala (Ud.). 3. Póngalo (Ud.) en el banco. 4. Factúrelo (Ud.). 5. Empiécela (Ud.). **PRÁCTICA D.** 1. (Sres. Corral,) No lo recomienden (Uds.). 2. No la abran (Uds.) muy tarde. 3. No la pidan (Uds.). 4. No la paguen (Uds.). 5. No lo traigan (Uds.). **PRÁCTICA E.** 1. No la toque. 2. Cómprelo. 3. No lo compre. 4. Léala. 5. No lo lea. 6. Véala. **PRÁCTICA F.** 1. Haga sus/las maletas. 2. Vaya al aeropuerto. 3. No llegue tarde. 4. Compre su/el boleto. 5. Facture sus/las maletas. 6. Haga cola. 7. Déle su/el boleto al camarero. 8. Suba al avión.

GRAMMAR SECTION 35. PRÁCTICA A. 1. novecientos treinta años 2. siete mil trescientas cincuenta y cuatro personas 3. cien países 4. cinco mil setecientos diez habitantes 5. doscientas cuarenta universidades 6. seiscientos setenta pasajes 7. dos mil cuatrocientas ochenta y seis mujeres 8. mil dólares 9. quinientos veintiocho pesetas. 10. ochocientas sesenta y tres pesetas 11. ciento una niñas 12. un millón de dólares **PRÁCTICA B.** 1-e, 2-d, 3-a, 4-f, 5-g, 6-c, 7-b

UN POCO DE TODO. EJERCICIO A. 1. No sean Uds. demasiado serios. 2. No les hagan eso. 3. ¿Les gusta todo eso? 4. No nos digan Uds. las respuestas.

5. No nos gusta nunca jugar al tenis. 6. No me gusta este asiento. 7. No le dé Ud. tanta comida al niño. 8. ¿Le gusta a Ud. aquella clase? 9. Tráigale el disco a él. 10. Me gusta comer tranquilamente. **EJERCICIO B.** 1. No le sirva Ud. vino al niño. 2. Léame Ud. las palabras en la página quinientos cuarenta y dos. 3. A Vicente le gusta llegar puntualmente a clase. 4. Háganlo Uds. rápidamente para mí. 5. A ti no te gusta eso, ¿verdad? **EJERCICIO C.** 1. prepárele sopa. 2. déles más exámenes. 3. cómprenles boletos. 4. ábrale la puerta. 5. tráigale las maletas. 6. toquen y cántenle una canción.

CAPÍTULO 8

VOCABULARIO: PREPARACIÓN. EJERCICIO C. 1. secar 2. refrigerar 3. cocinar 4. lavar 5. acondicionar

GRAMMAR SECTION 36. PRÁCTICA A. 1. yo me quito, Carolina se quita, nosotras nos quitamos, tú te quitas, todos los estudiantes se quitan, vosotros os quitáis 2. tú te acuestas, nosotros nos acostamos, Arturo se acuesta, yo me acuesto, Evangelina y Nati se acuestan, vosotras os acostáis 3. ellos se bañan y se visten, yo me baño y me visto, nosotros nos bañamos y nos vestimos, tú te bañas y te vistes, Ana María se baña y se viste, vosotros os bañáis y os vestís **PRÁCTICA B.** 1. me pongo 2. nos despertamos 3. se divierte 4. se sientan 5. me quito 6. lavarme **PRÁCTICA C.** 1. Despiértese más temprano. 2. Levántese más temprano. 3. No se acueste tan tarde. 4. Vístase mejor. 5. No se divierta tanto. 6. Quítese esa ropa sucia y póngase ropa limpia. 7. Báñese más. **PRÁCTICA D.** 1. ¿Me quito los pantalones? —Sí, quíteselos, por favor. 2. ¿Me quito la camisa/la blusa? —Sí, quítesela, por favor. 3. ¿Me quito el suéter? —Sí, quíteselo, por favor. 4. ¿Me quito los calcetines/las medias? —Sí, quíteselos/las, por favor. 5. ¿Me quito toda la ropa? —Sí, quítesela, por favor. **PRÁCTICA E.** 1. Voy a acostarme (Me voy a acostar) más tarde. 2. Voy a acostar a mi hijo más tarde. 3. ¡Despiértese ahora! 4. ¡Despierte a su esposa ahora! 5. se llama Agustín. 6. (Él) Llama a sus padres. 7. Se ponen los zapatos. 8. Ponen la cafetera en la estufa.

GRAMMAR SECTION 37. PRÁCTICA. 1. Estela y yo nos miramos. 2. Eduardo y Pepita se hablan. 3. El padre y el hijo se necesitan. 4. Tomás y yo nos conocemos. 5. Tú y Luisa se escriben (os escribís—*Sp.*). 6. La profesora y los estudiantes se escuchan. 7. Ud. y su esposo se quieren.

GRAMMAR SECTION 38. PRÁCTICA A. 1. yo estudié, Uds. estudiaron, tú estudiaste, Graciela estudió, nosotros

estudiamos, vosotros estudiasteis 2. Rosendo escribió, yo escribí, nosotras escribimos, ellas escribieron, Uds. escribieron, vosotros escribisteis 3. yo bailé y bebí, José bailó y bebió, nosotros bailamos y bebimos, tú bailaste y bebiste, Uds. bailaron y bebieron, vosotros bailasteis y bebisteis 4. yo (no) fui, Paula (no) fue, tú (no) fuiste, nosotros (no) fuimos, Estela y Clara (no) fueron, vosotras (no) fuisteis 5. yo (no) hice, nosotros (no) hicimos, Uds. (no) hicieron, tú (no) hiciste, Adolfo (no) hizo, vosotros (no) hicisteis **PRÁCTICA B.** 1. Julián hizo cola para comprar una entrada de cine. La compró por fin. Entró en el cine. Vio la película. Le gustó mucho. Regresó a casa tarde. 2. Yo llegué a la universidad temprano. Asistí a las clases. Fui a la cafetería. Almorcé. Estudié en la biblioteca. **PRÁCTICA C.** 1. Regresé, preparó, cenamos, empecé, salió 2. Pasé, pagaron, trabajé, viví, aprendí, Fui, escribieron 3. fue, hizo, comió, gustaron, dieron, salieron

GRAMMAR SECTION 39. PRÁCTICA A. 1. pan—Me lo pasas, por favor. tomates—Me los pasas,... tortillas—Me las pasas,... vino—Me la pasas,... jamón—Me lo pasas,... 2. ¿Las ventanas? Te las lavo mañana. ¿El refrigerador? Te lo lavo mañana. ¿Los platos? Te los lavo mañana. ¿La ropa? Te la lavo mañana. **PRÁCTICA B.** 1-e, 2-b, 3-f, 4-c, 5-d, 6-a, 7-g **PRÁCTICA C.** 1. No, no se lo vende a ellos. Sí, se lo vende a él. 2. No, no se la sirve a él. No, no se la sirve a ellos. Sí, se la sirve a ella. 3. No, no se las manda a él. No, no se las manda a ellos. Sí, se las manda a ella. 4. No, no se los recomienda a ellos. No, no se los recomienda a ella. Sí, se los recomienda a él. **PRÁCTICA D.** 1. No te lo escribo a ti. Se lo escribo a mis padres. 2. No te las pido a ti. Se las pido al profesor. 3. No te lo doy a ti. Se lo doy a Pepe. 4. No te los compro a ti. Se los compro a mi hermana menor. 5. No te la sirvo a ti. Se la sirvo a mis primos. **PRÁCTICA E.** 1. Acaban de decírmela. No me los lea Ud. 3. No tienen que pagárnosla. 4. Estoy guardándoselo. 5. Cómpreselos Ud. 6. ¿Me los quieres sacudir? 7. La camarera se las sirve. 8. Se la recomiendo, señor.

GRAMMAR SECTION 40. PRÁCTICA A. 1. Me gusta cuando mis amigos me invitan a jugar al volibol (comer, salir con ellos, visitarlos, bailar). 2. Mis profesores me ayudan a aprender... (comprender..., descubrir..., hacer..., expresar...). 3. En esta clase hay que estudiar... (conjugar..., estar..., escuchar..., saber...). B. *Note:* insistir en, empezar a, acabar de, desear (*no prep.*), venir a, tener que

UN POCO DE TODO. EJERCICIO A. 1. No sabemos cómo se llaman ellas. ¿Nos las presentan (presentáis—*Sp.*)? 2. Uds. vienen a leérnoslas, ¿verdad? 3. Uds. se despertaron a las seis, ¿no? Pues, acuéstense temprano esta noche. 4. Todavía estamos tratando de comprender los diálogos. No nos los explicaron bien los tutores. 5. No se levanten a las siete si no tienen que estar allí hasta las once. **PRÁCTICA B.** 1. ¿La cafetera? Yo se la di a mis padres. 2. Pablo y Claudia se conocieron en Buenos Aires, pero él nunca la invitó a salir. 3. Carlos empezó a vestirse a las ocho. 4. Yo traté de explicárselo a ellos, pero no me escucharon. 5. Pedro se afeitó, se bañó y se acostó. **PRÁCTICA C.** 1-c, 2-b, 3-g, 4-e, 5-d, 6-a, 7-f

CAPÍTULO 9

VOCABULARIO: PREPARACIÓN. EJERCICIO A. 1-g, 2-e, 3-f, 4-b, 5-d, 6-a, 7-c **EJERCICIO B.** 1. la directora o el empleado 2. la directora o el empleado 3. el empleado 4. la directora 5. la directora 6. el empleado **EJERCICIO C.** 1. un(a) mujer/hombre de negocios 2. un(a) comerciante 3. un(a) abogado/a 4. un(a) director(a) 5. un(a) empleado/a 6. un(a) plomero/a 7. un(a) obrero/a 8. un(a) siquiatra 9. un(a) enfermero/a **GRAMMAR SECTION 41. PRÁCTICA A.** 1. yo baile, cene, mire, llegue, busque, quite 2. tú aprendas, escribas, leas, asistas, respondas, sacudas 3. Ud. empiece, piense, vuele, juegue, se siente, se despierte 4. nosotros pidamos, sirvamos, prefiramos, muramos, nos divirtamos, despidamos 5. Uds. esperen, deban, se bañen, decidan, almuercen, cambien 6. yo conozca, haga, ponga, traiga, sepa, diga 7. ella sea, dé, venga vaya, oiga, salga **EJERCICIO B.** 1. Ana se despierte, nosotros nos despertemos, yo me despierte, ellos se despierten, vosotros os despertéis 2. nosotros durmamos, tú duermas, Paco y yo durmamos, Uds. duerman, vosotros durmáis 3. Ud. pueda, Emanuel pueda, nosotros podamos, yo pueda, vosotros podáis **PRÁCTICA C.** 1. Ojalá que yo pase... (tenga..., conozca..., encuentre..., gane...). 2. ¡Ojalá que hablemos... (no tengamos..., contestemos..., aprendamos..., no tengamos que escribir...)! **GRAMMAR SECTION 42. PRÁCTICA A.** 1. No, el/la profesor(a) no quiere que yo fume (que nosotros fumemos, que tú fumes, que los estudiantes fumen, que Lupe fume, que vosotros fuméis) en clase. 2. Mis amigos me piden que me vista... (salga..., les explique..., vaya..., no tome...). 3. La directora te recomienda a ti que trabajes (le recomienda a Mariana que trabaje, les recomienda a Uds. que trabajen, le recomienda a Ud. que trabaje, les recomienda a todos que trabajen, os recomienda a vosotros que trabajéis) el sábado. **PRÁCTICA B.** 1. pague 2. maneje 3. despida 4. vea 5. me levante 6. los

tome (*or*: tome ocho; tome tantos cursos) 7. dé **PRÁCTICA D.** Quiero que Ud. haga (hagas, Uds. hagan) el inventario. Insisto en que esté listo para mañana y si no puede (puedes, pueden) hacerlo/terminarlo para entonces, quiero que trabaje (trabajes, trabajen) este fin de semana. **GRAMMAR SECTION 43. PRÁCTICA A.** 1. Sí, esperemos. 2. Sí, bailemos. 3. Sí, comamos ahora. 4. Sí, leamos. 5. Sí, salgamos 6. Sí, divirtámonos. 7. Sí, acostémonos temprano. 8. Sí, levantémonos tarde mañana. **PRÁCTICA B.** 1. Sí, invitémoslo. No, no lo invitemos todavía. 2. Sí, escribámosela. No, no se la escribamos todavía. 3. Sí, vendámoselo. No, no se lo vendamos todavía. 4. Sí, digámoselo. No, no se lo digamos todavía. 5. Sí, ayudémosla. No, no la ayudemos todavía. 6. Sí, pongámoslo. No, no nos lo pongamos todavía. 7. Sí, sacudámoslos. No, no los sacudamos todavía. 8. Sí, quitémonoslo ahora. No, no nos lo quitemos todavía. **GRAMMAR SECTION 44. PRÁCTICA C.** 1. mi libro de español. 2. un día de otoño 3. nuestro/a profesor(a) de ciencias 4. su número de teléfono **UN POCO DE TODO. EJERCICIO A.** 1. Yo prohíbo que Uds. compren aquel anillo de plata. 2. Ojalá que Lauro venga al programa de música argentina. 3. Felipa prefiere que no la llame Carlos. Llamémosla nosotros. 4. Nosotros insistimos en que tú no dejes la universidad. (Nosotros) Queremos que tú te gradúes primero. 5. Yo recomiendo que Roberto trabaje. Divirtámonos nosotros. **EJERCICIO B.** 1. No quiero que María escriba la carta. Prefiero que la haga/escriba Juan. 2. Vamos a pedirles (Les vamos a pedir) que vengan. ¡Ojalá que vengan! 3. ¿Entonces Ud. recomienda (recomiendas) que visitemos Taxco? ¡Vamos!/Vámonos! 4. Ojalá que no sea demasiado tarde. Salgamos ahora. 5. Ojalá que Ana haga/prepare el postre. Pero si no lo hace ella, hagámoslo juntos/as. 6. ¿Por qué quiere Ud. (quieres) que vayamos en autobús? Volemos. **EJERCICIO C.** 1. Federico prepare una paella / la prepare / la prepara, preparémosla 2. la criada limpie el baño esta semana / lo limpie / lo limpia, limpiémoslo 3. los niños canten en la fiesta / canten / cantan, cantemos 4. Marcos escriba un poema para el cumpleaños de Andrea / lo escriba / lo escribe, escribámoslo 5. los señores Santana inviten a nuestro amigo Ramón a la cena / lo inviten / lo invitan, invitémoslo 6. Arturo les diga la verdad a sus padres / se la diga / se la dice, digámosela **EJERCICIO D.** 1. Quiero que Ud. lave... (limpie..., saque..., lo prepare todo...). 2. Recomiendo que Ud. llegue... (no deje..., siempre esté de acuerdo...). 3. Ojalá que nosotros trabajemos... (lleguemos..., no dejemos..., siempre estemos de acuerdo...). 3. Recomiendo que Ud. visite... (conozca..., compre..., hable...).

CAPÍTULO 10

VOCABULARIO   PREPARACIÓN. EJERCICIO B. 1-g, 2-h, 3-i, 4-d, 5b, 6-f, 7-c, 8-a, 9-k, 10-e, 11-j **EJERCICIO D.** agencia de automóviles, vendedor, ganga, pago inicial, pagar a plazos, firma, funcione **GRAMMAR SECTION 45. PRÁCTICA A.** 1. estén..., funcione..., vengan..., se diviertan..., estén... 2. haya..., venga..., tenga..., cueste..., haya..., les pase..., haya... 3. A mí me sorprende..., A todos los estudiantes les..., A ti te..., A nosotros nos..., A Armando le..., A vosotros os... **PRÁCTICA B.** 1. sea económico 2. lleguen 3. esté enfermo 4. haya un examen y que sean necesarios 5. haya 6. no me la vaya a poner/no vaya a ponérmela **PRÁCTICA D.** Siento que su/tu hija esté enferma y espero que el médico/doctor (la médica/doctora) pueda ayudarla (la pueda ayudar) pronto. Me alegro de que su/tu hijo se sienta mejor. **GRAMMAR SECTION 46. PRÁCTICA A.** 1. tú seas, el/la profesor(a) sea, ellos sean, nosotros seamos, Ud. sea, vosotros seáis 2. Creo que es, Dudo que sea, Estoy seguro/a que es, Niego que sea, No dudo que es, No estoy seguro/a que sea **PRÁCTICA B.** *Use subjunctive after* No creo que, Dudo que, Niego que, No estoy seguro/a que; *indicative after* Creo que, No dudo que, No niego que, Estoy seguro/a que. **PRÁCTICA C.** Hay un examen, pero no estoy seguro/a que sea mañana. Dudo que el subjuntivo entre en el examen y no creo que haya mandatos/imperativos. ¿Cree(s) que sea/va a ser fácil? **GRAMMAR SECTION 47. PRÁCTICA A.** 1. Sí, es mejor que compre... (es cierto que compra..., es posible que compre..., es seguro que compra..., es probable que compre...) 2. compre..., limpie..., busque..., invite..., traiga... **PRÁCTICA B.** *Use subjunctive after* Es importante que, Es terrible que, Es imposible que; *indicative after* Es verdad que. **GRAMMAR SECTION 48. PRÁCTICA.** 1. se anuncie 2. volvamos 3. esté viajando 4. se prohíba 5. visitemos 6. haga 7. sea 8. haya 9. tomen 10. se doble **UN POCO DE TODO. EJERCICIO A.** 1. Nosotros esperamos que Julio firme pero tal vez no quiera. 2. Ellos niegan que Adolfo sea buen mecánico. 3. Tal vez sea la batería. —Yo no estoy seguro/a. 4. El agente va a alegrarse (de) que nosotros le demos el pago inicial hoy. 5. Es evidente que Ud. no cree que yo sea buen(a) estudiante. **EJERCICIO B.** 1. Sentimos que no pueda(s) estar allí. Tal vez venga(s) el año que viene. 2. Dudo que sea necesario trabajar tanto. 3. Me sorprende que haya tanto sol ahora. Pero es posible que llueva más tarde. 4. Es verdad que la carretera es mejor, pero aquel (ese) camino es más interesante. 5. Estamos seguros/as que la conocen, pero dudamos que conozcan a su mamá/madre. **EJERCICIO**

C. 1. compre aquel carro tan barato / lo compre / lo compre 2. pueda arreglar el radiador / lo pueda arreglar / lo pueda arreglar 3. visite a Ramiro en el hospital / lo visite / lo visite 4. toque el piano en la fiesta / lo toque / lo toque 5. conozca a los padres de Evita / los conozca / los conozca 6. sepa el número de teléfono de Mateo / lo sepa / lo sepa

CAPÍTULO 11

VOCABULARIO: PREPARACIÓN. EJERCICIO C. El lunes (martes, miércoles, jueves, viernes, sábado, domingo) es el primer (segundo, tercer, cuarto, quinto, sexto, séptimo) día de la semana. Enero (febrero, marzo, abril, mayo, junio, julio, agosto, septiembre, octubre, noviembre, diciembre) es el primer (segundo, tercer, cuarto, quinto, sexto, séptimo, octavo, noveno, décimo, undécimo/onceno, último) mes del año. **EJERCICIO D.** 1. Manuel está en el quinto grado. 2. Teresa está en el tercer grado. 3. Eduardo está en el séptimo grado. 4. Jesús está en el primer grado. 5. Pablo está en el décimo grado. 6. Evangelina está en el segundo grado. **EJERCICIO E.** 1. Alicia es la décima persona. Raúl es la quinta persona. Jorge es la tercera persona. Teodoro es la novena persona. María es la segunda persona. 2. Ángela está en la cuarta posición. Cecilia está en la octava posición. Juan está en la séptima posición. Simón está en la primera posición. Linda está en la sexta posición.
GRAMMAR SECTION 49. PRÁCTICA A. 1. No gastes tanto. 2. No despiertes al niño. 3. No lo cierres, por favor. 4. No lo limpies. 5. No le arregles el carro hoy. 6. No escribas la carta a máquina. 7. No corras tanto. 8. No vengas tan tarde. 9. No lo leas, por favor. 10. No hagas tanto ruido, por favor. **PRÁCTICA B.** 1. No los dejes en el suelo, por favor. 2. No regreses tarde a (casa), por favor. 3. No lleves mi ropa (No la lleves), por favor. 4. No juegues/corras en la calle. 5. No vayas al parque todos los días. 6. No mires la televisión (No la mires) constantemente. 7. No le digas mentiras a papá. *Or:* No se las digas (a papá). 8. No te olvides de sacar la basura (sacarla). 9. No dobles en esta esquina (aquí). 10. No seas tan mala. **PRÁCTICA C.** 1. Llena la solicitud. 2. ¡Niégalo! 3. ¡Contéstale inmediatamente al aspirante. 4. Pregúntale su apellido. 5. Almuerza allí. 6. Apréndela bien. 7. Sal de aquí. 8. Sírvele el vino. 9. Ve al colegio. 10. Ven al aeropuerto. **PRÁCTICA D.** 1. Escríbele a Santiago. 2. Ayúdame. 3. Ten paciencia. 4. Desayuna. 5. Escúchame. 6. Termina tus proyectos. 7. Di la verdad. 8. Haz la ensalada. 9. Pon la mesa. 10. Sé buena. **PRÁCTICA E.** 1. Anita, habla español en la entrevista; no hables inglés. 2. Gilberto, lee una novela; no leas un periódico. 3. Nati, pregúntale la dirección a Lorenzo; no se la preguntes a Carmen. 4. Santiago, bebe una limonada; no bebas el café. 5. Maricarmen, cómpranos cuatro boletos; no nos compres tres. 6. Mariela, baila el chachachá; no bailes el tango. 7. Dolores, trae vino; no traigas cerveza. 8. Silvia, estaciona el carro en la calle Bolívar; no lo estaciones en el estacionamiento.
GRAMMAR SECTION 50. PRÁCTICA A. 1. Olga y Paula son las empleadas más trabajadoras de la oficina. 2. Es la plaza más pequeña de la ciudad. 3. El Brasil es el país más grande de Suramérica. 4. La Sra. Gómez es la mejor aspirante de la lista. 5. La lección once es la lección más importante del texto. 6. ¡Es la peor clase de la universidad! **PRÁCTICA B.** 1. importantísimo 2. dificilísimo 3. altísimo 4. pobrísimo 5. especialísimo 6. facilísimo 7. perfectísimo 8. atrasadísimo
GRAMMAR SECTION 51. PRÁCTICA A. 1. Quiero ir por barco. 2. Hablo (con mis amigos) por teléfono. 3. Me gusta caminar por la universidad. 4. Me gusta estudiar por la tarde. 5. Estoy tan nervioso/a por el examen. 6. Estudio (por) tres horas todos los días. 7. Pagué dos mil dólares por el coche. 8. Los padres se sacrifican por los niños. 9. El secretario de estado habla por el presidente. 10. Volví a la tienda por vino. **PRÁCTICA B.** 1-f, 2-g, 3-d, 4-b, 5-e, 6-c, 7-a
GRAMMAR SECTION 52. PRÁCTICA A. Pues... me gusta más la roja (me gustan más los rojos, me gustan más las rojas, me gusta más el rojo, me gusta más la roja, me gustan más los rojos). **PRÁCTICA B.** 1. Debo comprar el barato (el caro). 2. Prefiero las grandes (las más pequeñas). 3. Voy a comprar la verde (la amarilla). 4. Me gusta más la española (la mexicana). 5. Me da el americano (el japonés), por favor.
UN POCO DE TODO. EJERCICIO A. 1. No compres el primer carro que ves. Compra el mejor. 2. La primera película de aquella actriz fue/es buenísima, pero la segunda fue/es malísima. 3. Raquel, dobla en la segunda esquina. No dobles en la primera. 4. Dime tus apellidos. No me digas tu nombre. 5. Vende tu casa grandísima y compra esa pequeñísima. **PRÁCTICA B.** 1. Lee la lección quinta, pero no leas la sexta. 2. Me gusta más el último aspirante por su experiencia. 3. Por la mañana llené una solicitud larguísima. 4. El primer aspirante me cayó pesadísimo. 5. Preséntame a ese panameño altísimo. **EJERCICIO C.** 1. ¿Escribiste el primer ejercicio? Sí, y también escribí el segundo. Fueron complicadísimos, ¿no? El primero no fue tan complicado como el segundo. 2. ¿Renunciaste tu primer puesto? Sí, y también renuncié el segundo. Fueron pesadísimos, ¿no? El primero no fue tan pesado como el segundo. 3. ¿Te preparaste para la primera clase? Sí, y también me preparé para la segunda. Fueron aburridísimas, ¿no? La primera no fue tan aburrida como la segunda. 4. ¿Aprendiste el primer diálogo? Sí, y también aprendí el segundo. Fueron larguísimos, ¿no? El primero no fue tan largo como el segundo. 5. ¿Hablaste con el primer aspirante? Sí, y también hablé con el segundo. Fueron listísimos, ¿no? El primero no fue tan listo como el segundo. **EJERCICIO D.** 1. Jacinto, no estudies por la tarde; es malísimo para la salud. Estudia por la tarde. 2. Carlota, no vayas a Europa por barco; es carísimo. Ve por avión. 3. Pedro, no tomes el autobús; es pesadísimo. Toma el tren. 4. Consuelo, no compres la blusa amarilla; es feísima. Compra la azul. 5. Anamari, no llenes la solicitud blanca; es viejísima. Llena la nueva. 6. No juegues en la calle; es peligrosísima. Juega en el parque.

CAPÍTULO 12

VOCABULARIO: PREPARACIÓN. EJERCICIO A. 1. La señorita está riéndose. Se siente bien (feliz, contenta). 2. La señorita está llorando. Se siente triste. 3. La señorita está enojándose (está enojada). Se siente enojada (furiosa). 4. La señora está sonriendo. Se siente feliz (contenta, bien). **EJERCICIO E.** 1. peso 2. ¡Felicidades! 3. regalaste 4. niño/varón 5. bebé/niño 6. bautizar
GRAMMAR SECTION 53. PRÁCTICA A. 1. Raúl (no) tuvo, yo (no) tuve, nosotros (no) tuvimos, tú (no) tuviste, nadie tuvo, vosotros (no) tuvisteis 2. yo (no) estuve, nosotros (no) estuvimos, Soledad (no) estuvo, tú (no) estuviste, Carlos y Fidelia (no) estuvieron, vosotras no estuvisteis 3. Silvia se puso furiosa. Mi esposo/a se puso furioso/a. Uds. se pusieron furiosos/as. Nosotros nos pusimos furiosos. Tú te pusiste furioso/a. Vosotros os pusisteis furiosos. 4. yo quise, pude; ellos quisieron, pudieron; Eloísa quiso, pudo; tú quisiste, pudiste; Ud. quiso, pudo; vosotras quisisteis, pudisteis 5. tú dijiste, el/la profesor(a) dijo, Ud. dijo, nosotros dijimos, todos los estudiantes dijeron, vosotros dijisteis 6. Ud. no vino. Nosotros no vinimos. Uds. no vinieron. Tú no viniste. Rosalba no vino. Vosotros no vinisteis. **PRÁCTICA B.** En 1969 los estadounidenses pusieron un hombre en la luna. Adán y Eva supieron que las serpientes son malas. Jorge Washington estuvo en Valley Forge con sus soldados. Los europeos trajeron el caballo al Nuevo Mundo. Stanley conoció a Livingston en África. María Antonieta dijo "que coman pasteles." **PRÁCTICA C.** 1. vino, se portó, estuvo, dijo, se fue. 2. hicieron, pusieron, tuvieron, pudieron 3. quise, pude, vino, tuve, trajeron
GRAMMAR SECTION 54. PRÁCTICA A. 1. librito 2. angelito 3. autorcito

4. jovencito 5. hombrecito 6. laguito 7. botita 8. varoncito 9. chiquito 10. perrito **PRÁCTICA B.** 1. Carmencita 2. Juanita 3. Xaviercito 4. Rafaelito 5. Alvarito 6. Sarita 7. Anita 8. Lolita **GRAMMAR SECTION 55. PRÁCTICA A.** 1. (No) Estamos aquí para aprender español (para divertirnos, para conversar, para escuchar). 2. Para mi madre, el pescado. Para mi hermanito, el bistec. Para mi abuela, la paella. Para mí, el pollo. 3. Colón salió para la India. Los astronautas salieron para la luna. Lewis y Clark salieron para el oeste. Hernán Cortés salió para México. **PRÁCTICA B.** 1. No, para mañana hay que leer el diálogo 12. 2. No, esa camisa es para mujer. 3. No, para niño, Juanito pronuncia muy bien. 4. No, para la semana que viene, tenemos que aprender el pretérito. 5. No, trabajé para la señora Hernández el año pasado. 6. No, para mí, el español es muy fácil. **PRÁCTICA C.** 1. para, por 2. por, para 3. por, para 4. por, para 5. para *or* por, para 6. para, para 7. para, por, para, por 8. por **UN POCO DE TODO. PRÁCTICA A.** 1. ¿Por qué te pusiste tan triste, mi amorcito? 2. Rosita llegó a ser enfermera. 3. Se hizo maestra en un pueblito de asturianos. 4. Tuvo un niñito gordo. 5. Se enojó porque no hubo sidra en el bautizo. **EJERCICIO B.** 1. Ana me regaló una medallita de oro. 2. ¿Tu amigo vino a la fiesta con sus hermanitas? 3. La chamaquita dijo unas palabras en español para su/el abuelo. 4. El marido le trajo a su mujer un relojcito de oro para su cumpleaños. 5. Cuando la prima se hizo rica, compró una casita de verano para su/la familia. **EJERCICIO C.** 1. La semana pasada vinieron a vernos mis hermanos. ¿Qué tal su visita? Fue muy agradable. Se quedaron cinco días. ¿Cuándo se fueron entonces? Ayer, y cuando salieron, les regalamos un perrito para su hijo. 2. La semana pasada vinieron a vernos mis nietas. ¿Qué tal su visita? Fue muy agradable. Se quedaron dos semanas. ¿Cuándo se fueron entonces? Ayer, y cuando salieron, les regalamos unos libros para su biblioteca. 3. La semana pasada vinieron a vernos mis abuelos. ¿Qué tal su visita? Fue muy agradable. Se quedaron una semana. ¿Cuándo se fueron entonces? Ayer, y cuando salieron, les regalamos una foto de toda la familia para su álbum. 4. La semana pasada vino a vernos nuestro amigo Julio. ¿Qué tal su visita? Fue muy agradable. Se quedó seis días. ¿Cuándo se fue entonces? Ayer, y cuando salió, le regalamos un radio para su cumpleaños.

CAPÍTULO 13

VOCABULARIO: PREPARACIÓN. EJERCICIO A. 1. pegó 2. distraído 3. llaves 4. brazo/pie, daño 5. duele,

aspirinas **EJERCICIO C.** 1-e, 2-d, 3-c, 4-b, 5-f, 6-a **GRAMMAR SECTION 56. PRÁCTICA A.** 1. tú no te acordaste, Raúl no se acordó, nosotros no nos acordamos, Ud. no se acordó, ellos no se acordaron, vosotros no os acordasteis 2. todos perdieron, tú perdiste, Horacio y Estela perdieron, yo perdí, Ud. perdió, vosotros perdisteis 3. yo pedí, Jacinto pidió, tú pediste, nosotros pedimos, Uds. pidieron, vosotros pedisteis 4. nosotros nos reímos, yo me reí, Esteban se rió, tú te reíste, todos se rieron, vosotros os reísteis 5. yo dormí, todos durmieron, tú dormiste, Irma durmió, Uds. durmieron, vosotros dormisteis **PRÁCTICA B.** La primavera pasada llovió mucho. Romeo murió por Julieta. La Segunda Guerra Mundial empezó en 1939. Rip Van Winkle durmió muchos años. Los turistas se divirtieron en Acapulco. Los estudiantes se acordaron de todo el vocabulario en el último examen (se divirtieron mucho, durmieron mucho, siguieron muchos cursos el semestre pasado). **PRÁCTICA C.** 1. se sentó, pidió, se acordó, sirvió 2. se acostó, apagó, durmió, se despertó, se vistió, salió 3. me vestí, fui, me divertí, volví, decidió, se divirtió, perdió, sintió **GRAMMAR SECTION 57. PRÁCTICA A.** 1. A mí se me olvidó el libro. A nosotros se nos olvidó..., A Inés se le olvidó..., A ti se te olvidó..., A Héctor y Ramiro se les..., A vosotros se os... 2. A María se le olvidó tomar el desayuno (se le olvidaron las llaves, se le olvidó estudiar para el examen, se le olvidaron los cheques, se le olvidó venir a clase). 3. Se me olvidaron (rompieron, cayeron, quedaron en casa) los vasos. Se me olvidó (quedó en casa, acabó) el champán. Se les olvidó (acabó) el champán en la tienda. **PRÁCTICA B.** 1. A Jorge se le rompieron los vasos. 2. A Roberto y Jacinta se les olvidó cambiar el carro de lugar. 3. Se me olvidó tomar las aspirinas. 4. Se nos quedaron en casa los boletos. 5. Se me perdieron las llaves. 6. Ayer se me rompieron varias cosas. 7. Se les acabó el pan. **GRAMMAR SECTION 58. PRÁCTICA A.** 1. yo cantaba y jugaba, Uds. cantaban y jugaban, tú cantabas y jugabas, nosotros cantábamos y jugábamos, Demetrio cantaba y jugaba, vosotros cantabais y jugabais 2. todos los niños bebían y dormían, tú bebías y dormías, nosotros bebíamos y dormíamos, Alicia bebía y dormía, yo bebía y dormía, vosotros bebíais y dormíais 3. Anoche, yo (no) estaba leyendo (mirando la televisión, escribiendo, llorando, comiendo, apagando las luces). 4. tú veías, yo veía, Uds. veían, Pablo veía, ella veía, vosotros veíais 5. Tú ibas a acostarte, yo iba a acostarme, nosotros íbamos a acostarnos, Pablo iba a acostarse, ella iba a acostarse, vosotros ibais a acostaros **PRÁCTICA B.** O. J. Simpson

jugaba al fútbol. Todos los niños creían en Santa Claus (se acostaban temprano, estudiaban mucho/poco). Elvis Presley cantaba música popular (cantaba mucho). Elizabeth Taylor era guapa. Burt Bacharach tocaba el piano. Chris Evert-Lloyd jugaba al tenis. Yo... **PRÁCTICA C.** 1. iba, asistía, preguntaba, era, estaban. 2. trabajaba, se llamaba, hacía, almorzábamos, jugábamos 3. vivía, llovía, gustaba, estaban, podía **PRÁCTICA D.** Eran las ocho y yo leía mientras mi amigo escribía cheques. Había poco ruido y nevaba afuera. No esperábamos a nadie y creíamos que iba a ser una noche tranquila. **UN POCO DE TODO. EJERCICIO A.** 1. Se divirtió mucho porque la película era muy cómica. 2. Durmieron hasta muy tarde porque estaban muy cansados. 3. ¡Casi se murieron de hambre! No había nada de comida. Se perdió en el centro cuando buscaba su casa. 5. Pidió paella porque su amigo le dijo que estaba buena. **EJERCICIO B.** 1. Ella sirvió la cena temprano porque todos tenían hambre. 2. Nosotros apagamos las luces porque teníamos sueño y queríamos dormir. 3. Lorenzo se despidió temprano porque tenía que levantarse a las siete. 4. Nosotros no fuimos a las montañas esta mañana porque nevaba mucho. 5. El hombre se rió mucho aunque estaba triste. **EJERCICIO C.** 1. ¿Por qué te quedaste en casa? → Sabía que no me iba a gustar aquella película. 2. ¿Por qué durmieron ellos tanto? → Tenían mucho sueño. 3. ¿Por qué olvidaron Uds. los regalos de los primitos? → Estábamos (muy) distraídos/as por el examen. 4. ¿Por qué te reíste tanto? → Horacio se portaba como un loco. 5. ¿Por qué se te cayó el vaso? → Pensaba en otra cosa. 6. ¿Por qué se equivocó Ud. tanto en los detalles del examen? → No sabía bien las fórmulas.

CAPÍTULO 14

VOCABULARIO: PREPARACIÓN. EJERCICIO A. 1. los pulmones 2. el ojo 3. la nariz 4. el corazón 5. la boca 6. la garganta 7. el estómago **EJERCICIO E.** 1. resfriado 2. respira 3. enfermo; enfermero/a 4. tos 5. dolor **EJERCICIO F.** siento; fiebre, temperatura; enfermera; mareado/a; congestionado/a; pulmones; cuerpo; boca; garganta; respire; receta; jarabe; aspirinas, antibiótico

PRONUNCIACIÓN. PRÁCTICA. 1. atención 2. amoníaco 3. teología 4. oposición 5. seudo- 6. correcto 7. fotografía 8. innumerable 9. exagerar 10. clasificar 11. caos 12. fosfato 13. físico 14. teoría 15. progreso 16. arquitecto 17. anual 18. clorofila 19. afirmar 20. colección 21. patético 22. arcángel 23. químico 24. accidente 25. alianza 26. fotosíntesis 27. (p)sicólogo 28. ateísmo

GRAMMAR SECTION 59. PRÁCTICA

A. 1. vivíamos 2. tomé 3. nos quedábamos 4. se enfermaron 5. Eran 6. se resfrió 7. estaba 8. viste 9. tosía, hablaba 10. se apagaron 11. tomó, examinó, dio 12. trabajaba **PRÁCTICA B.** 1. No podía leer (el) español en la (escuela) primaria. 2. Cuando lo conocí, ya conocía a su hijo. 3. Quisieron hacerlo pero no pudieron. 4. Sabía tocar el piano cuando tenía cinco años. 5. Tenía que estudiar pero no quería. 6. ¿Cuándo supo tú (supiste) eso? **PRÁCTICA C.** were walking → imp.; saw → pret.; looked, were → imp.; asked, gave → pret.; had, was → imp. **PRÁCTICA D.** estaba, entró; preguntó, quería; dijo, sentía; salieron; vieron, se rieron; hacía, entraron, tomaron; eran, regresaron; se acostó, estaba, empezó **PRÁCTICA E.** conocí; hicimos; era, daba; venían; había, cantaba, bailaba; llamaron, dijeron, hacíamos; vino, dijo, estaba; queríamos, podíamos; despedimos, eran; aprendió; tiene, invita

GRAMMAR SECTION 60. PRÁCTICA A. 1. Vinieron los primos, el tío y la abuela (los padres, los abuelos y [los] otros parientes; los primos, las hermanas y los esposos de ellas). 2. Sí, el doctor está los miércoles (los viernes, los sábados, los martes, los jueves). 3. Sí, y me puse el abrigo (el sombrero, las botas, los calcetines) porque hacía tanto frío. 4. Sí, le duele el estómago (le duelen los pulmones, le duele la cabeza, le duelen los ojos, le duele la nariz). 5. Sí, Antonia habla muy bien el francés (el inglés, el japonés, el chino, el ruso, el portugués). Tomó muchos cursos de francés (de inglés, de japonés, de chino, de ruso, de portugués) en la secundaria. 6. Sí, (la) Argentina es..., No, (el) Japón no es... Sí, (el) Brasil es..., No, Francia no es... Sí, (el) Paraguay es..., Sí, México es..., Sí, (el) Ecuador es..., No, (el) Canadá no es..., Sí, Colombia es..., No, los Estados Unidos no es... **PRÁCTICA B.** El Dr. García es cubano (tiene cincuenta y siete años, tiene una familia grande, habla español, es de la Habana). Dr. García, ¿es Ud. cubano? (¿cuántos años tiene Ud.?, ¿tiene Ud. una familia grande?, ¿qué lenguas habla Ud.?, ¿de dónde es Ud.?) **PRÁCTICA C.** (No) Creo que el dinero (la amistad, el amor, la salud, el matrimonio, la educación, la libertad) es/sea importante. **PRÁCTICA D.** El señor Radillo nos buscó en la estación el domingo. Pusimos/Metimos nuestras/las maletas, nuestros/los regalos y nuestros/los abrigos en su coche/carro y caminamos a un restaurante. La comida argentina es excelente y pedí en español. No necesitaba ayuda de nadie. Creo que nos va a gustar la vida en (la) Argentina.

GRAMMAR SECTION 61. PRÁCTICA A. 1. lo divertido 2. lo peor 3. lo interesante 4. lo curioso 5. lo necesario 6. lo bueno **PRÁCTICA C.** 1. lo bueno 2. lo

importante 3. lo peor 4. lo triste es (que) **UN POCO DE TODO. EJERCICIO A.** 1. Rómulo tomó el jarabe. Dijo que no le gustó/gustaba el sabor. 2. Me explicaron/ explicaban que lo mejor era quedarme en cama. 3. Lo peor era que me resfrié durante mis vacaciones. 4. Ellos se quitaron/quitaban el abrigo porque tenían calor. 5. Los martes y jueves lo más interesante era la clase de portugués. **PRÁCTICA B.** 1. El Dr. Matamoros le dio al niño un antibiótico porque tenía una fiebre alta. 2. El atleta dijo que lo fundamental era hacer ejercicio. 3. Eran las cuatro de la mañana cuando por fin el niño enfermo empezó a respirar sin dificultad. 4. Cuando nosotros éramos niños, pensábamos que lo mejor de la escuela eran las vacaciones. 5. El lunes yo fui al centro con la Sra. Medina, aunque yo no quería comprar nada. **EJERCICIO C.** 1. Para ti, ¿qué fue lo más interesante de tu cumpleaños? Comí en El Toledano. ¿Por qué comiste allí? Porque quería comer comida española. 2. Para ti, ¿qué fue lo más interesante de tu niñez? Viví en el Perú. ¿Por qué viviste allí? Porque mi padre trabajaba allí. 3. Para ti, ¿qué fue lo más interesante de las/tus vacaciones? Fui a esquiar en las montañas. ¿Por qué fuiste allí? Porque quería descansar y divertirme. 4. Para ti, ¿qué fue lo más interesante de la escuela secundaria? Estudié español. ¿Por qué estudiaste español? Porque mis abuelos hablaban español en casa. 5. Para ti, ¿qué fue lo más interesante de la fiesta? Bailé la noche entera. ¿Por qué bailaste la noche entera (bailaste tanto)? Porque tenía ganas de bailar.

CAPÍTULO 15

VOCABULARIO: PREPARACIÓN. EJERCICIO A. 1. Paga al contado. 2. Lo carga a su cuenta. 3. Paga con cheque. **EJERCICIO D.** 1-f, 2-d, 3-e, 4-c, 5-a, 6-b

PRONUNCIACIÓN. PRÁCTICA. 1. ¿Cuál es tu profesora? ¿Cómo se llama ella? 2. Uno, dos, tres, cuatro. ¡Caramba!, él compró cuatro trajes. 3. ¡Qué ejercicio más fácil! 4. ¿Fue Juan al mercado? 5. ¿Dónde estuviste ayer? 6. Ja, ja. (Or: ¡Ja, ja!) Tú no hablas en serio, ¿verdad? 7. ¿Quiénes vienen? Luisa, María y Juan.

GRAMMAR SECTION 62. PRÁCTICA A. 1. yo hablaré, Uds. hablarán, nosotros hablaremos, el/la profesor(a) hablará, tú hablarás, vosotros hablaréis. 2. tú insistirás, Elena y Miguel insistirán, yo insistiré, nosotros insistiremos, Ud. insistirá, vosotros insistiréis. 3. el/la profesor(a) se levantará, yo me levantaré, nosotros nos levantaremos, tú te levantarás, Uds. se levantarán, vosotros os levantaréis **PRÁCTICA B.** Note the irregular future stems of querer (querr-), tener (tendr-), and poder (podr-). **PRÁCTICA C.** 1. Yo también

me mudaré (de apartamento). 2. Yo también haré un presupuesto y lo seguiré. 3. sabré todas las respuestas... 4. saldré... 5. iré... 6. le diré a Graciela que vaya a la fiesta (también). 7. me casaré... 8. pondré... **PRÁCTICA D.** El Sr. Adams dice que pagará al contado. La Sra. Walsh usará su tarjeta de crédito. La Srta./Sra. Smith dice que tendrá que cobrar un cheque en el banco. El Sr. Collins dice que la tienda tendrá que mandar la factura a su casa.

GRAMMAR SECTION 63. PRÁCTICA A. 1. Serán las cuatro. 2. Será (un) paciente. 3. Sabrán la respuesta. 4. Estará en Phoenix. 5. Tendrán muchos hijos/niños. 6. ¿Dónde vivirá (ella)? 7. ¿Cuántos años tendrá (él)? 8. ¿Quién tendrá las tarjetas de crédito? **PRÁCTICA B.** 1. La doctora le dará un antibiótico. 2. Cobrarán mucho en aquella tienda. 3. ¿Cuánto será...? 4. Habrá... 5. Tendrá... 6. Saldrán... 7. ¿...tendrá? 8. No vendrán... 9. ¿Estará...?

GRAMMAR SECTION 64. PRÁCTICA A. 1. yo (no) iría, Ud. (no) iría, tú (no) irías, Uds. (no) irían, nosotros (no) iríamos, vosotras (no) iríais 2. tú dijiste que lo harías, Armando dijo que lo haría, yo dije que lo haría, Uds. dijeron que lo harían, nosotros dijimos que lo haríamos, vosotros dijisteis que lo haríais 3. los astronautas (no) estarían, nosotras (no) estaríamos, yo (no) estaría, Ud. (no) estaría, tú (no) estarías, vosotros (no) estaríais **PRÁCTICA B.** 1. Saldríamos pronto. 2. Diría que sí. 3. Lo sabrían... 4. ¿Podrías... 5. No tendría... 6. No te quejarías... 7. Uds. deberían... **PRÁCTICA C.** ¿Te gustaría cenar con nosotros/as esta noche? Sé que te divertirías y que conocerías a algunas personas interesantes.

UN POCO DE TODO. EJERCICIO A. 1. Gastarían mucho, no ahorrarían y nunca pagarían sus facturas. 2. Habría gente de todos los países en el banco. 3. ¿Tendría una cuenta corriente o una cuenta de ahorros? 4. ¿Qué harían con el dinero? 5. Dejaría de usar mi tarjeta de crédito. **EJERCICIO B.** 1. Alicia dijo que haría calor mañana. 2. Tomás y Ana dijeron que se mudarían para reducir sus gastos. 3. Mis padres y yo dijimos que estaríamos allí a las ocho en punto. 4. El empleado dijo que lo cargaría a la cuenta de la Sra. Pérez. 5. Los Sres. Delgado dijeron que sería necesario abrir otra cuenta. **EJERCICIO C.** 1. Estaré en el bar a las dos. ¿No dijiste que estarías allí a las doce? ¡Que no! Dije que estaría allí a las dos. Entendiste mal. 2. Estudiaré con Juan. ¿No dijiste que estudiarías con Juana? ¡Que no! Dije que estudiaría con Juan. Entendiste mal. 3. Iré de vacaciones en julio. ¿No dijiste que irías en junio? ¡Que no! Dije que iría (de vacaciones) en julio. Entendiste mal. 4. Te veré en casa. ¿No dijiste que me verías en clase? ¡Que no! Dije que te vería en casa. Entendiste mal.

5. Compraré la blusa rosada. ¿No dijiste que comprarías la (blusa) roja? ¡Que no! Dije que compraría la rosada. Entendiste mal. **EJERCICIO D.** *Note: Use conditional forms to tell what you would do.*

CAPÍTULO 16

VOCABULARIO: PREPARACIÓN. EJERCICIO A. Campo: 1, 2, 4, 7, 8; Ciudad: 3, 5, 6, *possibly* 7. **EJERCICIO B.** Cierto: 1, 3, 5, *possibly* 6 (*opinion*); Falso: 2, 4, *possibly* 6 (*opinion*), 7. **EJERCICIO D.** Pancho: 3, 6, 7; Gabriela: 1, 2, 4, 5. **EJERCICIO E.** muuu—vaca; ahiii—caballo; guau guau—perro; miau—gato; cua cua—pato; pío pío—pajarito; cloc cloc—gallina; qui-qui-ri-quí—gallo; grrr—león. **EJERCICIO F.** 1. hora 2. vez 3. tiempo, rato 4. vez, veces 5. rato 6. hora 7. tiempo **GRAMMAR SECTION 65. PRÁCTICA A.** 1. Aquí tengo un libro usado (mandado, recomendado, pagado, comprado, leído, traído) por Eugenio. 2. Tengo un vestido hecho (una figurita hecha, unos vasos hechos, unas florecitas de papel hechas) en el Ecuador. **PRÁCTICA B.** 1. La carta no está escrita todavía. 2. La tienda no está abierta todavía. 3. David y Marta no están casados todavía. 4. La ventana no está cerrada todavía. 5. El equipaje no está facturado todavía. 6. La mesa no está puesta todavía. **PRÁCTICA C.** 1. dinero ahorrado 2. un cheque firmado 3. las facturas pagadas 4. el equipaje perdido 5. una frase repetida 6. el/la empleado/a despedido/a 7. moscas muertas **GRAMMAR SECTION 66. PRÁCTICA A.** 1. Sí, he escrito (he empezado, he estudiado, he comprendido, he aprendido, he olvidado) la lección. 2. tú te has preparado, el/la profesor(a) se ha preparado, los estudiantes se han preparado, Luis se ha preparado, Carmen y Pilar se han preparado, vosotros os habéis preparado. 3. Esta mañana Lidia se ha levantado (se ha bañado, se ha vestido, se ha desayunado, ha corrido, ha leído, ha reído). 4. yo no he vuelto, ellos no han vuelto, Carlos no ha vuelto, nosotros no hemos vuelto, tú no has vuelto, vosotros no habéis vuelto **PRÁCTICA B.** 1. Hemos recorrido el rancho entero. 2. Hemos visto las vacas y los toros. 3. Hemos montado a caballo. 4. Hemos hablado con los campesinos. **PRÁCTICA C.** 1. Estarás cocinando, ¿no? —No, ya he cocinado. 2. Estarás descansando, ¿no? —No, ya he descansado. 3. Estarás lavando los platos, ¿no? —No, ya he lavado los platos. (*Or:* No, ya los he lavado.) 4. Estarás leyendo el periódico, ¿no? —No, ya lo he leído. (*Or:* No, ya he leído el periódico.) 5. Estarás poniendo la mesa, ¿no? —No, ya la he puesto. (*Or:* No, ya he puesto la mesa.) 6. Jorge dice que le mandes la invitación a Pablo. —Pero ya la he mandado. (*Or:* Pero ya se la he mandado.) 7. Jorge dice que

hables con Concepción. —Pero ya he hablado con ella. 8. Jorge dice que pases por casa. —Pero ya he pasado por (su) casa (*or:* por allí). 9. Jorge dice que veas _____. —Pero ya lo he visto. 10. Jorge dice que escribas la composición esta tarde. —Pero ya la he escrito. **PRÁCTICA D.** Ha habido mucho trabajo en clase. Todavía tengo tres ejercicios que escribir para mañana. Acabo de hacer/terminar el primero, pero no he terminado (ni) el segundo ni el tercero. **GRAMMAR SECTION 67. PRÁCTICA A.** 1. tú (no) habías estudiado, yo (no) había estudiado, Armando (no) había estudiado, nosotros (no) habíamos estudiado, Ud. (no) había estudiado, vosotros (no) habíais estudiado 2. Antes del año pasado, no habíamos asistido a la universidad (no habíamos montado a caballo, no habíamos visitado Patagonia, no habíamos viajado a Moscú, no habíamos comido flan, no habíamos conocido a Rita Moreno). 3. Jaimito le dijo que su hermana había mirado la televisión toda la tarde (había perdido sus libros, había roto un vaso, había faltado a clase, había comido todo el pastel). **PRÁCTICA B.** 1. Estabas escuchando las noticias, ¿no? —No, ya las había escuchado. 2. Estabas bañándote, ¿no? —No, ya me había bañado. 3. Estabas preparando la cena, ¿no? —No, ya la había preparado. 4. Estabas haciendo las maletas, ¿no? —No, ya las había hecho. 5. Estabas mirando _____, ¿no? —No, ya lo había mirado. **UN POCO DE TODO. EJERCICIO A.** 1. Yo he madrugado esta mañana. Nunca me había levantado tan temprano antes. 2. Ellos han depositado todo el dinero en el banco. Nunca habían depositado tanto antes. 3. Hoy Juan ha faltado a clase por primera vez. Nunca había faltado antes. 4. Nosotros nos hemos reído tanto hoy. Nunca nos habíamos reído tanto antes. 5. Tú has pedido pollo. Antes siempre habías pedido bistec. **EJERCICIO B.** 1. Siempre hemos vivido en casas bien construidas. 2. Nunca he oído una canción escrita por José Feliciano. 3. ¿Te ha gustado el flan? ¿Nunca lo habías comido antes? 4. Me habían dicho que la tienda estaba abierta por la mañana. 5. Nunca había recorrido el rancho entero antes. Hoy lo he hecho. Todo me ha encantado. (*Or:* Me ha encantado todo.) **EJERCICIO C.** 1. ¿Ya están hechas las maletas? No, no las he hecho todavía. Ah, creía que ya las habías hecho. 2. ¿Ya están pagadas las facturas? No, no las he pagado todavía. Ah, creía que ya las habías pagado. 3. ¿Ya está preparada la paella para la cena? No, no la he preparado todavía. Ah, creía que ya la habías preparado. 4. ¿Ya está facturado el equipaje? No, no lo he facturado todavía. Ah, creía que ya lo habías facturado. 5. ¿Ya está abierta la cuenta en el Banco Nacional? No, no la he abierto todavía. Ah, creía que ya la habías abierto.

6. ¿Ya están sacudidos los muebles? No, no los he sacudido todavía. Ah, creía que ya las habías sacudido. **EJERCICIO D.** 1. ¿Has recorrido unos países latinoamericanos este año? Y antes de este año, ¿habías recorrido unos países latinoamericanos? 2. ¿Has montado a caballo este año? Y antes de este año, ¿habías montado a caballo? 3. ¿Has viajado a España este año? Y antes de este año, ¿habías viajado a España? 4. ¿Has hablado con una persona de otro planeta este año? Y antes de este año, ¿habías hablado con una persona de otro planeta? 5. ¿Has ahorrado mucho dinero este año? Y antes de este año, ¿habías ahorrado mucho dinero?

CAPÍTULO 17

GRAMMAR SECTION 68. PRÁCTICA A. 1. Es posible que tú hayas encontrado (que Uds. hayan encontrado, que Roberto y Hernando hayan encontrado, que nosotros hayamos encontrado, que yo haya encontrado, que vosotros hayáis encontrado) un apartamento. 2. Espero que ya haya visto el agua (que ya haya descubierto el problema, que ya haya llamado al plomero, que ya haya hecho los arreglos). **PRÁCTICA B.** 1. Dudo que (Armando) haya alquilado... 2. Tal vez hayan vendido... 3. Sí, y me alegro mucho de que nos hayamos mudado... 4. No creo que ellos hayan pagado... 5. Sí, es probable que (los vecinos) se hayan sentado... 6. Es probable que hayan subido... 7. Espero que hayan alquilado... 8. Sí, es probable que ya hayamos perdido... 9. Siento que se haya muerto... 10. No, no creo que Julián haya puesto... **PRÁCTICA C.** Me alegro de que (él) haya vuelto/regresado de su año en (el) Uruguay y espero que nos haya traído un recuerdo. No creo que haya encontrado (un) apartamento todavía. **GRAMMAR SECTION 69. PRÁCTICA A.** 1. Voy a buscar un apartamento que tenga tres alcobas (que tenga una vista magnífica, que esté en el centro, que tenga un garaje amplio, que sea cómodo, que tenga por lo menos dos baños). 2. No hay nadie en clase que sea actor/actriz (que hable chino, que sepa tocar la viola, que coleccione insectos, que sepa preparar comida turca, que monte a caballo muy bien). **PRÁCTICA B.** 1. Buscamos un secretario que sepa escribir... 2. No hay nada aquí que me guste. 3. Quieren bailar con alguien que sepa... 4. He encontrado a un dentista que no cobra mucho. 5. No hay nadie que pueda... 6. Aquí no hay ningún vecino que se queje... 7. Aquí tenemos un sillón que es... 8. No hay nada de su personalidad que me encante. **PRÁCTICA C.** 1. Tengo un(a) médico/a (un[a] doctor[a]) que habla español. 2. Necesitamos un(a) médico/a (un[a] doctor[a]) que hable español. 3. Conozco a alguien que juega bien al tenis. 4. No conozco a nadie que juegue bien al tenis. 5. ¿Hay alguien aquí que pueda arreglarlo? 6. No hay nadie aquí que pueda arreglarlo. **GRAMMAR SECTION 70. PRÁCTICA A.** No salgo esta tarde a menos que llame Luis (antes de que llame Luis, en caso de que llame Luis, sin que llame Luis). 2. Sí, quiero que vengan todos para que naden en la nueva piscina (para que se diviertan, para que vean la casa, para que conversen, para que celebren conmigo). **PRÁCTICA B.** 1. Vamos a las montañas a menos que llueva. 2. Voy al centro con tal que tú me acompañes. 3. En caso de que Jaime regrese, dígale que he salido. 4. Los padres trabajan tanto para que sus hijos vivan cómodamente. 5. Alquilemos aquella casa antes de que otra persona la alquile. 6. No me caso contigo a menos que vendas tu motocicleta. 7. Voy a alquilar el apartamento con tal que tenga dos alcobas. 8. Compre Ud. pan ahora en caso de que no tengan pan en la otra tienda. 9. Les doy tanta tarea para que Uds. aprendan. 10. Ojalá que lleguemos a la casa (pronto), antes de que nieve. **PRÁCTICA C.** 1. Vamos allí para divertirnos. 2. Vamos allí para que los niños se diviertan. 3. Van a nadar antes de limpiar/arreglar el garaje. 4. Van a nadar antes de que limpiemos/arreglemos el garaje. 5. No salga(s) sin hablarle a ella (sin hablar con ella). 6. No salga(s) sin que ella hable con Ud./contigo.

UN POCO DE TODO. EJERCICIO A. 1. Busco un secretario que haya vivido en Venezuela. 2. Aquí no hay nadie que haya visto la nueva casa de Carmen. 3. El trato está hecho con tal que el dueño haya firmado el contrato. 4. No lo alquilamos sin que hayan instalado el ascensor. 5. Con tal que lo hayan terminado, pueden irse. **EJERCICIO B.** 1. No empieces antes de que te lo hayamos explicado. 2. No hay ninguna tienda que tenga el estante. 3. Llame Ud. más tarde en caso de que haya vuelto. 4. ¿Prefieres una mesa que tenga sillas de plástico o sillas de madera? 5. No cierres la puerta a menos que hayas apagado la lámpara. **PRÁCTICA C.** 1. Buscamos una casa que tenga piscina. ¿Para qué? Para que los niños aprendan a nadar. 2. Buscamos una casa de apartamentos que tenga ascensor. ¿Para qué? Para que el abuelo no tenga que subir las escaleras. 3. Buscamos un apartamento que tenga un garaje doble. ¿Para qué? Para que Ramón no tenga que dejar el carro en la calle. 4. Buscamos un apartamento que esté cerca del centro. ¿Para qué? Para que Elena llegue más rápido al trabajo. 5. Buscamos una casa que esté cerca de la universidad. ¿Para qué? Para que Catalina no tenga que usar tanto el carro.

CAPÍTULO 18

VOCABULARIO: PREPARACIÓN.

EJERCICIO A. frontera, aduana; inspector (de aduanas), pasaporte; nacionalidad; declarar; extranjero; derechos; registra; multa. **EJERCICIO E.** Hotel: 1, 2, 4, 5, 7, 9, 10. Pensión: 3, *possibly* 5, 6, 8. **GRAMMAR SECTION 71. PRÁCTICA A.** 1. No voy en autobús aunque Ramón siga insistiendo (aunque tú sigas insistiendo, aunque Ud. siga insistiendo, aunque Catalina y Juan sigan insistiendo, aunque vosotros sigáis insistiendo). 2. No hay habitaciones, aunque Ud. prometa pagar el doble (aunque espere aquí en la recepción toda la noche, aunque insista en quedarse aquí, aunque me dé una propina enorme, aunque haya reservado una habitación, aunque haya(mos) confirmado su reservación, aunque se queje a la policía). **PRÁCTICA B.** 1-b, 2-f, 3-c, 4-g, 5-d, 6-a, 7-e **PRÁCTICA C.** 1. Aunque es un huésped 2. Aunque sea un huésped 3. Aunque cruzamos la frontera 4. Aunque crucemos la frontera 5. No tomaré el tren (No iré en tren) aunque tenga que ir a solas. **GRAMMAR SECTION 72. PRÁCTICA A.** 1. Entregan las planillas tan pronto como aterrice (cuando aterrice, después de que aterrice, en cuanto aterrice) el avión. No entregan las planillas hasta que aterrice el avión. 2. Le entrego el pasaporte tan pronto como yo lo encuentre (tan pronto como encuentre la llave de mi maleta, tan pronto como cierre mi maleta, tan pronto como me lo dé mi esposo/a, tan pronto como recuerde dónde lo tengo). **PRÁCTICA B.** 1. Voy a decidirlo cuando cruce la frontera. 2. Juana va a mudarse después de que su amiga regrese del Perú. 3. No digas nada hasta que Julio pague el billete. 4. El inspector va a registrar la maleta en cuanto mi esposo la abra. 5. Van a construir una nueva casa de apartamentos tan pronto como el gobierno les dé el permiso. **PRÁCTICA C.** 1. Mi hijo nacerá después de que mi esposo vuelva de Guatemala. 2. Vamos a caminar mucho cuando cambiemos de tren. 3. En cuanto sepas la respuesta, dímela. 4. Este año llamaremos con dos días de anticipación cuando confirmemos las reservaciones. 5. Hoy compraremos el billete en cuanto se abra la taquilla. **PRÁCTICA D.** Tomaremos la habitación sin ducha hasta que la habitación con ducha esté desocupada. Avísenos, por favor, en cuanto (tan pronto como) salgan los otros huéspedes. ¿Nos ayudará el mozo (el botones) cuando cambiemos de habitación? **GRAMMAR SECTION 73. PRÁCTICA A.** 1. ¿Las lámparas mías? Ya las he arreglado. ¿El estéreo mío? Ya lo he arreglado. ¿La cámara mía? Ya la he arreglado. ¿Los frenos míos? Ya los he arreglado. ¿La transmisión mía? Ya la he arreglado. 2. El maletín de Juan, sí, pero las maletas suyas (las maletas tuyas, las maletas nuestras, las maletas suyas, las

maletas mías, las maletas vuestras), no. **PRÁCTICA B.** No, no es suya (suya, suya, suya, tuya, vuestra). 2. ¿La guitarra? No, no es mía. La mía es más pequeña. ¿Los zapatos? No, no son míos. Los míos son más pequeños. ¿La llave? No, no es mía. La mía es más pequeña. ¿El televisor? No, no es mío. El mío es más pequeño. ¿Las maletas? No, no son mías. Las mías son más pequeñas. ¿El diamante? No, no es mío. El mío es más pequeño. **PRÁCTICA C.** No puedo pagar mis facturas este mes, pero tú puedes pagar las tuyas. 2. No han confirmado sus reservaciones, pero yo he confirmado las mías. 3. ...pero Rafael no ha dejado el suyo. 4. ...pero ellos (sí) pueden encontrar las suyas. 5. ...pero Ud. no puede usar el suyo. 6. ...no hemos declarado todas las nuestras. 7. ...pero ellos (sí) perdieron el suyo. 8. ...pero los señores Benítez no han reservado la suya. **PRÁCTICA D.** 1. Es una amiga suya. 2. Éstos son los billetes/boletos nuestros. 3. Ésta es mi litera, no la suya. 4. Ése no es su asiento; es mío. 5. Ella tiene su pasaporte y yo tengo el mío.

UN POCO DE TODO. EJERCICIO A. 1. Esta semana vamos a visitar a los abuelos cuando tengamos tiempo. 2. Todos los veranos recorremos el rancho suyo tan pronto como empieza el buen tiempo. 3. El dependiente trajo nuestra alfombra cuando te trajo la tuya. 4. En cuanto terminaron nuestro garaje, empezaron el tuyo. 5. Aunque haya una demora, nuestro autobús va a llegar a tiempo. **EJERCICIO B.** 1. Aunque tú no tengas nada importante que decir, llámanos. 2. Nosotros vamos a mandar las cartas en cuanto tú termines la tuya. 3. Nosotros pensamos confirmar nuestro horario después de confirmar el tuyo (or: después de que confirmes el tuyo). 4. Tú no vas a salir con tus maletas hasta que yo tenga la mía, ¿verdad? 5. Se llega a su finca pero no a la nuestra por autopista. **EJERCICIO C.** 1. ¿Te confirmamos la reservación cuando confirmemos la nuestra? No, gracias. Yo voy a confirmar la mía en cuanto pueda llamar. 2. ¿Te compramos un billete cuando compremos el nuestro? No, gracias. Yo voy a comprar el mío en cuanto vaya al banco. 3. ¿Te reservamos una litera cuando reservemos las nuestras? No, gracias. Yo voy a reservar la mía en cuanto se abra la taquilla. 4. ¿Te entregamos la planilla de inmigración cuando entreguemos las nuestras? No, gracias. Yo voy a entregar la mía en cuanto conteste la última pregunta. 5. ¿Te compramos un periódico cuando compremos el nuestro/los nuestros? No, gracias. Yo voy a comprar el mío en cuanto facture el equipaje. **EJERCICIO D.** 1. El inspector va a registrar mis maletas en cuanto registre las tuyas. 2. ...tan pronto como lleve el tuyo. 3. ...cuando compremos los nuestros.

4. ...en cuanto preparen la tuya. 5. ...tan pronto como te entregue el tuyo.

CAPÍTULO 19

VOCABULARIO: PREPARACIÓN. EJERCICIO A. 1-b, 2-c, 3-a, 4-c, 5-a, 6-c **EJERCICIO B.** emigró; necesidad; refugiado; raíces; idioma; mantener; acostumbrarse; costumbres; su tierra natal; bilingüe; acostumbrado; añorarán. **EJERCICIO C.** *Answers on same page as exercise.* **EJERCICIO D.** 1. sino 2. sino 3. pero 4. sino 5. pero 6. sino 7. pero 8. pero 9. sino 10. sino

GRAMMAR SECTION 74. PRÁCTICA A. 1. Ojalá que tú te acostumbraras (que Uds. se acostumbraran, que Juan se acostumbrara, que Ángel y Ana se acostumbraran, que tus padres se acostumbraran) sin problemas. 2. El Sr. Meléndez quería que Juan conociera (que ellos conocieran, que yo conociera, que todos conocieran, que María conociera) algunas de las costumbres de su familia. 3. Tú no creías (Ellos no creían, Ud. no creía, Yo no creía, Nosotros no creíamos, Vosotros no creíais) que pudiéramos hacerlo. 4. Me gustaba que nosotros estudiáramos idiomas (leyéramos libros interesantes, viéramos películas en la clase de historia, hiciéramos experimentos en la clase de física, bailáramos durante el almuerzo, nos divirtiéramos después de las clases). Cuando yo era niño/a, mis padres querían que yo fuera bueno/a (que yo estudiara mucho, que yo creyera en Santa Claus, que yo me pusiera la ropa vieja para jugar, que yo no jugara en las calles, que yo no comiera tantos dulces, que yo tuviera amigos que se portaran bien). **PRÁCTICA B.** 1. Pablo insistía en que yo le diera consejos. 2. Preferíamos que dijeras la verdad. 3. Me alegraba de que lo supieras. 4. Sentía que no tuvieras tiempo de visitar tu tierra natal. 5. Dudábamos que emigraran por necesidad. 6. No creían que te doliera mucho. 7. Era probable que un profesor chicano enseñara la clase. 8. No me gustaba que durmieran tanto. 9. Necesitaban un secretario que fuera bilingüe. 10. No había nadie que añorara su patria como él. 11. Tal vez estuvieran allí ayer. 12. Aunque tuviera el dinero, no iría. **PRÁCTICA C.** 1. Nunca corría allí a menos que el perro me acompañara. 2. Me escribieron en cuanto se establecieron. 3. Me lo ofreció antes de que yo pudiera pedírselo a él. 4. Luis dijo que me despertaría con tal que yo lo despertara al día siguiente. 5. No pasaron a la sala de espera hasta que el maletero facturó su equipaje. 6. Se casaron después de que sus padres anunciaron su noviazgo. 7. Te lo dije para que te rieras. 8. El refugiado no quería perder sus costumbres en caso de que volviera a su patria. 9. Se sorprendieron cuando vieron a su hijo en aquel lugar. 10. Nunca comían en aquel restaurante sin que el Sr. Gutiérrez les pagara la cuenta. 11. Salimos tan pronto como vinieron. 12. Les dimos una fiesta antes de que fueran a España. **PRÁCTICA D.** 1. Debiera(s) visitar a los Jiménez en El Paso. 2. ¿Podría(s) llamarme esta noche? 3. Quisiera ver la falda verde.

GRAMMAR SECTION 75. PRÁCTICA A. 1. Si yo fuera tú (estuviera allí, tuviera ese problema, tuviera que decidir, viviera allí), no lo haría. 2. Si estuviéramos de vacaciones, nosotros tomaríamos el sol en la playa (no tendríamos que estudiar, podríamos pasarlo bien, no vendríamos a clase, estaríamos en un café, mandaríamos unas tarjetas postales). 3. Carlota habla como si fuera rica (siempre tuviera razón, fuera un experto en todo, lo supiera todo). **PRÁCTICA C.** 1. Llegaríamos más rápidamente si doblaras en esta esquina. 2. Si te equivocaras, perderías todo el dinero. 3. Si no ganaran, se enojarían. 4. No te lo perdonaría si me interrumpieras. 5. Si te estacionaras aquí, no tendríamos que cruzar la calle. 6. Dejaría de fumar si se enfermara.

GRAMMAR SECTION 76. PRÁCTICA A. 1. Carmen no permite que sus niños jueguen (no permitirá que sus niños jueguen, no permitió que sus niños jugaran, nunca ha permitido que sus niños jueguen/jugaran) en la calle. 2. Era necesario que se acostumbraran (Será necesario que se acostumbren, Fue necesario que se acostumbraran, Sería necesario que se acostumbraran, Ha sido necesario que se acostumbraran) a la vida allí. 3. Esperan que salga (Esperarán que salga, Esperaron que saliera) el vuelo. **PRÁCTICA B.** 1. añoren, añoraran 2. aprenda, aprendió 3. conozcan, conocieran 4. sea, fuera 5. te acostumbres, te acostumbraras **PRÁCTICA C.** Sentimos que tuvieran que dejar todos sus bienes. Insistimos en que acepten nuestra ayuda. Será fácil que ellos se mantengan tan pronto como (en cuanto) hayan encontrado empleo (trabajo). **PRÁCTICA D.** llegó; entró, viera; preparaba, pidió, quedara, terminaran; tuviera; pueda

UN POCO DE TODO. EJERCICIO A. 1. Si se estableciera pronto, estaría contento. 2. Seguían negando que fueran los ladrones. 3. No creía que lo conocieras tú. 4. Era muy probable que ya te extrañaran. 5. Sentía que no pudieran mantenerse fácilmente. **EJERCICIO B.** 1-b, 2-c, 3-b, 4-a, 5-b, 6-b **EJERCICIO C.** 1. Yo quería que fuéramos a ver (que viéramos) una película latina. 2. Yo prefiero que vayamos a la playa. 3. Yo quería que emigráramos más temprano. 4. Yo prefiero que vayamos en autobús. 5. Yo quería que alquiláramos una casa nueva y con todas las comodidades. 6. Yo prefiero que los niños sean bilingües.

CAPÍTULO 20

EN EL EXTRANJERO: PALABRAS ÚTILES. PRÁCTICA B. 1. falso (Se pueden comprar pastelitos...) 2. falso (...iría a un café/un bar). 3. falso (Se va al correo...) 4. falso (Es más rápido tomar el metro que ir a pie). 5. falso (Se va a una farmacia...) 6. falso (...iría a una farmacia) 7. cierto 8. falso (...con leche)